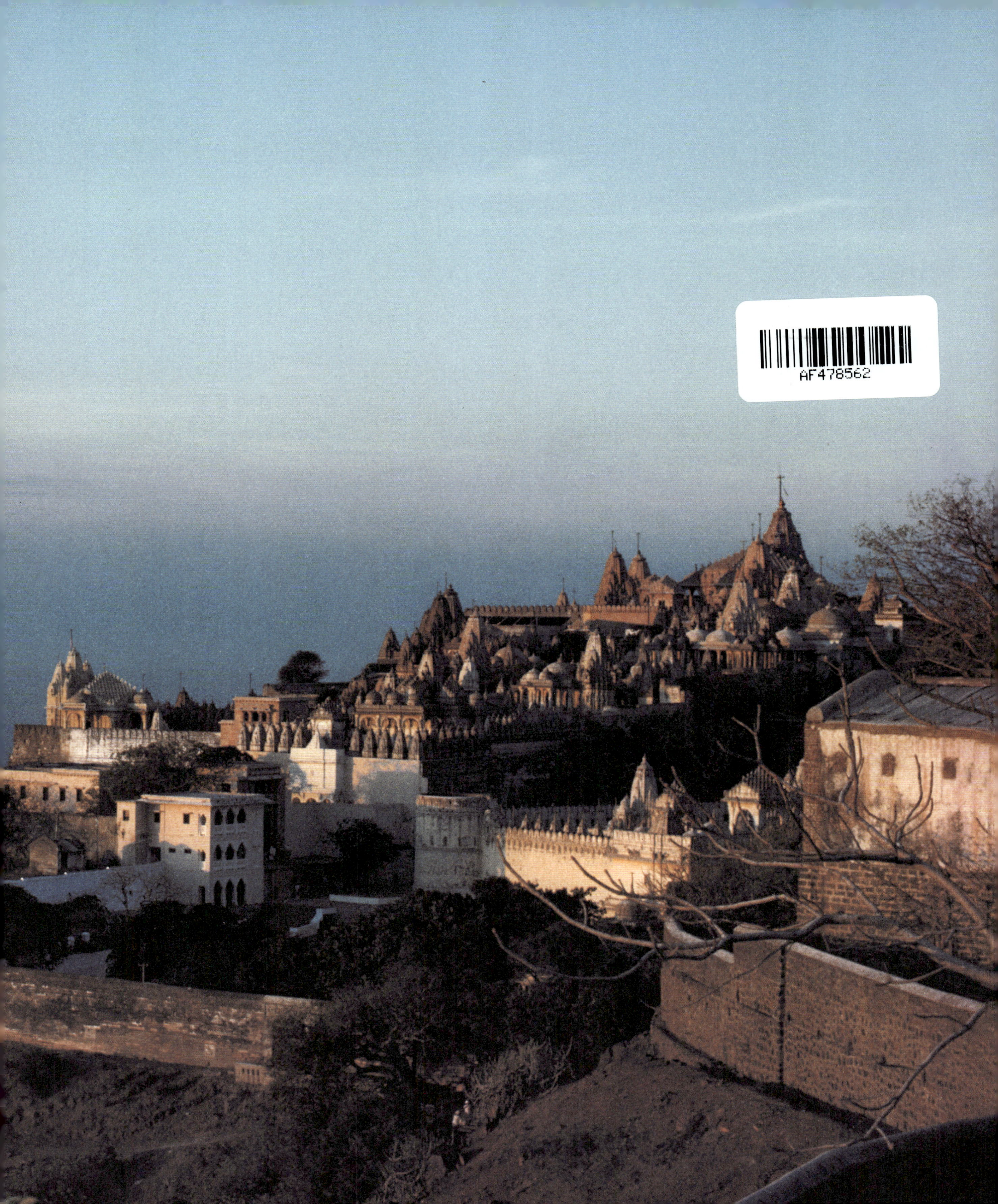
AF478562

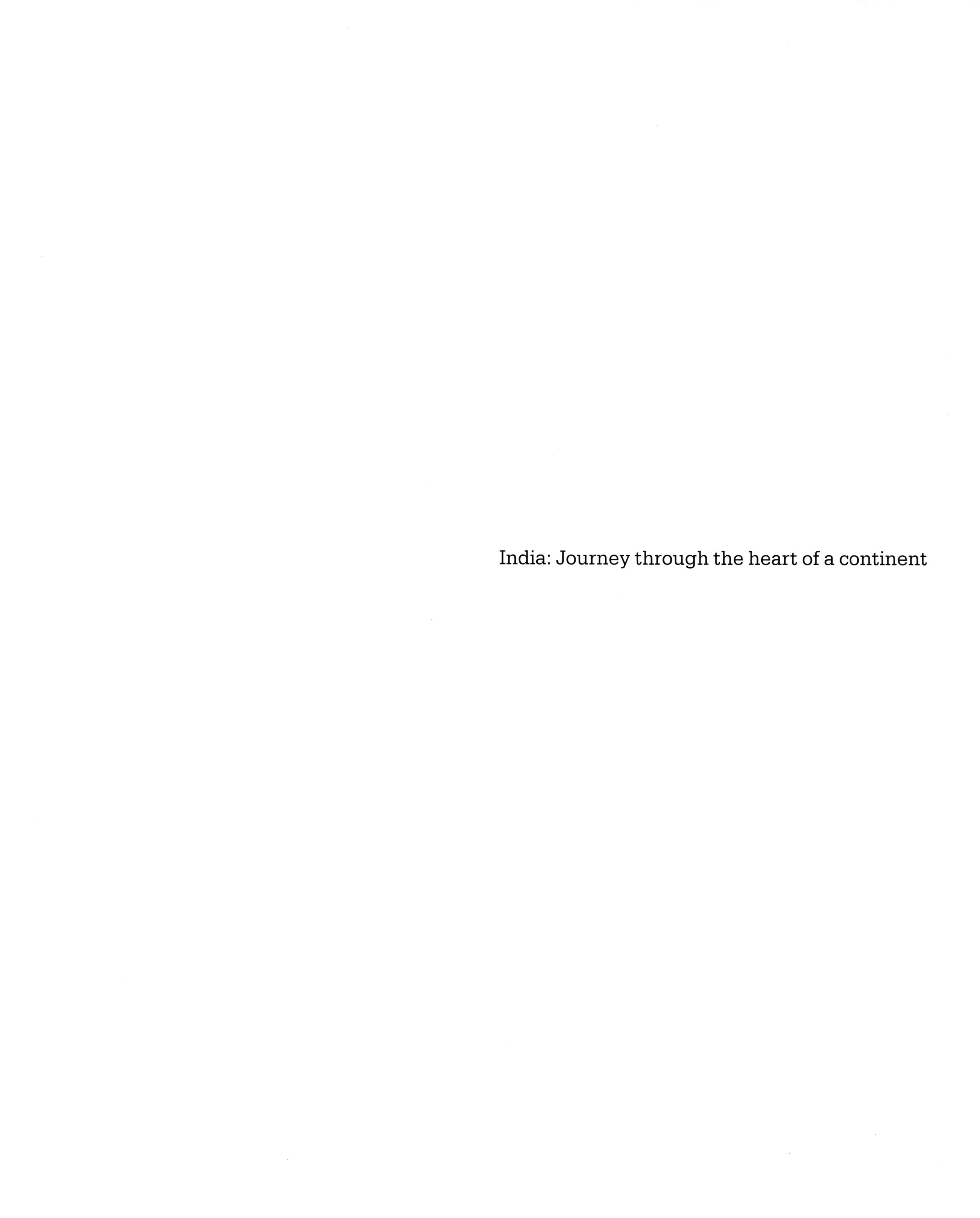

India: Journey through the heart of a continent

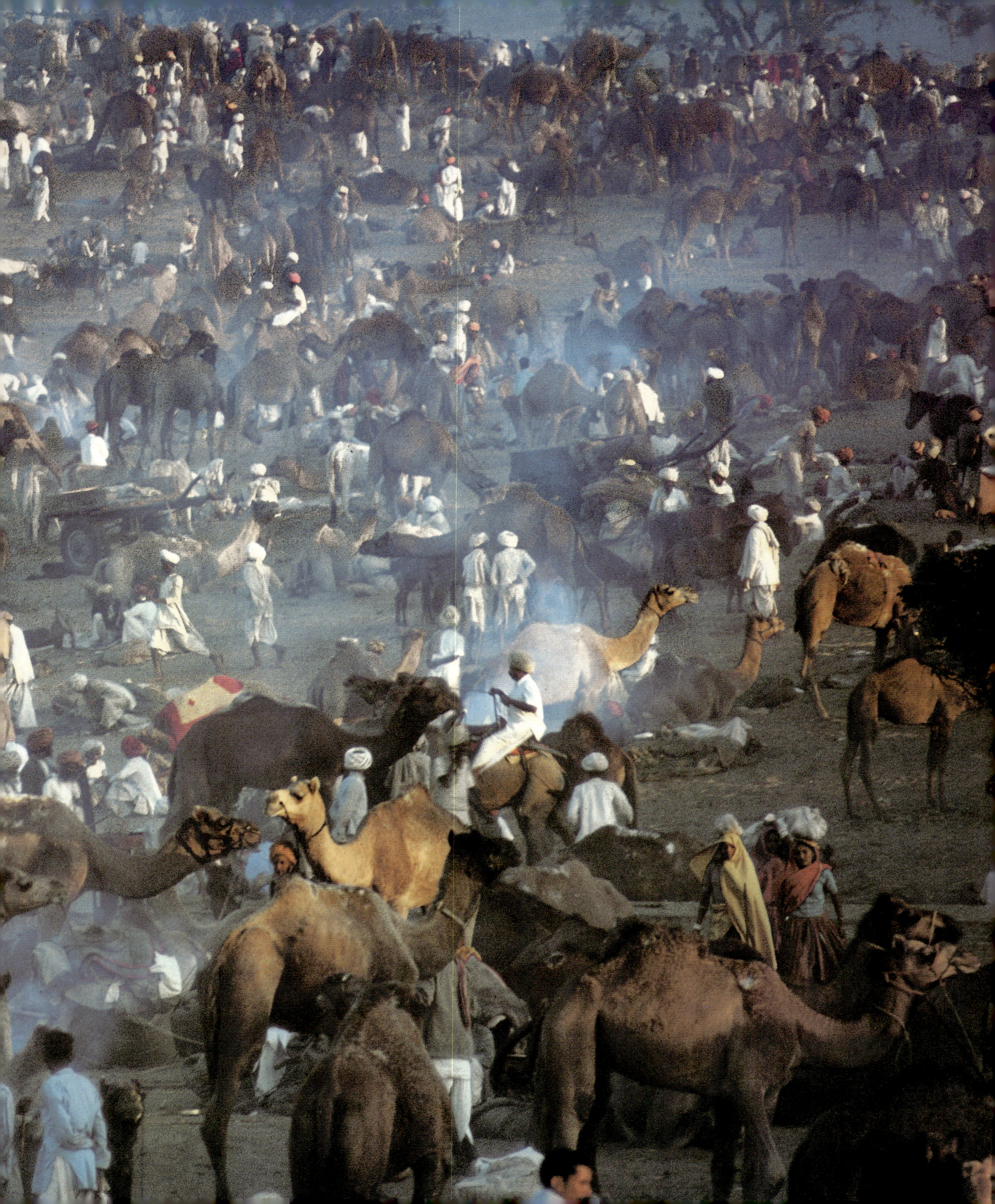

india: journey

through the

heart of a

continent

Photographs: Roland and Sabrina Michaud · Text: Olivier Germain-Thomas

Abbeville Press · Publishers   *New York · London*

For the English edition:
Editor: Susan Costello
Copy editor: Mary Christian
Production manager: Louise Kurtz
Production editors: Molly Dorozenski, Marie Dessaix
English translation: Josephine Bacon
Image layout: François Chevret
Map: Cartographie
Jacket design and interior typography: Maxim Zhukov

First Edition
10 9 8 7 6 5 4 3 2 1
ISBN: 0-7892-0869-5

Library of Congress Cataloging-in-Publication Data
Michaud, Roland.
India: journey through the heart of a continent /
photography by Roland & Sabrina Michaud;
text by Olivier Germain-Thomas.— 1st ed.
p. cm.
1. India—Description and travel. 2. India—Pictorial works.
I. Michaud, Sabrina. II. Germain-Thomas, Olivier, 1943– III. Title.
DS414.2.M53 2005
915.404'53'0222—dc22
2005014434

Contents

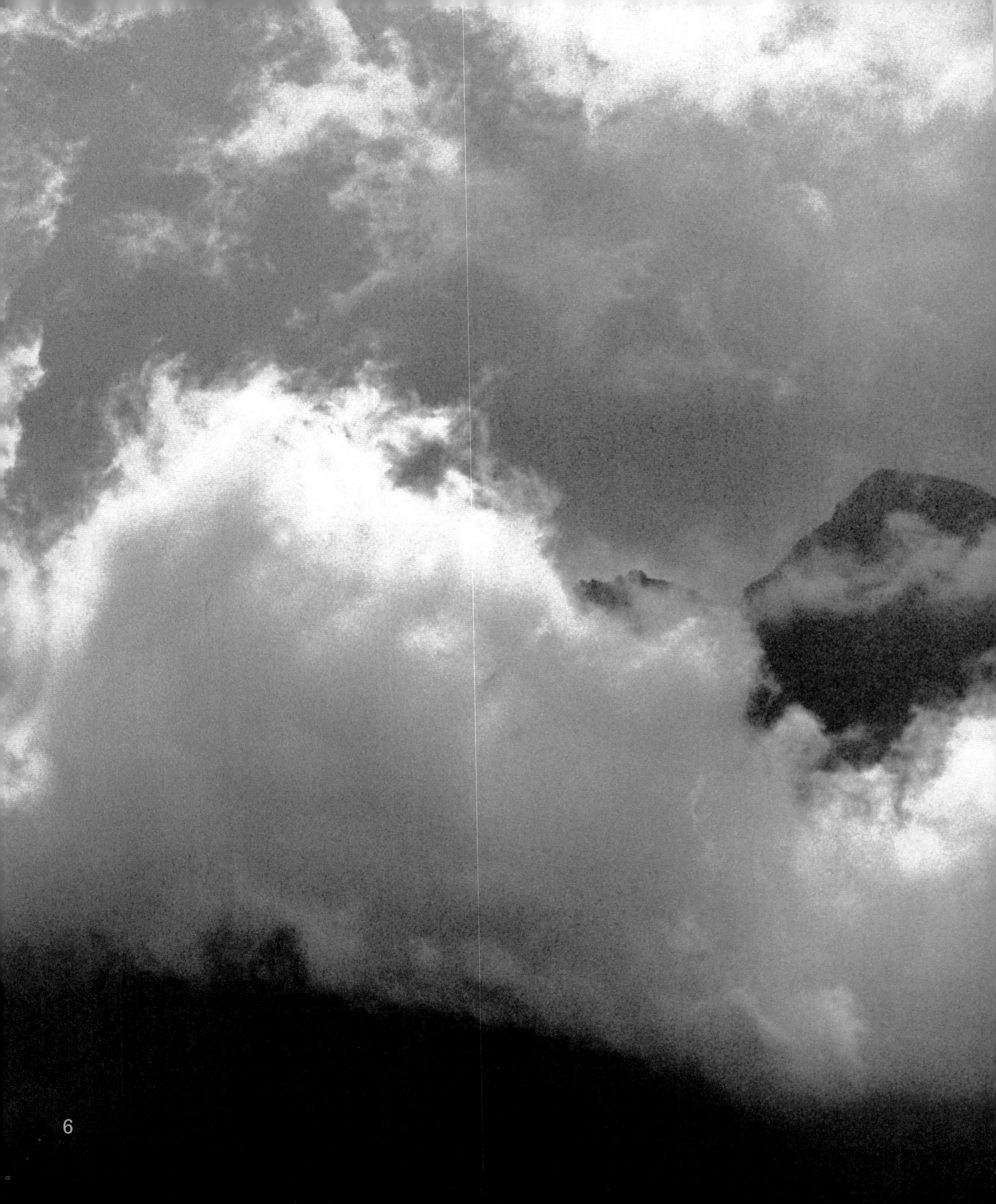

From 1965 through 2001 we traveled through India, sometimes for a whole year at a time. We photographed it constantly. Why India? Because it has everything. It is in a state of constant change; it fascinates and amazes us. India operates at two speeds: a modern speed, in which the problems are the same as our own, and another speed that is so traditional it seems to have emerged from the mists of time.

It is a whole world of its own; if it didn't exist, it couldn't be imagined.

India is a magical place that at every moment is bursting with the most vibrant life, in which the worst and the best, the sacred and the profane, reality and fantasy are combined. It continues to fascinate us even after thirty-six years of so many trips. It feeds our fantasies, heightens our feelings, revives our emotions, questions our certainties, and reconciles opposites.

Isn't Shiva both the master of eroticism and the god of ascetics? We need at least a lifetime simply to understand India a little and love it a lot. But what is one life on earth when compared to the whole of eternity?

Roland and Sabrina Michaud

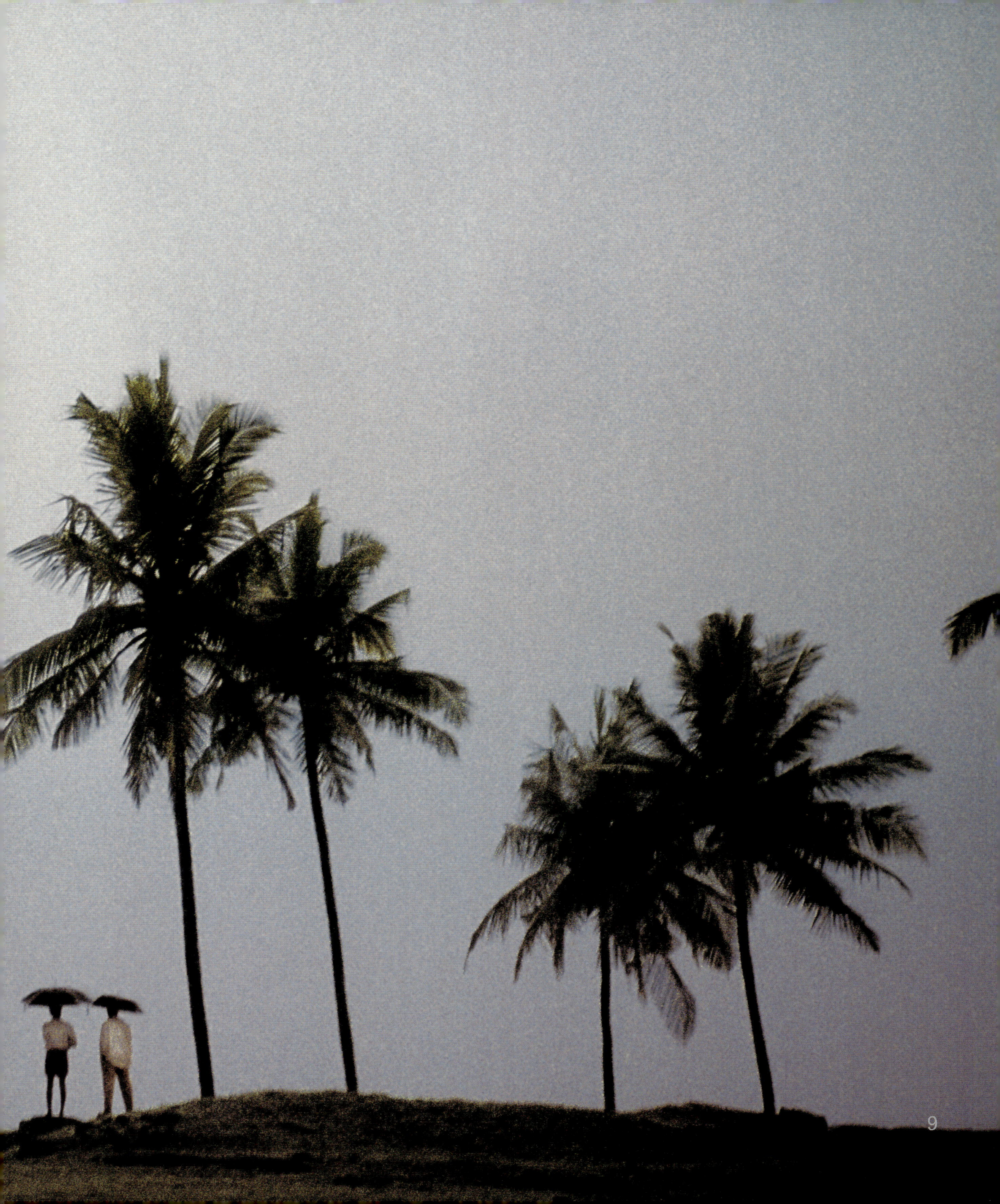

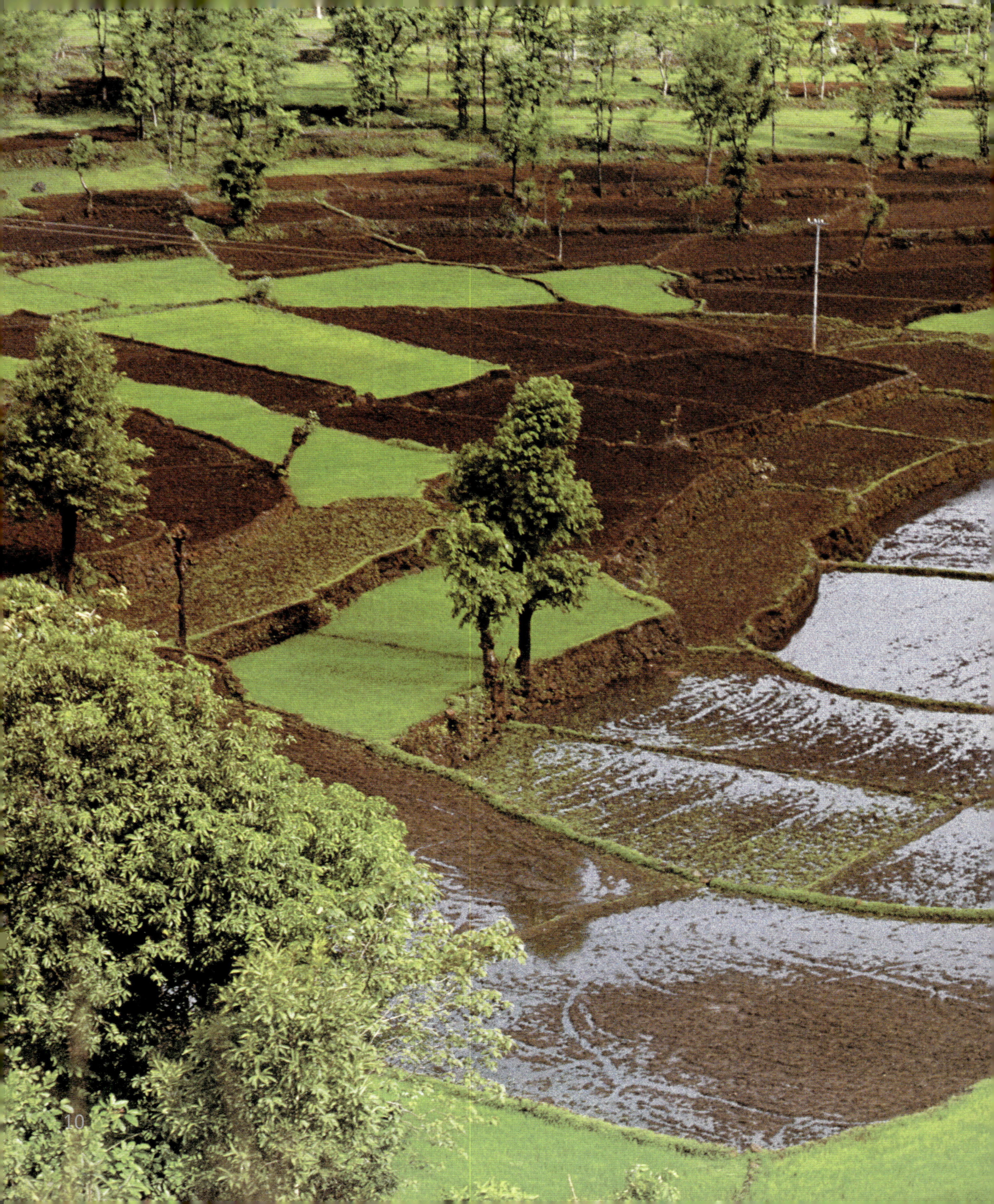

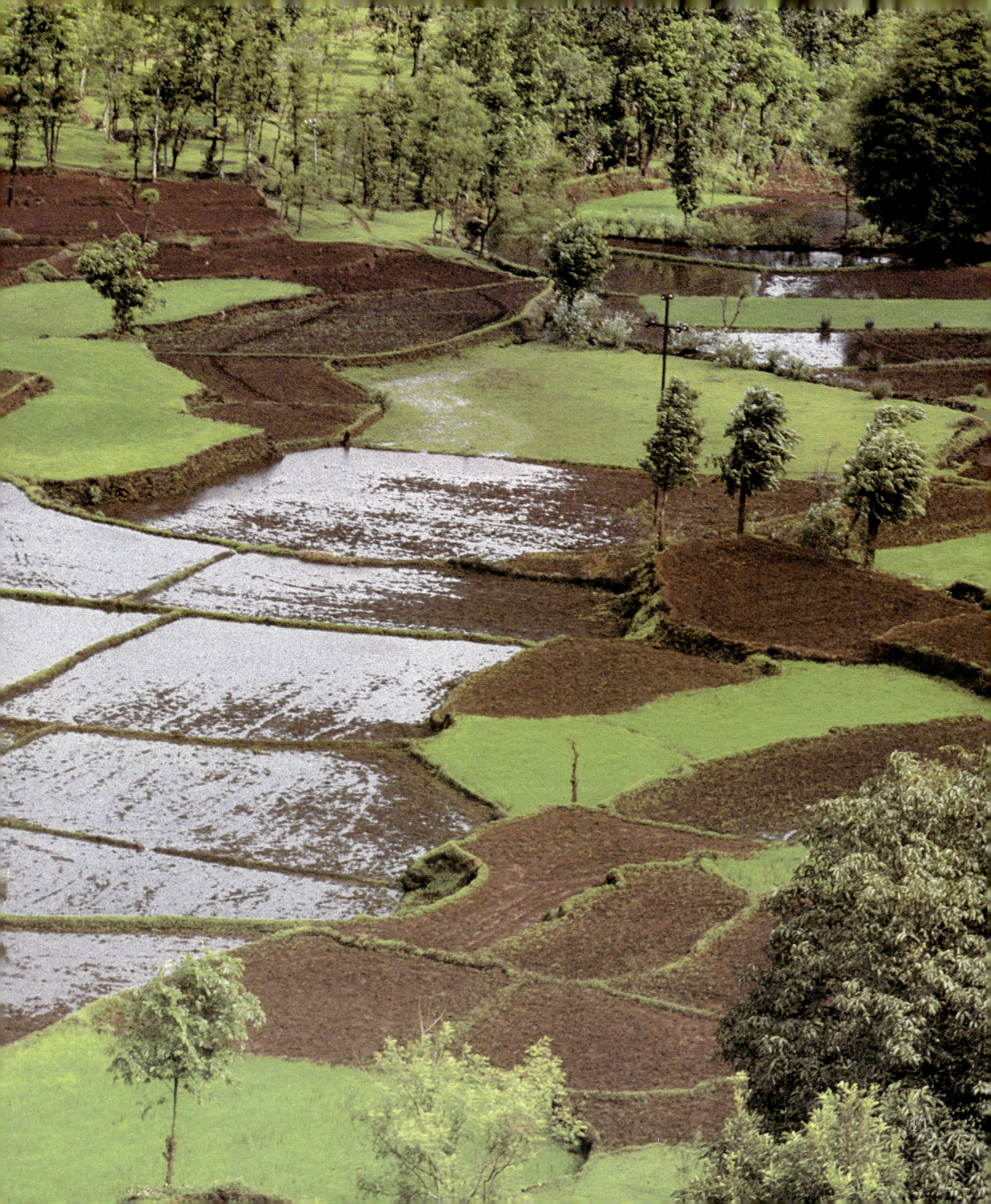

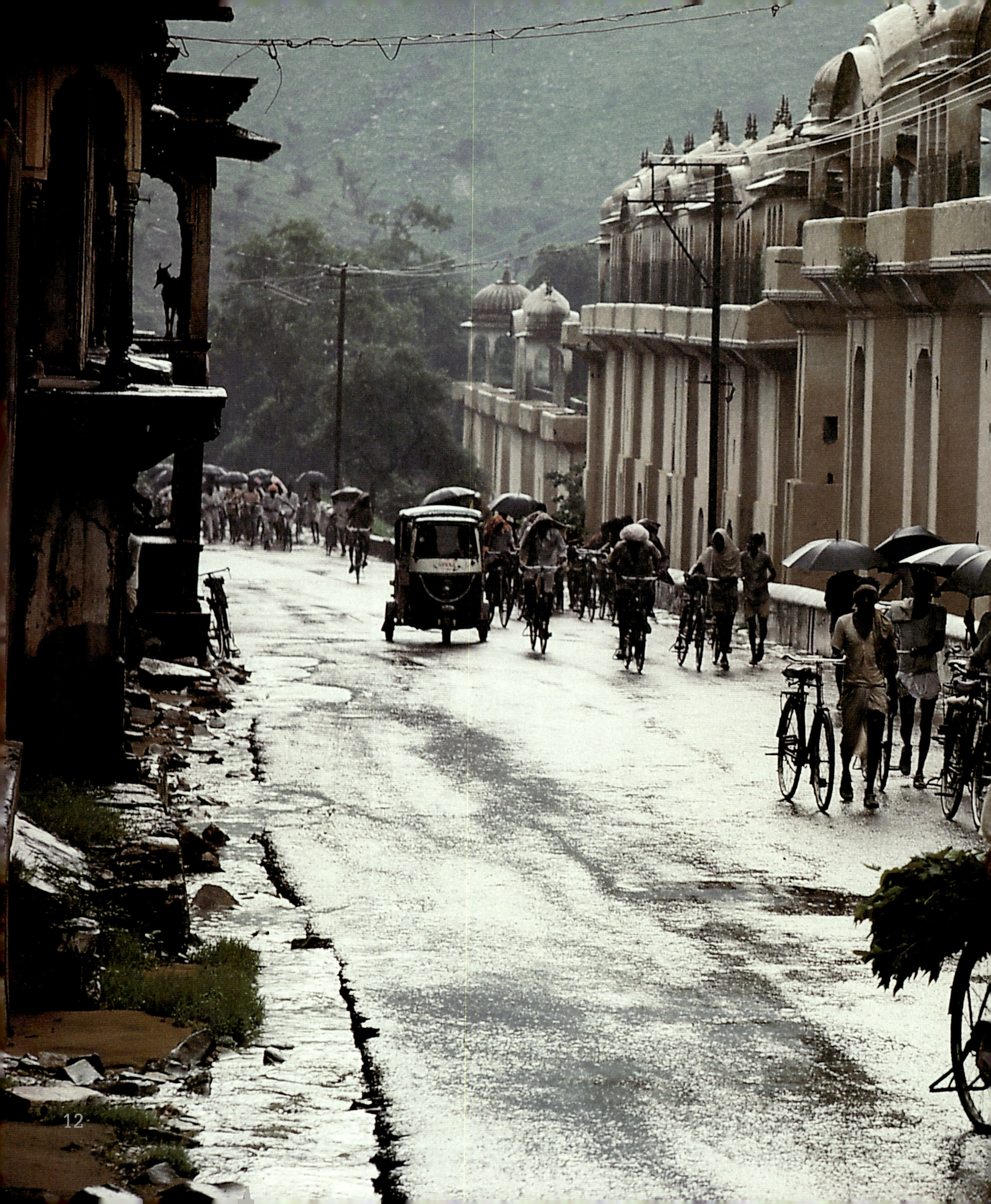

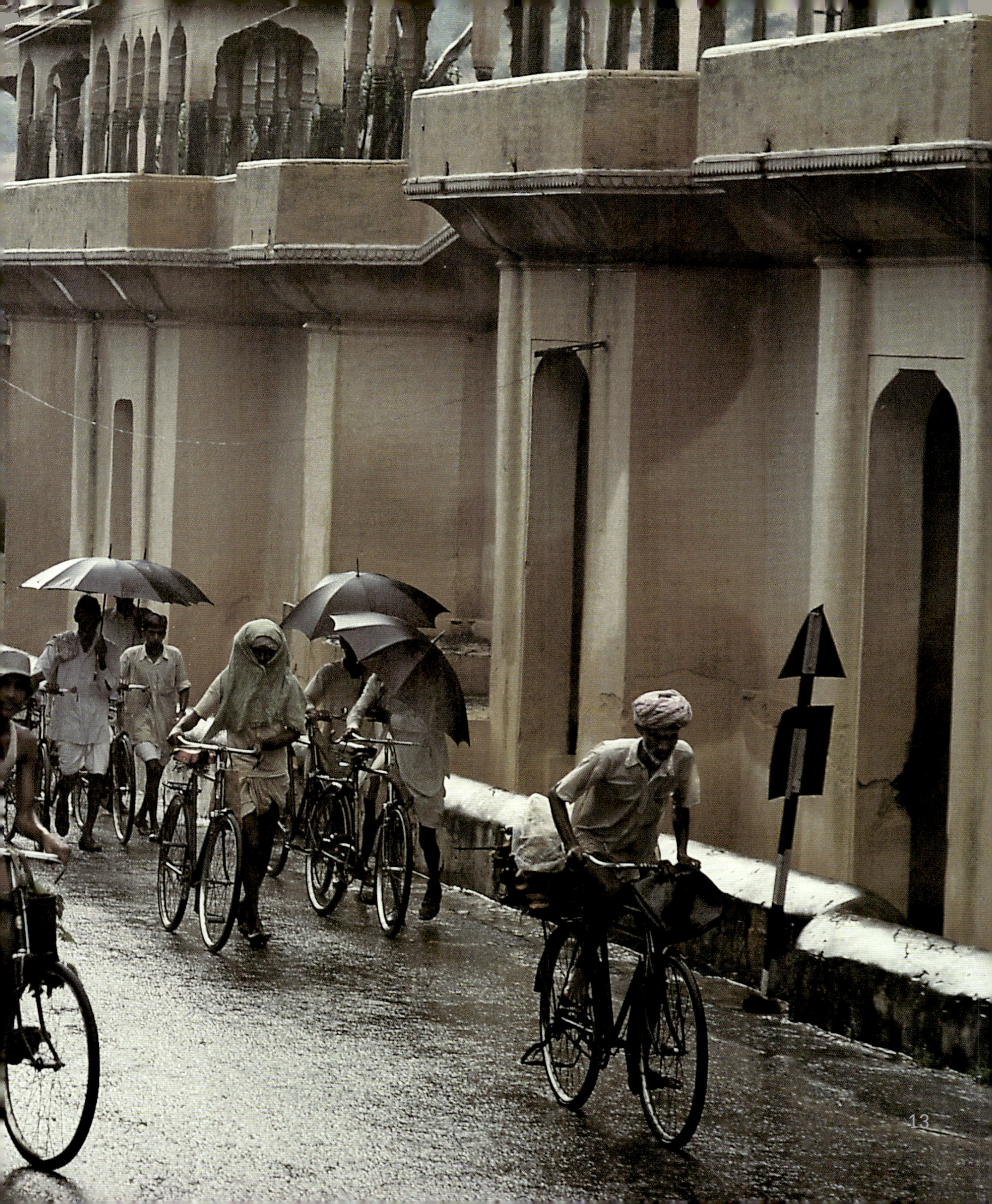

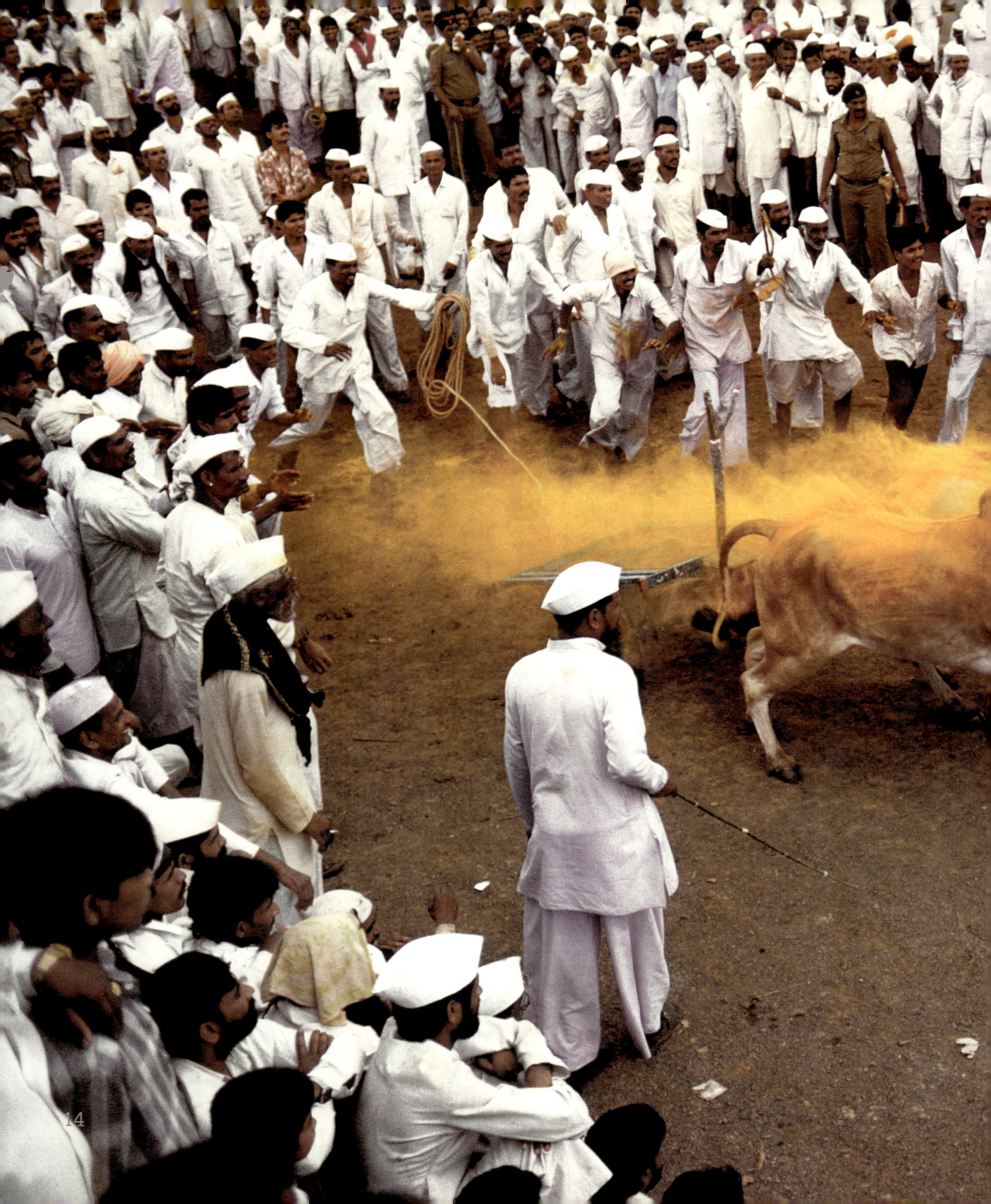

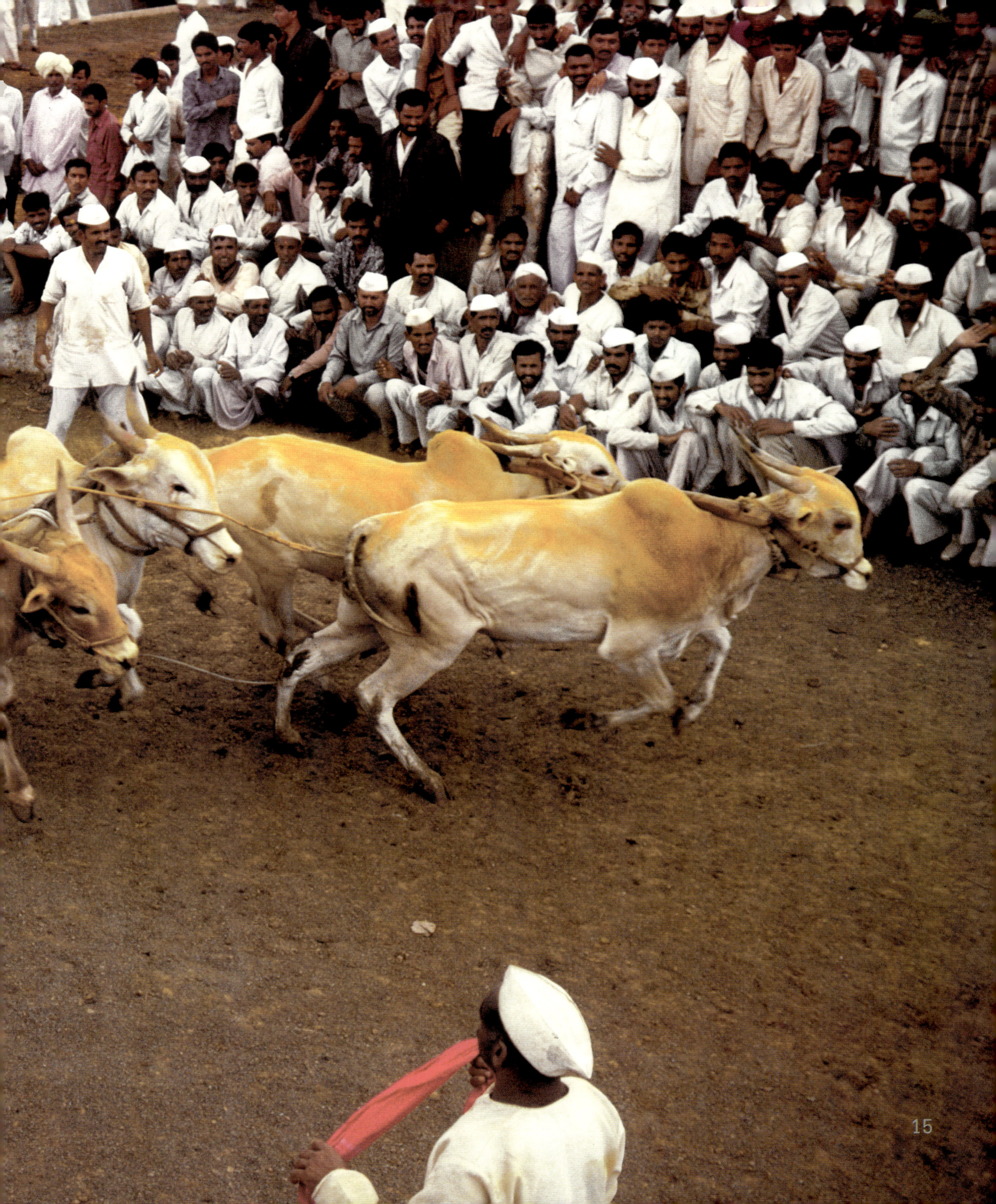

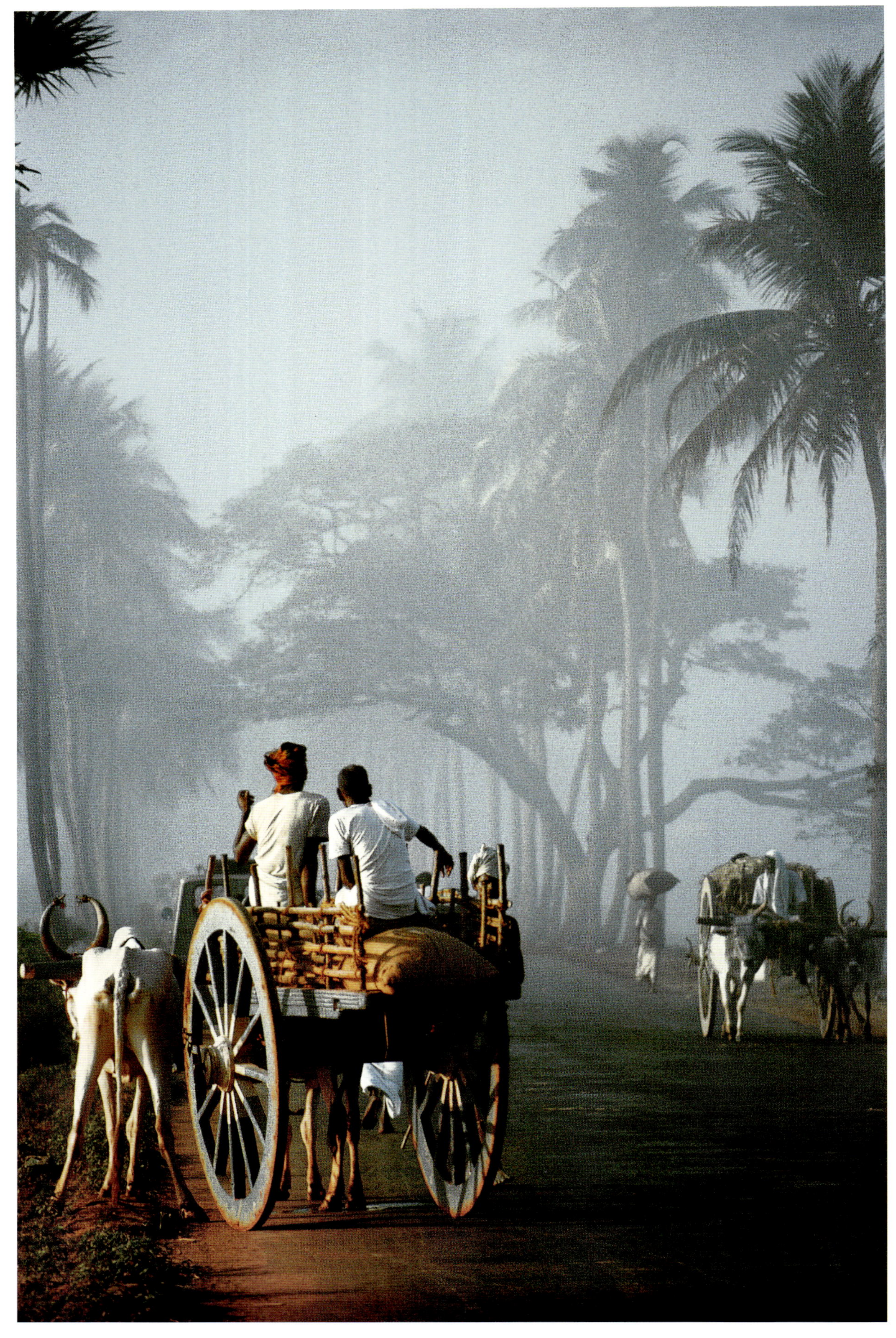

16   A Road in Tamil.

Desire came upon that One in the beginning;
That was the first seed of mind.

Rig-Veda

This text is a ramble through India written by a traveler who has explored India for more than thirty years. India has shaped his mind and reached depths of sensitivity hidden away since his childhood.

While still helping to contribute to an encyclopedic knowledge of the country, the route draws on experiences that will start to enlighten you about what distinguishes India from other great civilizations. Extracts included from the founding literature and from India's great writers will expand on these points of view, and at the end of the book the detailed captions for the photographs by Roland and Sabrina Michaud are supplemented by a map, a glossary, a chronology, and a bibliography to enrich the impressions you receive from the images and the text. Is it important to learn more to see better, or to see without knowing too much to get a better sense of place? The spirit of this book enables all readers to dip into it as they see fit.

India has always preferred to represent statues of a divinity as having both a male and female aspect. Can these photographs and words be assembled to form a single figure? They should be understood in this way. While the text clearly cannot serve as a commentary on the photographs, it has been written to provide insight about them. The metaphors are sometimes obvious, as if the same scene had been lit in two different ways; sometimes they are subterranean, playing on indirect relationships.

As for the way the chapters are arranged, although there is a certain order to the book, it has been produced in a way that takes into account the propensity for a reader to open an illustrated book at the end. The book can thus be started from several points. Remember that the mandala is circular and that the divinity is at its center, not at the edges. It is the genius of India to conceive of a multiple center.

Olivier Germain-Thomas

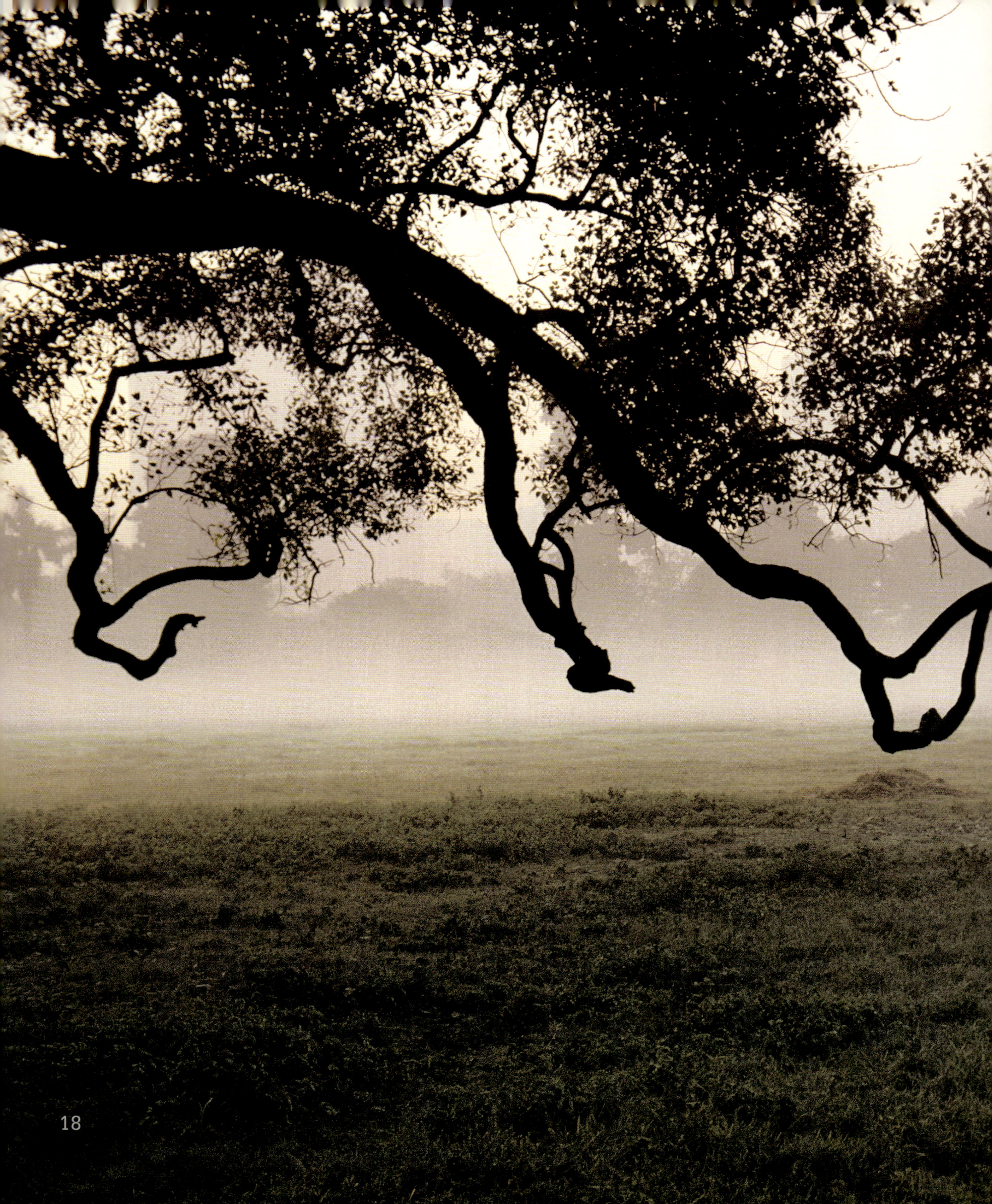

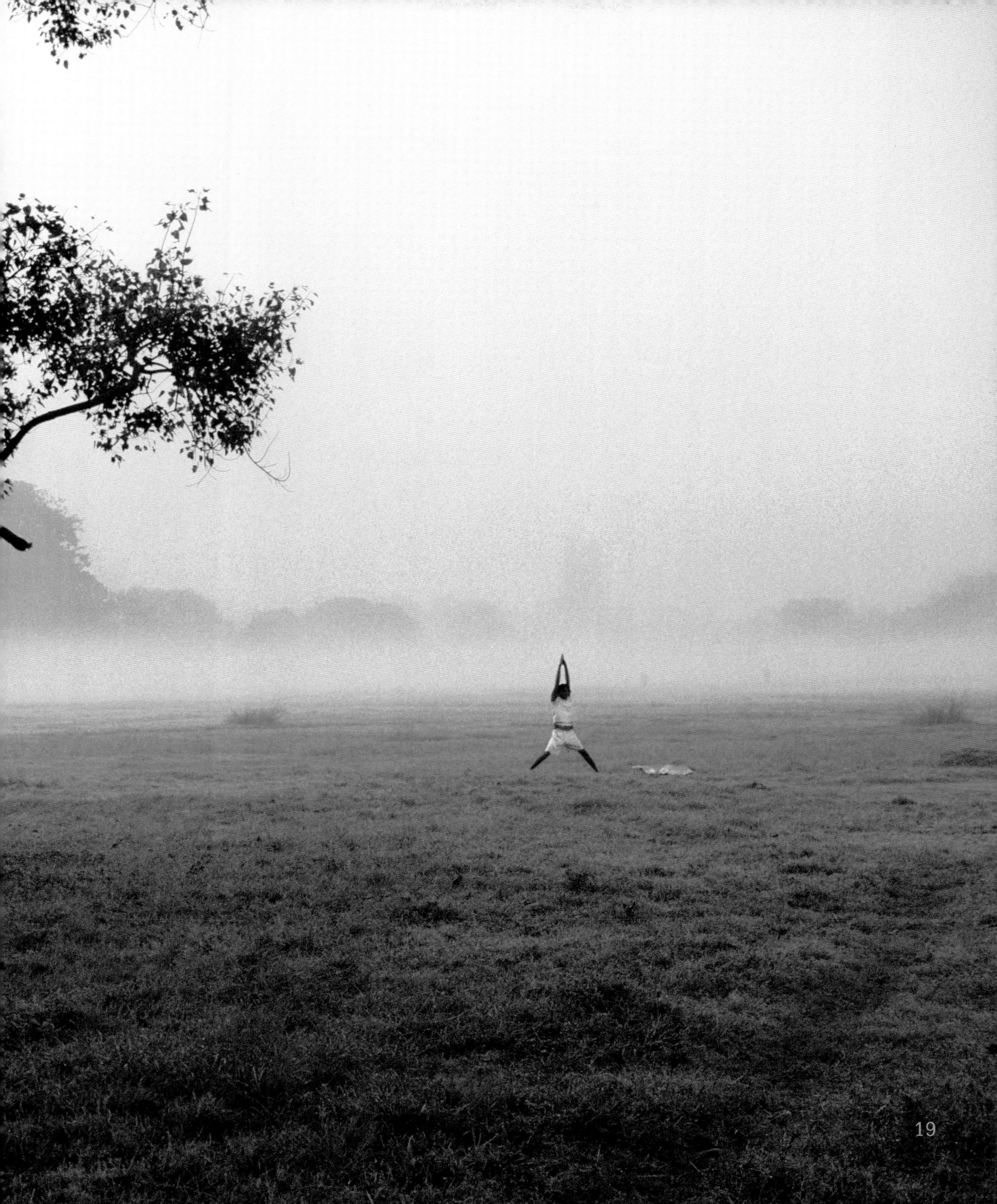

Fire and water

*All that is, all that was, and all that will be, all that moves and
all that is immobile: The Sun [Surya] is the origin and the end.*

Shaunaka, *Brihaddevata*, 1:61

For B.

The earth is like the skin of a mummy. We walk on parched earth from which a fine brown dust rises, known as time. Behind its veil, the sun admires the damage it has caused—the scorched plants, parched cattle, dried-up ponds. No adoration can calm the ardor of the sun. A stray dog still moves along the dried-up river bed. It is waiting for night, when it dies. Is there a part of consciousness that remembers past lives and hopes for a future life that is better than its present miserable condition? First this creature will have to submit to the fire of heaven, celebrated in anthems. Know that one does not worship what is good, one worships what is there; as it is with the sun, the serpent, with Kali and her necklace of skulls, with Shiva dancing around the flames, or with the two sexes in one.

There is a banyan tree on this bare plateau. It looks as if it had fallen from the sky rather than born of this dead land. The tree has genius, being cunning enough to understand the capriciousness of the seasons. In order to protect itself, it puts out new roots from amidst its branches and these go in search of the water that the earth conceals. The trunk and dozens of roots form a colonnade, or rather, a temple. There you have it. No opportunity to worship is ever missed in India. The goats are aware of it. They sit in the circle of shade provided by the banyan tree. Their panting breath resounds like a prayer. India has always venerated the tree. It has been a sanctuary from the very beginning and the house of divinity. It still houses the statues that can cure us. While awaiting his Awakening under a tree, the Buddha elevated it into a master. Seated against a tree trunk, man finds the means to rediscover his true nature, a nature that is hidden like water under the earth or like the permanent beneath the apparent, something that is repeated in multiple forms in Indian philosophy.

From the shade to the horizon where sky and earth merge in a yellowish dust, there is death. The sun's pressure is so great that nothing can move, as if gripped in a vise.

As if to contradict me, a truck jolts along a road leading eastward. Its windows and metalwork intermittently reflect a brilliant flash of sunlight. Who is the madman who thinks he is above the power of the burning fire? He has no face. He leaves behind him a black trail that is soon replaced by the yellow that sucks up all life. The put-put of the engine is also swallowed up by the dust. And now we are floored by the silence. It is reassuring to believe that there is an absolute here, and to seize it as if it were a condition of life. We find ourselves in conflict with that Indian wariness of illusion that consists in believing in the reality of the world. The forms of "reality" are mere outward appearances: wide expanses, light, open space, silence.

As if to reinforce this teaching, an ascetic (*sannyasi**) would have to appear, walking forward covered in ashes, with a shock of hair like that of John the Baptist. Impossible! Those who fear neither hunger nor wild beasts have no love of the sun. Detachment is practiced with keen attention to the rhythms of life. The bells in the temples that herald the fire-offering ceremony have never required us to burn ourselves. It's about taming the fire, something that is impossible at this time of year. Although there is not a human soul about, in the distance a shape shimmers in the dust. It is a rocky hillock rising from the plain. Holy from the beginning, it is naturally adorned with a shrine so burning hot that it can only be claimed by the imagination. Seen from above, the sun, sky, and earth appear to be forced into matrimony in the same land that resounded to the delicate love songs of Krishna and Radha.

What will be the condition of the first village inside this burning brazier? Has it been abandoned? No. It is serene, man and beast together under the thatched roof, waiting for the (feeble) respite that the night will bring.

Are the people anguished? Not at all. For millennia they have been used to the brutality of the seasons, and they wait with serenity for the moment when the sun will change its mood. Nothing is fixed, according to the founding texts. How is it possible not to be turned upside down by the movement of the world? Stability is to be found in oneself. The Indian peasant knows it by instinct. Sitting beside him in the dog days of

**This and other Sanskrit terms are defined in the glossary on page 302.*

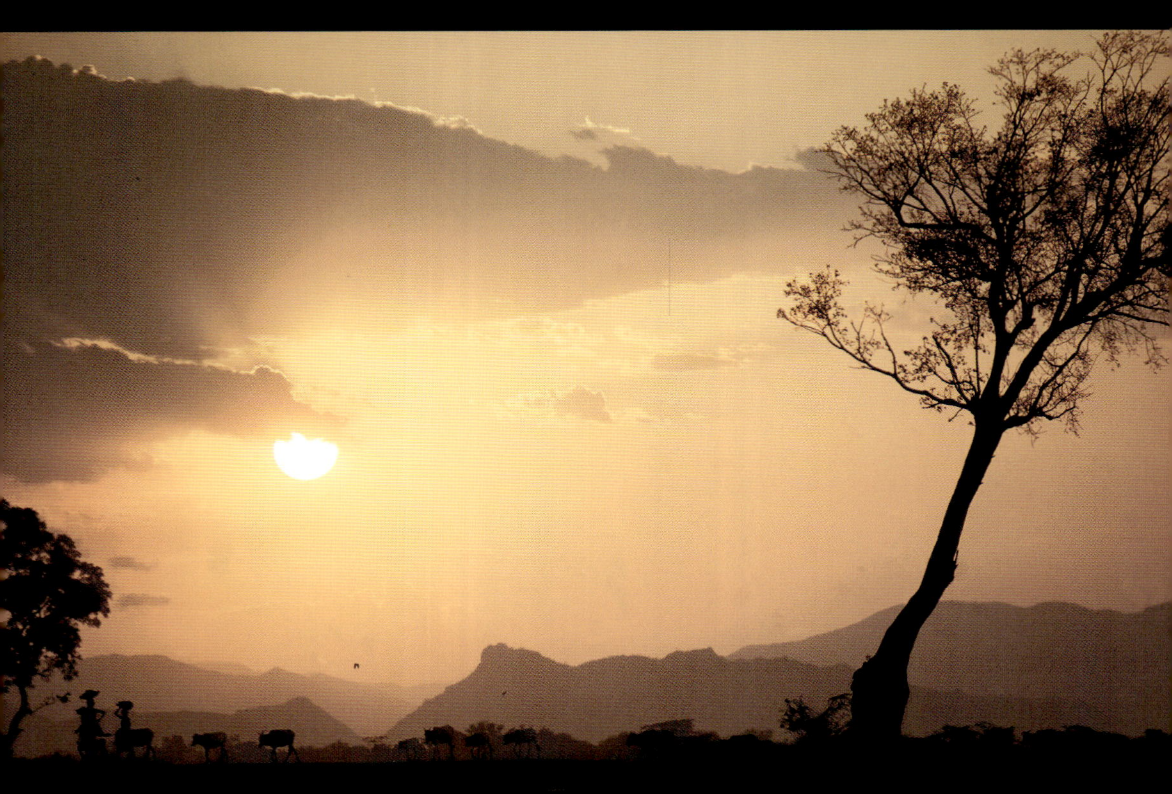

Above: Sunrise over the trees.
Opposite: Pastoral scene.

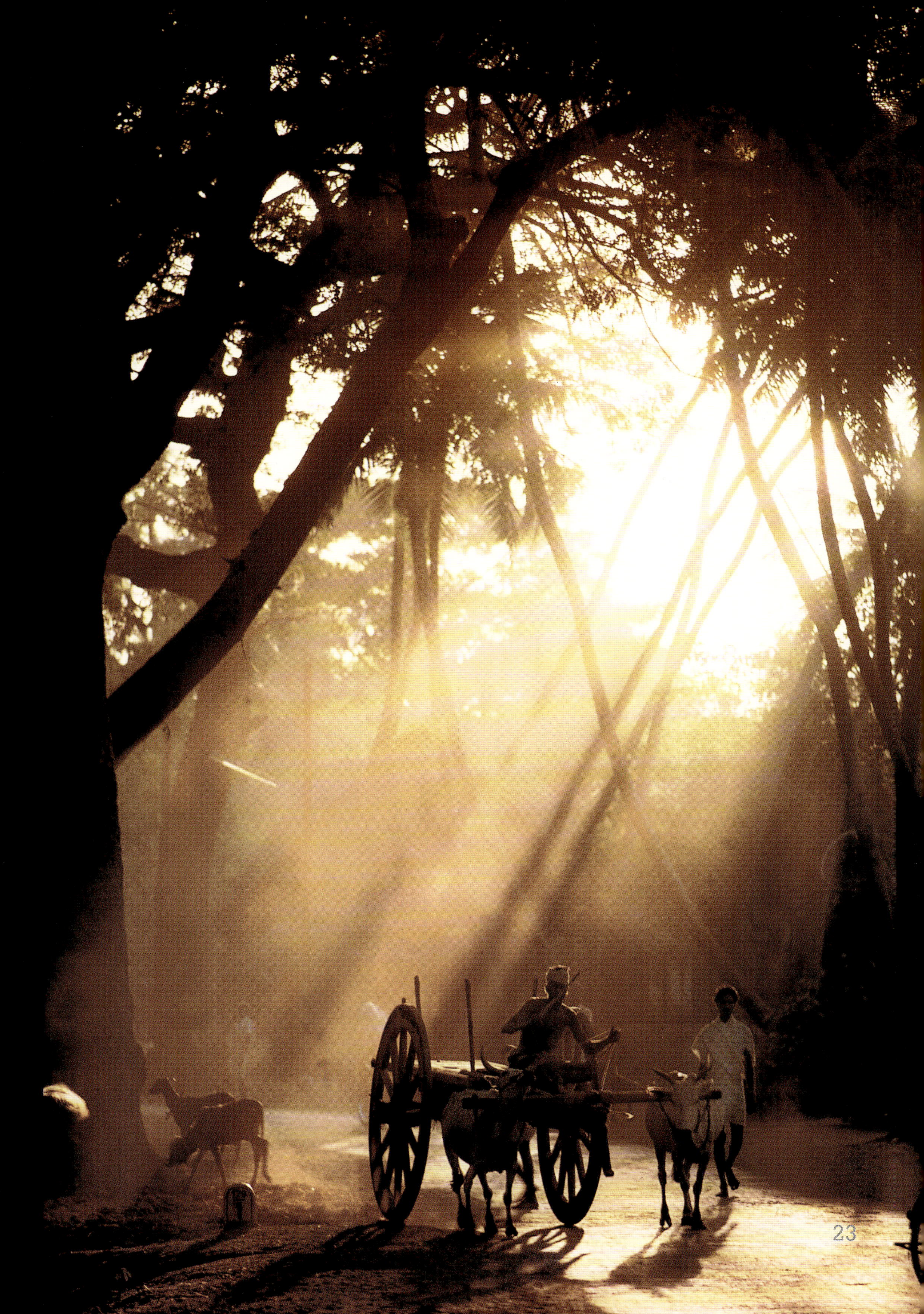

summer or in a storm is to comprehend his strength. To call it indifference is a misnomer. It is, in fact, a permanent bond with a different reality. It is late afternoon in the village. Sunset is short but of such magnificence as to make the most stubborn of skeptics into a believer. The women are at the riverside. Slip, slap—they beat the red and green cloth against the stones, while the laughter of the naked children is ignored by the cattle who are drinking from the trickle of water. The earth from above has taken on a moribund face that attempts a last smile: a trace of water.

Waters, source of happiness,
pray give us vigor so that we
may contemplate the great delight!

Rig-Veda, 10:9

As night falls, the sounds of the village become sharper. The cry of an infant, the grinding of a wheel, the bleating of a goat. A few hours before dawn, sleep takes over and man and beast sleeping outdoors have a short respite before the red horsemen arrive.

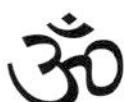

Violence is sleeping on the earth. Might it be possible to reach the tree, merely experiencing a simple shower, although the stinging rain is hard enough to throw bodies into the mud. Over there, the path has become a raging torrent. The waters sweep the earth away and it is impossible to see more than a few feet ahead. It's as if a madman had streaked a drawing of the creation with angry lines. In this village, all the roofs have collapsed and the waters that have collected on the paths are sweeping along pieces of wood, bloated rats, peelings, dishes, a hen cackling helplessly, a blue sari. From the top of the hillock (the same one), sky and earth invent shades of gray. Land? Land is a mass of gyrating water. Sky? A burst bladder with infinite reserves.

The river has swollen to six times its size before the monsoon. It rumbles in shades of brown and beige, sweeping away soil, ox carts, and, this morning, a lost child. There was no one to hear his cries.

The roads are deserted, the trains have stopped running, the iron bridge has collapsed, just as it did last year, carrying train number 6043, from which most of the passengers emerged unharmed, thanks to their prayers.

The uproar is even greater in the cities where you move through calf-deep water, while the tin roofs clatter in response to the squalls of rain. Life outside—that is, almost all of life—carries on or ceases as is dictated by the clouds. From the shoeshine boys to the fortune-tellers, those who ply their trade on the sidewalks have been chased away while the children and the elderly wait for a respite that will restore their territory to them. They laugh. Why are they laughing when everything around them is gray? They laugh because life is laughter and it is particularly amusing to find oneself beneath the water of a river. Without electricity, the night again learns the power of darkness, unless a gust of wind sets the moon free. It then becomes a fairyland of thousands of pearls running off the roofs and silver filaments snaking through the streets. You stop and are captivated. Who is there to thank?

Another cloud. Once again you have to stretch out your arms to move forward, watch out for potholes, walls, planks of wood. Lightning. Oh! The nakedness of the city—it has never looked so beautiful. Praying hands. Splash! Suddenly, you find yourself in the midst of a putrid swamp. Invoke the *Veda*:

O farseeing Sun, bearer of Light,
The joy of every single eye,
May we live to see your glorious radiance
Flooding in as you ascend on high!

Rig-Veda, 10:37

There is one certainty: properly recited prayers are always answered—if not today, then in a hundred years' time.

The sun returns five days after the vomiting of the sky. It makes no excuses. It brings down on everything a liquid, trembling light that brings proof that if the gods have brought the world out of the shadows, it was to admire the liquid gold coursing down from the banyan tree after the rain. They are rightly said to be disgusted with the human race. But Krishna has recovered his flute in the forest in which these shiver.

In the beginning, the whole was enveloped in utter darkness.
Nothing was discernible.
By the great power of Warmth was born the One. . . .
Who knows then whence it first came into being?

Rig-Veda, 10:9

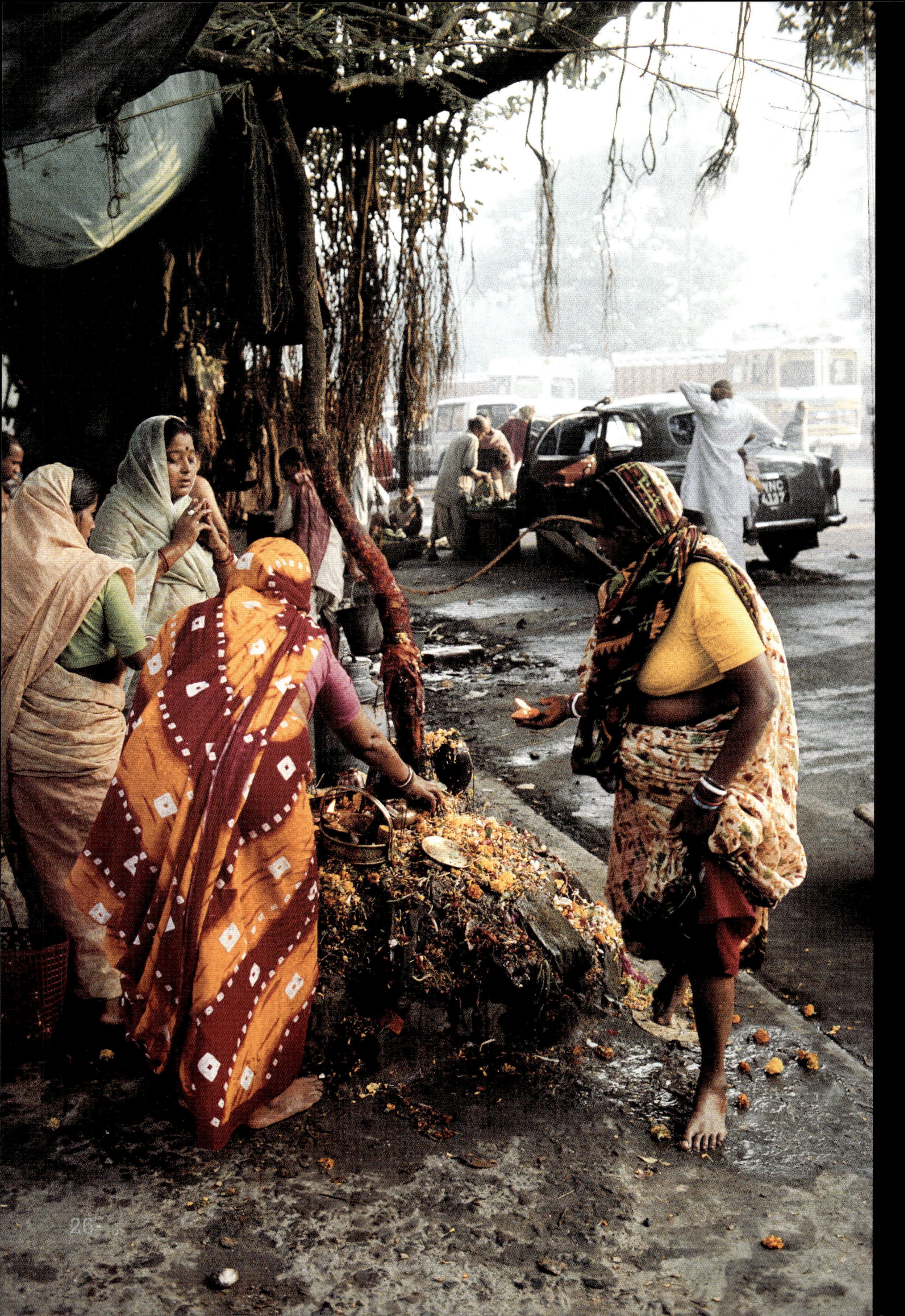

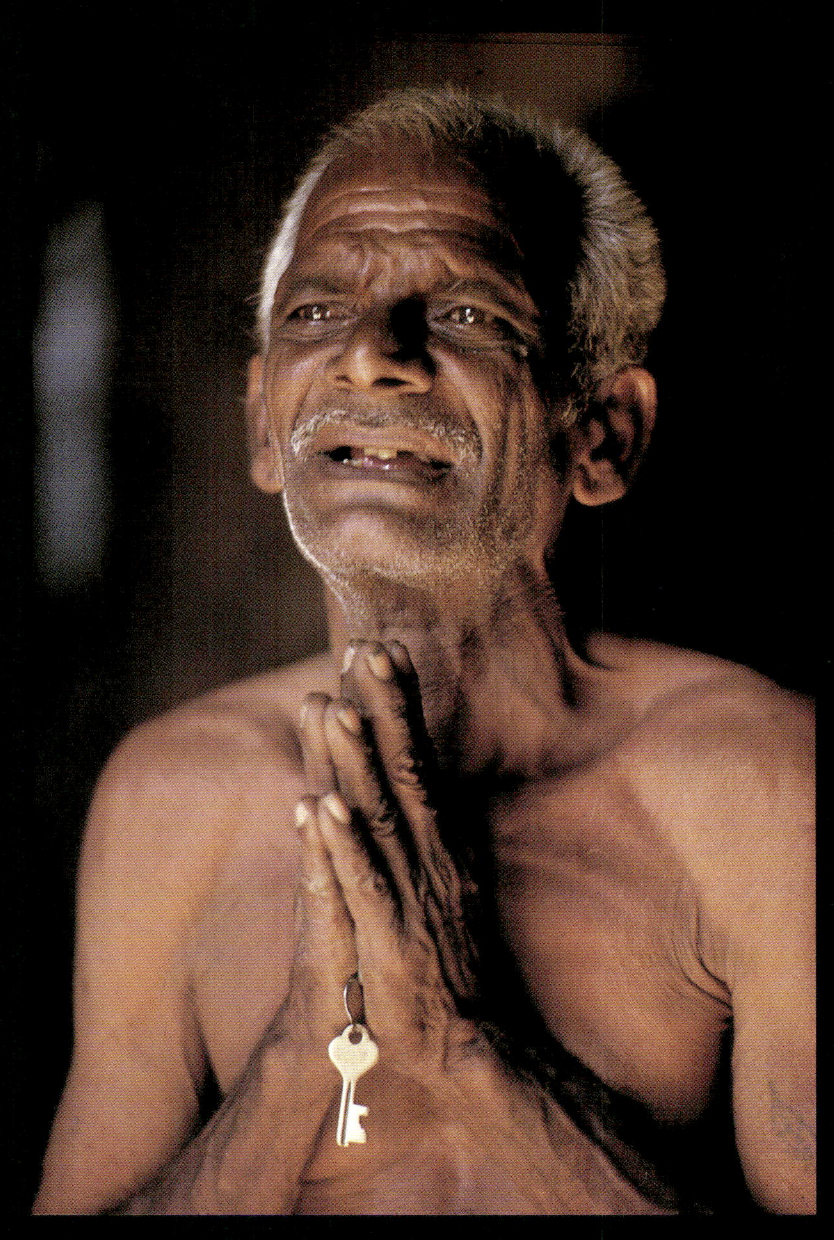

Opposite: Street scene in Calcutta.
Above: Traditional greeting.

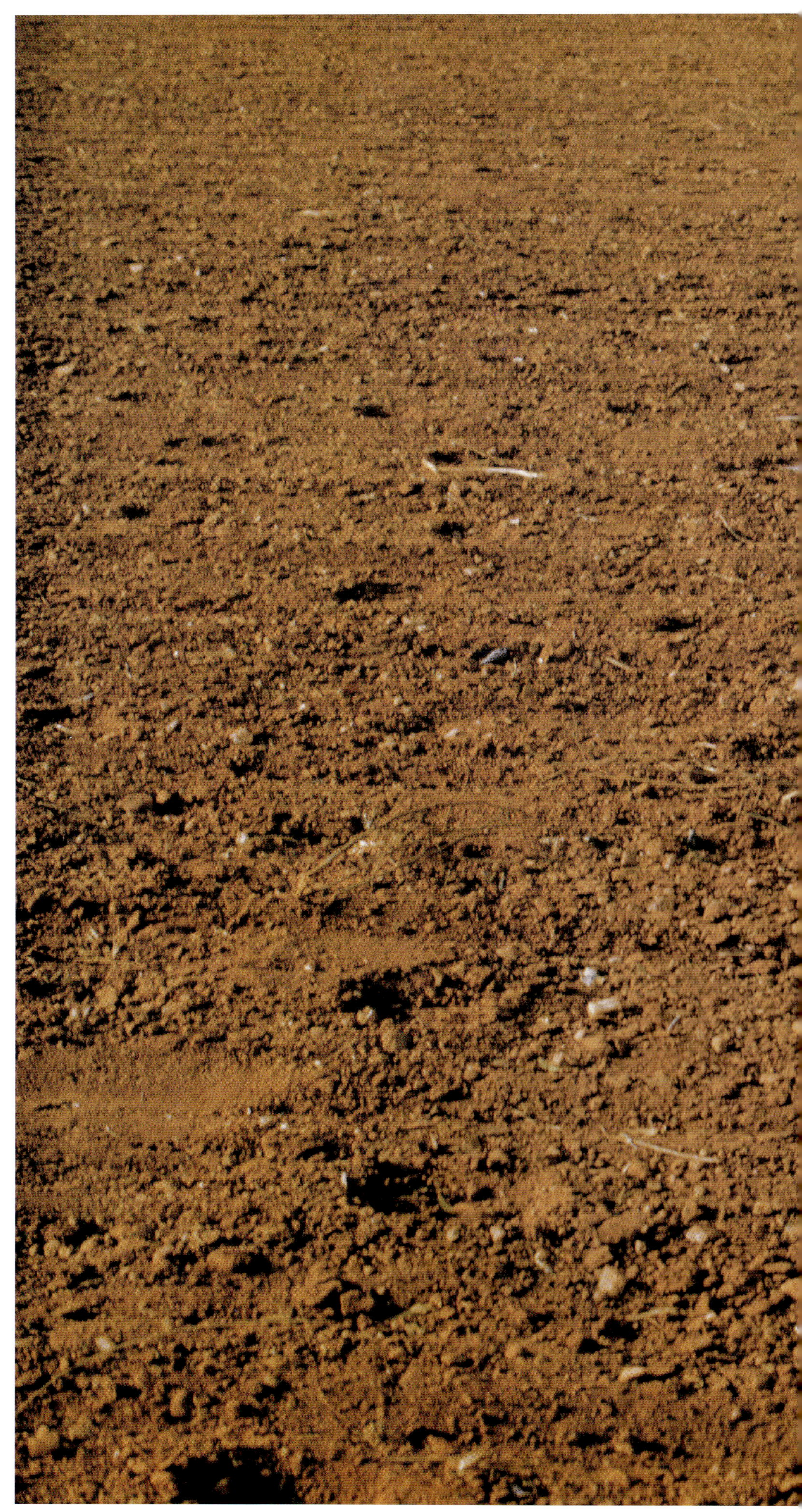

Peasant woman
in Karnataka.

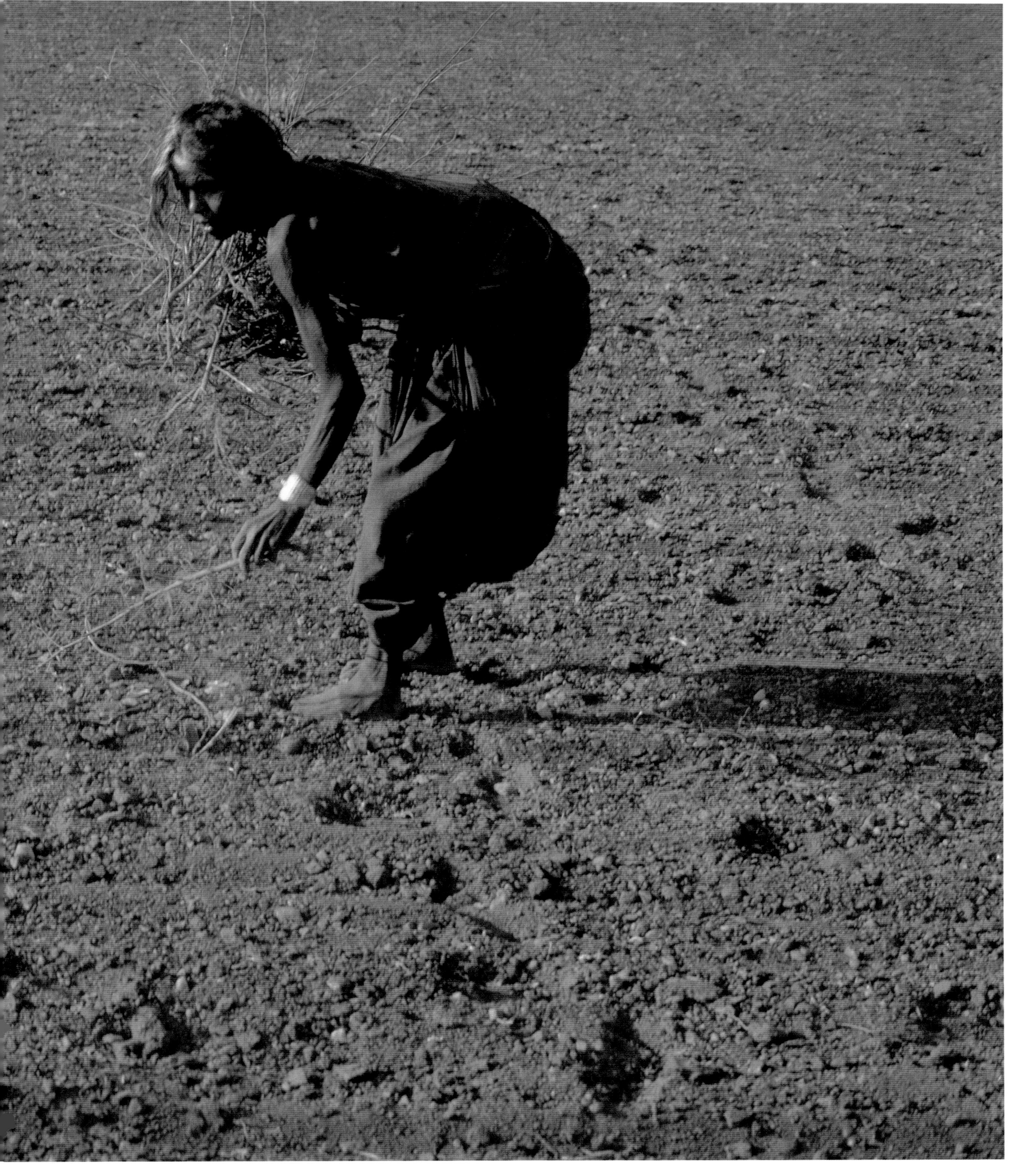

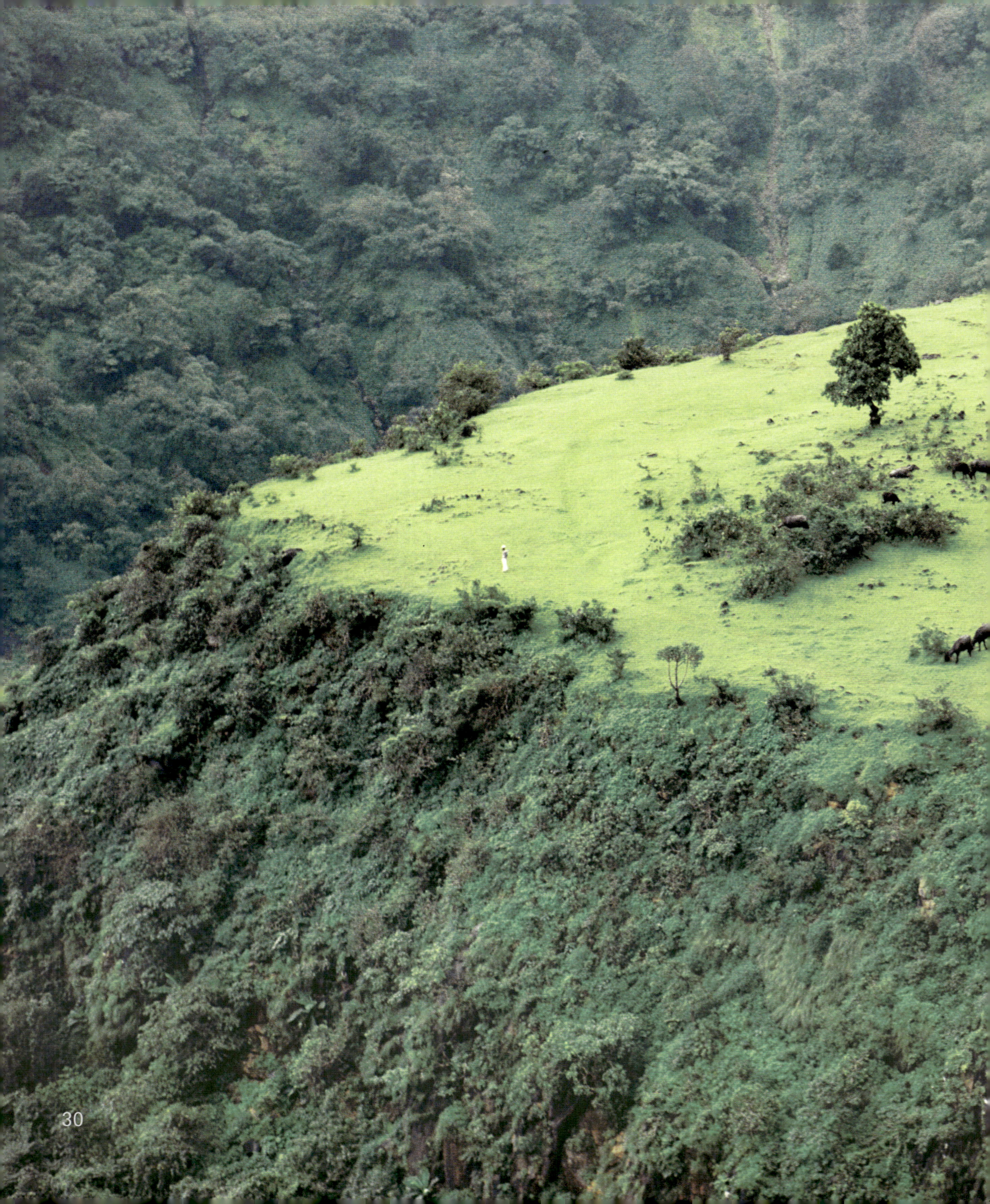

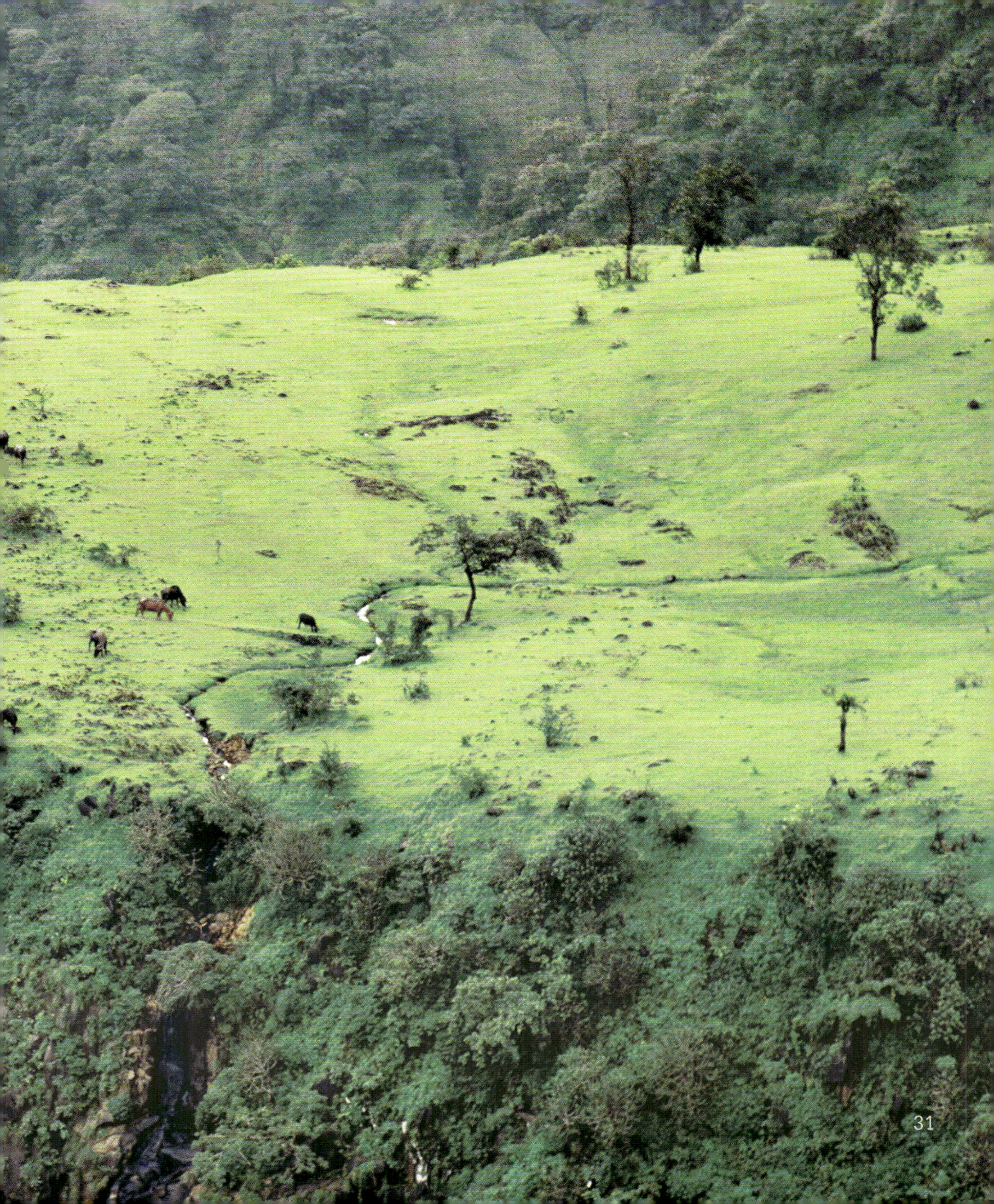

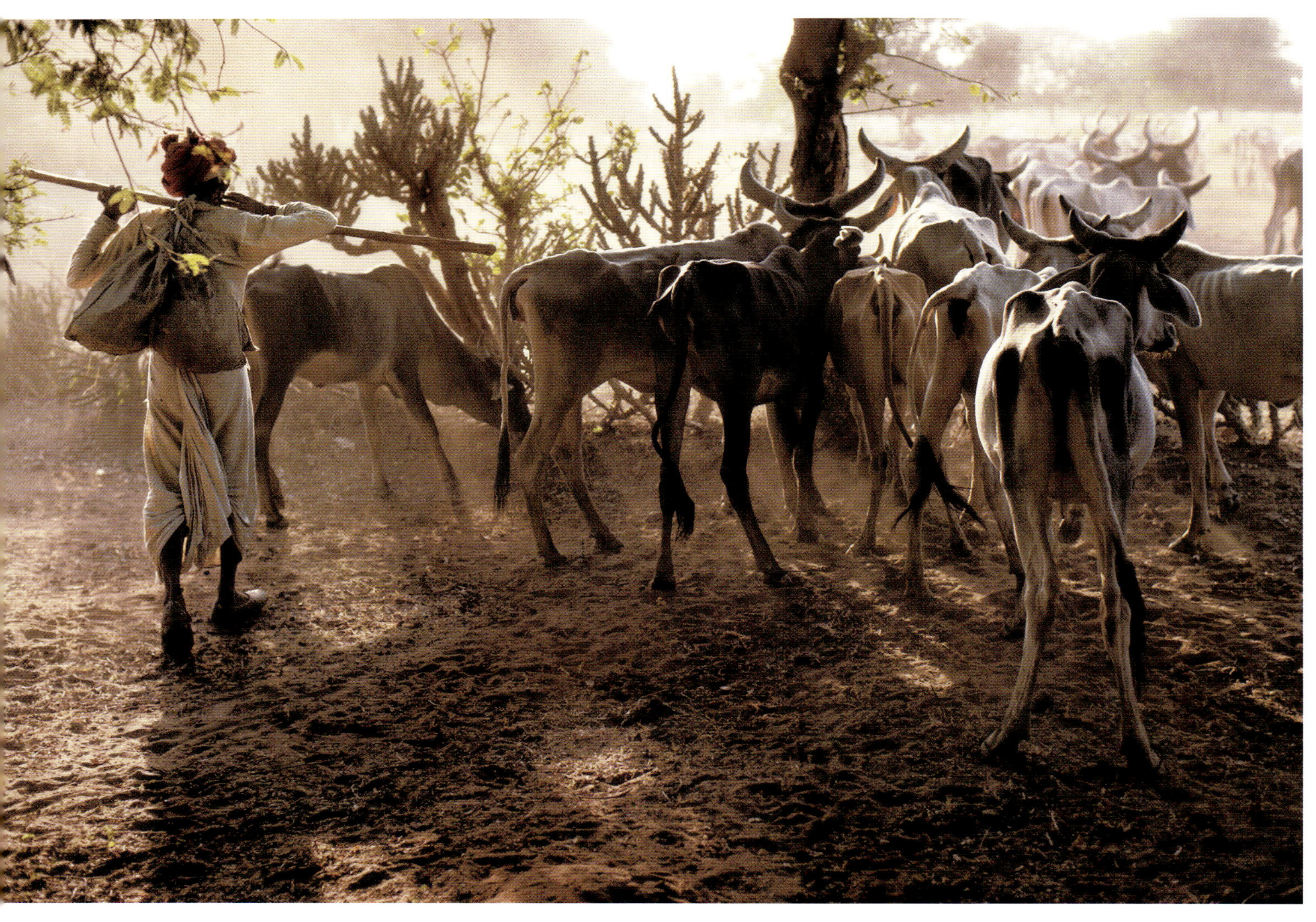

Above: Herd of cattle. Opposite: Children.
Pages 30–31: Pastoral scene in Maharashtra.

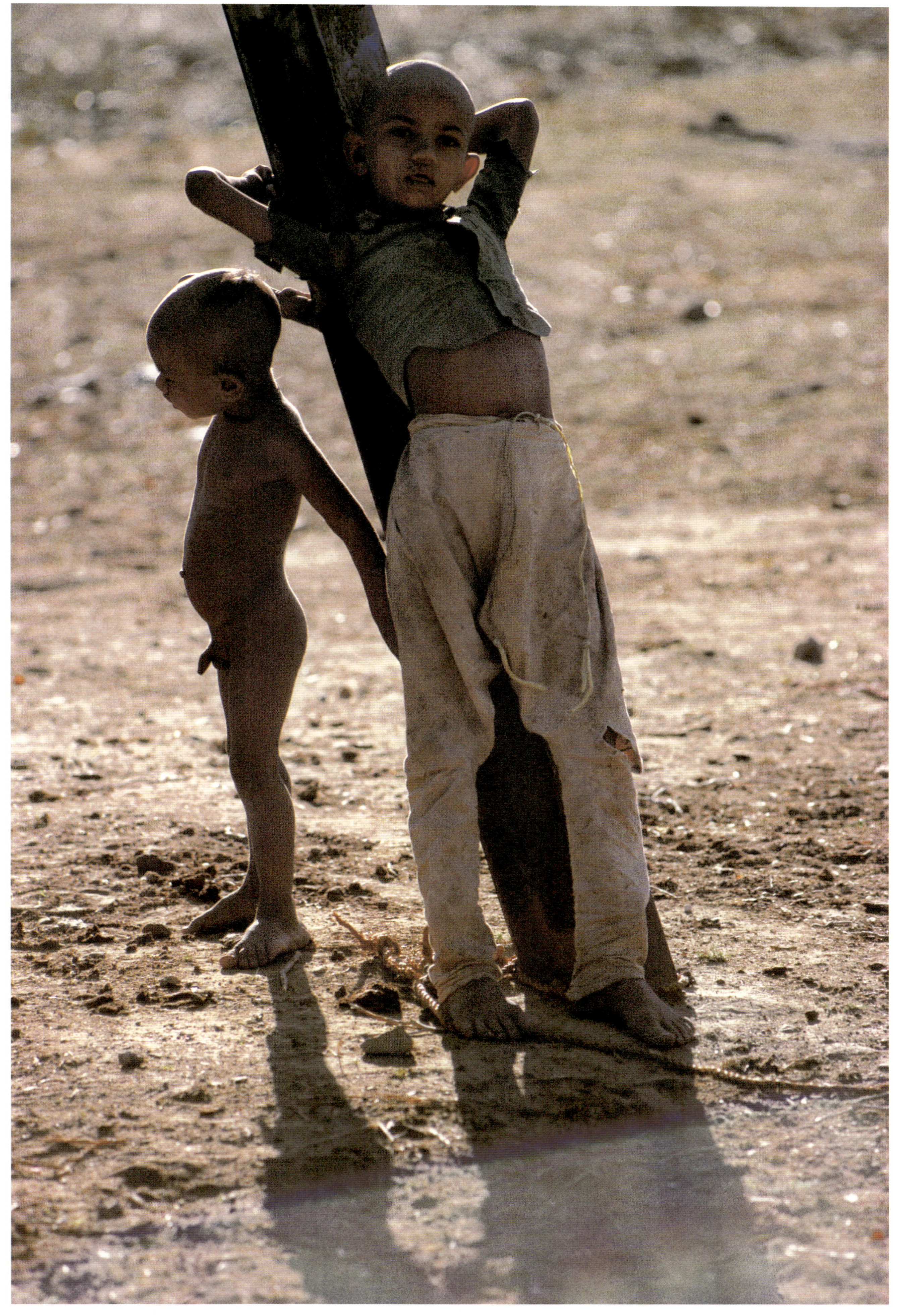

Capturing the essence of India

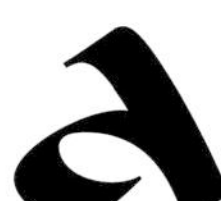clear night, that Indian night that shows the other half of the sky. The constellations are clearly delineated. Leo and Capricorn are recognizable. But this is an arbitrary perspective, since the stars are not on the same plane. Between the closest and the most distant star of Ursa Major, there is a distance of 1,270 light years. So it is with civilizations that are reduced to a diagram by compacting space and time. Any glimpse must attempt to find the whole in relief, complex and uncertain, that no formula can ever reduce to a reassuring principle. This is a territory as varied as Europe, stretching from the Himalayas to the tropics of the south, with more than fifty centuries of history, multiple invasions, several religions born on its soil, others imported, more than 1600 languages, and ethnic origins of every color—forming a country that definitely has a very special nature but no consistency.

India itself invites one to object to unilateral responses with a story that that is supposed to serve as the introduction to any approach to knowledge. It is taken from a sutra in the Buddhist tradition:

One day a rajah brought together all those in his kingdom who had been born blind and asked them if they wanted to know what shape the elephants had. The blind were eager to know: The rajah ordered his servants to bring an elephant for the blind, so they could feel it for themselves with their hands. Among them were some who felt the elephant's trunk and the king said to them: "This is an elephant." Others touched the elephant, seizing an ear, or its tusks, or its head, its back, its side, its thigh, a hind leg, its footprint, or its tail.

To all of them, the rajah said: *"This is an elephant."*

Then the rajah ordered the elephant to be taken away and asked the blind: *"What is an elephant like?"*
The blind people who had taken hold of the trunk said: *"An elephant is like a curved plow beam."*
Those who had grasped the ear said: *"An elephant is like a basket."*
Those who had grasped a tusk said: *"An elephant is like a plowshare."*
Those who had felt the head said: *"An elephant is like a cooking pot."*
Those who had felt the back said: *"An elephant is like a hillock."*
Those who had felt the flank said: *"An elephant is like a wall."*
Those who had taken hold of the thigh said: *"An elephant is like a tree."*
Those who had taken hold of the hind leg said: *"An elephant is like a column."*
Those who had felt the footprint said: *"An elephant is like a mixing-bowl."*
Those who had taken hold of the tail said: *"An elephant is like a rope."*
Each accused the other of being wrong. Some said: *"It is like this!"*
Others replied: *"No, it isn't!"*

Instead of calming down, their discussion turned into a quarrel.
When the rajah saw this, he could not stop laughing.

Dirghagama Lokaprajnapati Sutra

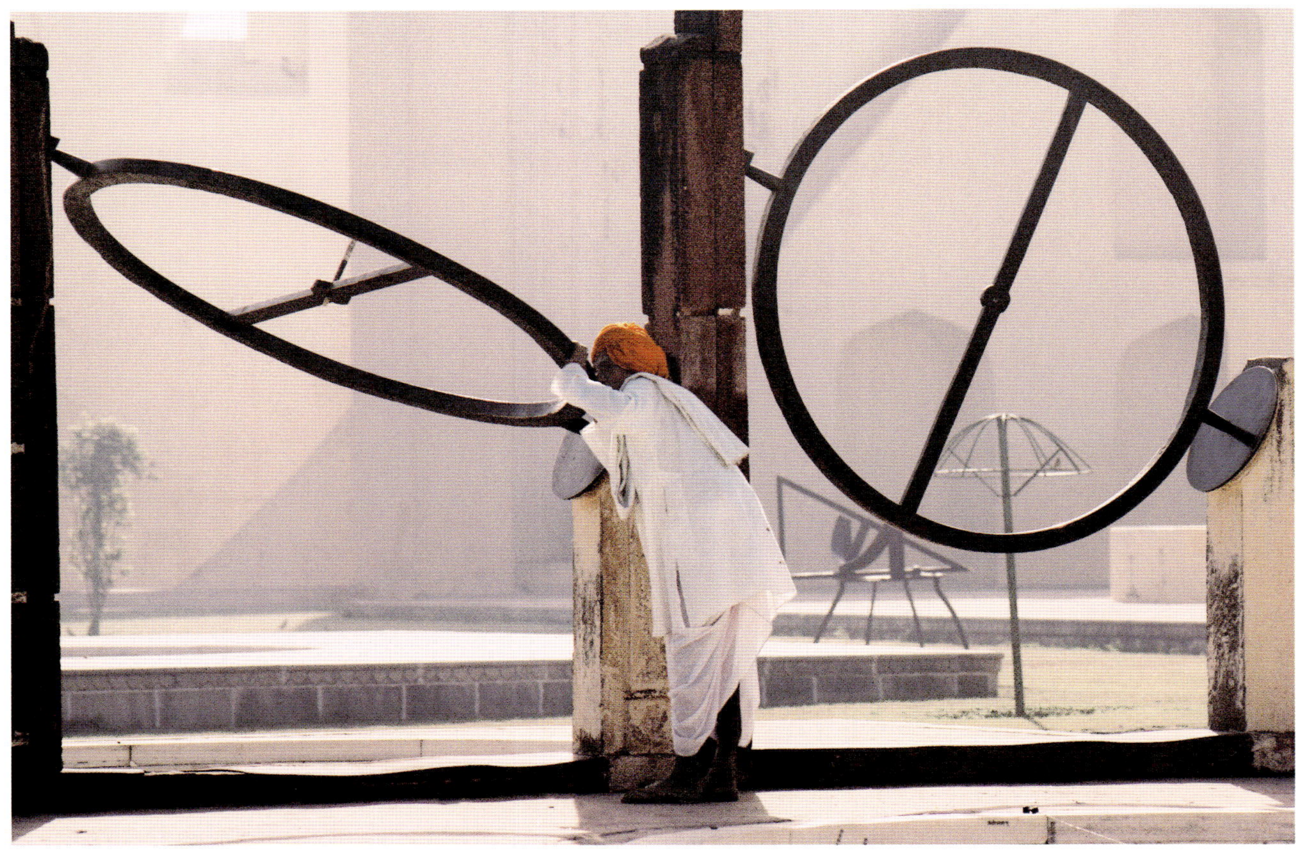

36   Above and opposite: Jaipur Observatory, Rajasthan.

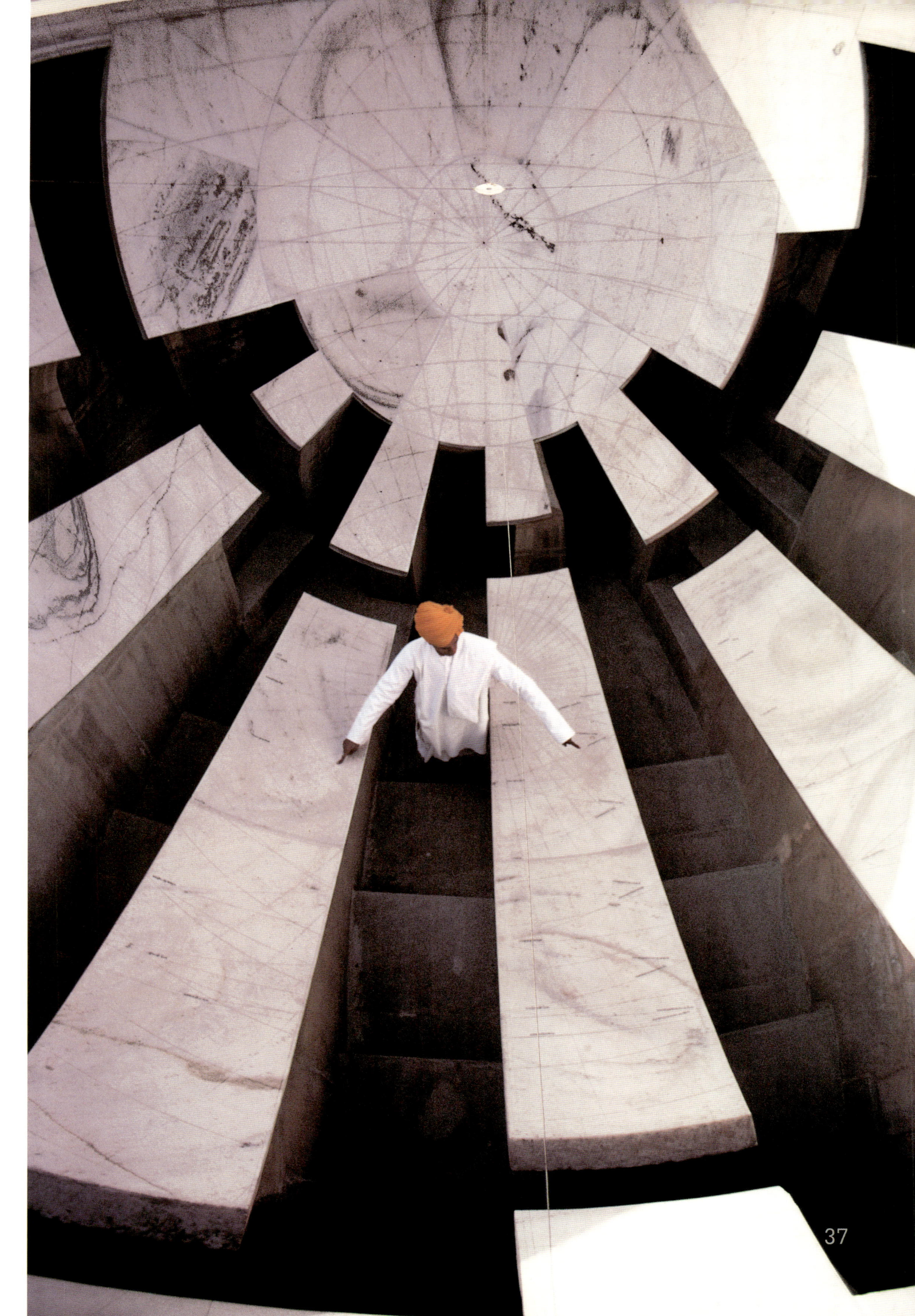

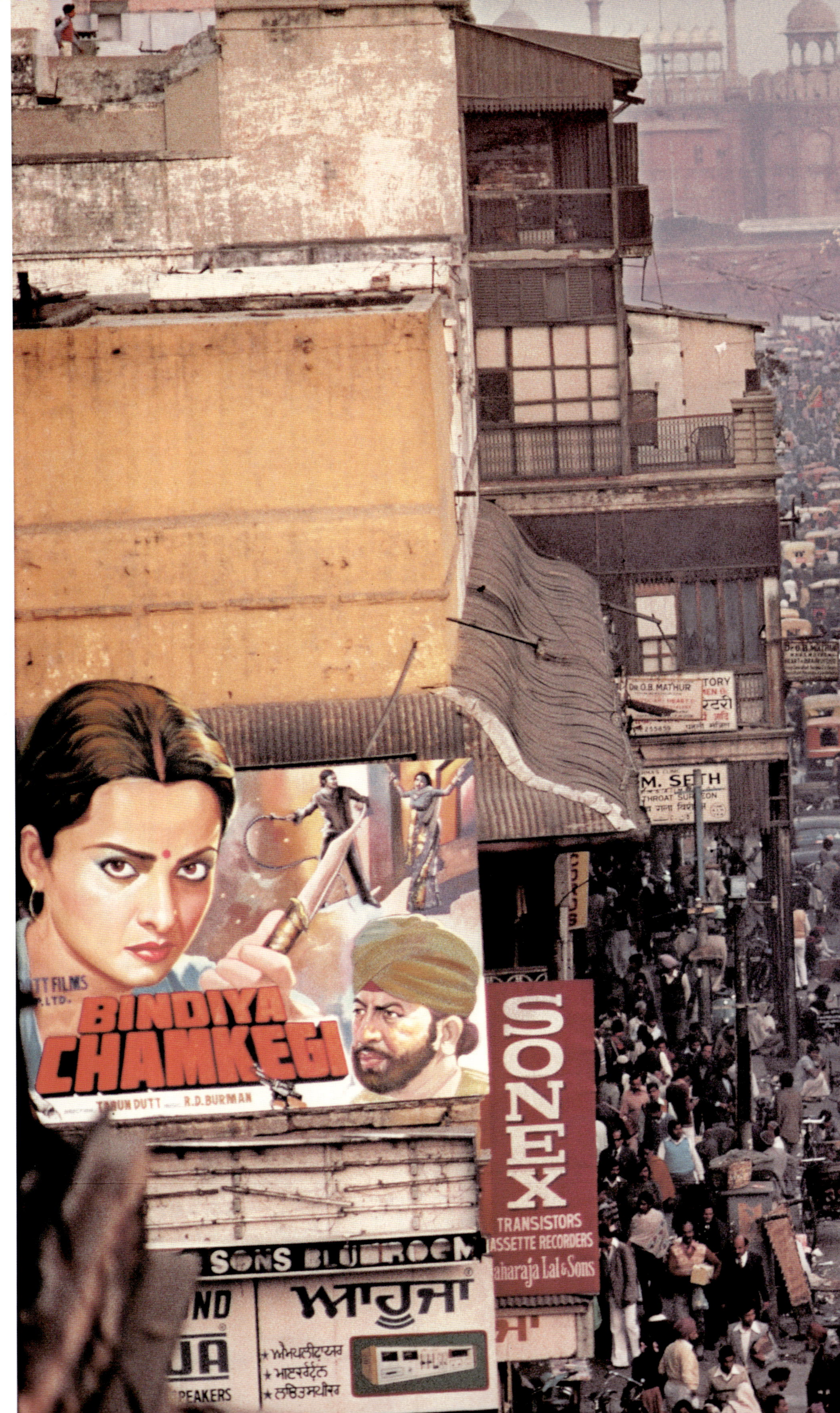
BINDIYA CHAMKEGI
TARUN DUTT   R.D. BURMAN
DUTT FILMS
PVT. LTD.
Dr. O.B. MATHUR
M. SETH
THROAT SURGEON
SONEX
TRANSISTORS
CASSETTE RECORDERS
Maharaja Lal & Sons
SONS BLUE ROOM
आहूजा

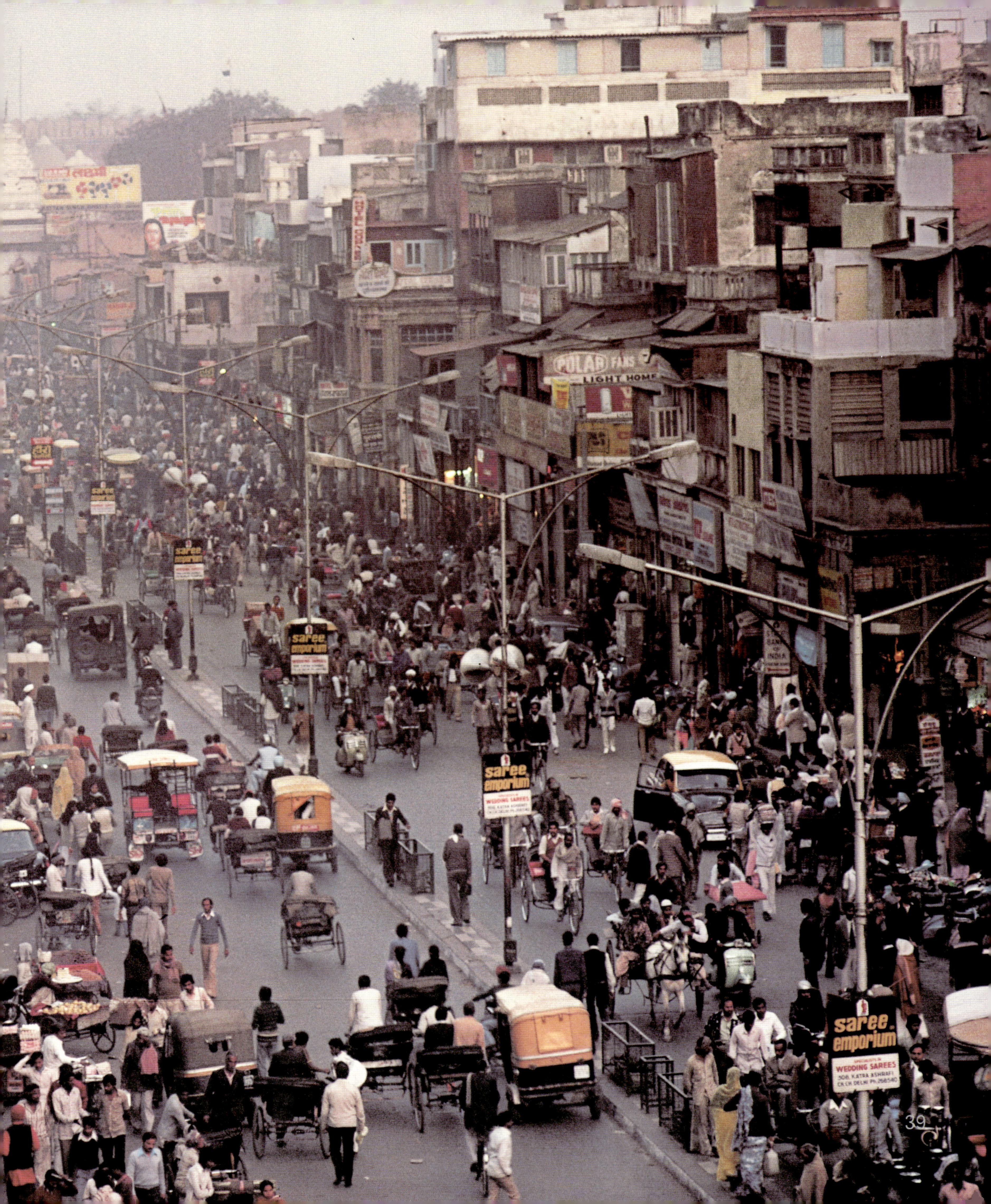

POLAR FANS
LIGHT HOME
saree emporium
saree emporium
WEDDING SAREES
saree emporium
WEDDING SAREES
saree emporium
SPECIALISTS IN
WEDDING SAREES

Was the rajah aware that there reigned over him an emperor who laughed heartily when he realized that the rajah himself had thought that what was a true elephant was merely a small part of it? Did the emperor know that there was one who reigned over him... ?

This story should encourage us to say nothing. If that isn't possible, we should at least avoid repeating: "India is like a..." This is necessarily, though unfashionably, abstemious. Claims that are as peremptory as they are empty are made from all quarters, in a way that they are made for few countries because here, more than anywhere else, the network of causes remains hidden.

Listen to the rumors: India is a poor country; Indians bury themselves in mysticism; they are irrational (the connection is made between two phenomena); the gurus are frauds; the castes an abomination; the destitute die in the street; women are the slaves of men; the Hindus and Muslims hate each other. Such confusion prevails, such corruption, that India will never be able to escape from it—and as for this polytheism, can't you see that it belongs to a different age? And so on, and so on.

Any effusive praise in the opposite direction would be just as ridiculous. It should be reaffirmed that Indian democracy is not exemplary; Indian women are not the most beautiful in the world; the caste system is not an ideal community system; true spiritual masters are extremely rare; indifference to money is almost nonexistent; nonviolence has been as rare in the history of India as loving one's neighbor as oneself has been in Christianity; sacred prostitutes have not practiced their art for centuries; dowries are ruinous; religion has been eroded by urbanization; pilgrimages are not mystical; the poor limping orphan who holds out his hand has been sent by tricksters who will take the money away from him.

Once one embarks on the process of denigration or idealization, arguments are both easy and futile. To get an equitable vision, rid oneself of preconceptions, and try to forget the models that shape our way of thinking. When contemplating the *jati,* forget our own class system; when hearing prayers recited, forget the Lord's Prayer; when seeing the gods, forget Greece; when contemplating Eros, forget psychoanalysis; when viewing the erotic sculptures, stay cool-headed; and when confronted with a pushcart piled high with fruit, hide your camera.

The worst temptation is to believe there is a key. There is no key with which to open India, not the key of the seasons, nor the key of myths or beliefs, nor that of history. Having no key, try the number of gods, of whom there are 330 million.

    Pages 38–39: Street scene, Old Delhi.

While it is impossible to say that "India is..." let's just say "India is."
And leave it at that.

Having emphasized that, remember that one of the reasons for the complexity of
India is the result of the fascination that it has always exercised over us, and
thus the variety of nations who have invaded it, most of whom stayed and settled there. The Aryans who brought the Veda, the Persians, Greeks, Scythians,
Huns, Arabs, Turks, Afghans, Moguls, and finally, the Europeans: Portuguese,
Dutch, French, and British. Ever since the advent of the Aryans (the story of
which is only evoked in myths), India has had rulers who practiced the Vedic
religion as well as Brahmanism, Buddhism, Hinduism, Islam, and Christianity.
It also gave rise to various forms of shamanism, to Jainism, and to the Sikh
religion. Jewish communities have long had a presence on the west coast, and
eastern Christians have lived here since the dawn of Christianity. The Parsees
(worshipers of Zoroaster) found refuge, as did the Tibetan Buddhists more
recently. The single word India (taken from the name of the River Indus that now
flows through Pakistan) embraces such multiple realities that before it can be
used, the place and time should be specified. Let us remember the image of the
multiple arms and heads that change their shape depending on how they are lit.

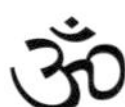

The "mystical" tag attached to Hindu India distorts our perception of it. The
hordes of Indians who regularly go on pilgrimages are no more mystical than their
medieval counterparts who thought they could buy salvation for the price of a trip
on foot to a holy place. The first stage in religious fervor, and often its only visible
manifestation, is physical in nature. The living world (humans and all other crea-
tures) is governed by immutable laws that are expressed in the revealed texts to
which the centuries have patiently added multiple commentaries. These must be
obeyed to the letter, just as a mountain climber or atomic engineer would do. The
recitation of prayers and the performance of a rite affect the order or disorder of the
world. Our own culture has made us so accustomed to the primacy of intention
that we have discarded the idea that sacred words have a power of their own. It is
a serious offense to spoil a recitation of the *Veda*, one that must be atoned for if one
wants to avoid disaster. That which is mistaken for a cumbersome formality is
actually a technique of propitiation. At the heart of the sanctuary, the god or goddess (or both in one) is a radiating source of energy. Crowds stand in line for a
whole day in searing heat before they can enter the sanctum sanctorum, the place
of the cure where they will be anointed with the magical vibrations of the divinity.

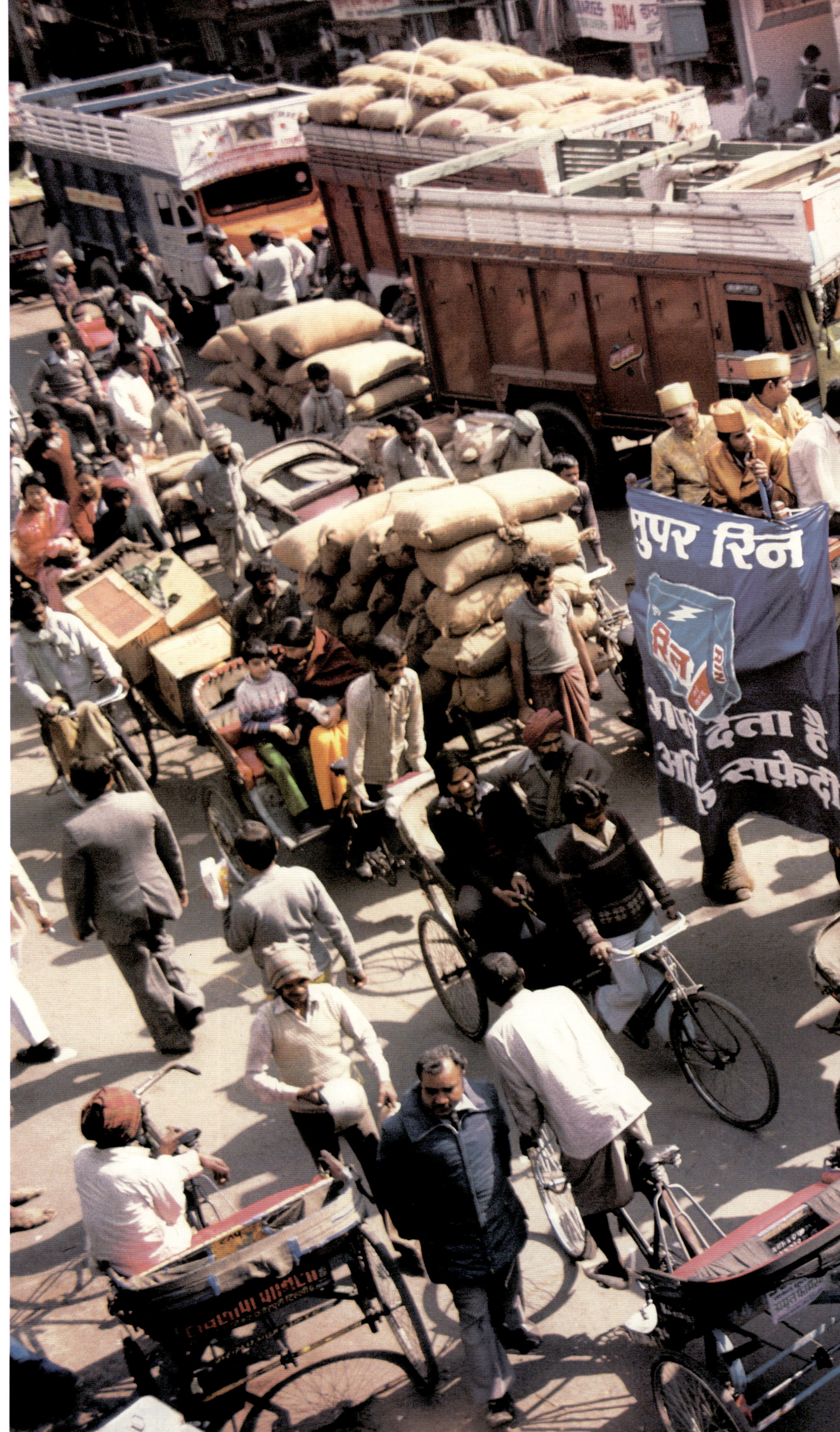
सुपर रिन
RIN
आपको देता है
आई सफ़ेदी

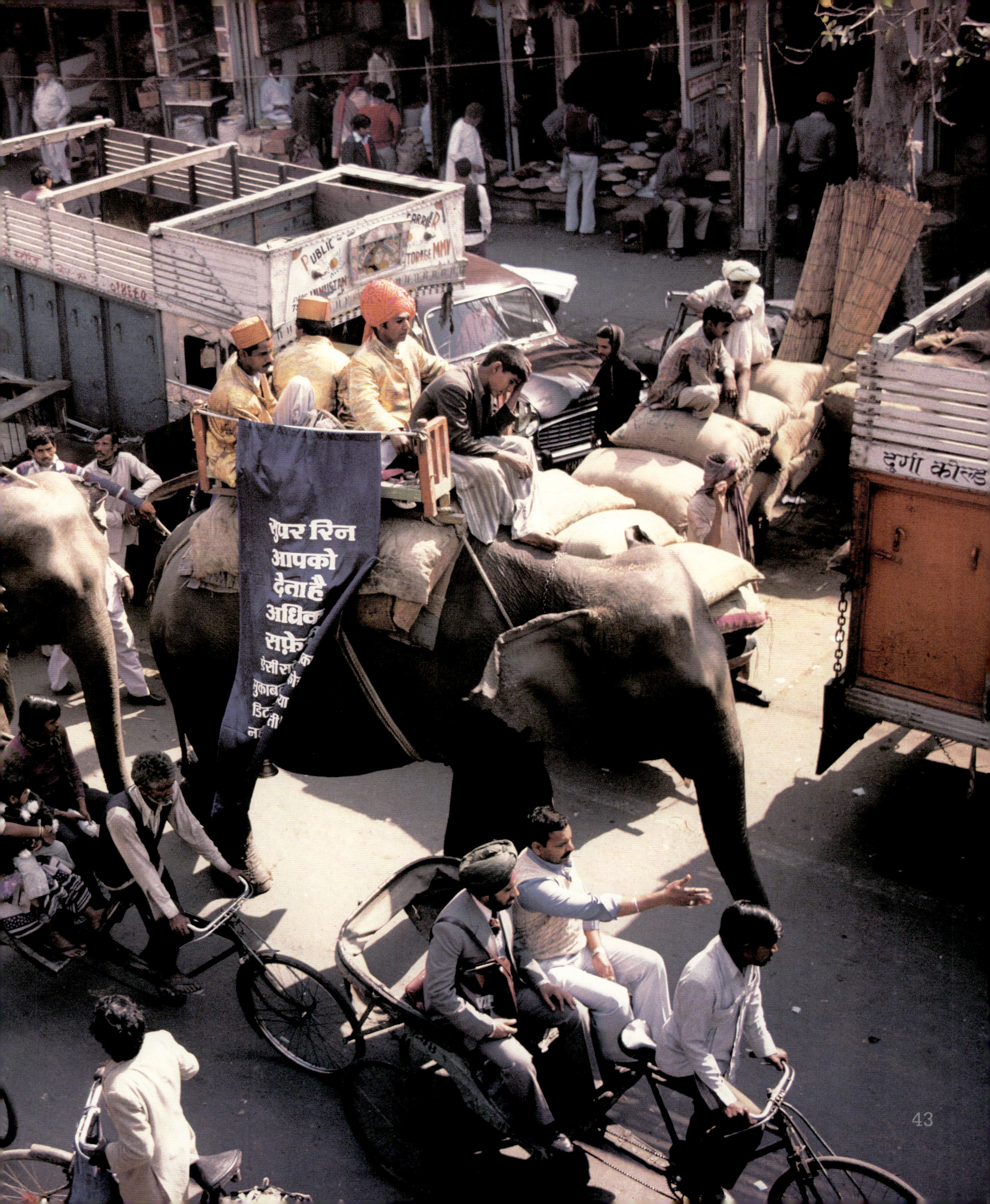

सुपर रिन
आपको
देता है
अधिक
सफेद

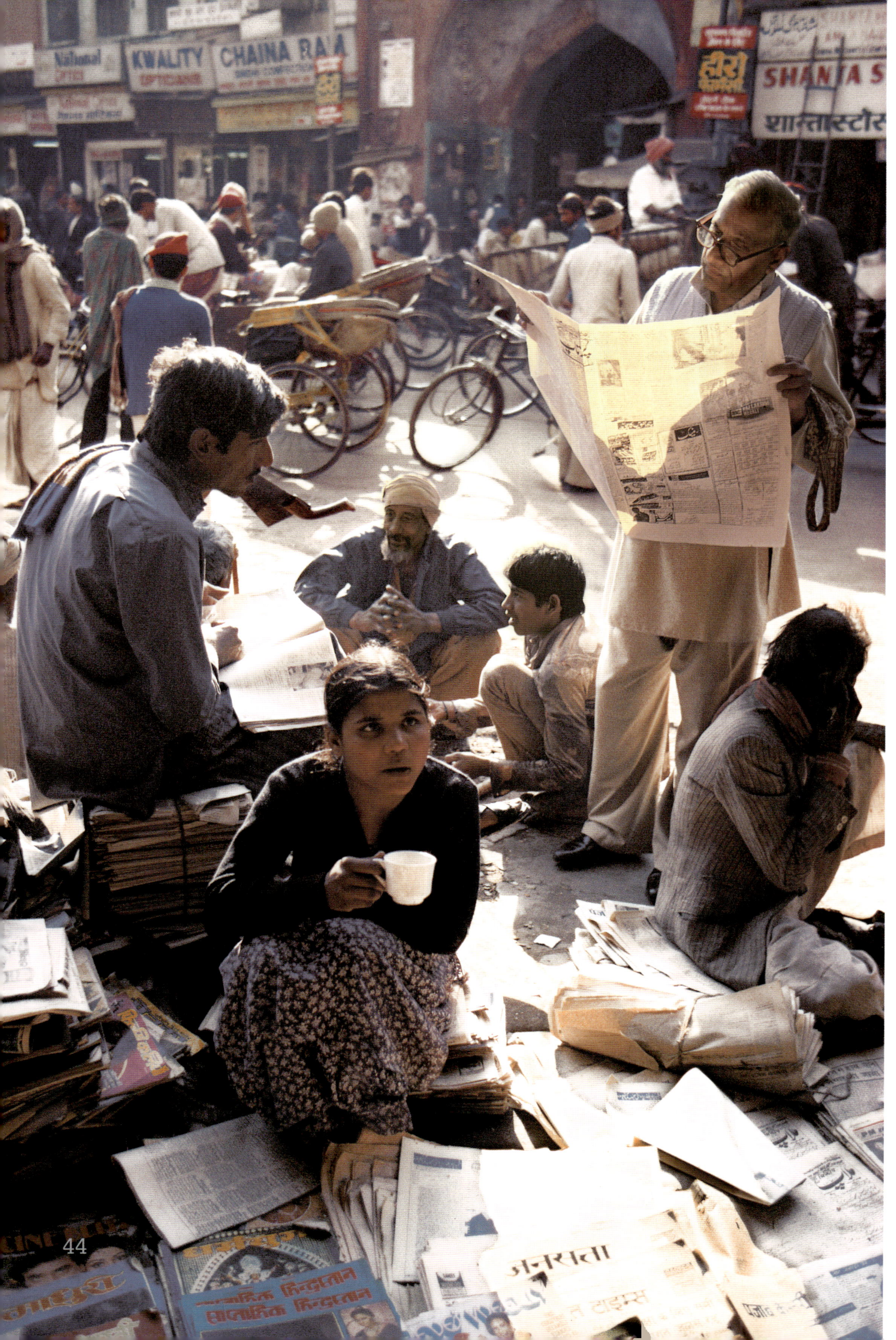

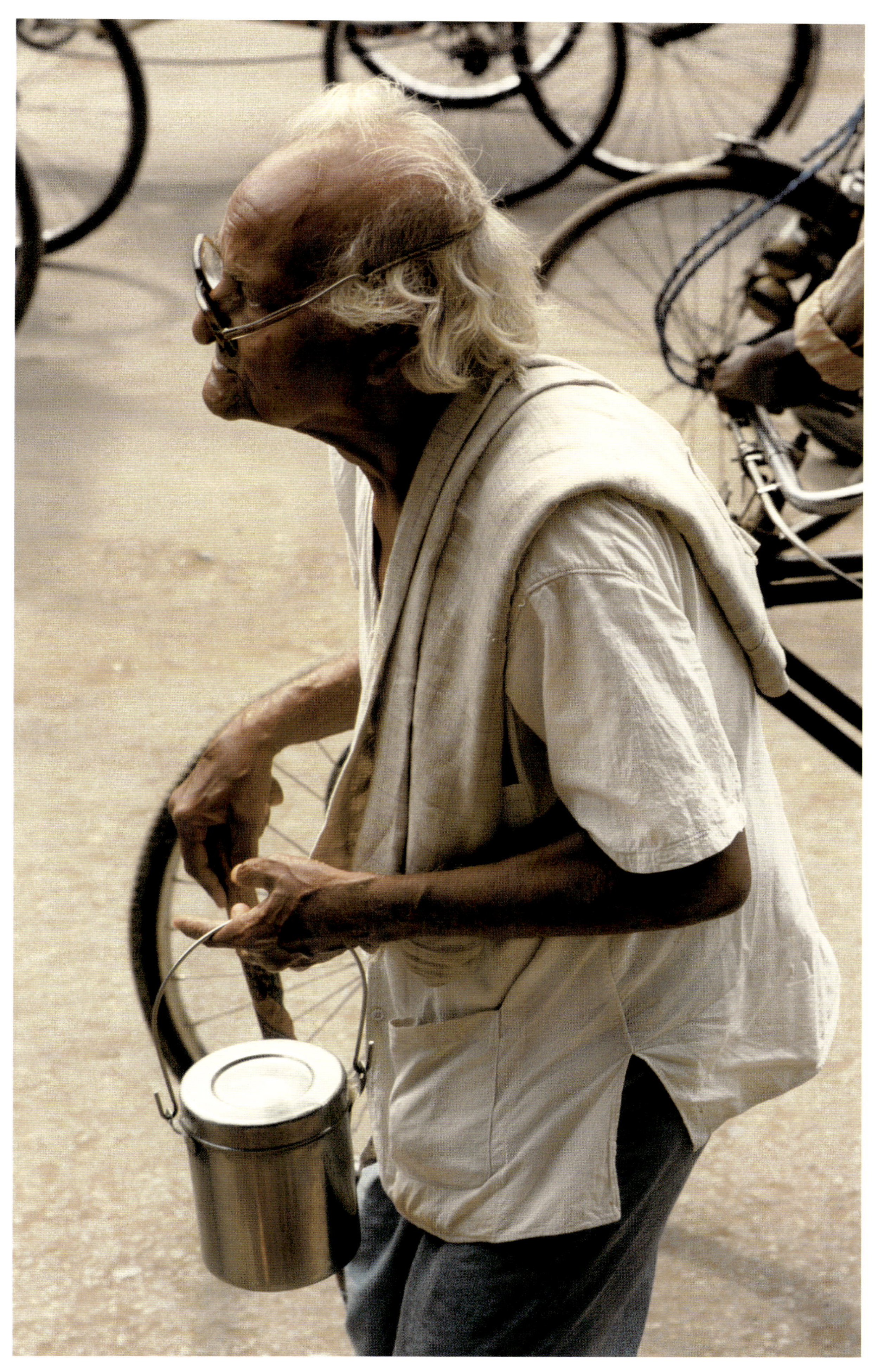

Beggar
in Old Delhi.

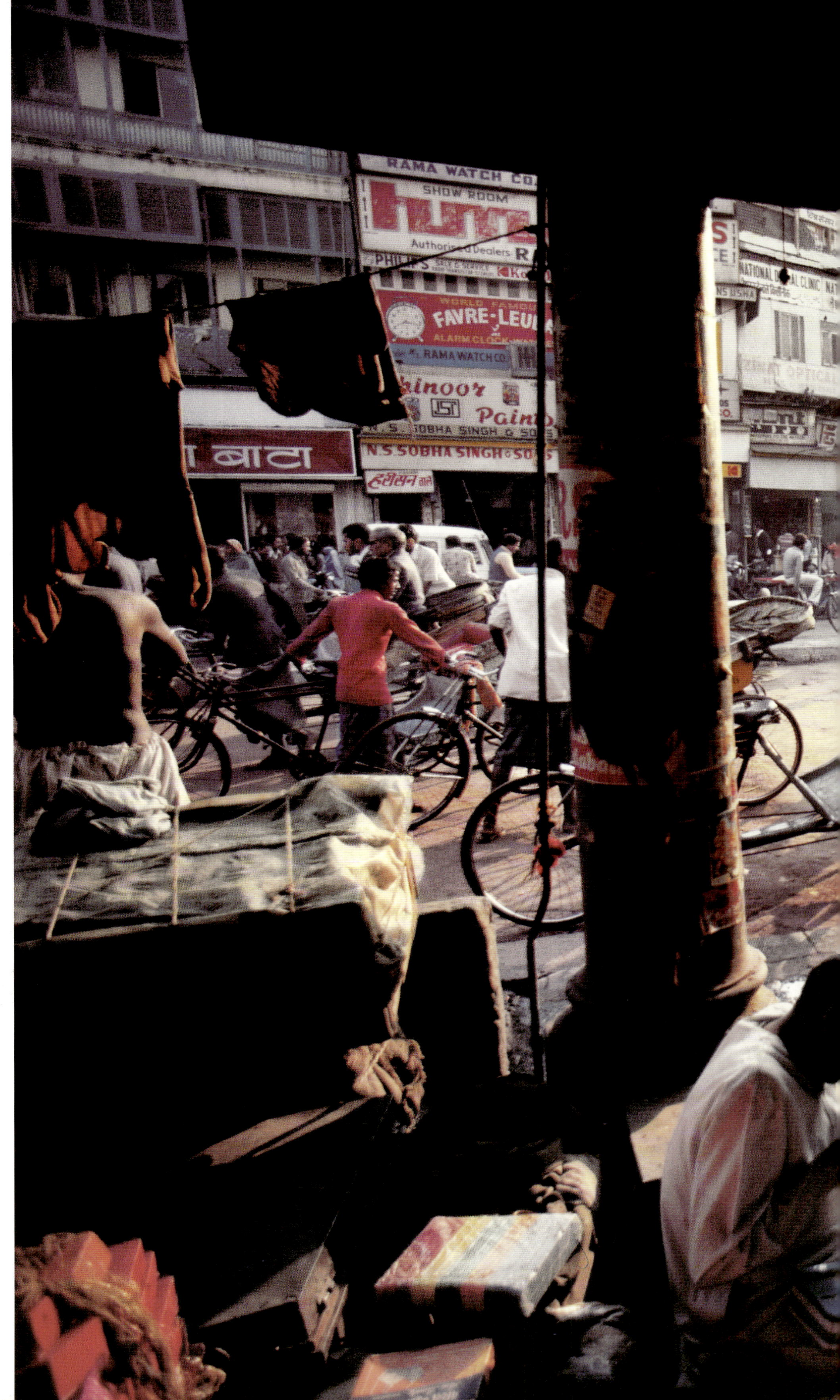
RAMA WATCH CO.
SHOW ROOM
Authorised Dealers
PHILIPS
WORLD FAMOUS
FAVRE-LEUBA
ALARM CLOCK
RAMA WATCH CO.
Kohinoor
Paints
N.S. SOBHA SINGH & SONS
बाटा
NATIONAL DENTAL CLINIC

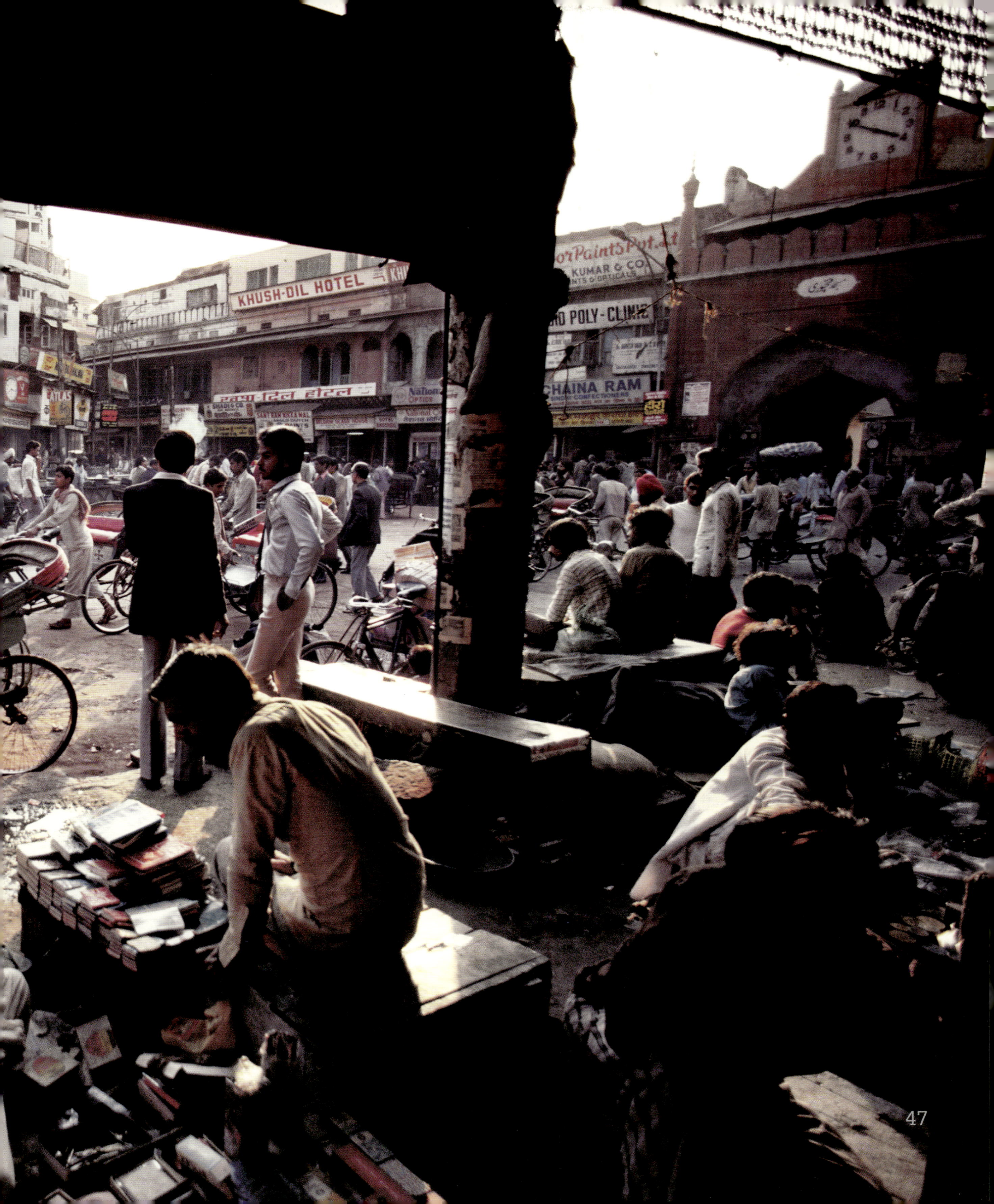

KHUSH-DIL HOTEL
ATLAS
KUMAR & CO
POLY-CLINIC
CHAINA RAM
CONFECTIONERS
National Optics

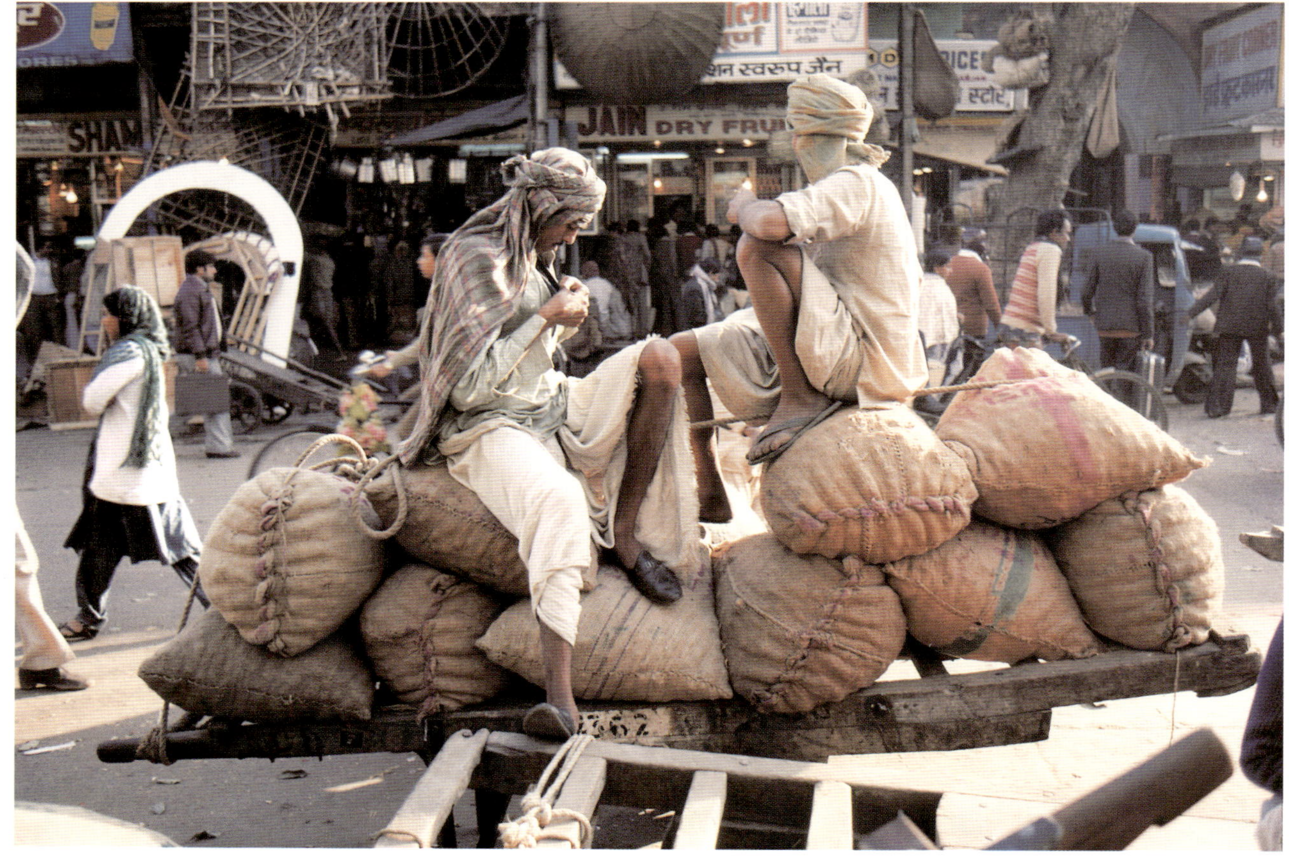

Above: Porters resting on their pushcarts, Old Delhi.
Opposite: Pontoon bridge over the Ganges, Delhi.

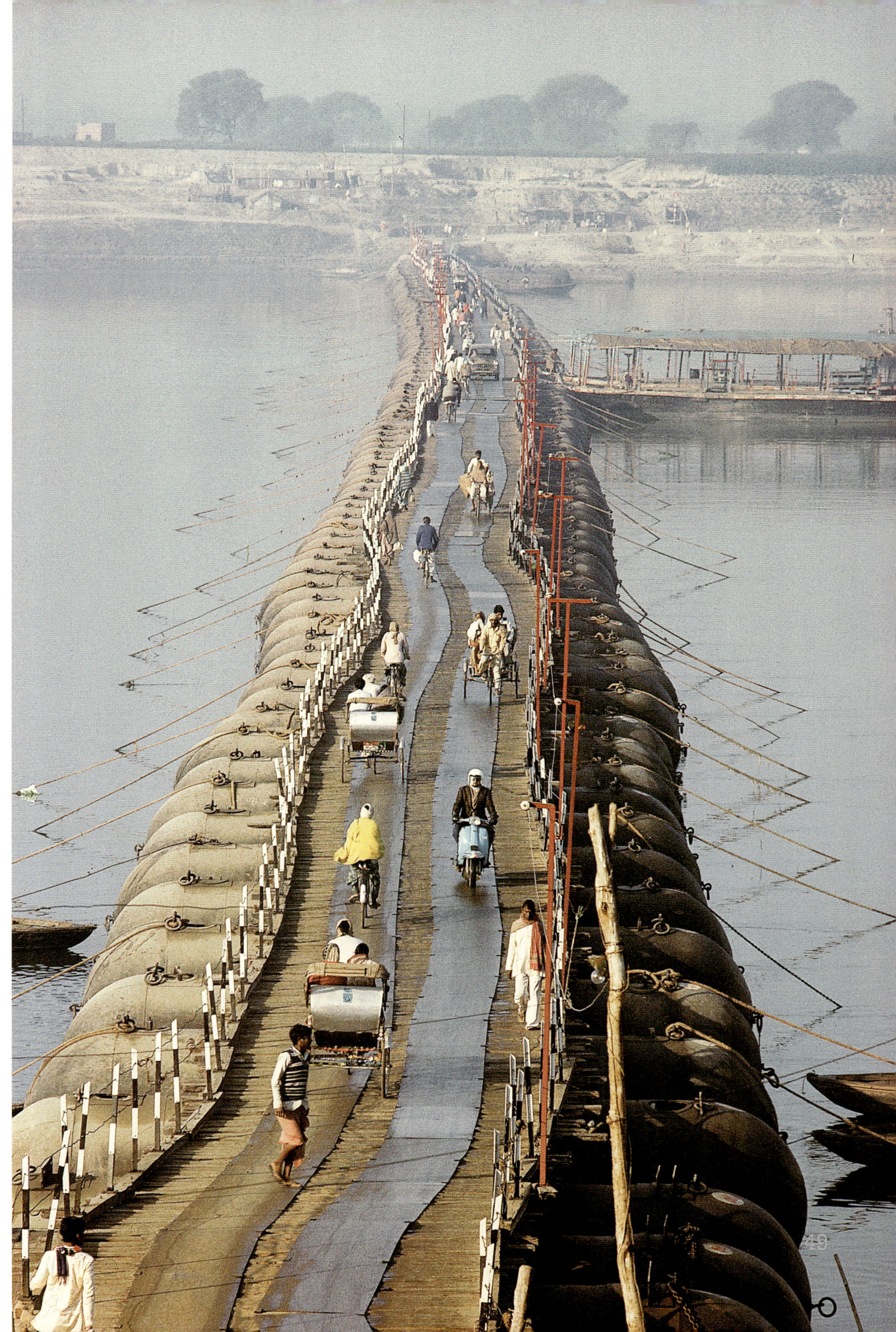

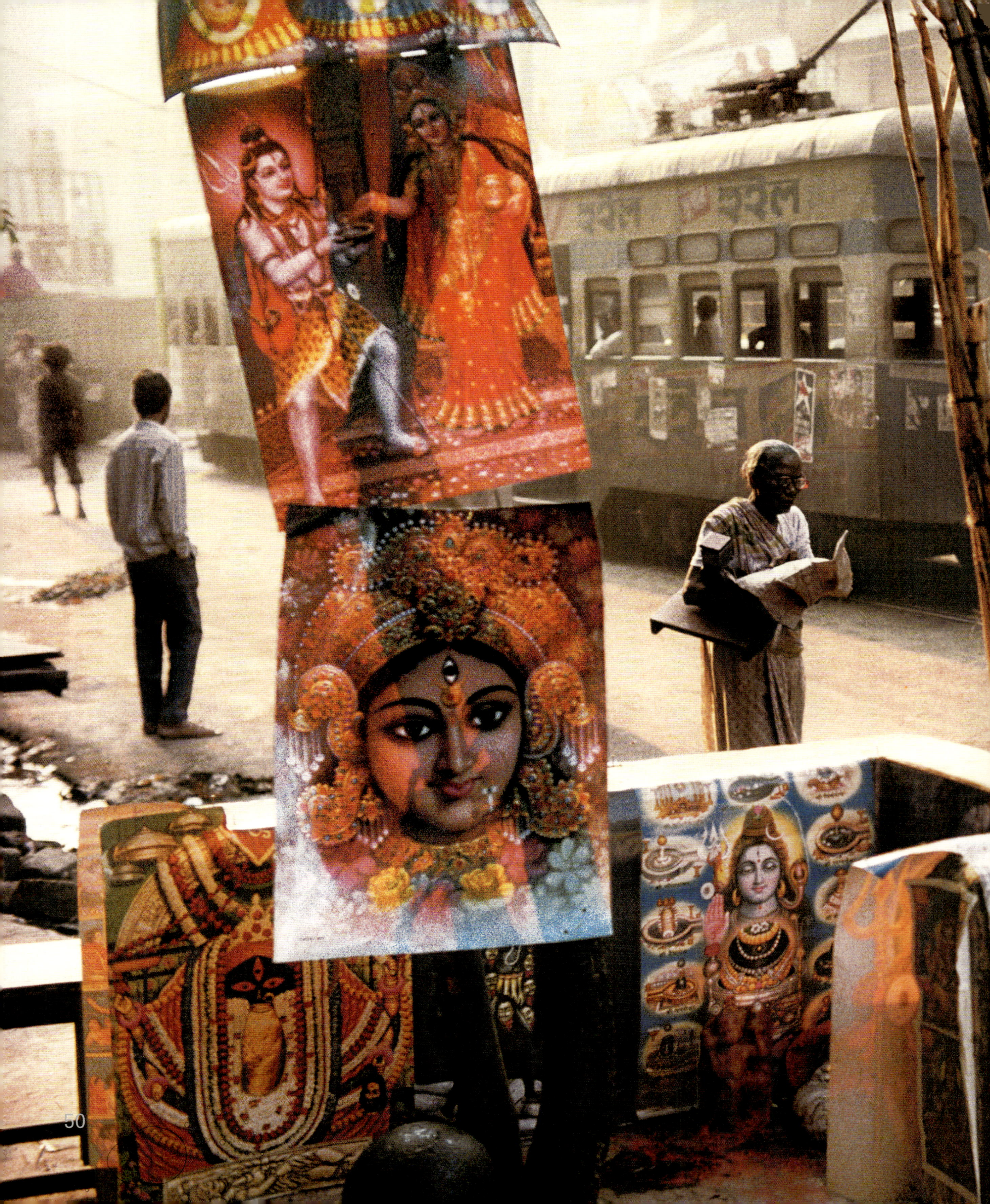

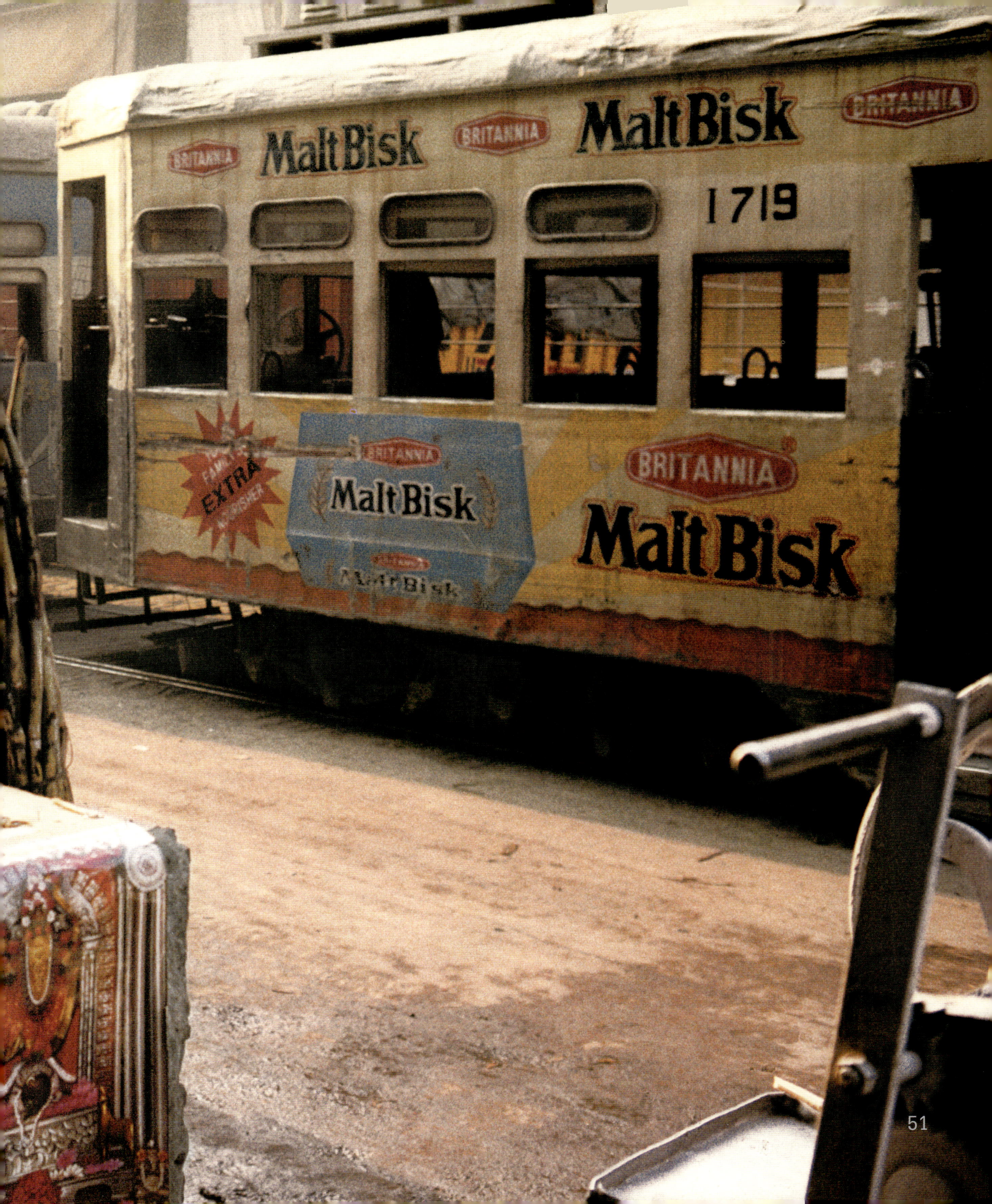
Malt Bisk
BRITANNIA
Malt Bisk
BRITANNIA
Malt Bisk
BRITANNIA
1719
EXTRA
BRITANNIA
Malt Bisk
BRITANNIA
Malt Bisk
BRITANNIA
Malt Bisk

The word "polytheism" is confusing. While there are innumerable gods, just as there are numerous rules that organize the material world—gods for desire, for inspiration, for fertility, or the invention of the lute—there is also an all-embracing principle of faith. Since the post-Vedic era, the sacred texts have established the *Brahman* (neuter), as the Supreme Self, cause and energy. It cannot be represented or defined in words. The yogis use the Sanskrit expression *neti neti* to try to explain it. It is neither-nor . . . neither this nor that. It must be approached through intermediaries. At the cutting edge of mystical experience, the ego disappears, becoming one with the *Brahman*.

The sun does not shine there, neither the moon
Nor the stars. There these lightenings shine not—
How then by this fire?
Because He shines
Everything shines after Him.
By His light
All this shines.

Svetasvatara Upanishad, 6:14

The Muslim invaders, who mercilessly attacked the idols, were at first horrified by the external manifestations of this religion, just as it would subsequently provoke titters among travelers from the West, though in a simplistic reaction some became infatuated with them, seeing them as the answer to everything they lacked.

If the multiplicity of religious figures originates in the realization that a multiplicity of rules and tendencies govern life—from Eros to the merging into one—there is another reason that explains the profusion of approaches: history.

The religious and cultural forms that were born in India did not reject the previous layers; they merely added to them. The Aryan gods did not eliminate the pre-Vedic divinities, no more than Buddhism eradicated the gods of Brahmanism; Hinduism victoriously incorporated part of the metaphysics of Buddhism; Tantrism contributed to both Buddhism and Hinduism; Sikhism attempted a synthesis between Islam and Hinduism; etc. The *ashrams* of neo-Hindu inspiration that place the Buddha and Christ alongside Rama, Parvati, or Vishnu are merely adopting in their simplistic manner a tendency that India has always had.

If a comparison is needed, the Hindu religion, as practiced in India today, represents a variety of religious tendencies of which the equivalent in the Mediterranean world would be the cohabitation, under a single name, of the cults of Ancient Greece with Judaism and several forms of Christianity. Consider thus the astonishment and rage of the Hindus when Islam came along with one book and one truth. At least in the case of Christianity, which did not have a strong base, and especially in its most ancient form, the saints partially compensated for the absence of gods, which is why it was more readily accepted.

Of course, all religions, even those of one book, incorporate previous beliefs, but no Christian could accept kneeling in a cathedral before the naked body of Aphrodite. In the case of the Hindu religion, what the Westerner or Muslim mistakes for confusion is this propensity of the Indian mind never to reject anything. It should be considered a sign of realism and the reason for an excellent state of mental health. If life requires a god figure, that is because it is necessary. Let the sun, the wind, the river, the *lingam,* the *yoni,* fire, asceticism, death, the dance, compassion, or meditation find a home here!

In the case of India, the "or" should be replaced with an "and." "Are you a woman or a goddess?" inquires Ulysses when confronted with the troubling apparition of Aphrodite. Goddess *and* woman, would be the answer here. The contrasts that have produced our vision of the word—profane versus sacred, good versus evil, body versus soul, polytheism versus monotheism, human versus animal, and so on—do not work when applied to this civilization that is the only one to have retained the manner of approaching reality that existed within the human race until the death of the "Great Pan."

Honoring multiplicity in no way implies rejecting the order of things. Few philosophical traditions have been as fond of classifications. The sacred texts abound with interminable lists that order states, stages, and trends with a rigor that we do not possess and it leaves us stupefied. Hence it can be seen that encountering Indian thought begins with a struggle against a part of oneself.

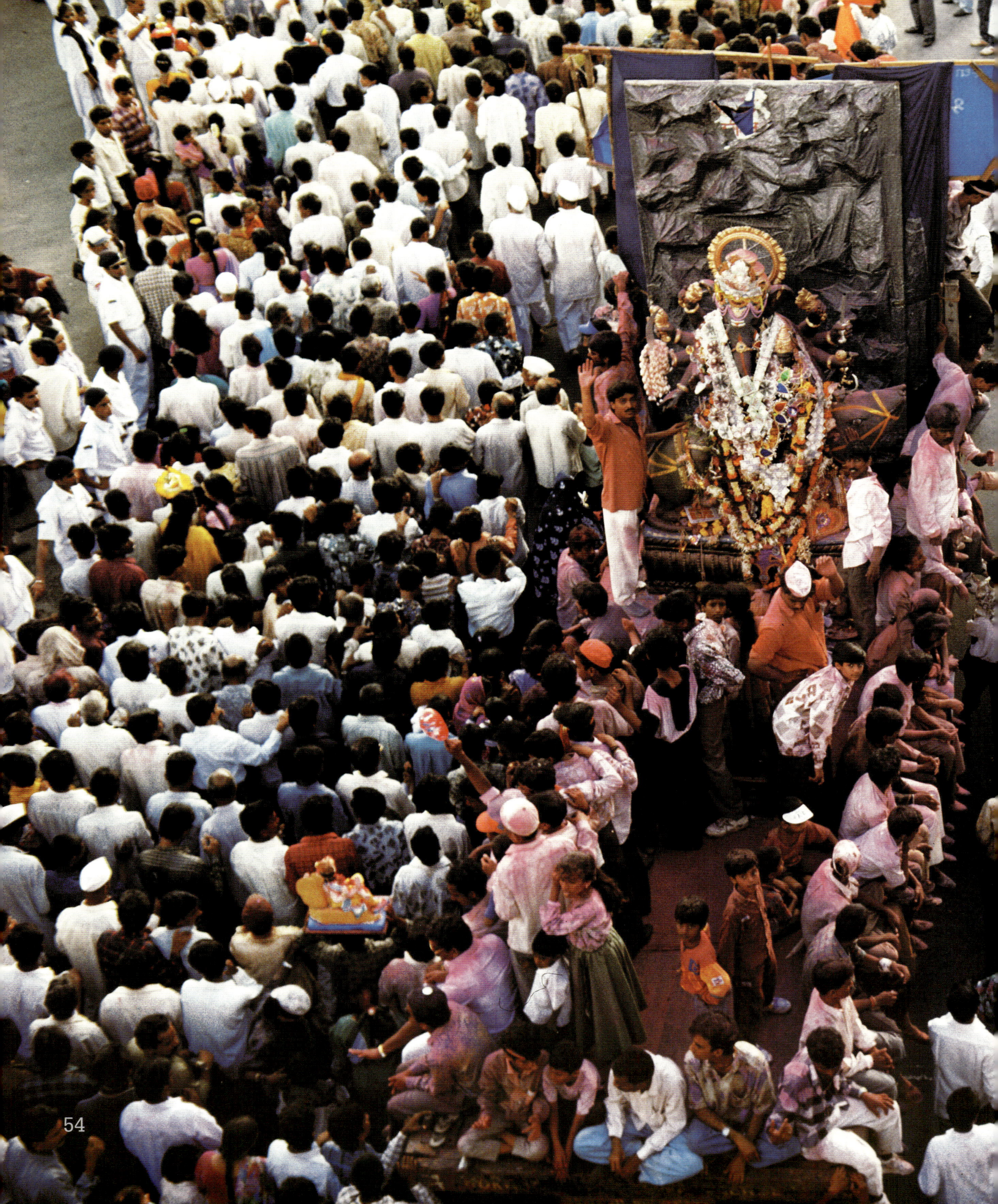

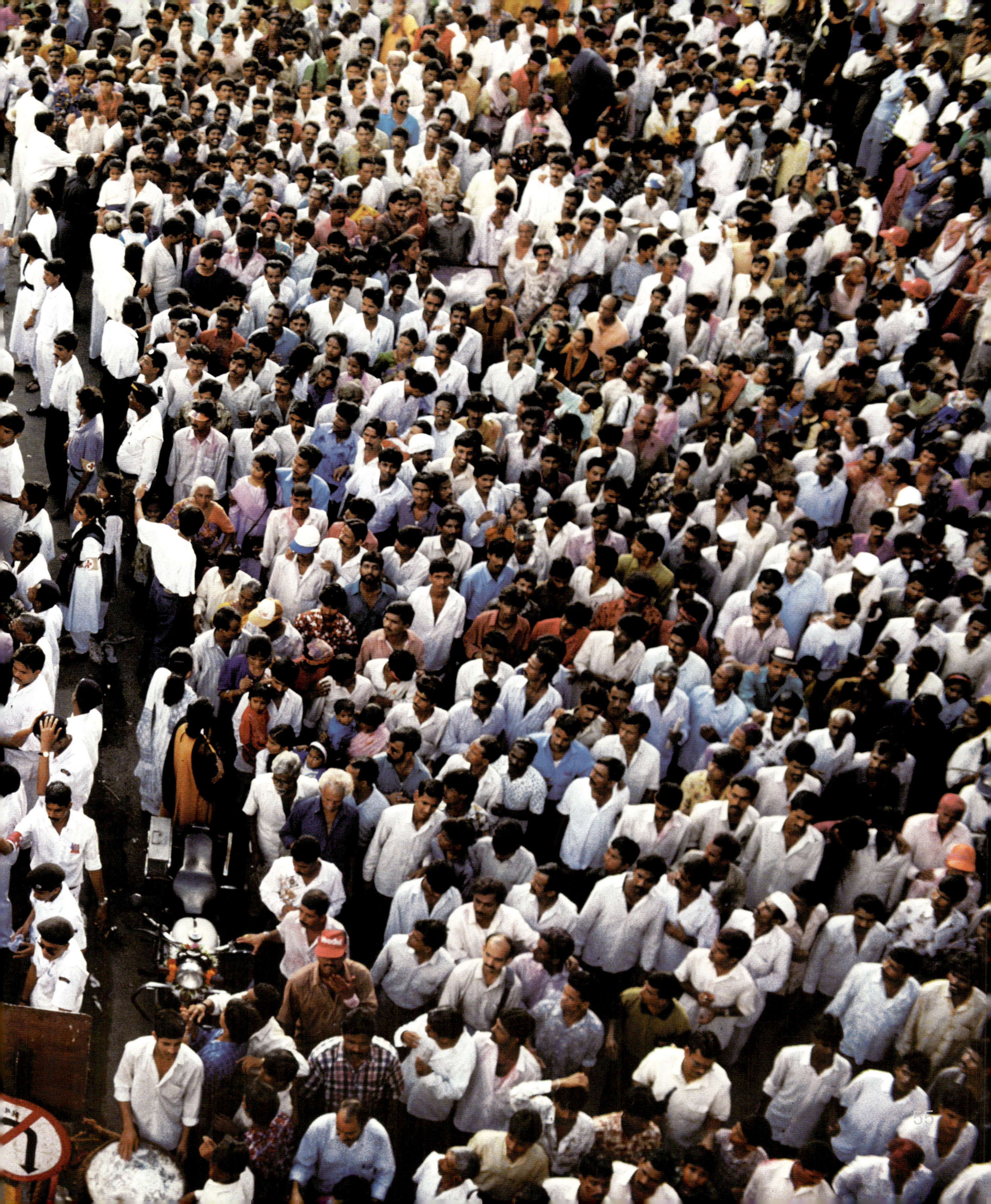

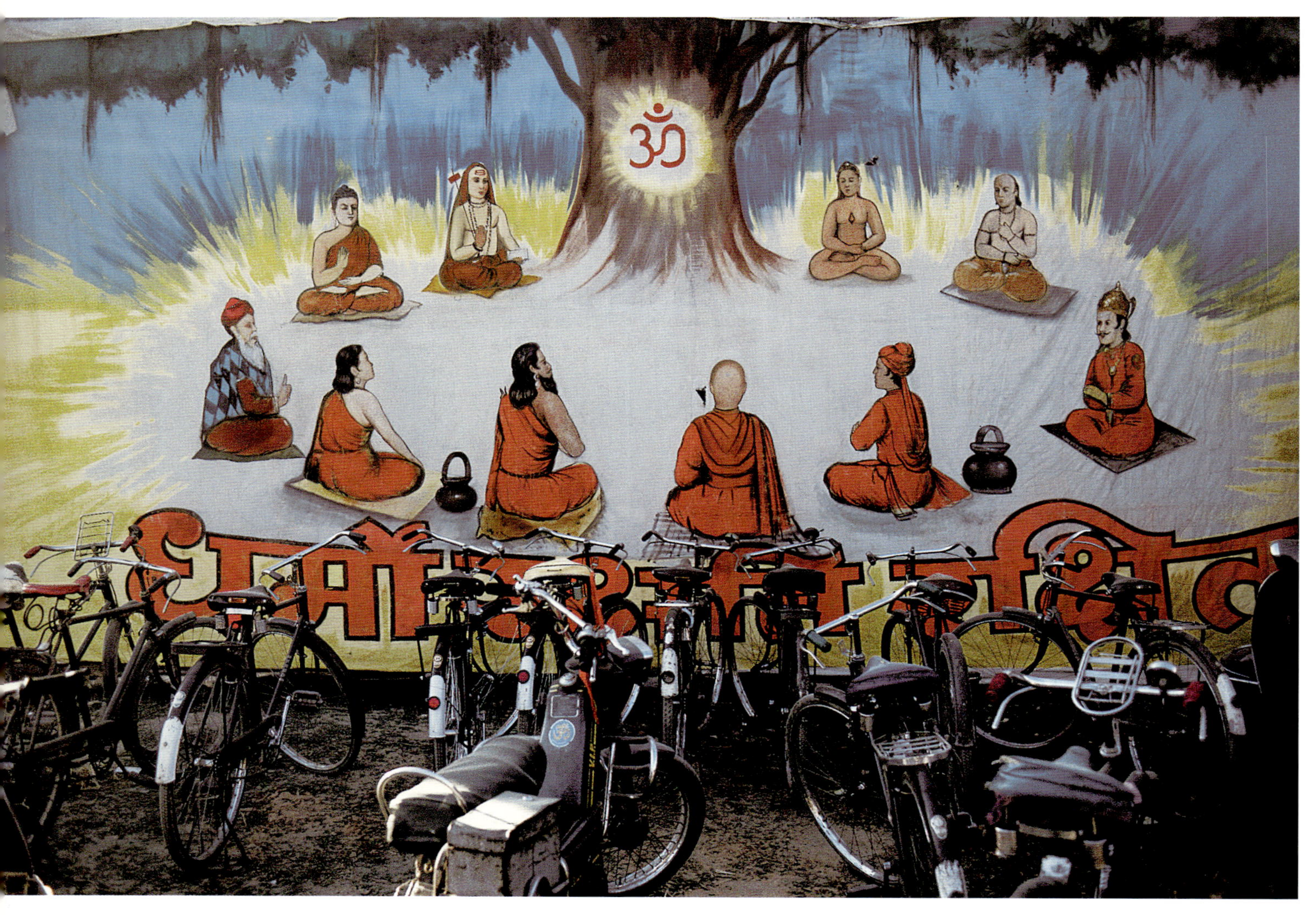

Above: Ecumenical poster, Allahabad.
Opposite: Holy man and police officers, Benares.

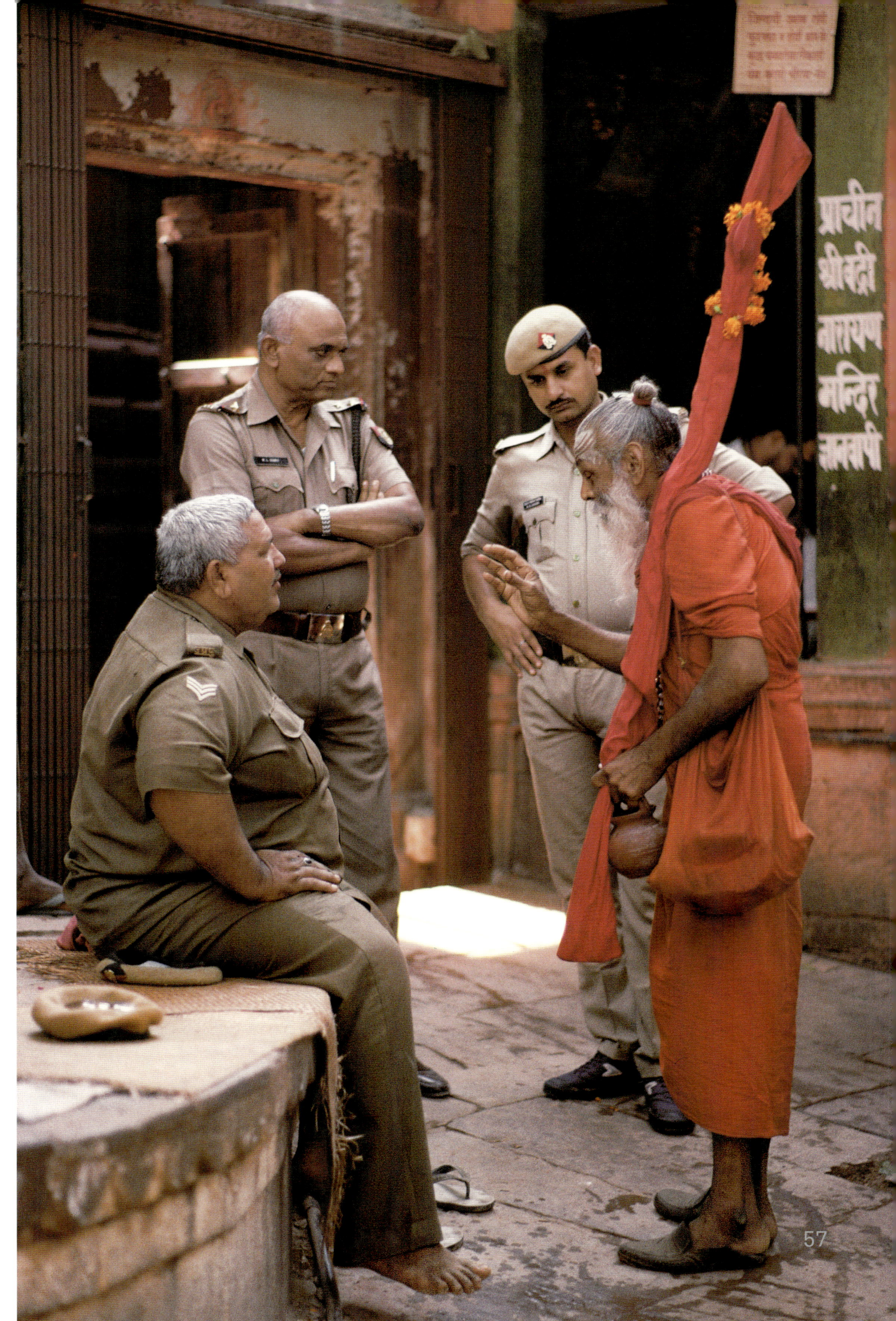

प्राचीन
श्रीहरि
नारायण
मन्दिर

India does not place importance on chronologies. Unlike China or Greece, it has never compiled a single version of its history. Although archaeology, epigraphy, and the analysis of myths have provided indications, the historian lacks certainties, especially concerning the Aryan invasion and the nature of the civilization that preceded it, concerning the origin of the caste system, or much later, the reasons why Buddhism gradually disappeared in India. By drawing a veil over numerous periods in its history, did India want to teach a lesson in *māyā*? Or did it want to help us to enter into its cyclical concept of time?

One certainty: India, which has had a realistic view of the human psyche and of nature, is not interested in the passing of time in the historic sense. This is not a matter of denying reality, it is simply placing importance on a different perspective.

Four points about its history (so as not to wander too far from the subject):

- India was only completely united by its colonizers: first the Moguls, then the British. The first attempt at unifying the whole of the Indian subcontinent dates from the Mauryas (325–185 B.C.), the second was made by the Guptas (4th–8th centuries A.D.). In both cases, this only involved part of what is now India.

- By taking India over from the Moguls, the British merely substituted one colonization for another. There were two notable differences, however. The British did not seek to convert the population, and the center of power remained in London; the British were merely passing through.

- Northern India and Southern India do not share the same history or the same organization of society; although these two halves of India, whose borders fluctuated, were part of the same civilization.

- For centuries India was the richest region on earth.

> *Listen, o my brother:*
> *The Ganges is not water,*
> *The fig-tree and the pipal are not trees,*
> *The tulsi and the rudraksha are not herbs,*
> *They are the most beautiful limbs of God.*

Tukaram, *Psalms of the Pilgrim*, XLIII

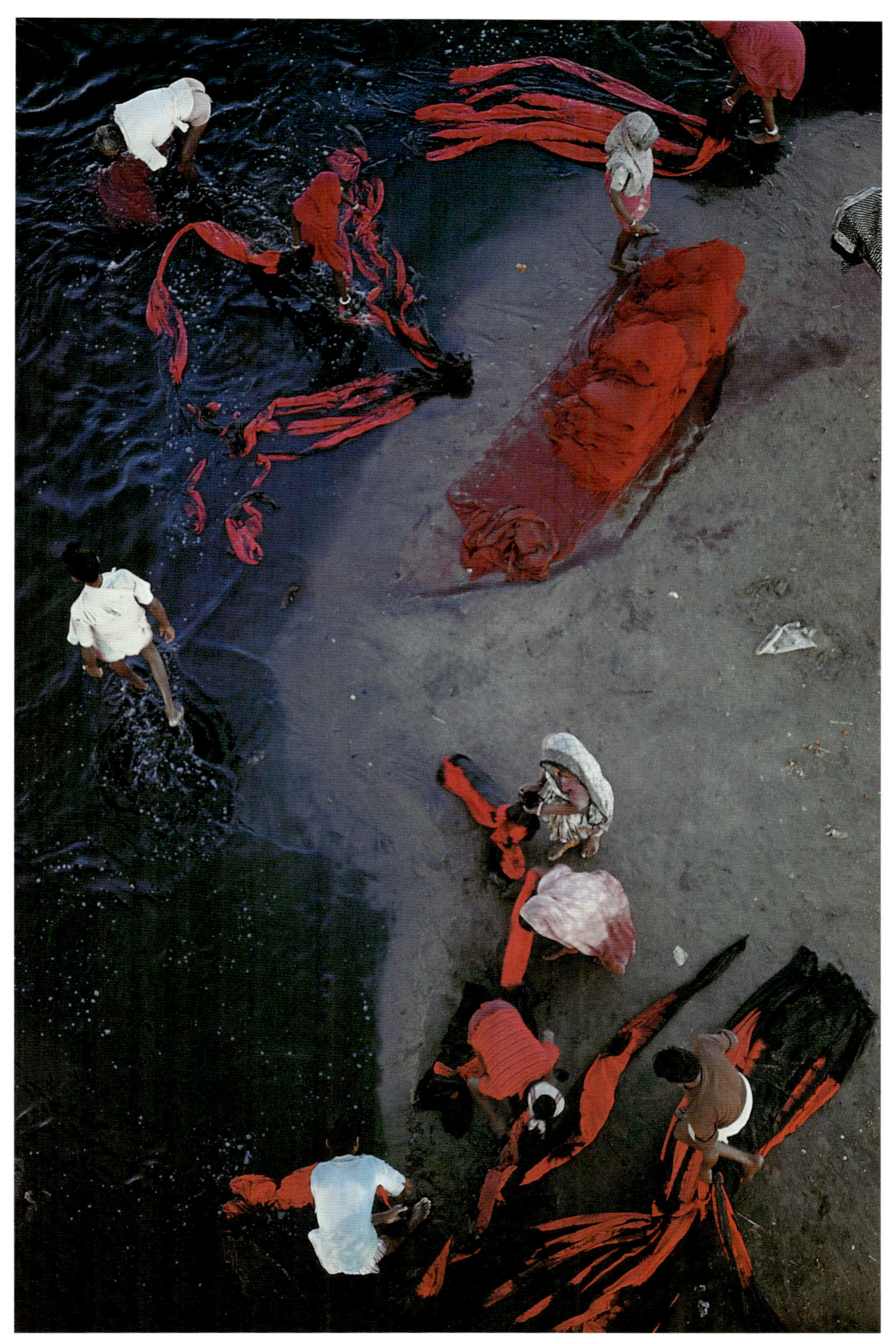

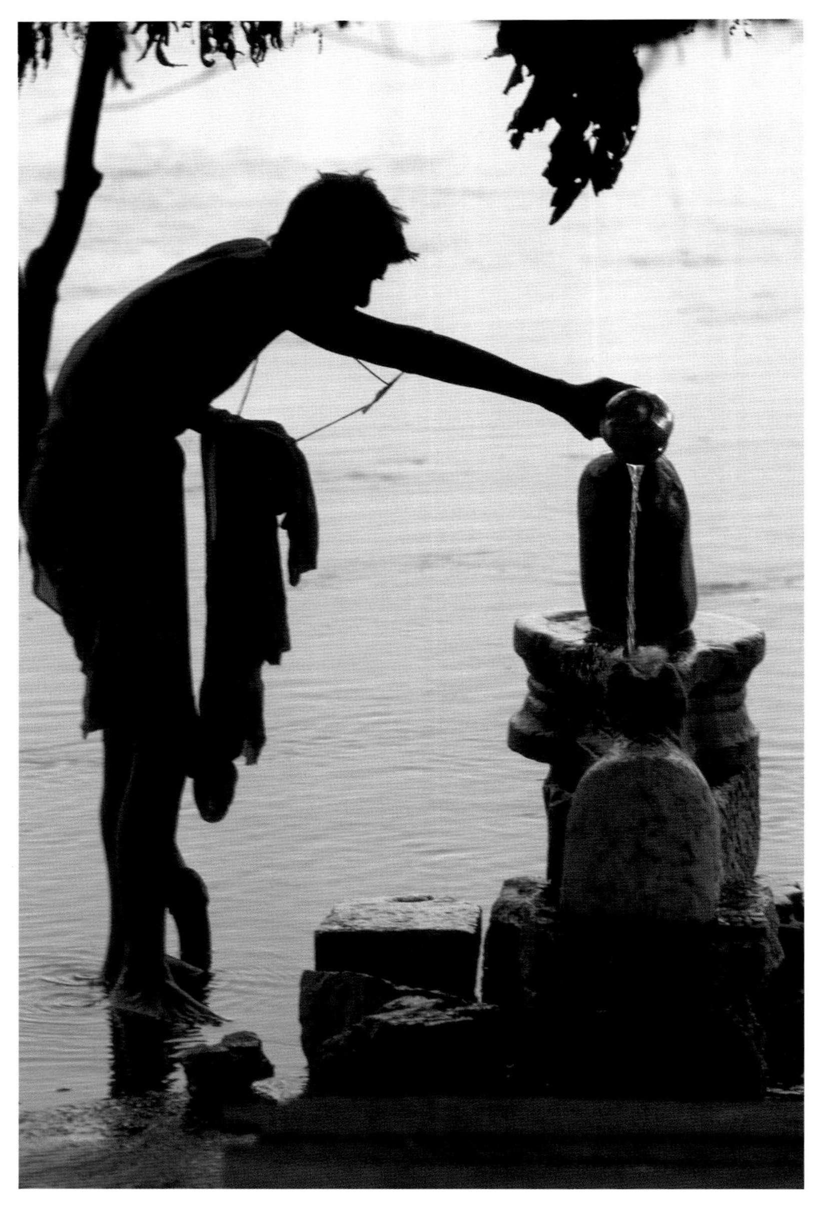

Above: Offering in honor of Shiva.
Opposite: A sadhu meditating.

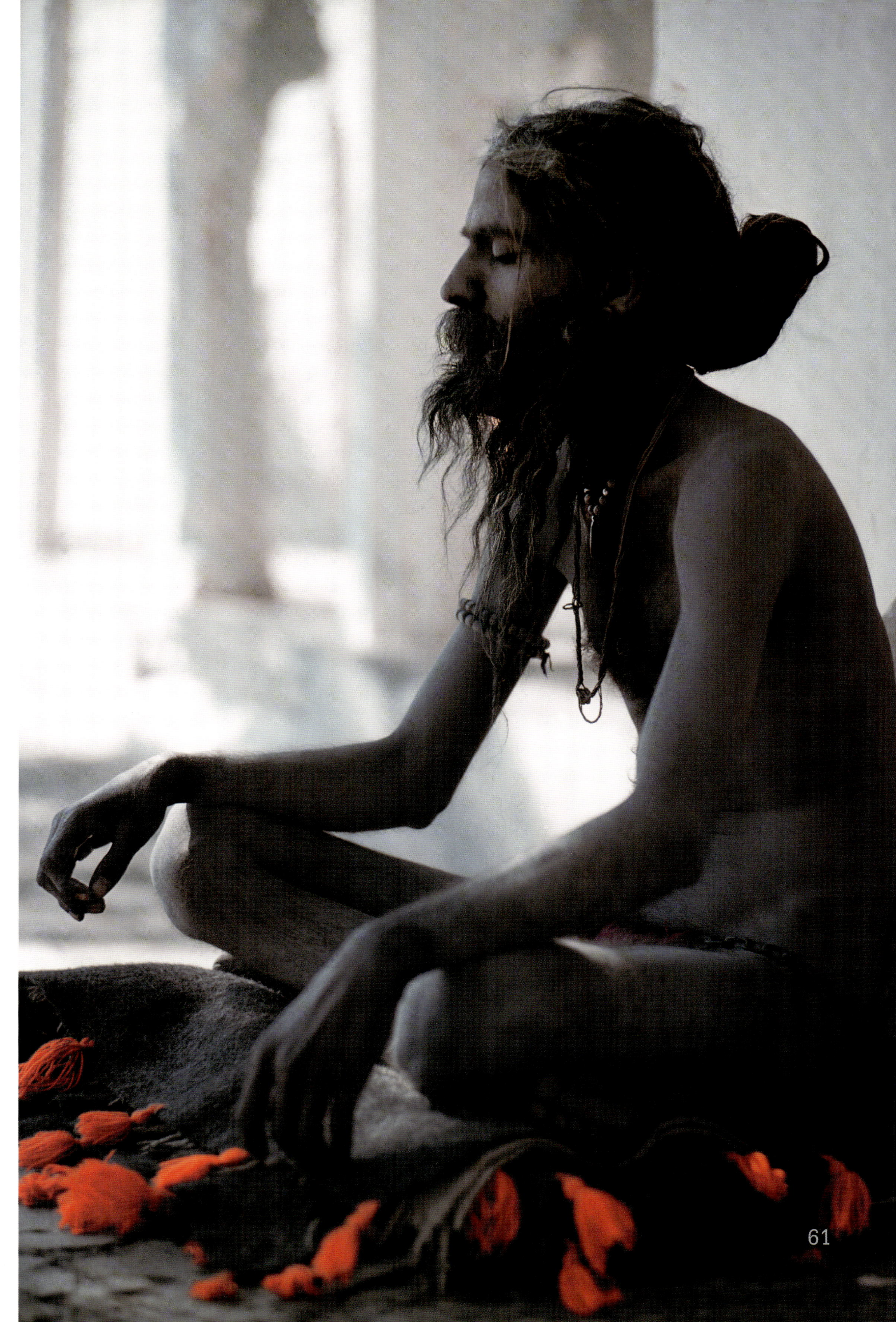

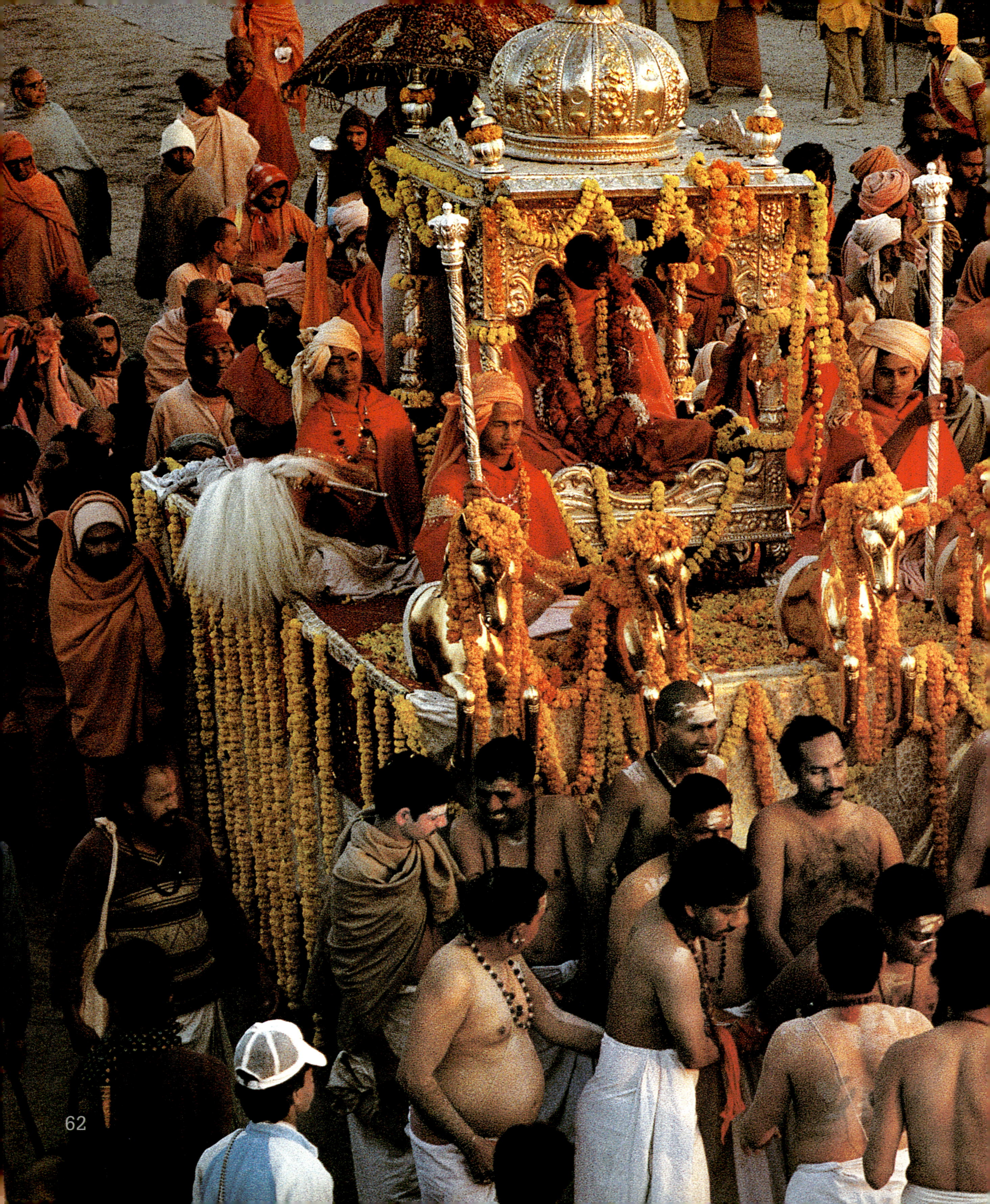

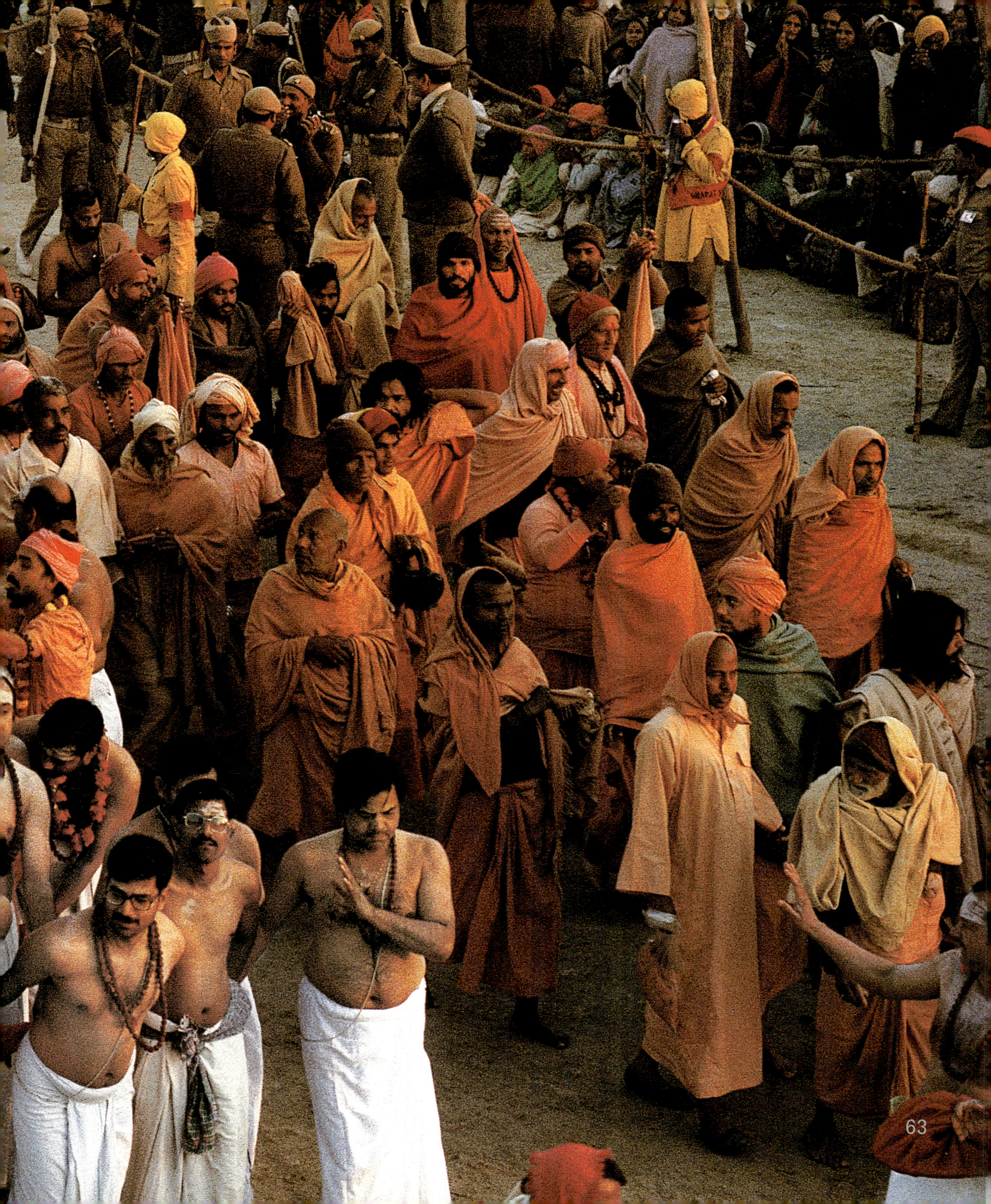

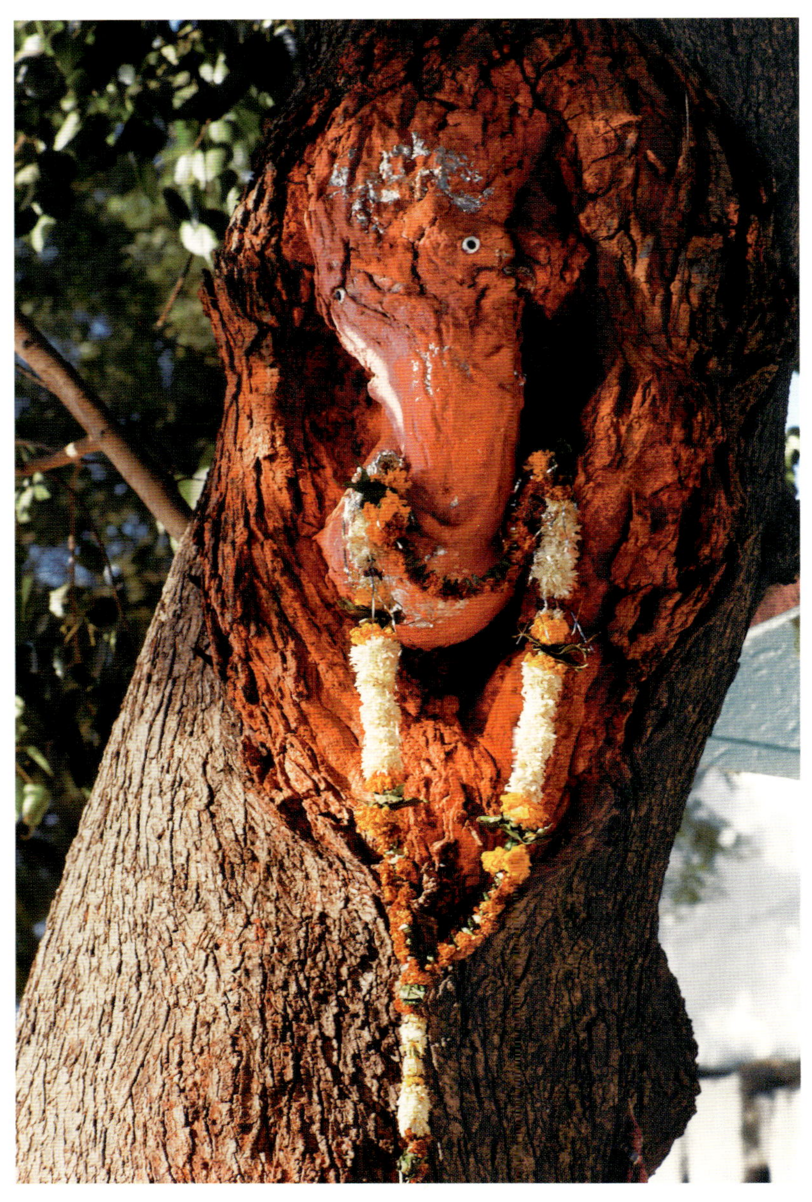

Above: Tree trunk representing Ganesh.
Opposite: Wayside shrine, Calcutta.
Pages 62–63: Hindu procession, Allahabad.

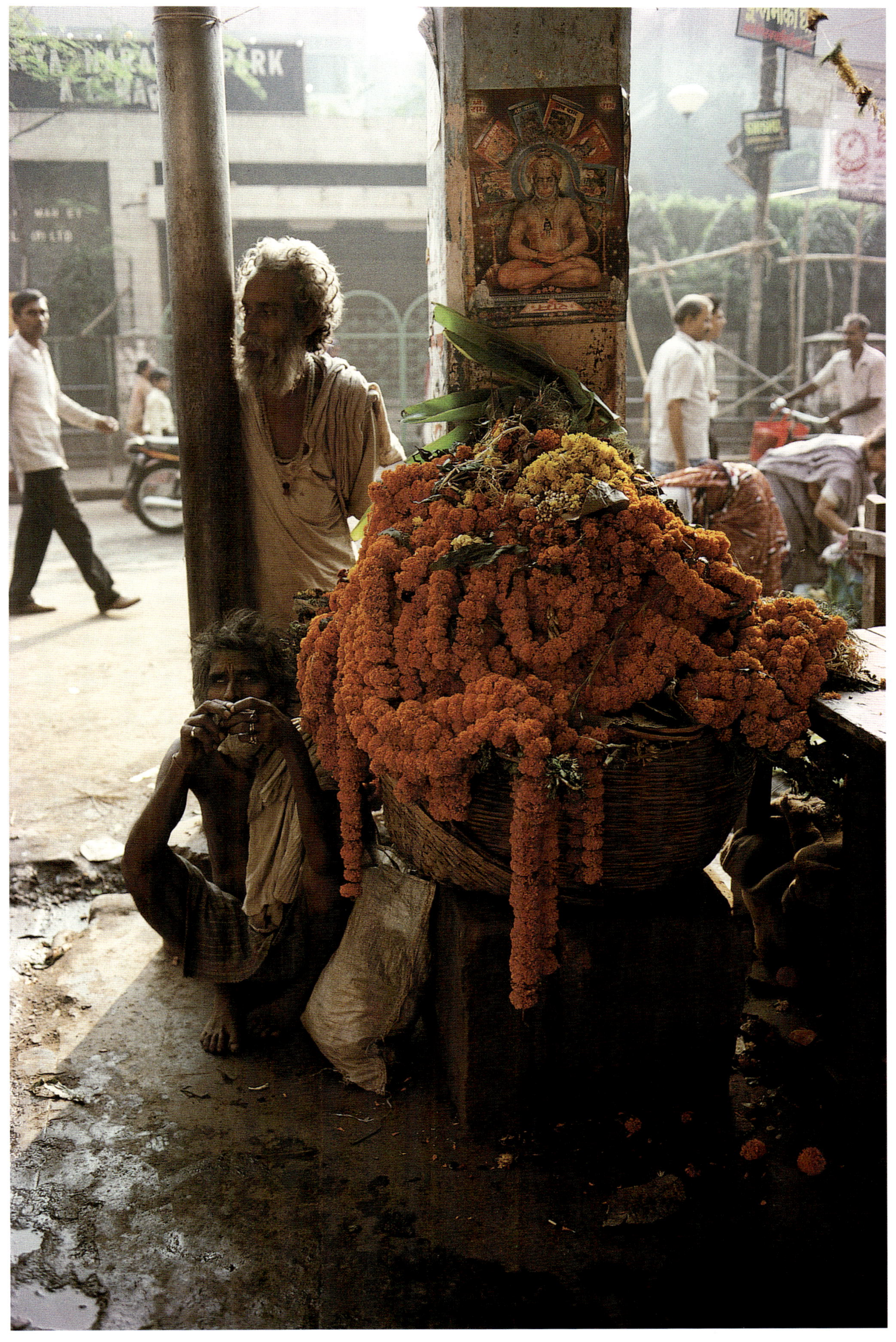

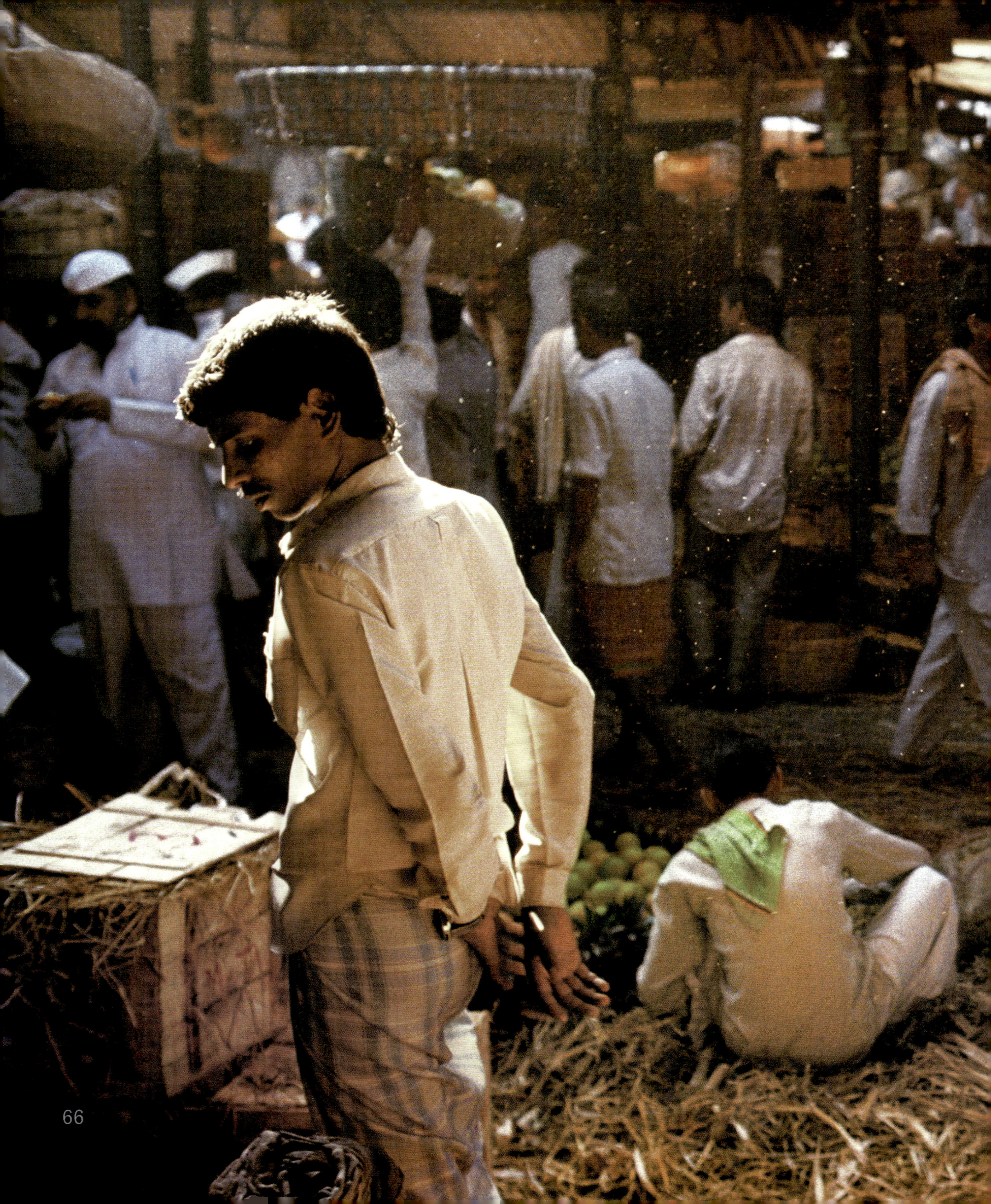

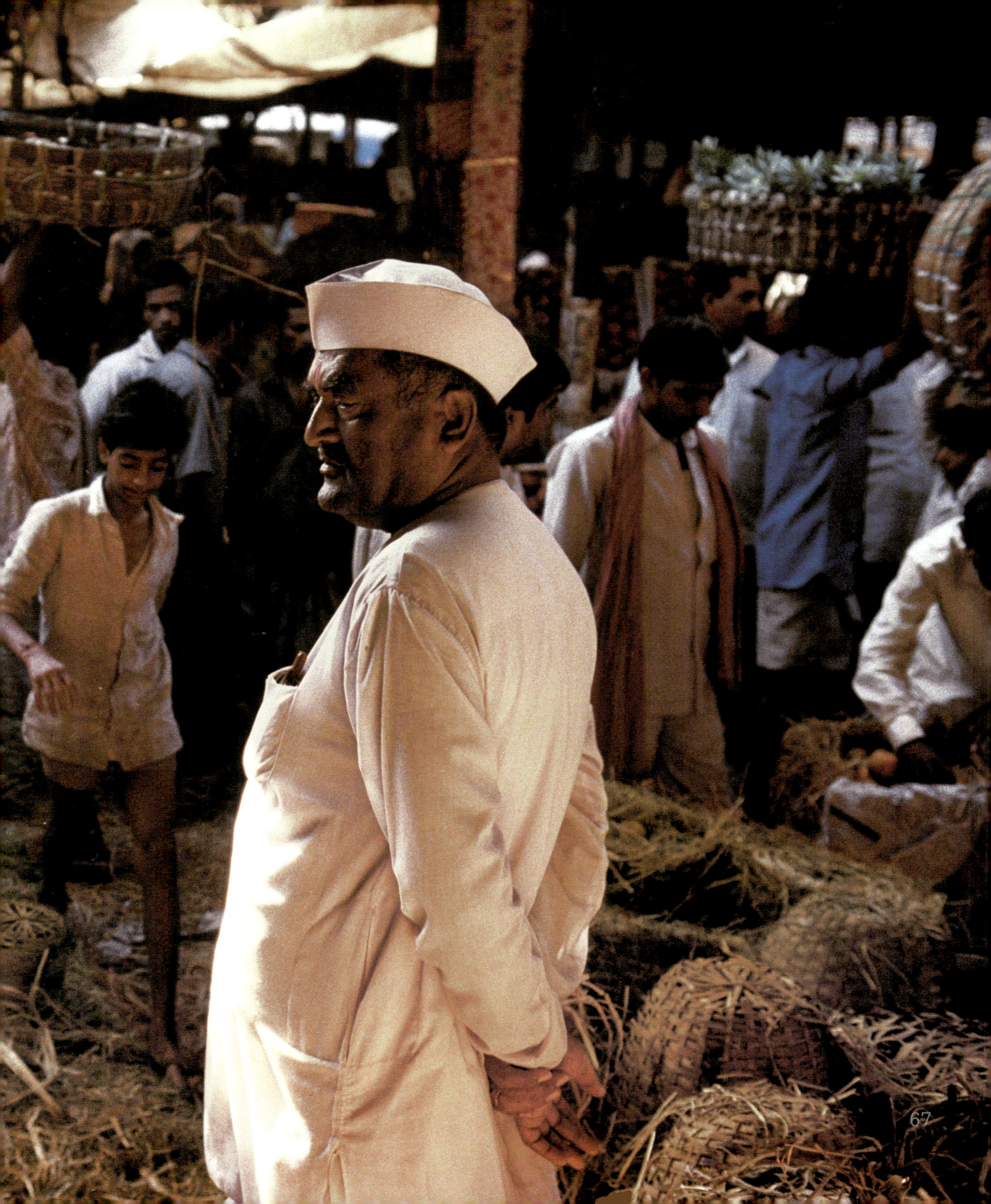

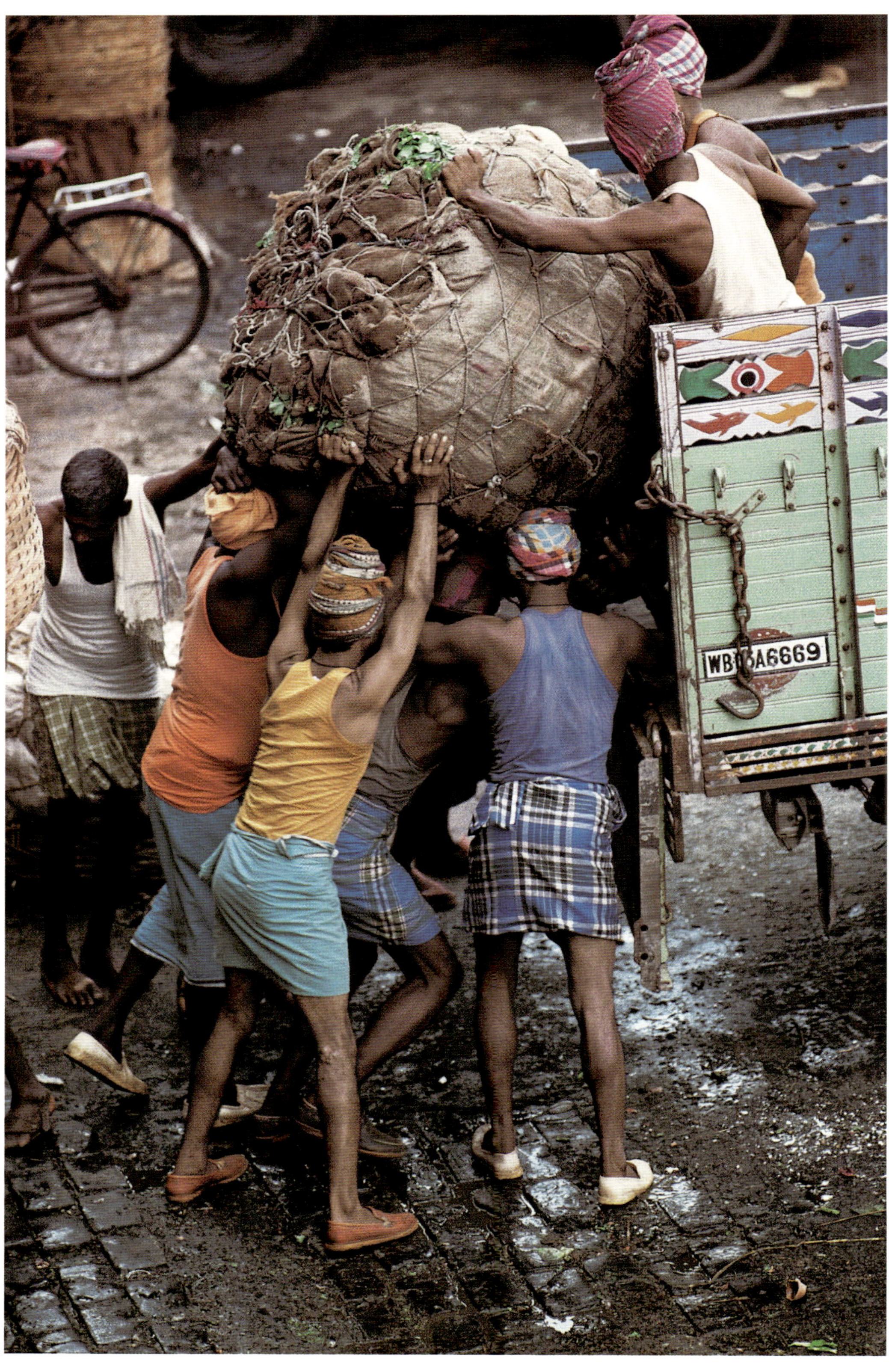

Above and Opposite: Porters, Calcutta.
Pages 66–67: Market in Bombay.

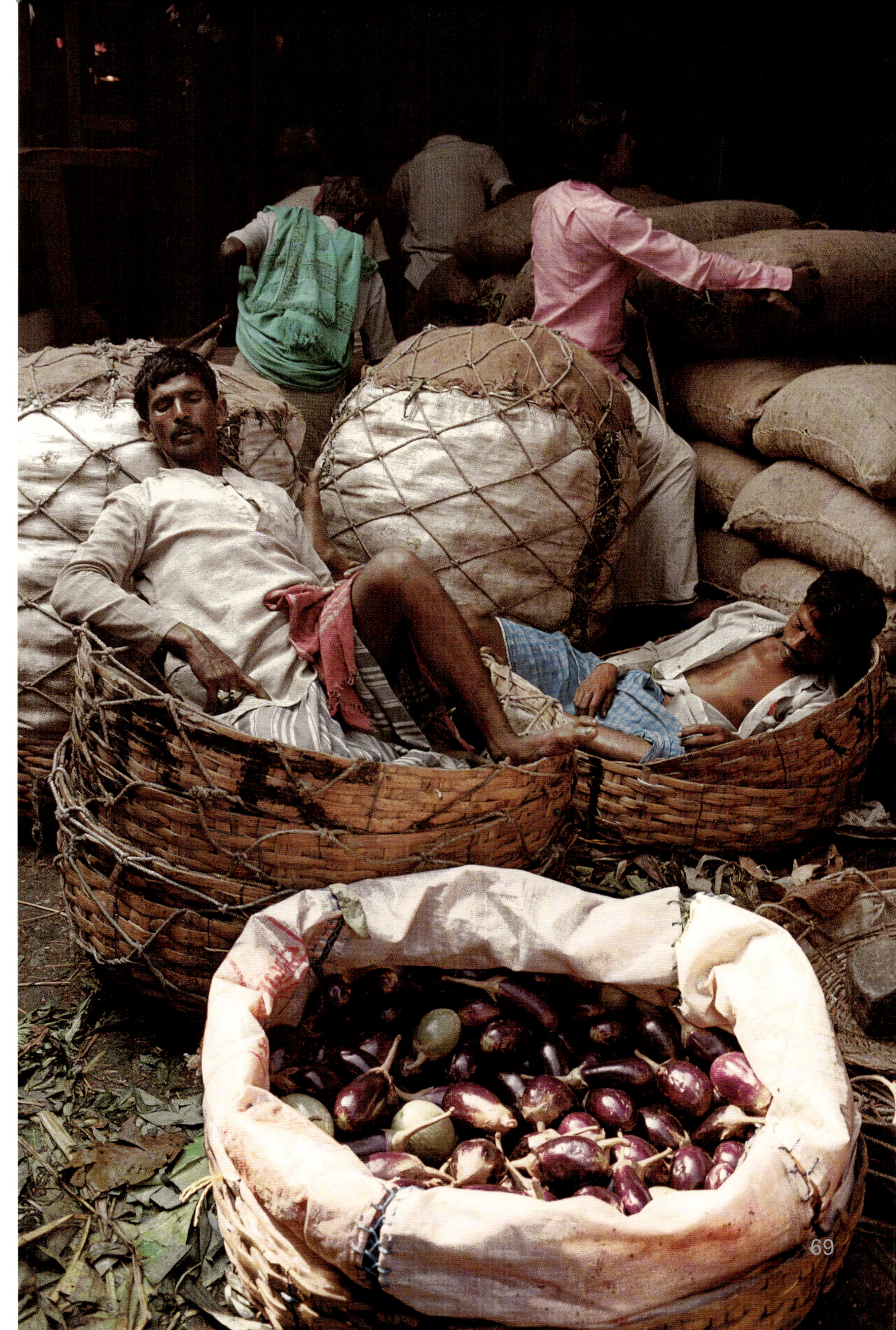

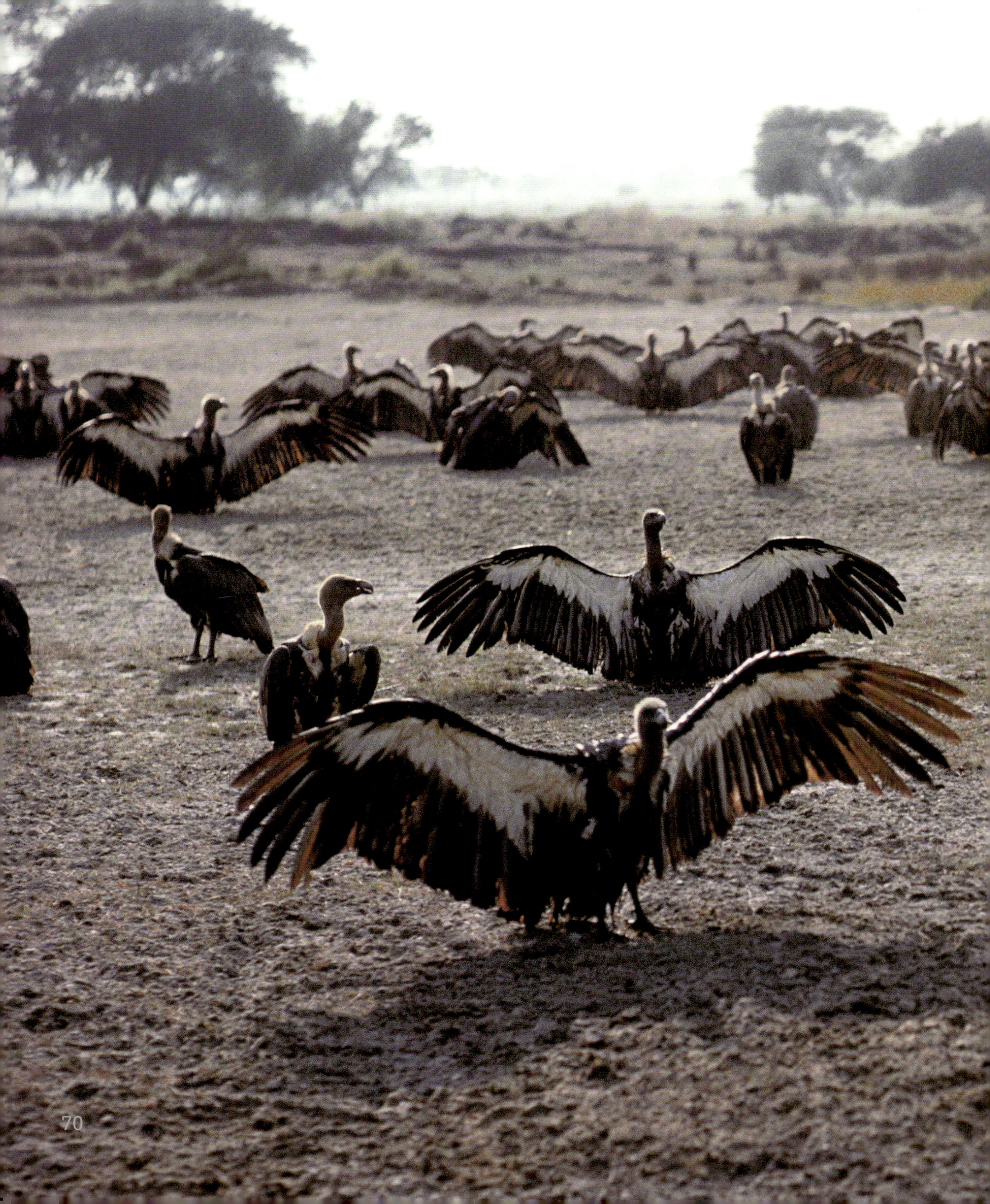

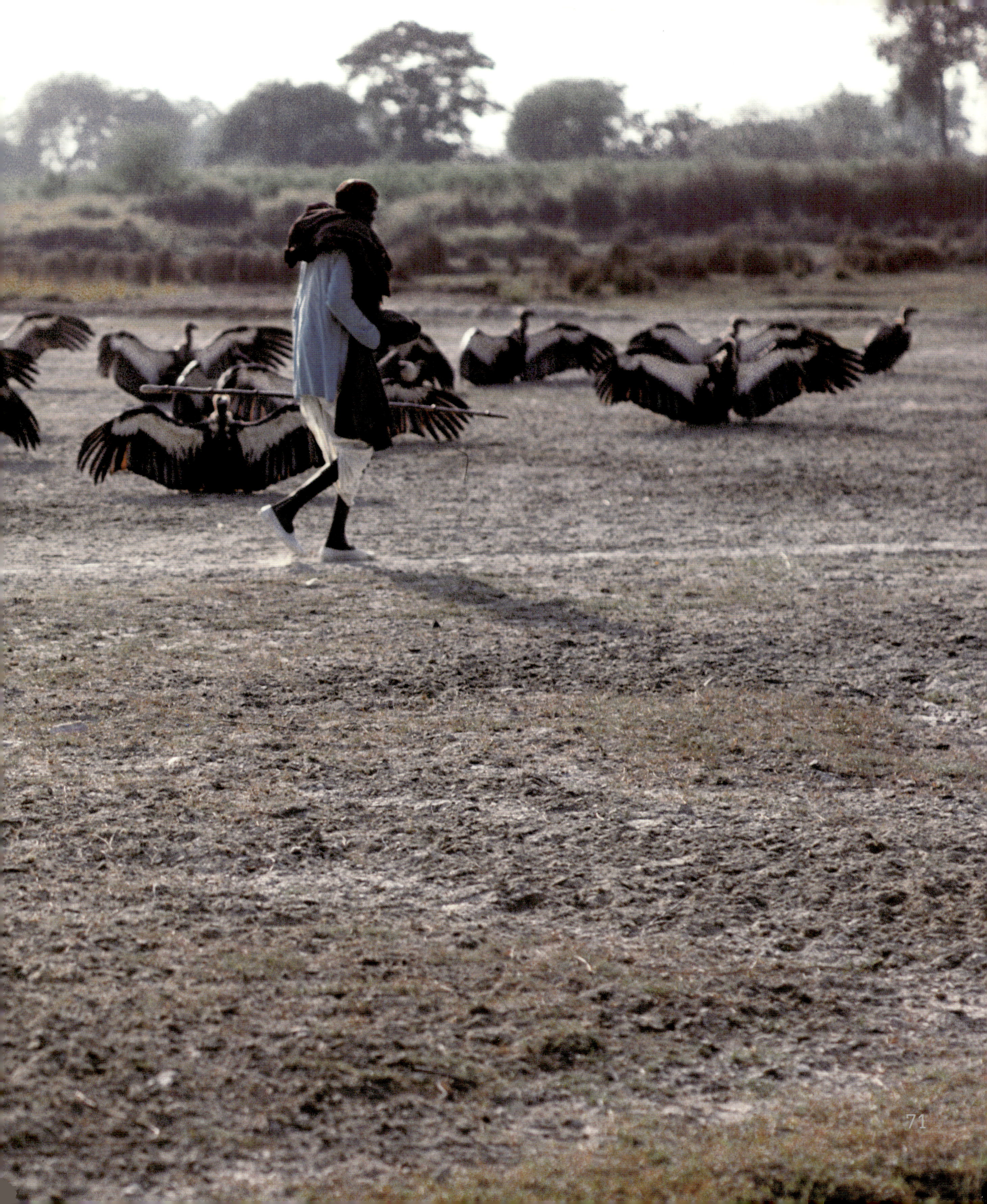

The village

Early in the morning we find ourselves on a local bus that stops at the railroad station. The haze of dust, pierced by the cries of peddlers, partially conceals tricksters, shoeshine boys, soothsayers, inquisitive cows, booths selling flowers and fruit, animal droppings. If the town is a tourist attraction, urchins crowd around the bus, eager to act as guides. If it isn't, we find ourselves lost in the milling throngs, being given the wrong directions. It is a satisfactory situation, to the extent that an attempted experience is subjected to chance.

The bus we have chosen is ancient, and it contains travelers lugging huge suitcases or bales of dried herbs. We shall have to endure a few hours of overcrowding in the chaotic vehicle before we arrive in a small farming village. After wandering about, soaking up the atmosphere of the place, we find a young man whom we commission to find us two bicycles. People here do not understand the inclinations and strange notions of travelers, so our request is rejected. But in India, a "no" is as ineffectual as a "yes." Two bicycles finally arrive and are even found to be in working order.

When we set out, we have to firmly refuse to reveal where we are going. On leaving the village, trailed by a horde of playful children, we assume a determined look as we choose a dirt road at random. Fate is kind, and we soon find ourselves among brilliant green paddy-fields, plowed by oxen harnessed to a swingplow, guided by a shirtless chocolate-colored farmer.

A brightly dressed group of women are beating sheaves of rice in a timeless gesture. They are pleased to see us. We exchange smiles and looks before we resume our route with intense pedaling. We encounter paths that lead into a bucolic landscape. We choose each path at random as our inspiration leads us. We have to watch out for large stones, potholes, the sharp points of agave leaves, and goats herded by a biblical-looking patriarch. We are sure to reach an Indian village, since there are 600,000 to choose from. If it is of average size, it will have between 300 and 500 inhabitants.

As soon as we enter a village, we see a likeness of the Samaritan woman at the well, a jar on her head.

Of course, each village differs in the types of buildings it contains, the activities of the villagers, and the number of *jatis* present. No village resembles any other in this country because India claims diversity as a way of life. And yet there are constants, such as include the certainty that village life revolves around the temple. We seat ourselves on a burning hot low wall. We don't have long to wait. The children at first keep their distance. They are unfamiliar with the sight of strangers in this village. But with a few little gifts, the ice is soon broken.

The children press around us, but the women still stare at us from a distance and ask themselves the age-old question—is our arrival a good or a bad omen? An offering placed before the statue of the god and a (sincere) prayer will settle the question. We find ourselves led to a house where we are served *chai*, milky tea perfumed with cardamom.

The one-story adobe house has a roof of rice straw that will be swept away by the monsoon; the roof will have to be rethatched every year, a task that is accepted without complaint. We are welcomed in a clean, cool room. A portable stove and a few cooking utensils that have been polished a thousand times stand on the earthen floor. Behind a tattered veil there are two more rooms, one for men and one for women, each just as plain as this.

Washing facilities are outside, and consist of a bowl and a thin trickle of stagnant water. For more substantial ablutions there is the well or, better still, the river. The tall *jatis* are higher up the village, the low *jatis* below it. As for latrines, look to Mother Nature. The state of cleanliness varies depending on whether you are in a private home that is well-kept or a public place treated with indifference. Thus, the village paths, the city streets, and the Indian-style hotels are strewn with detritus that is moved about from time to time by miserable, bowed wretches in this country that is unaware of the garbage can and the handkerchief.

Sleeping at a railroad station in the company of other Indians enabled us to discover the contradiction of clean bodies and clothing, but filthy latrines and waiting-rooms. Does this mean that Indians do not have the same perceptions and sense of smell that we have? Yes, it does. They do not seem to see that the delightful tourist bungalow located between the sea and the palm trees is spoiled by the presence of garbage on the avenue leading to the beach—no more than we realize how disgusting it is to collect our snot in a piece of cloth, or the ambiguity of the kisses exchanged in greeting between men and women. Every situation has its blind spots. Thus, we might be shocked by the close living conditions of this seven-member family (including the grandmother), while an Indian could not bear to sleep alone in a bedroom. We are surprised at the absence of intimacy between husband and wife. So where do they practice the ritual through which life is perpetuated? We need reassurance!

Now, in this darkened room, no one seeks to make conversation because it is enough just to be together; we are patient because someone has gone to find a young man who is reputed to speak English. There are silent smiles; no one is worried. Is this brotherhood

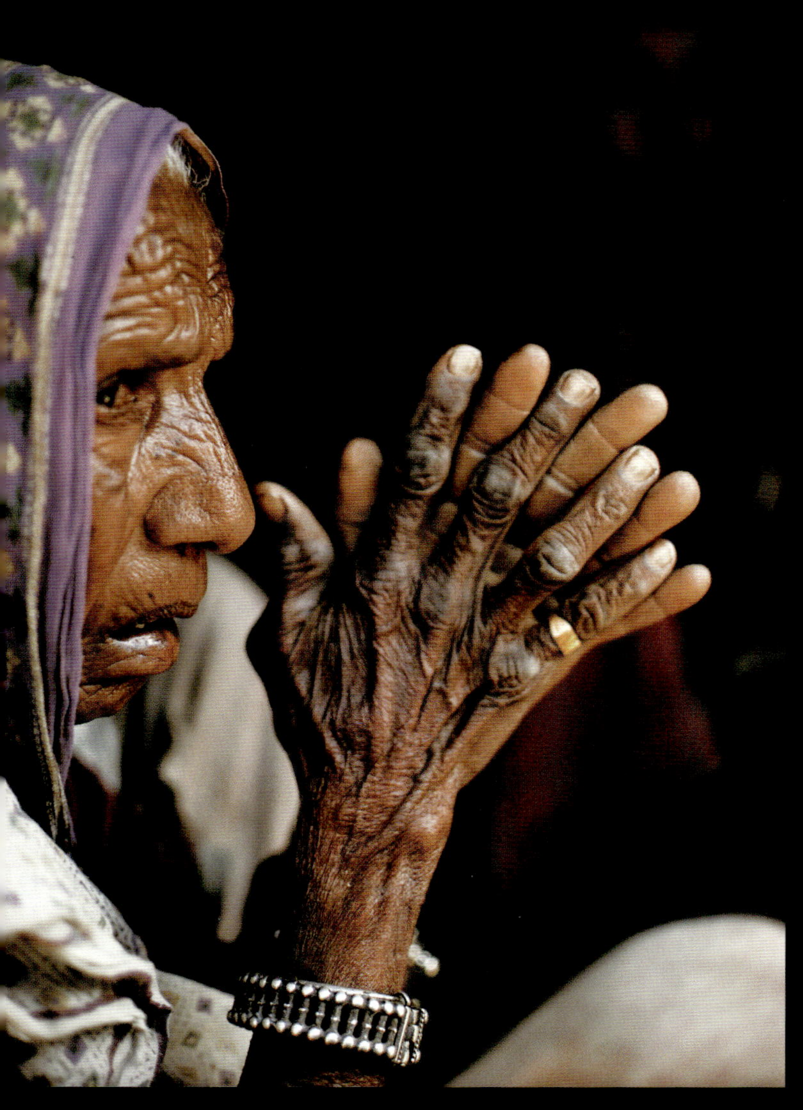

Above: Old woman.
Opposite: Returning home from the fields.

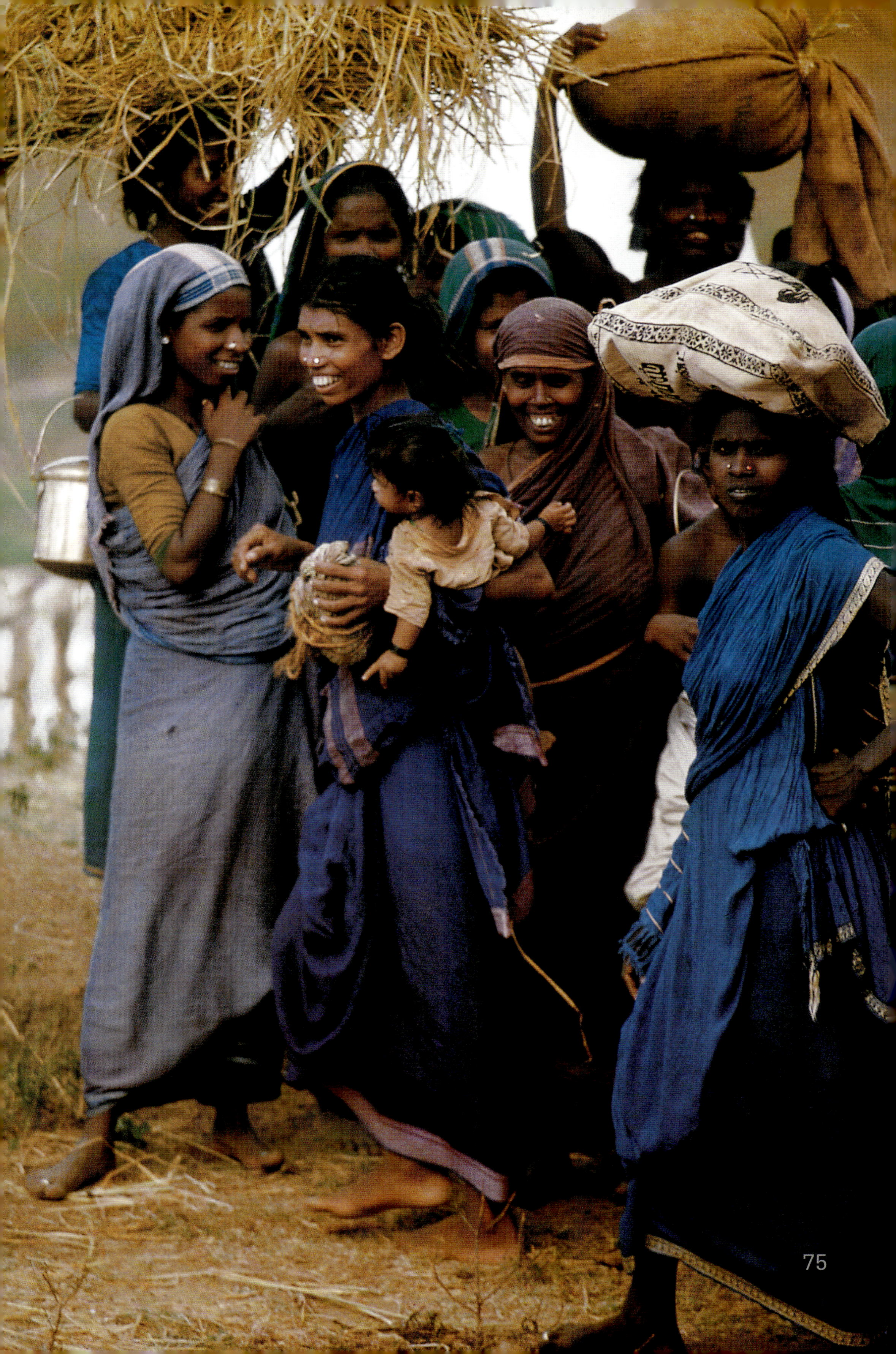

an illusion? Only partially. The consciousness of belonging to a common humanity is real, despite the gulf between mentalities and social situations. An interpreter could contribute nothing more than facial expressions.

Here he is, the young man we so eagerly awaited! He is awkward, timid, and his English is gibberish. But it is preferable to be able to deal with a boy like this who is unspoiled rather than a westernized Indian who will present a doubly distorted picture of India through his desire to conceal the poverty, the child labor, or the fate of the "untouchables," and the prejudices that he imagines we have against polytheism, animal sacrifice, arranged marriages, the importance of astrology, and so on. At any event, whatever the naïveté or malice of our guide, it is obvious that years of observation would be needed to fully understand the complexity of this village. And again, personal perception does much to alter the object that is perceived.

Yet, by paying attention and using intuition, some aspects of it are revealed. For instance, a village is usually organized in a very rigorous structure around the *jatis*, each of which plays a specific and indispensable role in community life. The functions of men and women are strictly delineated. At no time does the question arise as to who should do what.

The potter, the slaughterer, the *Brahman*'s daughter, the daughter-in-law of the sorghum field owner, the goatherd, and the son of the latrine emptier—each has his role that has been predetermined for generations; each will marry in his or her own *jati*; the boys will stay home; the girls will go live with their in-laws, who may come from this village (what luck!) or from another, depending on the availability of husbands of the same origin, but certainly not from the neighboring village since it has been judged to be "impure" even in the eyes of the little community of untouchables.

This pecking order does not operate on criteria based on money and temporal power. It all depends on the nature of one's work and the purity that this implies. For reasons that date far back in history, though probably after the Vedic era, there is a hierarchy of jobs—from the pure to the impure—that no one has ever challenged before modern times. It is pure to handle milk, impure to handle leather. Although the modern economy and a new way of thinking are overturning these preconceptions in the cities, the villages perpetuate this system among organically linked communities; Indian society does not create exclusion in the same way as modern Western society; it simply sends to the bottom of the pecking order certain people who are in other ways integrated into it.

After a few meaningless exchanges and a first visit to the neighborhoods surrounding the temple, we are invited to visit another house. The laughing children are already waiting for us. This brick building appears to us to be in the worst possible taste, with shocking pink and pistachio green frontage, excessive decoration, and a large sofa in the reception room, representing modernity. The owner is a farmer who owns more land than most and who controls the distribution system. We are served tea once again, and again little is said.

Another trip around the village. First to the basket makers' neighborhood, then to a few houses in which clay pots are made before the plastic containers from the city intervene, killing off this ancient art that carries sacred associations due to its contact with fire. Over there, tailors labor over antique Singer sewing machines from a home of the conquerors; here there are mothers nursing their babies and with flies swarming overhead. Women sort grain on the steps. Behind a cowshed, lower down the village, there are some wretched hovels. "Is this the *harijan* neighborhood?" we ask the young man who has never before felt so important.

Harijan, or "children of God," is that name that Gandhi gave in 1929 to those previously known as untouchables. His genius was to give them a just name. They are members of the lowest *jatis*, and condemned to pursue impure occupations.

"Yes," replies our guide, quite unruffled because for him, the *jati* reflects the natural order of things. We wouldn't be worried about admitting that we had a school for the blind in our neighborhood. These unfortunate villagers, whose skin is blacker than the others, watch us anxiously; their astonishment rises to a crescendo when we offer them gifts under the disapproving eye of the people accompanying us, for whom our gesture is incomprehensible. Here is the sanctuary in which the *harijan* worship their own special divinity; here is the well from which they alone draw water; and here is the pile of garbage on which their children play. We pick up a child and stroke his silky cheek, leaving before there can be any embarrassing outpourings of gratitude.

Here is a comparison based on tradition: the untouchables are part of the human community in the same way that certain lower parts of our body are just as much part of the human organism as the mouth. The *Brahmans*' calling is to recite the sacred texts; the "untouchables" occupation is emptying the latrines. Each is indispensable to the other.

Nothing can justify such a situation. Fortunately, it is in the process of change. Few societies have worked so hard to help the least favored members of society for the last three generations. Firstly, there was Gandhi's universal compassion, the incarnation of India's greatest virtues. Successive governments after Independence claimed that they wanted to abolish the caste system, a pious wish in this country that remains so attached to this system of solidarity. By introducing quotas in favor of untouchables in the public service and the universities, some members of these communities were able to better themselves, allowing the rest not to feel forever overwhelmed by fate. In 1997, an untouchable became president of the republic, a symbolic gesture.

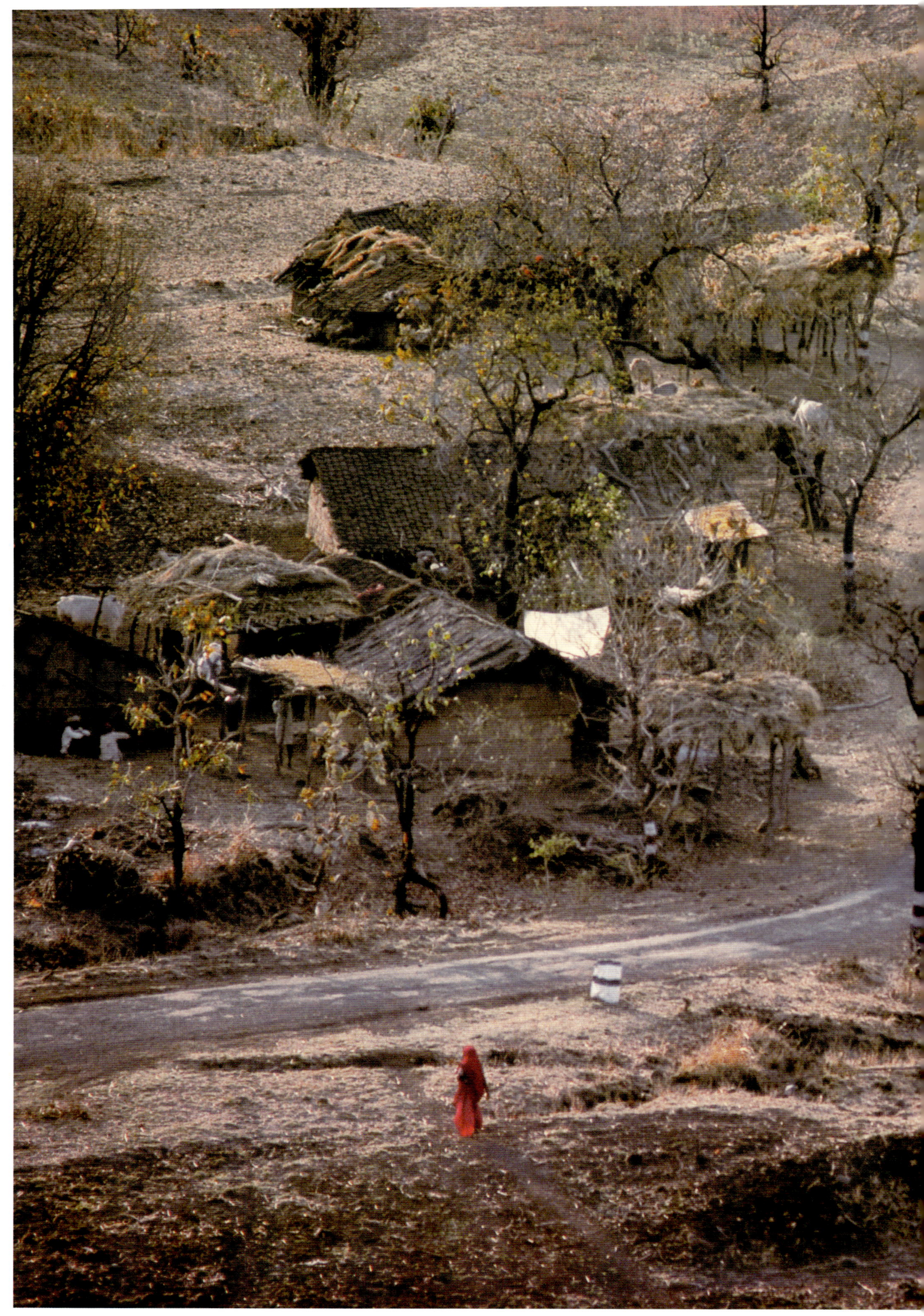

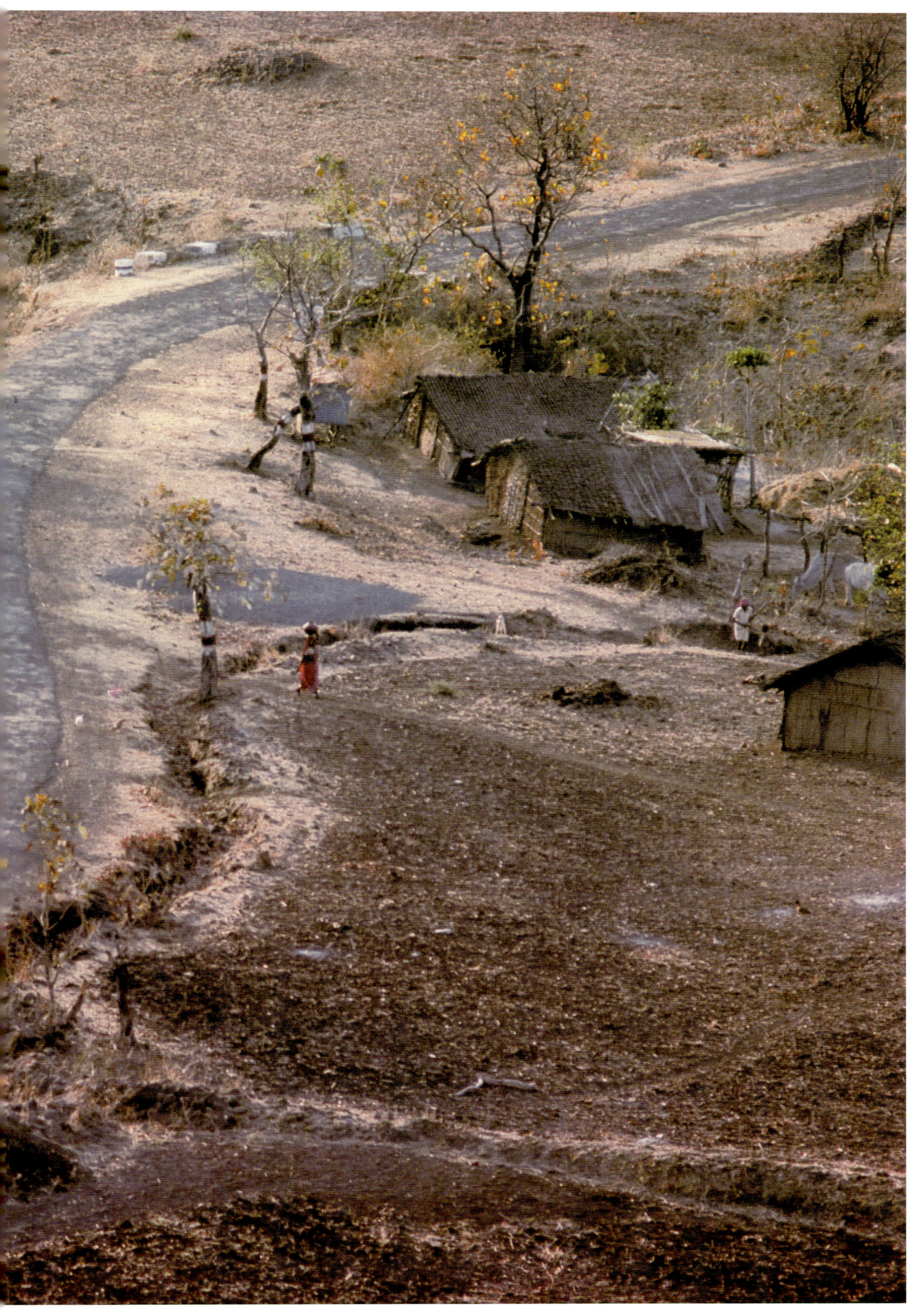

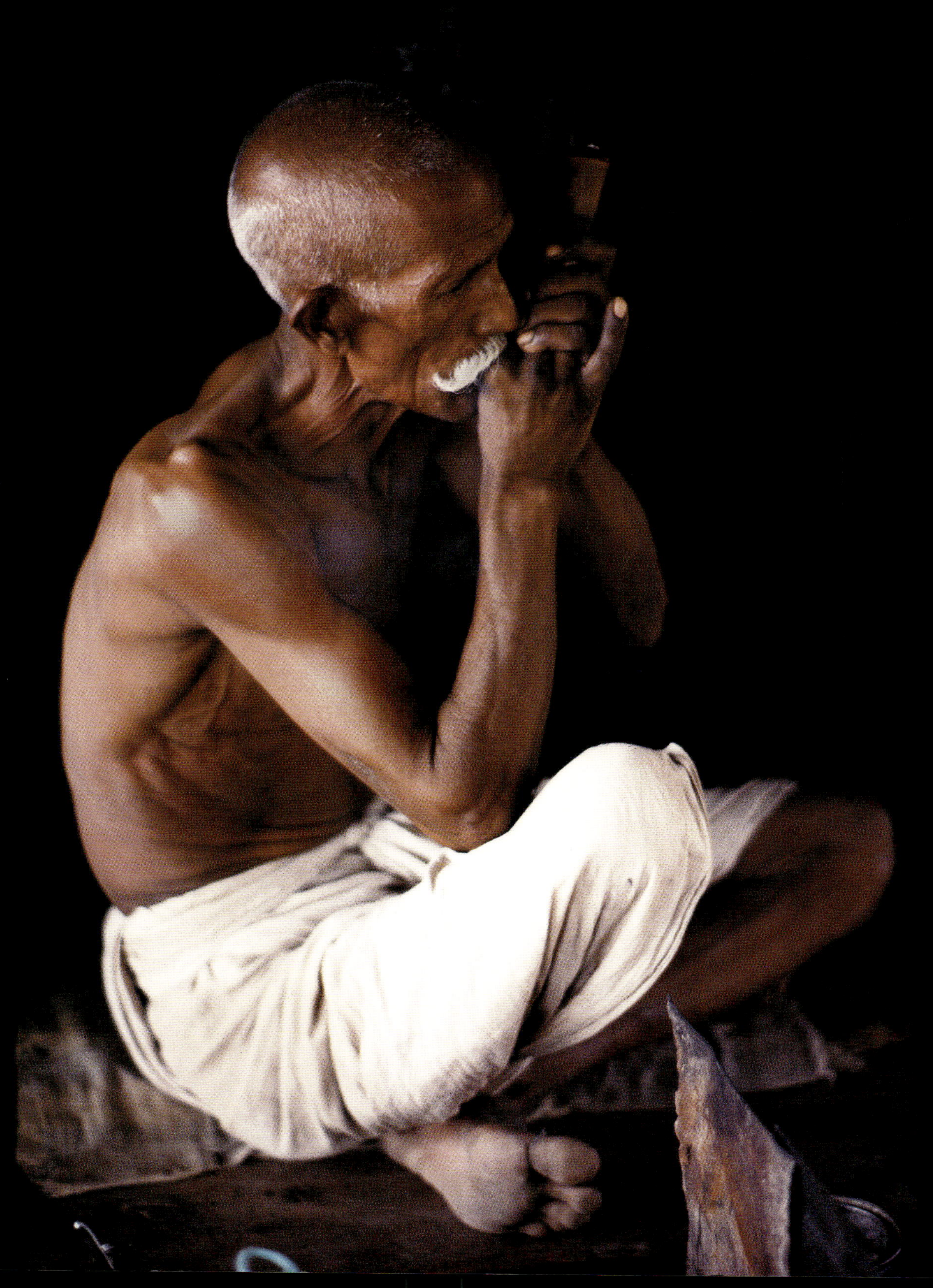

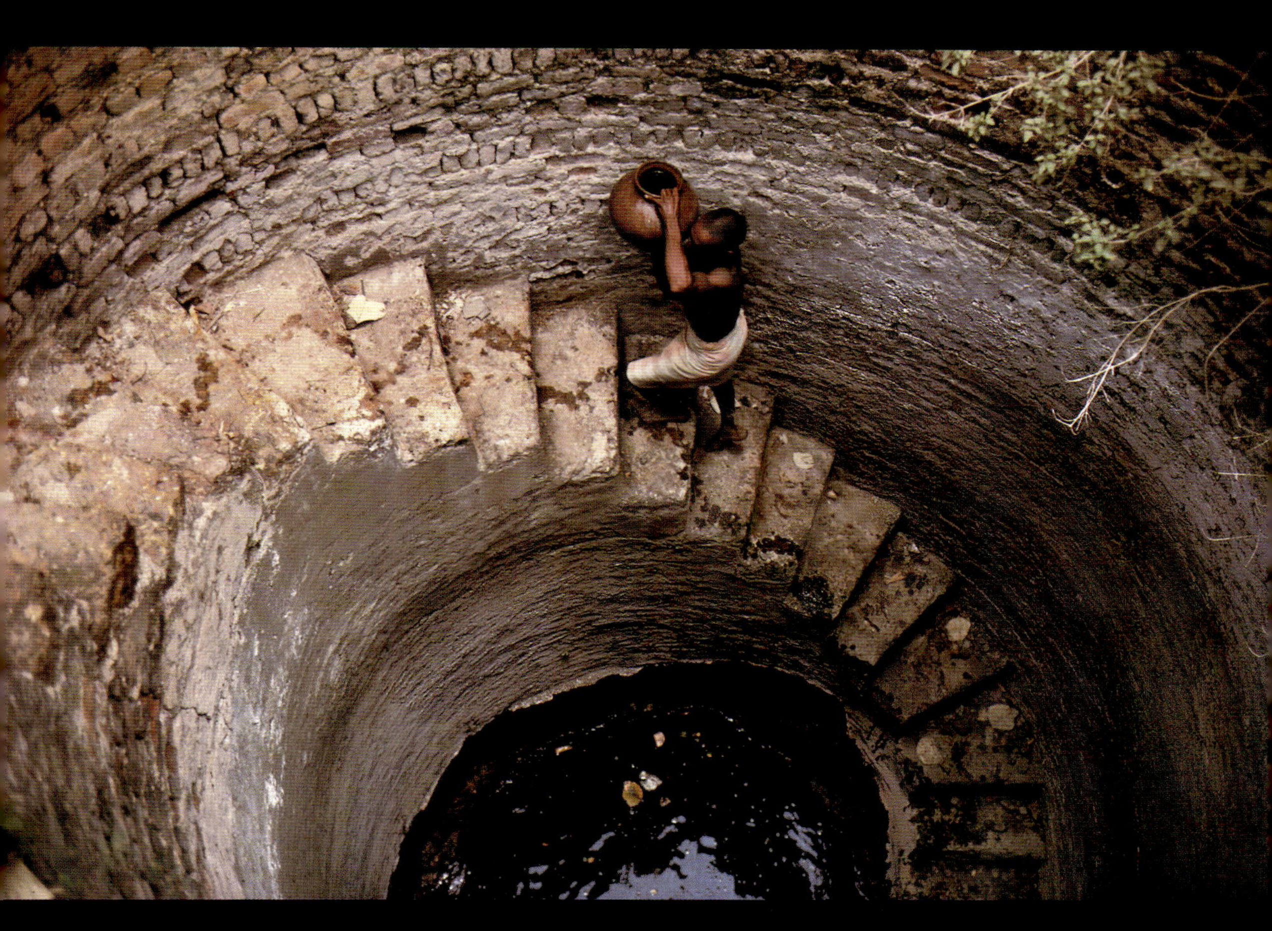

Opposite: Pipe smoker, Rajasthan.
Above: Returning from the well.

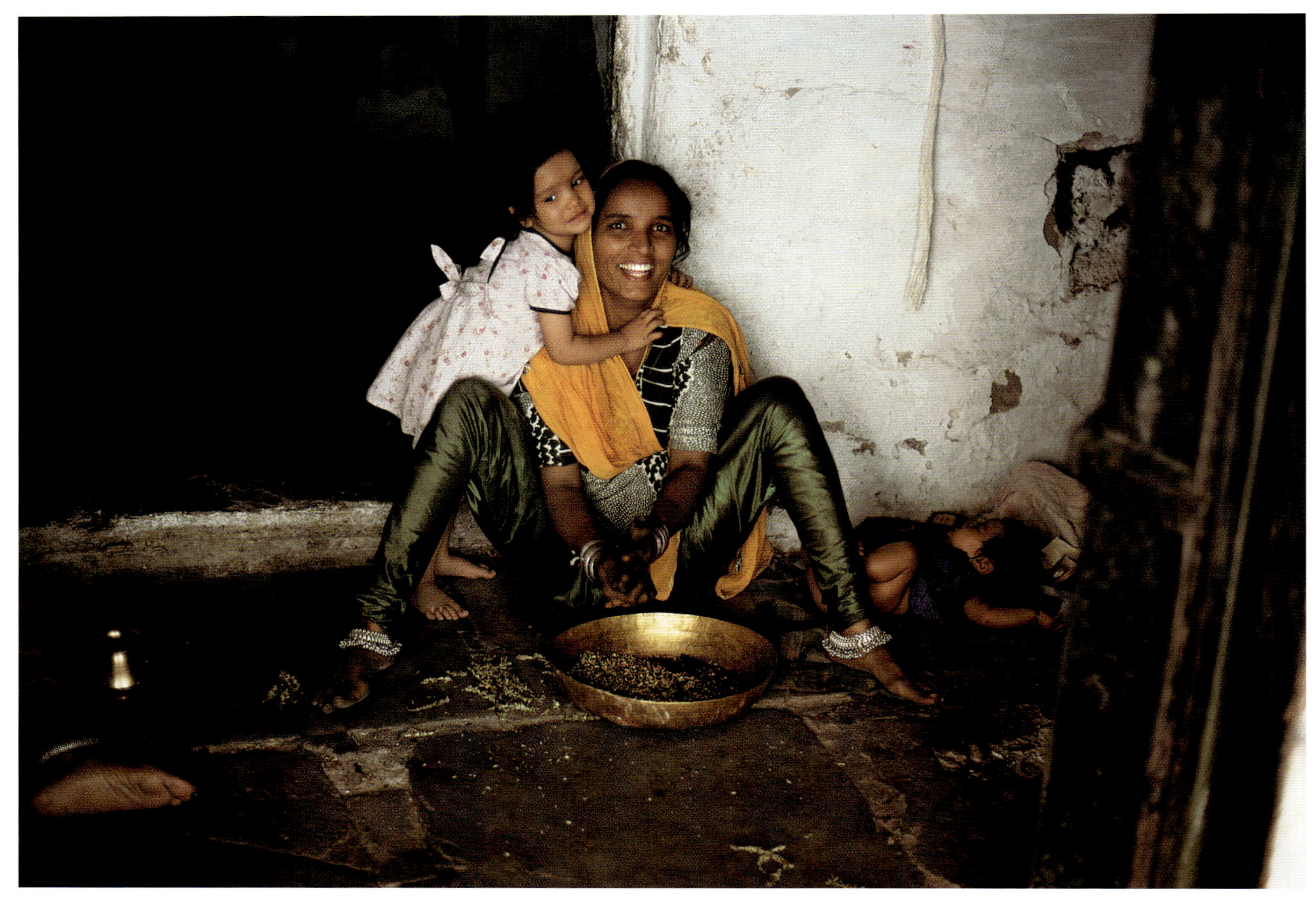

Above: Village interior.
Opposite: Winnowing in Kerala.

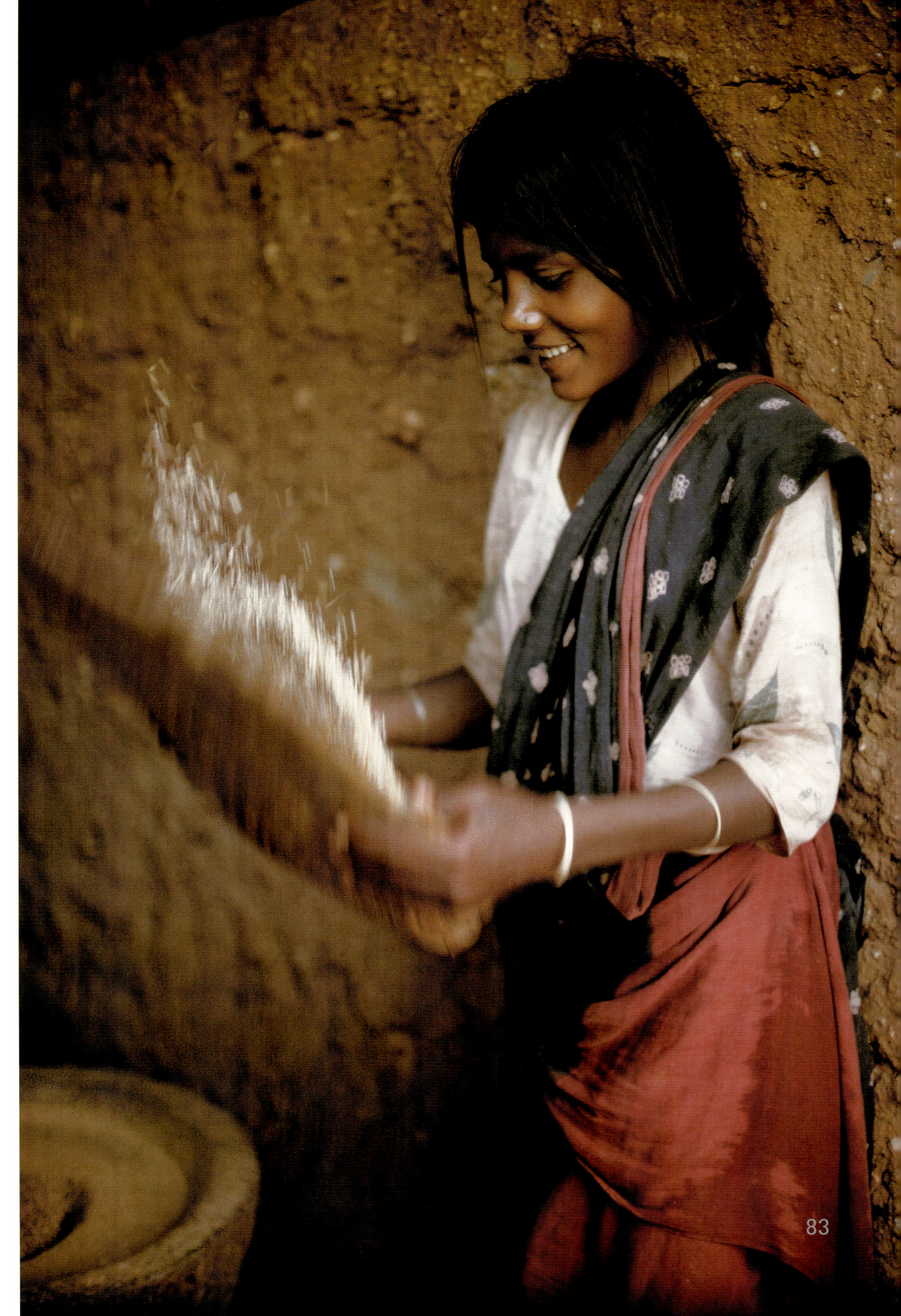

The untouchables represent 22 percent of the population of the Indian Union; 15 percent are from the lowest *jatis* and 7 percent are tribal peoples who have not been included in the Hindu system and who still live separately, often in remote regions in the center of India or in Orissa state.

The modern Western mentality is offended by the caste system, which they wrongly attribute to a social order based on money or race; there are poor *Brahmans* and dark-skinned *Brahmans*. In fact, the issue is so complex that we should forget our criteria and reject any simple explanation, even though "purity" in relation to sanctity obviously plays a fundamental role. There are four traditional *varnas*: *Brahmans* (those who have access to knowledge and are permitted to approach that which is holy), *Kshatriya* (warriors and politicians), *Vaisya* (merchants and peasants), *Sudra* (servants of the first three castes who are not considered as being *dvija* or "twice born"), followed by the *panchama* ("fifth member"), the untouchables. These divisions are not based on the real situation that is actually founded on the *jatis* ("births" or castes), of which there are 3,000 or more, that still constitute the basis of the Indian social order. By far the majority of marriages take place within the same birth *jati*.

Western studies of the caste system are contradictory on many points. There are many reasons for this. The texts of the tradition provide different answers depending on the era in which they were written, which proves to what extent the principle has constantly changed, as with so many aspects of Indian culture. On the other hand, a field study requiring time and finesse has resulted in observations that vary from one region to another. The ardent desire to find constants that are applicable regardless of the era and region has encountered, and will always encounter, the extraordinary accumulation of special cases that is India. To avoid becoming blind men faced with elephants (see page 35), a few simple ideas should be accepted. Indian society has been and will remain strongly hierarchical based on a scale of values that does not correspond to any of our own categories. There is a "purity" of which we are unaware and that, if strict rules concerning food and customs are obeyed, makes it possible to approach the domain of the gods at the source of life. The determinism that causes one to be born a *Brahman* or a *Sudra* is only restricted to one life. Each person can improve his or her karma with the hope of being reborn into a purer *jati* and, from life to life, coming closer to liberation. The Western materialist sees this concept as a trap for the unwary, designed to maintain social inequalities. But it's not as simple as that. The life of a *Brahman* is beset with cumbersome restrictions. This separation into endogamous communities may shock the Western egalitarian and homogenizing mentality, and yet it possesses some appreciable advantages because it contributes solidarity with the sick, the old, widows, and orphans that no other body would care for. When the egalitarian principle encounters the reality of a living community, the choice should not be made based on an abstraction.

Like the tongues in Aesop's fable, the *Brahmans* are the subject of both admiration and disapproval. In a culture in which oral histories prevailed for centuries, they ensured that knowledge was handed down. But, of course, any dominant position can give rise to abuse. The *Brahmans*, who are not saints, jealously guard their privileges. They cherish and protect them, and yet they never abuse them to the extent of playing a political role, a function that has always been left to the *Kshatriya*.

Without this being either an exportable model nor one adapted to the modern economy and the massive urbanization that this heralds, the system of *jatis* has made it possible for the Indian mentality to survive two colonizations, so that today it remains a solid bulwark against the model of bloodthirsty dictatorships that attempt to eradicate any differences, dictatorships that have arisen at the very gates of India.

The fact remains that the existence of *jatis* decreed to be impure should be intolerable for anyone with a conscience, whether they were born on the banks of the Potomac or the Ganges. This has been just as much the case in India. From the Buddha to Mahatma Gandhi, and from Bhimrao Ramji Ambedkar through Kabir, Nanak, and Tukaram, not forgetting the anonymous opponents, there has been a powerful desire running through India to restore to the untouchables the human dignity that a perverse system has denied them.

It is evening in the village. We have gone to visit the sorghum fields and the terraces where the spices that are the genius of Indian cuisine are grown—cardamom, basil, garlic, pepper, ginger, cinnamon, saffron, cloves, and the indispensable chili peppers that are often abused, since there is a tradition of Indian cuisine that is spicy without being too hot. The women preparing dinner survey their spices like a painter choosing his colors, selecting the perfect complements for their art. But innovation is rare. For a few minutes, the thatched roofs blaze in the setting sun. The smoke is tinged with orange bringing a new touch of color before its descent into gray. We are moved by it and are grateful for the cooler air, as a discussion begins around us. It concerns who is going to take us in for the night. It turns out to be one of the *panchayat* ("five sages") who has returned from the fields, a man in his fifties with an alert expression and sober speech. We are once again welcomed into a newly built home that conforms to the idea that the villagers have of our tastes, unaware of our penchant for a thatched cottage of the kind found in the frescoes of Ajanta. The *panchayat* is a five-man council of village elders to which a variable number of ad hoc participants are added. The way in which members are selected, appointed or elected varies from one region to another. The *panchayat* is the product of ancient and long practice of direct democracy, and deals with the widest range of problems that arise in a village, from rights to use the village well to disputes of a much more serious nature (theft, rape, fighting, etc.) between villagers. The member who greets us does not answer the questions we ask him as to how often the *panchayat* meets and the most recent matters discussed. He would answer

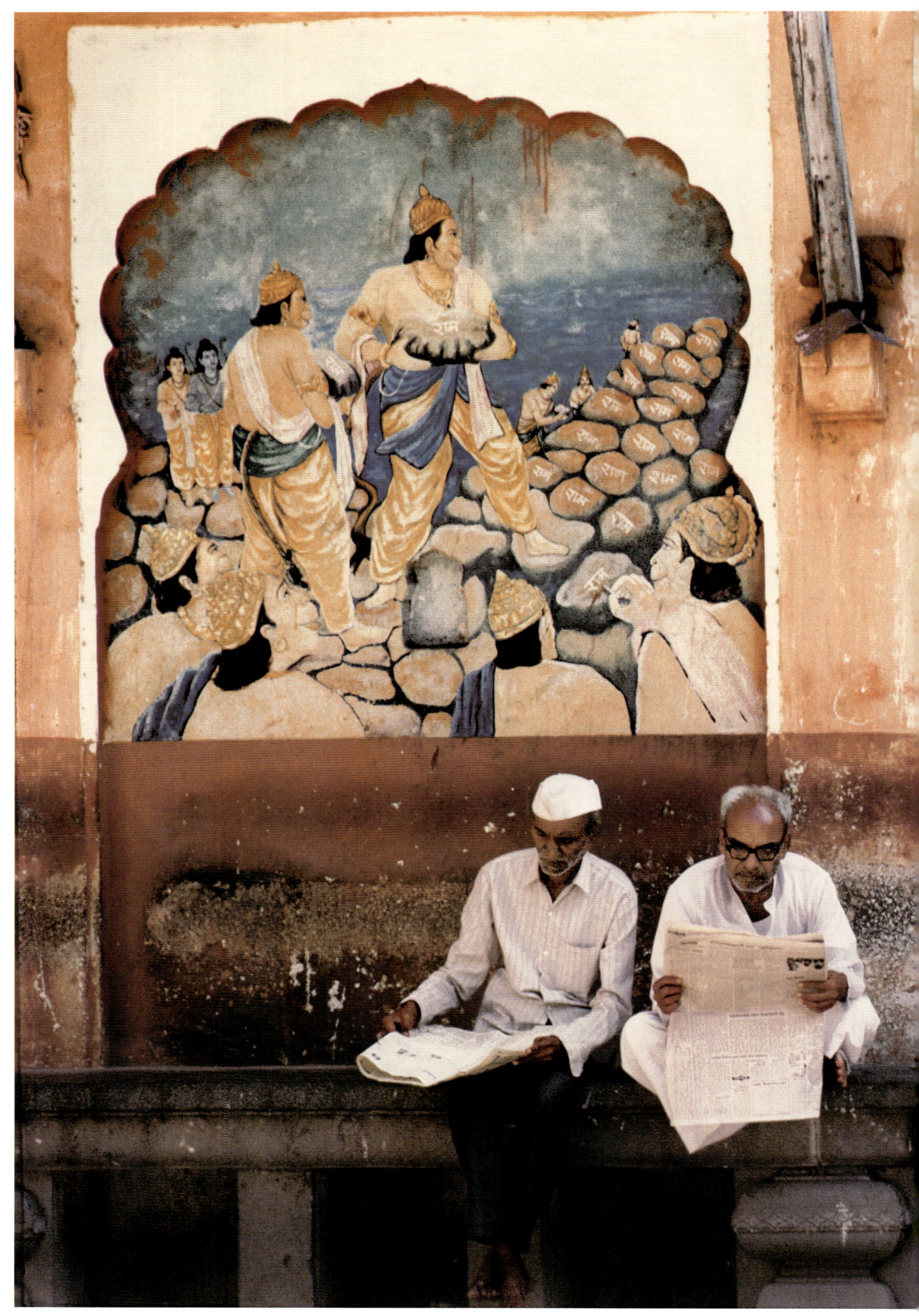

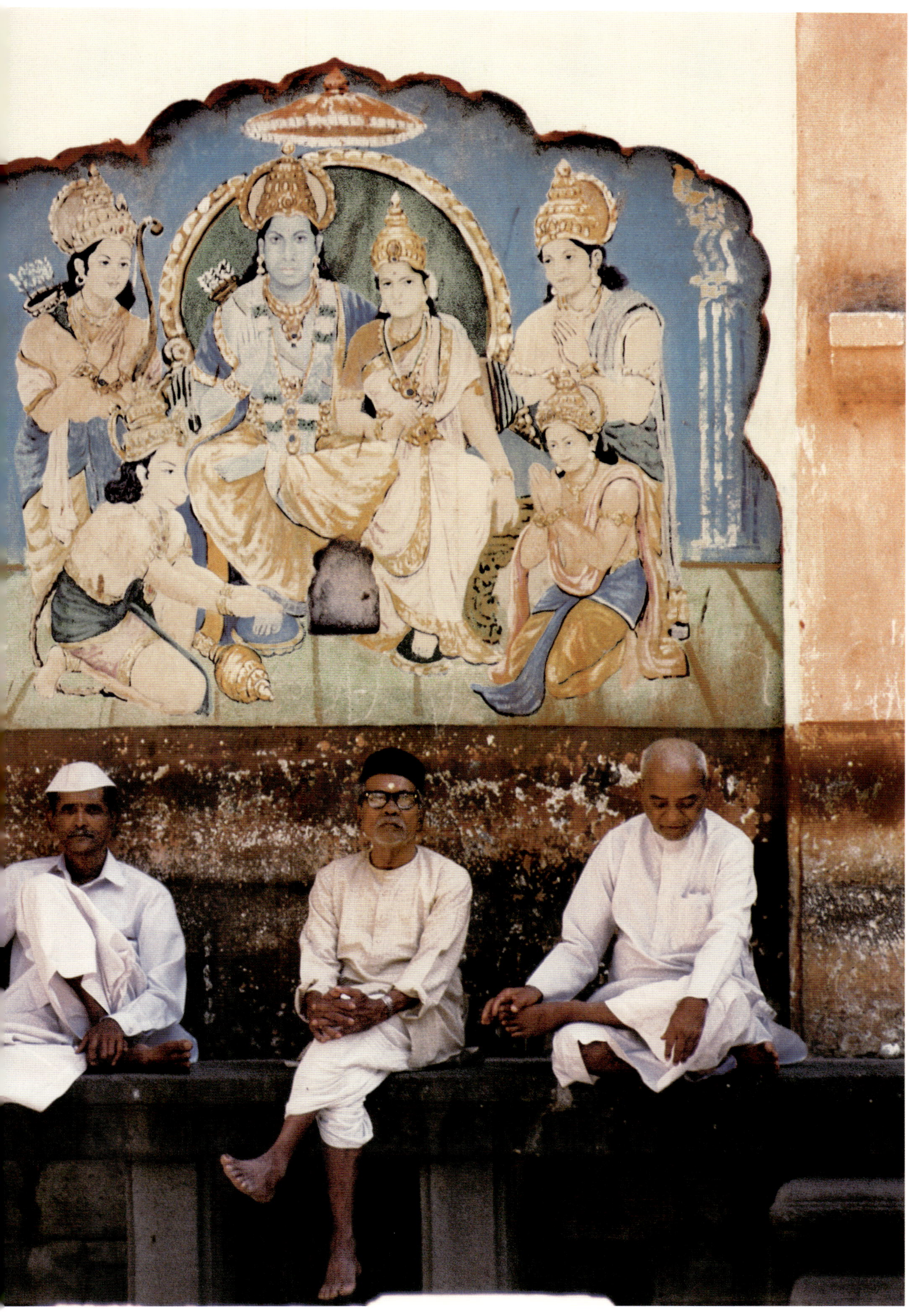

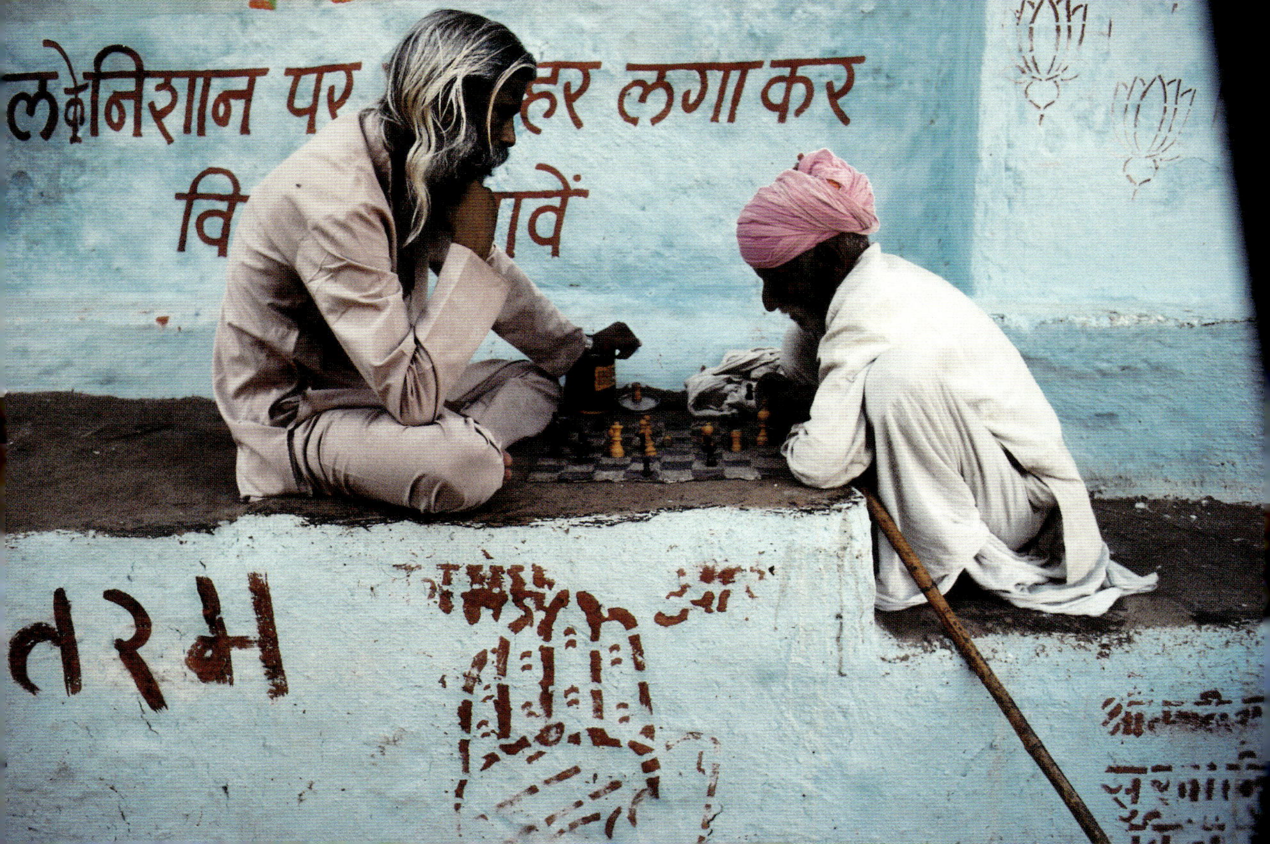
लेनिशान पर हर लगा कर
वि वें
तरम

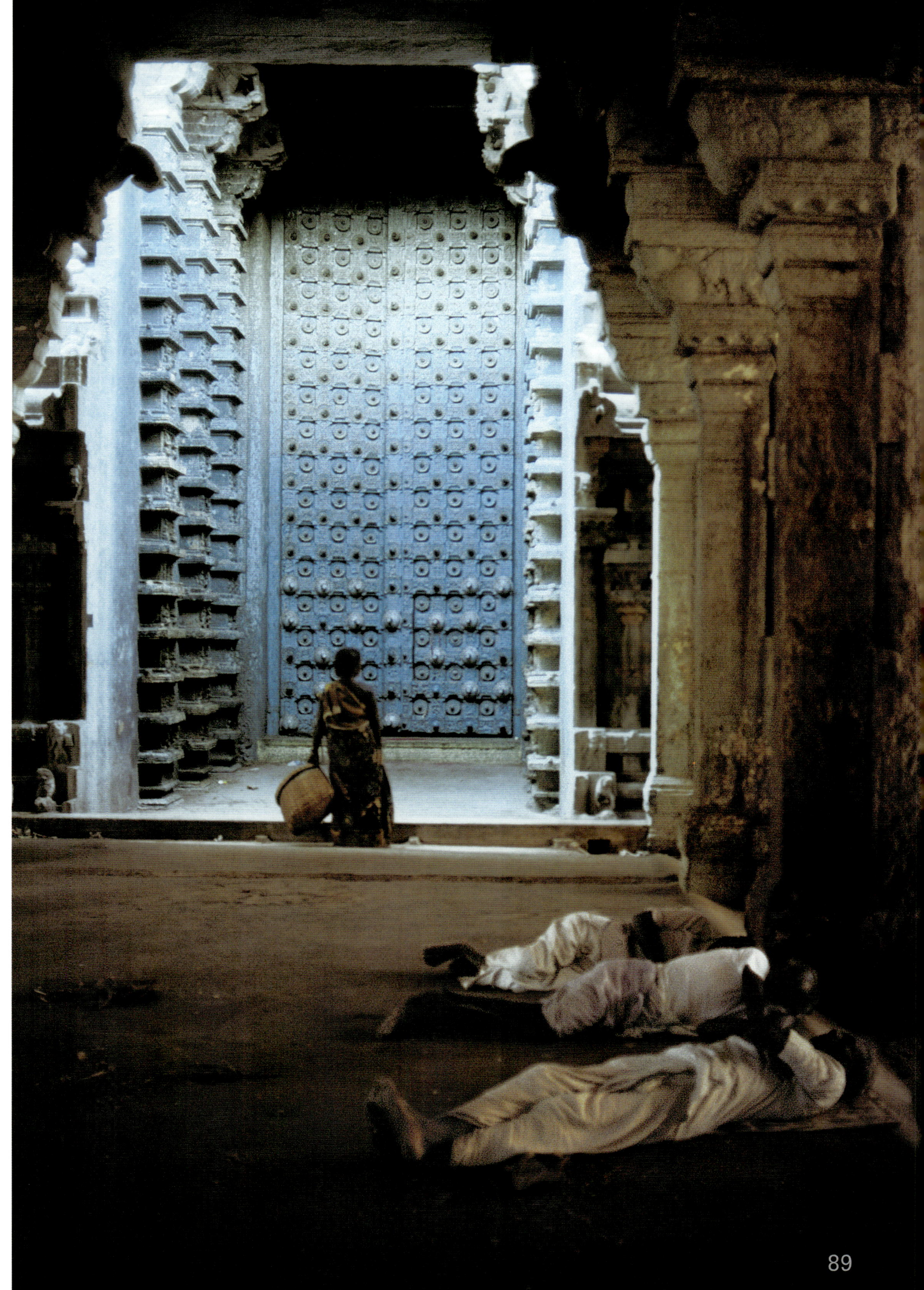

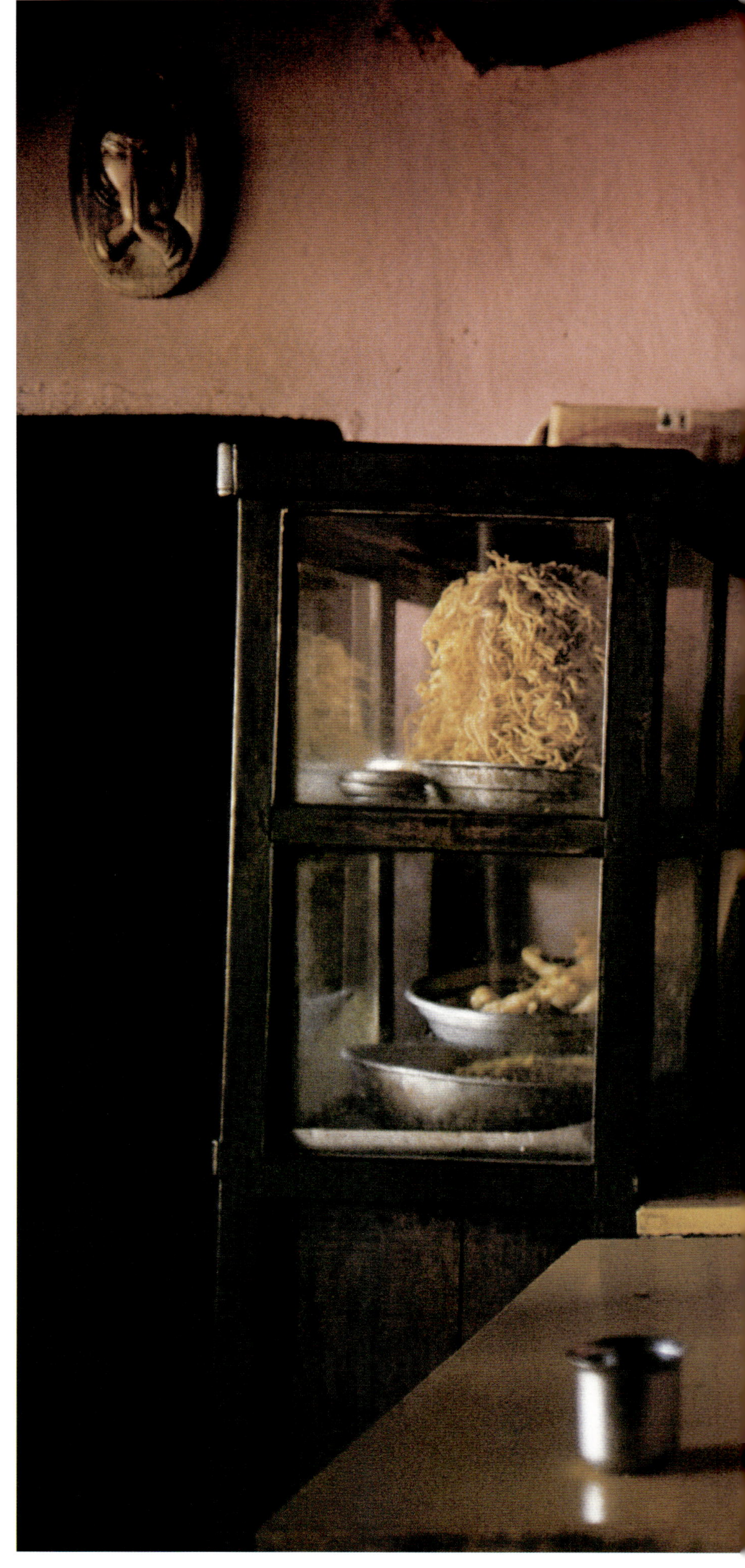

90 Inn in Karnataka.

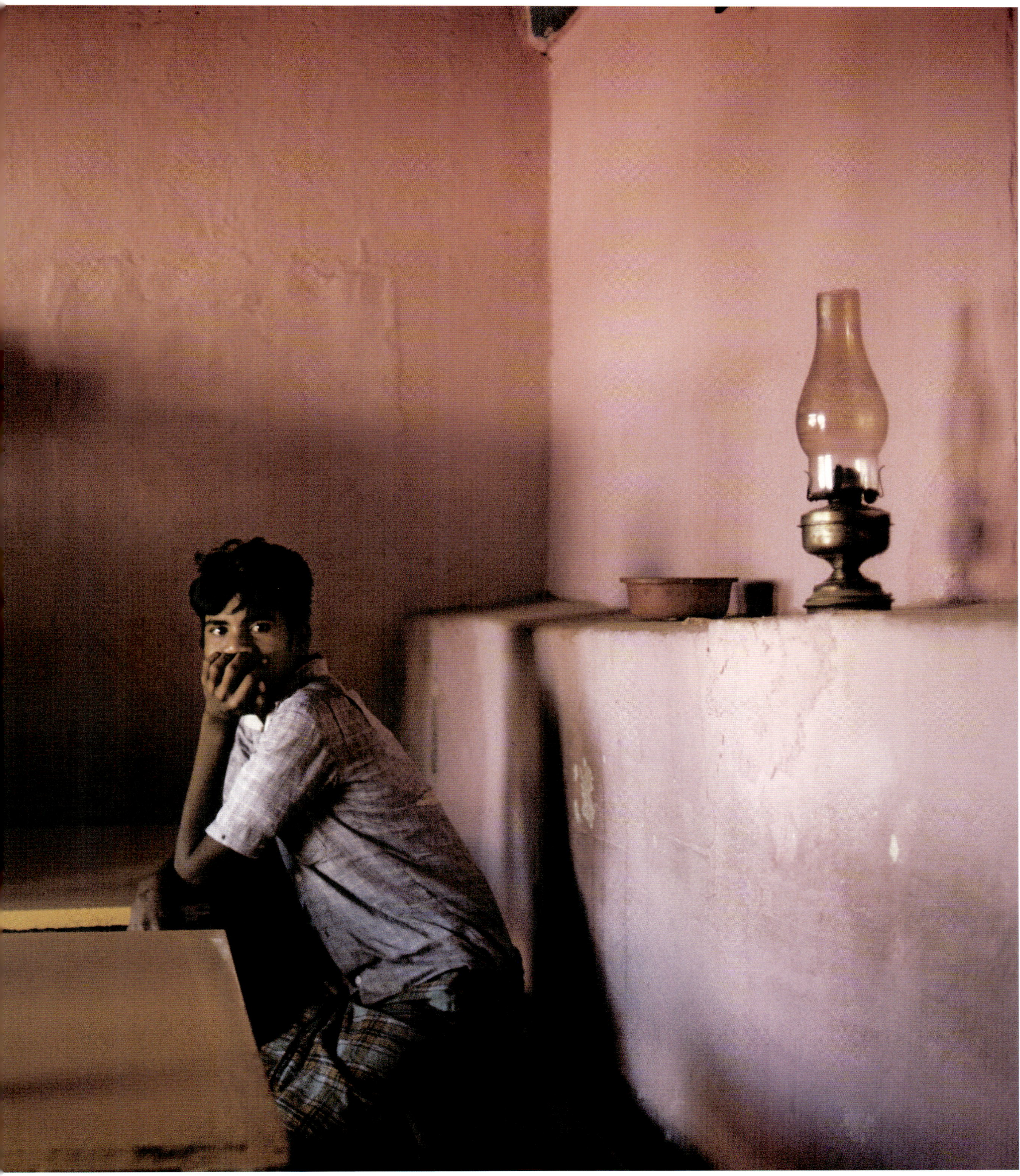

that witness testimony is of little value; certain questions of morality or violence toward women who have no children are not discussed with strangers. The man repeats the word "democracy" several times even though we have discovered that in this village, the members of the *panchayat* are appointed without their legitimacy ever being discussed. We are introduced to the other members (all of whom are male, although women are frequently made members now). They are country dwellers whose serene expressions are evidence of their satisfaction with their condition.

We are served the frugal dinner by the wife of our host, assisted by his daughter-in-law, who displays a childlike curiosity. After dinner we take a stroll through the moonlit village. Here and there, men sit around talking and smoking cigarettes or *bidis.* It is very peaceful, like walking through a painting of rural life in which the figures are slightly animated by an invisible thread. Each of them—men, women, children—occupies a position dictated by custom. The weave is tight. Alienation from the criteria of modernity, harmony for those who live here. But how fragile this existence has become! It requires just one television set for desire to emerge. After talking and smoking, the men, and more rarely the women, slowly lay their bedrolls outdoors and lie down on wood-framed beds sprung with knotted ropes. The heavenly sky watches over them. We return to our host. Two beds await us, covered in clean sheets, in the room in which we ate. When all noise has ceased in the village and the houses seem to be covered with a veil, one needs to go outside alone with the desire to answer this question. What is it that makes this village different from those in another developing country? Lying on the ground, palms upward, one can hear the answer:

> *For four thousand years*
> > *I have welcomed,*
> *I remain.*

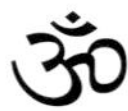 *The sophists (Brahmans) live naked, exposed to the sun in winter, and in summer, under the burning sun, they live in the fields and in damp places under large trees whose shade, according to Cretan admiral Nearchos, extends to form a circle of five plethora; a crowd could shelter under a single one of them, they are so big. . . . One is not permitted to take a wife outside one's own class, for example, farmers cannot take a wife from among the artisans or vice versa. Nor is it permitted for the same person to pursue two occupations nor to change class, for example to move from the shepherd class to the farming class or from the artisan class to the shepherd class. One only has the right to become a sophist if one is from any class, because the life of the sophists, far from being sweet, is the harshest of all.*

Arrian of Nicomedia, *The Indica,* XI:7–XII:8–9 (2nd century A.D.)

The "Children of God"

In Madhya Pradesh, a state in the center of the country, I visited the Sanchi *stupa,* a stone mound that is a reminder of Buddha's Nirvana, a jewel nestling amid balustrades and porticos covered in sculptures representing scenes from the life of the Master who, not being shown in human form, is represented by a symbol, such as a tree, footsteps, a wheel. Above are the lascivious *apsaras,* celestial nymphs who have come from the waters and who are ready to take flight. In the plain that surrounds the *stupa,* the landscape is crushed by the sun's heat at this time of year; there are hills in the distance.

I rent a bicycle, trying to remember a long-abandoned pursuit. Over here, a cloud of dust has been raised by a herd of destructive goats. Over there, there is a dry river bed in which a few mud puddles remain, enabling us to admire the substance of which we were made. A young man breaks the silence on his moped. I ask him the location of the *Harijan* village. He pretends not to understand. I pursue the matter. He points vaguely southward. "Is it far?" He looks disparagingly at my conveyance. "Ten minutes," he says over his shoulder as he rides off.

Pages 94–95: Saffron fields in flower, Kashmir.

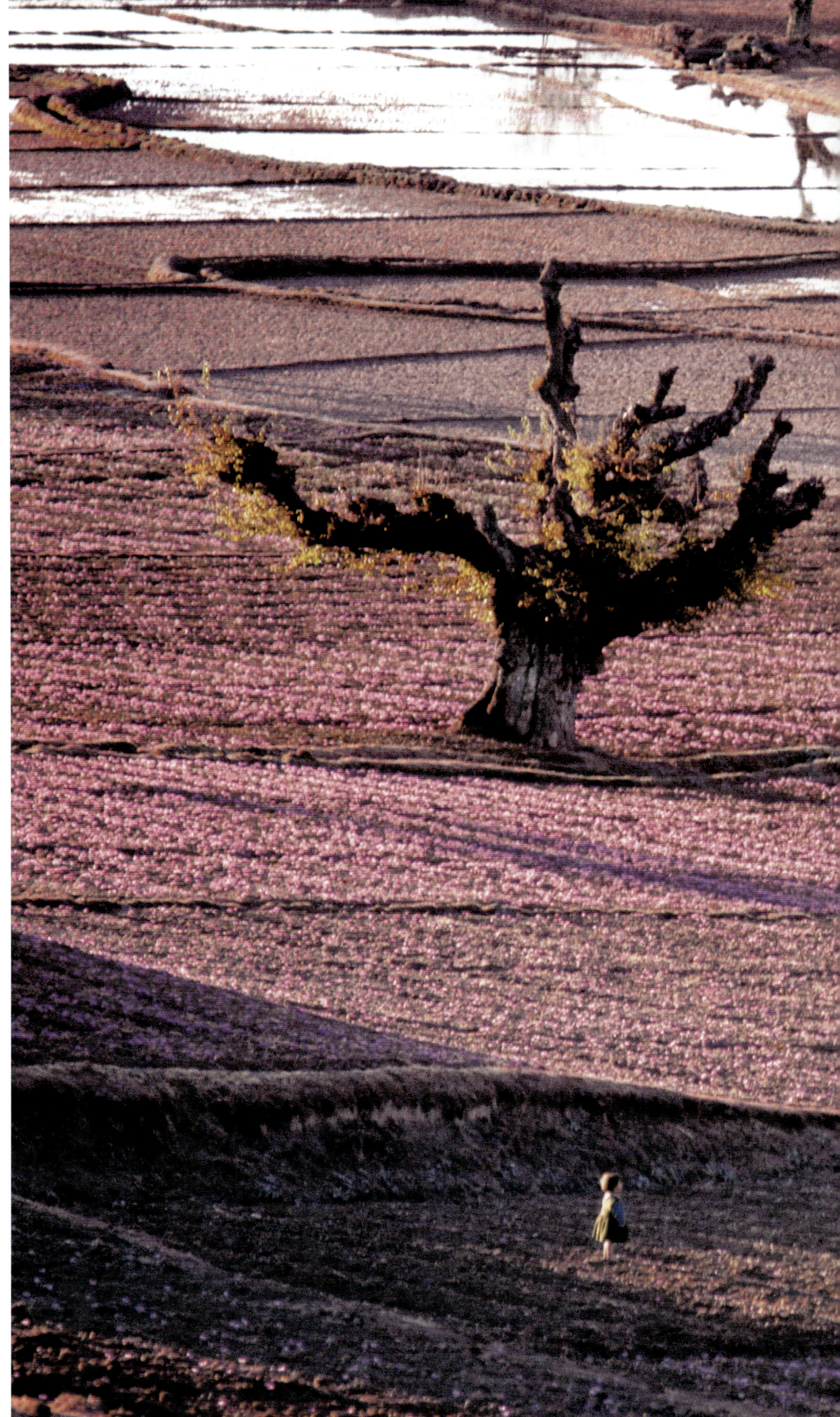

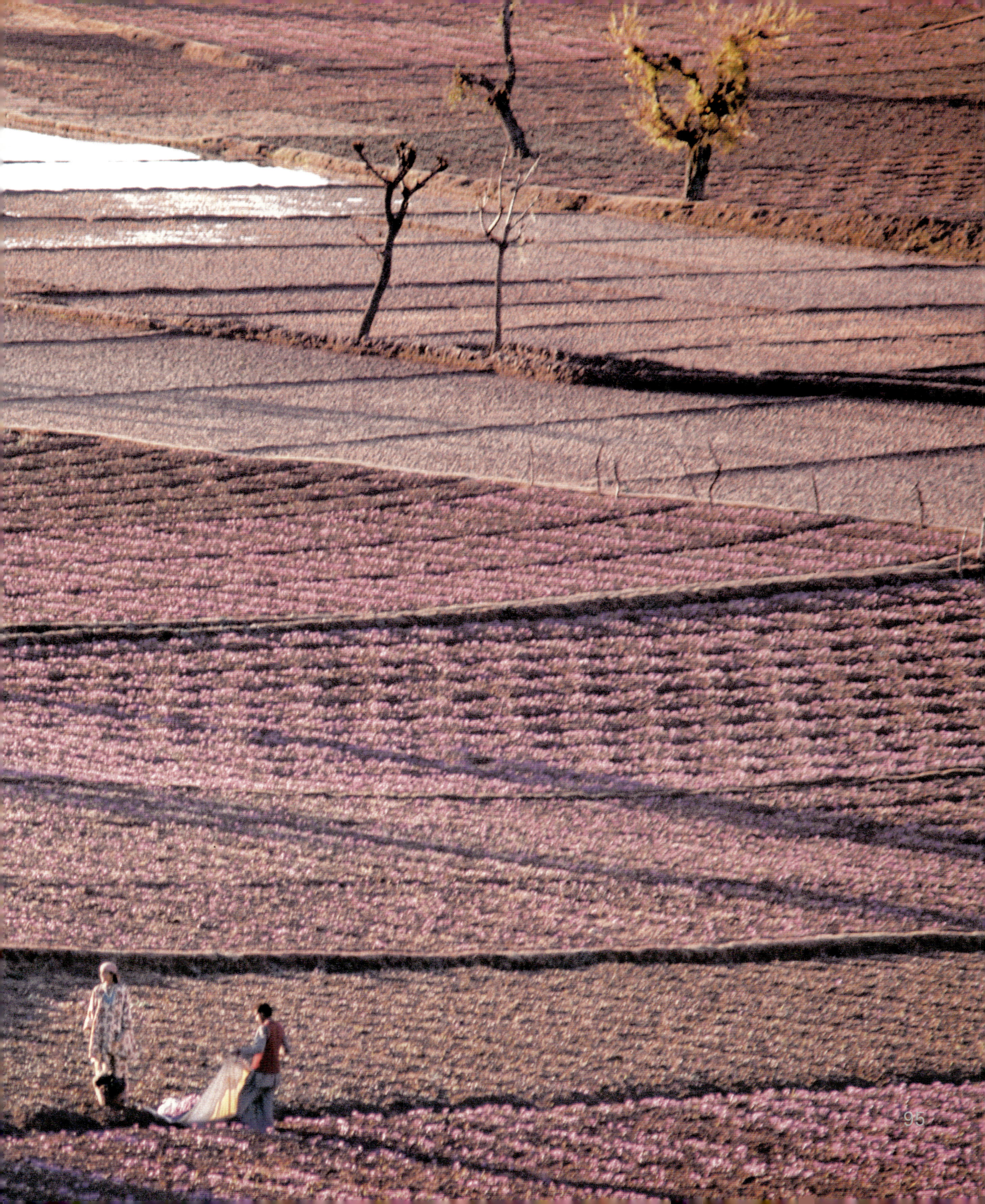

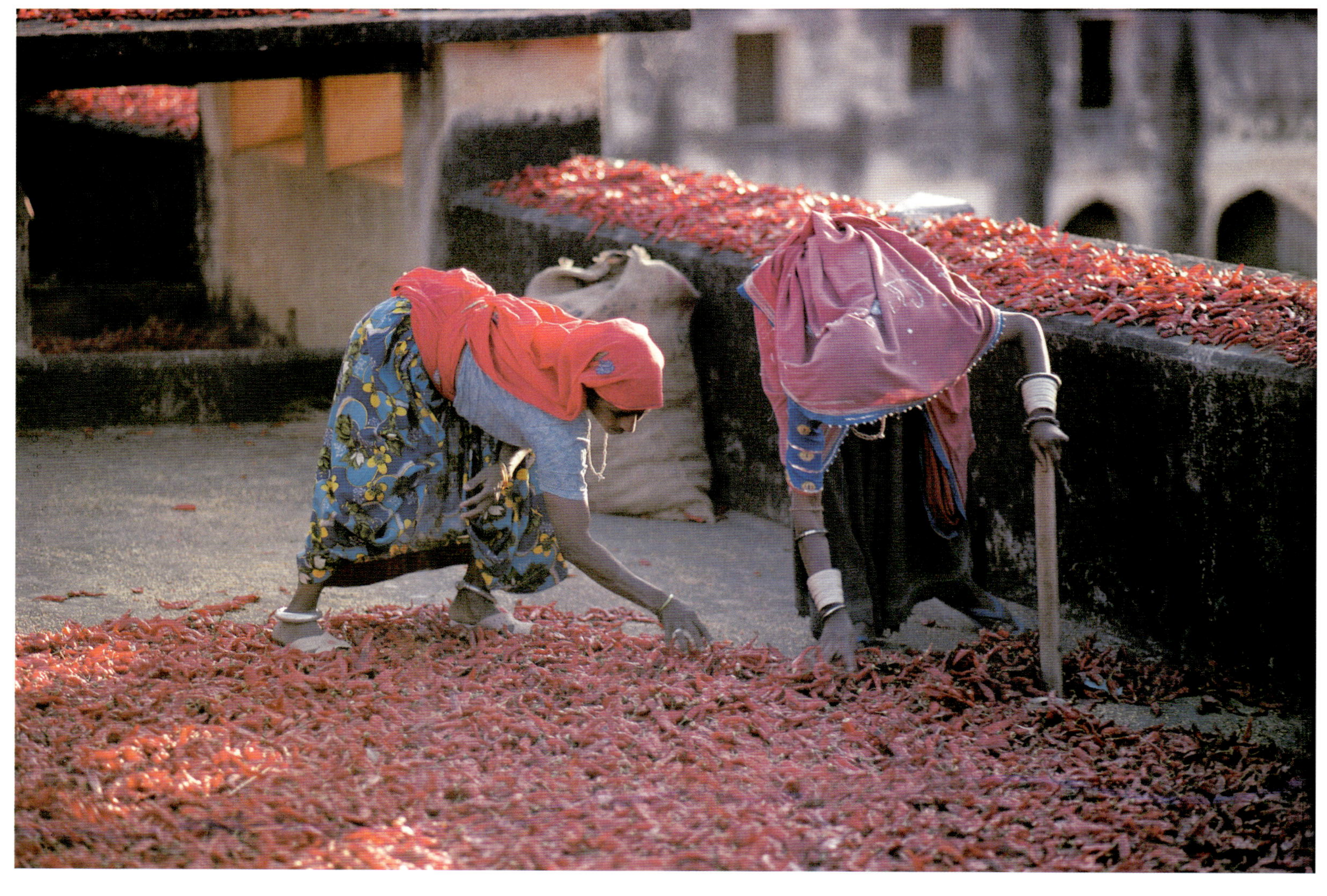

Above: Chile pepper harvesting, Rajasthan.
Opposite: Village women, Rajasthan.

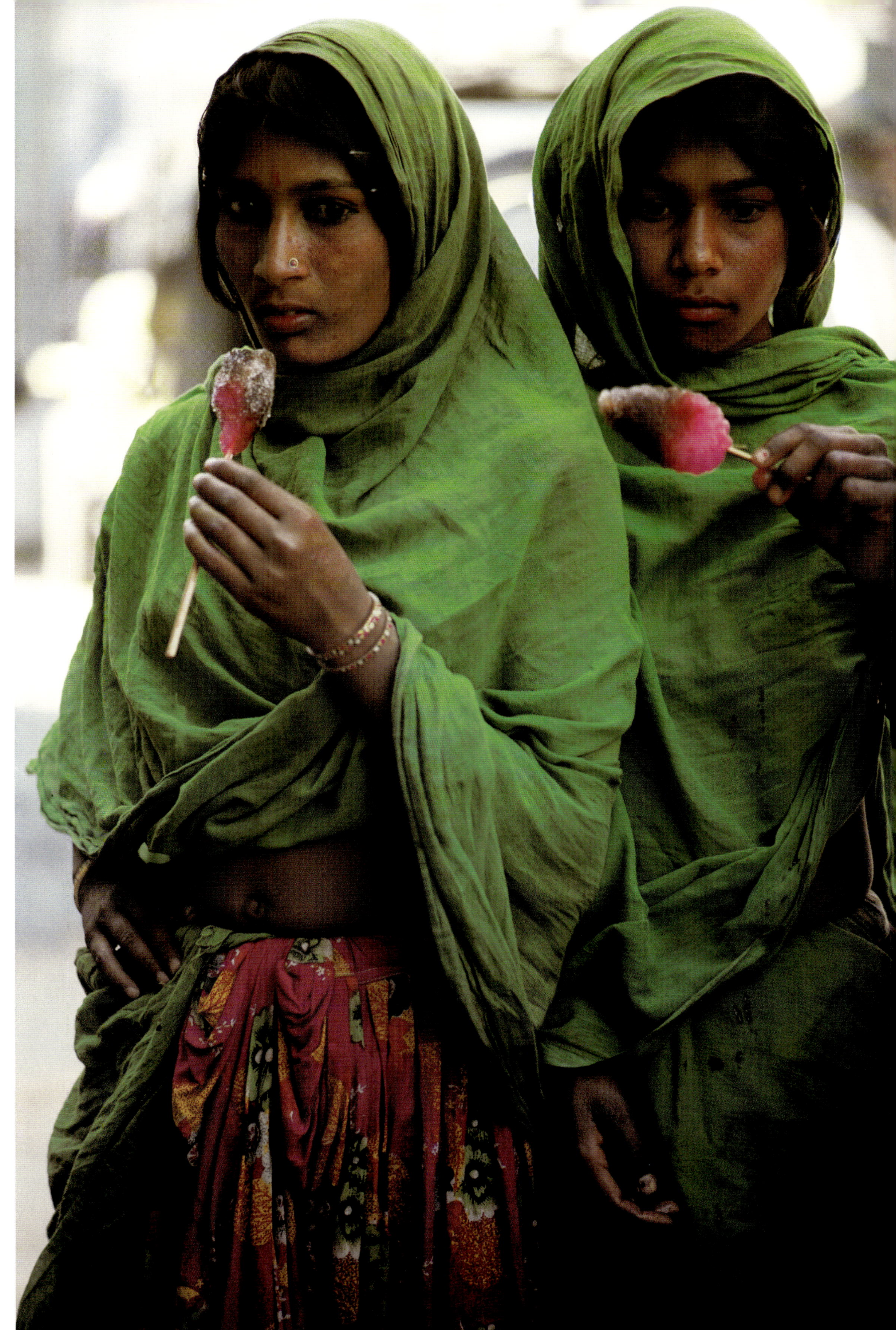

Gandhipuram consists of fifty or so houses, some of which were built recently. This is one of many villages inhabited by untouchables. As its name indicates, this village was created out of nothing by the government. How can I make the amazed and delighted children who surround me realize that I am not there as a "voyeur." I take out a camera of the type that develops photos instantly. A boy takes a photo. Another takes his place so as to be able to take a picture of the first one along with all the children in the village. There is general pandemonium when the photos emerge. They depict boys and girls with dazed expressions, looking like millions of other boys and girls who are still at an age when they can laugh, before they get to the age when they are conscious of inequalities. They surround a stranger with respect. Here is someone like no one they ever saw before, who has come to their village for reasons of which they are unaware, but who reassures them. Another photo is then taken of the stranger, showing him on all fours and imitating a pig, almost plausibly but incomprehensibly for someone who represents the powerful nations of the earth. I would like to continue these encounters, as would all the children. I hold the braid of a little girl in a red dress that matches the beauty of her dark skin and whose shy smile is the touch of an artist. To avoid solemnity, I pull her braid.

As I am leaving Gandhipuram, I am accosted by a skinny man in a tattered garment who introduces himself as the village teacher. Although he does not come from an untouchable *jati*, he has chosen to dedicate his life to giving children the means to leave their condition behind. It is like hearing a European teacher talk a century ago. He is flattered by my visit and wants to please me. He asks me what I like. "To be surprised," I reply.

My wish is not well received. Surprises are not India's strong point, here everything is accounted for. He clears his throat, spits, and suggests that I meet him again tomorrow to witness a very special ceremony performed by the inhabitants of Gandhipuram in order to fertilize the earth. Meanwhile, I take a stroll through the countryside, surveying the fields of millet, lentils, wheat, and pasture in which skinny goats are grazing. In the evening, I return to Gandhipuram, approaching it from another side, from the west. A road lined with trees blooming with red flowers leads to an abandoned temple that has been reclaimed by the vegetation. Here and there, heaps of stones indicate former dwellings, near which crudely carved door frames add a note of incongruity. After a patient search and crawling among spiny undergrowth and stones, I find a suitable hiding-place beside a kiosk. Clearly the children who are playing this evening on the road leading to the entrance to the village, along with the ruins covered in foliage, create a harmony that I am ready to settle for. Lying on my stomach, I clutch the camera that will capture the moment. It all seems so easy. Let's go! But here are two children who are running after a ball with the grace of dancers but who move out of the frame, and a herd of cows returning home at an unhurried pace is ruined by the presence of a teenage biker wearing a hideous helmet.

And now a goat comes and stands squarely in the foreground of my shot. Then a patriarch with a long beard and a staff moves forward between the patches of light on the road, but a truck raises a hellish dust storm. As soon as the dust has settled and silence begins to reign harmoniously once again, the graceful children, the old man, the cows—have all gone! Finally, while the light is still favorable, a woman carrying a tub of laundry on her head rests a bare arm decorated with three bracelets on the column of the kiosk with the elegance of a statuette by Mohenjo-Daro. I enjoy the sight for two seconds, and then I aim, raise my finger over the shutter release button and—for no reason, the woman abandons her pose and starts walking, but this time she is hidden by the bushes. And now the real culprit is the sun, which no longer accentuates colors; the last lingering light merges with the shadows. The rejects of creation are now understandable.

I have learned my lesson. I emerge from my hiding place. With my eyes, I photograph a reflection on a pond, the gray and white wreaths of smoke from a house in which the evening meal is being cooked, a sari hung out to dry, a woman shelling beans on her doorstep and three furtive children. I shake my head having made only a single image from all that I saw. Who is this crazy guy? the residents of western Gandhipuram ask themselves.

The next day, I meet the teacher once again beside the other entrance to the village. I follow him along a path leading to the plateau. The men of the village have gathered in a circle around an ugly statue that must be appeased. She is the mistress of the rains.

Since very ancient times, like us, the gods have lusted for blood. The circle opens to let in a goat that is neither inquisitive nor anxious, but rather submissive. Fistfuls of grass are thrown at her, and she devours them greedily. The trembling of her fur is merely a sign that life is still pulsating confidently within her.

A man approaches the goat and sprinkles red powder on the back of her neck then, without visible pleasure but also without hatred, he raises a cutlass that he has kept hidden. He brings it down in a lavish gesture, extinguishing life. The body of the goat is seized with stupefaction. She moves away, stops, seeks to regain a precarious balance, takes a few more faltering steps, lacking a piece of herself.

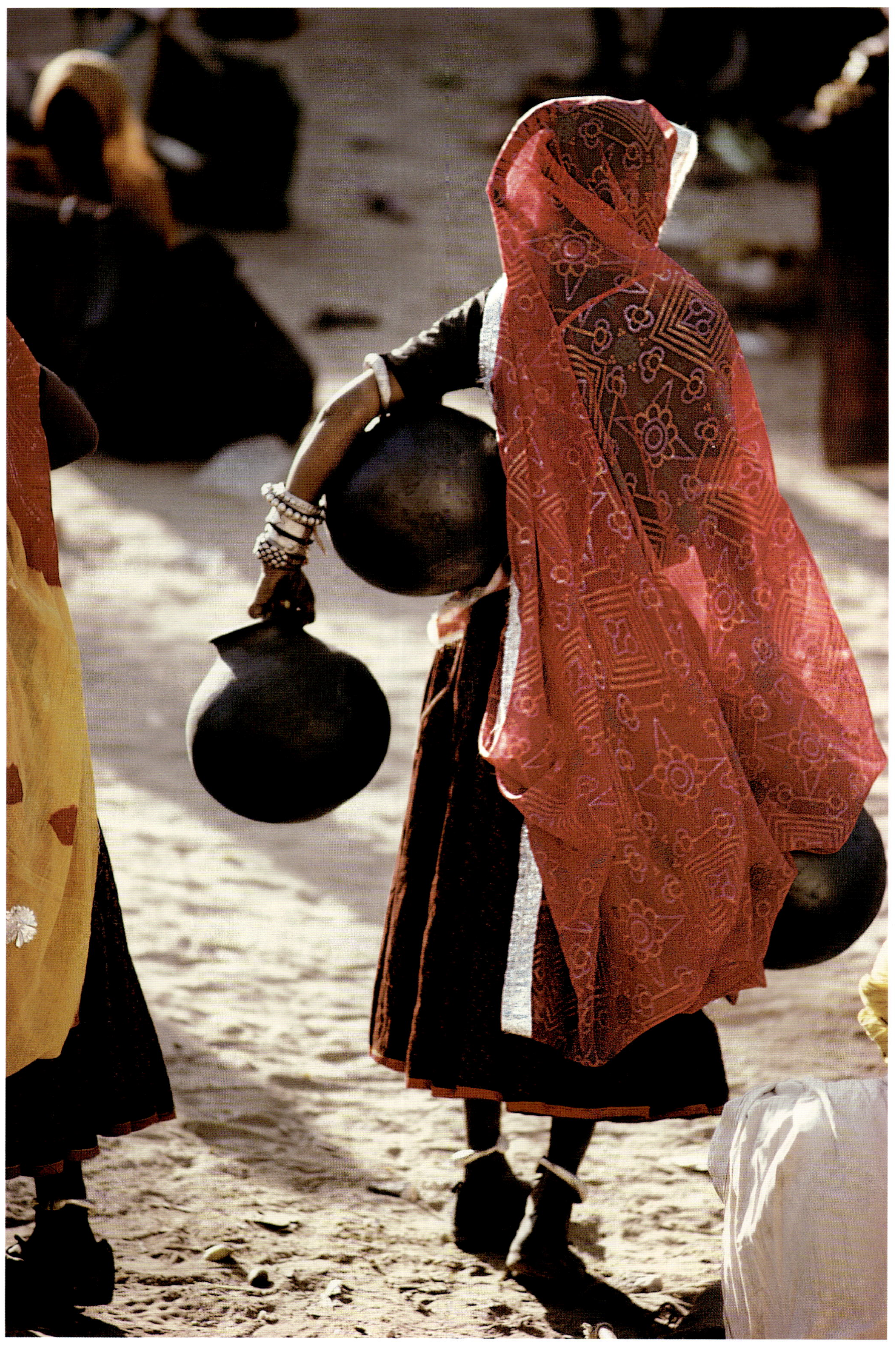

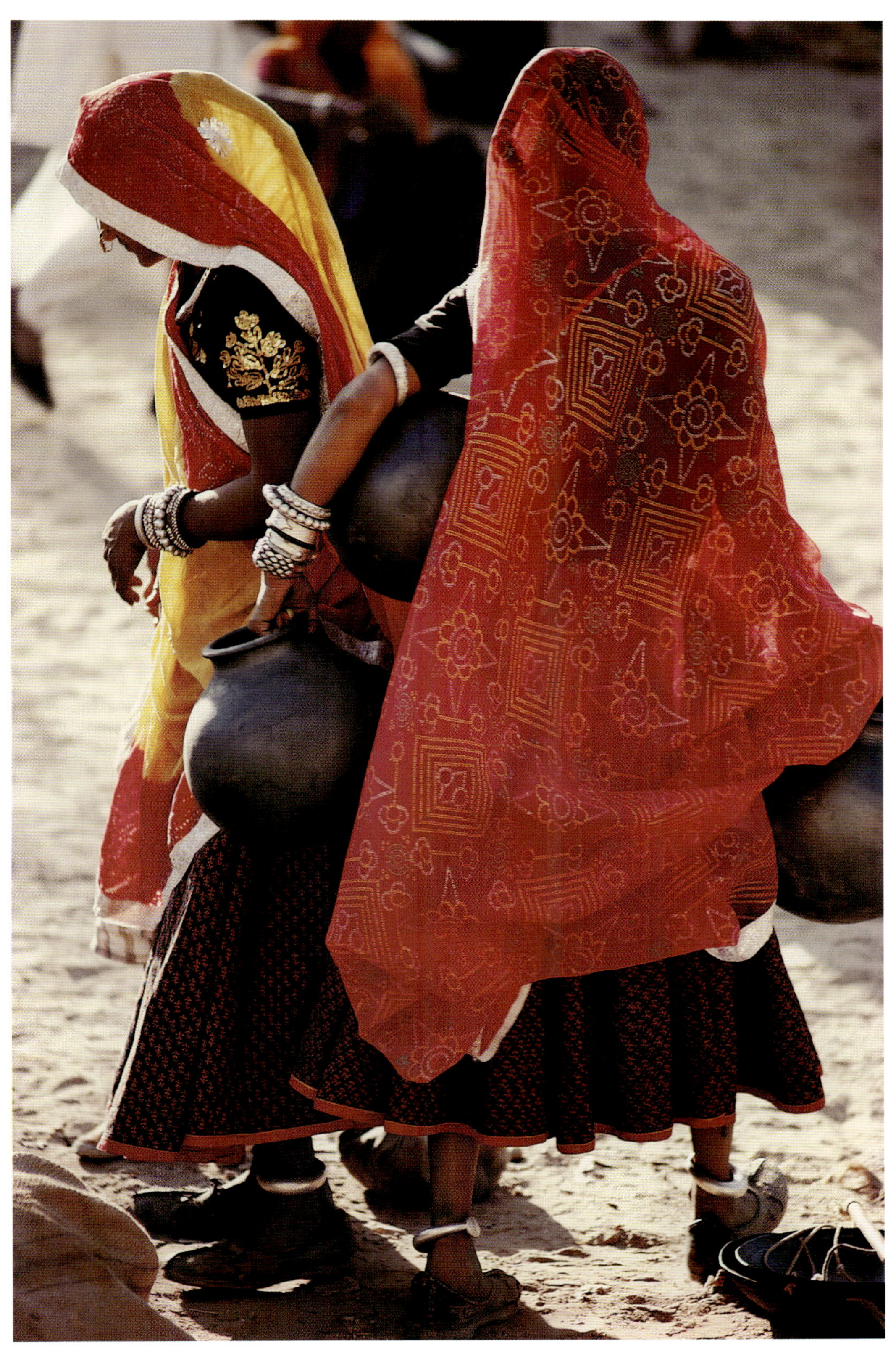

Above and Opposite: Village women at the fair, Rajasthan.
Pages 102–103: Camel fair, Pushkar, Rajasthan.

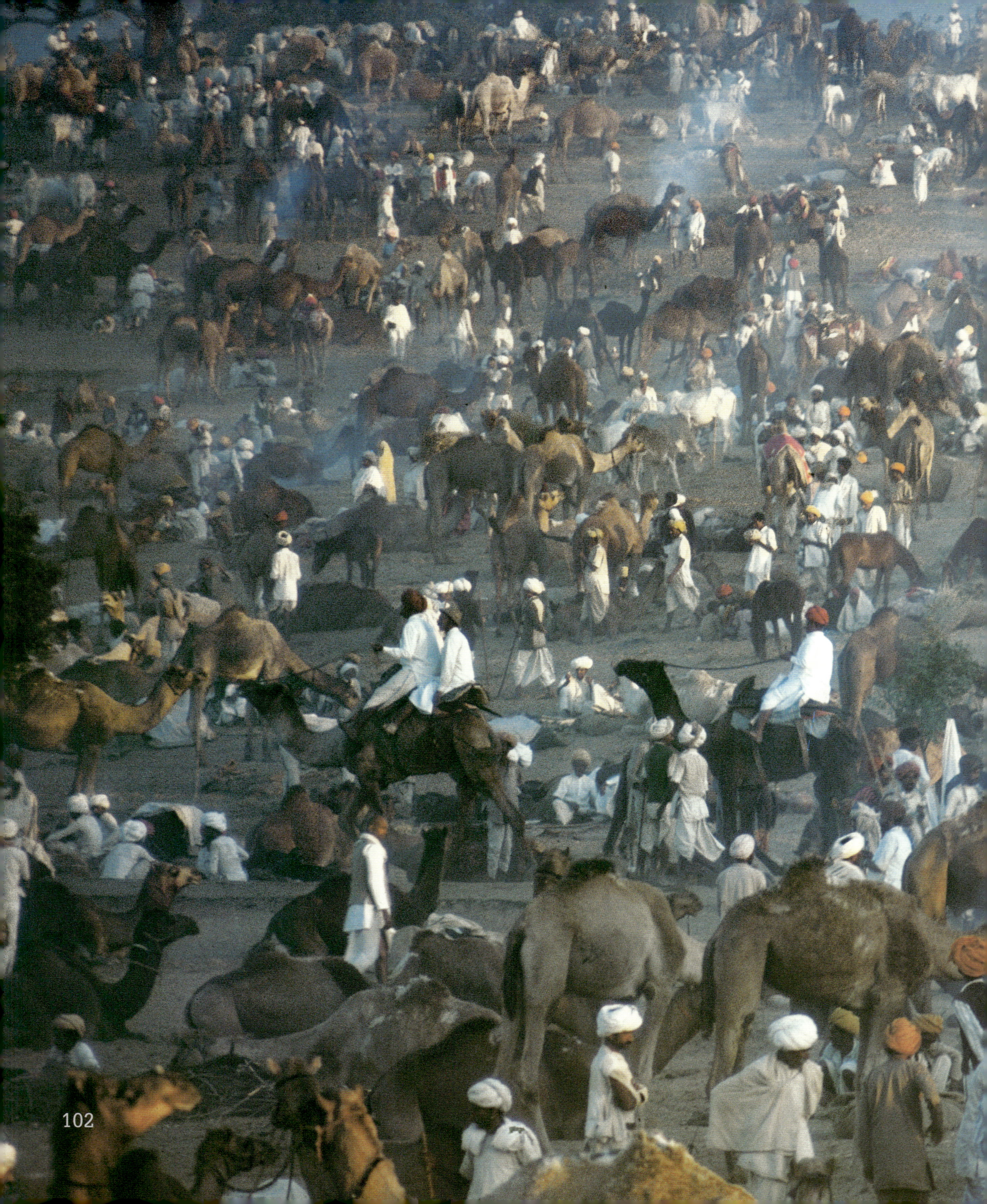

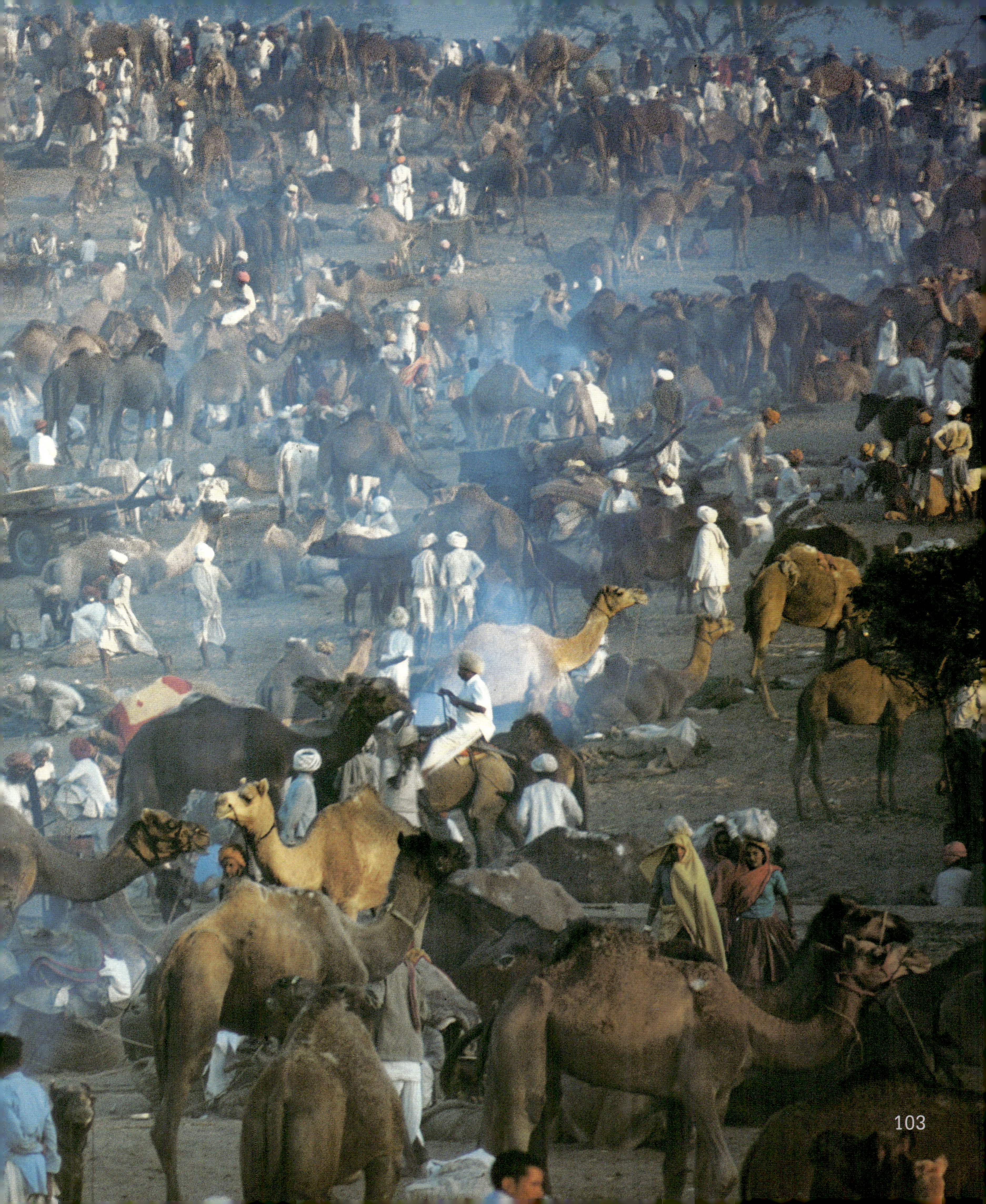

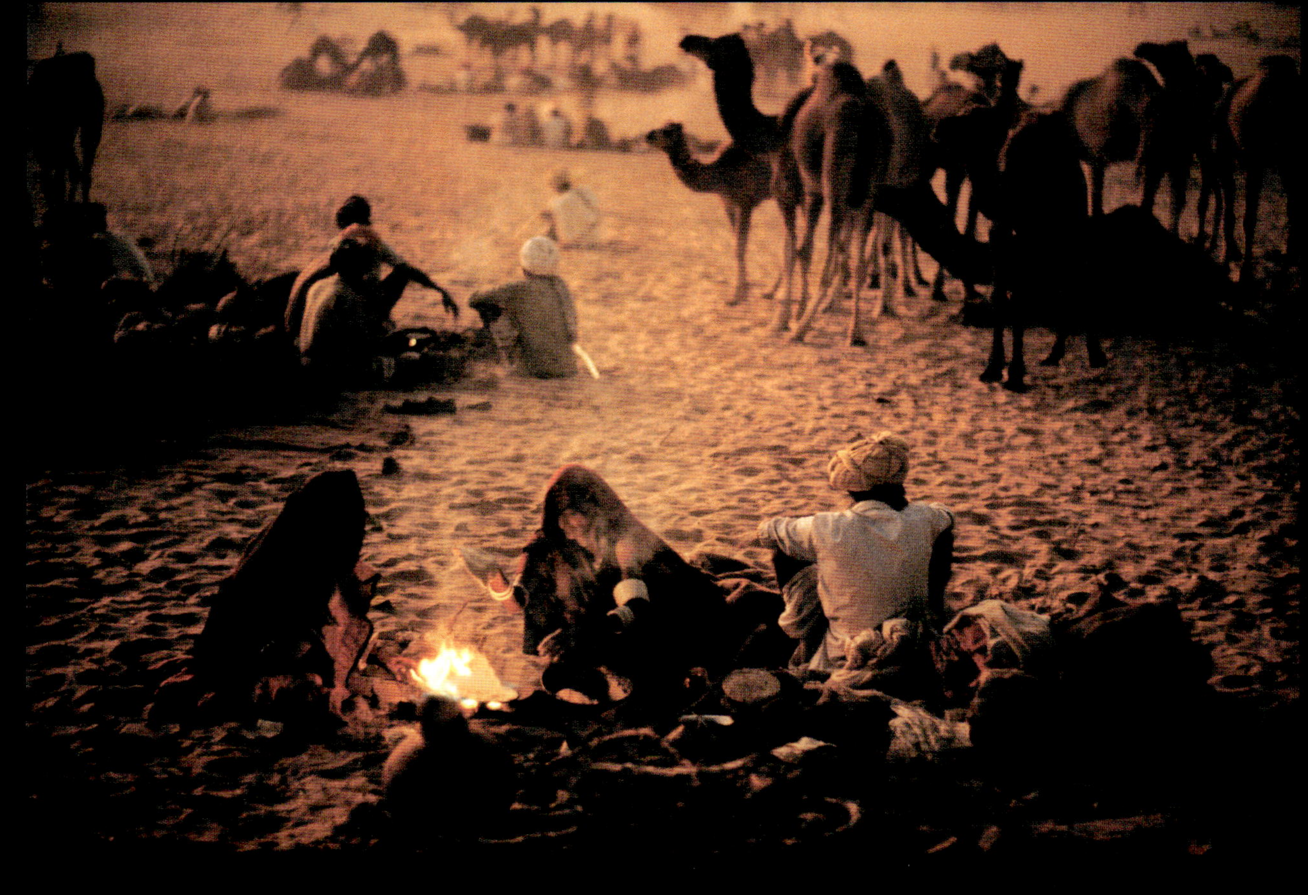

Above: Village encampment, Pushkar, Rajasthan.
Opposite: Portrait of a villager, Rajasthan.

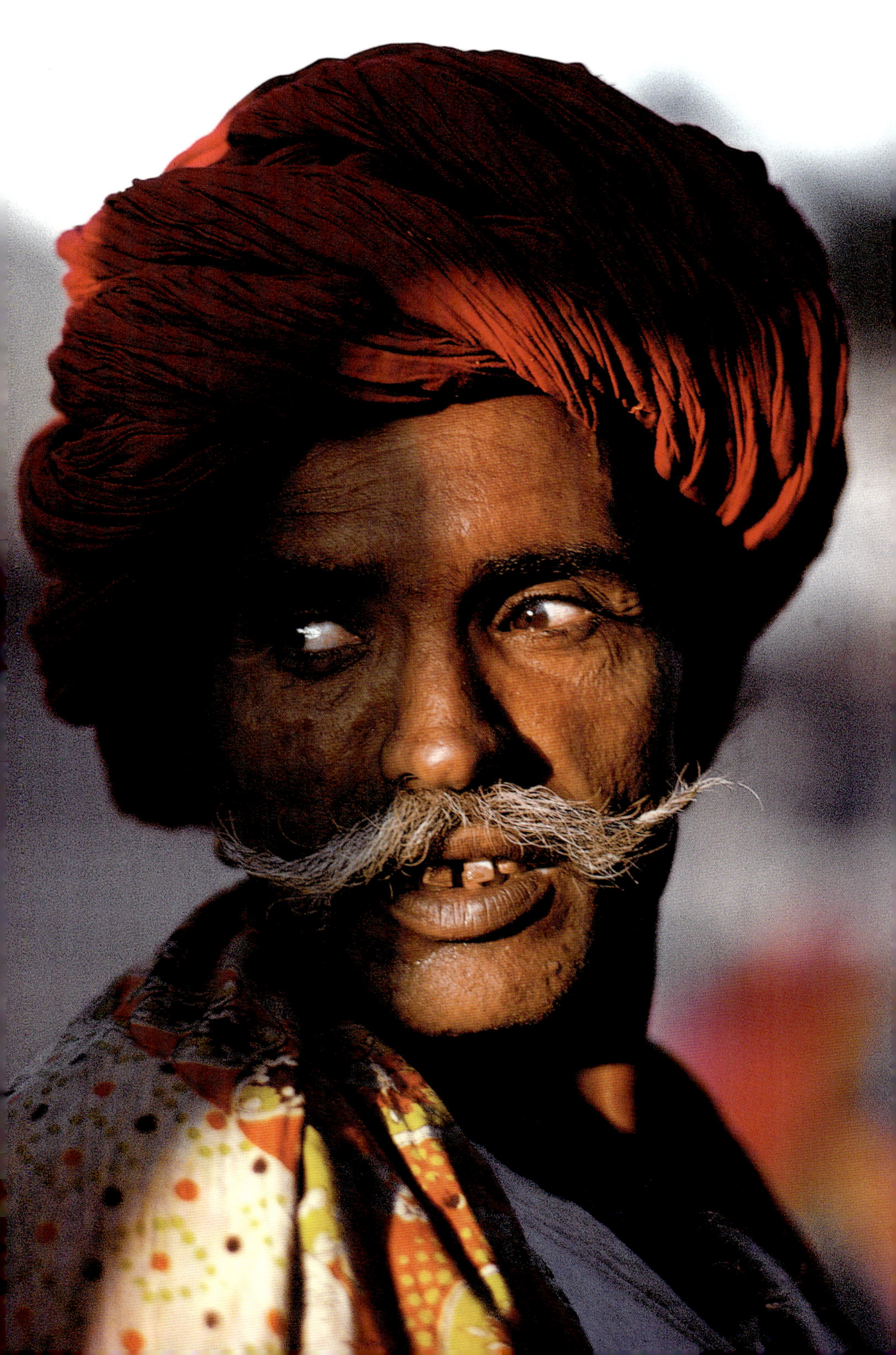

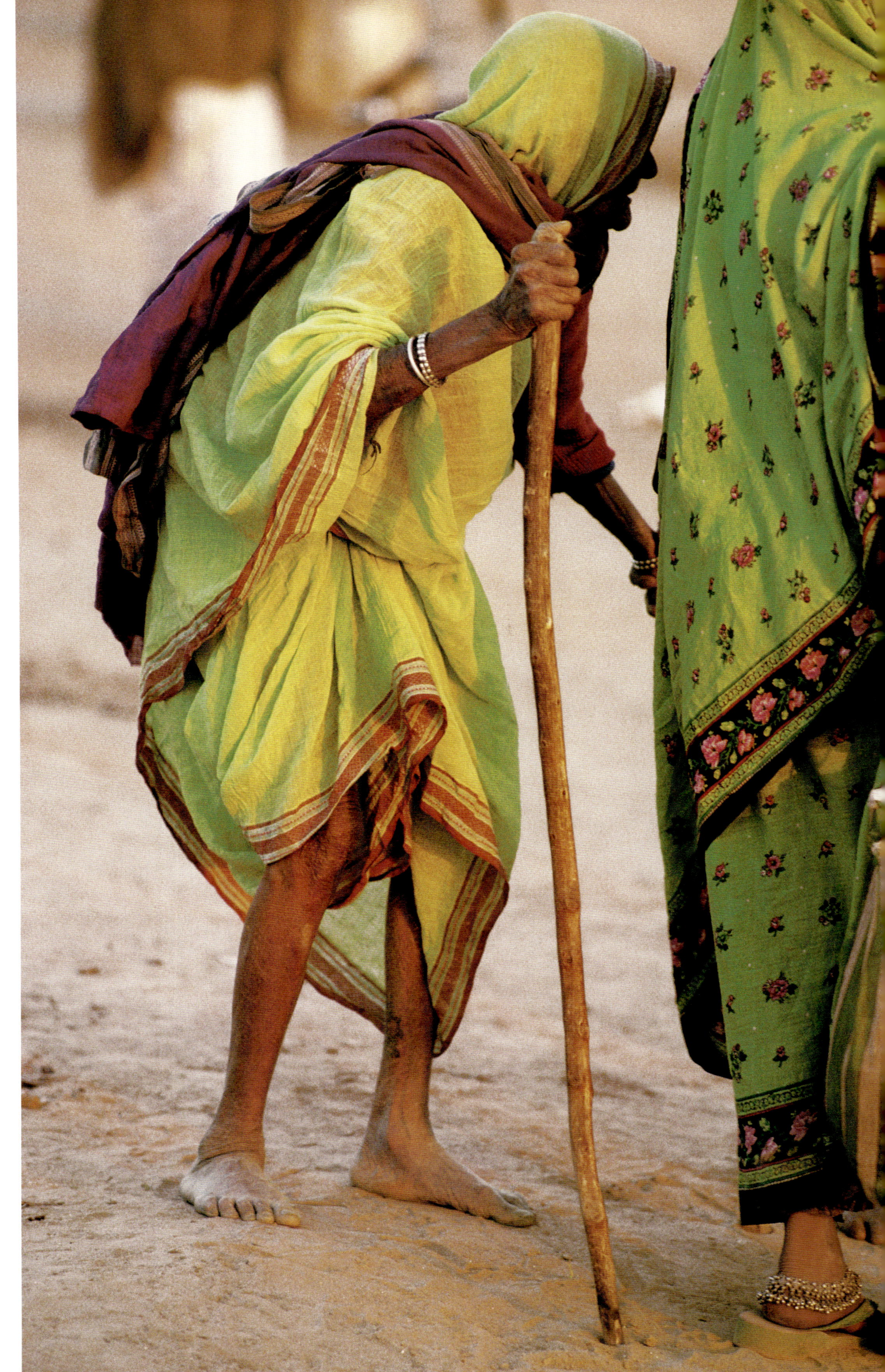

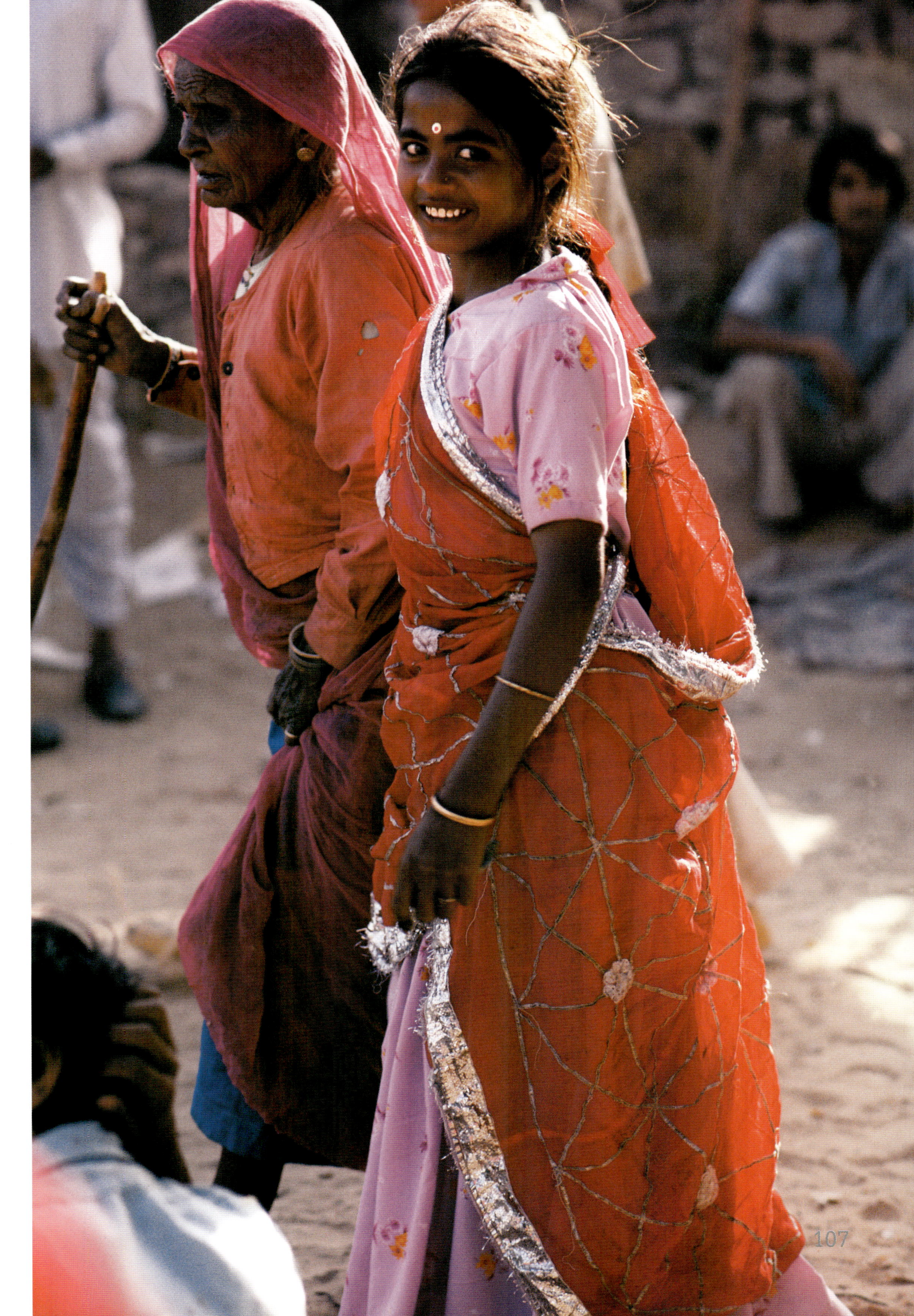

Women on
a pilgrimage.

The goat is disoriented by this condition that she has always tried to run away from without knowing why. Now she knows. She totters, then collapses a few yards from the place of the discovery. Her neck turns scarlet with the blood that pours out of it. The severed head has rolled away to the other side. The eyes have remained open, surprised that this time they have not been able to trick death. It cannot be said that the hen is more rebellious than the goat when faced with the raised blade, and yet here she is before the operation, in a state of useless agitation.

Of course, this is an age-old reaction in this unpredictable creature that moves so jerkily. The dignity of the goat is missed. Perhaps the hen understands nothing of holiness? She is annoyed merely by being interrupted in her pecking habit. As soon as the man of steel approaches her, she swears at him with her beak, wings, and cackling. Why don't you let me peck in the dust as I am used to! How can she be made to understand that there is no question of her being let go? When the knife plunges through her neck and she is, as it were, left to herself, she is seized with a strange rage. She runs away, tries to open her wings as if to eradicate—are we not all like this?—an action that has become irreversible. She shakes her bleeding neck while her last attempt at flight ends with an inglorious flop. Still trembling, but already becalmed, the neck pours a trickle of blood which mixes on the ground with that of the goat who now lies immobile. Small insects come to refresh themselves in this red manna. Attentive and silent, those assembled who have witnessed the sacrifice let out a sigh— of what?—at the moment when life still throbs before the last somersault.
I leave without a word, incapable this time of reconciling the images within me.

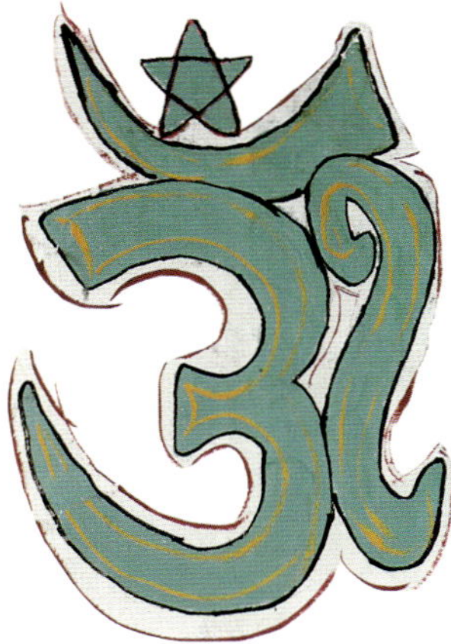

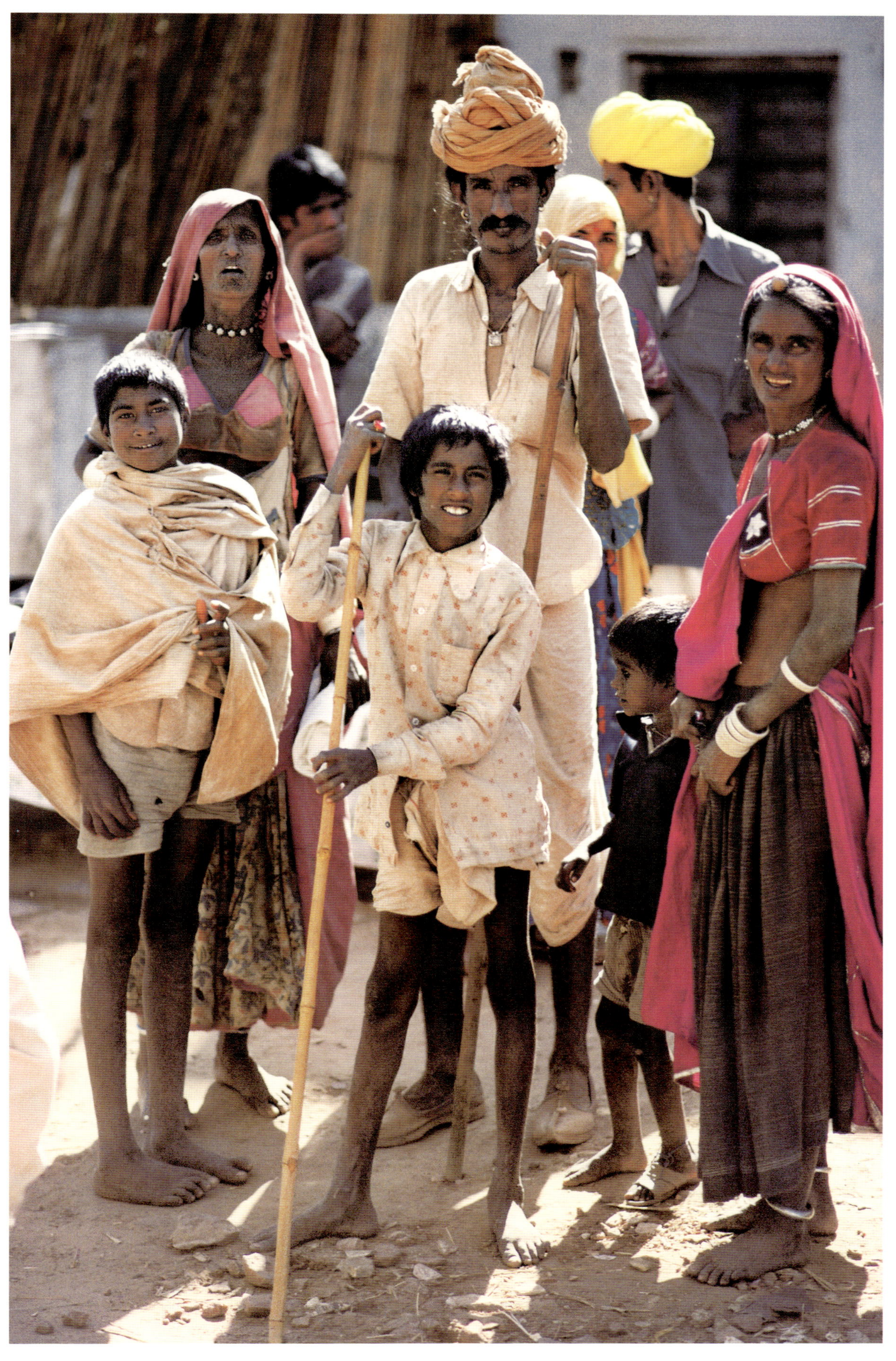

Farmers, Rajasthan.

Interlude

Imagine what the world would be like without India. We could live, think, love, walk, all in the same way, but there would be parts of our consciousness that would never have been raised. We would have fewer reasons to rejoice in living.

Without India, there would be no natural and supernatural figure of the Buddha in his meditation pose, the embodiment of human tranquility. There would be no god dancing in a circle of fire, creating worlds, destroying them in order to recreate them, making them into one, upon occasion, with his *shakti.*

Without India, what other culture would have elevated the naked ascetic as the model to be emulated by all as soon as they reached the right age? Would there be raga music to bring down the gods and cause the nymphs to leave the kingdom of the dead?

Two bodies united in sensual pleasure, two bodies moving toward spiritual fulfillment. Cries of abandonment, prayer. To start over the divine creation as a couple. This alchemy is unique to India.

And what about yoga ? And the sacred dances, the vibration of the *vinas,* the festivals of the full moon? And *ayurvedic* medicine? The *kalarippayat*? The myths, temples beside the sea, the mosques, abandoned palaces, the tigers who refuse to eat holy men, holy men who eat nothing but guavas?

Now let's imagine what it would be like if there were nothing but India. The collection of gods would be complete, as would that of facial expressions. Thought would have explored every possibility. But something would be lacking, the contribution of the West—the human scale as a yardstick for creation.

In the bus station there is a little girl with a metal rod inserted into her tongue, in order to benefit her parents. She is forced to keep her mouth open. How easy it is to understand the great minds of the eighteenth century in the way they thought of religion! Yet—let's go back to the story of the blind men and the elephant.

On the high tower (*gopuram*) that serves as the gateway to the temple, A man is cleaning the brightly colored statues of the gods. No one pays attention to him.

One more, one less.

Reality without the world of fantasy is a truncated reality.

Let India teach us this at least; as long as the world has not relearned enchantment, neuroses will multiply.

Of all the religions, Hinduism is the one that accords the greatest respect for desire, for the multiplicity of life's aspects, including dancing and eroticism.

In the *Bhagavad-Gita*, Krishna (the incarnation of Vishnu) speaks to Arjuna, who must fight his cousins:

He whose thought is not troubled by suffering,
Who has no desire for pleasure,
Who has neither fear, nor passion, nor anger,
Is said to be a sage possessing light

and later on:

When one has lost all desire
And lives thereafter without ties,
Without possessions, freed from oneself,
One then attains serenity.

Bhagavad-Gita, II:56, 71

How can detachment and sanctified eroticism be reconciled? There is no contradiction here for the Indians.

Two paths.

A religion without symbols—such as ours today—has nothing but morality or dogma with which to grapple. It rushes to its doom.

India (and much of Asia that has been influenced by Buddhism) takes instability into consideration. The West has been obsessed with the fixed point. Believing in permanence is to make a bed of nails for oneself. Each defeat (and especially death) produces rebellion. Here a serene detachment replaces the anguish of loss because the act of ownership is a mere puff of smoke. Mourning becomes less burdensome if "reality" is only an ephemeral game.

The *maya* and *samsara* that dominate our lives are not taken from the *Brahman*. So something that is immutable exists. But it does not concern that which we hold dear—our lives, our feelings, our loved ones.

There is no act of faith for a Hindu. His religion expresses a natural truth, like that of the laws of physics. The law of actions, karma, is considered to be a natural phenomenon. The same applies to *samsara*. Only the *Brahman* has been discussed by a fairly important school of thought, often referred to as "materialistic."

There is no need for ecumenical councils or synods in Hinduism. The sacred texts, myths, and rituals express the order of the world.

A discussion of the comparative merits of Indian and Western philosophies would be endless. From the outset, however, it must be realized that there is one irreconcilable difference: the concept of self. On the one side there is smoke, on the other a unique entity.

The impression of remoteness that an Indian always conveys, whether one is talking to him or doing something with him, comes from the fact that at the same time he is engaged in a different conversation. He is in a dialogue with the order of the world (represented by god), and for him this transcends everything else.

Death? It underlies all thought. The funeral pyres are a reminder. Yet it is not represented, not spoken of, no one takes any pleasure in its company. The aim of Hinduism is to have progressed by the time it intervenes. It is awaited without anxiety. An eclipse.

Above: Ceiling decoration in a temple in Tamil Nadu.
Pages 114–115: Paddies in Kashmir.

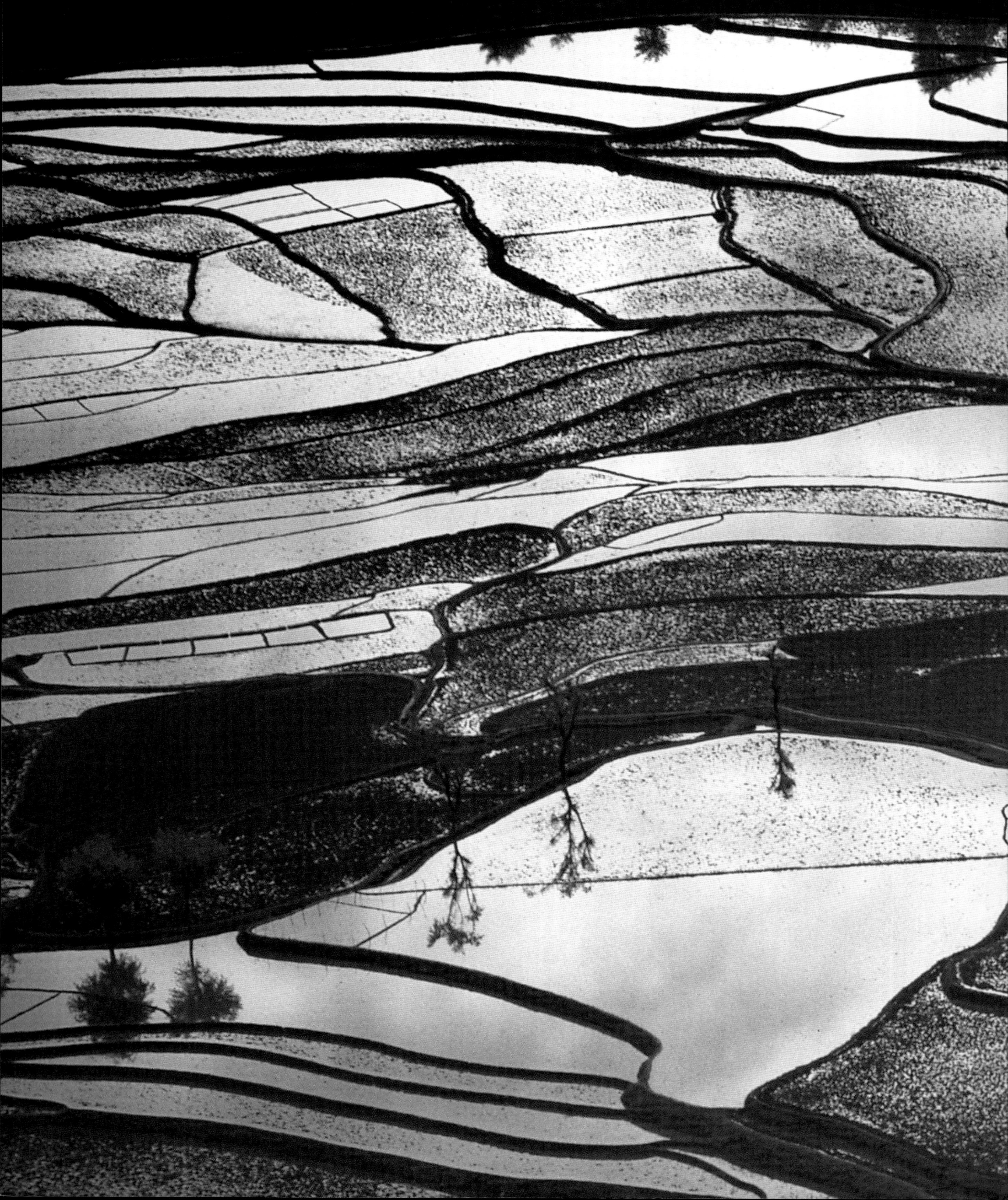

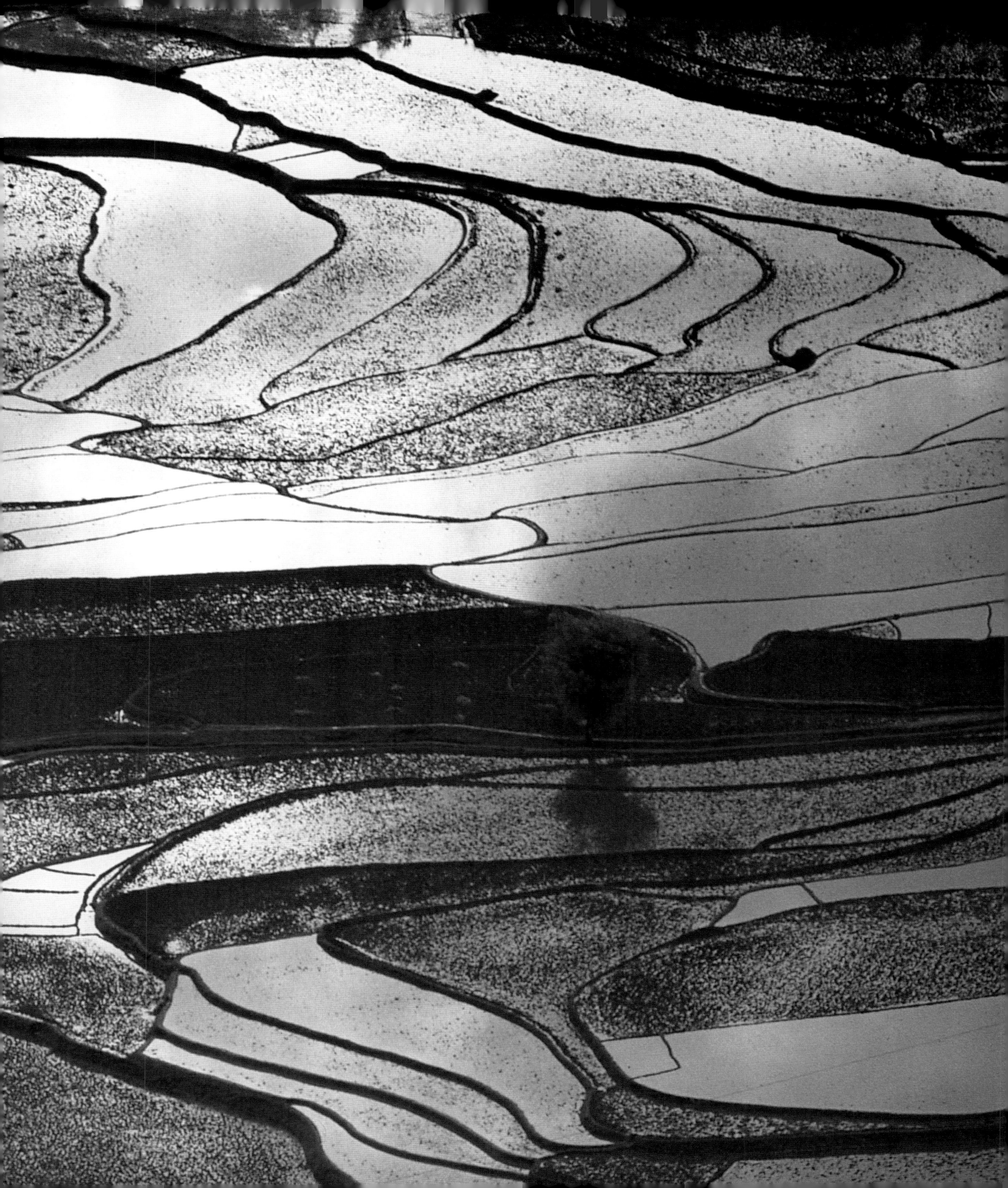

Sometimes a feeling of strangeness appears to us as if the result of our mental processes. We rebel against it: the children playing are like all other children, these women are suckling their babies with the same naturalness as our own women, these men in the city are dressed like us, rush around just as we do, trying to save time; they are as crazy as we are. As for the *sannyasis*, if you take away their staffs, long hair, and ashes, what remains?

It is within this small space that India can be found.

The smoke endures.

Something essential is happening in India. Not in the temples, at the railroad stations, at the palaces, in the street markets, on the narrow roads, in the jungles, or on the long, deserted beaches. It is happening in the heart of the Indian man-woman.

One day, a king asked a *Brahman* where his freedom came from. The *Brahman* replied that his masters were many, and all of them were clairvoyant. He listed them:

Earth, wind, sky, water, fire, moon, sun,
The pigeon, the python, the ocean, the butterfly,
The bee, the elephant,
The honey-eater, the doe, the fish,
The courtesan Pingala,
The white-tailed eagle, the child,
The maiden, the bowmaker, the serpent,
The spider, and the wasp
These are the twenty-four masters, O King,
To whom I have turned.
And it is from their behaviors that I have learned my lessons.

Uddhava Gita, II:33, 35

Giving candy to children, smiles to young girls, a friendly
cuff to boys (rarely the opposite), admiring looks to the
elderly, while still leaving time for meditation.

Living in an *ashram* to get to know your body, its
riches, and its limitations better. Understand-
ing the flexibility of Hinduism, that is
capable of inclusion without denying
itself. Knowing one can remain
motionless for four hours, after
scrupulous preparation, and not
finding that time to be long.
For in this void each person
creates their own experi-
ence, that which cannot be
conveyed in words.

Meditating while waiting
for a train, at the beauty
parlor, in traffic jams in
ugly towns, mediating
naked, while breast-feed-
ing, while making love (it's
possible), while refusing a
glass of water, while defecat-
ing (difficult), while eating an
alloo gobi that is too spicy, while
being attacked (heroic), while climbing up to a temple, while bathing in the
river, while sitting under a banyan tree listening to the green parrots in the Theosophical
Society's Park in Madras, meditating while riding a bicycle,
in the moonlight, while riding in a horse-drawn carriage.
Meditating.

Hindus do not meditate much.

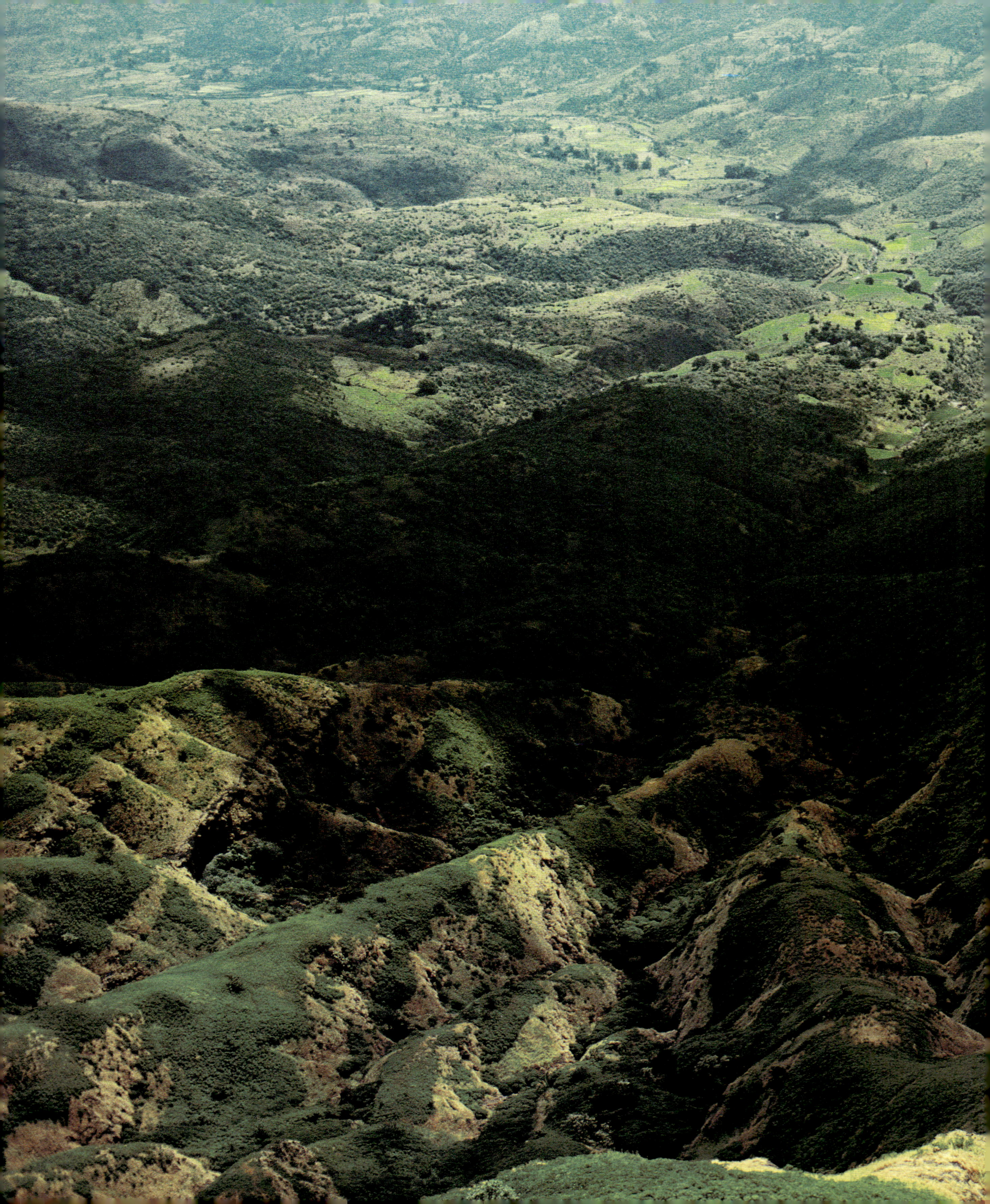

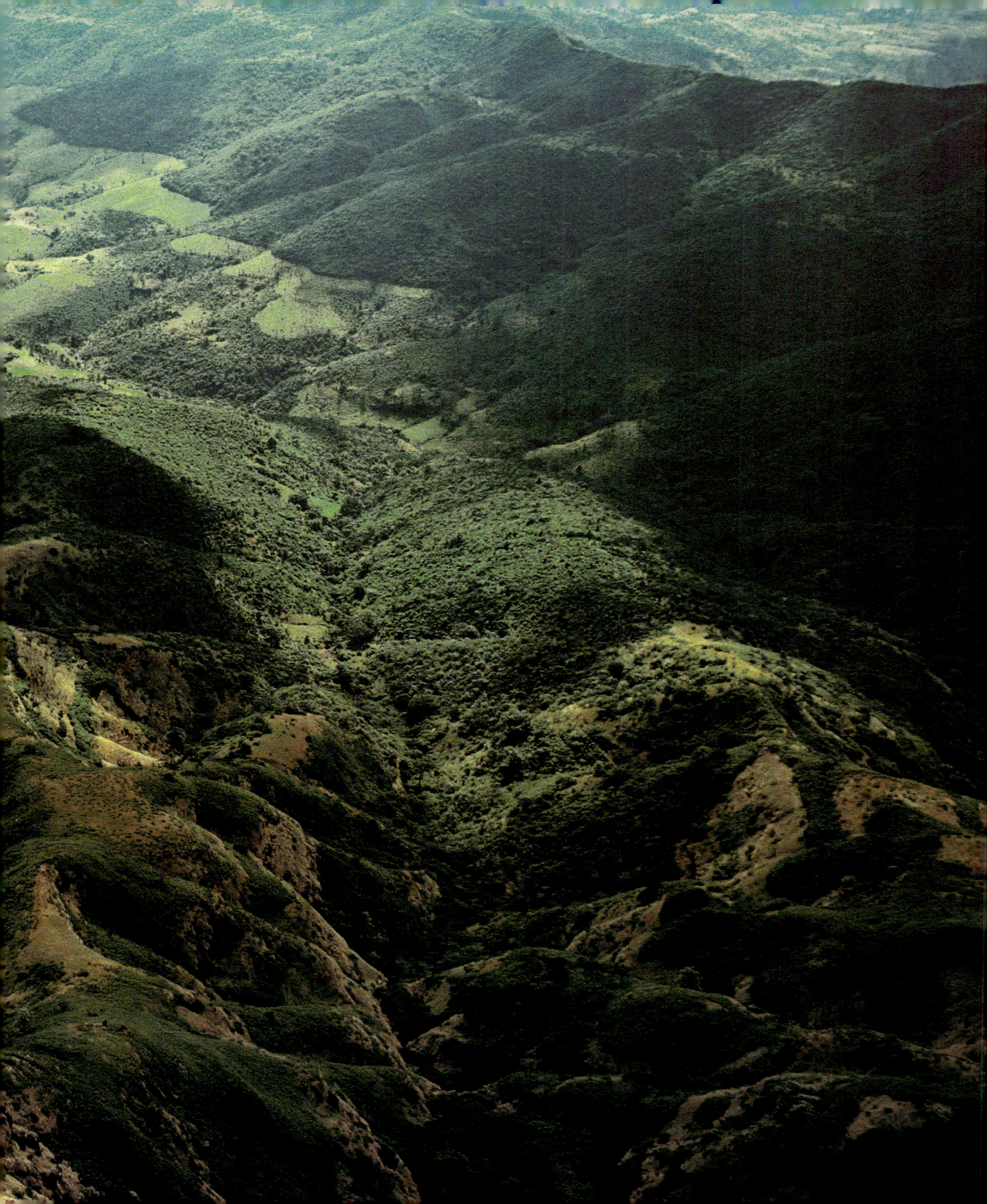

It is important to live in communion—with the world and with others, as well as with oneself, which means finding one's own deepest nature. Ritual is the medium through which these links are forged.

Few people practice yoga. Yoga owes its current expansion to Western enthusiasts. The mirror held up by powerful societies enables the colonized nations to rediscover a fashion for themselves. The word yoga is based on the Sanskrit root *yuj*, to harness, join, unite, based on an Indo-European root that has produced the word *jugum* in Latin, *joug* in French, and *yoke* in English.

"Unite" is the key word in Indian spiritual exercises. It applies just as much to one's own inner self as to the rest of the world. It is not a matter of creating a new state. In essence, man is united; it is a question of finding out what one is.

Each animal, each plant symbolizes a specific function in life. Thus, the elephant represents courage and intelligence, the palm tree signifies a link between man and God. Many yoga positions are aimed at enabling one to integrate one's own natural forces.

The lotus position, or the positions of thunder, the mountain, or the palm tree, the lion pose, and the poses of the vulture, the fish, the heron, the parrot, the turtle, the crocodile, the peacock, the cobra, and even the grasshopper, are like wings that enable a rather heavy body to fly, positions that affect the body's magnetism and that, according to certain texts, were advice given to the Sun (Surya) by Shiva.

It is important to specify here that the word yoga means the practice that we have adopted. In the Sanskrit texts, it has a much wider meaning.

The song of a boatman far out in the Ganges, suspended in the evening light. It is not the gods who appear, as in Greece, it is the river itself that carries divinity along with it.

Nighttime. A few reflections in the water. The frogs croak in the reeds. The gods are watching over us. What is the spirit of India? Just look into the faces of the old people. The sacred and the profane, which normally occupy two separate places in our minds, are not separated in India. The body is sacred, the act of love can also be, and people eat, sleep, talk, or play games in the sanctuaries. Yet the temple is a place apart, the dwelling place of genuine divinity. The ritual of *diparthamba* clearly shows that entering a temple implies a change of light. The devotee burns camphor beside a pillar located at the entrance. Thus he receives the inner light of the temple.

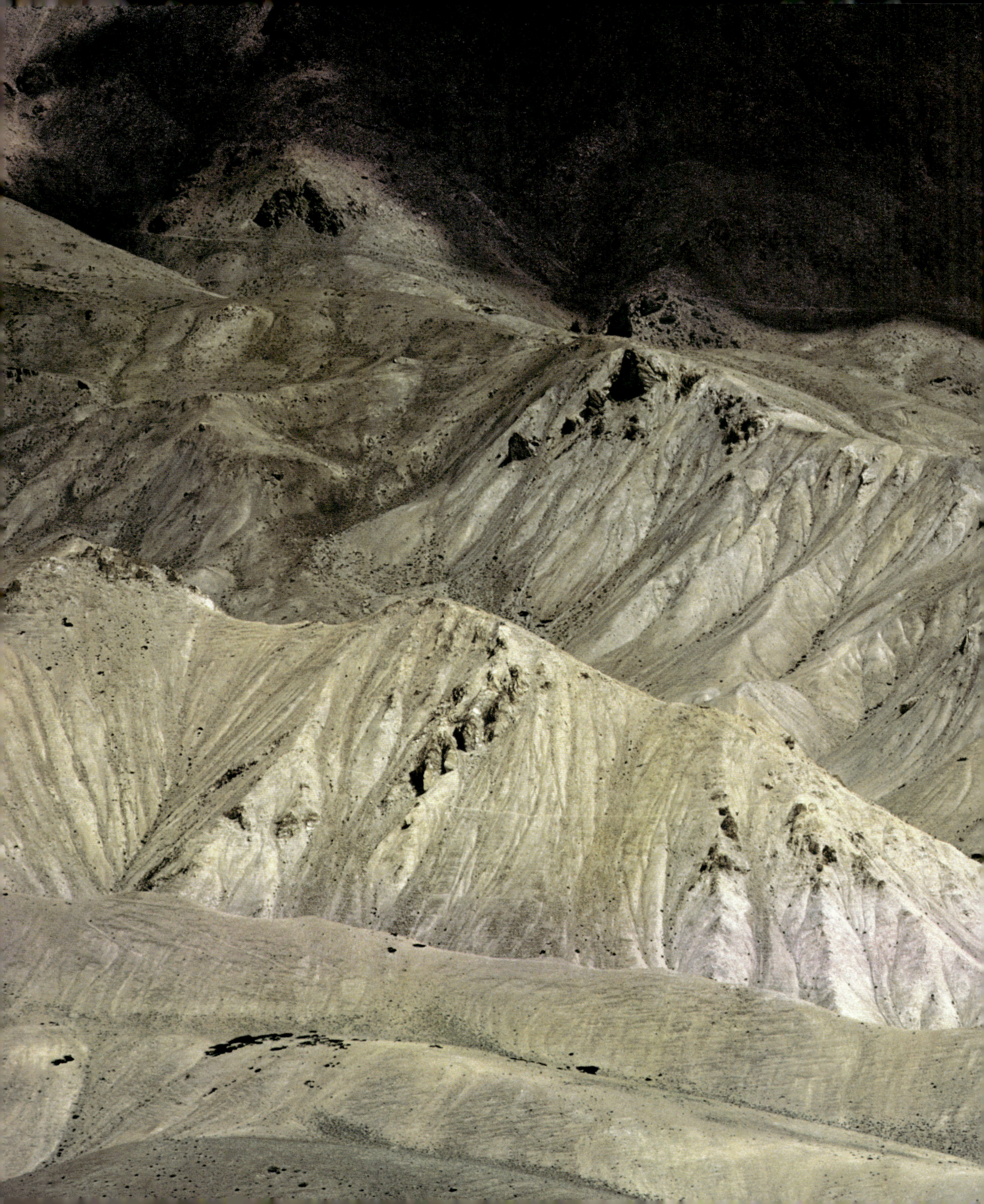

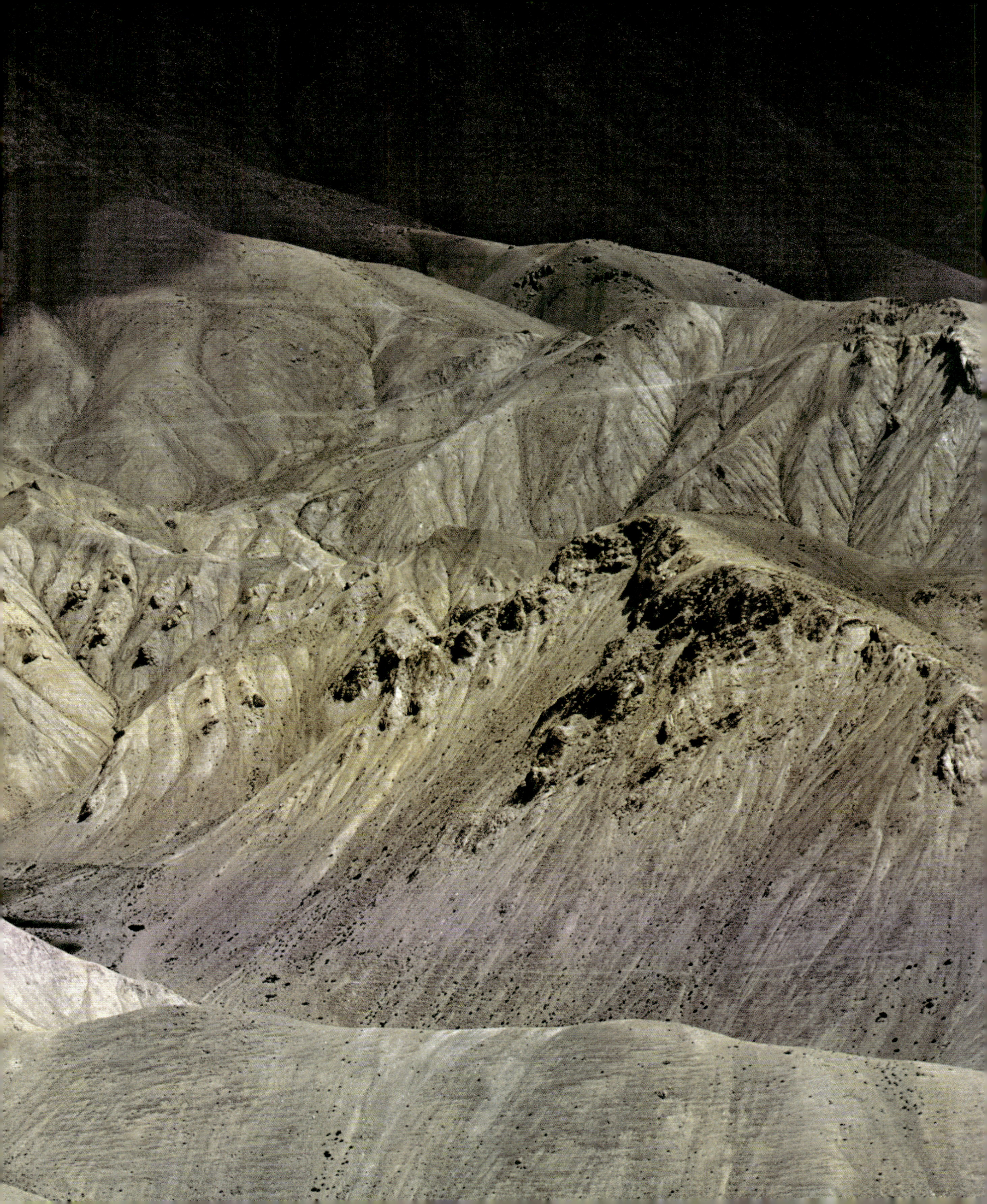

The goddess Kali, who is being venerated today in this village, is connected with and represents the energy of time (*kala*). According to the texts, she is even more closely linked to transcendental power. She has lent her name to the city of Calcutta. She is often seen represented in temples dedicated to Shiva. She is rightly disturbed when a person is overwhelmed by a fear of death, since her function is to release us from that fear. If she is welcomed into our psyche or our unconscious she elevates us above these suffocating dichotomies. In the Kali Tantra she is described as follows:

Frightening to behold, when she laughs she reveals her terrible teeth. She stands over a cadaver. She has four arms. In her hands she holds a sword and a severed head but gestures to us to dispel fear and to give of ourselves. She is the beneficent goddess of sleep, the companion of Shiva.

Naked, dressed in space, the goddess is resplendent. Her tongue hangs out of her mouth. She wears a necklace of skulls. This is the form that is worthy of meditation, of the power of time, Kali, who takes up residence beside funeral pyres.

Kali Tantra

There is no question of freedom in Hinduism. "Man is the cattle of the gods," as it says in the Brihadaranyaka Upanishad. One must become impersonal to leave all one's room for the god.

Are the Indians more spiritual than we are? No, religion is simply life. A smile always lingers at the edge of their expression. Anything can make it emerge. In certain nations, it is hidden behind walls.

In this darkened sanctuary incense sticks are burning. The smoke rises, twists, and vanishes. Nothing is left but the fragrance. So it is with our lives, as it is said.

There are no "pure ideas" in Indian philosophy, contrary to what one might think. The idea is everywhere associated with what is experienced. The cows wandering among the crowds in the market, the children sitting outdoors in school, a blind man humming to himself led by a little girl in rags, garishly painted gods invoked for a good harvest, boys, a cure, rain, the washerwomen who chatter around the communal washtub, a baby lying on straw. Dante would not feel out of place here. He watches Virgil from the undergrowth.

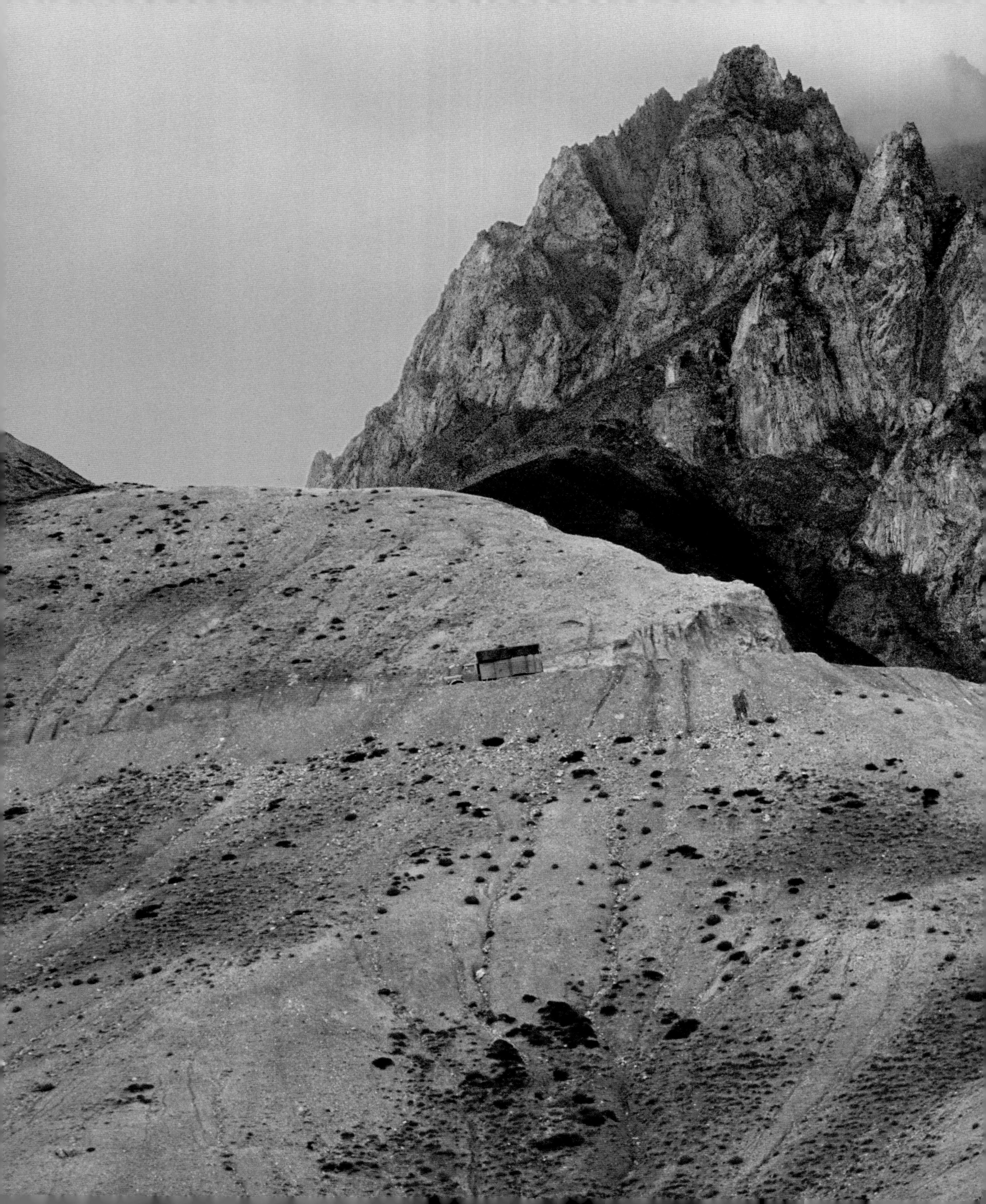

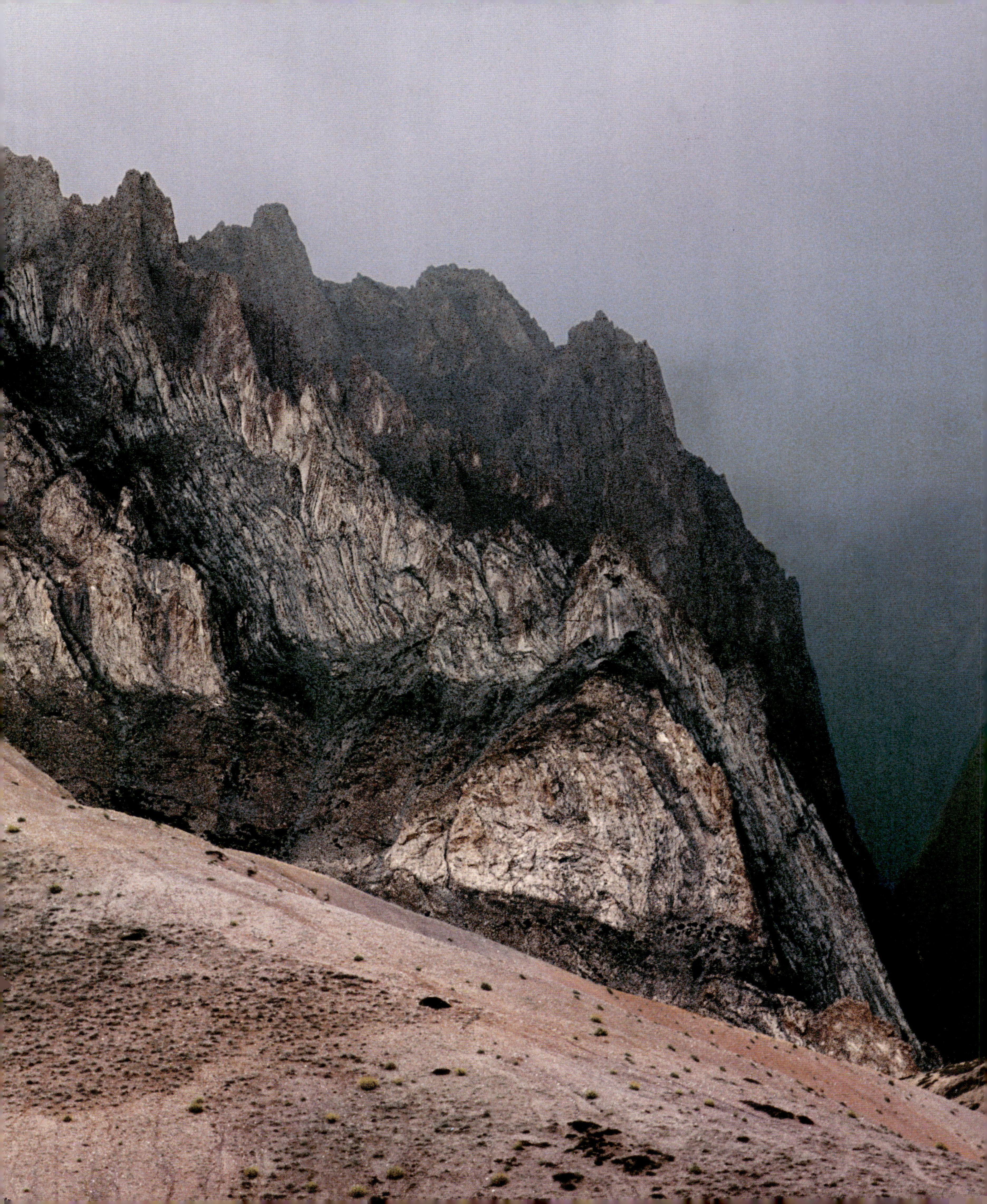

The tradition was once transmitted orally and continues to be. With our noses buried in books, we have forgotten the vitality of the spoken word. Furthermore, we have embraced Indian thought while forgetting that it needs to be practiced. We apply our manner of thinking to a culture that does things differently. And that is how so many silly things have come to be written. The Hindus are convinced that sacred words are a living organism. If you scratch one you are injuring a living thing and displeasing the gods. How hard one must toil to right the wrong! Sometimes one must start the recitation again from the beginning.

To repair does not mean to wipe out. Nothing is ever wiped out. We perform a bad action, we suffer the consequences for one, three, or seven lives.

Hindus walk around the temples in order to do themselves some good just as, in our culture, we go to the seaside, the mountains, or a spa to pamper ourselves and keep ourselves healthy. So why do foreigners make so many visits to the temples?

Sometimes a sigh, a word, a single note, a thin blade, opens up the sky. In this hilltop temple of pilgrimage, there is a cacophony of trumpets, tablas, and cymbals. Having an internal ear is useless.

Just follow the drain. Eventually you'll reach the sea.

If I had never encountered India, I would only have my childhood to teach me that myths can be touched and felt.

One day it happens, you get the Indian bug, your relationship to life itself has changed. "Modernity" takes on the appearance of a tiny adventure, a gray moth in a dismal season.

Progress is a partial and partisan idea. Religion is a necessity of life, even if God is no longer part of it. Beauty is the oxygen without which the days suffocate us. Time has changed our habits.

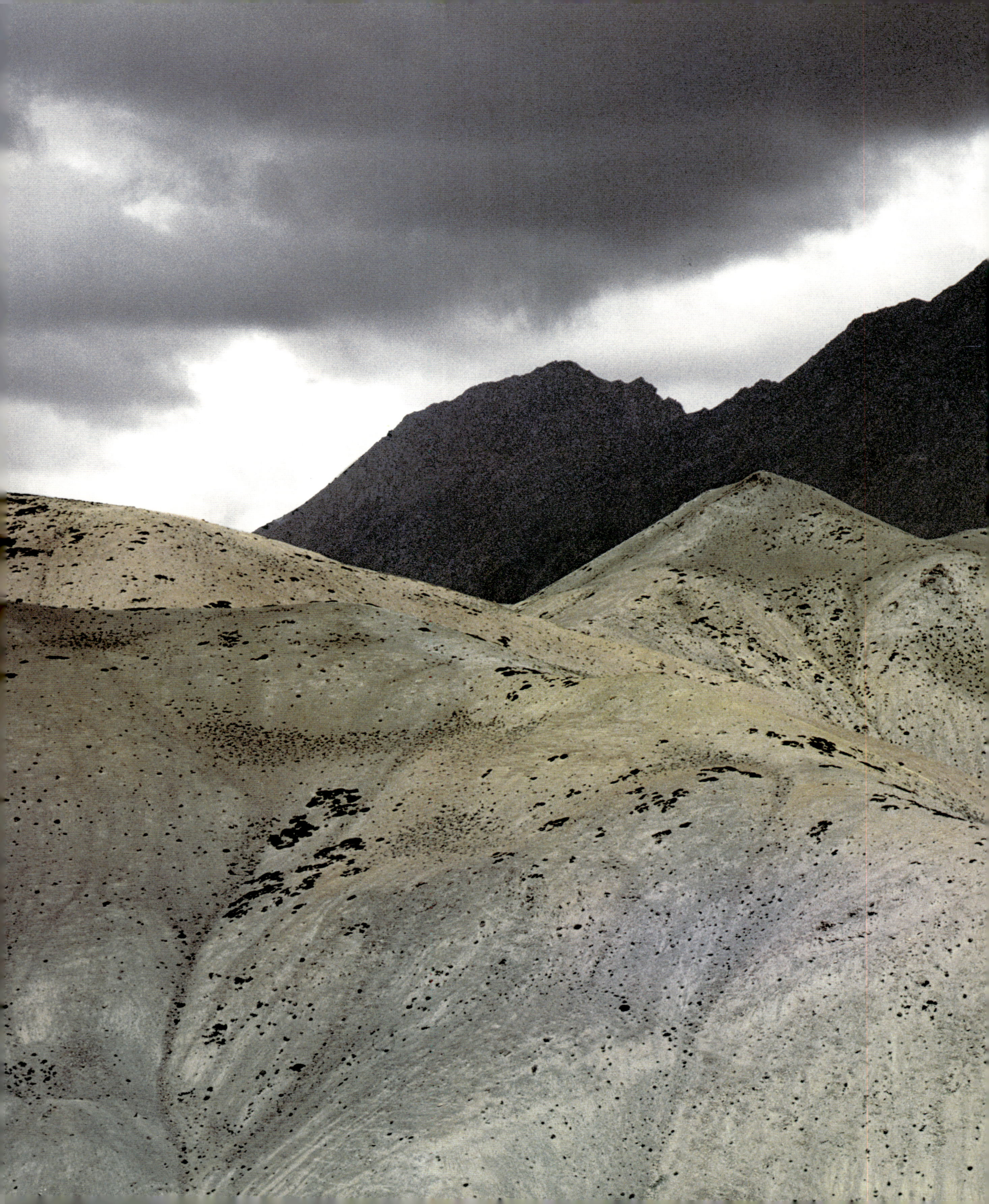

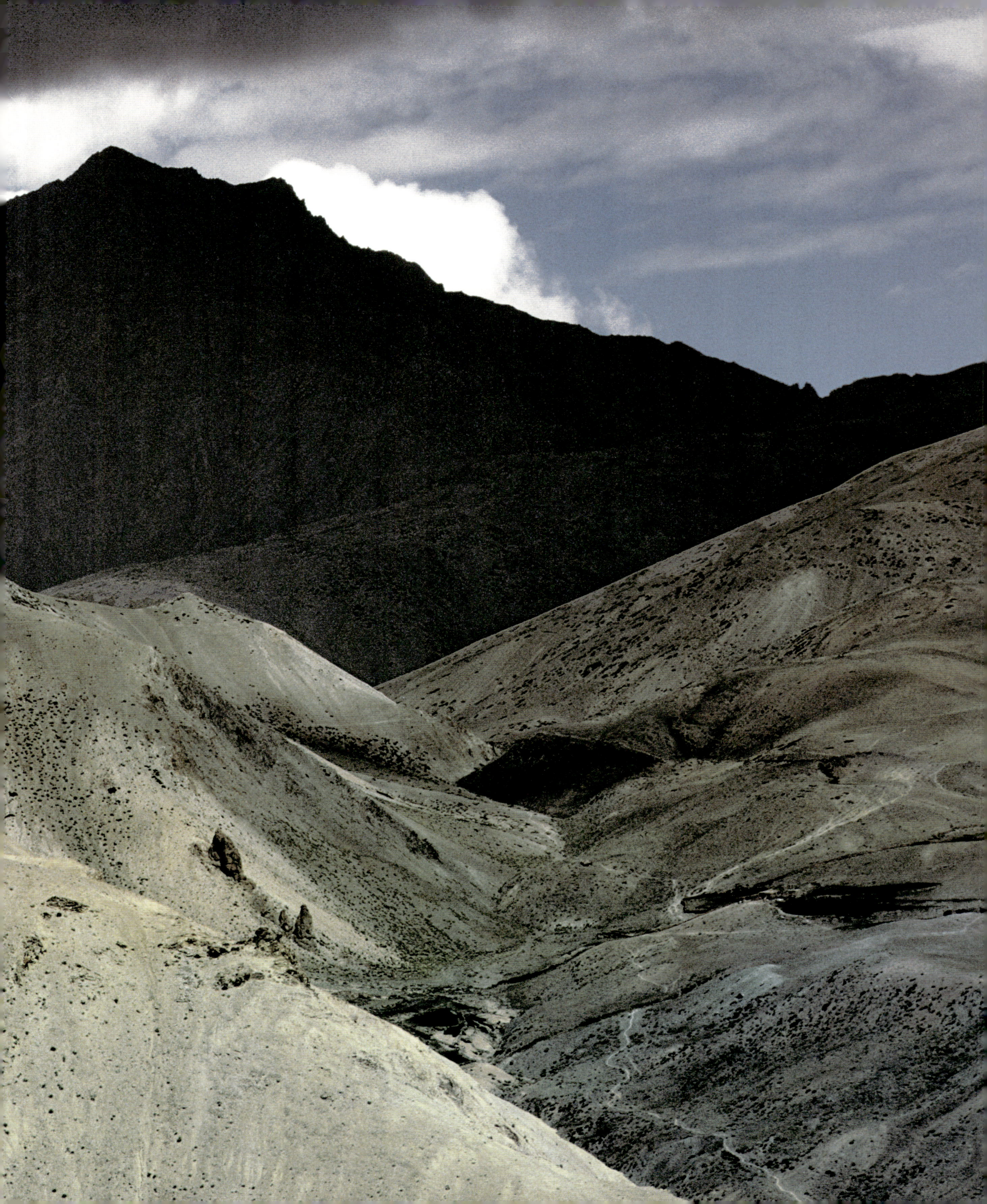

Other routes to divinity

The multiple arms of the gods are like the multiplicity of religions practiced in India. The relationship is not merely superficial. No other culture has been as welcoming to incoming religions from diverse sources. In addition to Hinduism—the religion of 80 percent of Indians, which alone accounts for a multiplicity of traditions, schools, and rites—Buddhism, Jainism, and Sikhism arose from the fertile soil of Indian philosophy. As a result of numerous invasions, Islam was grafted on, and is now linked to the destiny of the Indian Union. Prior to partition in 1947, one-third of the inhabitants of the empire that is now divided into India, Pakistan, and Bangladesh, were Muslims. An ancient Jewish community has lived in Cochin for many centuries; Christianity developed in the south as soon as it emerged as a religion, and was revived with the arrival of the Portuguese in the sixteenth century and, here and there, during the British raj. The Christian population of India represents only three percent of its inhabitants, but this translates into more faithful than there are in the whole of Italy. The Parsees, also known as Zoroastrians, were welcomed into India after Persia fell to Islam in the eighth century. Although they are few in number, many of them are powerful industrialists, especially in Bombay (Mumbai). Then there are the ancient religions that date from pre-Aryan times. These are difficult to define, being syncretic combinations of Hinduism and shamanism. They are practiced by the tribal peoples who live in the forests.

Although the distinction between religions born in India and those whose sacred books and beliefs arrived from distant shores is a historical reality, it does make some religions more legitimate than others. Did the Indo-Europeans, the original invaders, acquire greater legitimacy through the *Veda* than did other invaders, such as Muslims and Christians? While an ancient lineage may be admired, it does not imply greater proximity to the truth. On the other hand, let us not become confused as to chronology. The earliest Christian communities are almost two thousand years old, older than Christianity in France or the United Kingdom; Islam reached India ten centuries ago, even before it reached Istanbul or Jakarta. India is built on the circulation of peoples, beliefs, customs, and languages that constitute an inextricable network of mutual influences. This did not happen without conflicts and exclusions, especially between Hindus and Muslims, but Mother India is a reality who exists in everyday life from Kashmir to Kaniyakumari (on Cape Comorin). It is impossible to define her substance, yet it is palpable. An invisible thread links Ellora to the Taj Mahal, the same thread that can be found in the spirituality of Prince Siddhartha, Mahavira, Nagarjuna, Sankaracharya, Kabir, Guru Nanak, Tukaram, Dara Shikoh, Tagore, Ramana Maharshi, Gandhi, Sri Aurobindo, the Mother of Pondicherry, Anandamoyi Ma, Mother Teresa, and Amma.

The One, who is without nuance,
Appears through a secret design under diverse colors.

Svetasvatara Upanishad

The Buddha was an Indian

Buddhism is one the three great universal religions, along with Christianity and Islam, that exists on several continents. Is it a religion or a philosophy? The answers vary, depending on the definitions given to each word. Let's say that Buddhism is a path to freedom that has become a religion.

Shakyamuni (sage of the Shakya clan) or Gautama, known as Buddha (the enlightened one) after his "fulfillment" at Gaya, lived between the sixth and fifth centuries B.C. in northern India, in a location between the Himalayas and the plain of the Ganges. He revealed no sacred book, nor did he found a church. His teachings, which were oral, as were those of Socrates or Christ, were transmitted from master to disciple for five centuries before they were collected into an abundant corpus of literature, written in the Pali language. They were subsequently translated and adapted into several languages, including Sanskrit, Chinese, and Tibetan. A cross-check of the various sources tends to show that the Buddha's message has not changed down the centuries of oral transmission, even though the stories of his life have not escaped the human propensity for inventing miracles.

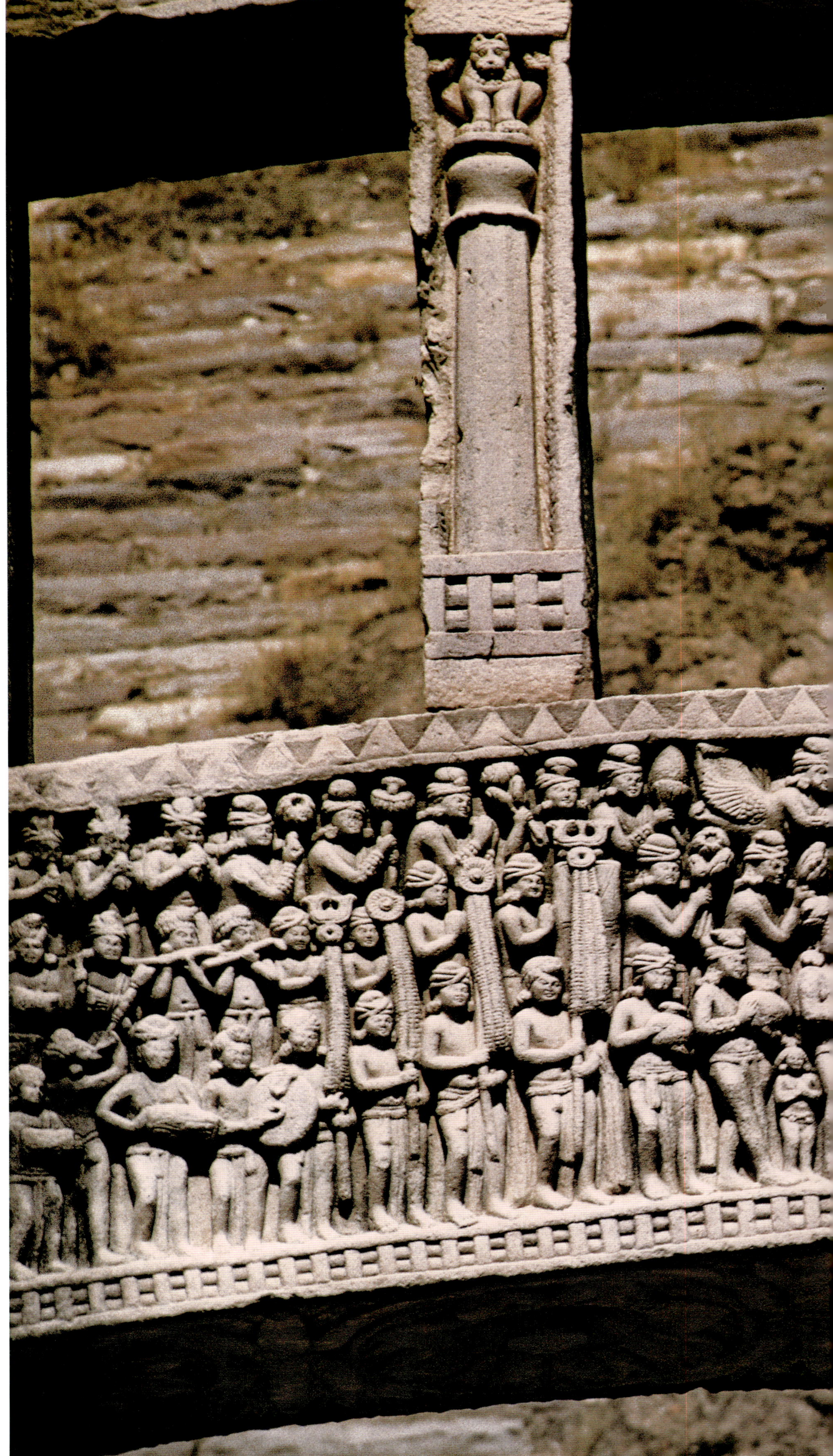

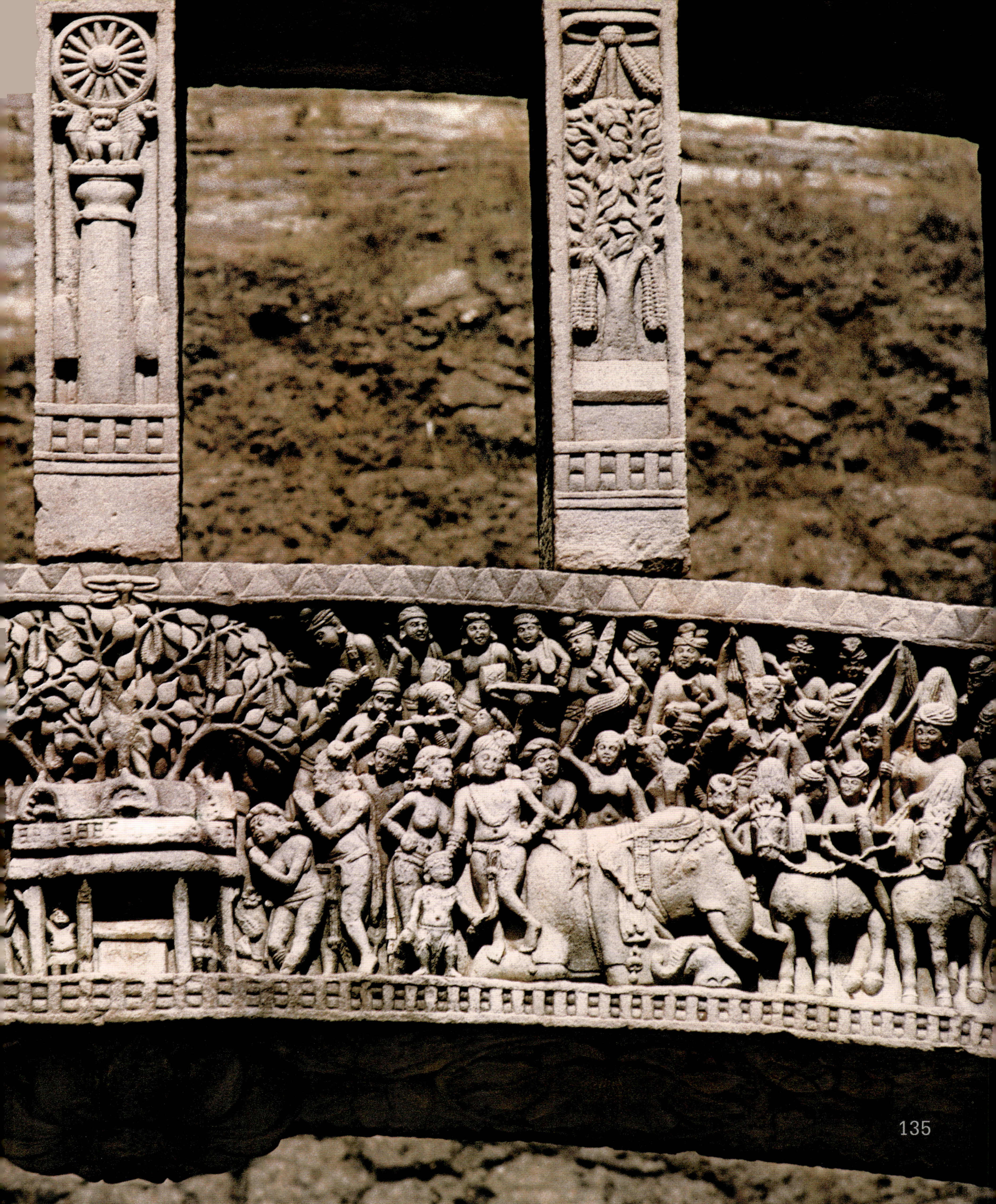

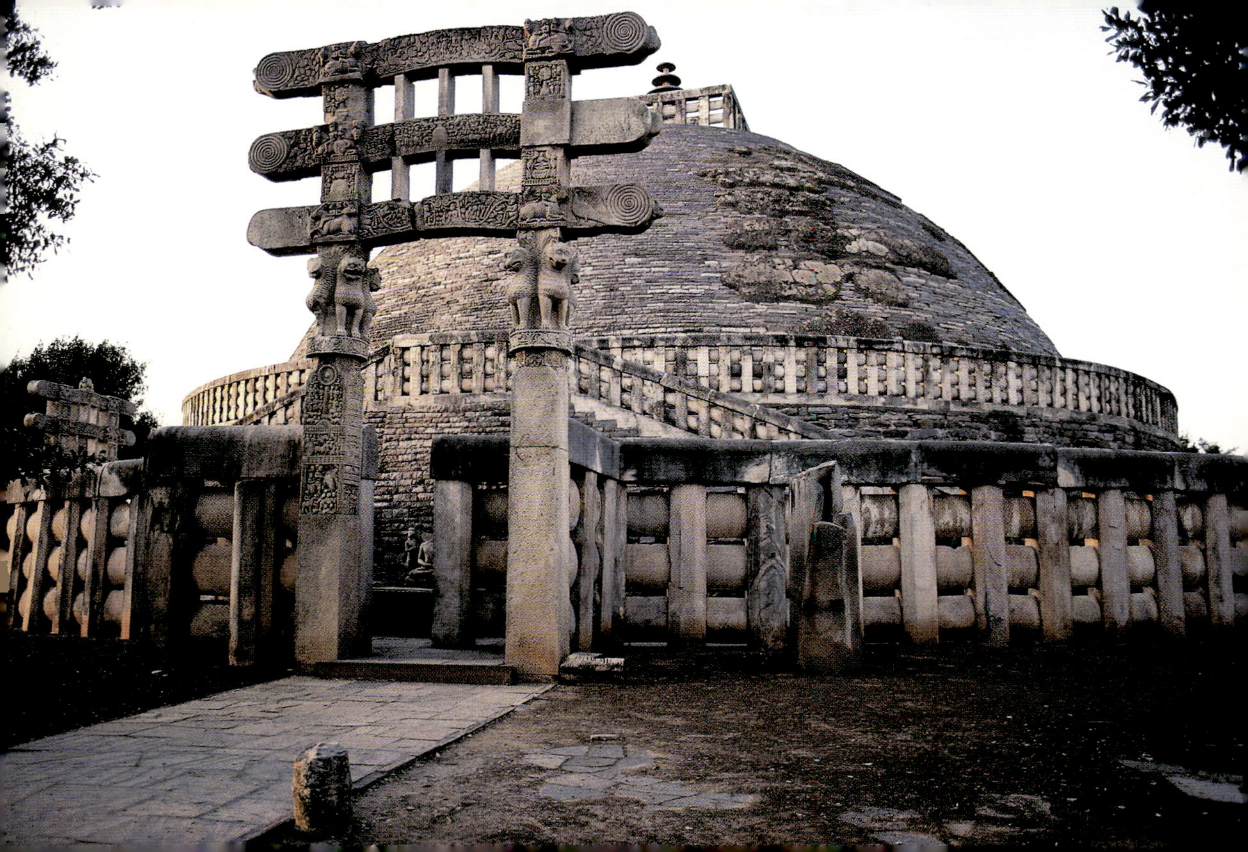

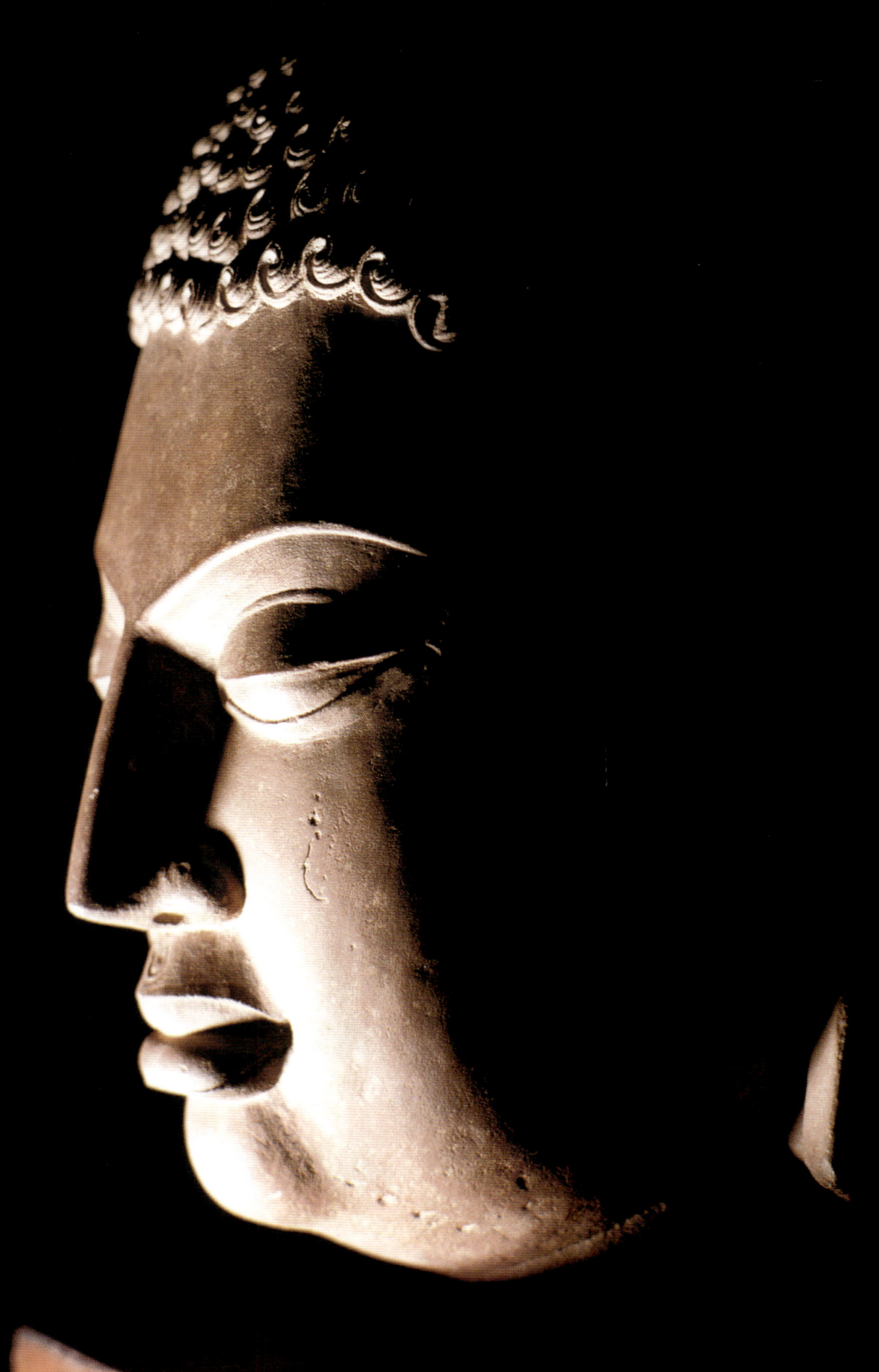

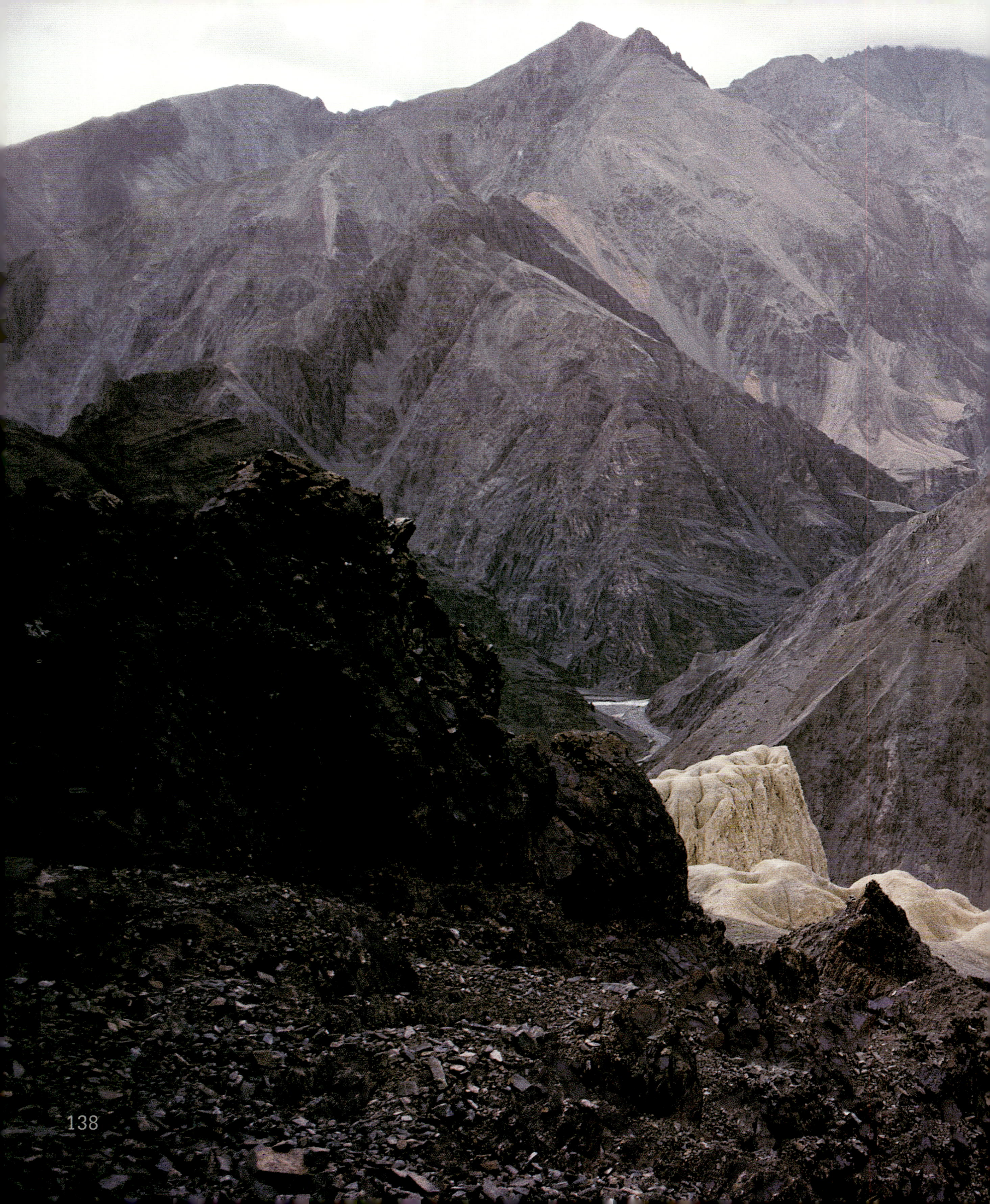

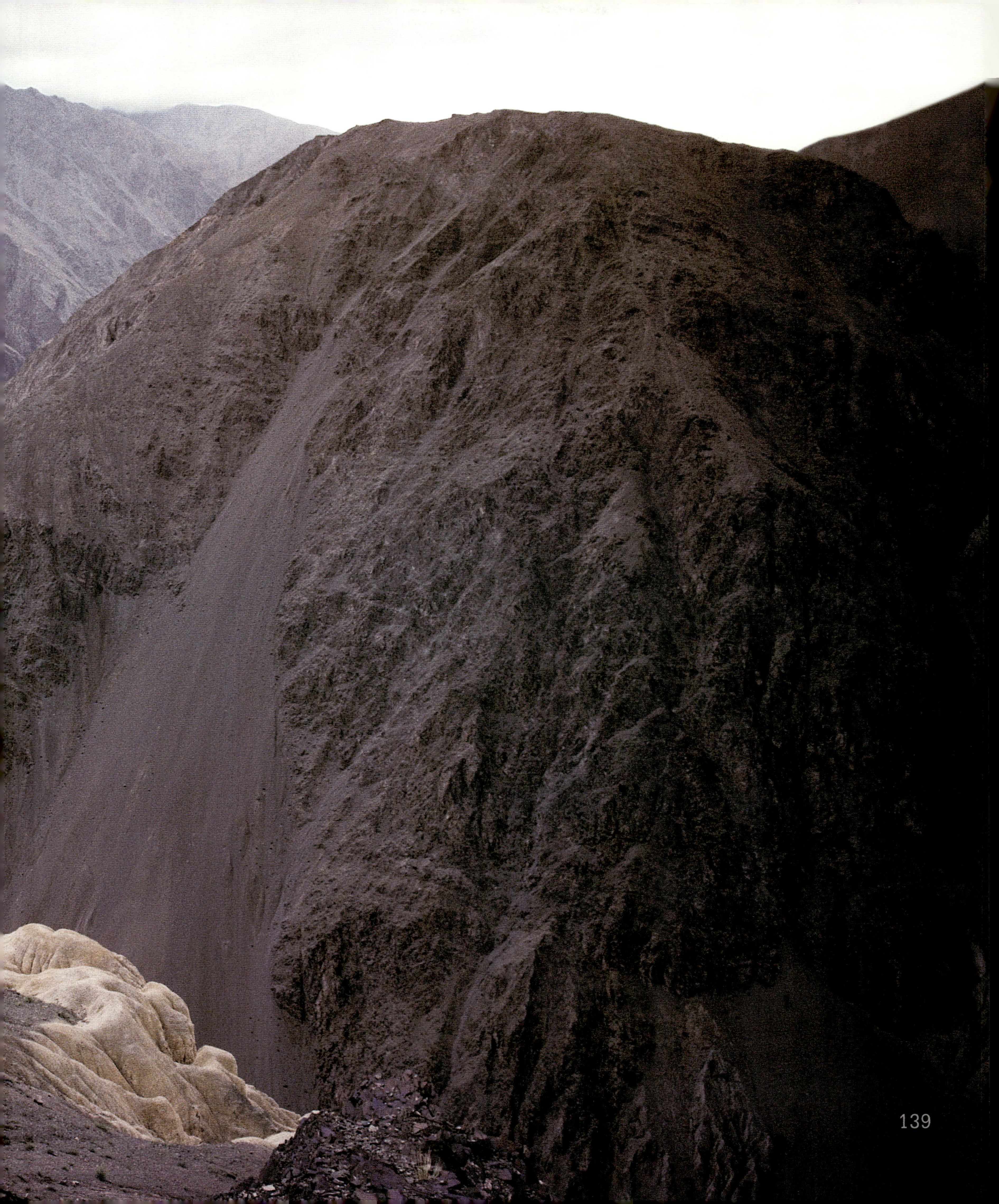

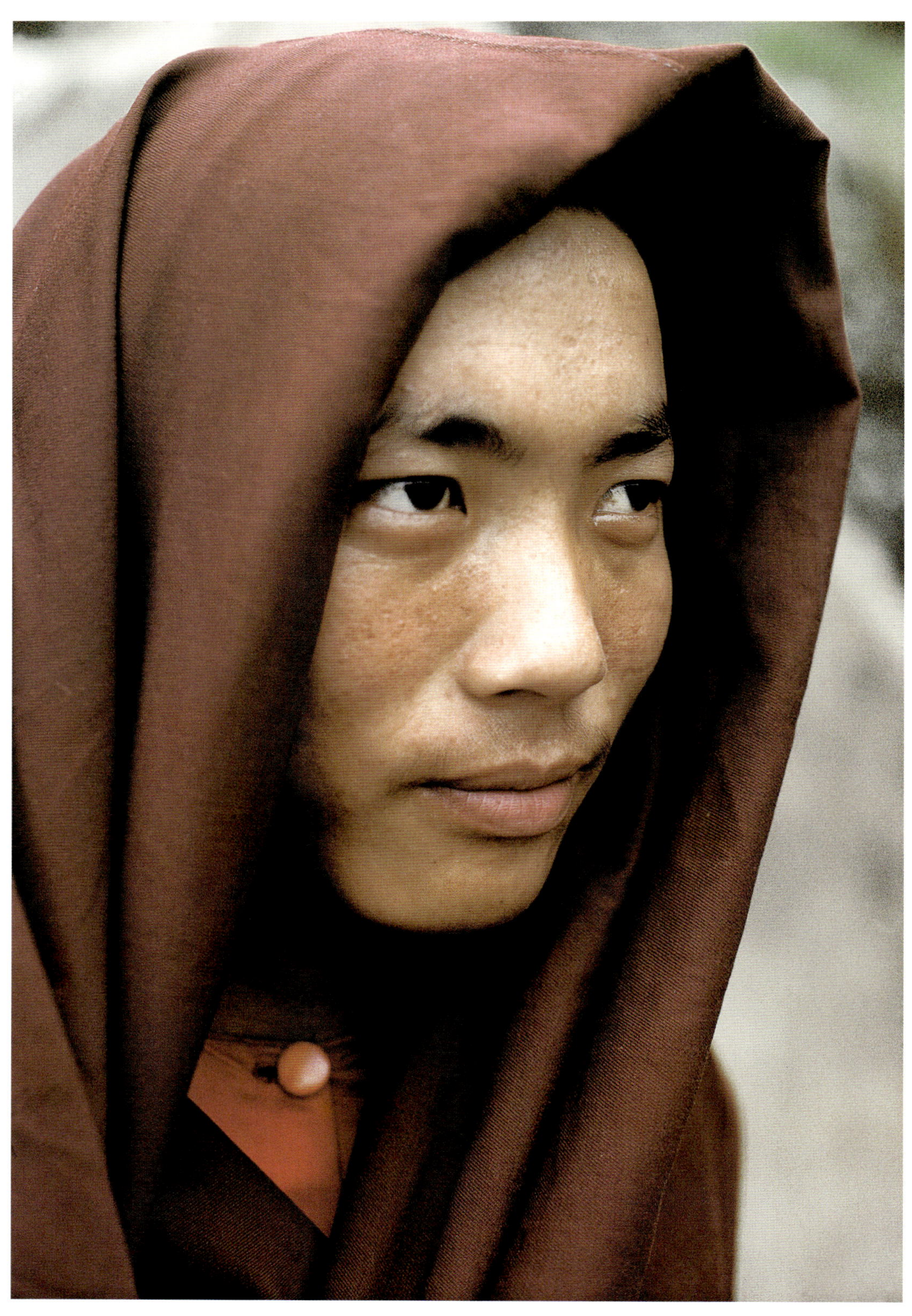

Above and Opposite: Tibetan monks.
Pages 138–139: The Karakorams, Ladakh.

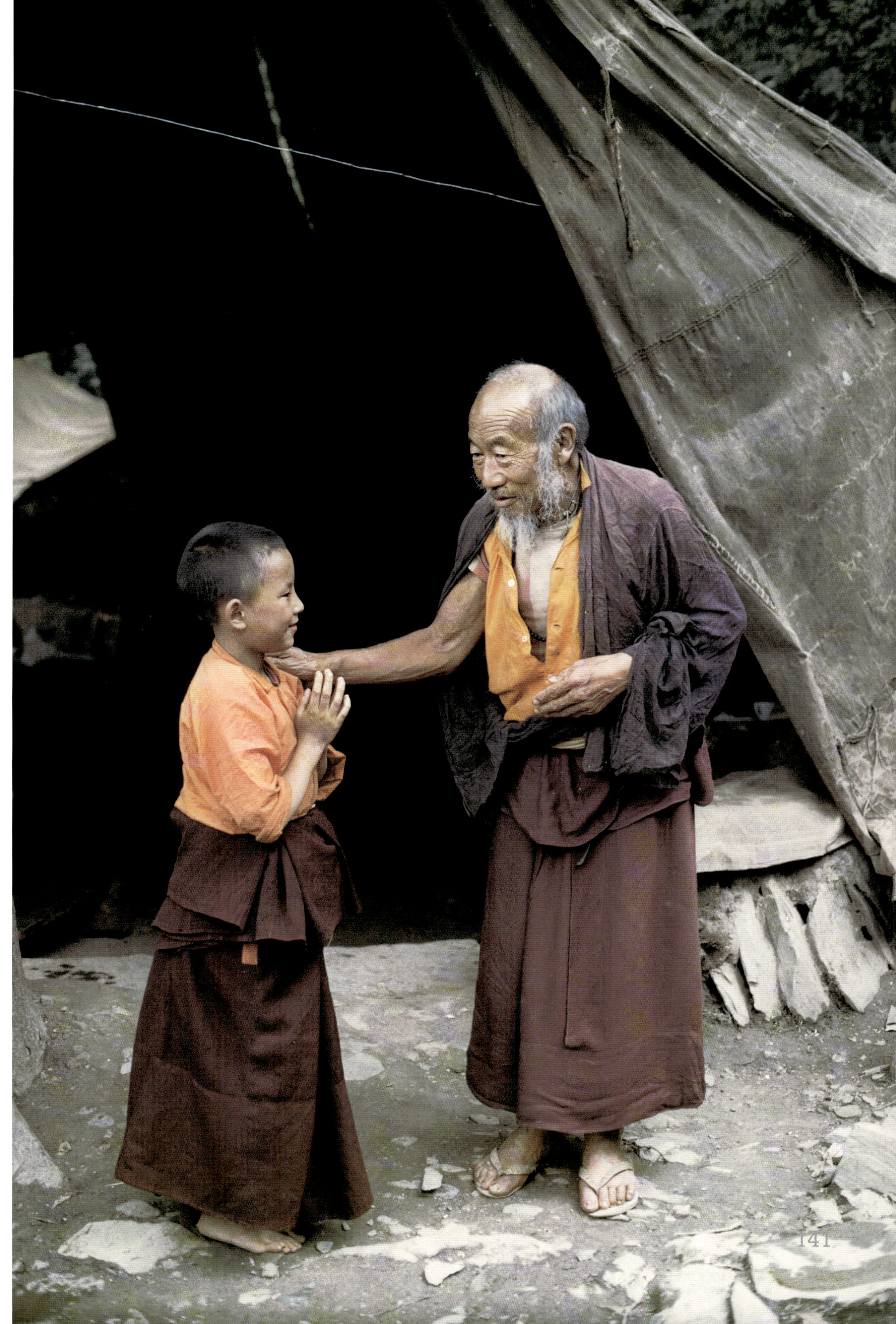

The Buddha contributed a method of salvation that is based on the simple inter-linking of four truths—suffering, the origin of suffering, an end to suffering, and the way that leads to the end of suffering. The stories, myths, and speculation that abound in the prolific Buddhist literature only have meaning as accompaniments on the road to self-transformation. If it were isolated from inner experience, Buddhism would be merely one more speculation in the graveyard of ideas that were never made flesh. Without meditation, there would be no Buddhism, amd there would no Buddhism without a master. For twenty-five centuries the essence of Buddism was transmitted from one human being to the next, from the one who was about to reach the goal to the one who had just chosen to follow the path. Without this flow, Buddhism would not have any vitality.

Buddhism has become an integral part of the culture of India by approaching it from an unusual angle. It incorporates *samsara* and *maya* but rejects the very existence of *alman* and denies man the possibility of replying to the question as to whether or not there is a God. Furthermore, it has no answer to the questions of caste, ritual, or multiple gods that require flattery. Salvation comes from within oneself.

Of course, as has been the case with the messages of so many masters who came to enlighten, Buddhism has become a religion, in a structure that is firmly implanted in the human psyche. Thus, in many Buddhist temples, the faithful can be seen imploring the Buddha (one can always hope) to help them acquire an automobile, a husband, money, a son, or a girlfriend.

The religion spread from India throughout east Asia, transforming itself and dividing into numerous paths. It should be noted, however, that if a monk from Sri Lanka (*Theravada* Buddhism), a Tibetan monk (*Vajrayana* Buddhism), a Japanese monk (*Mahayana* Zen or *Shingon*), and a monk from the West were to meet, and if they had practiced meditation with a strict master for many years, they would immediately understand the meaning of the blink of an eye or a burst of laughter among themselves. Based on physical and spiritual practice (that are treated as one) Buddhism is, in essence, flexible and welcoming. Wherever it has been accepted, it has coexisted happily with the other beliefs (often shamanistic in nature) that preceded its introduction, such as the Bön religion of Tibet, the Nats of Burma, the cult of the ancestors in China, and Shintoism in Japan.

In India, the movement developed somewhat differently. Thanks to the boost it received from Emperor Asoka (third century B.C.), it became firmly established. It then coexisted alongside what is by convention known as Hinduism until, very gradually, Buddhism began its decline. This happened between the seventh and twelfth centuries A.D., depending on the region. There is no really plausible theory in response to the eternal question of why Buddhism left India, where it had previously flourished for about fifteen centuries (longer than Christianity in Russia) before merging into Hinduism without any apparent conflict. None of the reasons generally offered—the advent of Islam, disappearance of the social class that had adopted Buddhism, incorporation into Hinduism of part of its metaphysics, the *Brahmans* regaining their former preeminence in society, incompatibility between the spirit of India and that of Buddhism, and so on—are sufficient in themselves to solve the conundrum, even if each of them separately, except the last, may contain a grain of truth.

In fact, the question that should be asked is different: Did Buddhism ever really leave India? It should be remembered that the Buddhist philosopher Nagarjuna, who lived in the second and third centuries A.D., influenced later Hindu thinking, especially that of Sankaracharya (ninth century A.D.) and the Advaita school of thought. After all, the *sannyasis* were the spiritual successors of the Buddhist monks who, for centuries, mastered their human frailties and held out their begging-bowls in the villages of India. The *sannyasis*, who are on the margins of Hindu orthodoxy, reject the exclusion of a person for reasons of birth, promote nonviolence, and practice forms of detachment that are close to those of Buddhism. Even in twentieth-century India, notable influences of Buddhism prevailed, embodied in the teachings of Gandhi, Sri Aurobindo, and Prajnanpad. Inside the white stripe of the Indian flag, between the orange of Hinduism and the green of Islam, there is the symbol of India, the capital of a column featuring the lions of Sarnath, a Buddhist sculpture.

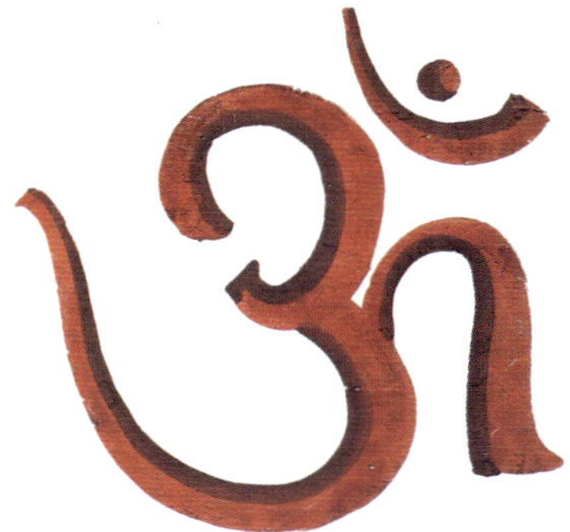

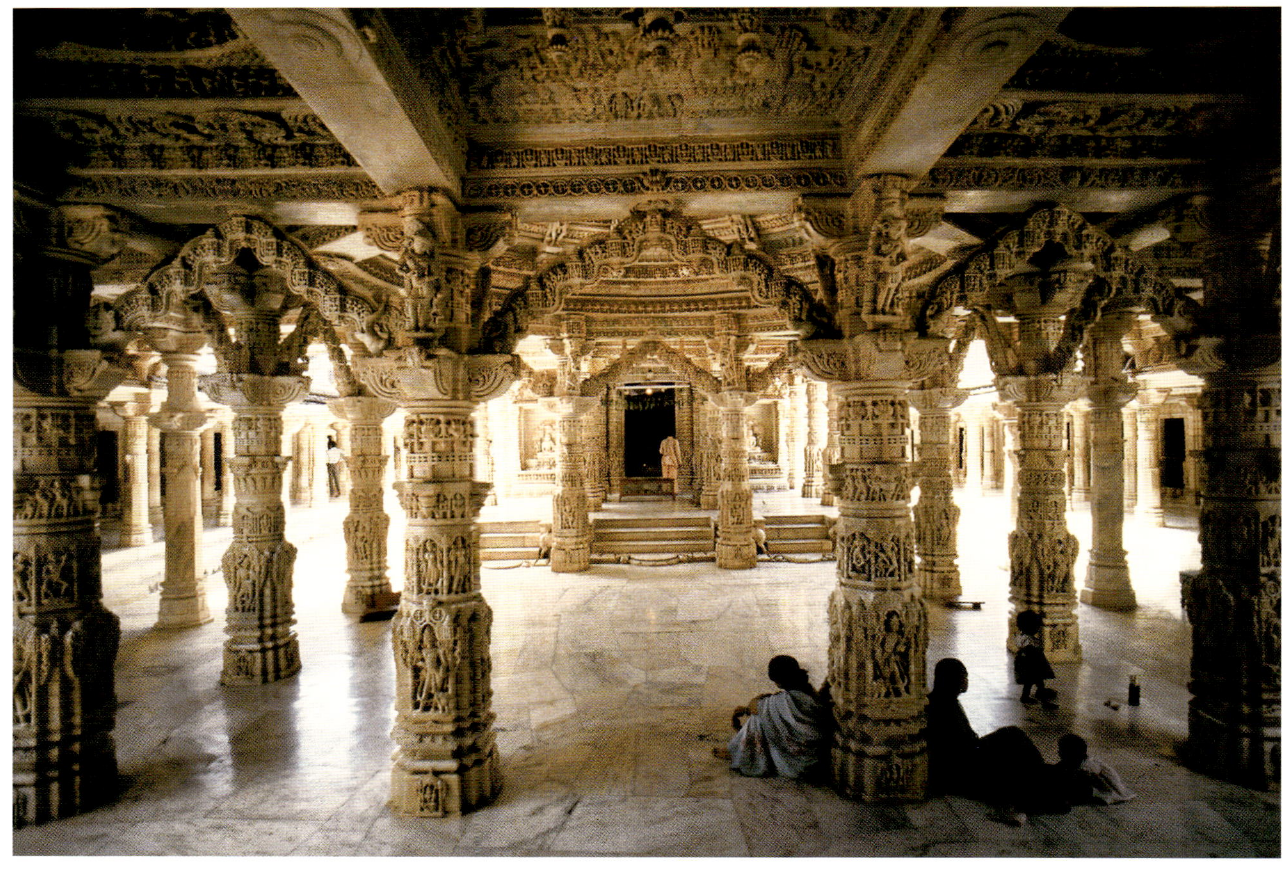

Above: Jain temple of Vimal Vasahi, Mount Abu, Rajasthan.
Opposite: Devotee in the temple of Luna Vasahi .

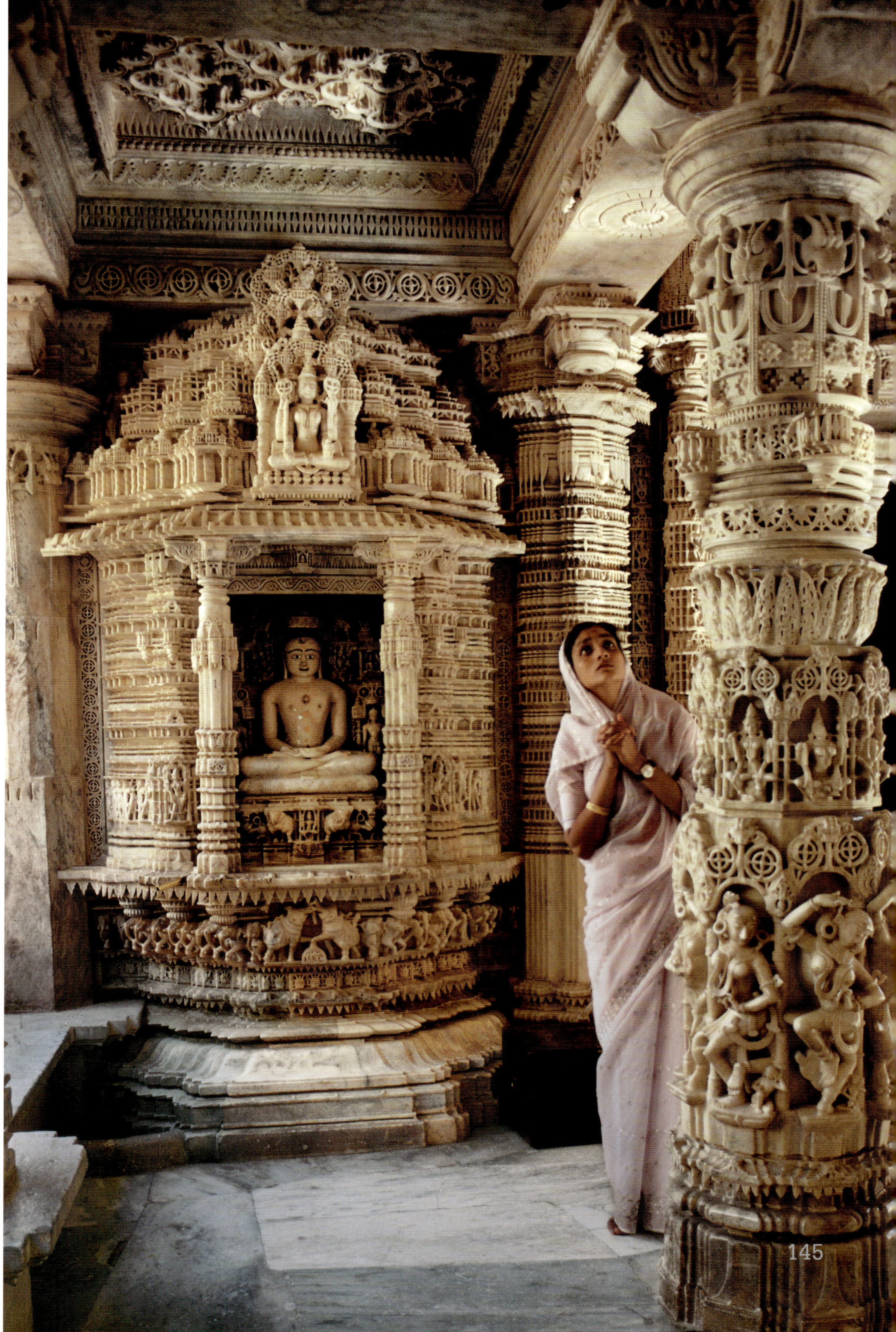

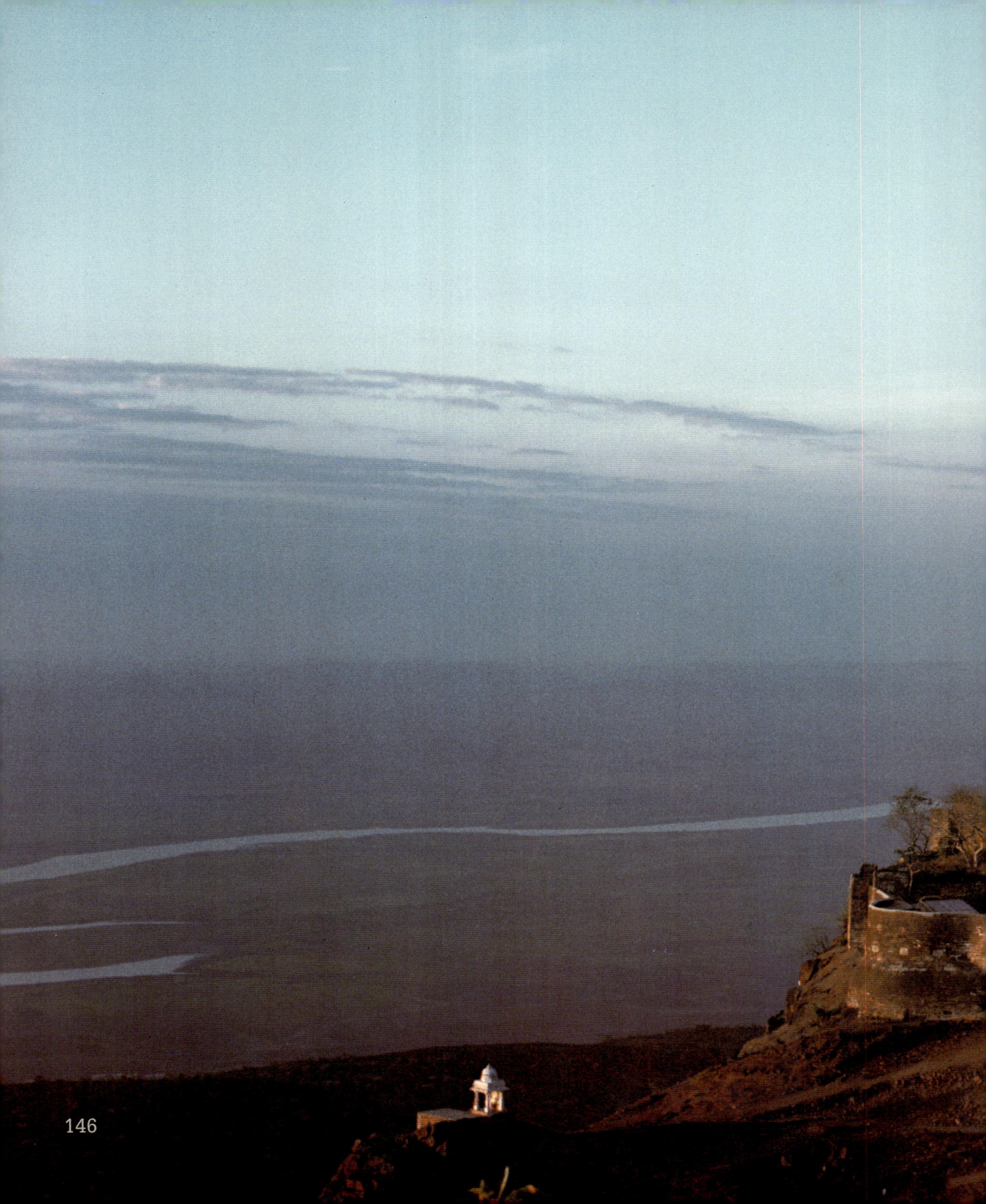

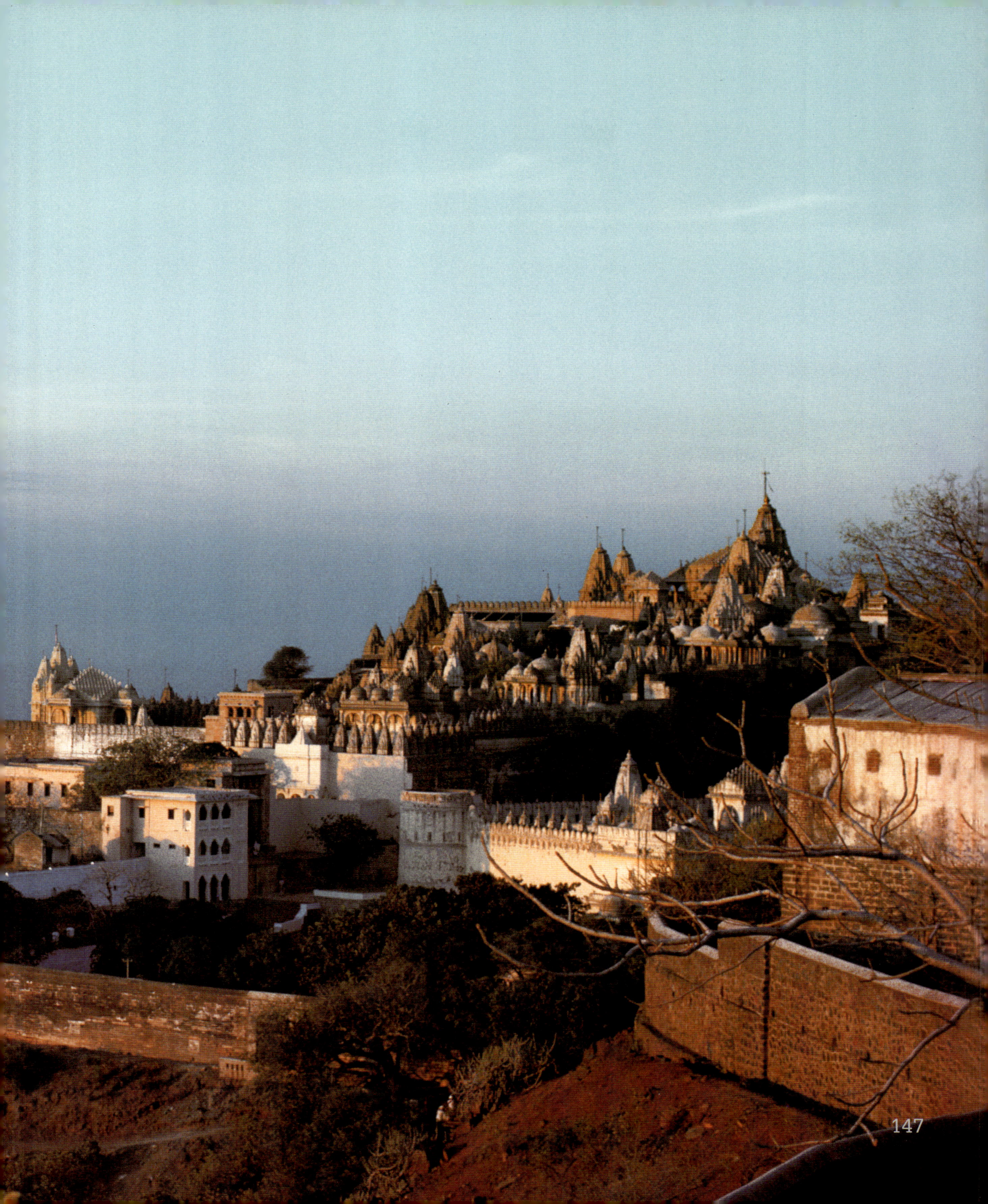

In addition, one of the greatest depictions of statuary throughout the world, the meditating Buddha, ceased to be represented more than a thousand years ago, yet no Hindu god usurped this spiritual accomplishment in the here and now.

Buddhist life prospered so greatly in India that the main schools of thought spread throughout the various other cultures that adopted Buddhism. They included Theravada, Madhyamika, Mahayana and its Dhyana (Zen) form, Tantrism, etc. In the same way, Buddhist statuary, whether from Sri Lanka or Japan, was inspired by India, in both the postures (*asanas*) or the symbolic gestures of the hands (*mudras*). What could be more universal than Buddhism? The simplicity of the four truths, to which could be added a fifth: there is a power that emanates from the life of the Buddha.

Strangely, Jainism, which resembles Buddhism in many of its aspects, has not spread beyond the shores of India. Jainism began to decline around the twelfth century, but it remains a living faith that surprises visitors. The founder of Jainism, Mahavira (or Vardhamana), lived in the sixth century B.C. Like Gautama, he abandoned his family to become a wandering monk. At the center of the rituals of Jainism there is a requirement for purity that is one of the foundations of Indian culture—hence the hackneyed image of the Jain who wears a veil over his mouth to prevent him accidentally swallowing an insect. Mahavira (which means "great hero") is often represented seated in meditation like the Buddha, or standing, depicted in monumental works of art that symbolize the three worlds: the lower world in the shape of the legs, the intermediary world in the shape of the body, and the higher world in the shape of the head. Jains constitute less than one percent of the population of the Indian Union, a paltry figure in comparison to the importance of Jainism in the history of Indian thought and art, not forgetting the effect of such holy places as Mount Abu or Palitana and its 863 temples with their strong vibrations. In fact, the many arms of Hinduism have been able to embrace the values of Jainism that have become common in India.

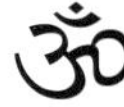

Buddhist statuary in India exists in two main phases. The early artists who illustrated significant moments in the life of Buddha never depicted the master himself. There is no explanation for this. Perhaps there was resistance to what might have become a deification of the master (which occurred in any case). What a lesson in impermanence it is that the form that represents Shakyamuni changes at the different stages of his life! When, after his four fateful encounters—with an old man, an invalid, a corpse, and an ascetic—he secretly escaped from his father's palace where his wife and son were sleeping, the sculptors represent his footprints. He wandered for many years before his awakening at Gaya under the fig tree, not far from the river. A tree is sculpted in stone to represent this moment. The fact that the Gautama chose to sit under a tree is significant in itself. The tree symbolizes a force that draws its sustenance from the soil and reaches toward the sky; it is permanent through its trunk but subject to the whims of the seasons through its leaves; it protects from rain and sun, and is potentially the substance of fire. It is patient and bows to the gusts of wind. Once he had been awakened, Gautama traveled to Sarnath (near Benares) where he delivered his first sermon. A wheel is carved to represent this stage, symbolizing the setting in motion of the Wheel of the Law. Would the sequel prior to his death be uneventful? The texts tell of a series of adventures that happened over many years when he taught, but none of them is consigned to the stone summaries of his life. The fourth stage, the culmination of his historic life, the Mahaparinirvana, was achieved at Kushinagara, and is symbolized by a *stupa*. A simplistic explanation for a *stupa* is a funerary monument designed to hold mortal remains. But it is, above all, the cosmic egg, a microcosm that radiates magical influences. As the Buddhist shape par excellence, it is a reminder that release from shackles makes it possible to rediscover the matrix of one's origins.

The second period of Buddhist sculpture in India, which is also the longest, is that in which the Gautama is represented in southeast Asia and the Far East as a man. These representations are based on the codes of Indian statuary, without the elements of fantasy that are characteristic of Hindu statuary. The first stage is his birth, in which he emerges from his mother's side or, as depicted by sculptors, he rides away from his father's palace on horseback after discovering the reality of life in the course of his four encounters. In the second stage, he is in Gaya, seated in the lotus position after the Awakening, taking some earth in his right hand as evidence that he has resisted the temptations of Mara. Only the position of the hands changes in the representation of the third stage, the teaching that sets the Wheel of the Law in motion. In the fourth stage, lying on his right side, he enters into the Mahaparinirvana that ends the cycle of reincarnations. All around him, his disciples are suffering, with the exception of one, who sits meditating serenely. Does this mean that the Buddha has only been understood by a single disciple after a life dedicated to teaching detachment? The sculptors had no illusions about the human capacity to leave behind the world of *maya*.

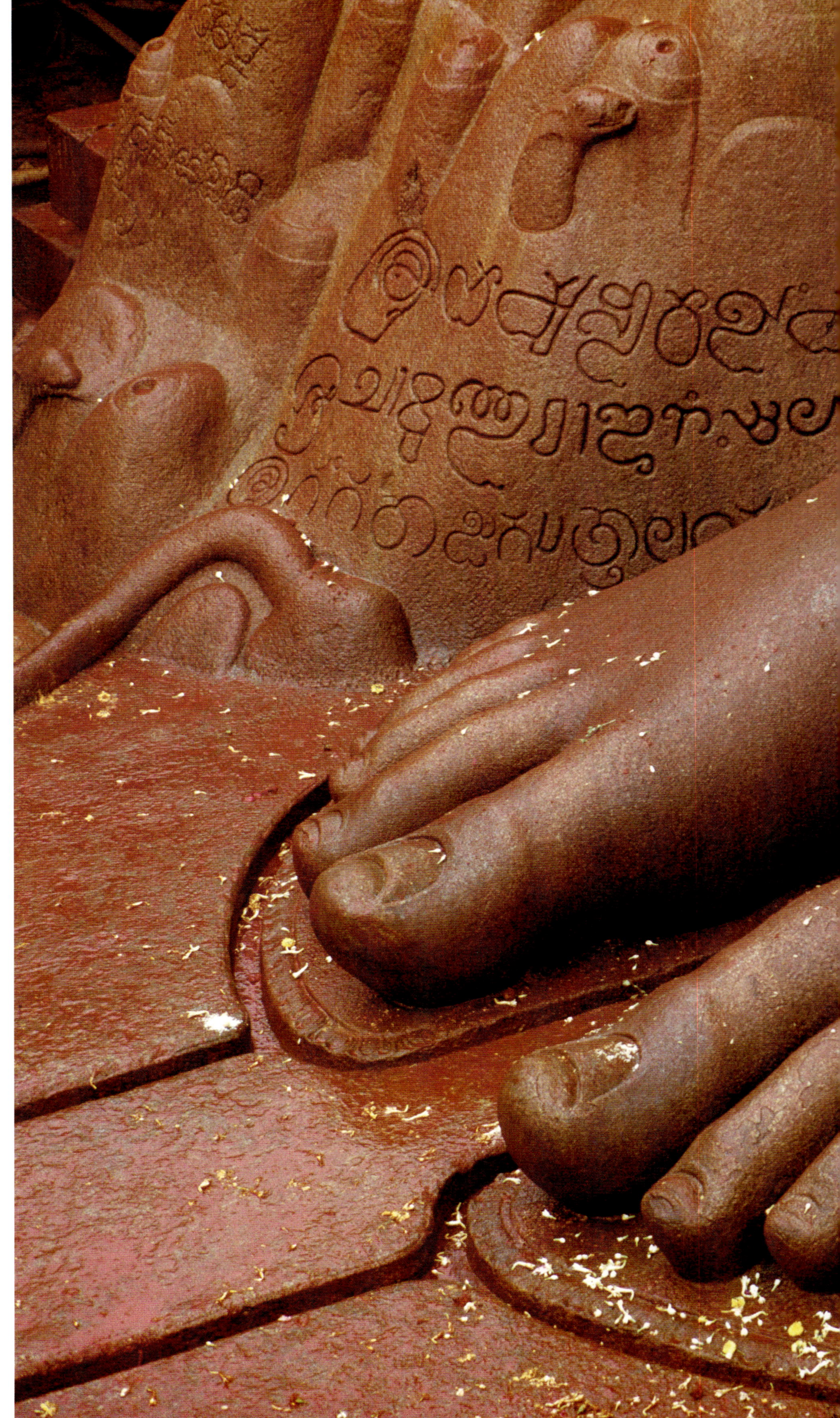

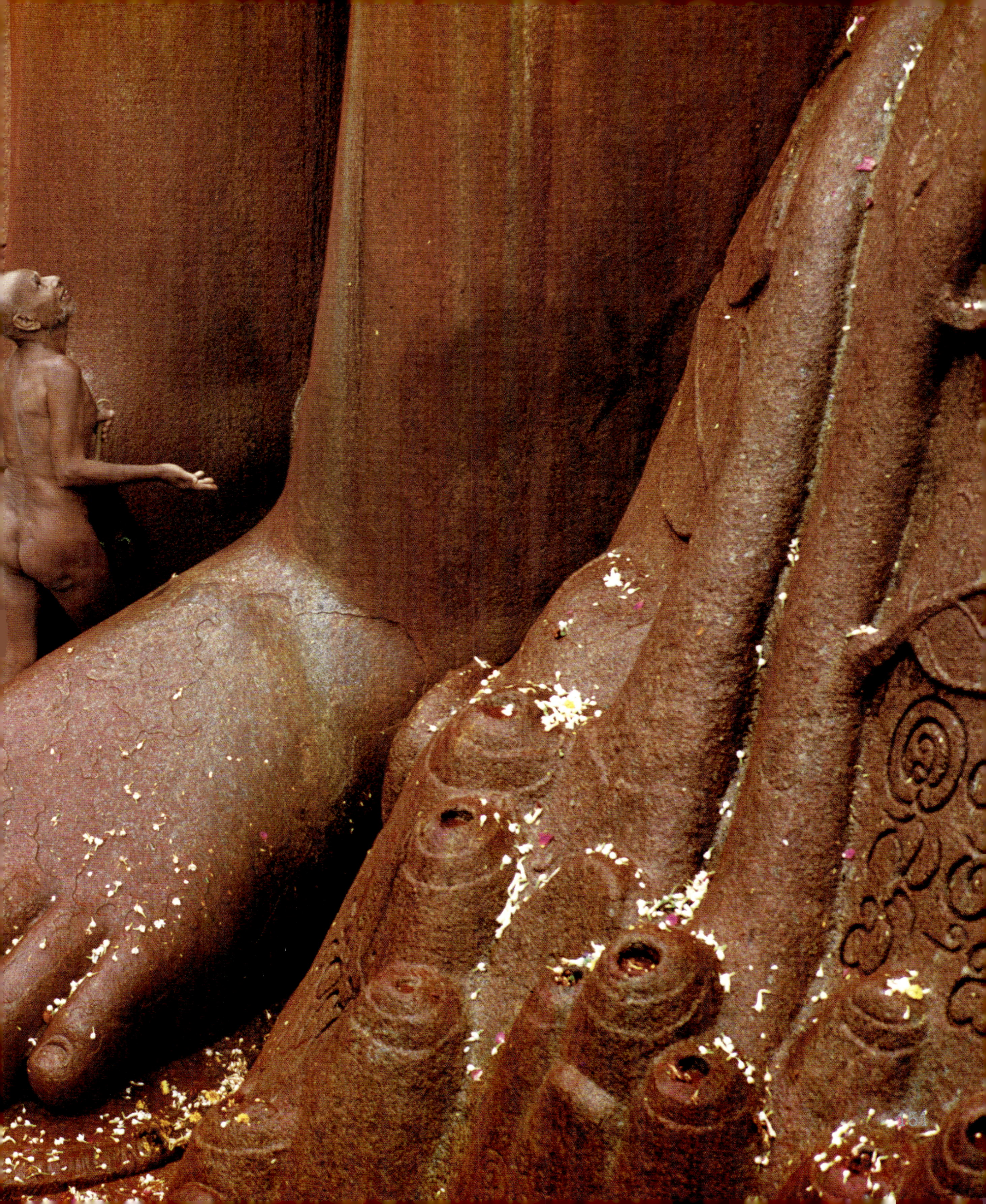

It is an extraordinary fact that twenty-five centuries after having preached and journeyed on foot throughout northern India, a prince to whom nothing extraordinary ever happened (nirvana is a natural state) spread a means of salvation that peacefully conquered the minds of more than half of Asia before taking root in the West, which was then in the throes of abandoning spirituality. Unlike Christianity or Islam, the spiritual journey is undertaken without the help of a powerful government or the crude arguments of the sword. The only weapon was and is the radiance of the masters. A single Indian monk, Bodhidharma, visited China in the early sixth century to preach the doctrine of Buddha, which then spread to Korea, then to Japan.

Siddhartha Gautama was born at Lumbini (c. 560 B.C.) a city currently located in Nepal, close to the Indian border, at the point where the valley of the Ganges rises in stages before encountering the Himalayas, which are inhabited by capricious gods who like to sing and dance. After the Awakening and the delivery of his first Sermon, the Buddha preached, walked, and must have had visions on a territory covering more than 3,860 square miles (10,000 km²) in what are now the states of Bihar (the name comes from that of vihara, a Buddhist monastery) and Uttar Pradesh. He attained Mahaparinirvana in Kushinagara, only forty miles (60 km) from Lumbini, a two-day walk.

Many pilgrims travel to the main sites connected with the life and preaching of the Buddha. They come from various Buddhist countries as well as from India, which has its own small Buddhist community whose numbers increased after the conversion of B. R. Ambedkar (1891–1956) in 1956. Dr. Ambedkar was an "untouchable" from Maharashtra who fought all his life for the rights of his fellow sufferers. His conversion to Buddhism was imitated by numerous fellow untouchables, and became a means of partially overcoming the caste barriers that had been erected against them by the Hindus.

The pilgrims lodge at inns but are also welcome to stay at monasteries that are often run by Singhalese monks, whose picturesque orange robes cause amateur photographers to believe they have talent. Here one can greatly enjoy listening to the birds twittering in the branches of the *bodhi* (pipal) trees, meditate on impermanence at the foot of *stupas* whose form is as rounded as a breast, pray before statues of the Master in dark alcoves, admire the lotus flowers that resemble those of the frescoes of Ajanta, philosophize before these same immaculate flowers that draw their sustenance from the nauseous depths of marshes, and sleep in one of the Buddha's favorite haunts, while everywhere absorbing his last words:

Listen to me carefully now, monks:
> *All the constituents of the human being are ephemeral.*
> *Fight with attention and ardor* [appamada].

Mahaparinibbana Sutta, VI:7

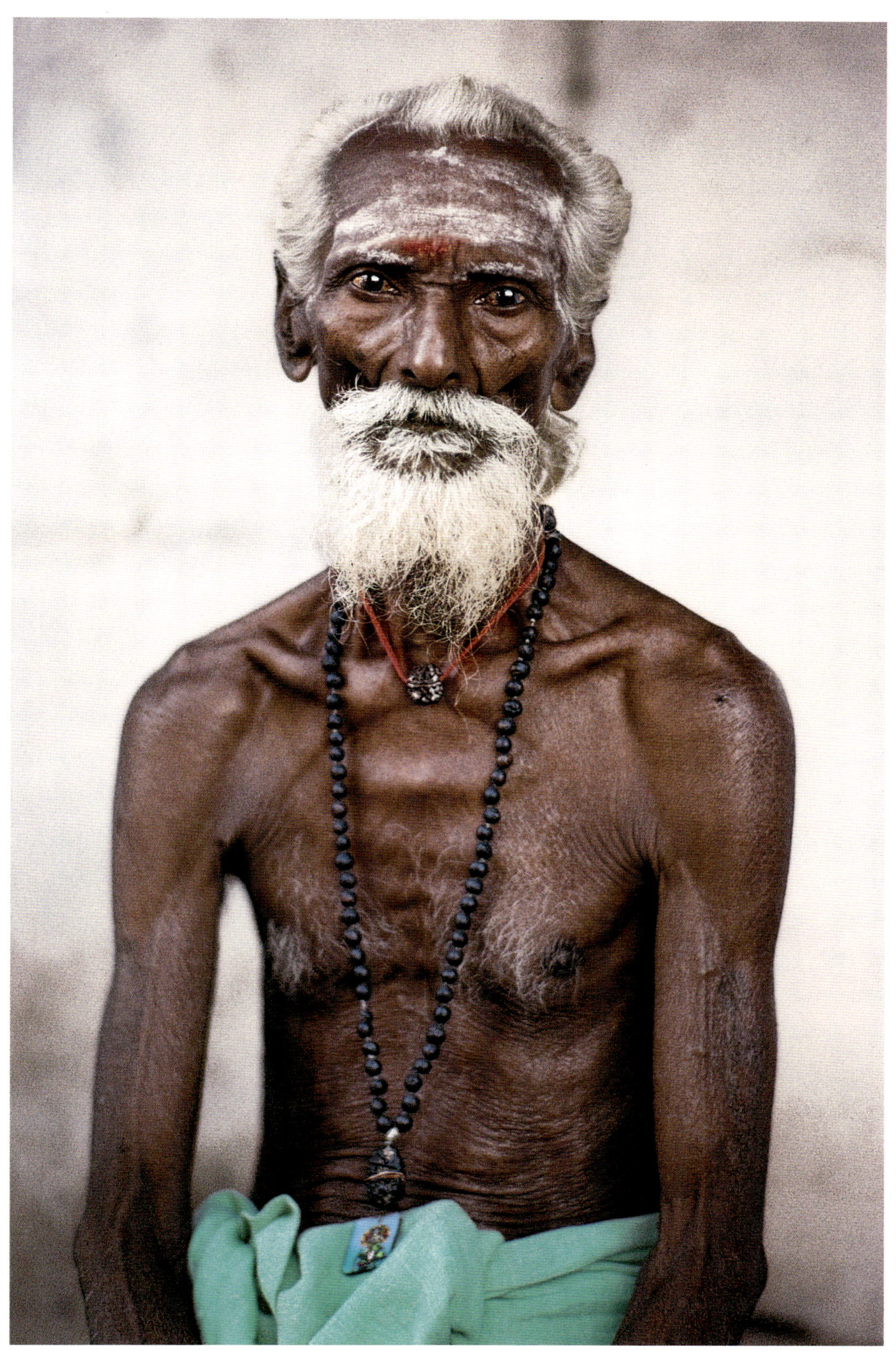

Pilgrim, Tamil Nadu.

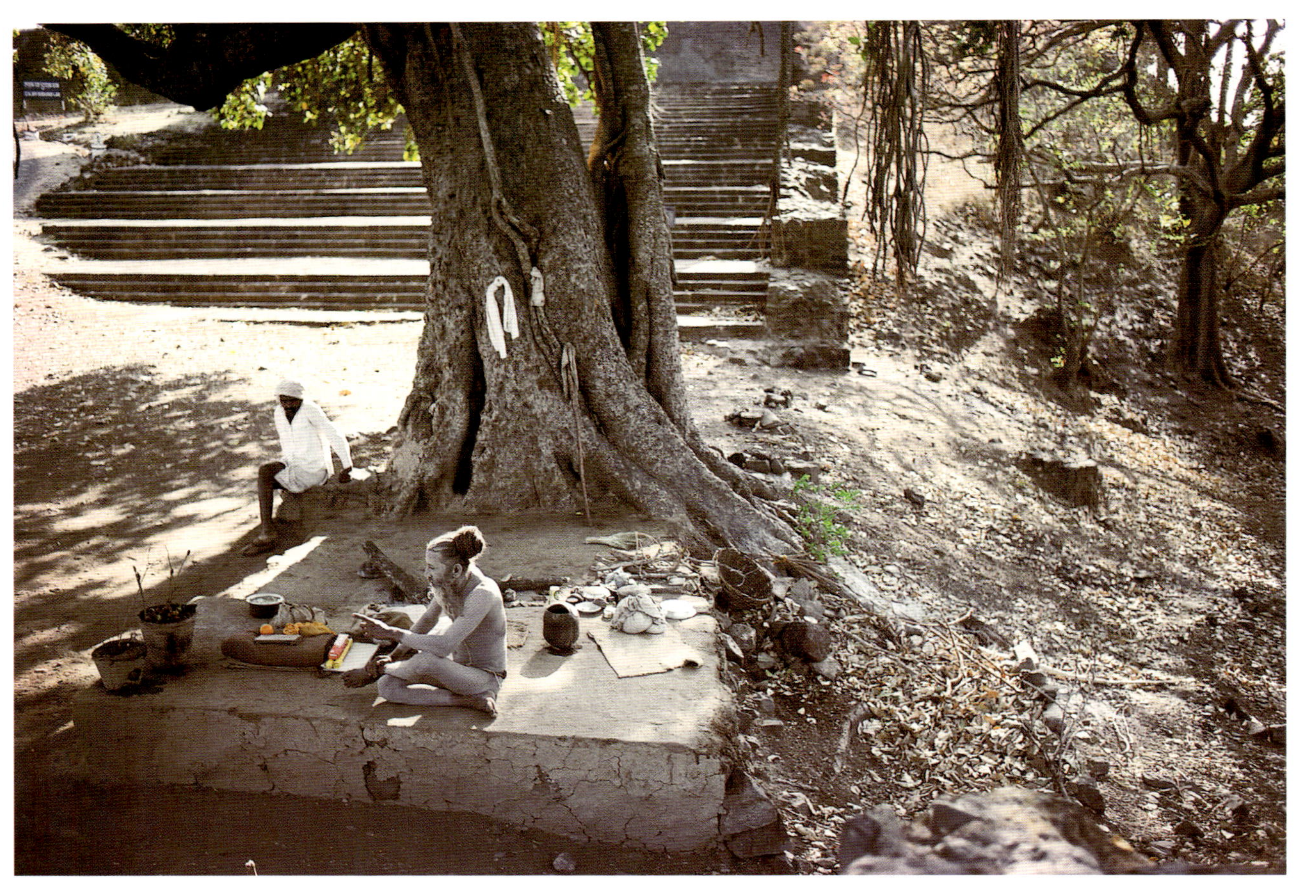

Sadhu sitting under a banyan tree.

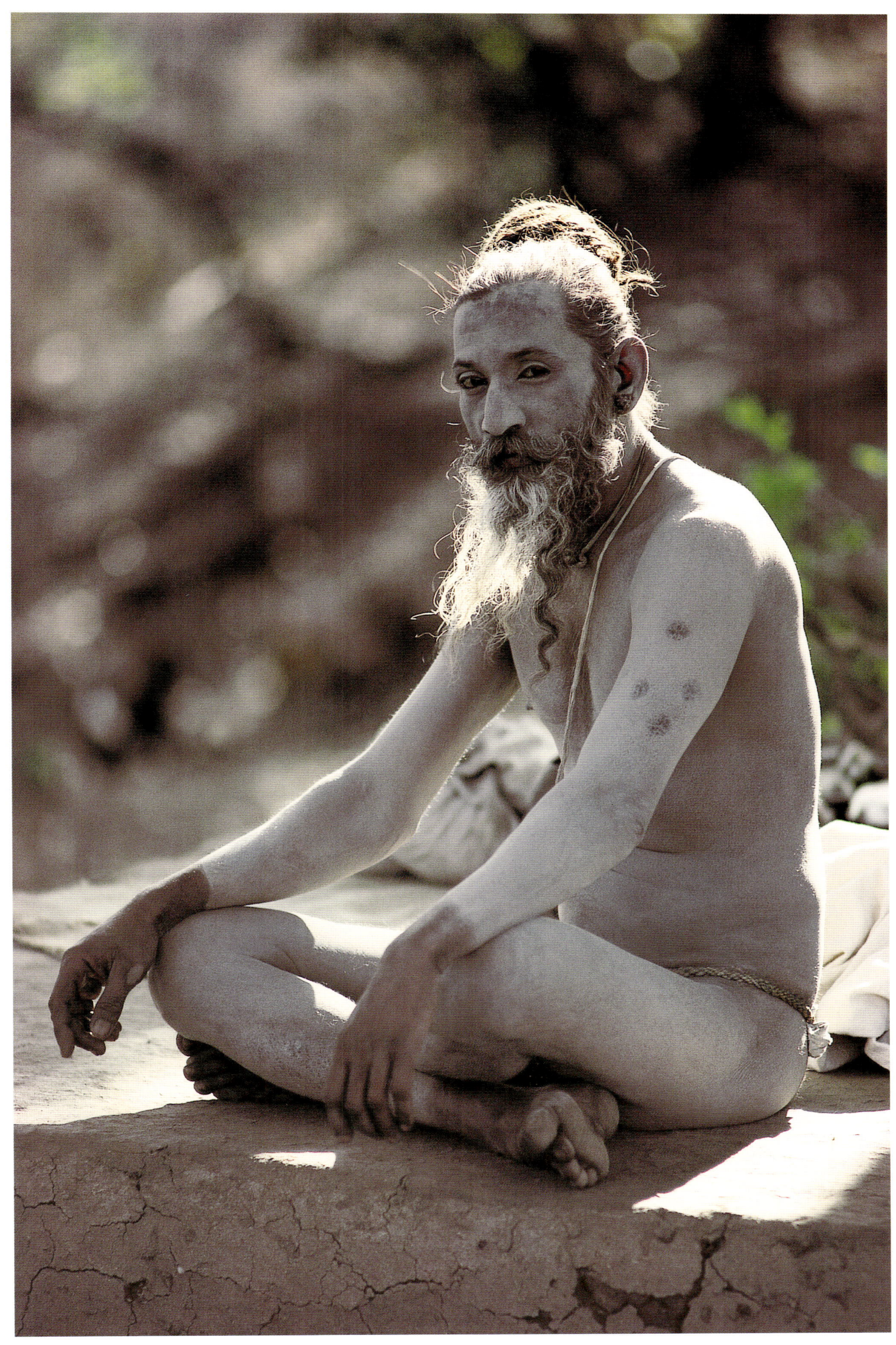

Islam and dialogue

For several centuries, Islam has been a fundamental component of Indian culture. Muslims represent 11 percent of the population of the Union. They are as numerous as the Muslims of Pakistan or Bangladesh and, after Indonesia, India has the second-largest Islamic community in the world.

The first Muslims were Arab traders who settled along the Malabar Coast, shortly after the Hegira. They were followed in the eighth century by invaders who colonized Sindh and, from the twelfth century onward, moved into Gujarat. From the late twelfth century through the sixteenth century, waves of invading islamicized conquerors descended from the plateaus of the northwest frontier. These warlike peoples, who were used to rugged landscapes and a harsh life, crossed the narrow Khyber Pass and suddenly discovered, stretching from the Indus to the Ganges, a country of flowers, rivers, beautiful women whom they sampled without restraint, and gods against whom they fought mercilessly. The Islamic tribes included Turkmen, Afghans, and Mongols—until the arrival in 1526 of a descendant of Timur, who soon restored order and created the Mogul Empire. The Moguls ruled most of India before being gradually defeated by the British in the eighteenth century. Although in purely chronological terms the Mogul Empire was short-lived, it had a profound effect on India by islamicizing a large section of the population, who converted voluntarily or through force. The Moguls embarked on a lavish building program, creating cities, palaces, mosques, and fortresses inspired by those of Persia. They also changed many customs—from dress to relationships with women—and imposed an administration that was partially taken over by their successors, the British, who granted India an empress who hailed from distant isles with incomprehensible customs.

Although the Muslims were builders, they were also pitiless destroyers. "Idolatry," or what they perceived to be idolatry, was judged to be intolerable by those who studied the Koran. The conquerors ravaged thousands of temples, a savagery whose scars are far from healed. Today's secular administration is much more respectful of the Muslim faith. In every town or city, and in many villages, mosques stand alongside Hindu temples without causing an incident, except in rare cases that are exaggerated by the media. Muslims occupy important positions in political life: two former presidents of India have been Muslim.

Indian Muslims are predominantly Sunni. Like the other religious communities, they freely advertise their faith in their dress and in depictions of the Ka'bah on market booths. As with other religions, there are no interfaith marriages, even though they are legally possible. Since the Muslim presence in India is too often associated with war and destruction, more must be said about those Muslims who were ready to have dialogue with the Hindus. One of the greatest poets of all time, Kabir, (1440–1518), a Muslim, was born in Benares where he worked as a lowly weaver when he was not going on long journeys on foot. He advocated a religious syncretism beyond the truths revealed by the scriptures. As a free man considered to be a saint, he was very popular among the simple people and openly rejected by the representatives of the established religions, who were unable to curb his influence. Upon his death, his devotees met to attempt to perpetuate his mysticism. His song of love in praise of the One mocked the *Brahmans* and the *mullahs* as "the purveyors of pious discourse [who] arise early every day to tell lies."

If Allah lived in a mosque,
>*To whom would the rest of the world belong?*
The Hindus say that He lives in the idol:
>>*Both of them are wrong!*

>*Satires*, VI

For so long people persisted in saying: "It's mine!"
>*For so long, nothing can be accomplished.*
When people stop saying "mine, mine."
>>*The Lord will come and grant your wishes.*

>*Spiritual Yoga*, LXV

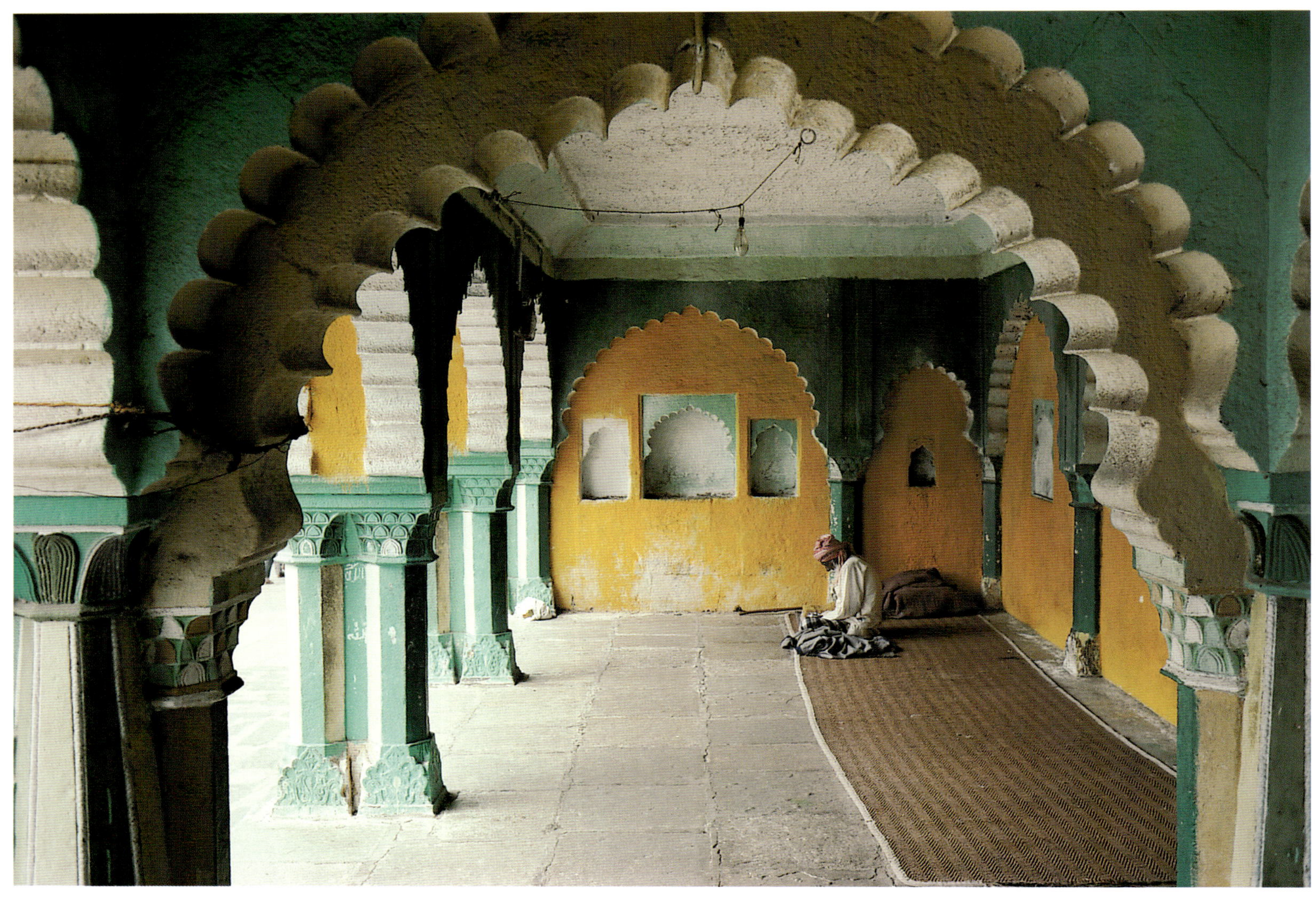

Above: Village mosque, Maharashtra.
Opposite: Muslim in Rajasthan.

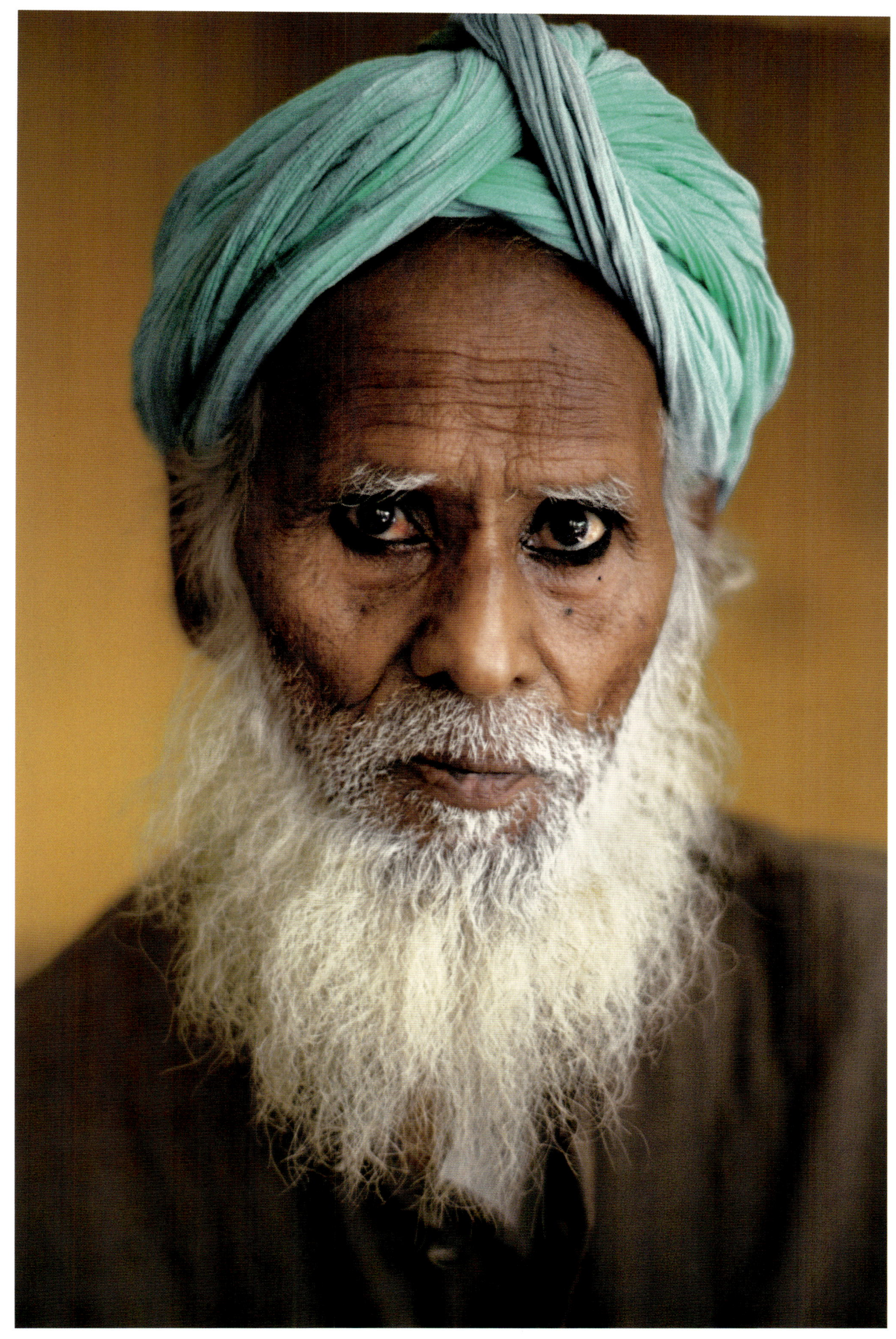

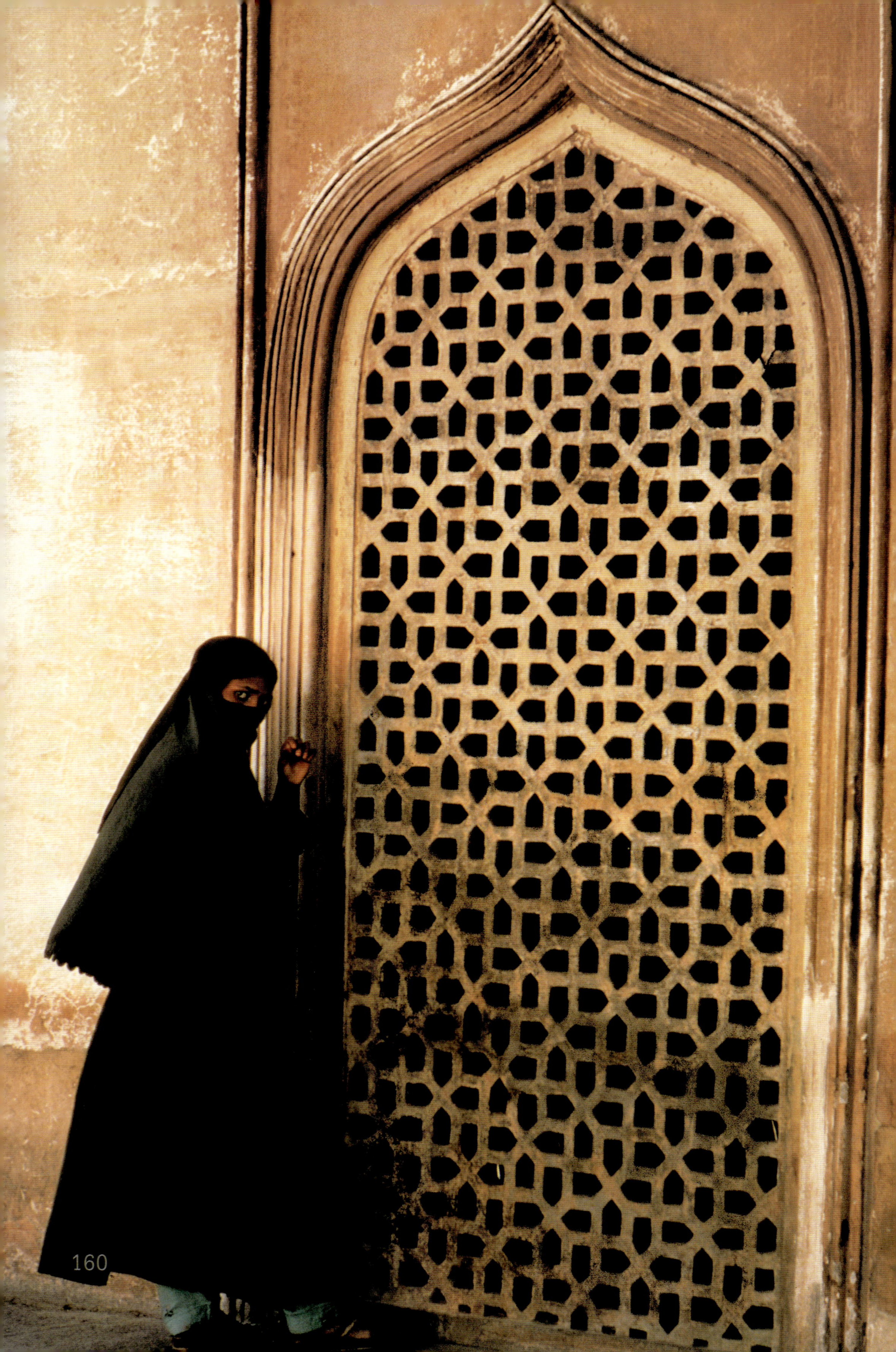
160

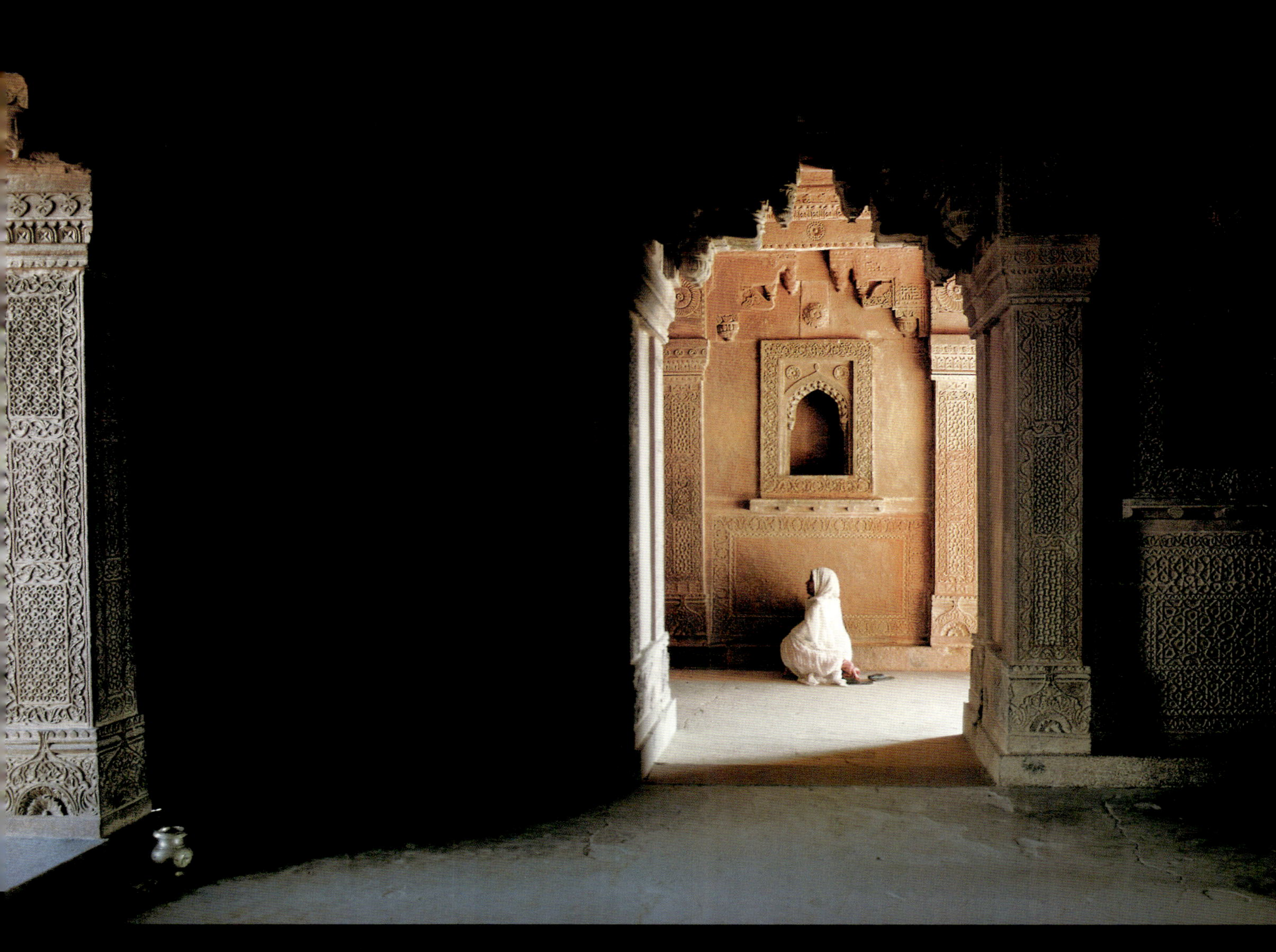

Opposite: Muslim woman, Hyderabad, Deccan.
Above: The Great Mosque, Fatehpur Sikri.

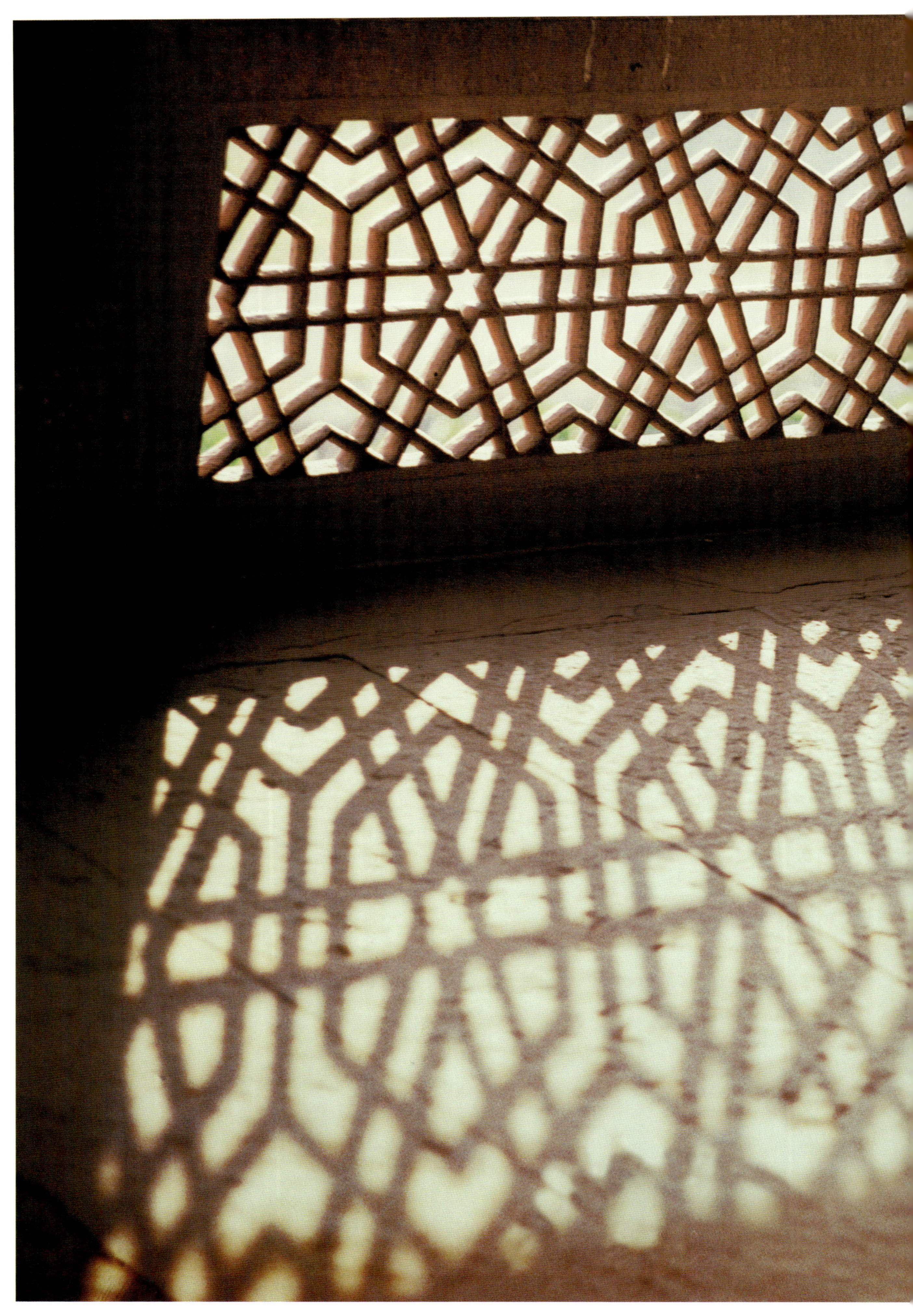

162 Fatehpur
Sikri.

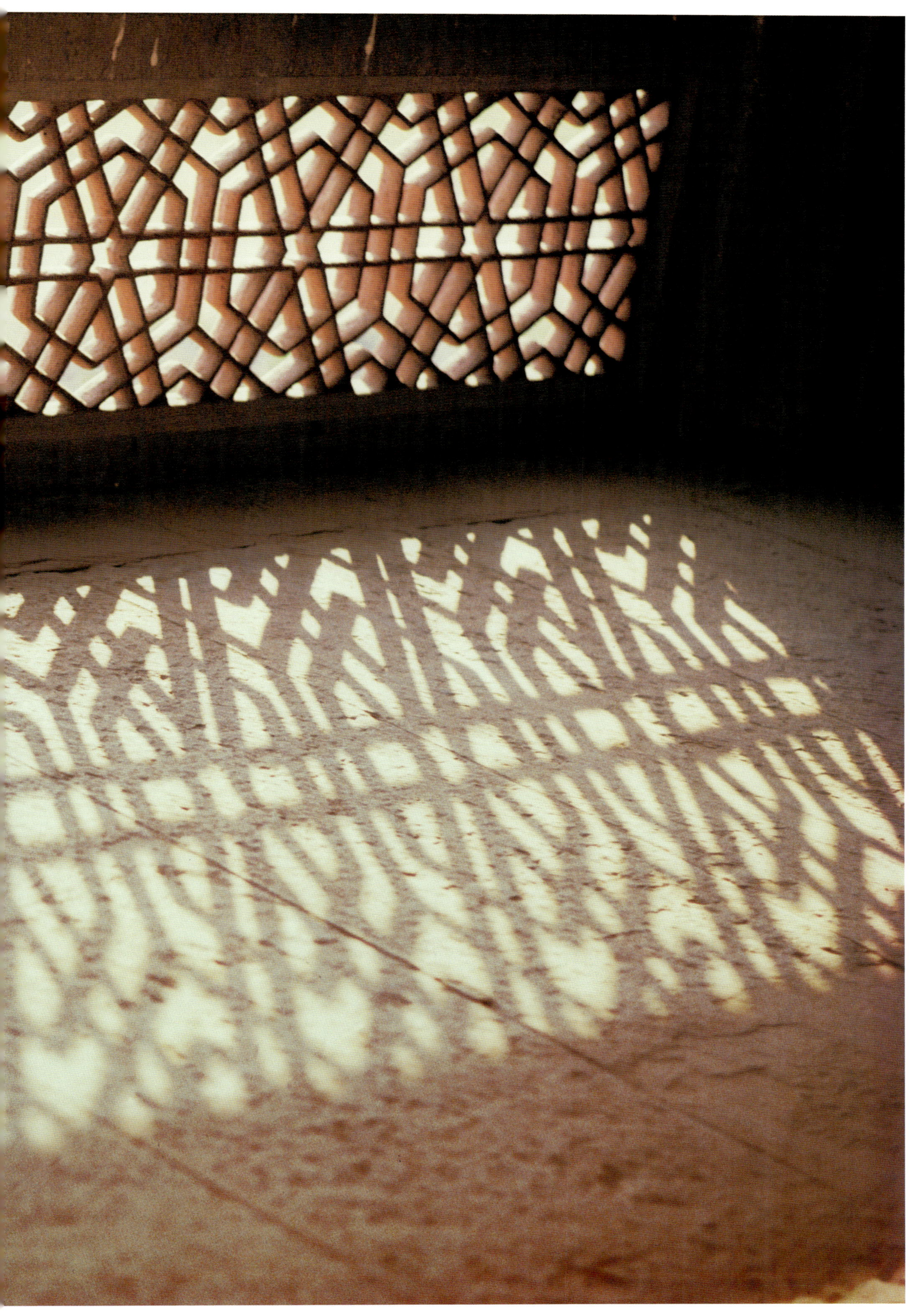

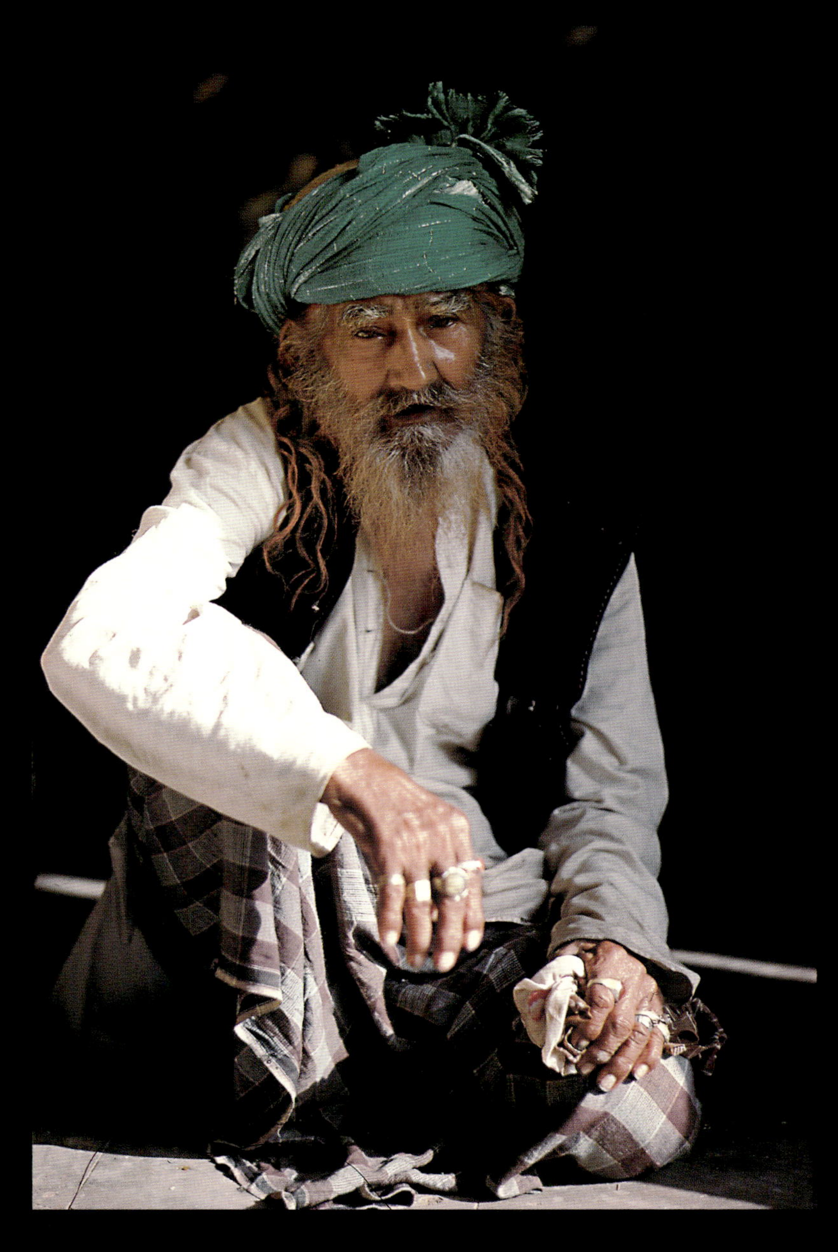

Above: Muslim, Ahmedabad, Gujarat.
Opposite: The Pearl Mosque, Red Fort, Old Delhi.
Pages 166–167: Lake Dal, Srinagar, Kashmir.

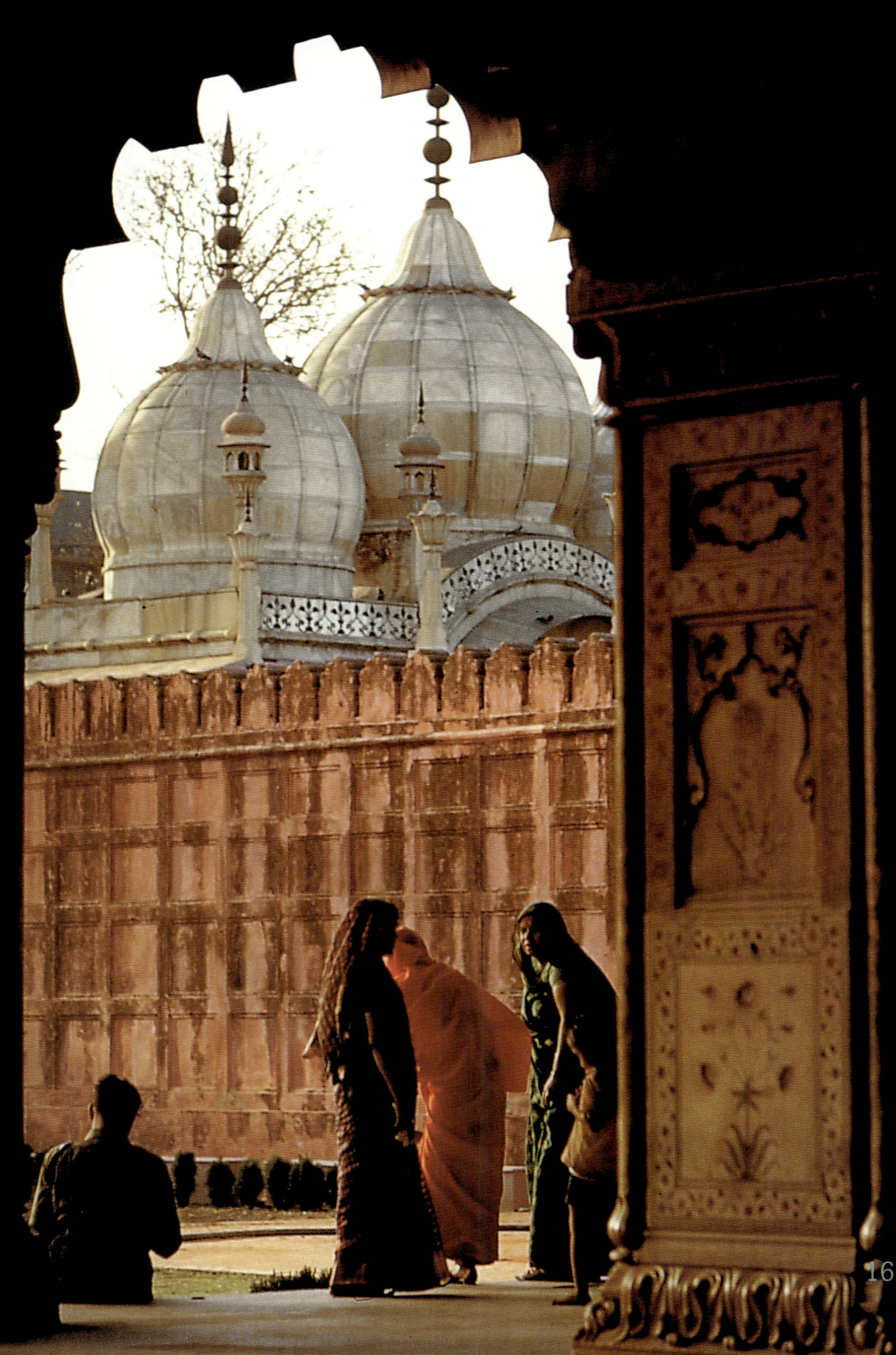

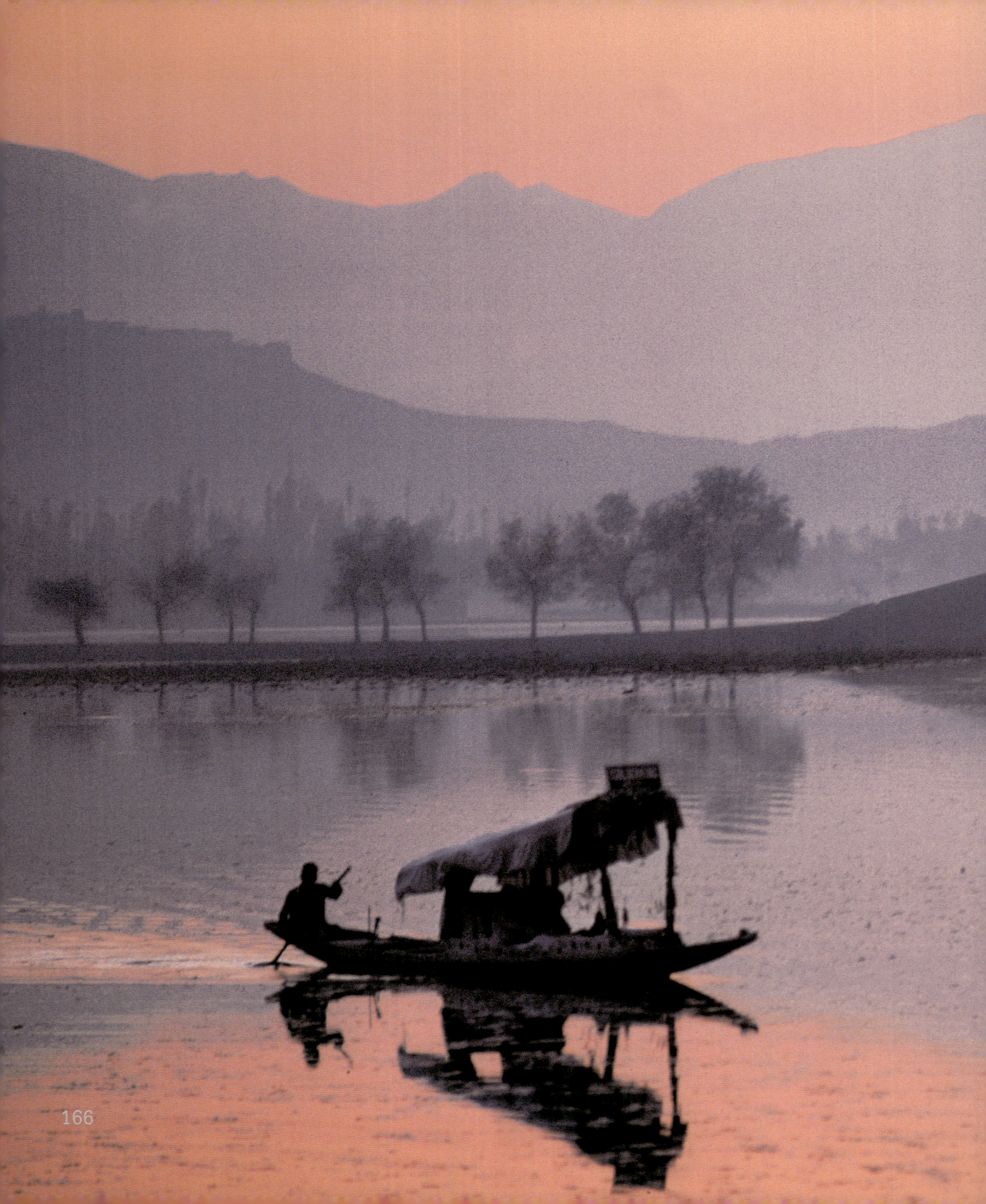

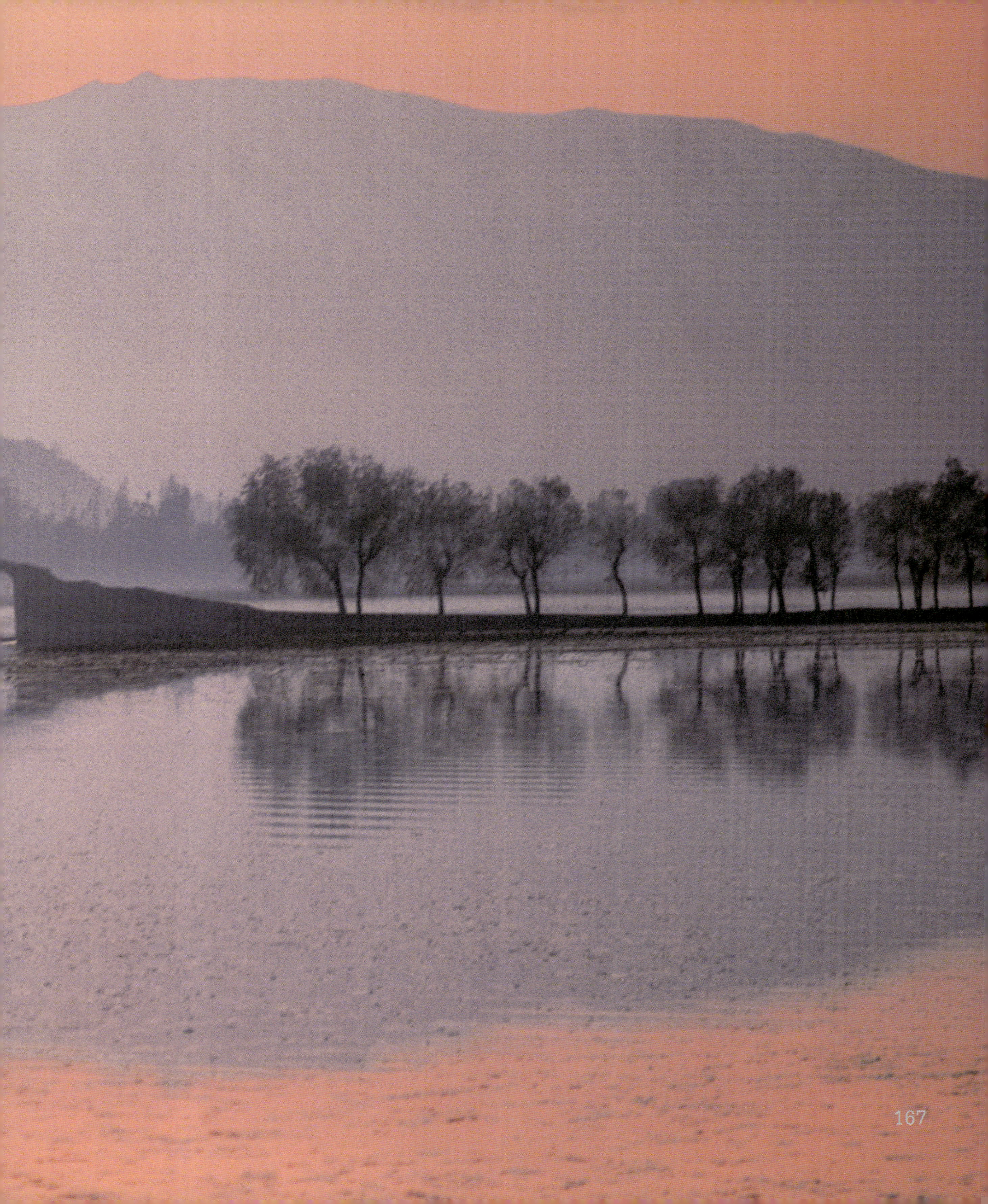

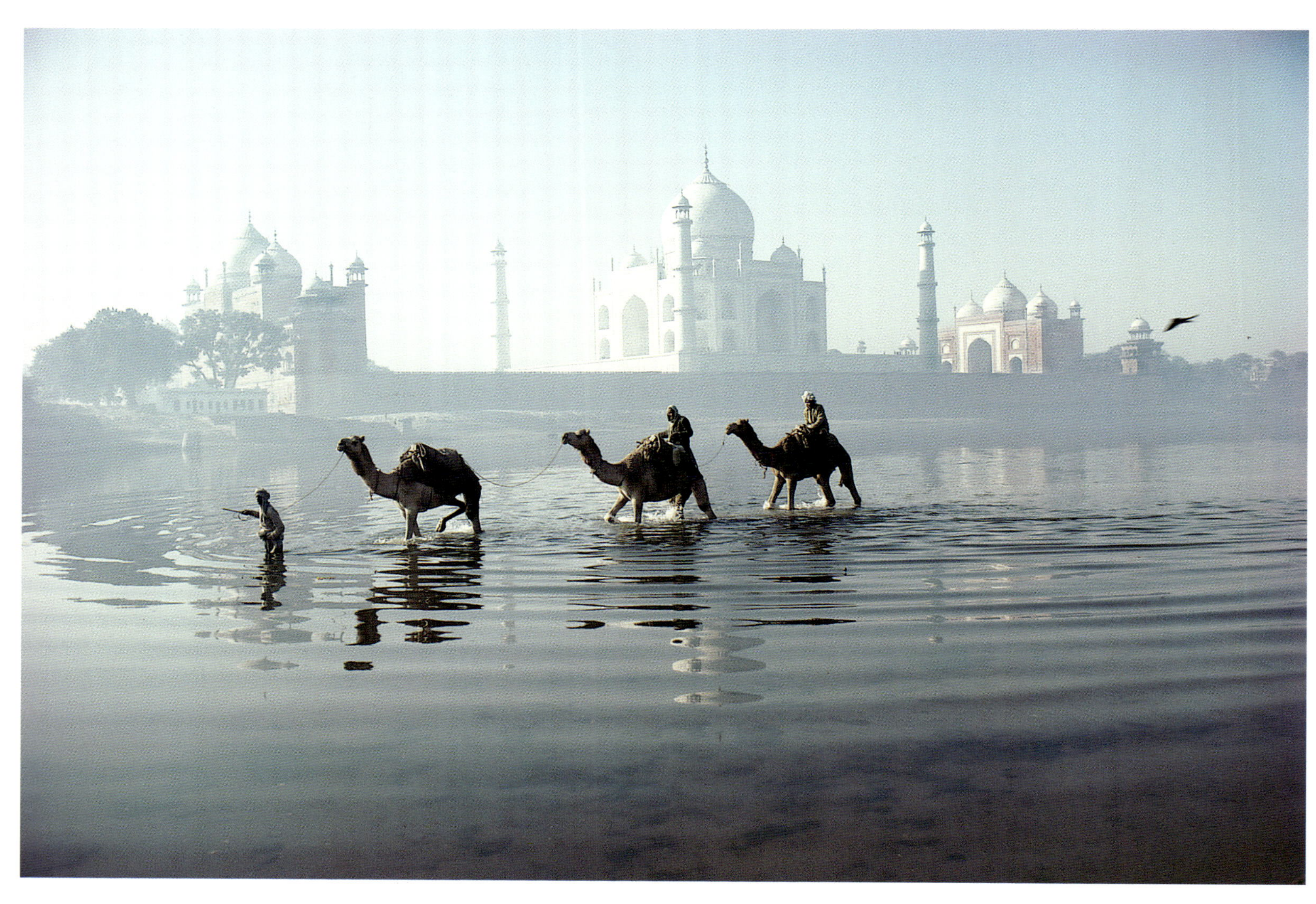

Above: The Taj Mahal, Agra.
Opposite: Muslim woman, Hyderabad, the Deccan.

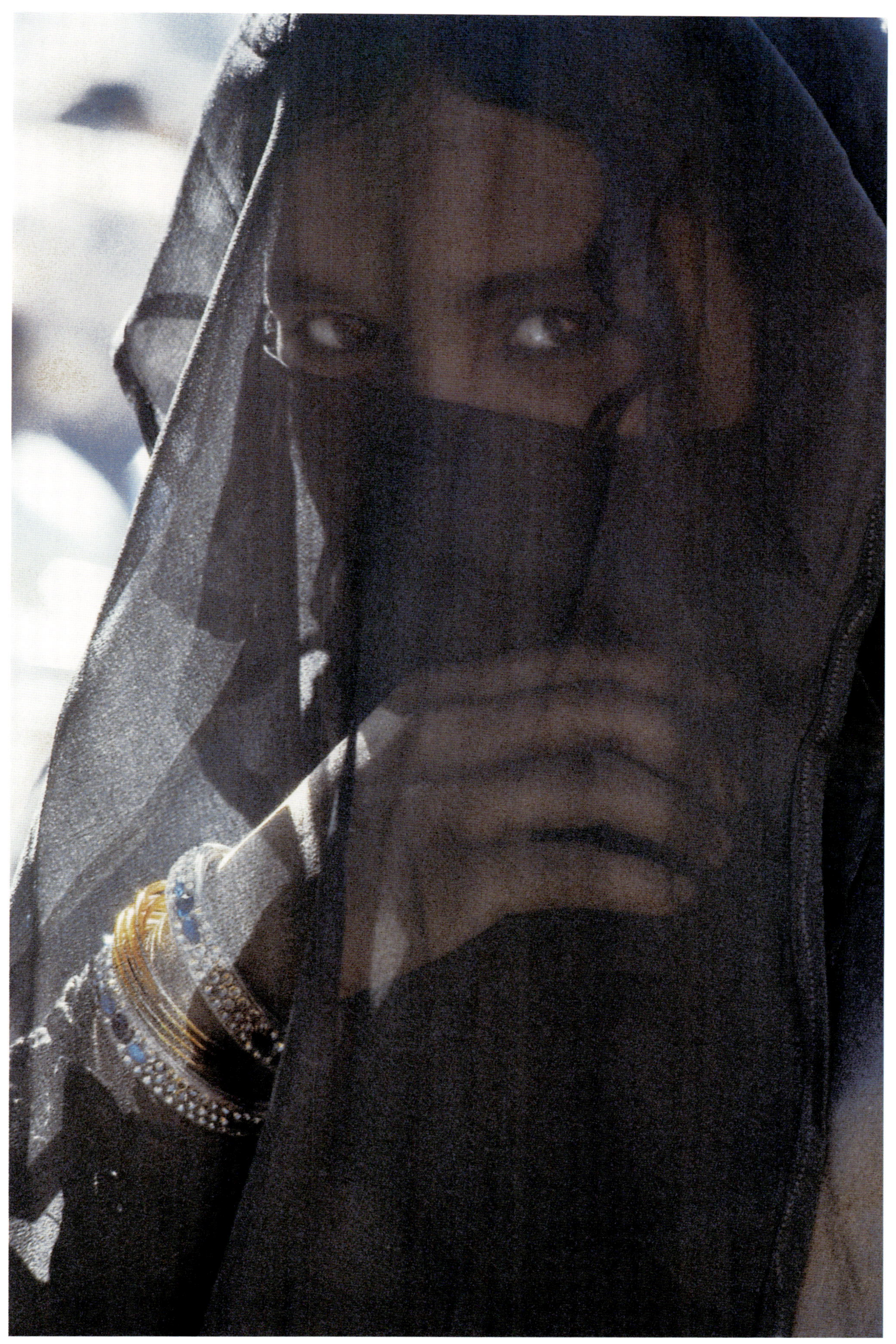

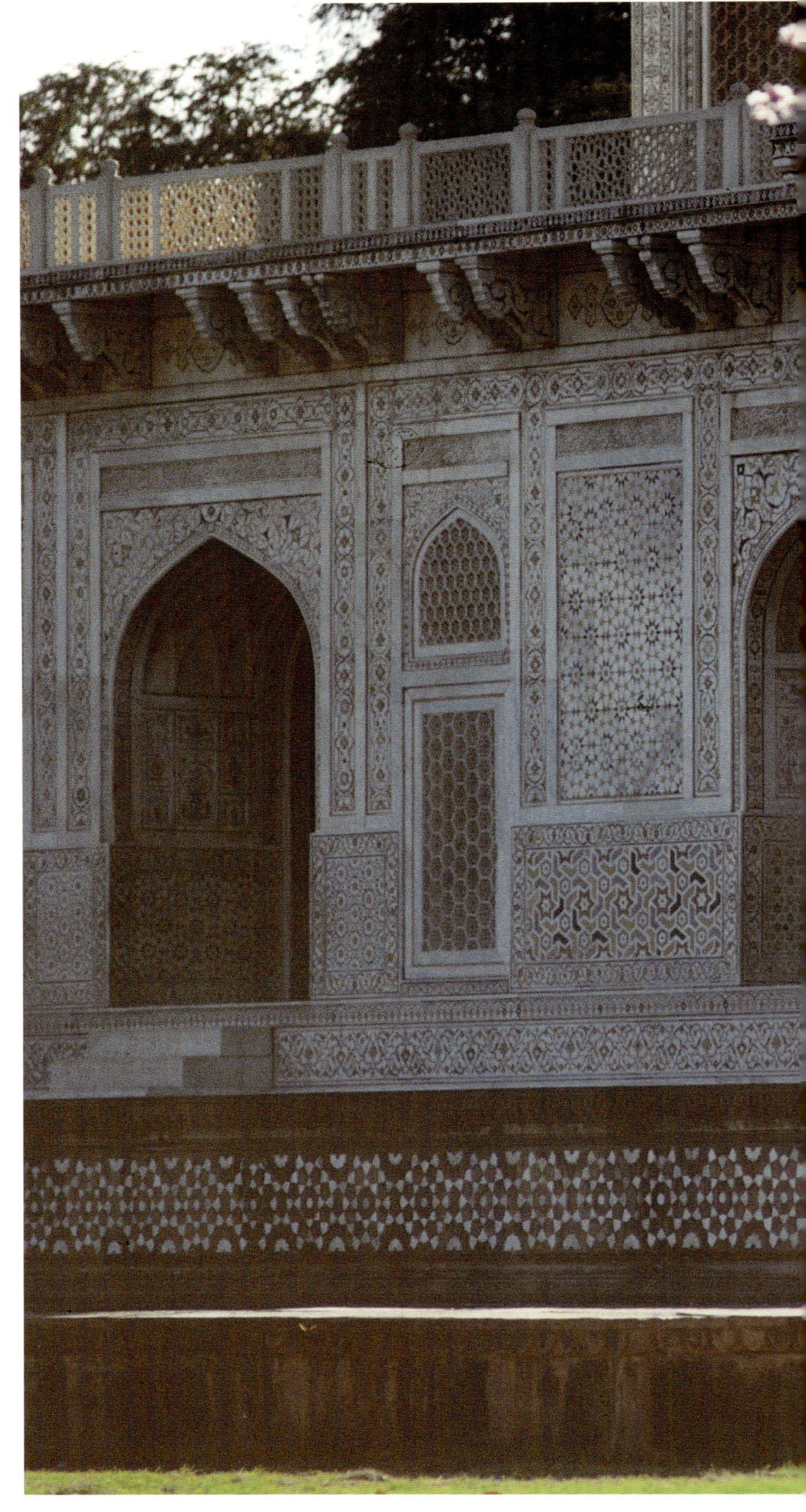

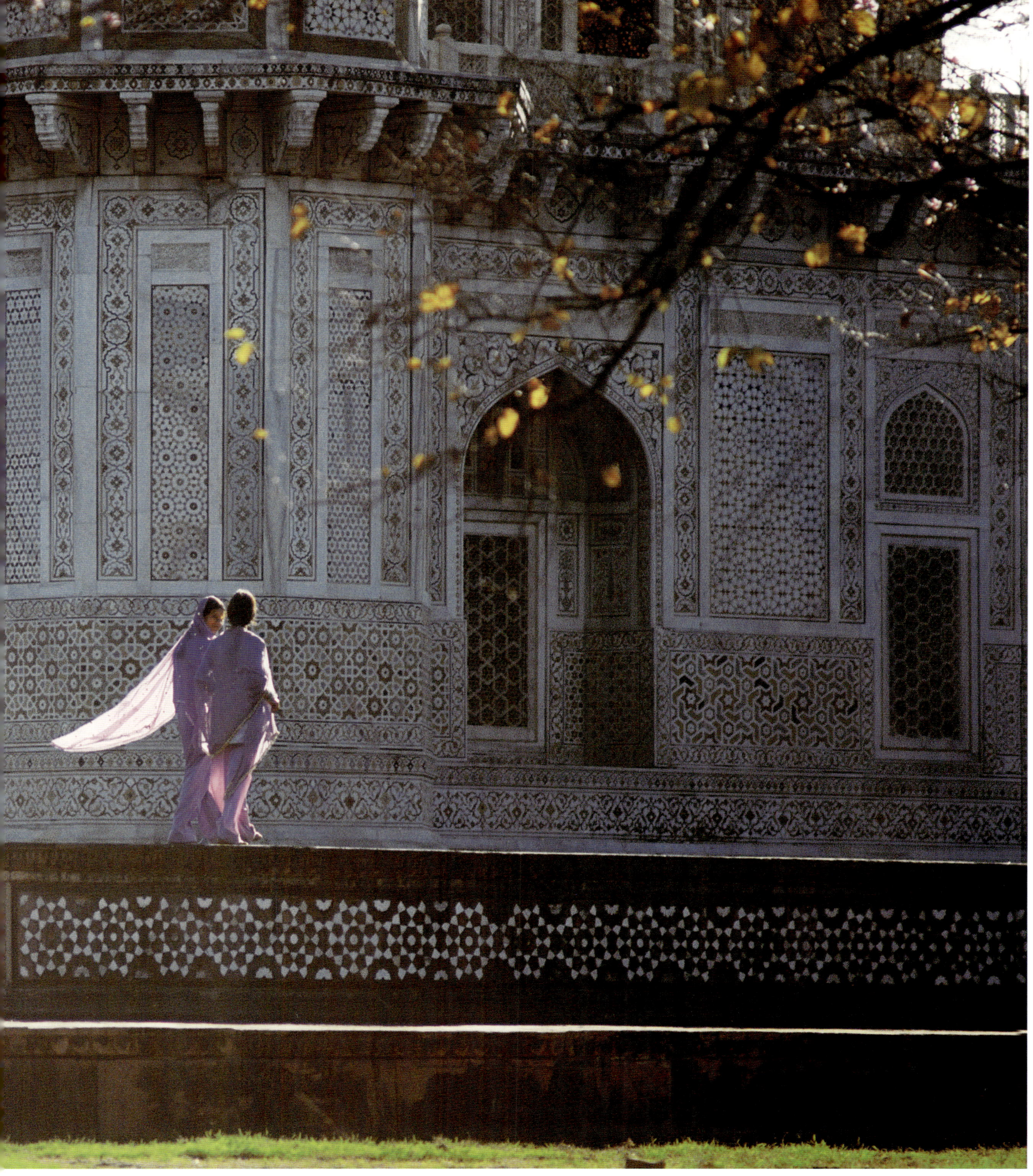

This world is a pantomime,
In which nothing ever stays still,
Travel straight along your path,
Or you'll suffer for it!
Children, old men or youths, O my Brother,
Death has taken them all!
Man is like a poor mouse,
And death is the cat that eats him! . . .

But for the servants of Hari [God] who please their Master
It is a very different story:
They do not come and go and they never die,
They are always with the Lord.

The Human Condition, XLIX.

During the same period, Guru Nanak (1469–1539) founded the Sikh religion, whose sacred writings are called the *Guru Granth.* Sikhism is something of a combination of Hinduism and Islam, with beliefs in a single deity, abolition of the caste system, and the affirmation of equality between the sexes. "Accomplish your labor, share its fruits, meditate on the Name," is the motto of this religion, which has a warlike reputation because the Sikhs are proud fighters; but which is, in fact, close to the *bhakti*, the devotion between the faithful and the godhead. Sikhism originated in the Punjab; Sikhs are active in northern India, representing less than 2 percent of the population.

In the seventeenth century, when the Mogul empire was at its height, the Muslim prince Dara Shikoh understood that Hinduism tended toward a unitarian principle, and that there was no unbridgeable gulf between Islam and the message of the Upanishads. Dara Shikoh was the eldest son of Shah Jahan, the emperor who had the Taj Mahal built in memory of his wife, who died in childbirth, the unforgettable Mumtaz Mahal. He wrote *The Confluence of Two Oceans*, an introductory text like few others in the history of religion. Sensing the danger for a power that needed to exclude in order to dominate, his younger brother, the cruel Aurangzeb, had Dara Shikoh executed in Delhi on September 10, 1659, as another proof of the unhappiness of the powerful.

     Pages 170–171: The mausoleum of Itimad-ud-Daulah, Agra.

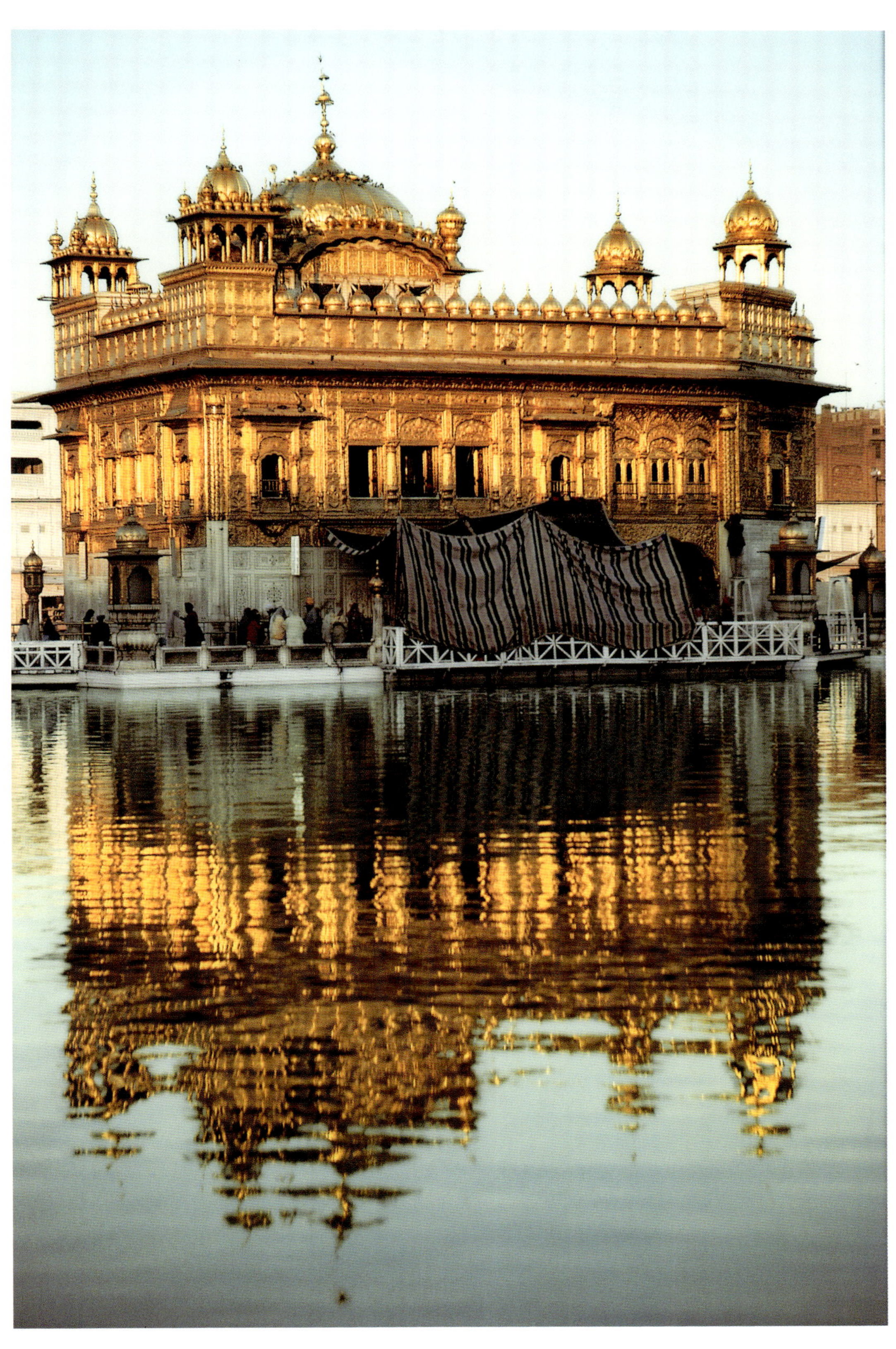

Above: The Golden Temple at Amritsar.
Pages 174–175: Guards at the Golden Temple at Amritsar.

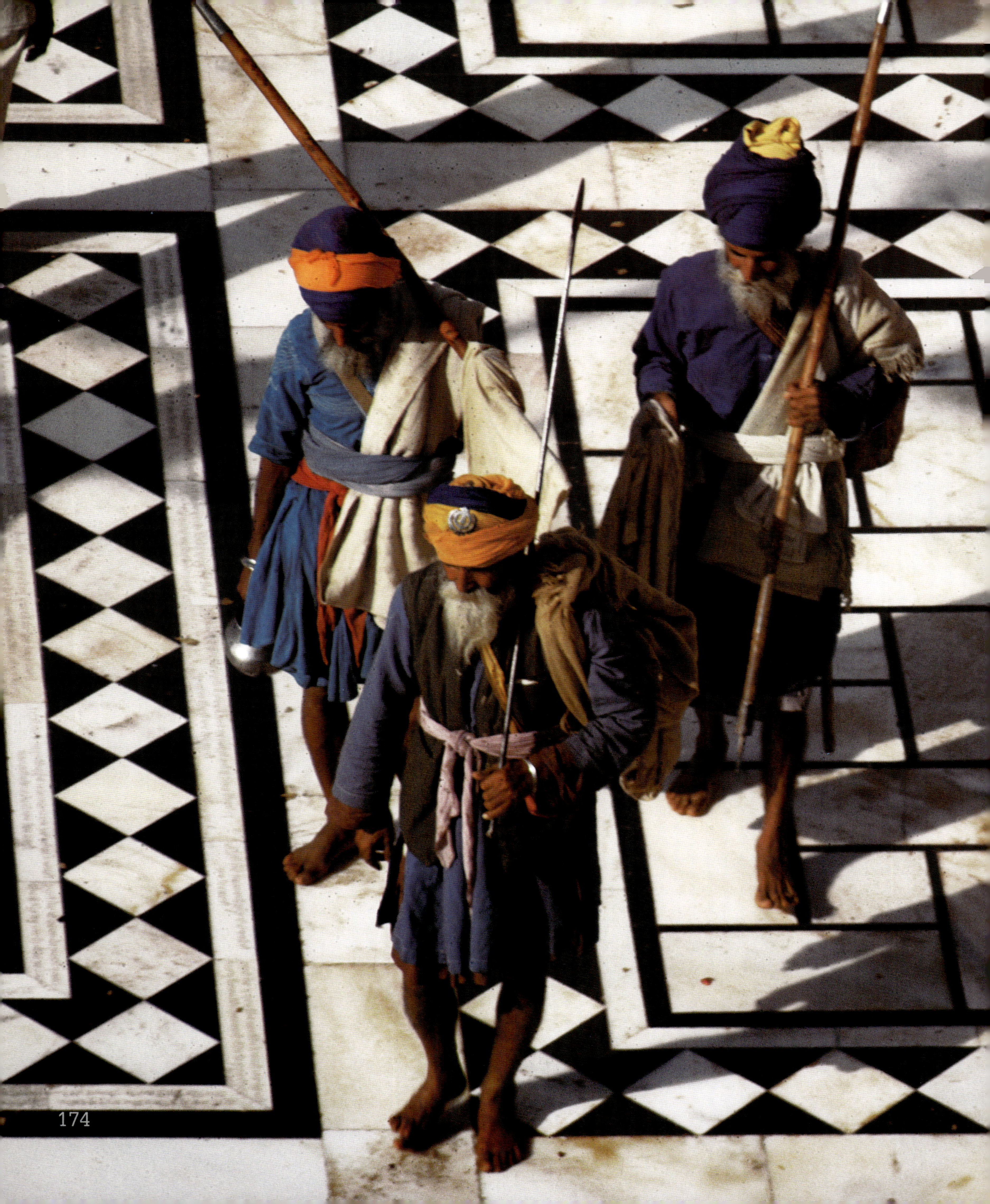

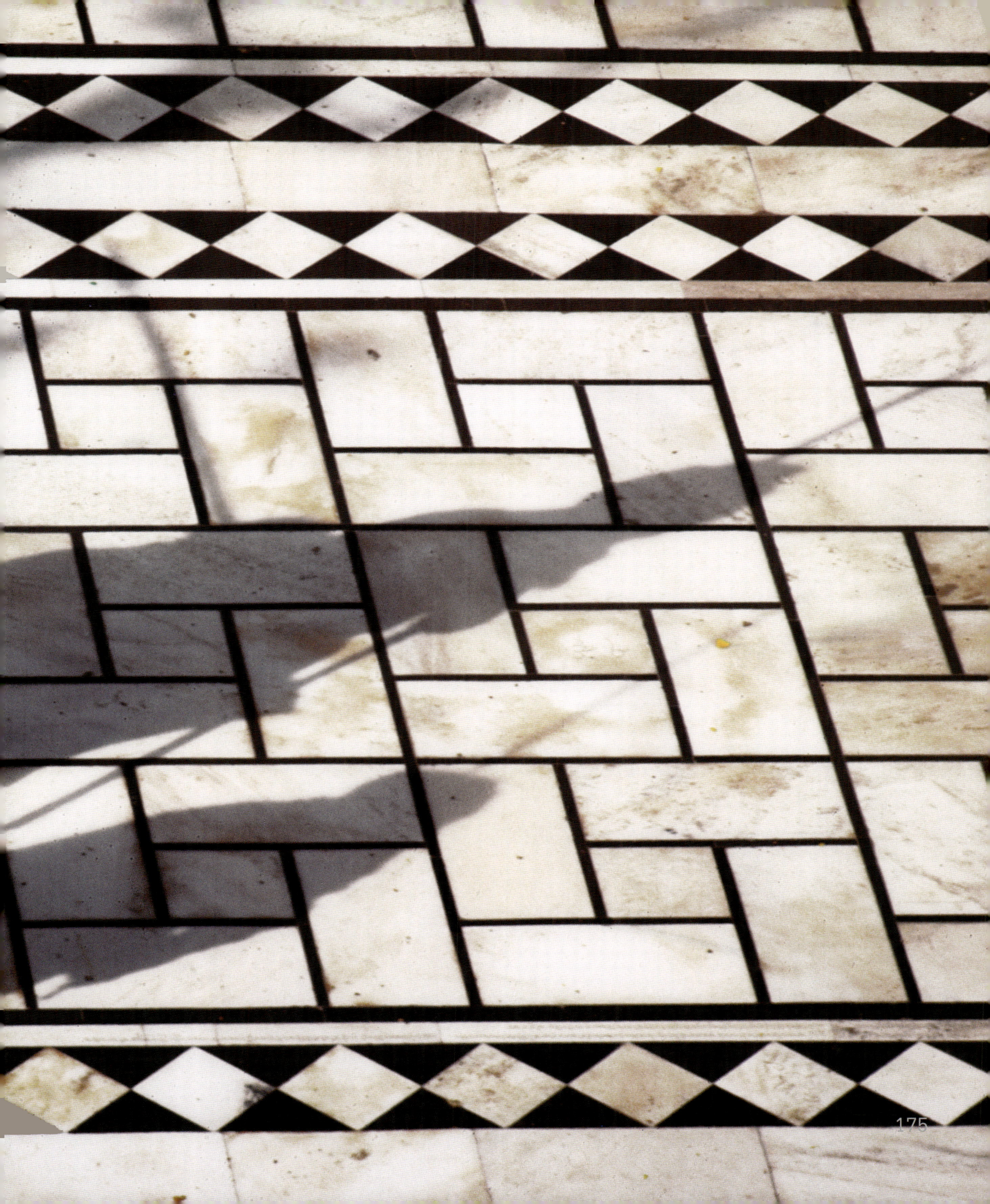

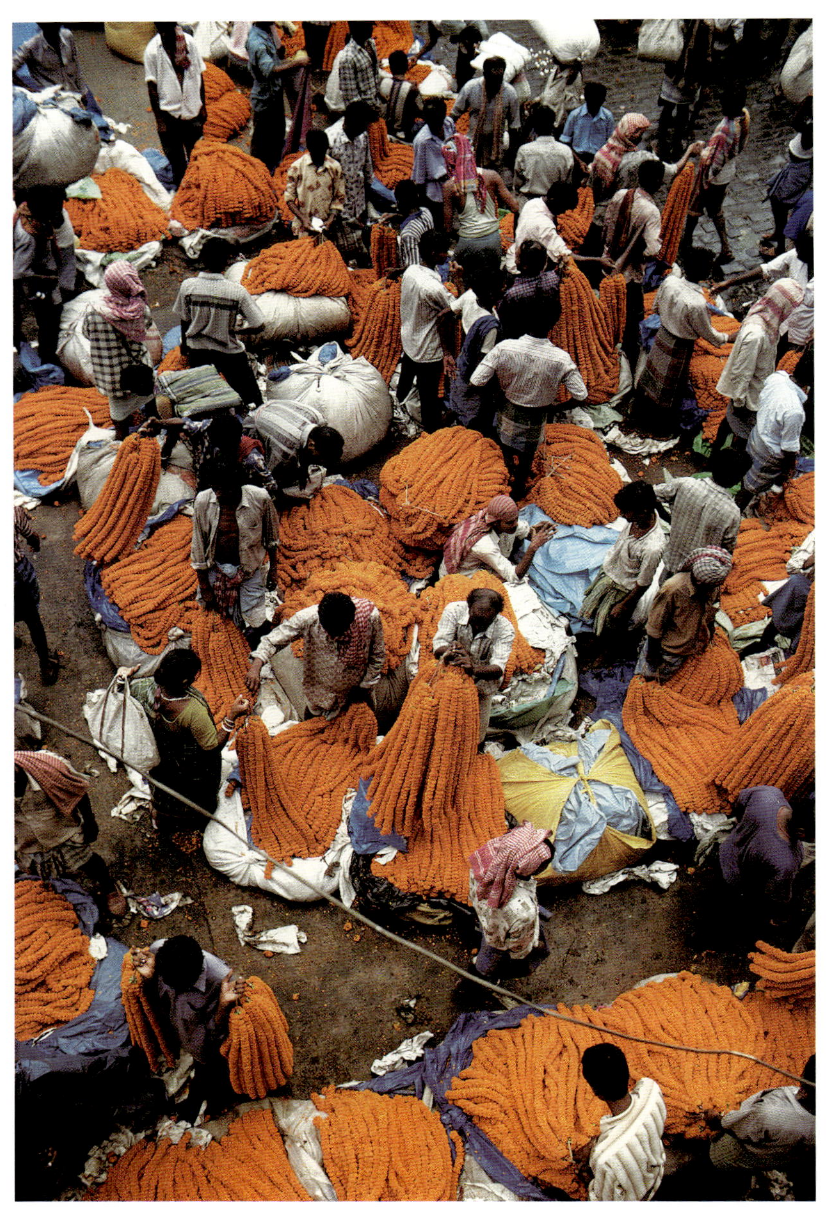

Above: The flower market, Calcutta.
Opposite: The Hooghly River, Calcutta.

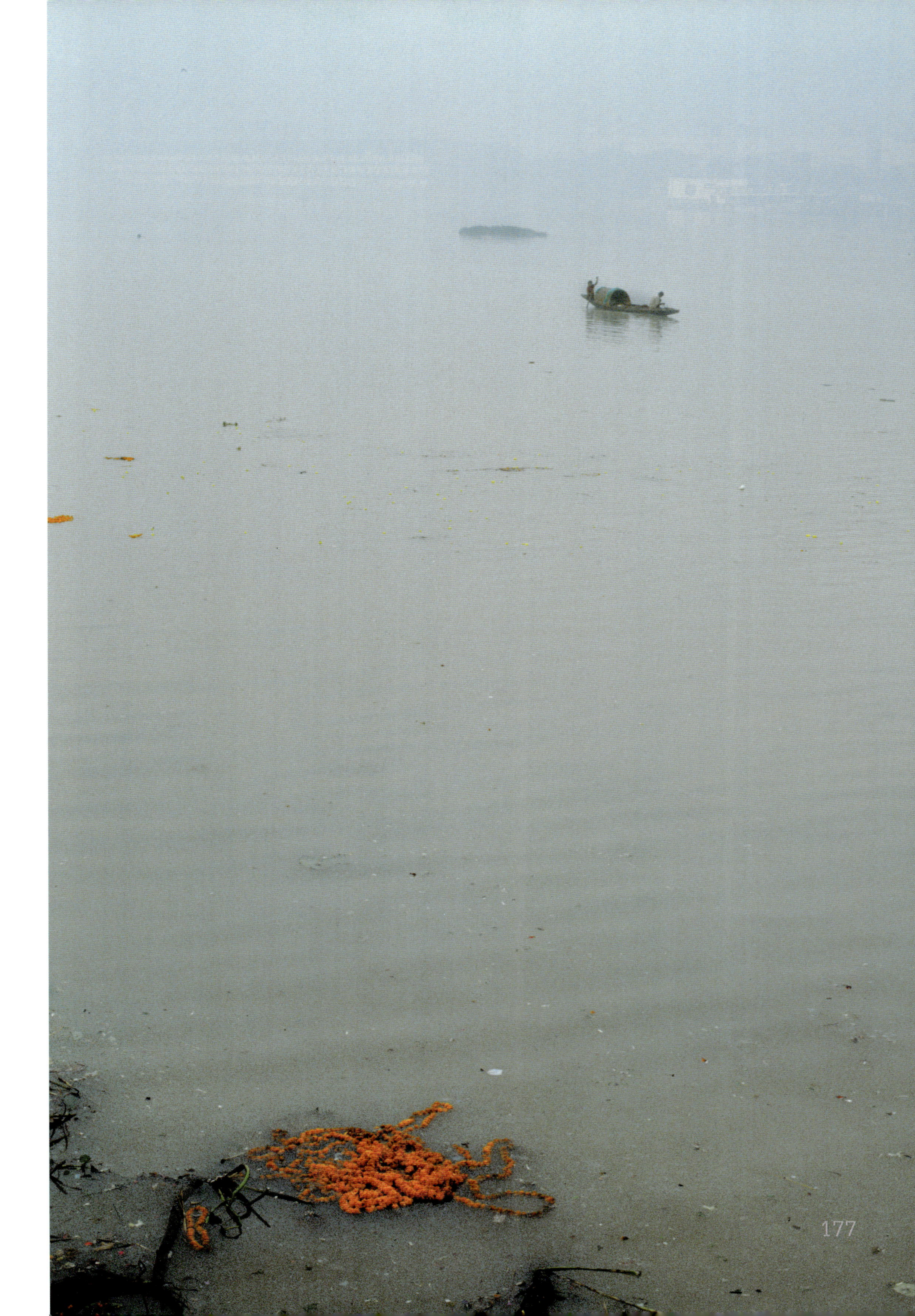

Indians—both Muslim and Hindu—have more in common than they realize. The vibrations of the Indian soil are so strong that they generate similar attitudes when faced with the rhythms of life. The peoples of India have always been organized into communities, so the cohabitation of several religions or origins is not such a problem as it is in Christianity or in the Islamic world. Nevertheless, the tension with Pakistan over Kashmir and the increasing fundamentalism on both sides of the border are fraught with danger. Will Mother India's generous embrace be sufficient this time?

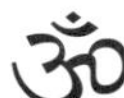

No culture in the world has been as sensitive to religious phenomena as that of India, which has generated or welcomed on its soil religions in their most diverse forms. These religious forms have constantly interacted with each other in a manner that those who adhere to orthodoxy in their own religions find completely disconcerting.

In the subcontinent, the spirit of classification and the spirit of logic have been pushed to extremes, but there is also a flexibility that arises from the confrontation of multiple aspects of reality, turning each philosopher or sage into a dancer, gyrating under the sky of illusion.

Since human nature is unique, all human beings
are the same, even if they seem different
due to various influences.

Guru Nanak

Do not go
To the flower garden!
Oh friend, do not go there,
Within you
There is the flower garden.

Kabir

Opposite: Funeral pyre, Gujarat.

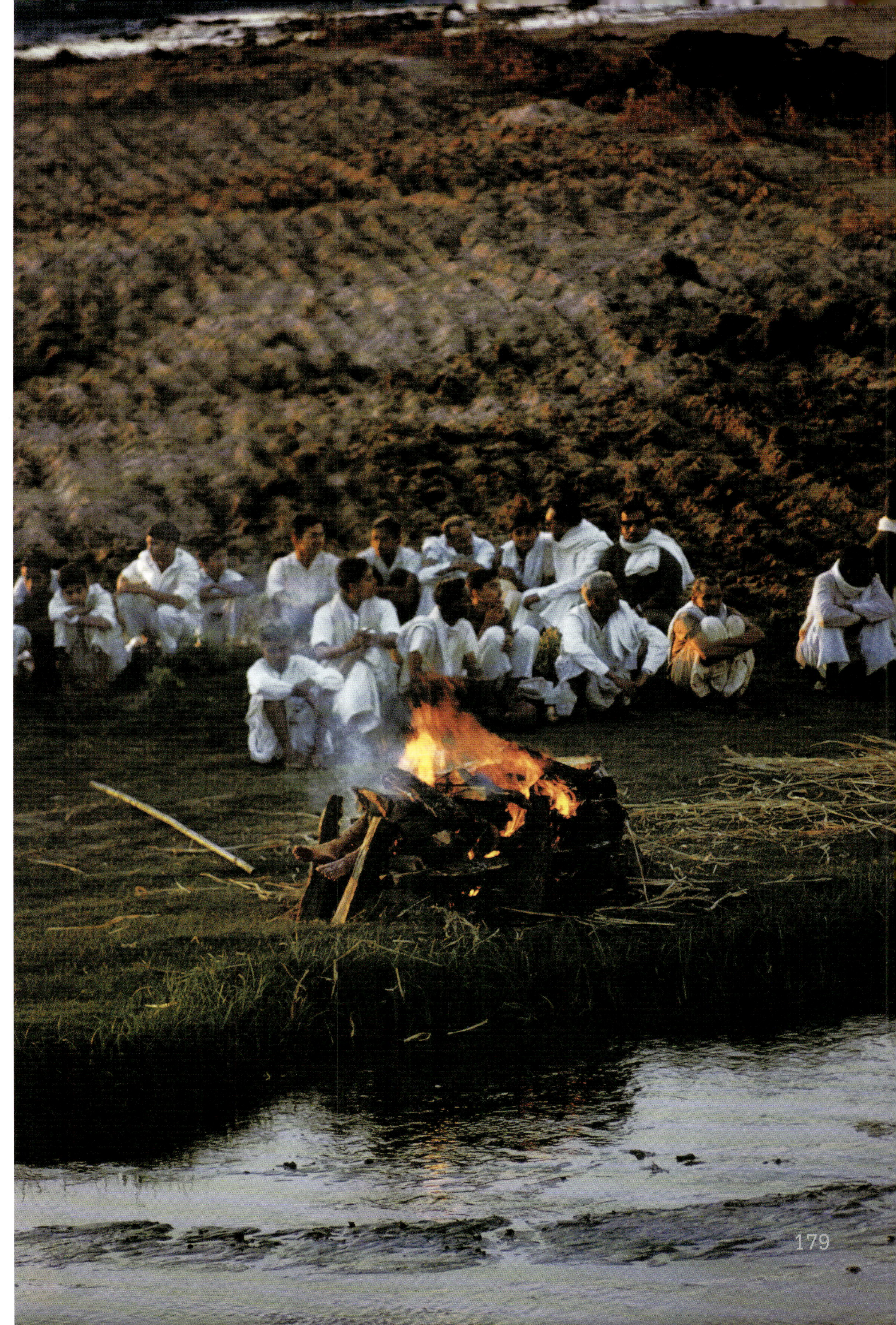

Travel

Traveling in India is like an inner revolution. Dung and jasmine, brilliant fire and shanty towns. The flame of saris, bunches of bodies, smoke slowly spiraling into the blue, burning paths between red rocks, long-drawn out chords: "Where are you coming from?" "Who are you?" "Give, since you possess!" But who am I now that I am no longer surrounded by that which gives me my identity? There have never been so many smiles, birds, gods, expectations, hands, dirt, fruits, so many threats, so much tenderness, milky sexuality, blood in the evening sky, black eyes analyzing, endings. Under a vanilla-colored morning sky, schoolgirls dressed in their best dance off to recite their lessons under a tree, cows have adopted the stately glide of philosophers, wagon-wheels grind, a fleeting reflection on the river lingers on and will linger on.

The wheel is known as a *chakra*. Our bodies have six *chakras* through which the kundalini energy rises. A seventh, flame-colored, *chakra* (*sahasrara*) hovers above the head. If traveling through India animates it, even slightly, it can at least dull the sound of cockroaches masticating in the sordid bedrooms of a dreary town (once again, a necessary initiation).

We do not have to make the choice between a night in a palace, two on the wooden benches in the packed trains that travel from the Ganges to the Dravidian lands, three of sleeping rough, or seven spent in an *ashram*. We should behave as India does with its gods—concatenate them. The purpose of travel in India is to expand the consciousness. Poverty with its appeal to pity or revulsion, the spirit of childhood (the dawn), the many arms, and wisdom that is free from fear open unoccupied spaces within us.

Go to the extremes, that is where the truth lies.

William Blake

How good it is to face the incomprehensible, and not to conceal new realities behind ancient facial expressions. Let them leave us voiceless, looking, feeling. Waiting. Our unconscious mind is perceptive enough to manage alone before the host of images it finds disturbing.

Haste is an obstacle, availability a source of discoveries. For example, take a passenger train, the slowest railroad train you can imagine, with the intention of reaching the main line, on which a better class of train, an express or mail train, runs. The passenger train arrives three hours late, so you miss your connection. Here you are, with a day lost in a city in which there is nothing to see. What luck, for the whole universe is in each piece of nothingness!

After you have worked off your irritation, wandering aimlessly through the streets of the city, a seated man beckons to you. He invites you to his little house where his astonished wife and excited children are waiting, thrilled that the "main attraction" is visiting their home. The grandfather has decided to retreat to the back room. After a few meaningless phrases are exchanged, there is a moment of silence. The whole family is seated on the ground, their eyes fixed on the ambassador. You are mute with stupefaction. Who are they? What is this life that pulsates within them, the same breathing in the silence, although their ways of loving, working, and dying are so dissimilar? For the first time you feel yourself free to become a stranger to yourself.

After that, there is the Taj Mahal, Elephanta, Khajuraho, Udaipur, and Madurai, they're all fine, yes they're fine, but...

In India everything is an allegory, but who will give us the keys?

J.-B. Le Gentil, *Voyage in the Seas of India,* 1761–69

The prescription: hiking through the countryside (for at least ten hours), meditating (for the same length of time), praying, fretting, celebrating, weeping, showing oneself to be more materialistic than the *Carvaka* (at least once), spending the night on a railroad train (three times), being thirsty, being hungry, waiting (for an indeterminate period), touching the fire of Shiva, the holy waters, the *yoni,* the *lingam,* loving, bargaining (a thousand and one times), not bargaining (no more than twice), carrying an untouchable on one's shoulders, feeding a baby by hand, drinking the waters of the Ganges (a few drops are enough), drinking mulligatawny soup without shedding a tear, not speaking for two days, living in a maharajah's palace (from one to five times), interrogating the red rocks, singing, watching the dawn, watching nothing.

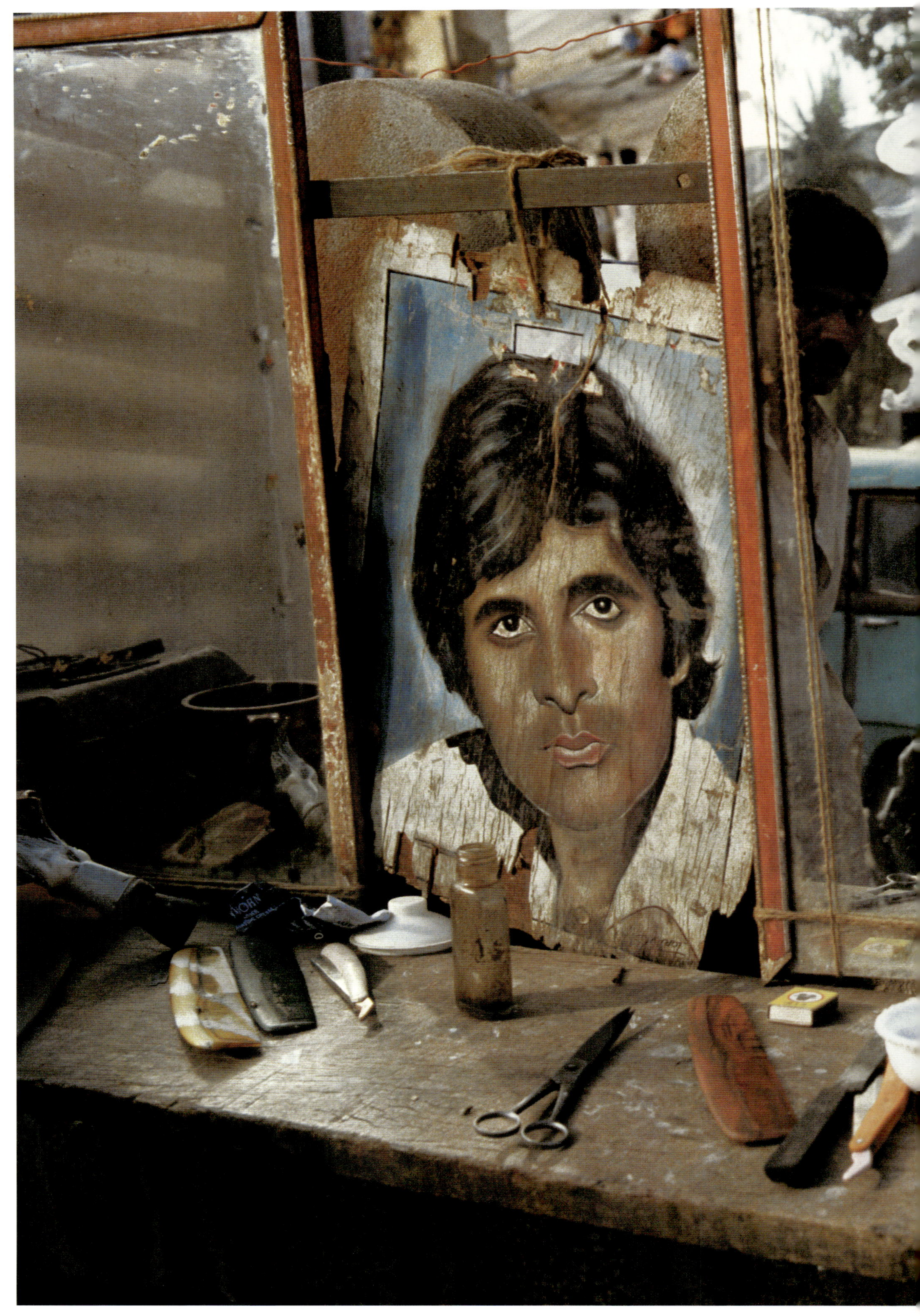

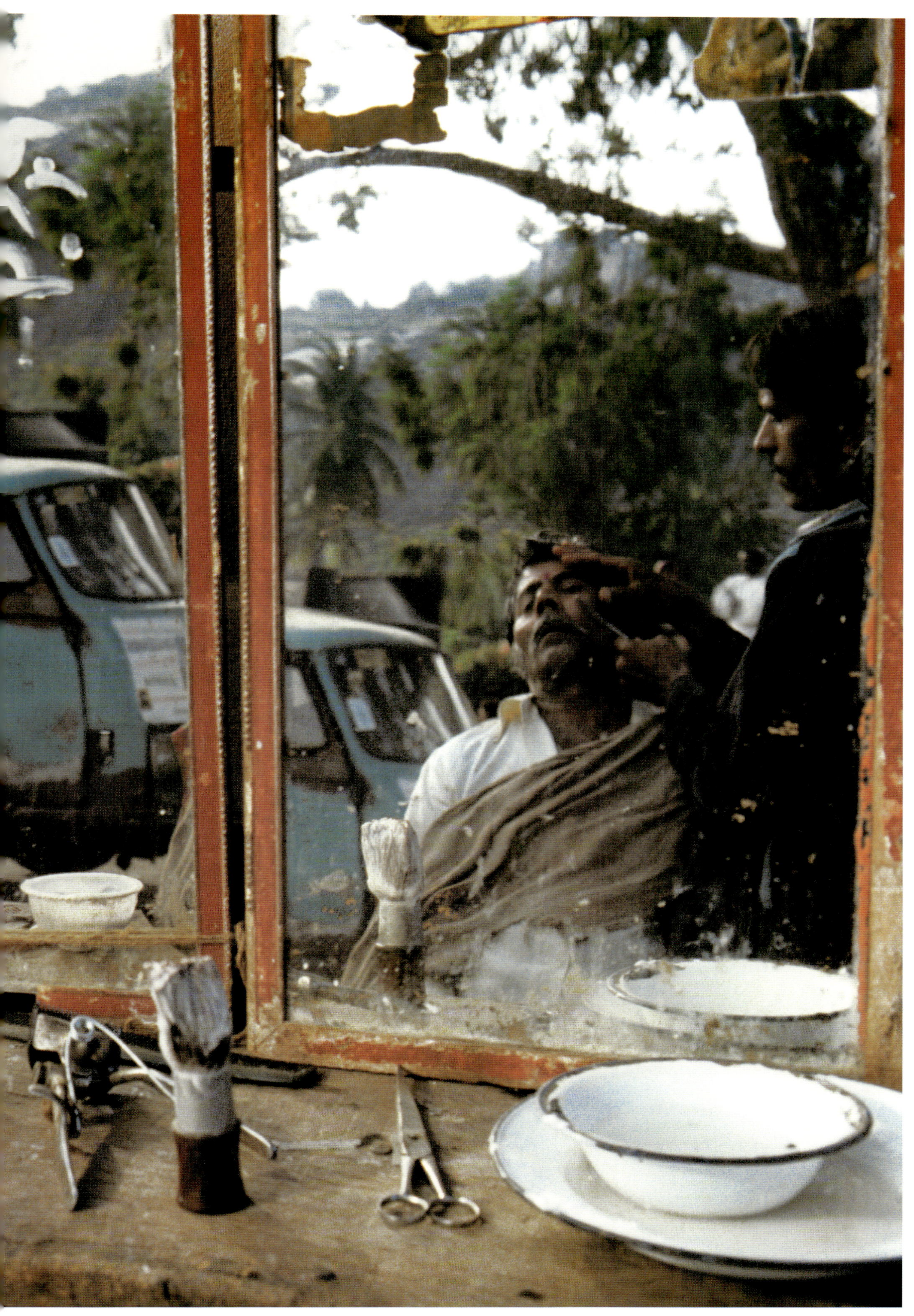

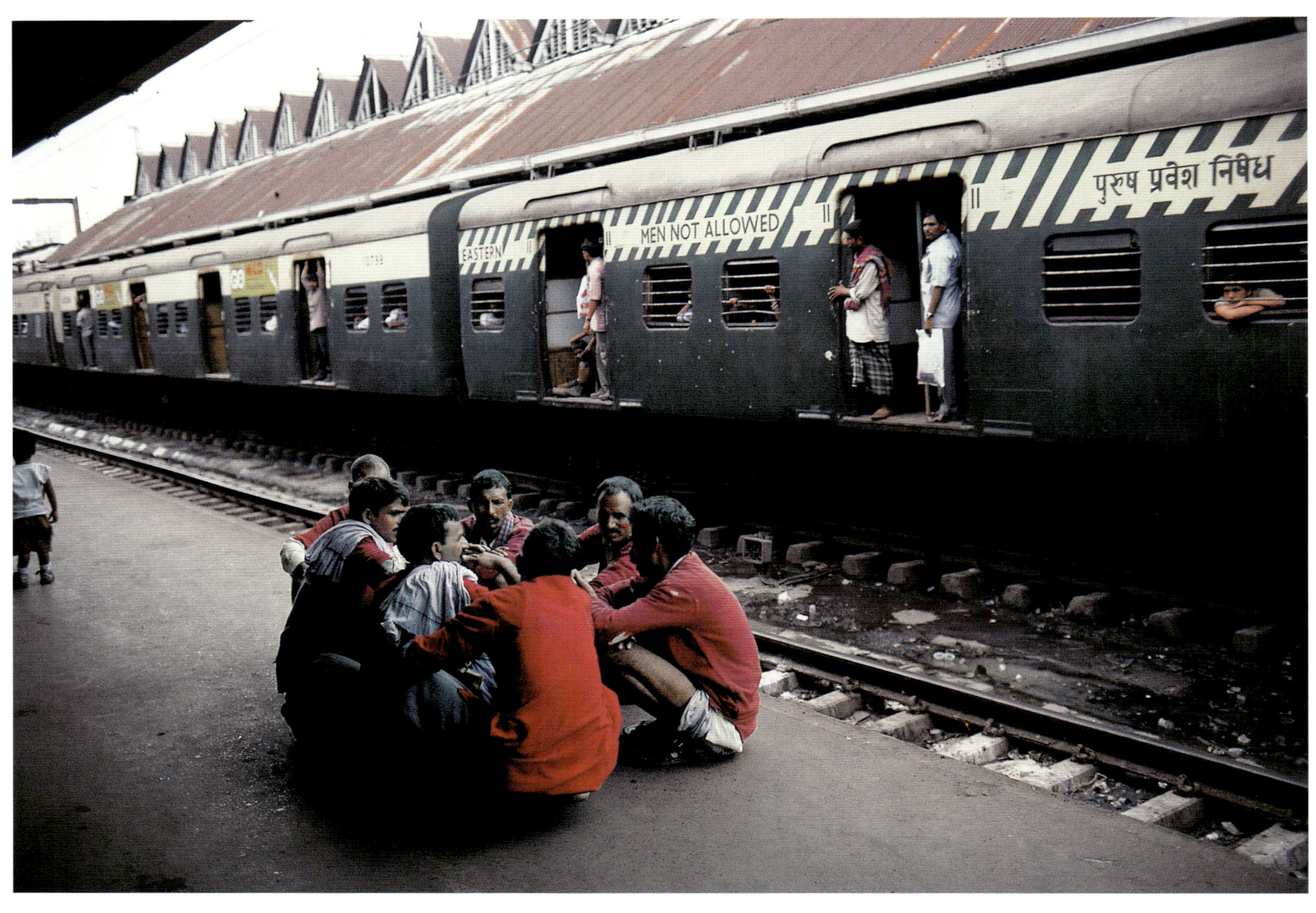

Above: Howrah Station, Calcutta.
Opposite: Muslim pilgrim.

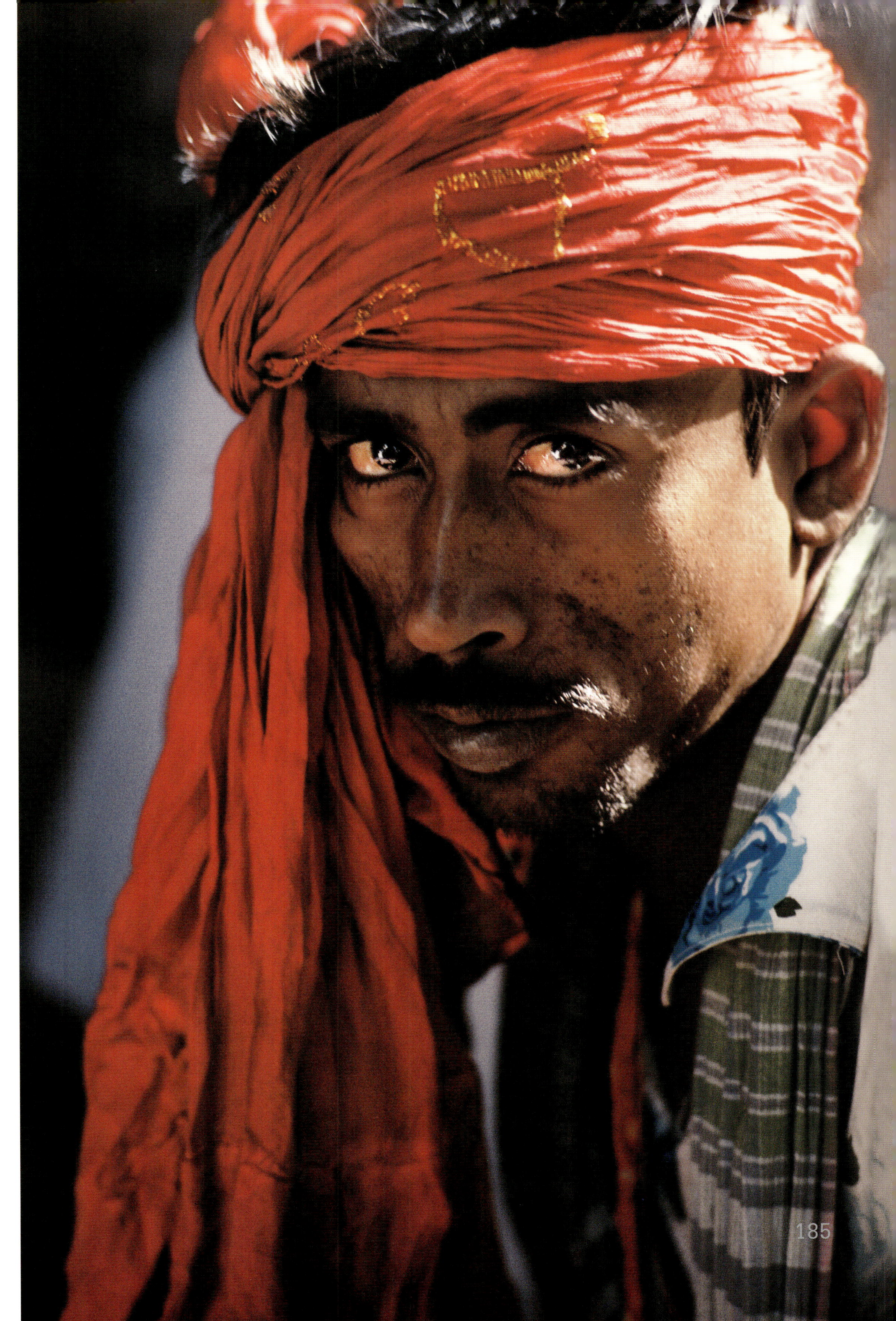

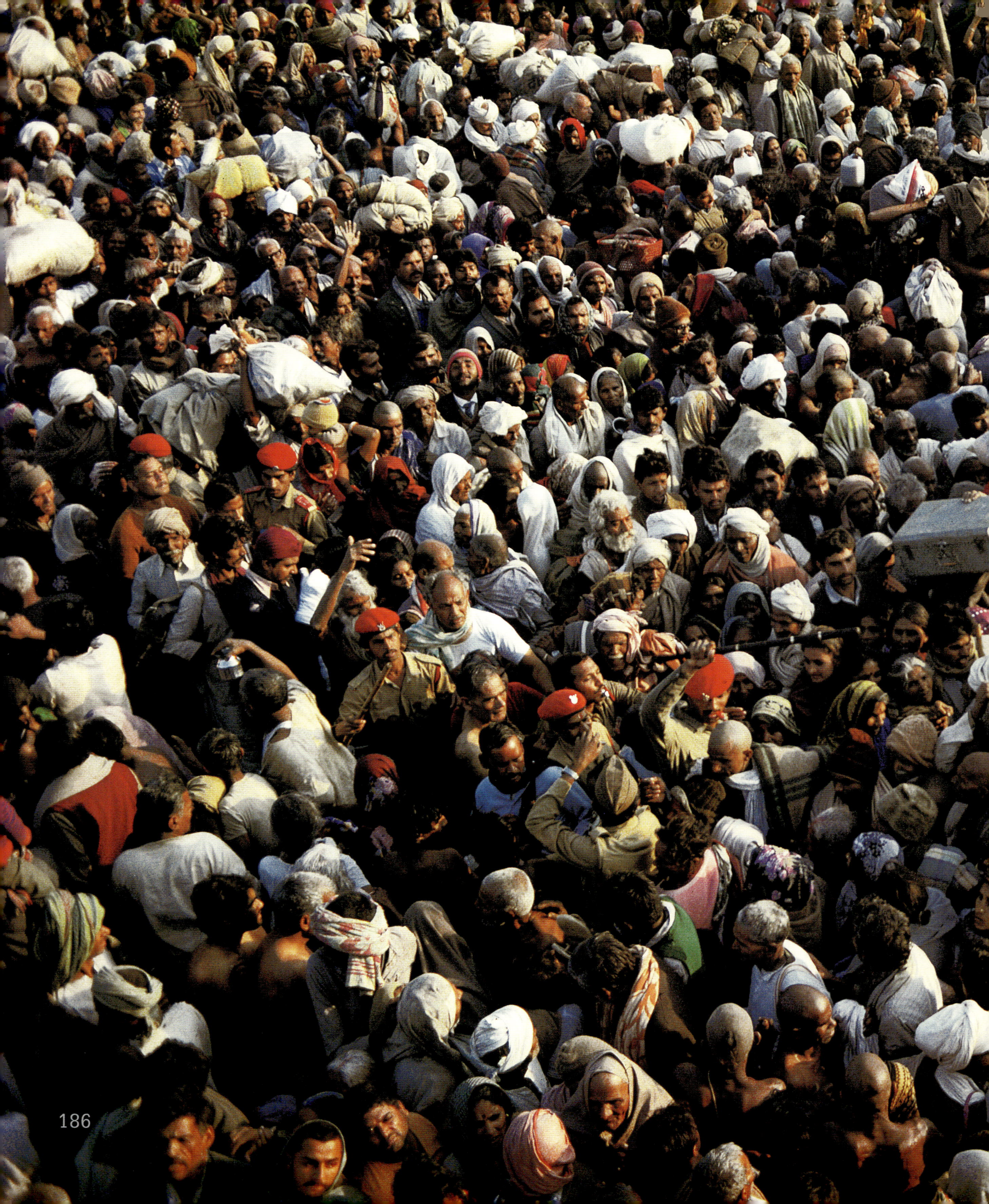

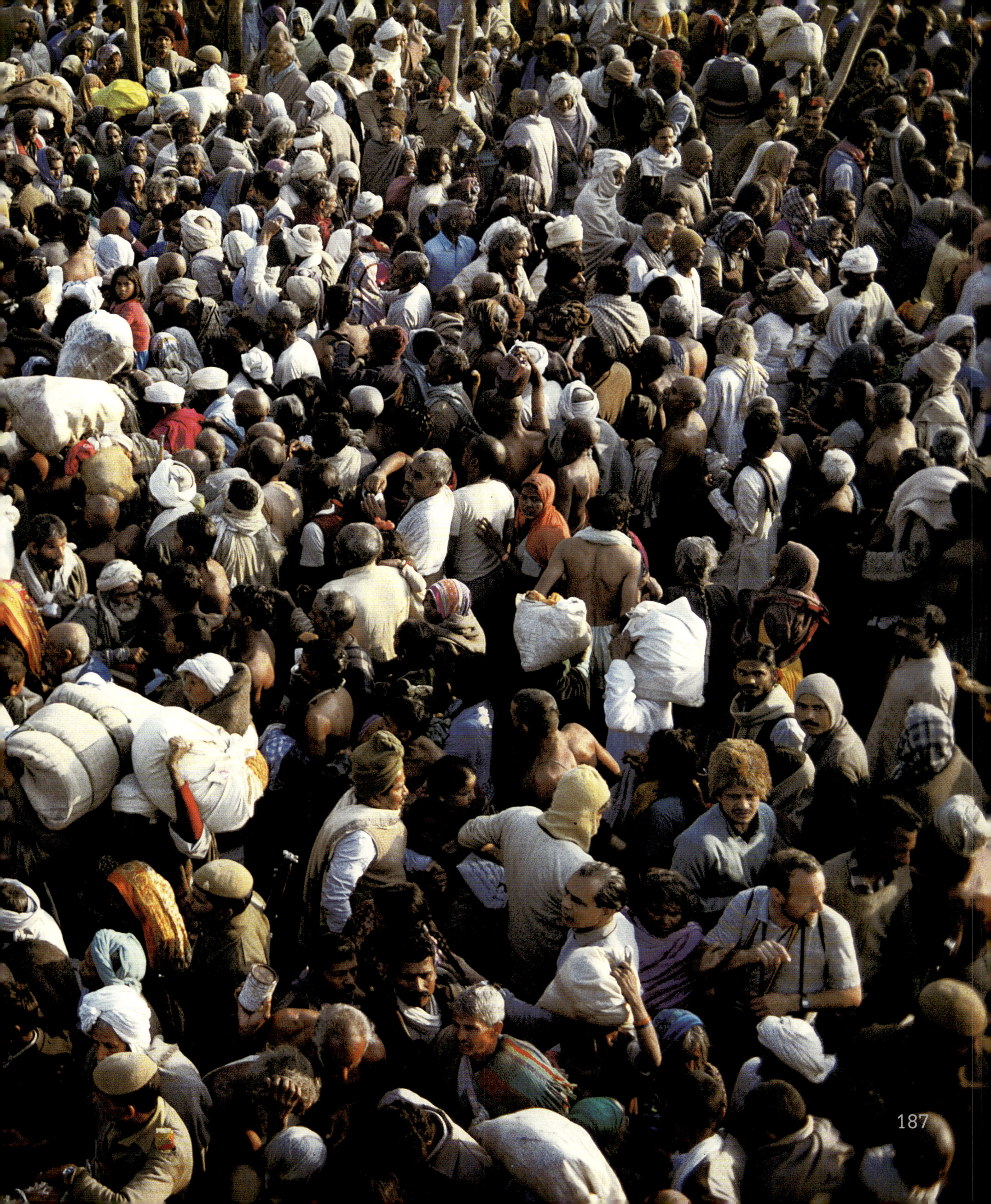

"Why are you standing here? There is nothing to see.
The temple is over there."

"I am watching the light on the trees."

"You...?"

I repeat what I have said, but it is untranslatable into Gujarati. The traveler more often drinks tea outdoors, standing or seated on rickety benches. Beside him sit his drinking companions, and a familiar link is established between them. Before him there unfolds the spectacle of the Indian street, which is known to be rich in philosophy. He is careful to drink his tea slowly and understand the meaning of the gesture.

Sometimes ancient sculptures are still fresh, although a building constructed four years ago is old.

The *mahout* makes the elephant urinate (such a shower!) and defecate before driving it to the temple gate so that it can pick up rupees in its trunk. It blesses the giver with an elegant movement of its trunk over its head before handing the coin to its master. The advantage of using an elephant instead of a slot machine is that each time one receives a benefit. But future generations will prefer machines.

The Golden Temple at Amritsar, is in the holy city of the Sikhs. In 1984 it was the scene of violent confrontations. The pools, the reflections, the marble, the copper, the gold, the mirrors, the mother-of-pearl, and the lapis lazuli of this temple-palace, with its beneficent welcome, cause the bloodshed to be forgotten and invite the visitor to contemplation. Through the orange glow of carnelian, the power is given to beauty, enough to tame even death.

Opposite: Tea break.
Pages 186–187: Crowd of pilgrims, Allahabad.

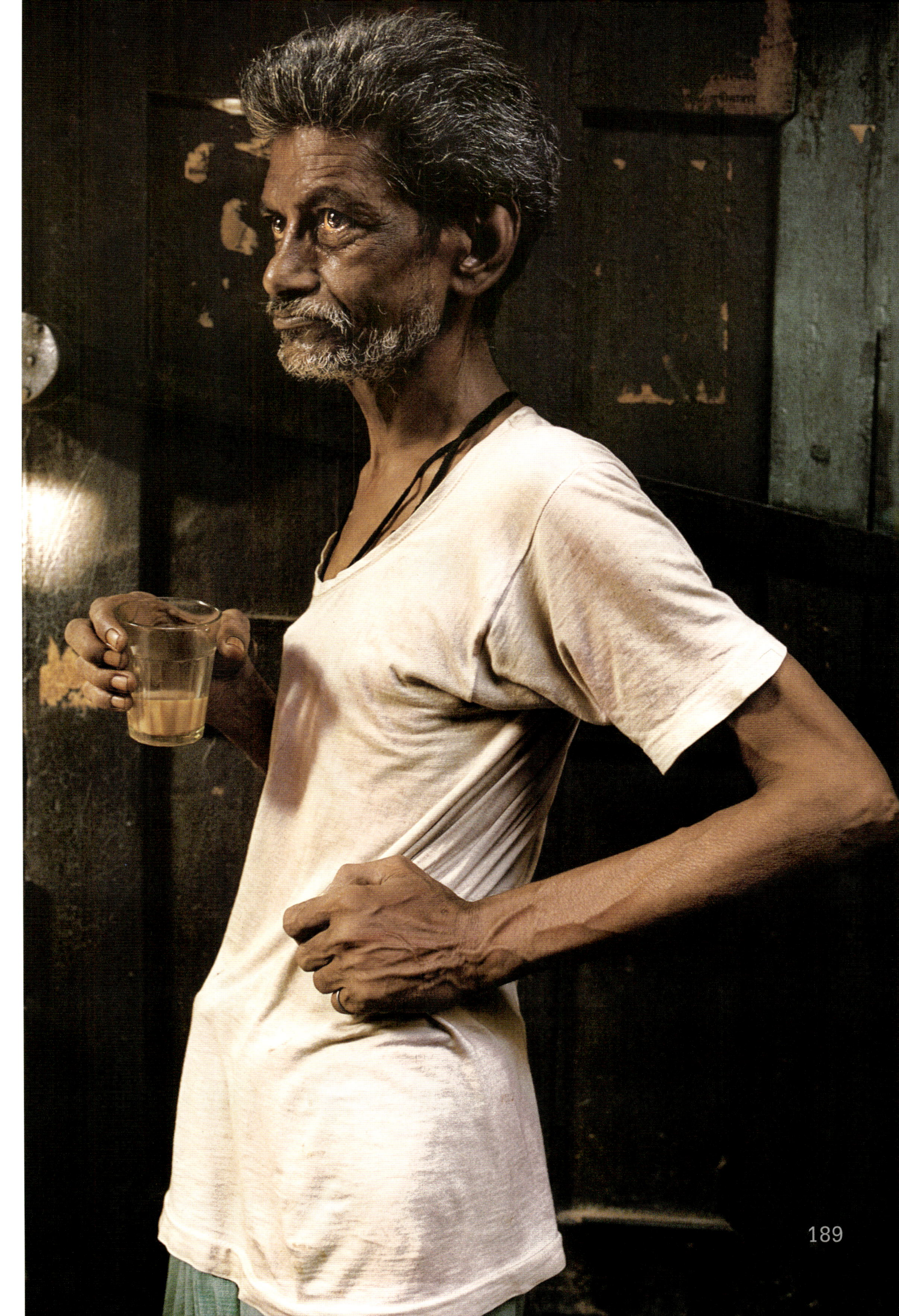

Le Corbusier's disaster at Chandigarh, with its streets built on the
block system and inhospitable buildings, is symbolic of one of the
catastrophes of the twentieth century: the refusal to take into consideration the meanderings of reality and human nature. At the Hindu University in Benares, a large hall is filled with young men and women
who sit silently behind computers. Is the spirit the same as in Berkeley
or Toulouse? No. Only part of their brain navigates the mortal canvas
with its beacon-covered pastures, the other part is still inhabited by
myths. A developed India will not become a slavish copy of the West.

There is a single stream
That runs through the small towns of India.
This open air drain receives the waste.
Each person washes in it and discharges into it.
There is no attempt to hide the dung,
The mucus,
Desires or evil thoughts.
The unconscious will be displayed.
And that is the odor of India.

If a European is questioned on his return from India,
    he replies unhesitatingly:
        "I have seen Madras, I have seen this, I have seen that."
  No, it is he who has been seen,
    Much more than he himself saw.

Henri Michaux, *A Barbarian in Asia*, 1933

The railroad stations of India are located like the *chakras*, distributed throughout the body in a network of energy. Some of them have a powerful energy that is well known, including Calcutta, Bombay, Benares, Simla, or Kanyakumari (Cape Comorin), the most southerly stop that faces the three oceans. Others are more discreet, such as Nalanda station, where only one train a day stops in what was once the Harvard of Indian Buddhism, but whose buildings are now reduced to a pile of bricks watched over by a Buddha secreted in an alcove. It is quite safe to go to sleep on the track. With luck and an art of abandonment, the ancient words of wisdom will emerge from their lethargy. Butterflies? They will flutter away to fertilize surprised corollas.

In stations of a certain size, you will always find families sleeping on the ground. The family is like a single body. A mother with the excrescence of her latest baby clinging to her breast; the father dressed in white, on his back, looking as if made of marble; the grandmother, almost mummified; four or five children laid out in folds of blankets, horizontal bas-reliefs carved by a sculptor who is already busy with another group, lie less compactly in a round lump. A little way away, several families belonging to a single *jati* silently munch wheat cakes from which a yellowish sauce trickles, a splash of light, a painterly touch. Remote, unlit platforms are dominated by rats, foraging urchins, and sometimes a Diogenes, whom death, too preoccupied with the blister-covered sucklings, appears to have forgotten.

For thirty years, how many places have I seen fall to the assault of tourists, beginning with Hampi, Jaisalmer, Jaipur, Khajuraho, Konarak, Mahabalipuram, and more! Many forgotten sites remain that are worthy of prayer. Some are only protected by a grove.

In the train moving slowly between Vizianagaram and Raipur, my neighbor, who is from a merchant *jati*, asks me in good English if I am a *Brahman* in my country. Replying in the negative, I add that there are no castes in Europe. He is so surprised that he asks the same question again. I repeat myself. His neighbor is intrigued and questions him to find out what we are saying. "No castes in Europe!" he repeats in astonishment. The information is passed around the car, to everyone's stupefaction.

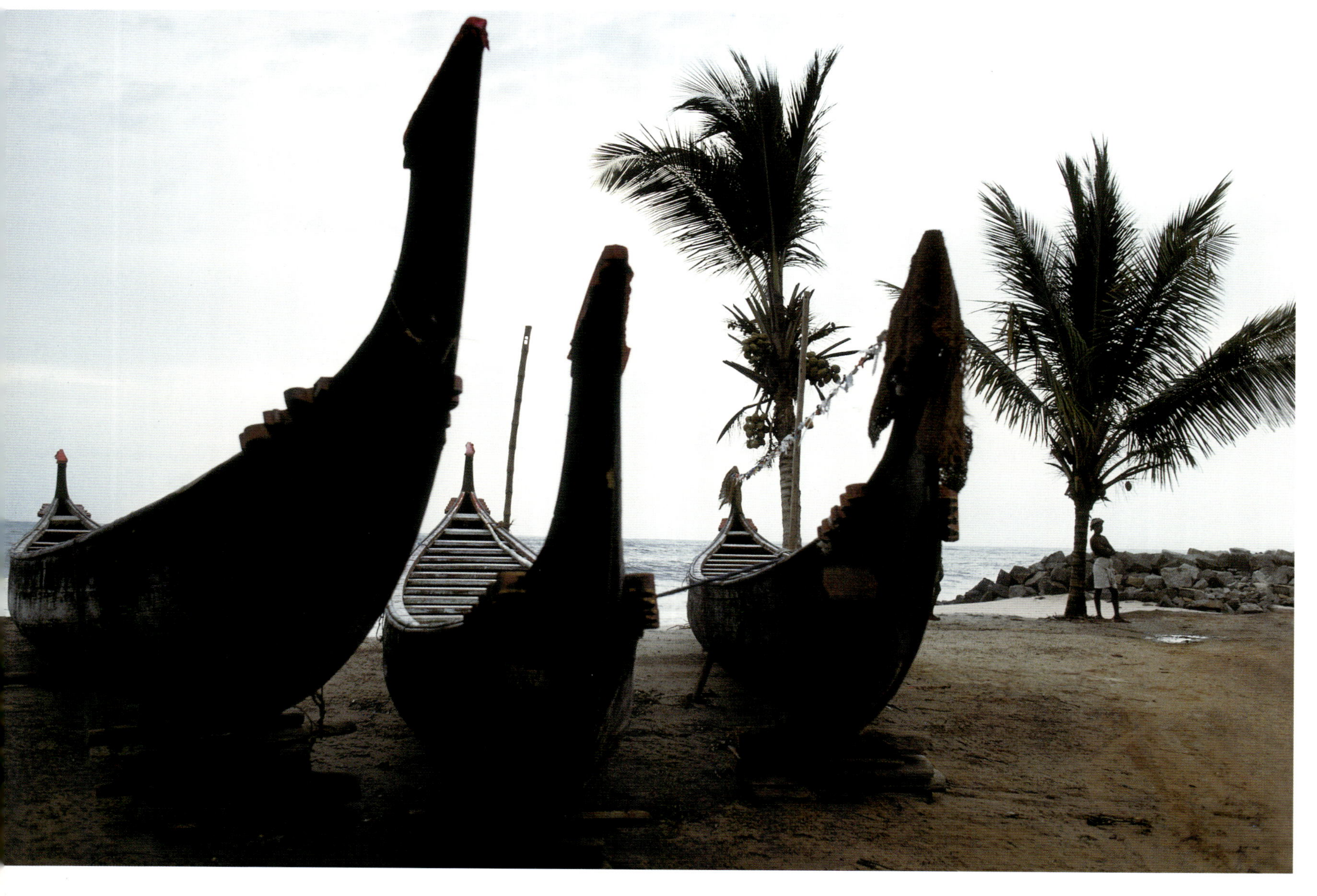

Above: Fishing expeditions, Kerala.
Opposite: Fisherman.

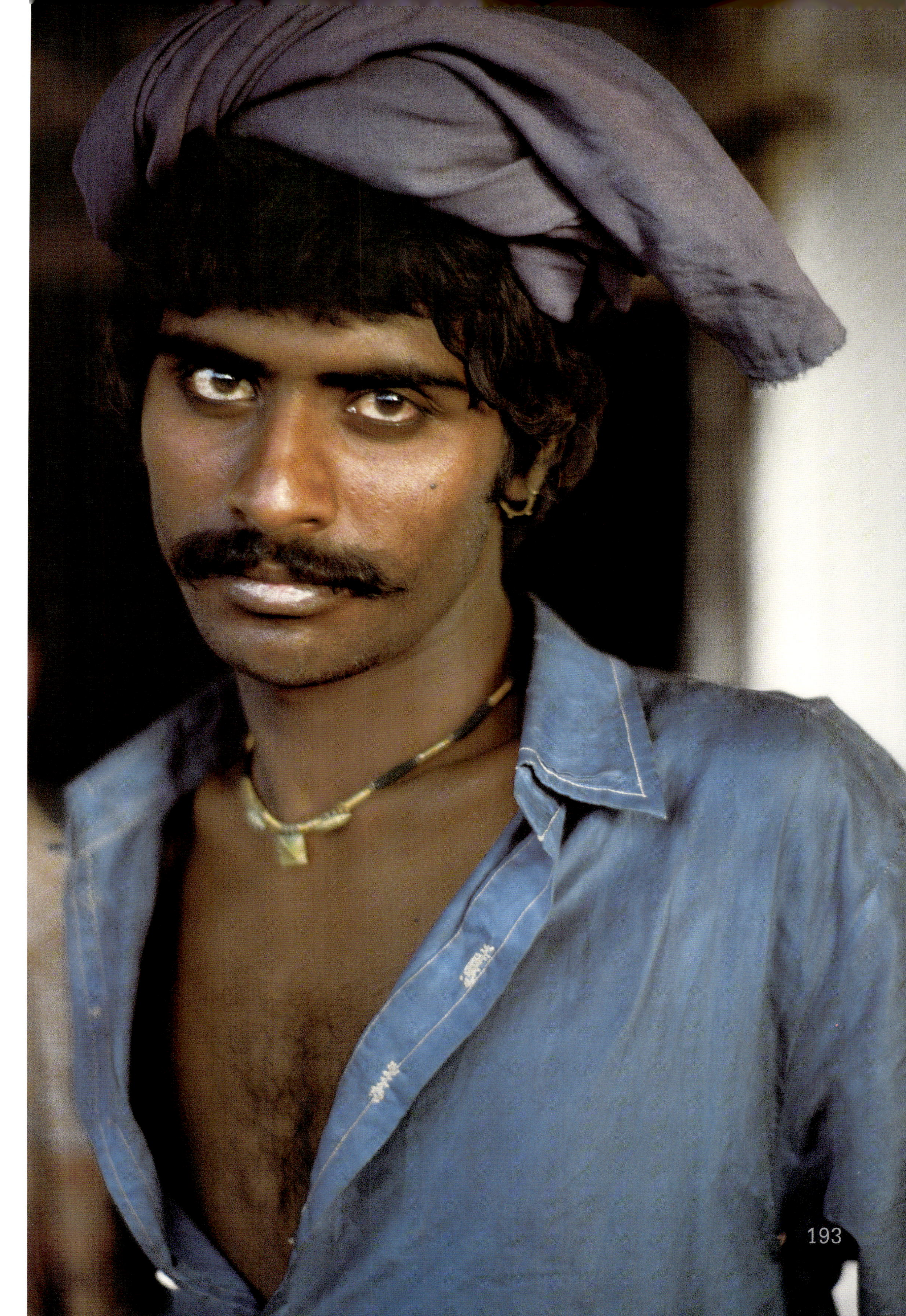

The disappearance of the sacred dances performed in the temples is an incalculable loss. If you rule out the displays put on for tourists that have lost their meaning, you can still have the experience of performances of dance for an Indian audience. On one of my first trips to India:

The costume of the dancer opens between her legs like a fan, closes and opens in a sacred breath. It is eroticism of course, but indirect eroticism, transposed to a different plane. Indian women, whether they are dancers or not, go to great lengths to protect their sexual organs. They know that the source is precious and not made to be seen. This does not stop them from recreating the source by means of gestures, mischievousness, or a flash of bare skin at the stomach.

Under the influence of a bourgeois society, we experienced a period of hypocritical prudery in the nineteenth century; under the influence of a commercial society we are now experiencing an era of obscene display. When will there be a return to sacred eroticism?

The dancer executes a very difficult pose that represents Krishna playing the flute to seduce the gopis. The audience holds its breath, then applauds enthusiastically. My neighbor leans toward me to give me explanations that I could happily do without. During a break between two dances and to stop his chatting, I take out a piece of paper and write on it:

The sacred dance is irresistible. Priests, faithful husbands, monks, swamis, ascetics, and even the pope and the emperor of Japan would be released from every vow of chastity and fidelity if they were seduced by an Indian dancer.

My intrusive neighbor asks me what I am writing.

An edict.

The dancer now creates another world. The music that enfolds her, rather than guiding her, is made by musicians and by the dancer herself with the irregular clinking of her wrist- and ankle-jewels.

Why introduce compunction into religion, when what it needs is art?

The Temptation of India

In the Westernized *ashrams* there are little booths selling "supreme love." There is nothing like this in traditional centers such as the *maths*, where the *Veda* is learned backward and forward. It is not a question of loving your neighbor, but of finding a way to unite with God.

The charm of the countryside lies in the encounter between a certain measure of amateurism and entrenched customs, an aristocratic charm. These humble farmers are the landlords. They have nothing to prove, they exist. When they come out to meet us, they do not humble themselves by aping us, as do the young city-dwellers. In cities or at tourist attractions, the Indians are tortured by a desire for possessions, a problem that is all too familiar to us in the West.

Philosophizing is the subject of small talk, just as a film shown the previous night on television or the menu for tonight might be in the West. My traveling companion in the first class berth on a train between Benares and Mathura, a fat man given to flatulence, after making three rather stupid generalizations about France and the United States, comes straight to the point: "Tell me, sir, what do you believe man's purpose to be on earth?" This sets us off on a long evening devoted to abstract thought. Then, beside a pool at a temple, a *Brahman*, naked to the waist, comes to sit beside me and addresses me thus: "How can you believe in the resurrection of the flesh?"

On another train, this one packed, a horde of teenagers climbing on top of each other assail me with: "Does God have a wife? What do you do to purify yourself? How much did you pay for your watch? What is Paradise? Do you have any fountain pens?"

Unlike those of today, Western travelers in the seventeenth and eighteenth centuries may well have known nothing about India when they disembarked there, but found many aspects of rural life that were familiar to them—religion as a part of daily life, the importance of religious festivals, the autarchy of the villages, the place occupied by women and children, and the man with the plow, not forgetting the Samaritan woman at the well.

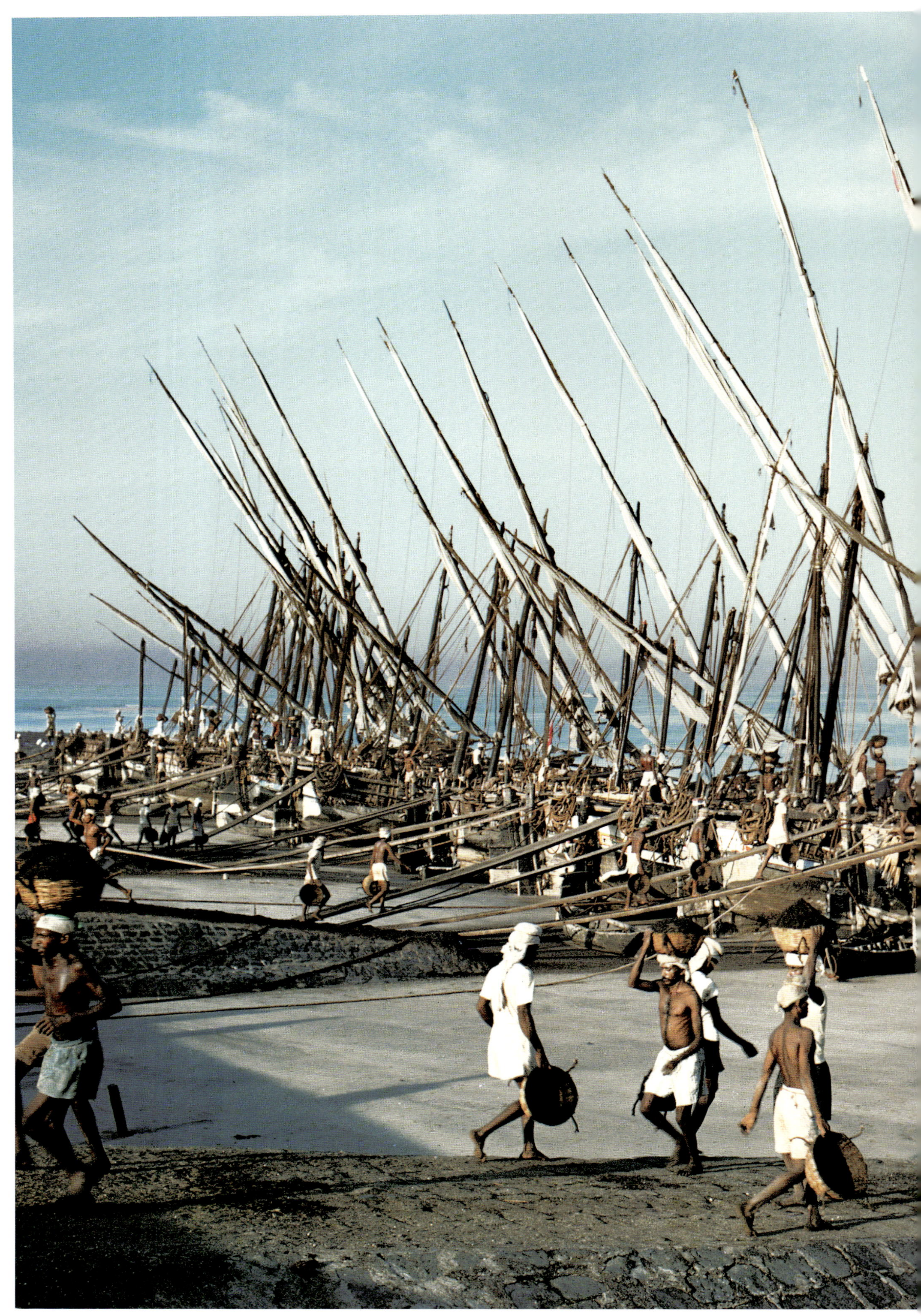

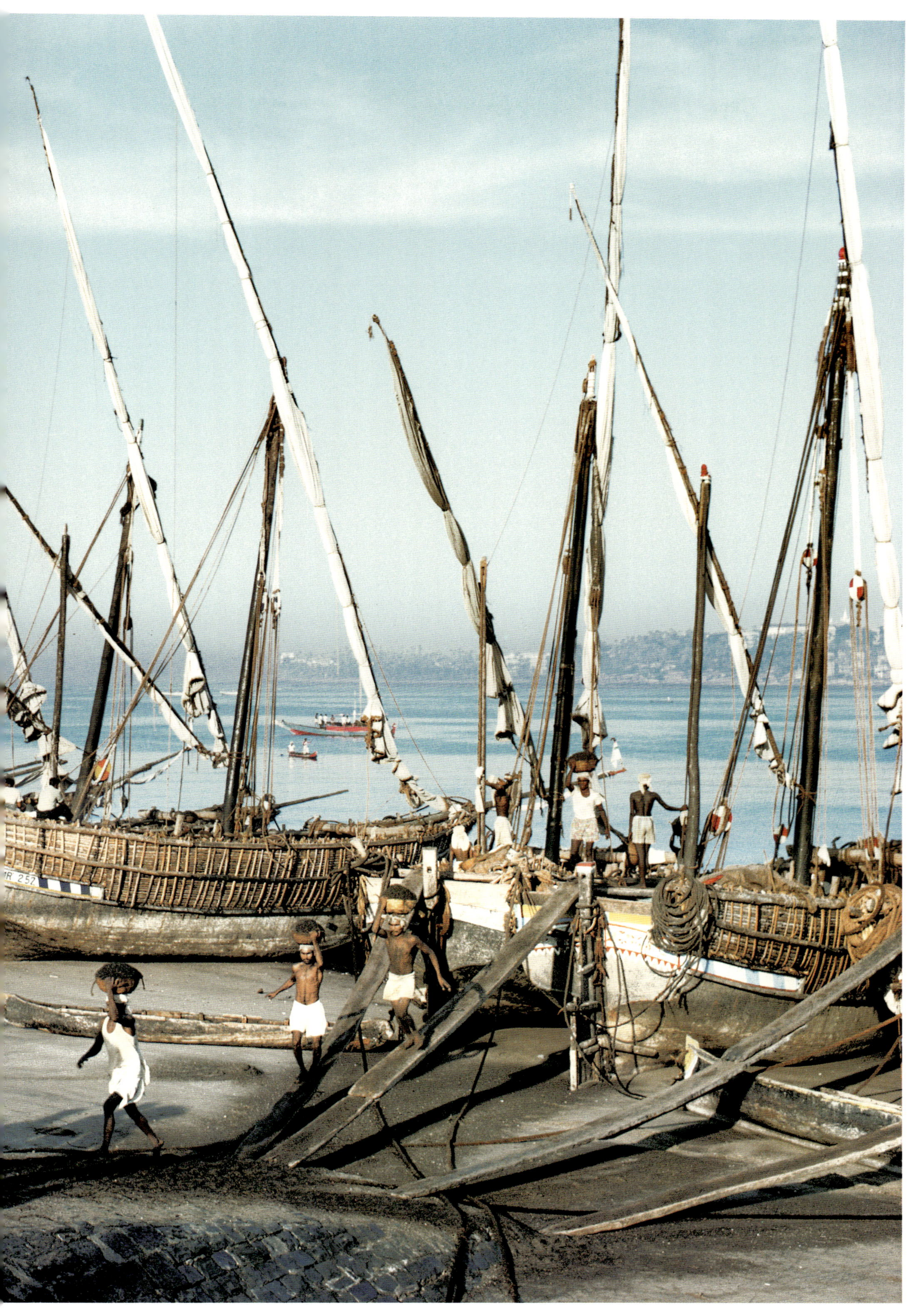

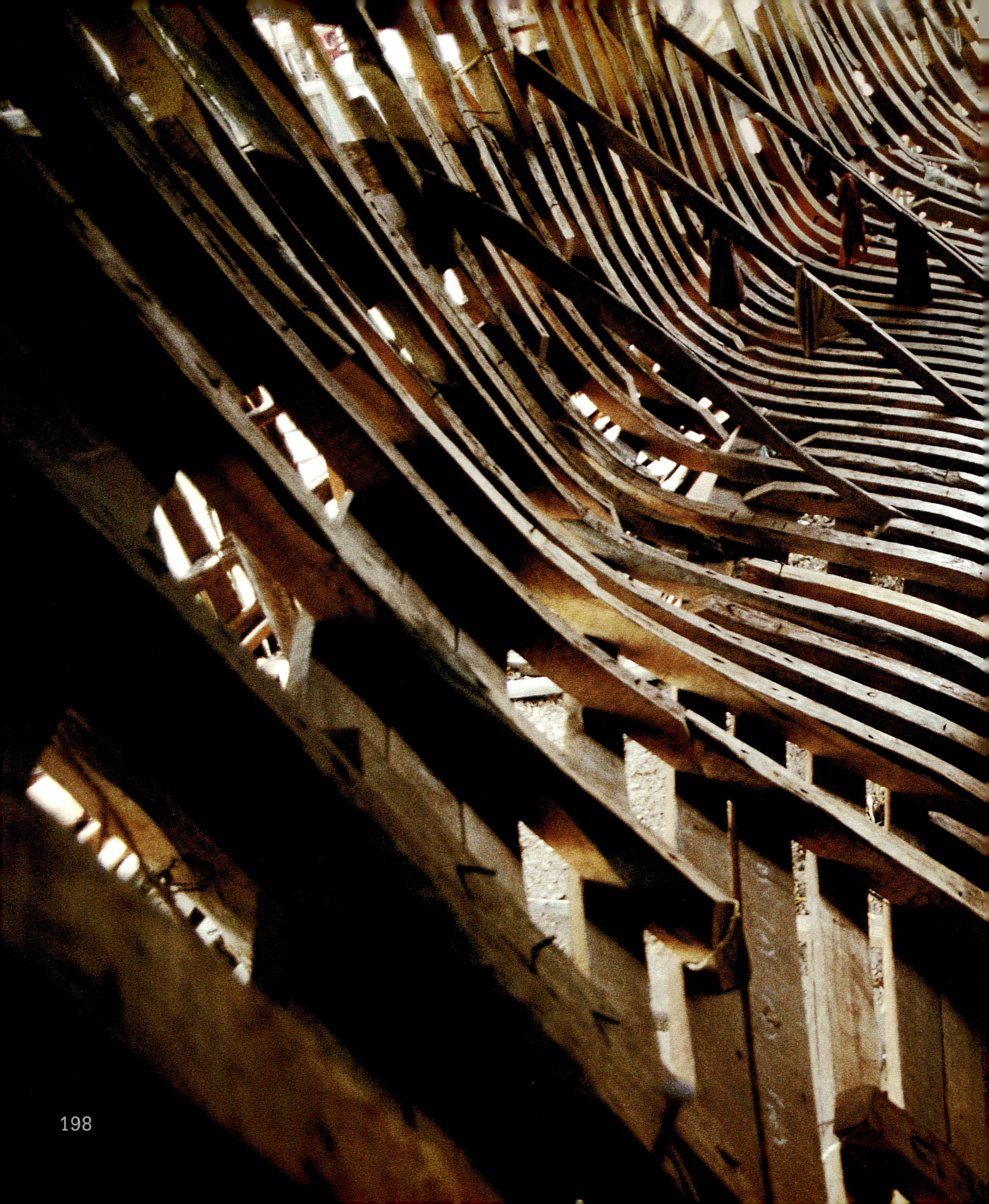

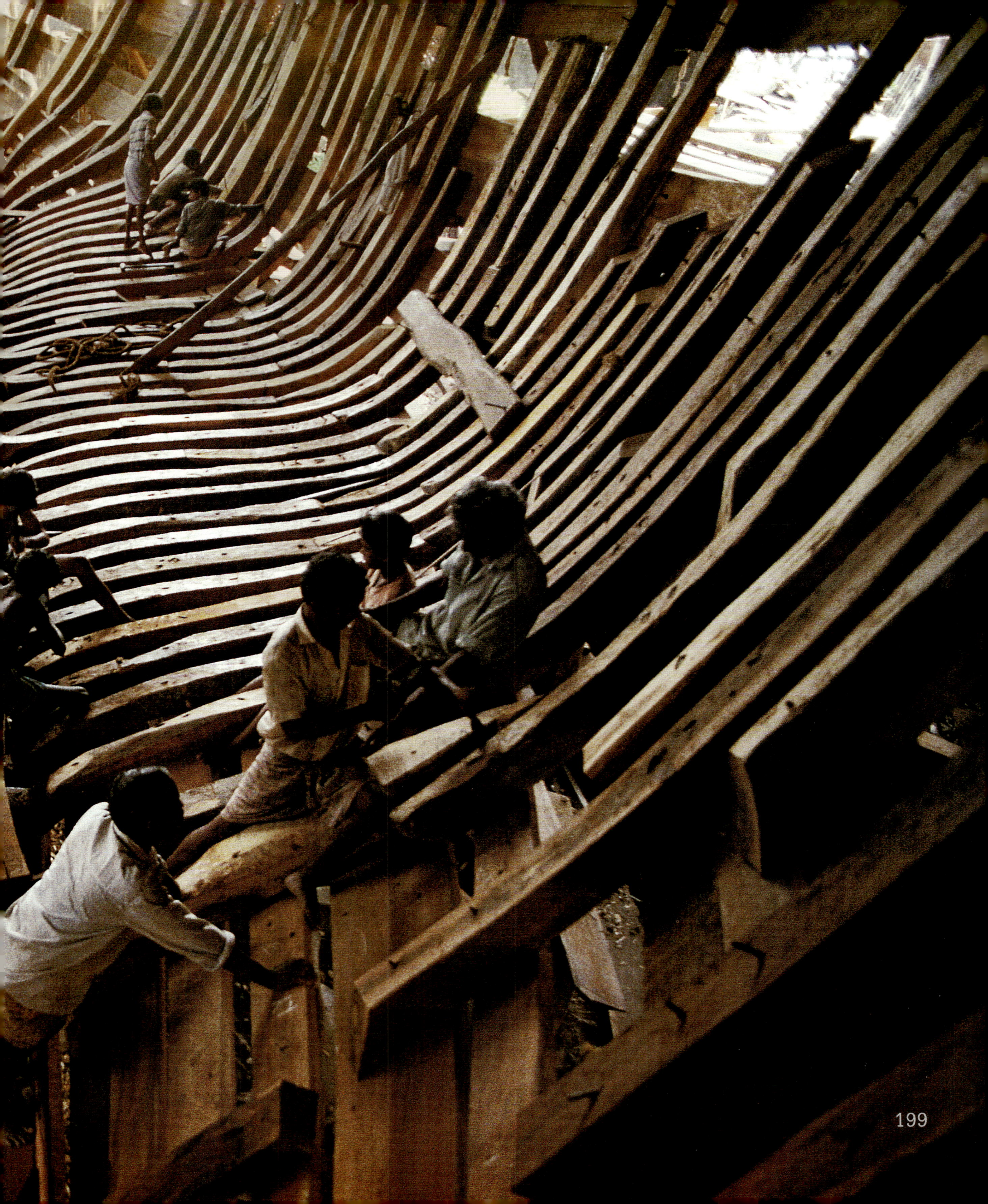

At Sravanabelagola, there is a statue of the Jain saint Bahubali that is the tallest monolithic statue in the world. It is fifty-seven feet (17 m) high, a great deal of space in which to express serenity, especially when one is at its feet. Afterward, it no longer seems so massive in the mind's eye. There remains the possibility of a man, standing naked and tall, his arms stretched down beside his trunk, to confront passions and serpents without blinking.

Rajgir. During the rainy season, the Buddha particularly liked to withdraw to Vulture Peak in Rajgir, a mountainous, wooded region. This is probably the loveliest location in the land of the Buddha. After climbing a long path that winds around the rocky outcrop, there is a view over the whole area that has remained in its wild state. The hills are covered in woodland as far as the eye can see. The vegetation appears to have fought for survival like a wild animal. Suddenly, the sound of a gong echoes across the plain. It comes from a Japanese monastery inhabited by gray-robed nuns. Here one of them is feeding a wild cat. After eating, the animal wanders away and the woman cleans the plate. Would she be willing to feed me? She is doing so already! She smiles at me, something with which to frighten away the powers of the night.

Since I do not have to pass a test, I make for the bamboo garden that the Buddha enjoyed. Thousands of leaves rustle in the wind and make the light dance. In the sky, birds pursue each other with cries of affection. The bamboos whisper over and over that which is most complex in Buddhism—to love creation while releasing oneself from its control.

The Madras (Chennai) museum is famous for its bronze statues representing the dancing Shiva and, an even more ancient art, the story of the Buddha told through the sculptures of Amaravati. There are also monuments, erected in memory of the women who threw themselves onto the funeral pyres of their husbands, in an act known as *suttee*. The woman's right wrist is adorned with bracelets that indicate that she is married to a man who is still alive, and not a widow. Western travelers, who witnessed these sacrifices before they were banned pretended to be disapproving but could not hide their fascination with it.

Pages 198–199: Boat building in Kerala.

Upon leaving the museum, I engage in conversation with a man of learned countenance in worn garments who seems sad. We talk about the state of the world, the evils of television, the necessity of having castes. Then he suddenly advises me to take a seven- or eight-hour train journey east of Madras to visit a city surprising for its—an inaudible word consisting of vowels that mingle with the stones of the waterfall. He hurriedly scribbles down the train timetable with very specific connections. He disappears as mysteriously as his explanations about the importance of the place he advised me to visit.

That month, I had plenty of time. The next day, in the train, I noticed that the information about the train times and connections was correct. Would this be my utopia? That evening, in a city mentioned in none of the guidebooks, I found a windowless room in a sordid "inn." In an attempt to hide my ignorance as to what I was looking for, I asked the innkeeper: "Where is it? How long will it take to get there on foot?" "Ten minutes," he replied with a vague, languid gesture. I ate in a little café still failing to understand the attraction of this place. I had been told of a temple on a hill, a beneficent statue, an incense factory.

The next day, what a disappointment! I should like to believe that the purpose of the scholar at the Madras museum was to make me understand that the only goal lies in travel itself. But that would be to suppose that this anonymous man was a master who understood the exaggerated tension for me—for us—in striving to reach a goal. It is a flattering explanation that I reject, due to a return of skepticism. Another theory is that the man sent me off to see something, but since nothing would interest me, I might as well benefit from receiving a teaching that, without having been forewarned, was the result of a misunderstanding. One can always see everything that way, which is what makes me stubborn.

I spent another dreadful night, learning a new lesson in patience at withstanding noise, heat, insects. I awoke before dawn. I cycled a few miles from the town through a jumble of granite boulders through which the sunrise revealed the plain. No longer seeking anything in particular, I rode peacefully through paddy-fields and villages, returning to the town at market time. Harmony between cauliflowers and guavas would have to suffice for me.

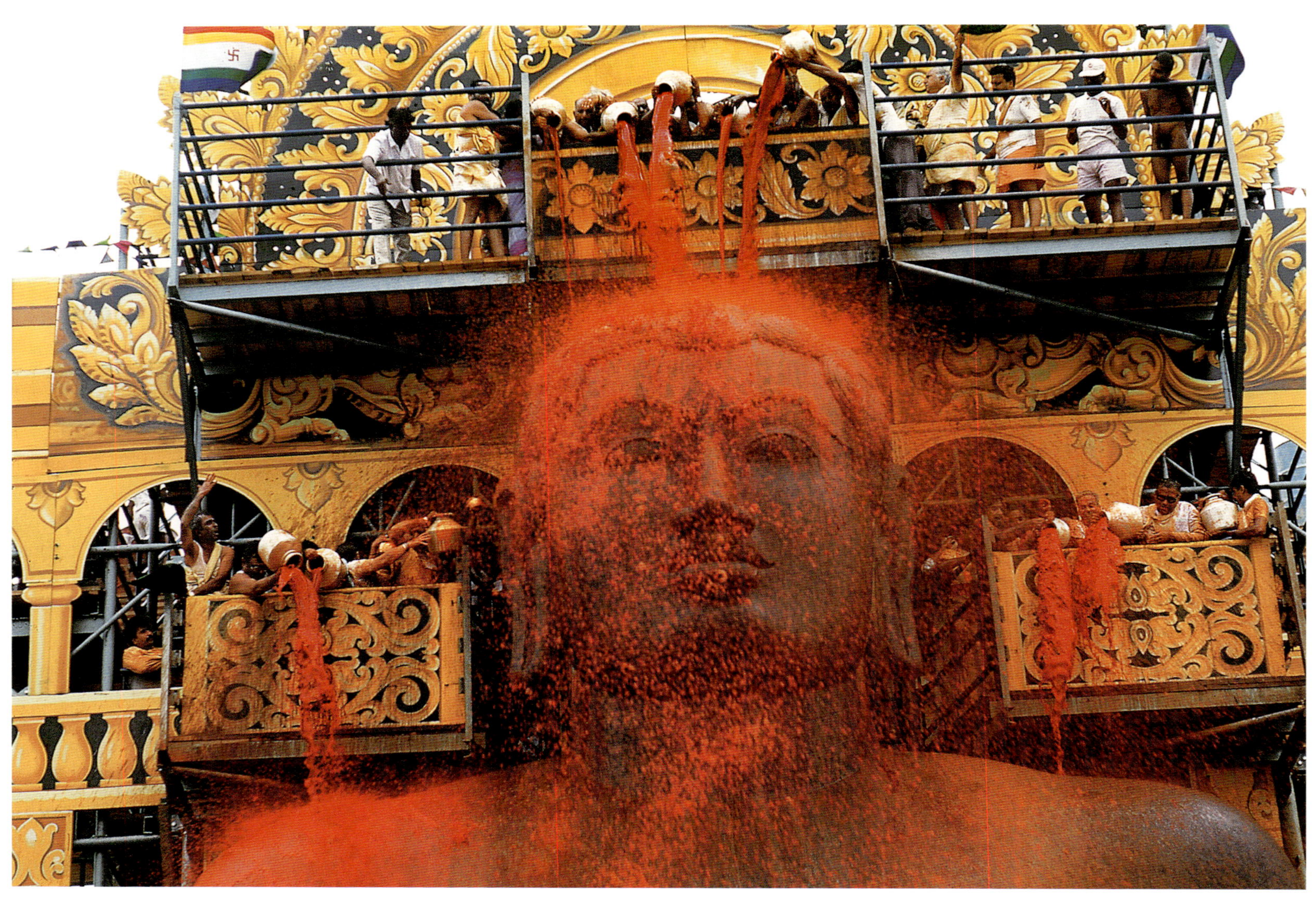

Ritual anointings, Sravanabelagola, Karnataka.

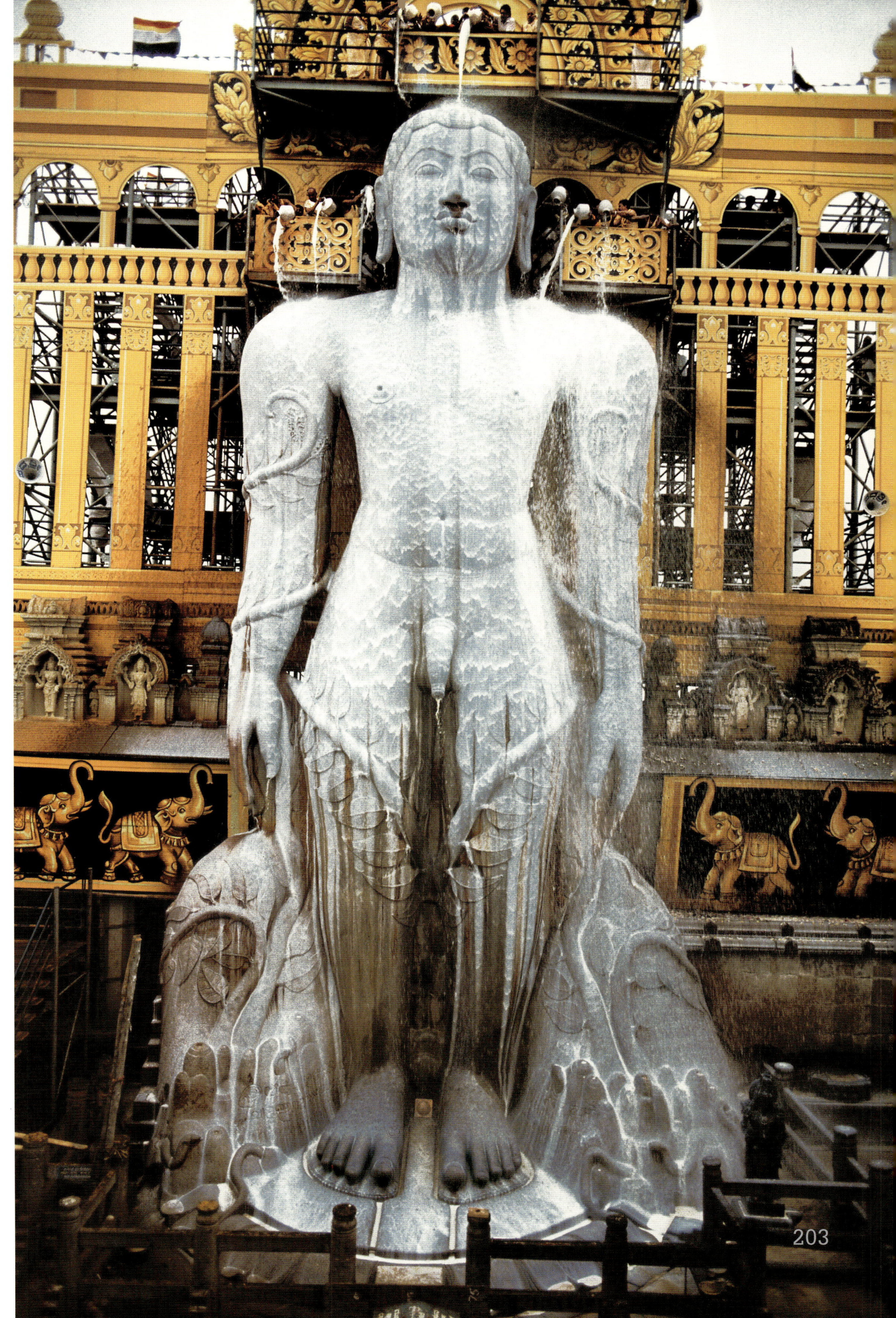

In the early afternoon I returned to the pile of rocks. I met three young men, who also had bicycles. I jokingly called to them "Where is it?" and they replied "Follow us!" After a moment or two, we left our bicycles and climbed along a cliff face.

"So you are interested in our caves?" they asked after a host of other questions. Here was the entrance, a narrow passage that had to be negotiated on all fours. "Didn't you bring a flashlight with you to come here?" asked Vinayak, who refused to lend me his. He came inside with me while the other two young men waited outside. I left my rucksack with them. After visiting two caves containing altars to Shiva and a long corridor with others branching off it, we entered a larger chamber decorated with rock paintings representing a ring of human figures about twenty inches high, their bodies consisting of two triangles in an hourglass shape, with stick arms and legs. "Wait!" I called to the boy who wanted to hurry me along. These human figures were an invitation to contemplation. Above them, was a stencil-like depiction of a man riding a buffalo.

There was nothing Hindu about these paintings; either they were a trick or a gesture from prehistoric ancestors who had discovered they were human. Still in a hurry, Vinayak took me into a new cave, then another. We were descending a long, narrow passage, and we eventually reached a cave in which he tapped the walls, looking for an exit that he couldn't find. We climbed along a wall, crawled into new places where I sensed something wrong. "Let's go!" I said to him. Without replying, Vinayak disappeared into a crevice. Was he trying to get rid of me? He was leaving me without much chance in this labyrinth, having only ten matches. I called to him the first thing that came into my head, "I have friends waiting for me, if they don't find me they'll come looking for me." Silence. The darkness gripped me like a vise.

A light shone from the other side. Vinayak reappeared. I sensed that he, in turn, was worried. We retraced our steps. I recognized a cave through which we had gone. "Let's leave traces," I said to him. He wasn't listening, but continued to search like a hunted animal. I no longer feared a trap, I feared stupidity. We were wandering around aimlessly. We went round the same route again which offered no way out. I became angry. He again escaped through a hole. The flashlight beam showed an alcove in which there was another painting of an upright man with long limbs. "That's all right," he said, without leaving me the time to look at the painting, which returned to the night. We wandered around for another five minutes, crawled up a sort of chimney, and found ourselves in the cave containing the triangular figures. I asked Vinayak to throw some light on the paintings. With a languid gesture he traced a quick flashlight beam over the wall as if he were rubbing out a stain with an eraser. The figurines leaped out, then went back into the rock.

Outside, under the fiery sun, Vinayak said something in Tamil to his friends. Did he say that we had gotten lost but he didn't dare leave me there? I laughed, a innocent laugh that communicated itself to the boys; they were abashed, as was I.

Other scenes from Indian life

This is what I have seen, though I do not know how to express it.

Beside a pond, within a stone's throw of the fort [of Pondicherry], there is a clump of trees through which stands a piece of wood eight inches high, representing the unclothed root of the human race. It is raised on a cube two feet high, and can be removed with the hand; and—it must be said—the libertines call it a dildo. It is naked, and not covered by satin or anything that is soft when rubbed, as are said to be those used by girls, by widows who are chaste against their will, and especially by nuns. This one is of wood and has nothing covering it. It is chained to its cube and rests on testicles that serve as its base. It is on this Priapus that the people oblige their wives who are sterile to rub a certain part of the body that I shall not name, because it is well enough understood; because, according to them, it renders them fertile. We Europeans are smarter: the original is always better than a copy.

Robert Challes, *Journal of a Voyage to India* 1690

Meanwhile, the woman arrived, mounted on a small horse, and followed by a large company. Her parents and those of her husband surrounded her, as did a few players of instruments. She stopped under a tree where I watched her attentively. She faced the pyre. She was speaking to those around her. She asked about the location of the pool where she was to perform her ablutions and as soon as it was pointed out to her, she urged her horse forward to go there.

Her son had been positioned so that she was unable to see him. He was then made to approach the pyre. The body of his father was brought to him on a stretcher decorated with little streamers. The body was wrapped in a shroud of daffodil-colored silk cloth. The son resumed the ceremonies of the logs, the straw, and the water. He then placed beside the corpse a few dishes of rice and of other foods, and then returned to the place he had left. The corpse was then laid out on one of the sides of the recess.

The woman returned from the pool and approached the pyre, still on horseback. I found myself standing beside her. She stopped, removed the cashmere veil she had been wearing on her head, and took a betel leaf and a few cardamom seeds from her pocket, which she proceeded to eat while talking to some people she knew.

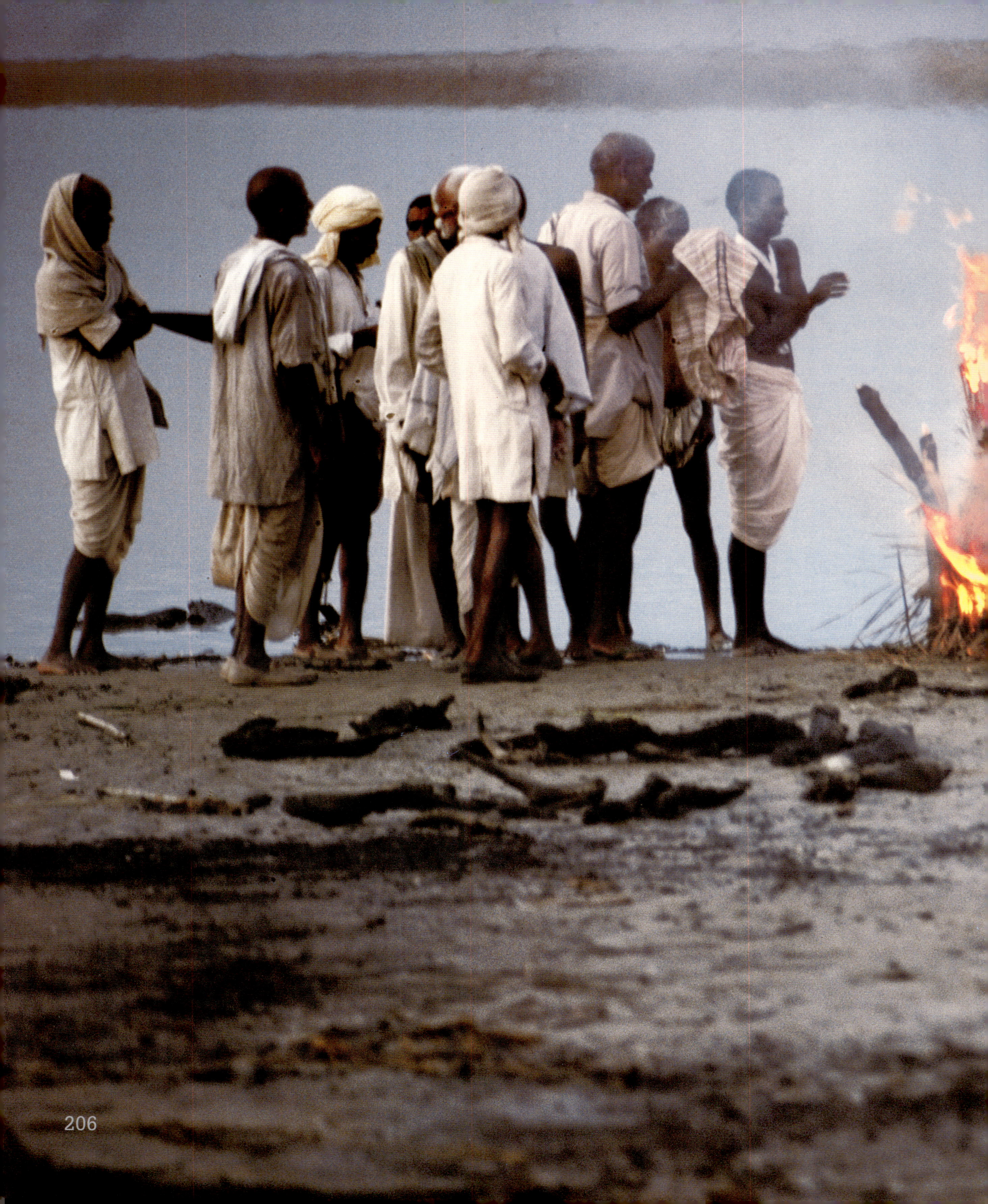

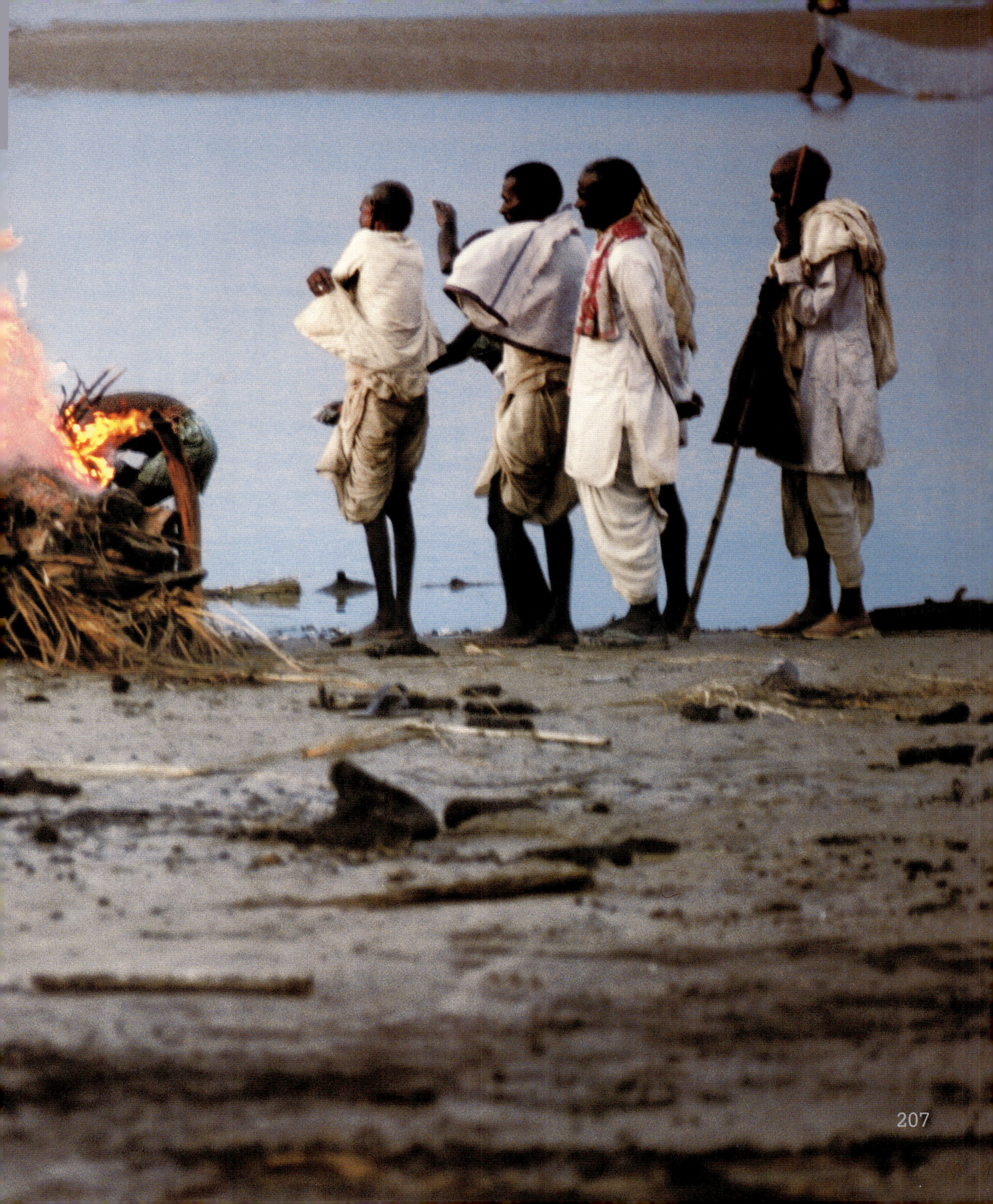

She asked for water twice and drank it. She then said that she wanted to mount the pyre. Several people helped her to dismount from the horse and took her to the recess, in which she sat beside the body of her dead husband.

The opening was then closed by slats of wood that were laid crosswise, along with bales of straw. Then the child was brought forward and given a burning brand. He walked around the pyre and then lit one side of it, and at the same time the other relatives performed the same ceremony so that in a flash, all the straw was alight. I forgot to mention that at the moment the wife wanted to enter the pyre, the nabob's choupdars *approached and tried to talk to her but the Kashmiris repulsed them with a great hue and cry. As soon as the pyre was alight, all these people began to run around it shouting and yelling. Musical instruments added to the hullabaloo.*

I noticed that two or three little girls aged three or four were being taken around the pyre in the arms of a few servants; they were no doubt intended to perform the same spectacle some day.

I could not see anything of the movements of this woman inside the pyre. The flames and smoke concealed my view, but seven or eight minutes after it had been set alight, one of my men whom I had sent as close as he could get, judged her to be dead and I think that she had suffocated in a few moments. The child was taken away as soon as he had done his duty. The spectators imperceptibly drifted away. I myself left at two o'clock, the pyre being just a pile of embers. It had been lit at midday precisely.

This horrible sight so preoccupied me that for two days I could not think of anything else. The image of that woman is so graven into my memory that she will never be blotted out. She appeared to be neither troubled, nor agitated, and performed all those frightful ceremonies as if they were the most indifferent thing in the world.

Louis de Federbe de Modave,
Voyage through India by the Comte de Modave, 1773–76

Whoever goes to the Mountains goes toward his mother.

They had crossed the Sewaliks and the half-tropical Doon, left Mussoorie behind them, and headed north along the narrow hill roads. Day after day, they struck deeper into the huddled mountains, and day after day Kim watched the lama return to a man's strength. Among the terraces of the Doon he had leaned on the boy's shoulder, ready to profit by wayside halts. Under the great ramp to Mussoorie he drew himself together as an old hunter faces a well-remembered bank, and, where he should have sunk exhausted, swung his long draperies about him, drew a deep double-lungful of the diamond air, and walked as only a hillman can. Kim, plains-bred and plains-fed, sweated and panted astonished.

This is my country," said the lama. "Besides Suchzen, this is flatter than a rice-field"; and with steady, driving strokes from the loins he strode upwards. But it was on the steep downhill marches, three thousand feet in three hours, that he went utterly away from Kim, whose back ached with holding back, and whose big toe was nigh cut off by his grass sandal-string. Through the speckled shadow of the great deodar-forests; through oak feathered and plumed with ferns; birch, ilex, rhododendron, and pine, out on to the bare hillsides' slippery sunburnt grass, and back into the woodlands' coolth again, till oak gave way to bamboo and palm of the valley, the lama swung untiring.

Glancing back in the twilight at the huge ridges behind him and the faint, thin line of the road whereby they had come, he would lay out, with a hillman's generous breadth of vision, fresh marches for the morrow; or, halting in the neck of some uplifted pass that gave on Spiti and Kulu, would stretch out his hands yearningly towards the high snows of the horizon. In the dawns they flared windy-red above stark blue, as Kedarnath and Badrinath—kings of that wilderness—took the first sunlight.

Rudyard Kipling, *Kim*, 1901

As night fell, the brahmans *signaled to me to enter the temple. I followed, without knowing what I was supposed to do. Then I perceived an infinity of pilgrims, hierophants, and servants of the temple who surrounded elephants decorated like icons, vehicles, and litters sparkling with gold, that were being prepared, by the light of flaming torches, for a solemn procession. Before I was even aware of it, I found myself at the head of it. The elephants, those most experienced bearers of tradition, marched in front of me at a stately pace; behind me, there followed the goddess, enthroned high on a precious palanquin. The procession carried on in this way, with the clashing of cymbals and the high-pitched notes of clarinets, until late into the night, in a solemn progress through the most magnificent cloisters in the world, against whose walls lines of devotees, lit intermittently by the torches, bowed in a murmur of respect.*

What a wonderful introduction to the land of the Hindus! The temple of Rameshwaram, isolated at the southernmost point of the peninsula, surrounded by the sea and framed by palm trees, is an edifice that is barely smaller than the largest of monasteries created in our early Middle Ages, with corridors that, for the beauty of their forms and colors, are probably unrivaled on earth; according to legend, the temple was founded by Rama himself, after had had abducted Sita at Ravana. It is considered to be the second most important sanctuary in Hindustan. Those who are able to do so make a pilgrimage to it, after visiting Benares.

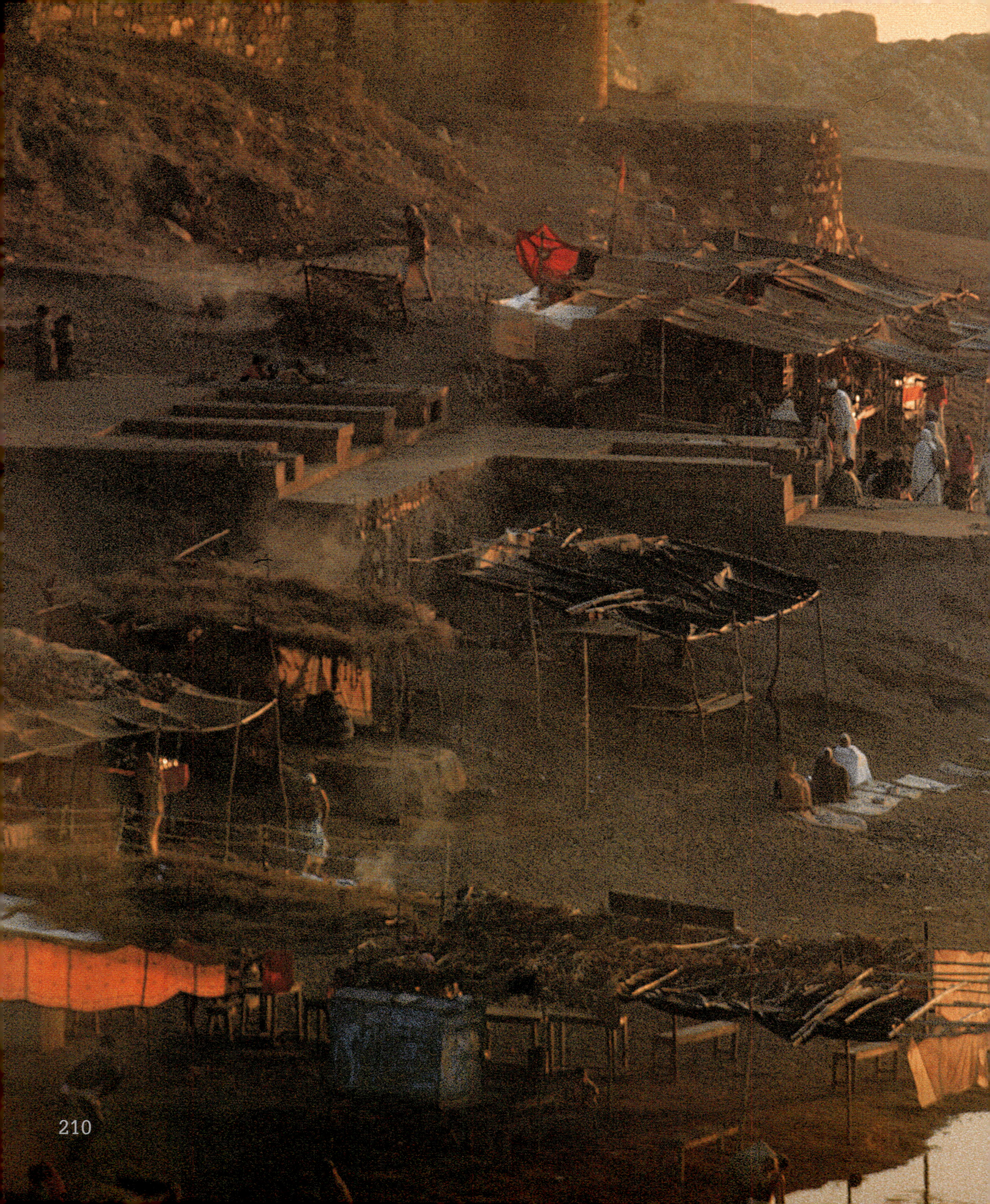

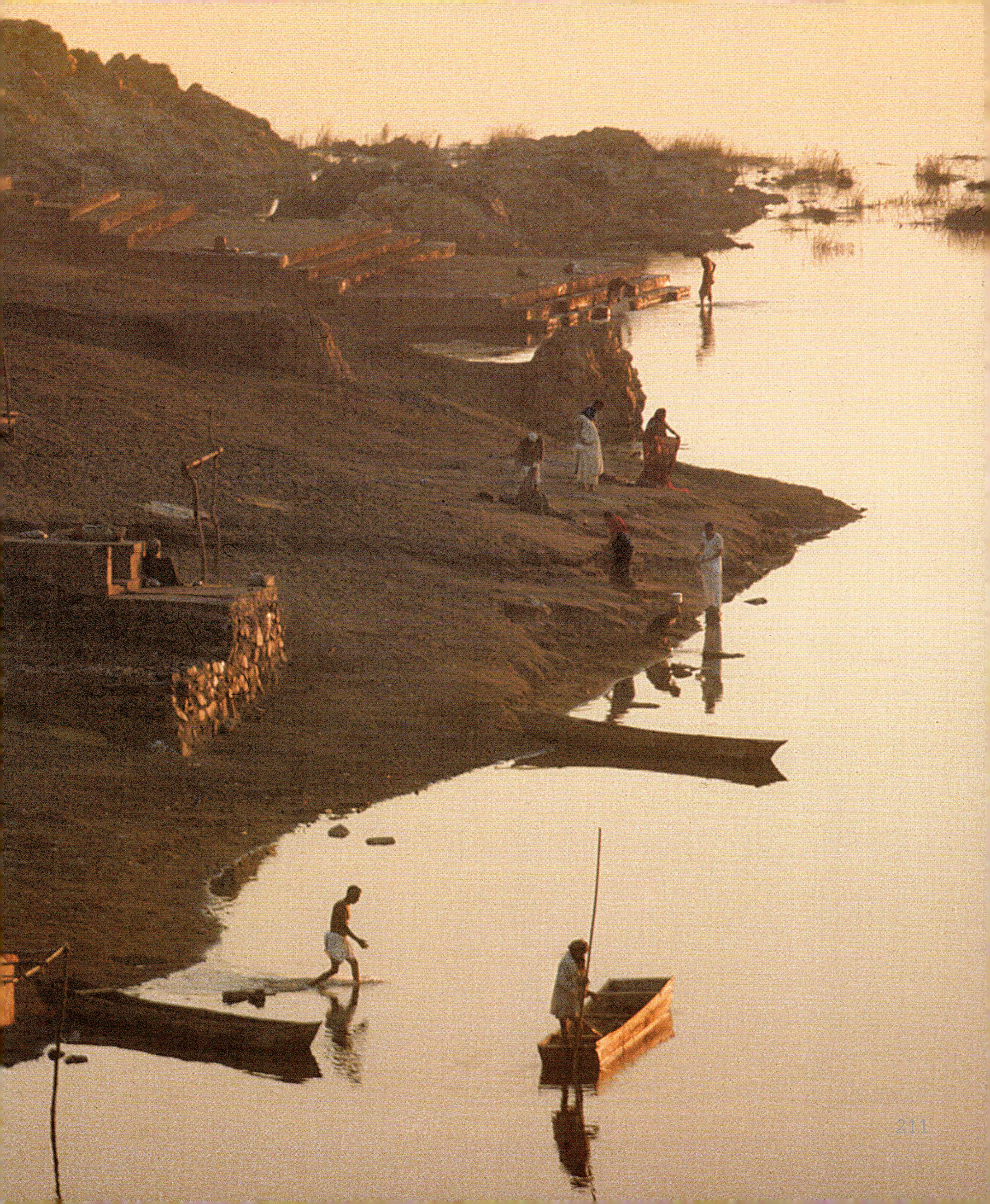

*And truly, the whole of India seems to be represented here. I note the presence of
all shades of complexion, all costumes, and all types, from the dark-brown Tamil
to the fair-complexioned Kashmiri, from the proud Rajput to the* sannyasin,
*whose hair is as matted as felt. Languages and dialects resonate in a hubbub; they
exhibit a hundred different facial expressions, caste stands cheek by jowl with
caste and prejudice stands shoulder to shoulder with prejudice. My eyes have
never witnessed such diversity among men.*

Hermann de Keyserling, *Journal of a Voyage of a Philosopher*, 1919

*Let us combine the apparent substance of white bread, milk, talcum powder, and
water, mix them together, and create out of them an excessive mausoleum, create a
gaping and formidable gateway, wide enough for a squadron of cavalry, but through
which only one coffin will ever enter. Do not forgot those utterly useless marble-lat-
ticed windows (because the material of which the building has been erected is an
extremely fragile, exquisite marble that looks as if it were suffering and made for the
swiftest dissolution, and that it would dissolve that very evening in the rain, but
which has remained intact and virginal for three centuries, with its irritating and
disturbing structure like something created by a young girl). Do not forget the point-
less marble windows at which the so intensely missed wife, the wife missed by the
Great Moghul, Shah Jahan, could come to cool herself in the evening.*

*Despite its rigorous, purely geometrical decoration, the Taj Mahal floats. The
bottom of the door is like a wave. In the cupola, the huge cupola, there is a super-
fluous nothing, a nothing that everyone feels, there is something sad about it.
Everywhere, there is the same sense of unreality. For this white is unreal, it is
weightless, it is not solid. False under the sun. False in the moonlight, a sort of
silver fish built by a man who overreacted.*

Henri Michaux, *A Barbarian in Asia*, 1933

Opposite: Temple servant, Nathdwara, Rajasthan.
Pages 210-211: The banks of the Narmada, Madhya Pradesh.

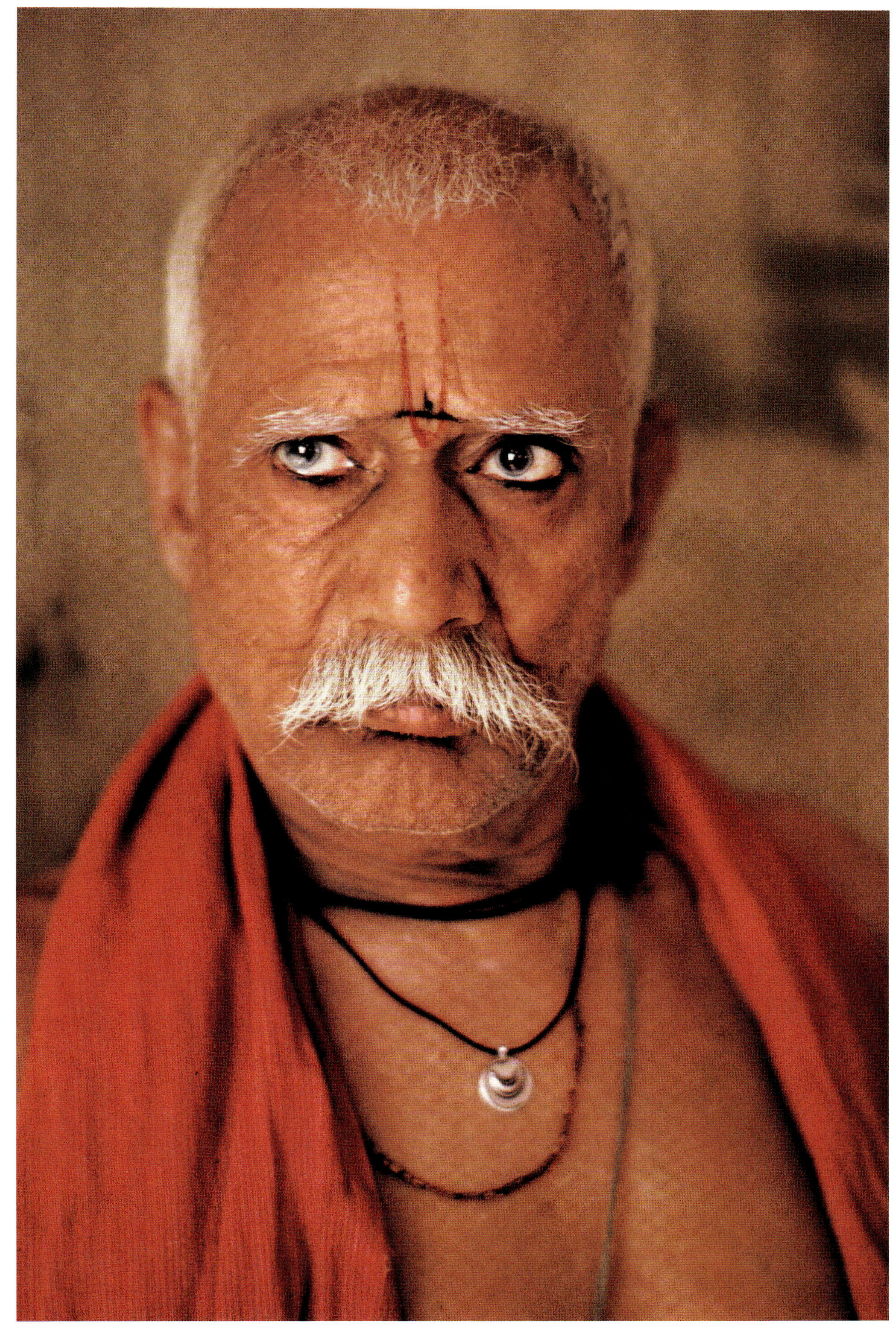

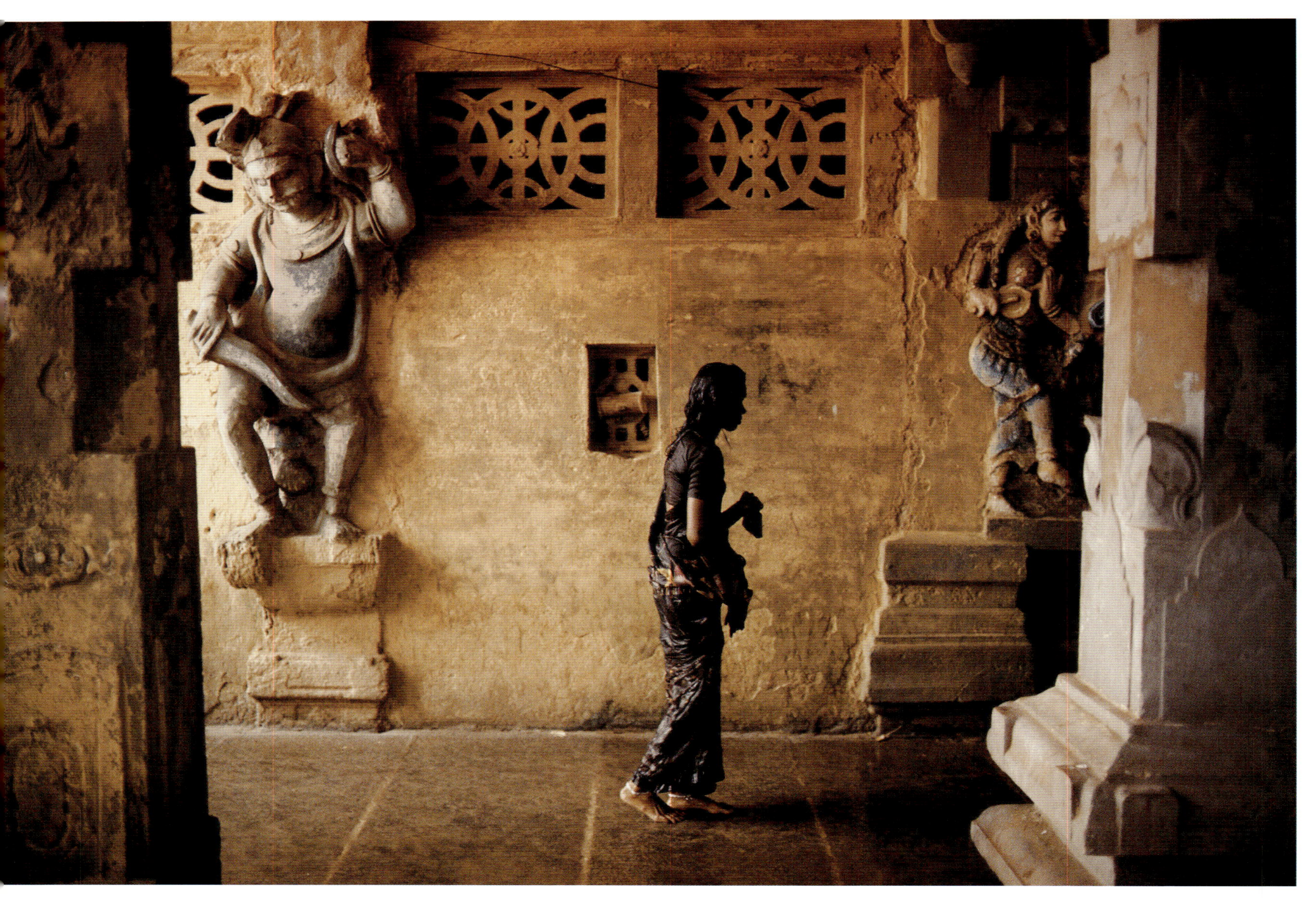

Temple of Rameshwaram on the Coromandel coast.

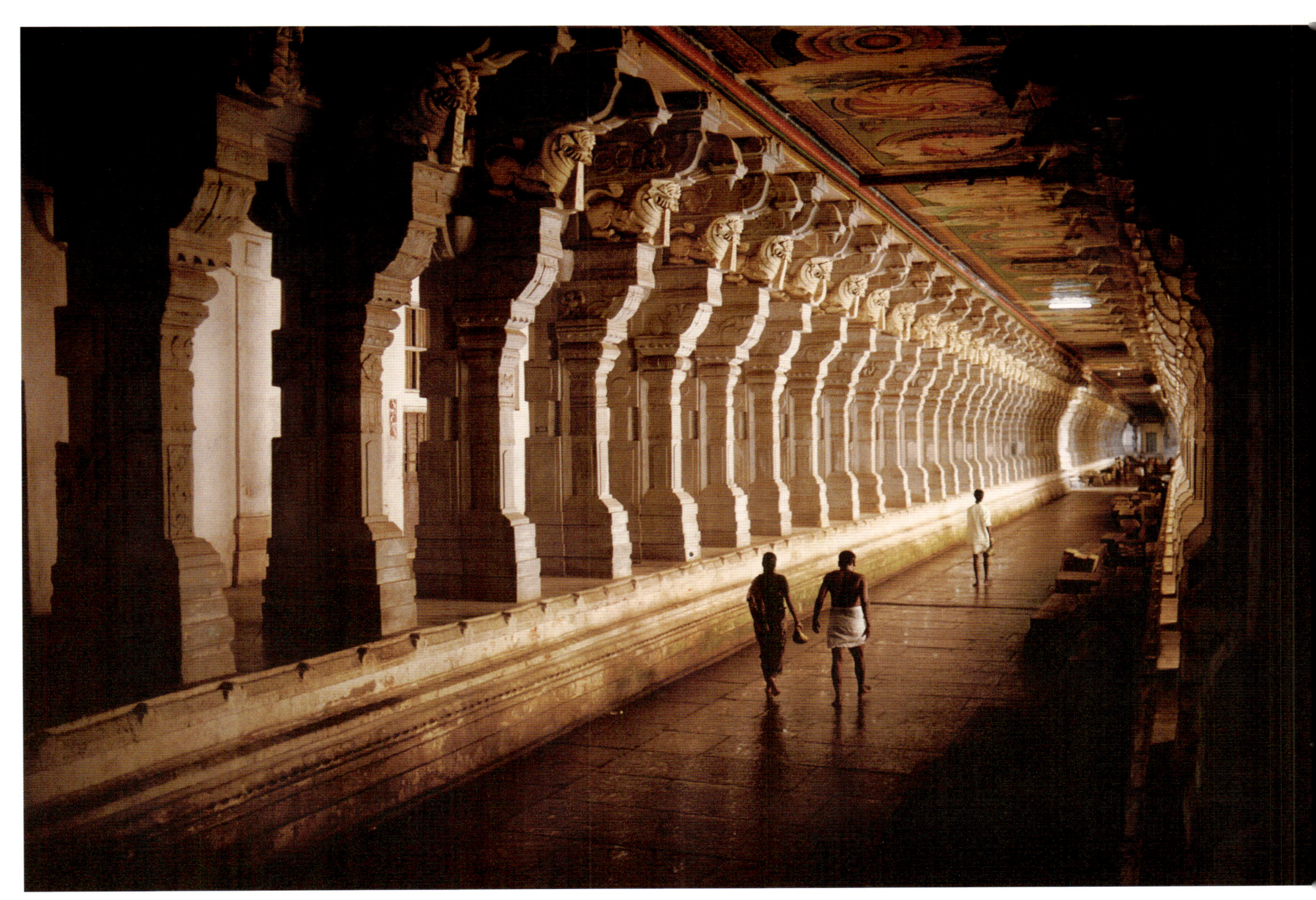

How cold the air was. Moravia and I instinctively moved closer to the burning pyre and as we drew nearer we soon felt the pleasant sensation that comes from warming oneself by a fire, in winter, our limbs frozen to the bone, happy to be there, amid a group of casual acquaintances, whose faces and rags were placidly mottled by a flame that was laboriously dying.

Thus comforted by the warmth, we stared more closely at those poor corpses who were being consumed without bothering anyone. Never, nowhere else, and at no time, in no act, throughout our stay in India, did we experience such a profound feeling of communion, of tranquility, and, almost, of joy.

Pier Paolo Pasolini, *The Odor of India*, 1961

In Madur, the sky was reflected in all the dark, water-filled, green-flecked holes of the ritual pools, three white flowers before an invisible divinity, a black Kali covered in partially bloodstained drapery, the odor of corruption masked by the heavy perfume of tuberoses, the oily, black brilliance of the galleries polished by human sweat and the passage of animals, of people walking by, silhouetted against the flaming lattices or lost in the obscurity. I discovered that our cathedrals are peopled with immobile Christians. I wandered through the endless galleries of this cathedral without a nave, whose nine towers rose unexpectedly, bombarded by swallows under the solemn flight of eagles. This architecture governed by so much severity, whose planes had been fixed by geomancers, seemed to be an epic chaos. The statues on its towers, in the caverns of its galleries, were of no more importance than the promenaders. Monkeys, as if being pulled by elastic, accompanied us and left us by turns. As I passed in front a bloodstained Durga, a black cat dropped from his shoulder and slowly walked into the shadows, under the rearing cavalry of divine horses, as if it had been the secret of the universe.

Andre Malraux, *Antimémoires*, 1967

For generations, the traders of Mahadeo have earned a living from the pilgrimage to Narmada, measuring piety against credulousness; I am amused to see them sitting cross-legged in little booths lit by kerosene lamps, supplying pilgrims with all their requirements, and persuading them to buy many items they do not need: another box of incense, the most expensive kind, and a few strips of saffron cloth, and a lucky stone, the most expensive one. And then, of course, at least a dozen clay lamps, isn't it?

I am always delayed by my fascination with these explosions of energy, and it is usually late by the time I reach the stone steps that extend the length of the thirty temples huddled tightly together along the shore.

These twenty or so low steps, that lead to the forecourts of the temple beside the river waters invite a whole world of human activity, like a bazaar. Beggars and holy men. Priests showing the faithful how to perform their act of submission to the river. Astrologers and fortune-tellers. Peddlers with baskets of marigolds to offer to the idols, or paintings on glass representing the gods, to keep as souvenirs. Women drying their saris after the ritual bath on stone steps that are still warm from the sun. Pilgrims pouring oil into the clay lamps that they will float on the river.

Above the steps, the temples rise like a city, their forecourts crowded with whole families who enter through the sculpted stone porches to make their offerings to the idols, and ring the temple bells as they leave, holding their children in their arms so that they can move the clapper. They descend into the darkness that still resounds to the ringing of the bell, to place food before the beggars and holy men sitting on the steps.

Gita Mehta, *Narmada Sutra*, 1993

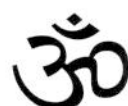

A Bombay shanty-town

I am walking amidst the *cloaca*, where the rejects of society linger far from sight. There are huts made of cardboard, alleys glistening with urine, oil, and dung, children covered in buboes ferreting in piles of reeking garbage. O wonderful progress! The dry lips of a suckling clinging to a furrowed breast, rats, menacing crows, flies, sewers, gutters, an old man so languid he does not even have the strength to die, pustules, laughter, teenage goddesses with apprehensive eyes. The worst thing about it is that they seem happy.

Why is that the worst? Their childhood, intelligence, movement has been stolen from them. All that is left to them is expectations, hunger, and innocence.

Can I continue to wander among them? Some of them see me passing as a hope, others look on me with fear. Only the toddlers throw themselves at my legs without seeing the difference. A strident cry rises from the depths of a hovel. Is it the throes of birth or death? I fall to my knees. Seeing how pale I look, a woman offers me a glass of water. I continue on. Between two areas, there runs a stream whose waters are as black as the skin of the children paddling in it. A child covered in sores is fighting with a dog. I sit down. A young man hones a knife intended for me. I wait. He approaches the children who are now still, waiting expectantly. I offer him a cigarette. He accepts it and sits down beside me. That's all.

As I leave the shanty-town a young girl follows me, her little brother in a sling on her back. She makes a gesture that is typical of India. She puts her little hand to her mouth and to the baby's mouth, then extends it to me, while murmuring. She will not let me go. An albino sitting in the dirt laughs. Here is a wide avenue with buses running along it. The little girl tries to hold me back by my shirt. Is that all?

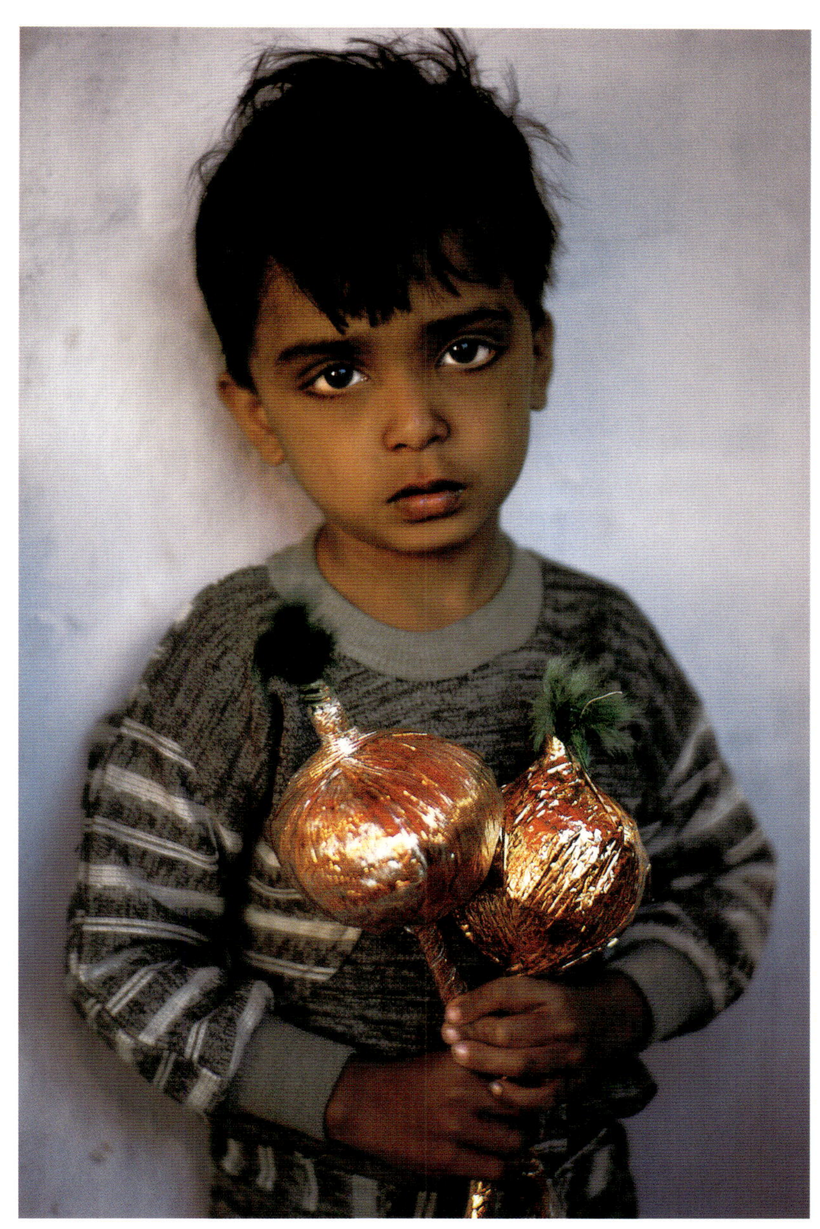

Young boy, Girnar, Gujarat.

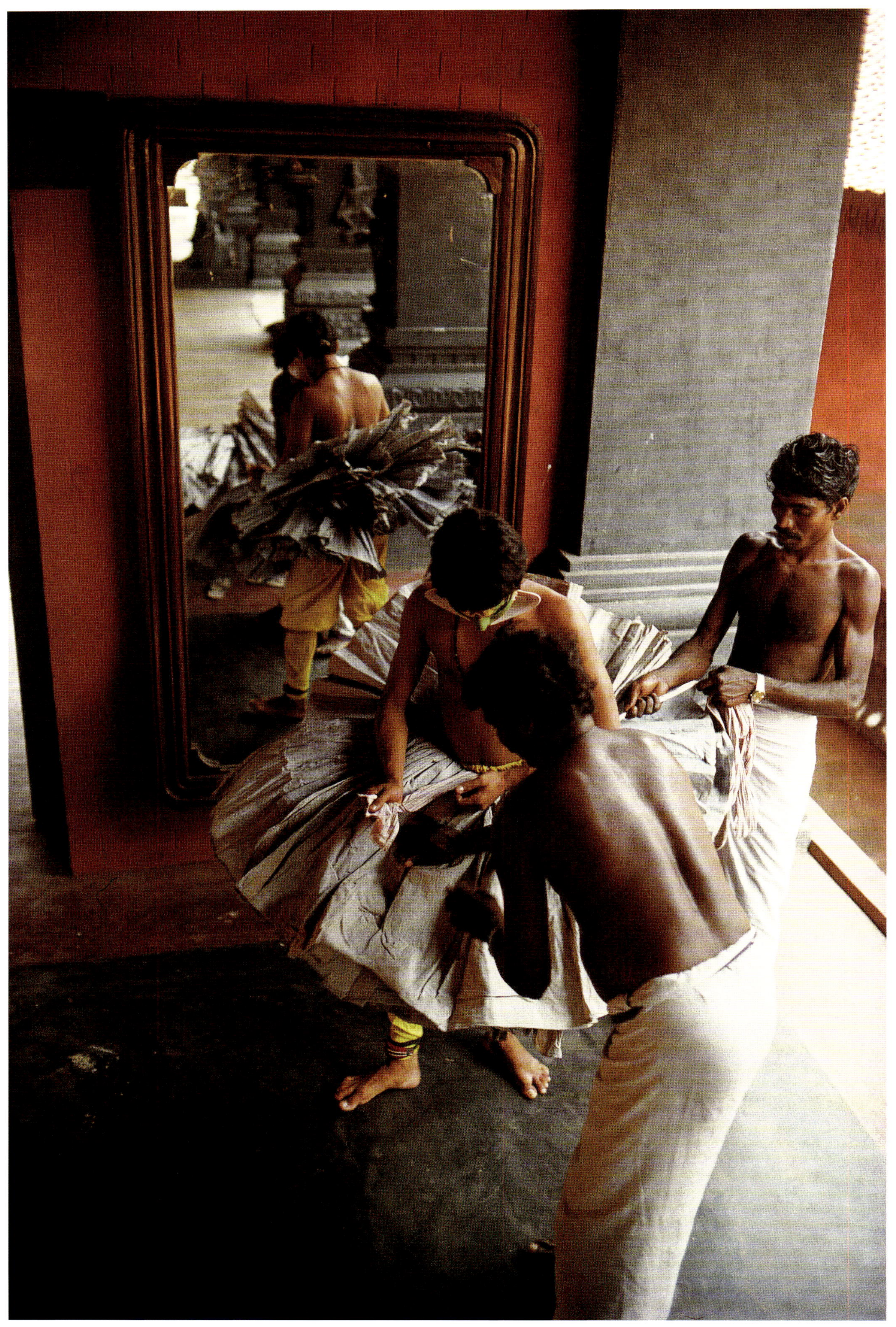

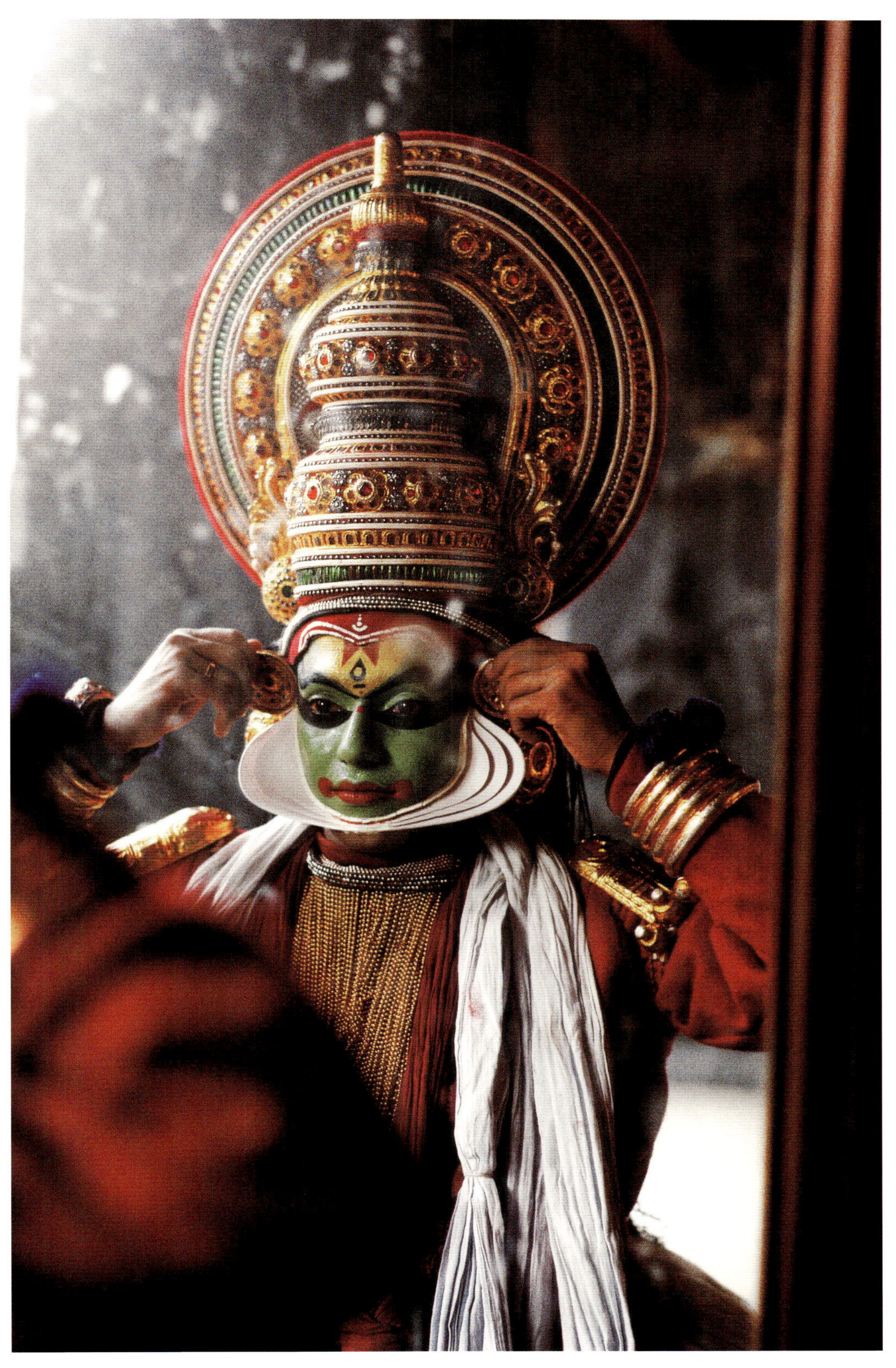

Above and Opposite: Preparing for Kathakali, Kerala.
Pages 222–223: The Kathakali ceremony, Kerala.

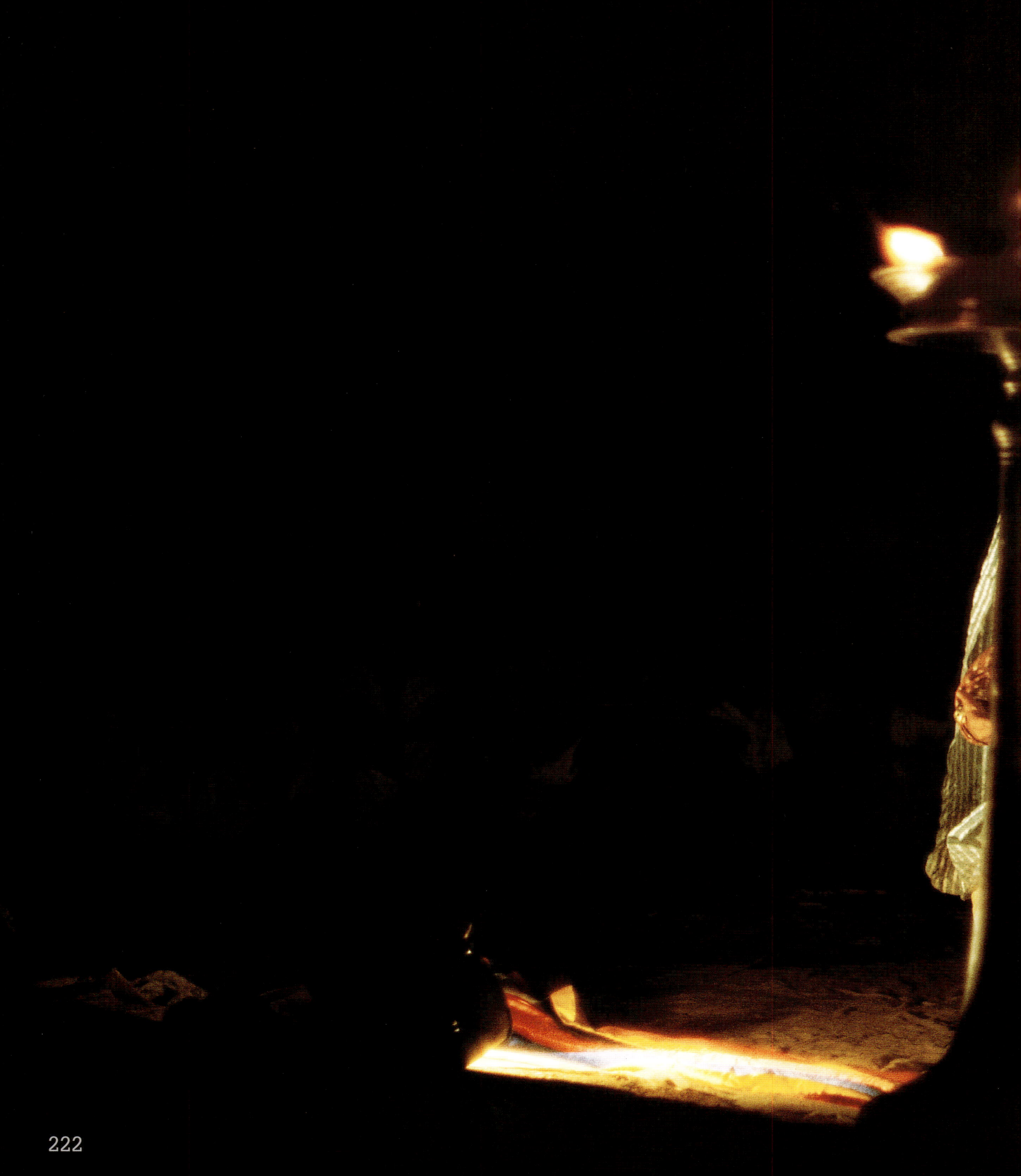

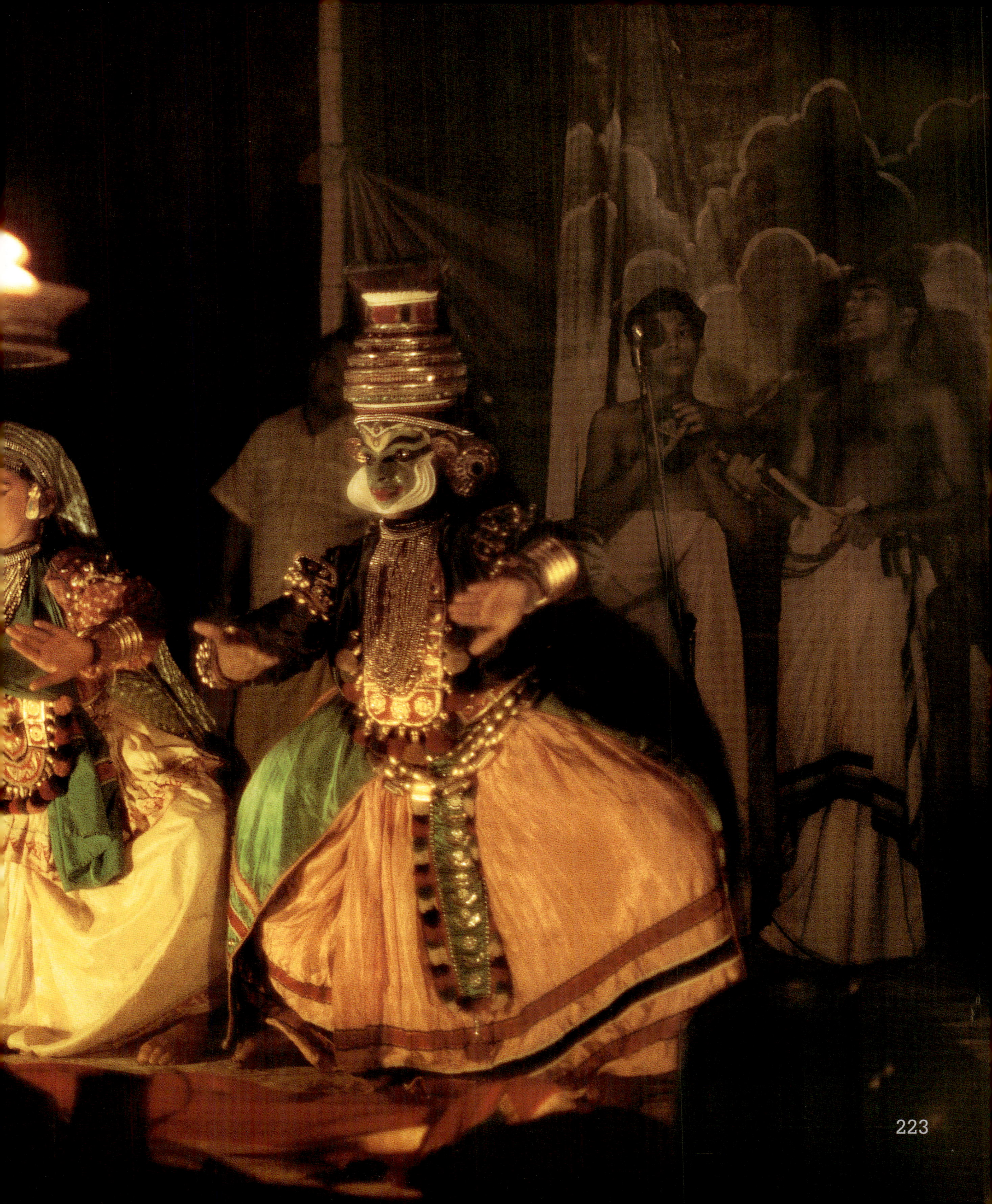

Dravidian women

our southern states—Karnataka, Andhra Pradesh, Kerala, and Tamil Nadu—
speak the so-called Dravidian languages. These do not belong to the same family
as the Indo-European languages spoken everywhere else in India (with the
exception of a few Sino-Tibetan languages in the Himalayas). The Dravidian
states represent 23 percent of the area of the union. The Aryans, like most of the
other conquerors, came down from the Afghan plateaus and moved southward,
and it is in southern India today that the earliest stages of Indian culture are best
preserved. Southern India also differs from the rest of the country in its tropical
climate, luxuriant lowland landscapes, greater wealth, less Muslim influence,
and distinctive architecture, sculpture, music, and dance. Its royal dynasties
were independent of the northern kingdoms. Karnataka is the birthplace of Carnatic music and Kerala is the home of the Kathakali dance, drama, and the less
well-known *kalarippayat*, a martial art that is the forerunner of the martial arts
practiced in China and Japan that have now spread throughout the world.

In southern India the atmosphere is lighter, communication is easier, and the
women are more independent and self-sufficient. Both coasts have always been
open to the outside world, from which contact was peaceful at first. The Romans,
Jews, early Christians, and Arabs came to trade and were fascinated by the sensu-
ality of the place. Waves of conquerors arrived—the Portuguese, the Moguls, and
the British—although they wrought far less destruction here than in the north.

At Hampi, in southern India, the kingdom of Vijayanagar held out for longest
against the Muslim armies. This spirit of resistance, combined with a sense of
openness, is still typical of the Dravidian lands. The scenery includes the noisy,
milling crowds of the great sanctuaries of Tamil Nadu (the magic circle includes
Kanchipuram, Tiruvannamalai, Madurai, Rameshwaram, and Chidambaram), the
picture postcard views of the backwaters of Kerala, a demonstration of *kalarippayat*, the poetry in stone of the ruins of Hampi at Karnataka, the pearly illusions

built in the name of Buddhism in Andhra Pradesh at Nagarjunakonda and Amaravati, and the sound of an evening *raga* played in a temple in the central mountains.

What do they have in common: the crowds of shaven-headed Hindus of Tirumalai, the aborigines of the Gond tribes that live on either side of the Godavari River, the student *Brahmans* reciting the *Veda* backward at Sringeri, churchgoers attending mass at the Syriac (Nestorian) church at Kottayam, the dancers of Madras, the "golden boys" of Bangalore, the "Afghan" streets of Kurnool, the ecologists of Auroville, Jain devotees rushing towards the huge stone figure of a man at Shravanabelagola, and the beggars of Vijayavada? There is a palpable unity of place here even if it neither obvious nor logical. It is rather a certain impetus symbolized by the crowd of faces in the *gopurams* and the dancing movements of the human body in motion. The people of southern India are artists, they practice an art form that has been neglected by modernity, art is a part of daily life, in their gait, the way they arrange vegetables on a banana leaf on a *thali*, the way the fishermen cast their nets into the sea, in a smile, in a bunch of flowers in the hair, and even in the way they engage in unarmed combat.

The women of southern India have remained free. Their feminism has been allowed to blossom without restrictions, without being smothered by fearful males, without needing to ape the masculine. Few, if any, places in the world offer the image of a culture in which male and female get along together as if they continued to be enchanted, at a distance, with the act that is the origin of life.

Telugu country

I have already inferred that no land in the world is more fertile than this one. Remember that the vegetation here is continual, that nature is always in action, that the sun powerfully attracts the sap, that it uses all its strength to germinate seeds, that the abundant dew at night constantly renders the soil light and friable, with just the right degree of humidity, and it can be imagined that the fields are constantly covered in greenery or crowned with ears of grain, all the time and at every season; that the trees are loaded simultaneously with fruits and flowers.

Father M. Perrin, *Voyage dans l'Indostan,* 1777–85

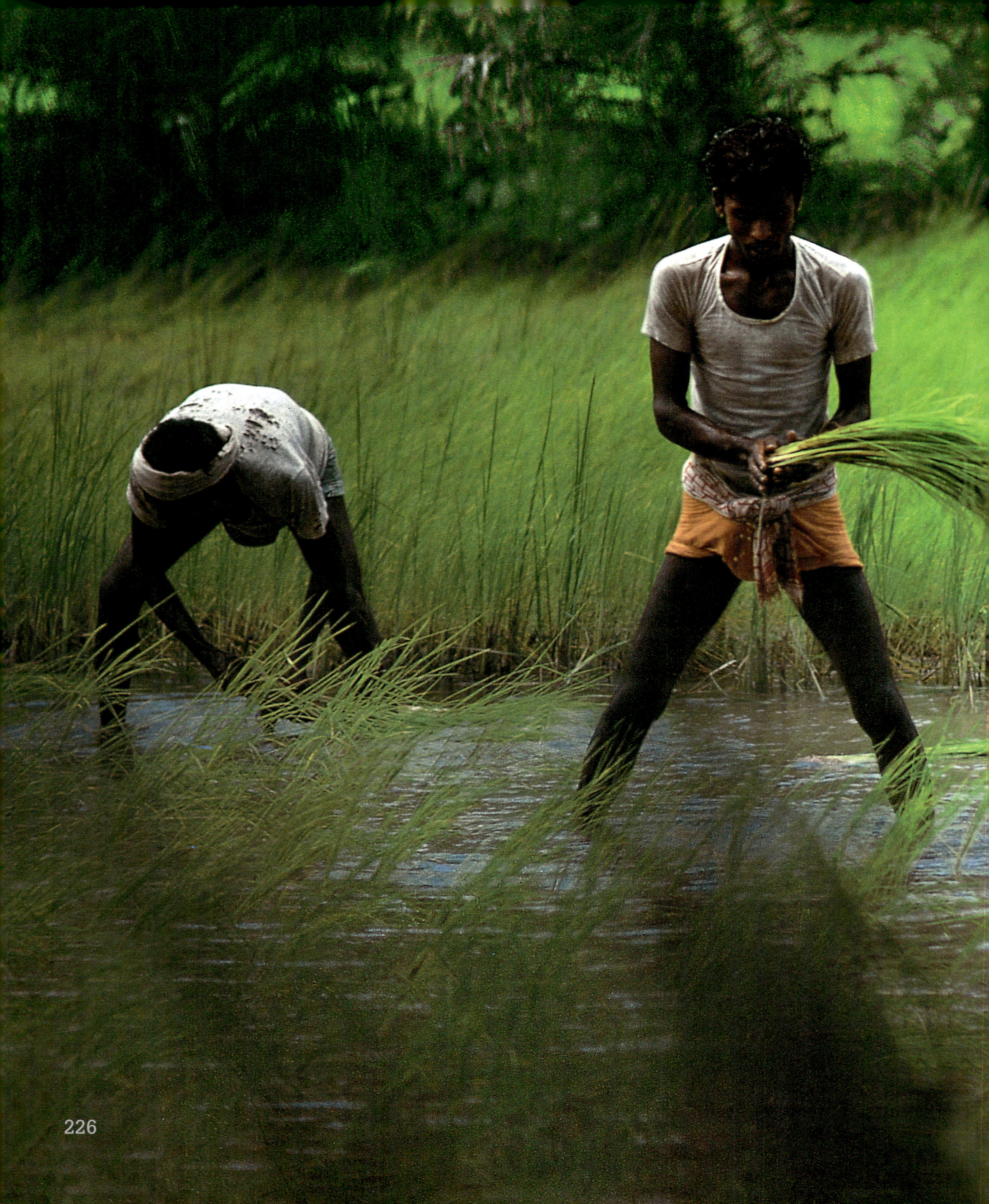

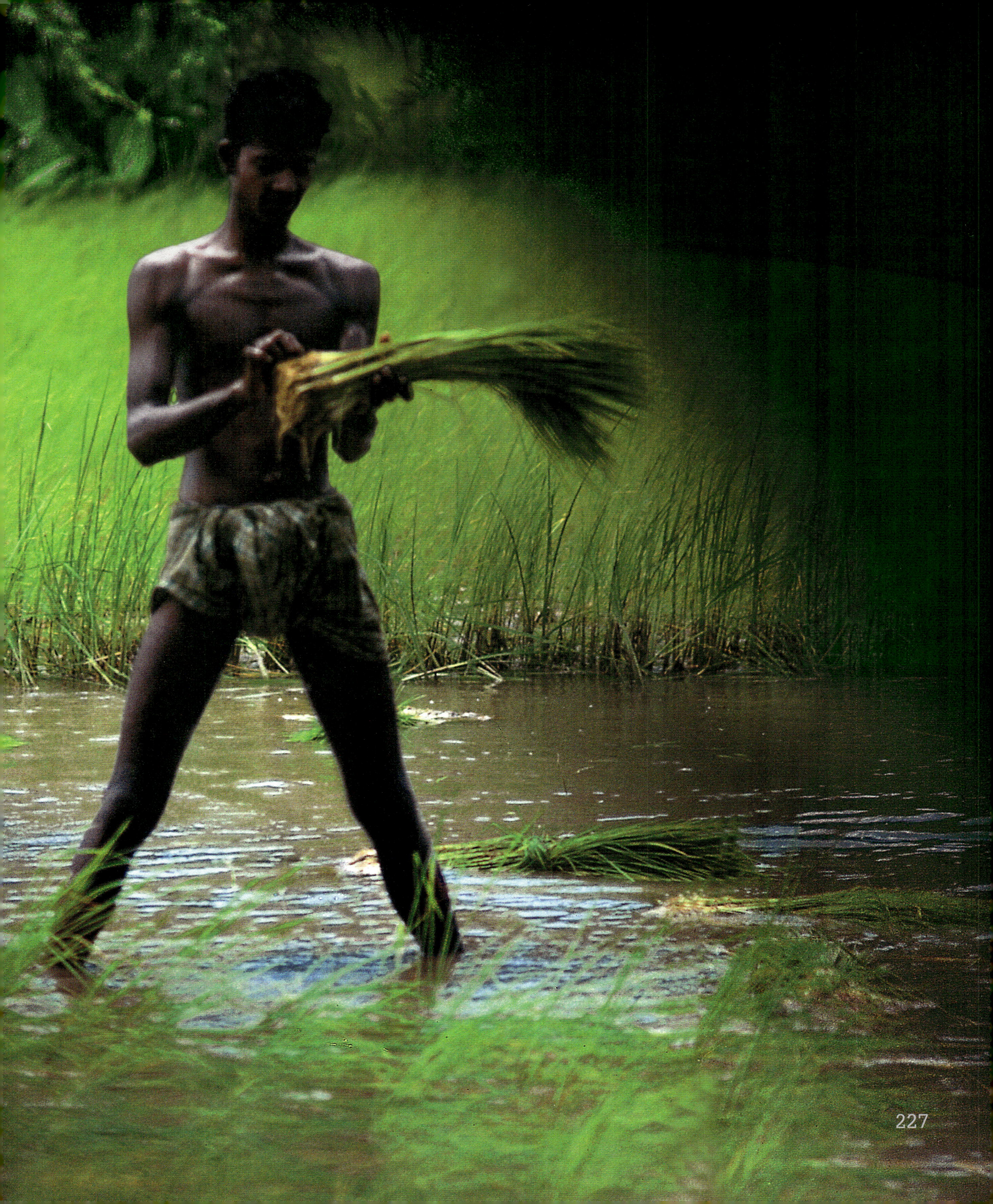

The multicolored temples of the South. Taking the bright colors and playful forms of Disneyland as a symbol of our time, the difference is that here there is also the metaphysical.

There is an engraving in the Tanjore museum representing the banks of the River Thames. The people wash themselves, sleep, and play there, wood and cattle are unloaded as on the rivers of India.

From a boat moving slowly along a canal between Quilon and Alleppey, tourists throw candy and ballpoint pens at the children on the banks as if they were apes. But who is aping whom?

At Rameshwaram, a temple beside the sea, the devotees take a ritual bath at the moment the sun rises from the water in the direction of Sri Lanka. I do not see the gods, but I hear the faint vibration at the same pitch of prayers and the world.

The forests of the Nilgiri. What substance, what principle, what subterranean arrangement has caused the stems of these yellow, indigo, carmine, orange, crimson, and (sometimes) blue flowers to emerge and shine more violently among the disorder of leaves, rings on the fingers of the jungle?

I do not weep because the children of Madras only have an old carousel to play with whose animals are broken and the bars twisted; I weep because our own children are indifferent to bright new carousels.

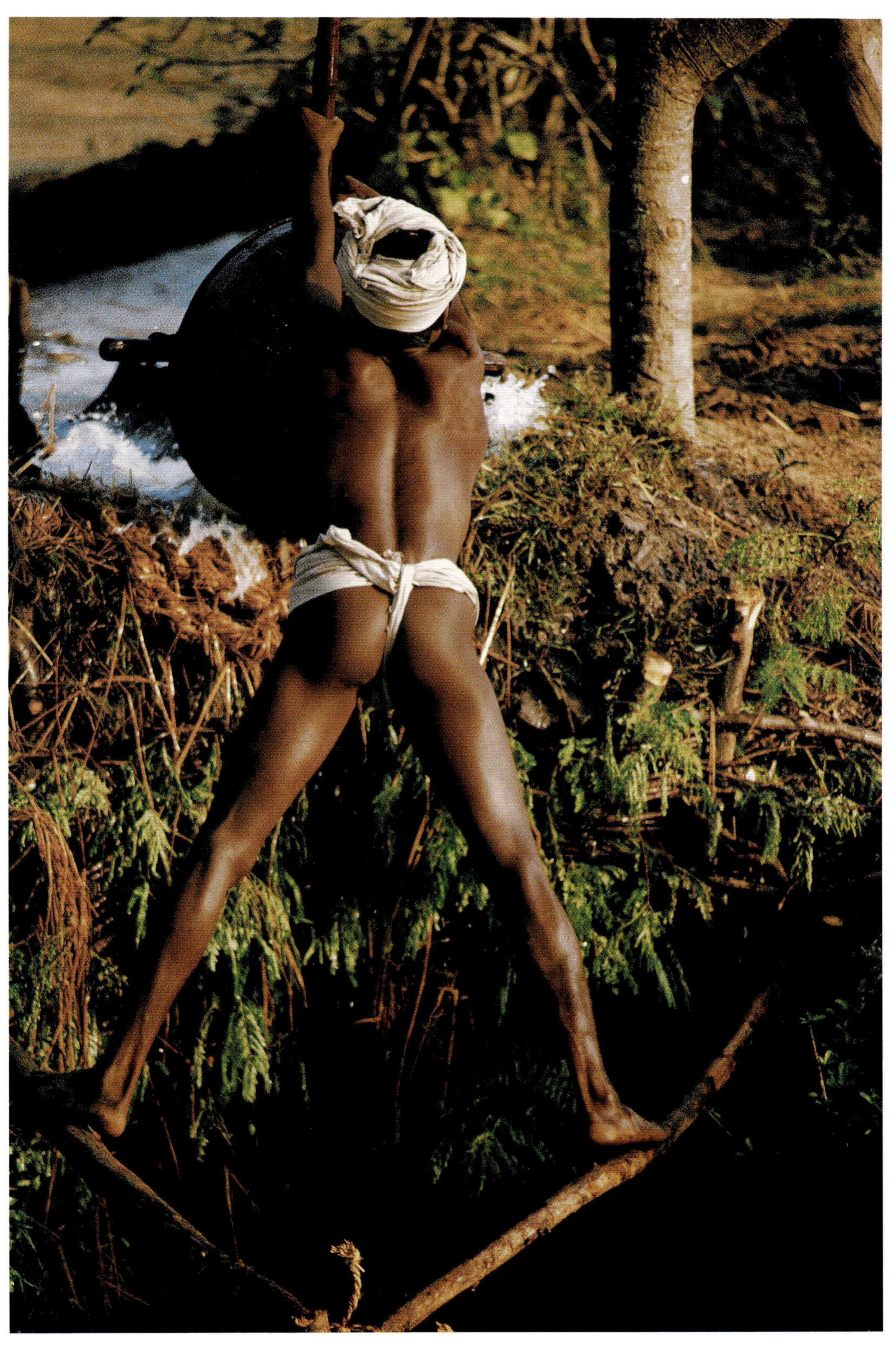

Above: Irrigation system, Kerala.
Pages 230–231: the backwaters of Kerala.

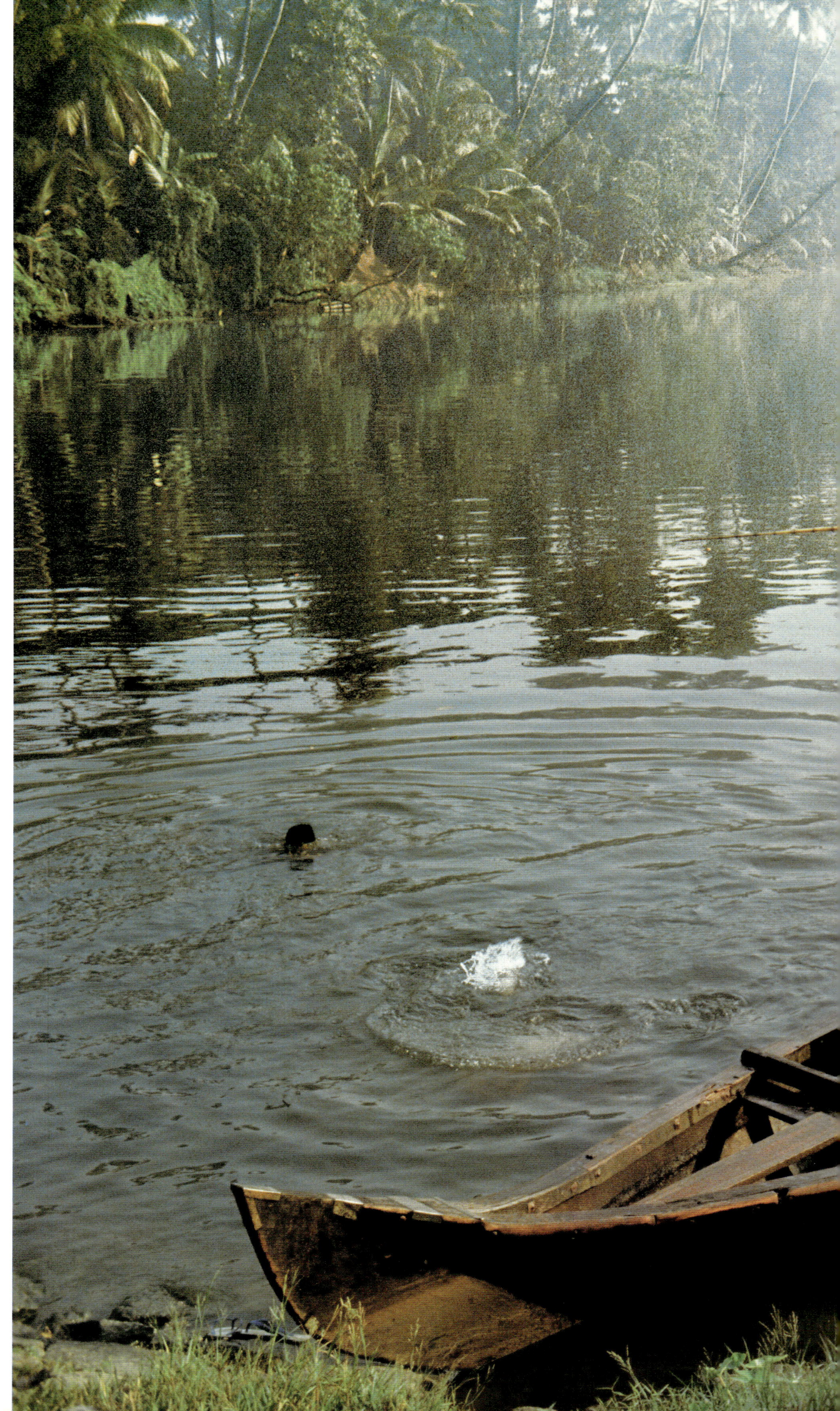

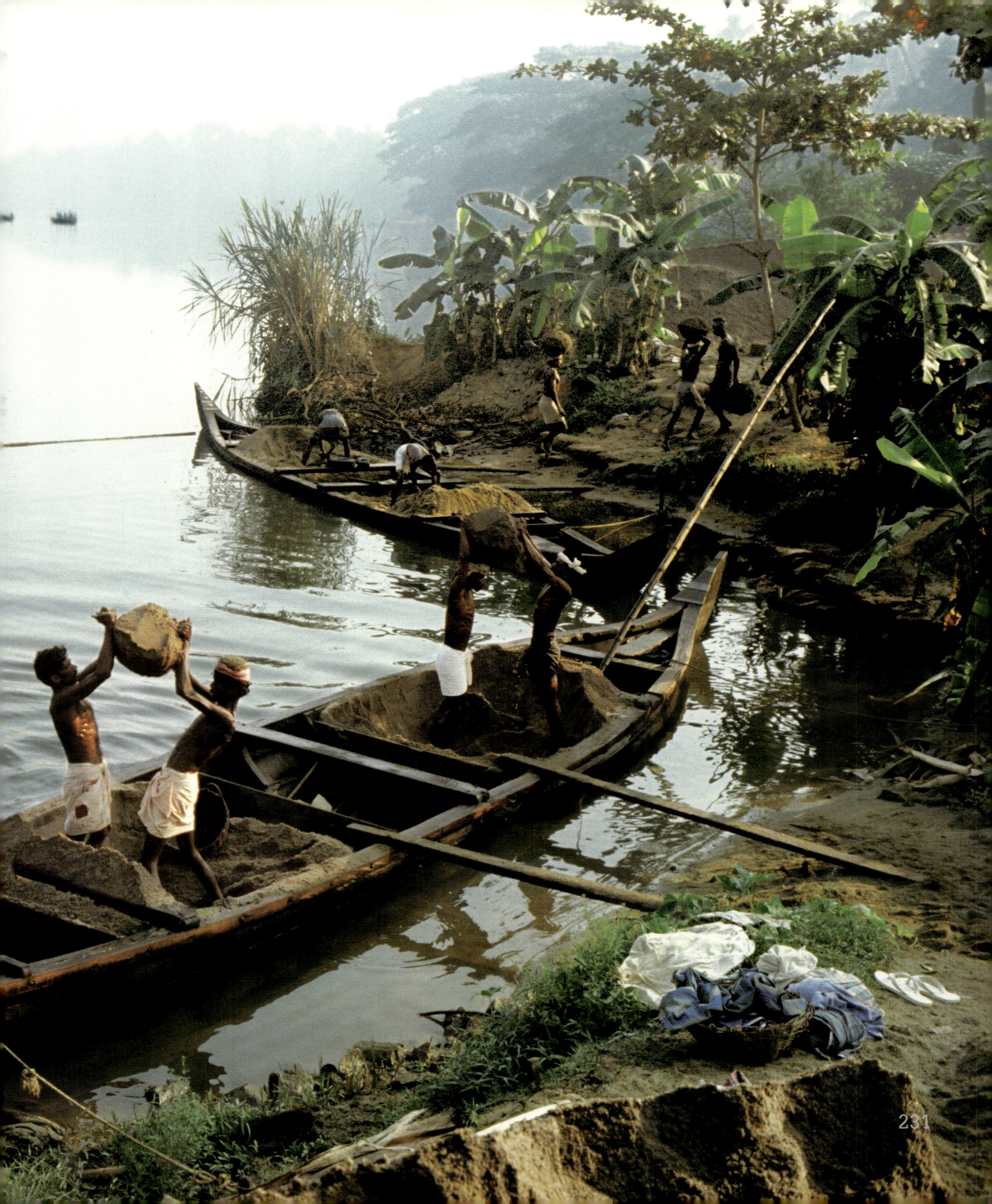

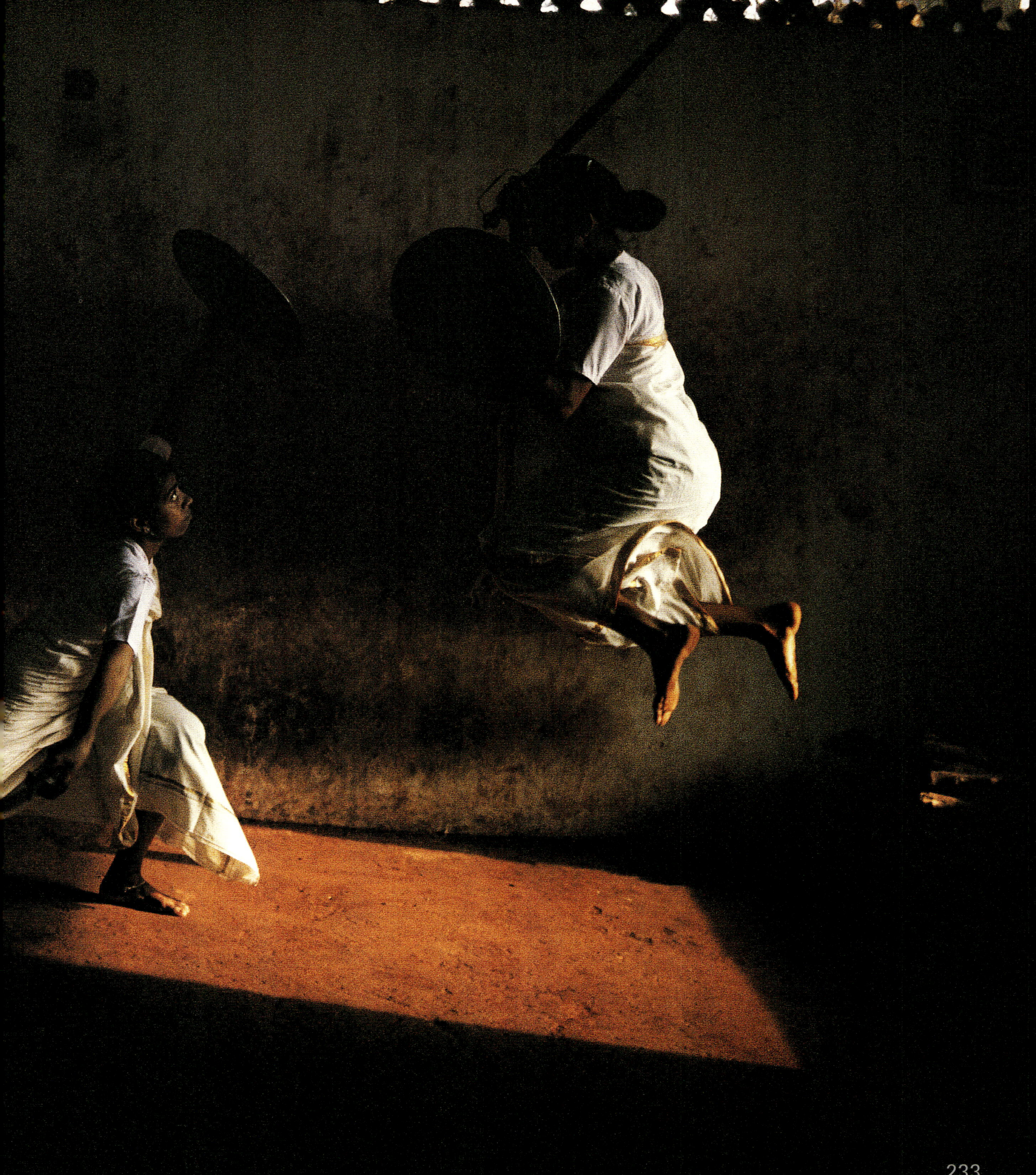

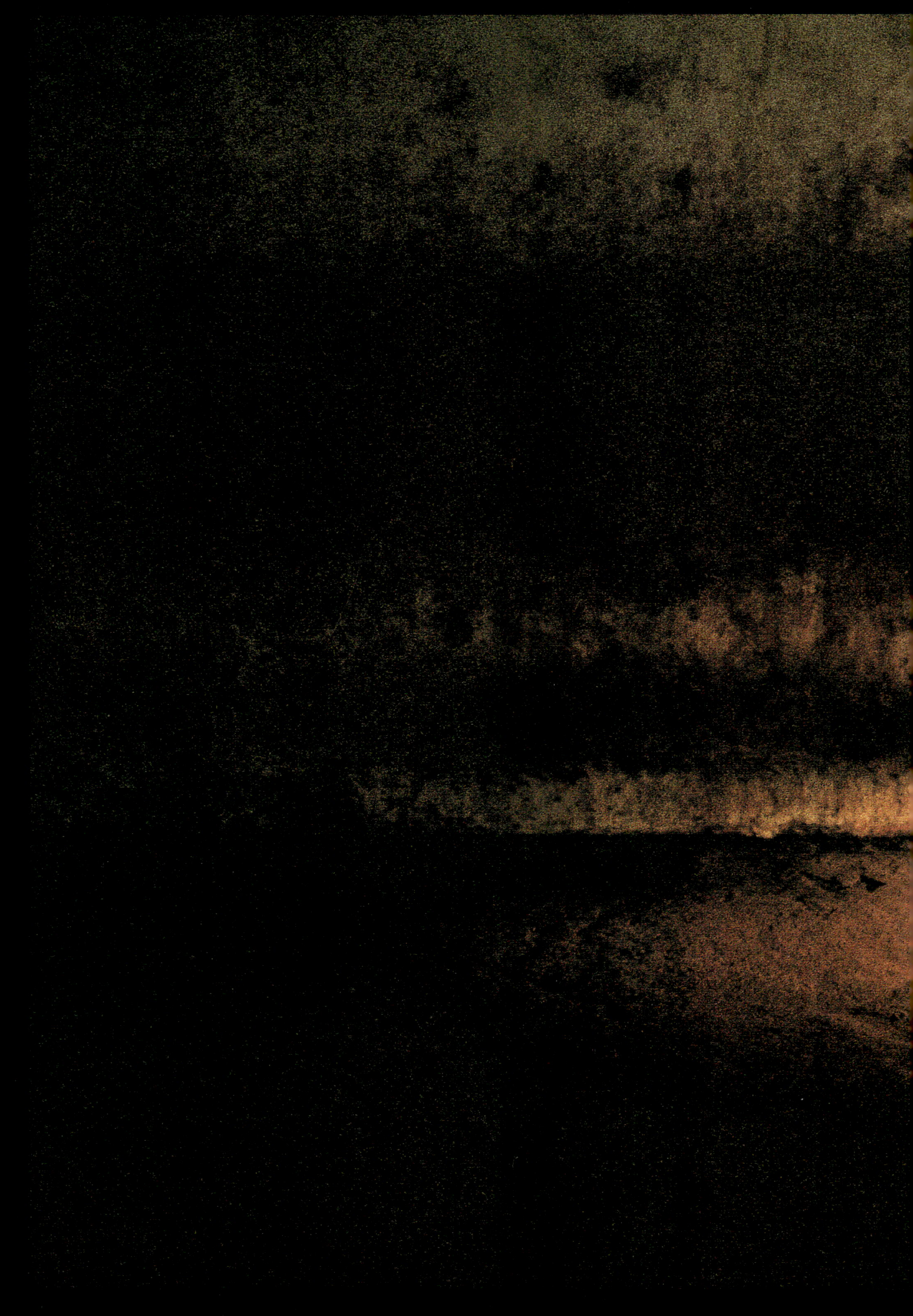

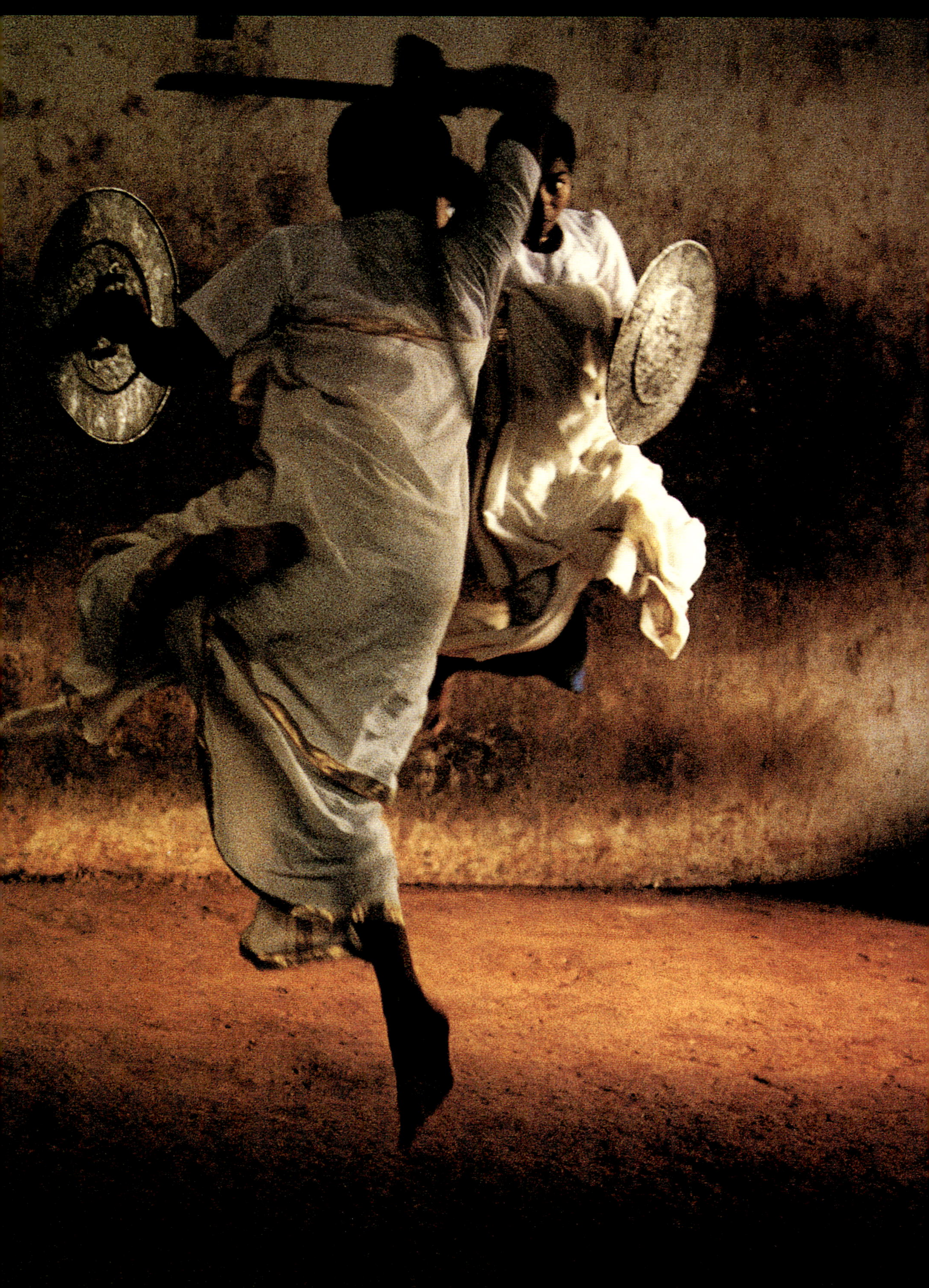

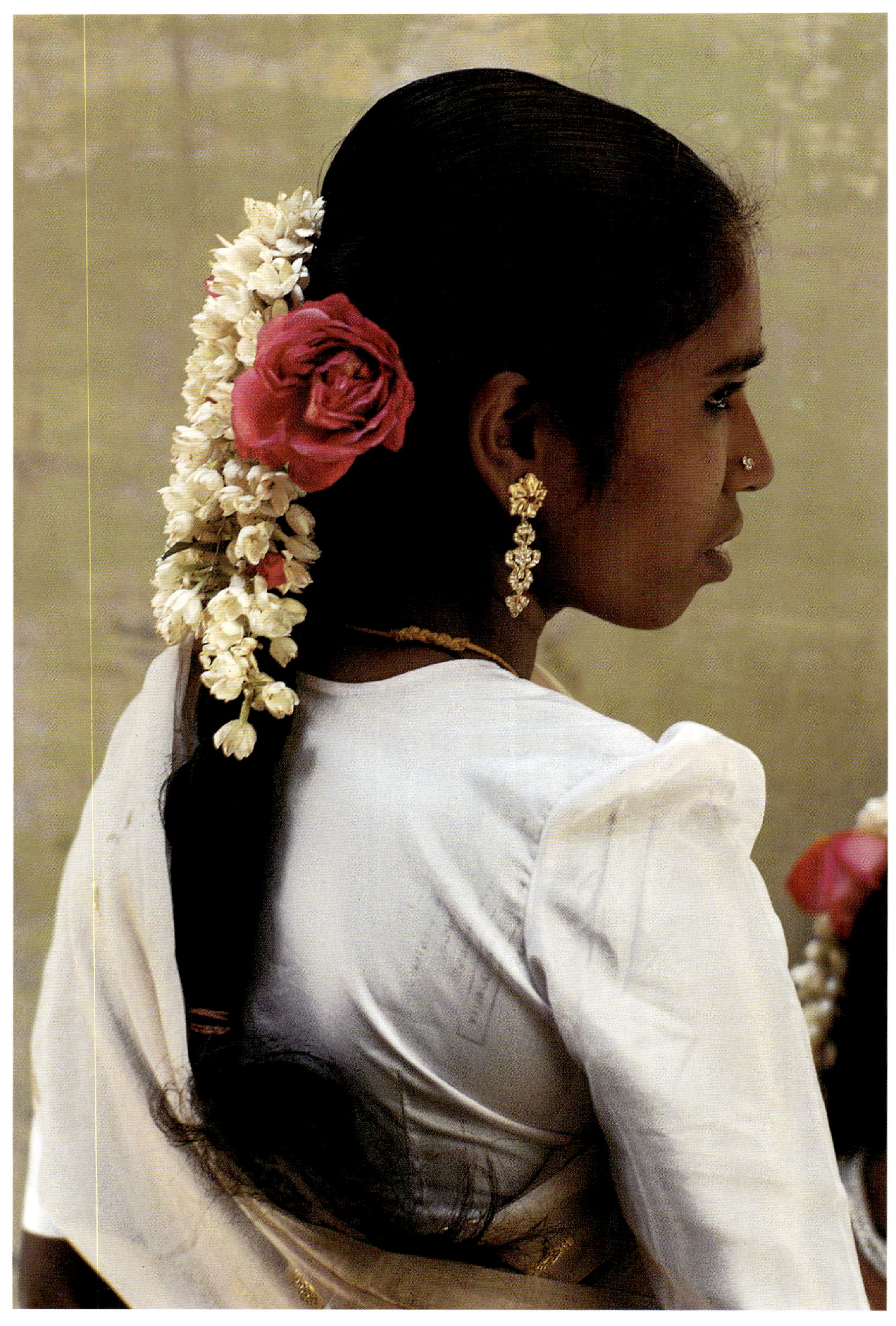

Above and Opposite: South Indian woman, Karnataka.
Pages 232–235: Martial arts in Kerala.
Pages 238–239: The backwaters of Kerala.

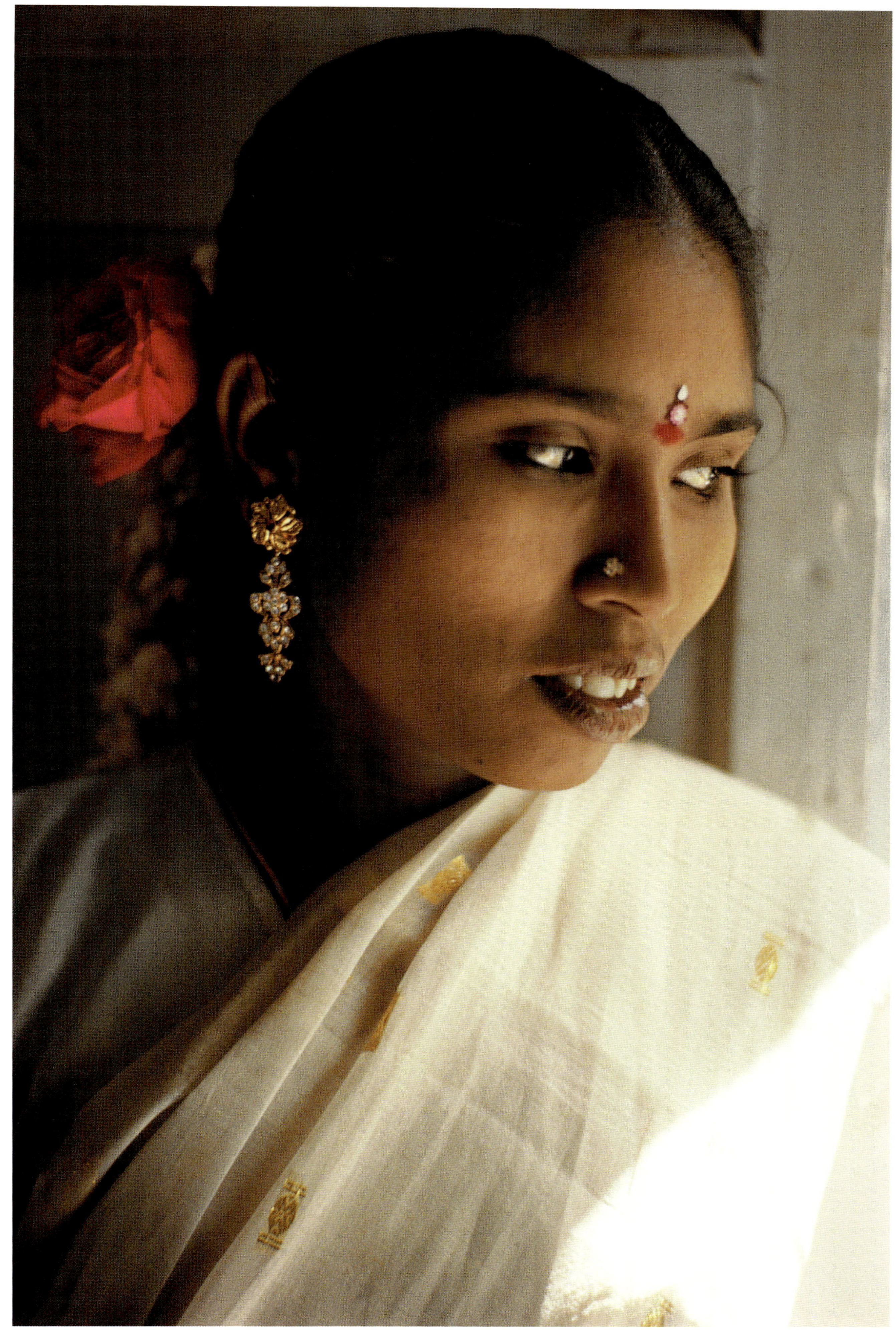

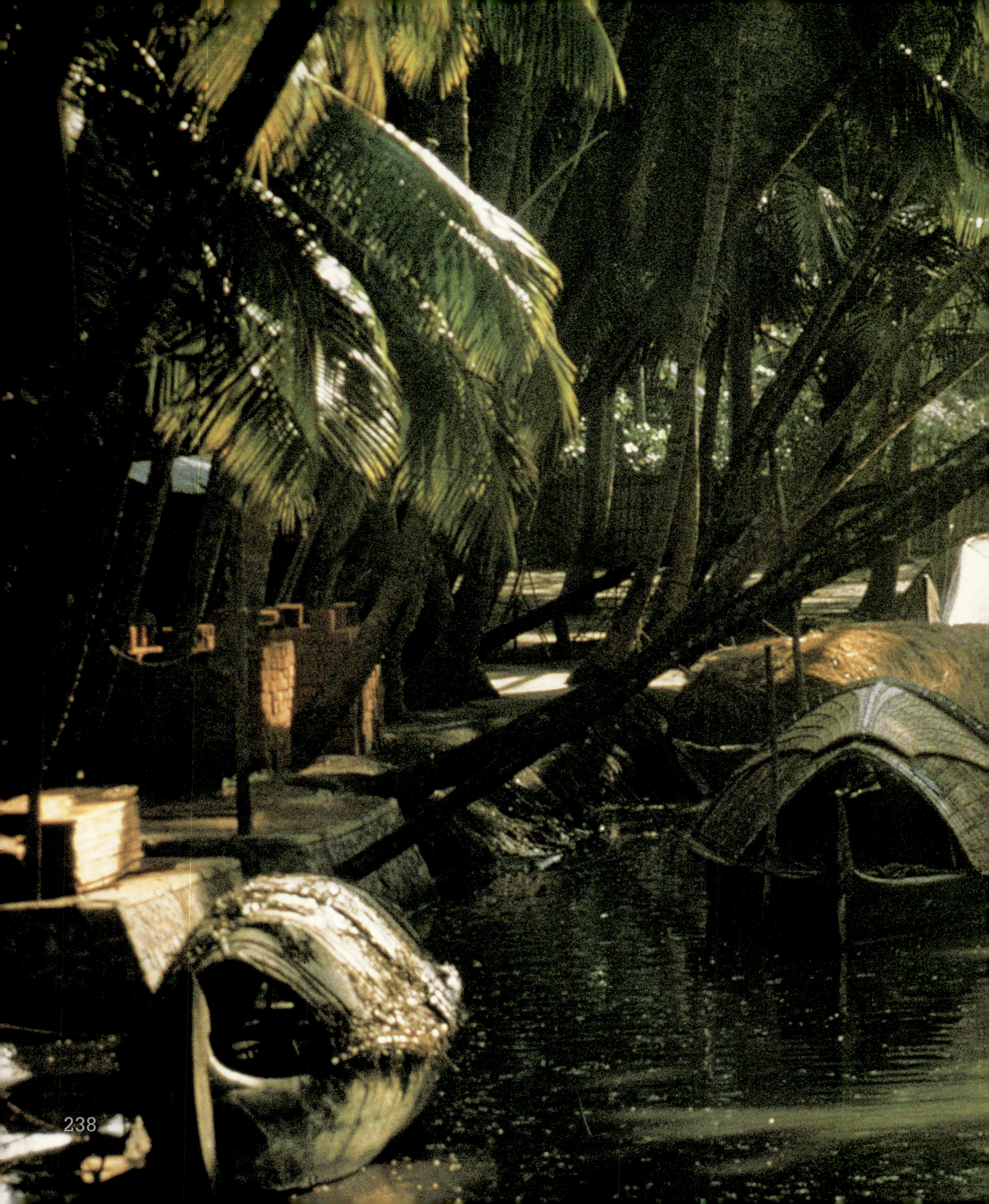

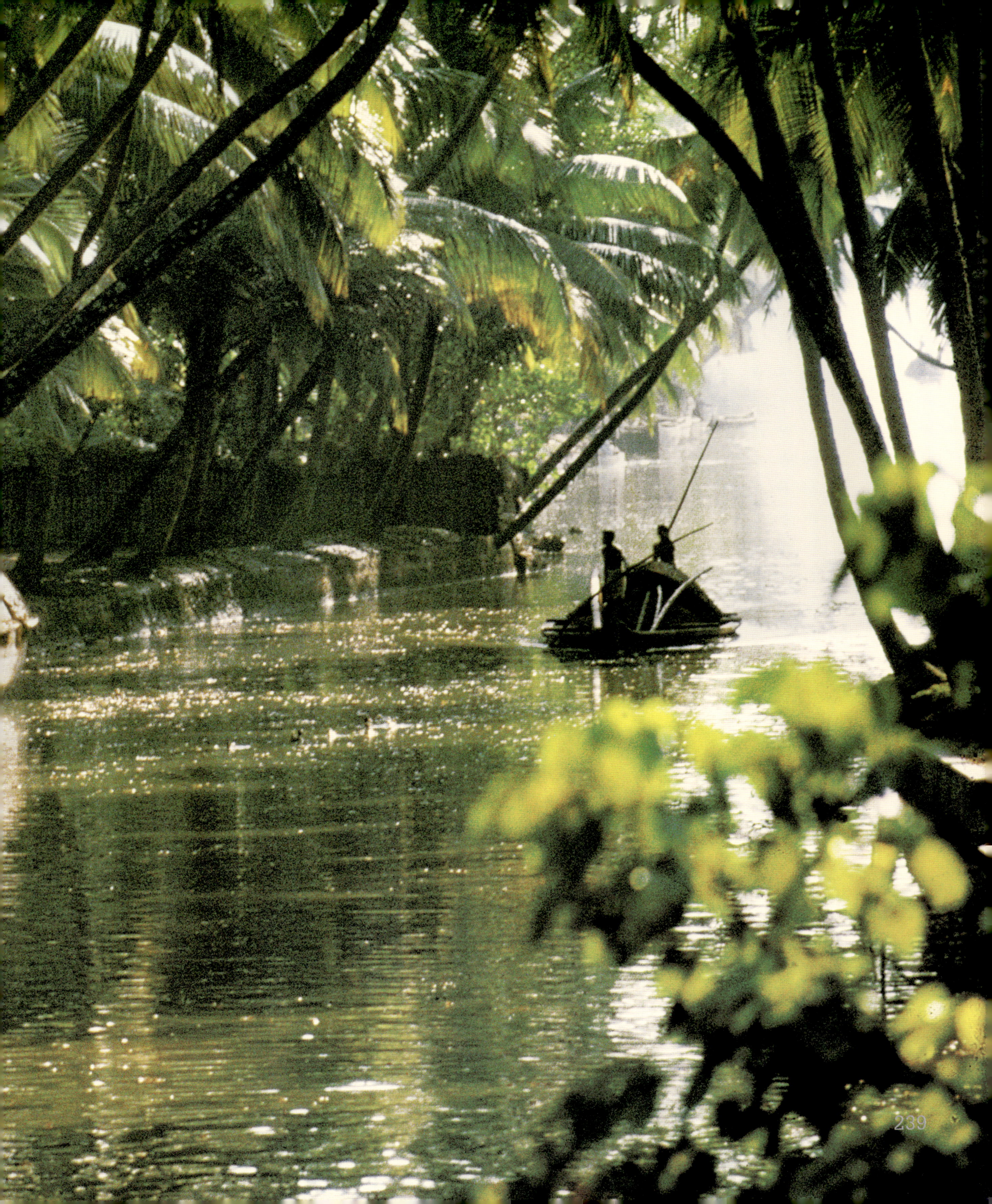

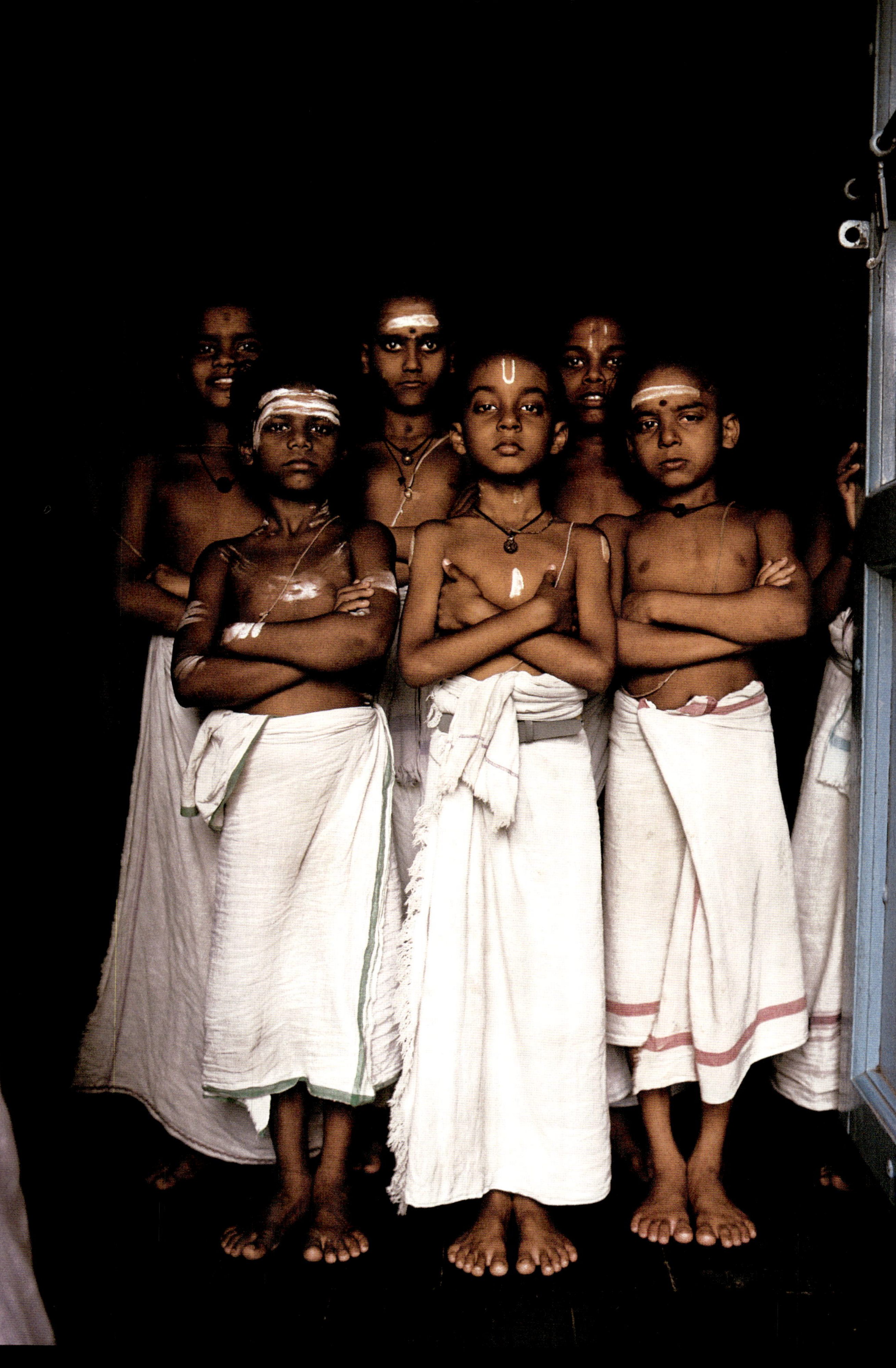

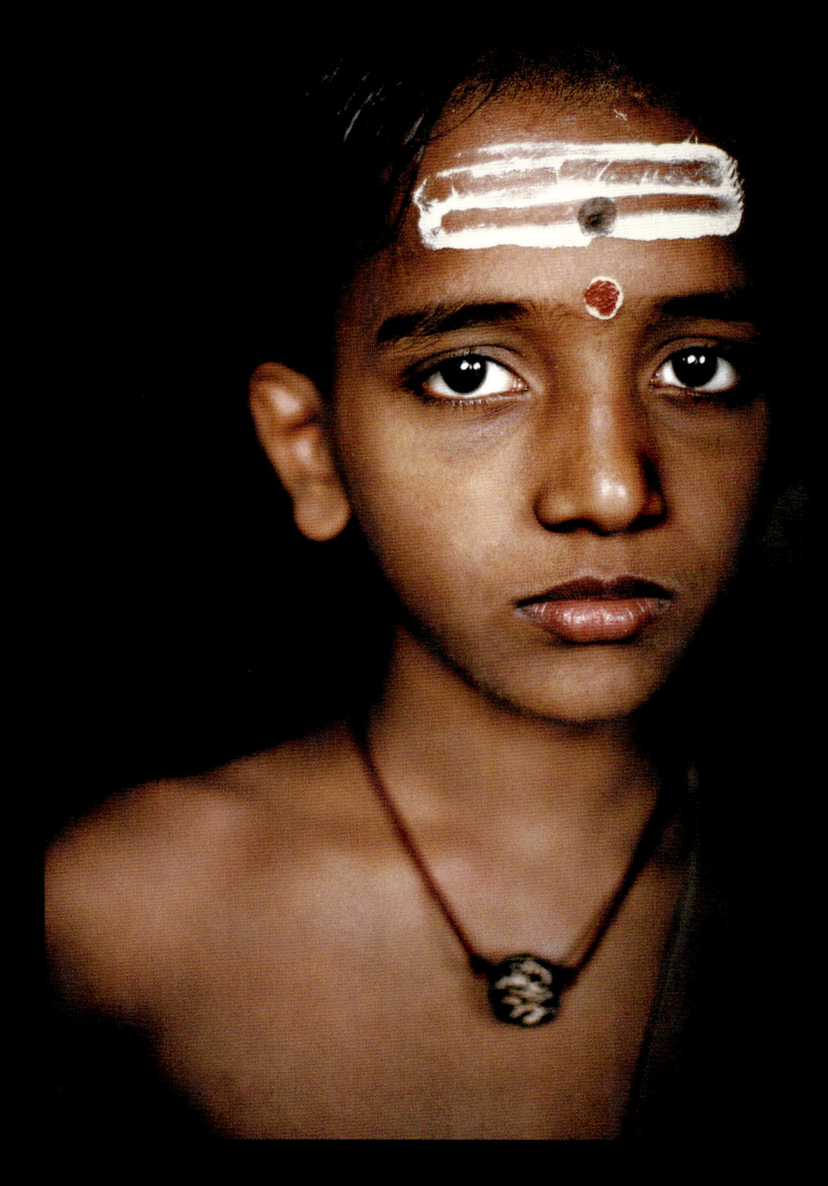

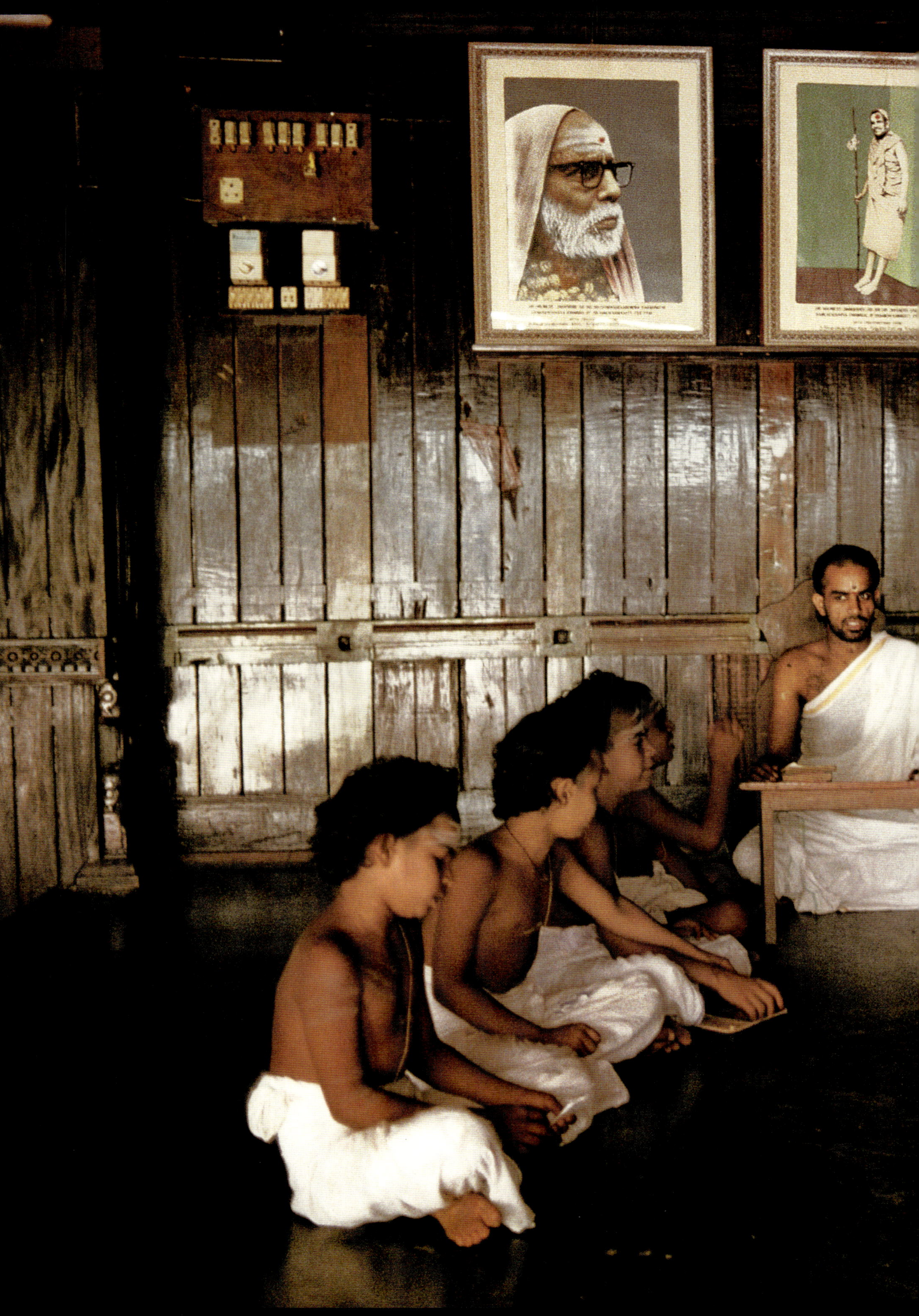

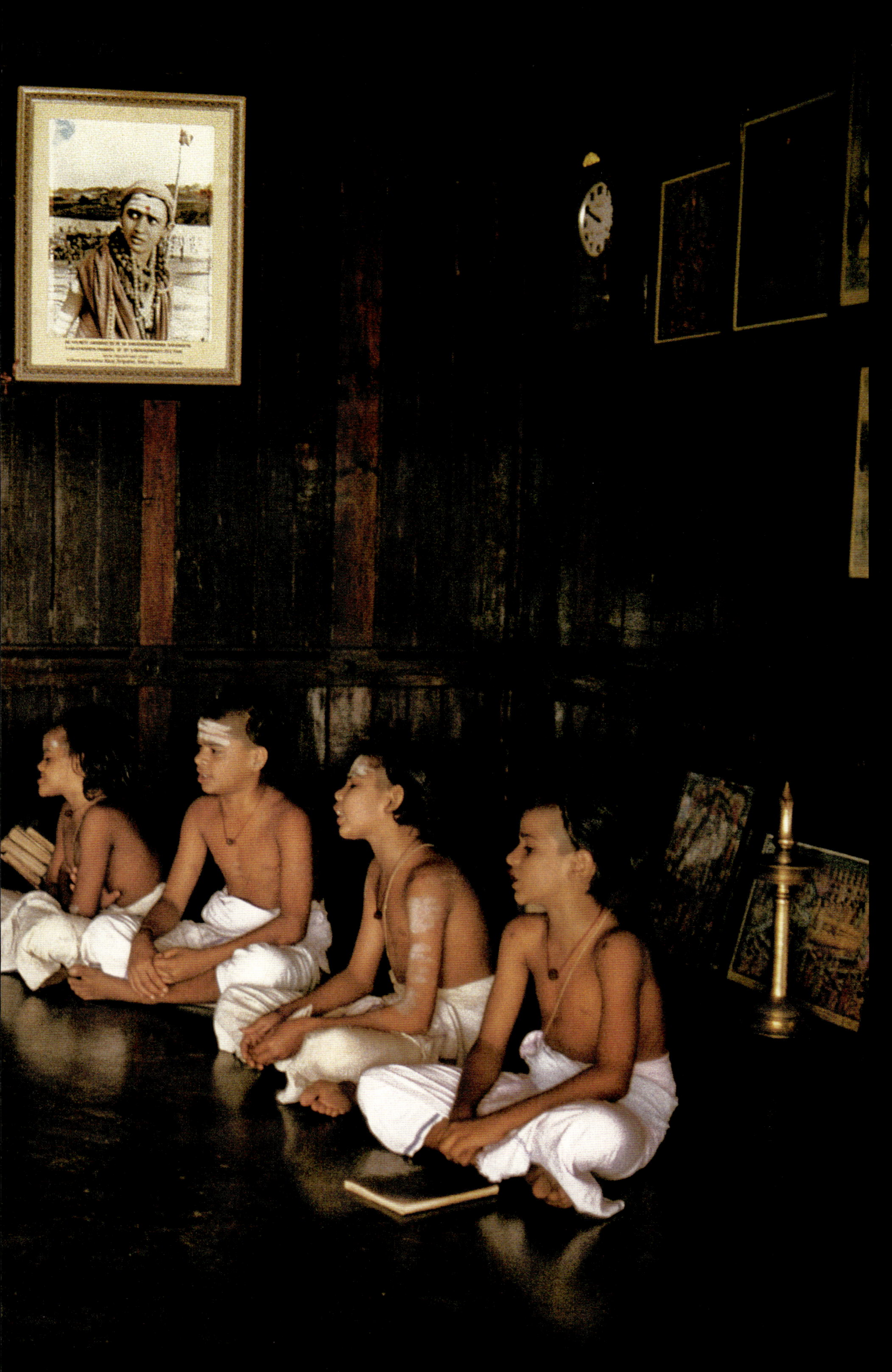

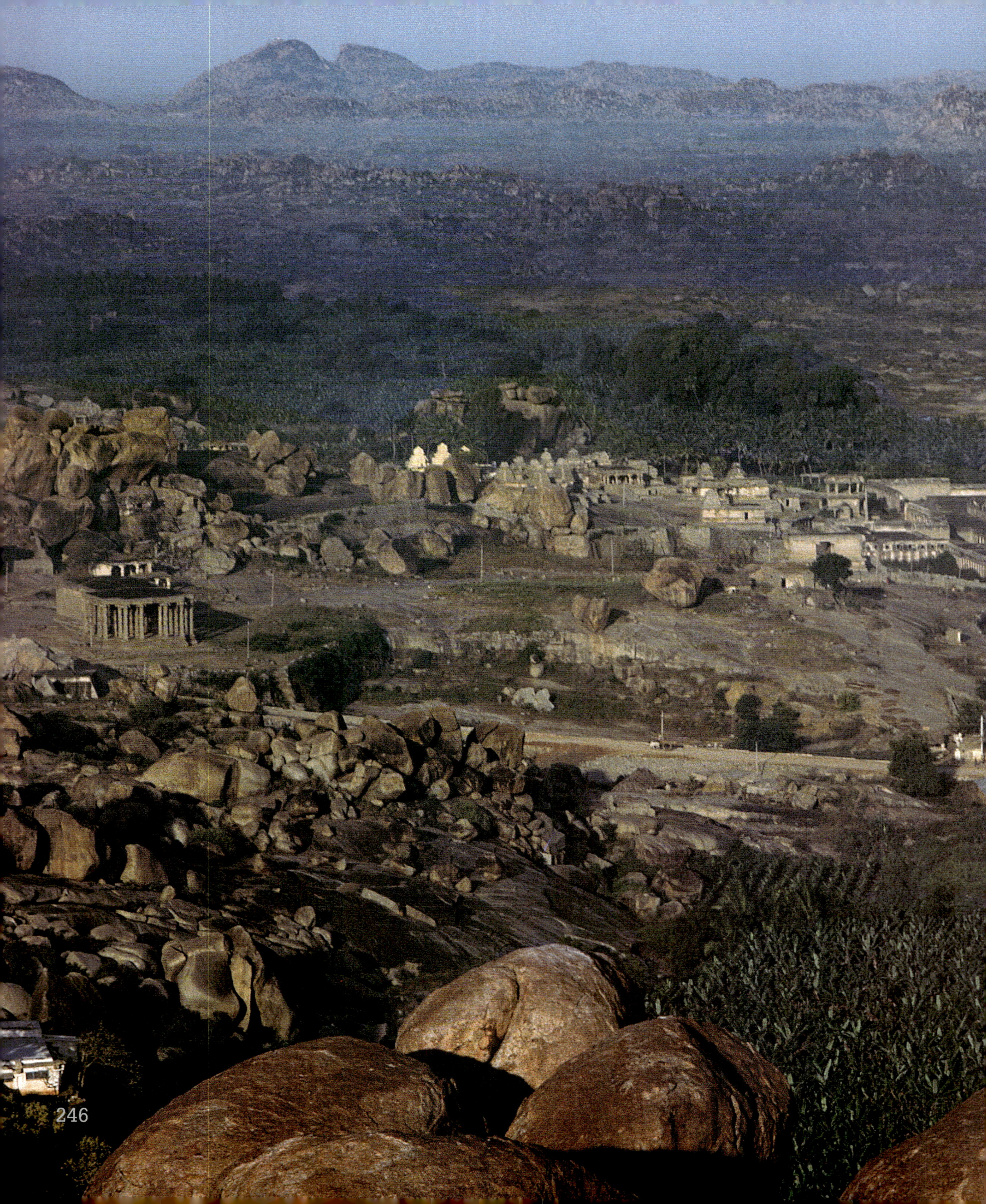

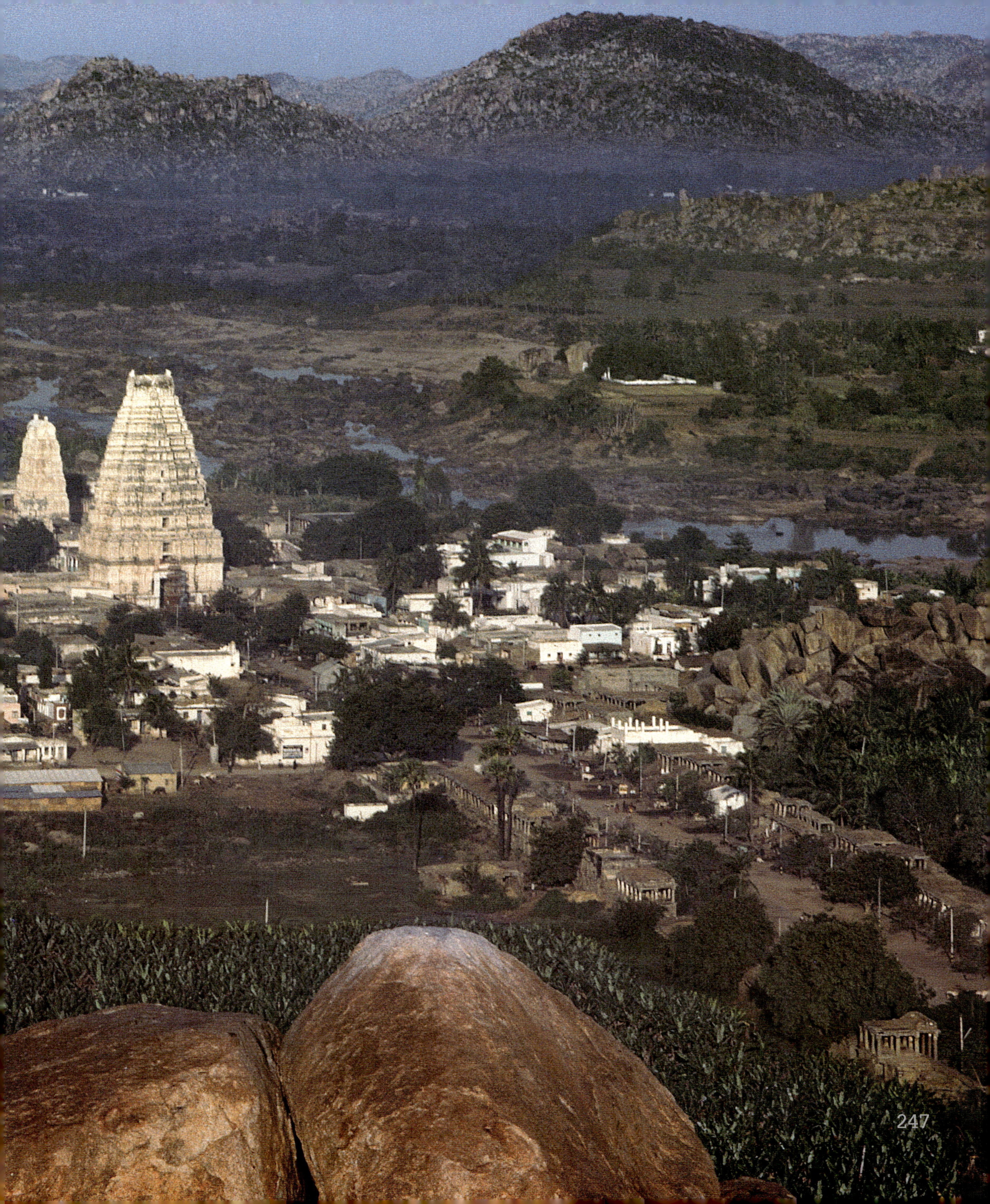

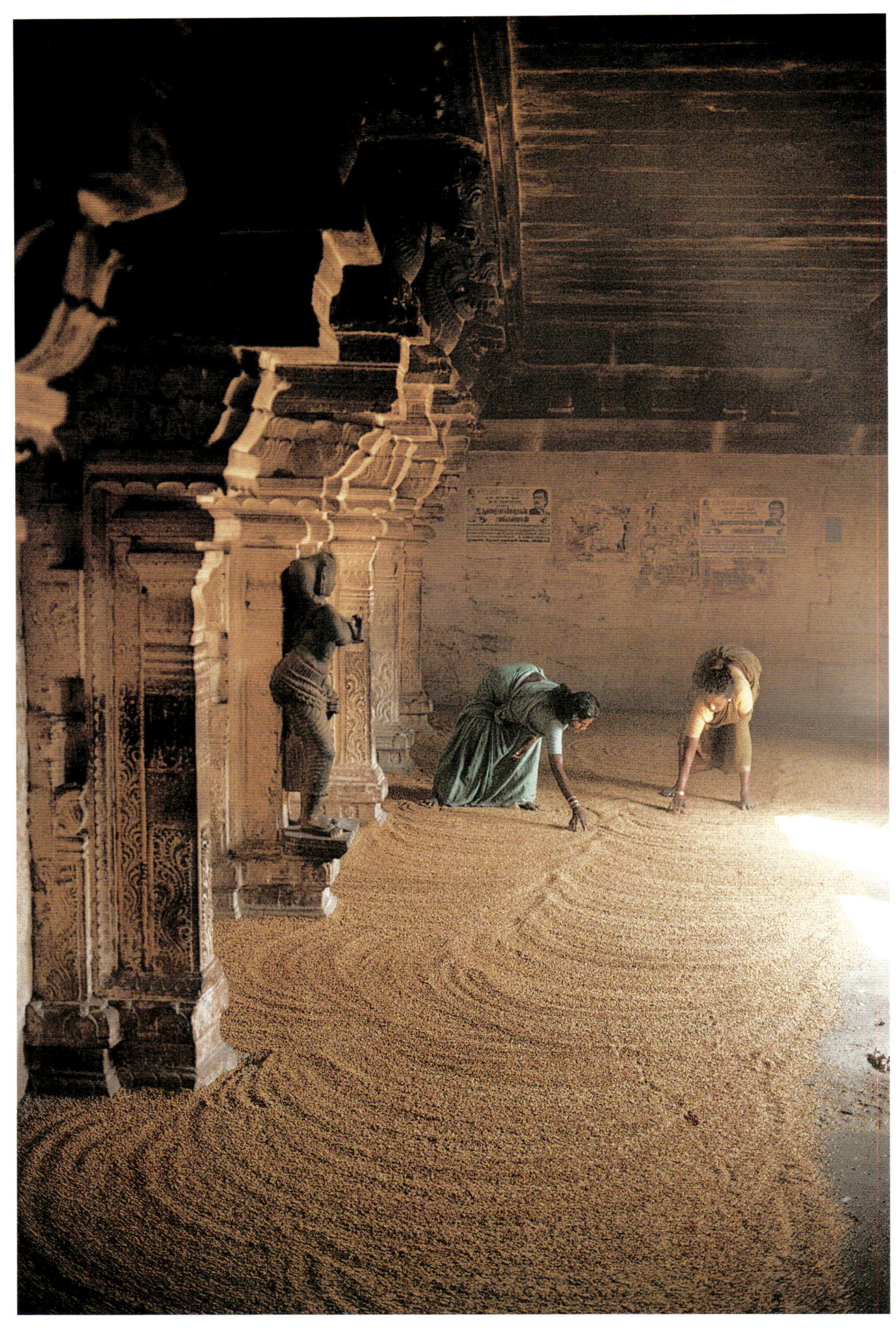

Above: Squatted temple, Tamil Nadu.
Pages 244–247: The Western Ghats, Kerala; the site of Hampi, Karnataka.

Hampi, capital of the Vijayanagar empire, is now the largest archaeological site in the world, along with Angkor. The Vijayanagar empire was founded here c. 1336, but fell in 1565 after the Battle of Talikota, which it lost to the Muslim armies. So the city, which was smitten with its own folly, lasted for around two centuries.

It took mystics to establish life in this rocky location. From the center to the outskirts, there are rocks here that are like no others. These are not timid rocks, in neat, well-behaved rows—there are thousand of rocks in the most extraordinary symphony of shapes, the most bizarre primeval chaos, a world petrified in a living eternity, lit by several suns, excavated by shade. The rocks that were the world before it was born, the world after it had lived, that witness the frozen cawing of rooks, the cry of death, the outpouring of thought, rocks that huddle around the site so as to form a chaotic jumble as far as they eye can see that flame in the setting sun.

Wait until evening to climb Matanga, a hillock rising above the paddyfields, where the world is set on fire, caught up in a yellow and red insanity that then turns brown, then gray, then black, and shines metallically in the moonlight. There are temple precincts, streets that lead nowhere, arcades, oratories, scattered fragments of sculpture, water tanks in which the water has been replaced by rice, the platform on which the royal palace once stood, the lazy and generous Tungabhadra River, which waters the plain, surrounded by the lunar landscape of the rocks.

The city was pillaged by the invading Muslims, who robbed it of its gold, then abandoned it. The Hindu peasants later returned to cultivate their land and plant new crops in the broad avenues, dried up water tanks, and on the sites of the houses. That is why sugar cane, cotton, and rice now grow wherever there is room between boulders and temples.

Life and death are thus intertwined, and their union is celebrated by the temple sculptures of thousands of dancers and male and female musicians. It is a silent universe of stone. The music that has now stopped is just as present as the thin stone of the columns that have the extraordinary property of producing musical notes when struck with the hand. In some temples the stone has been worn away from having served so often to delight the ears of the living. The children love it; here is the rhythm of a *tabla* emerging from a column.

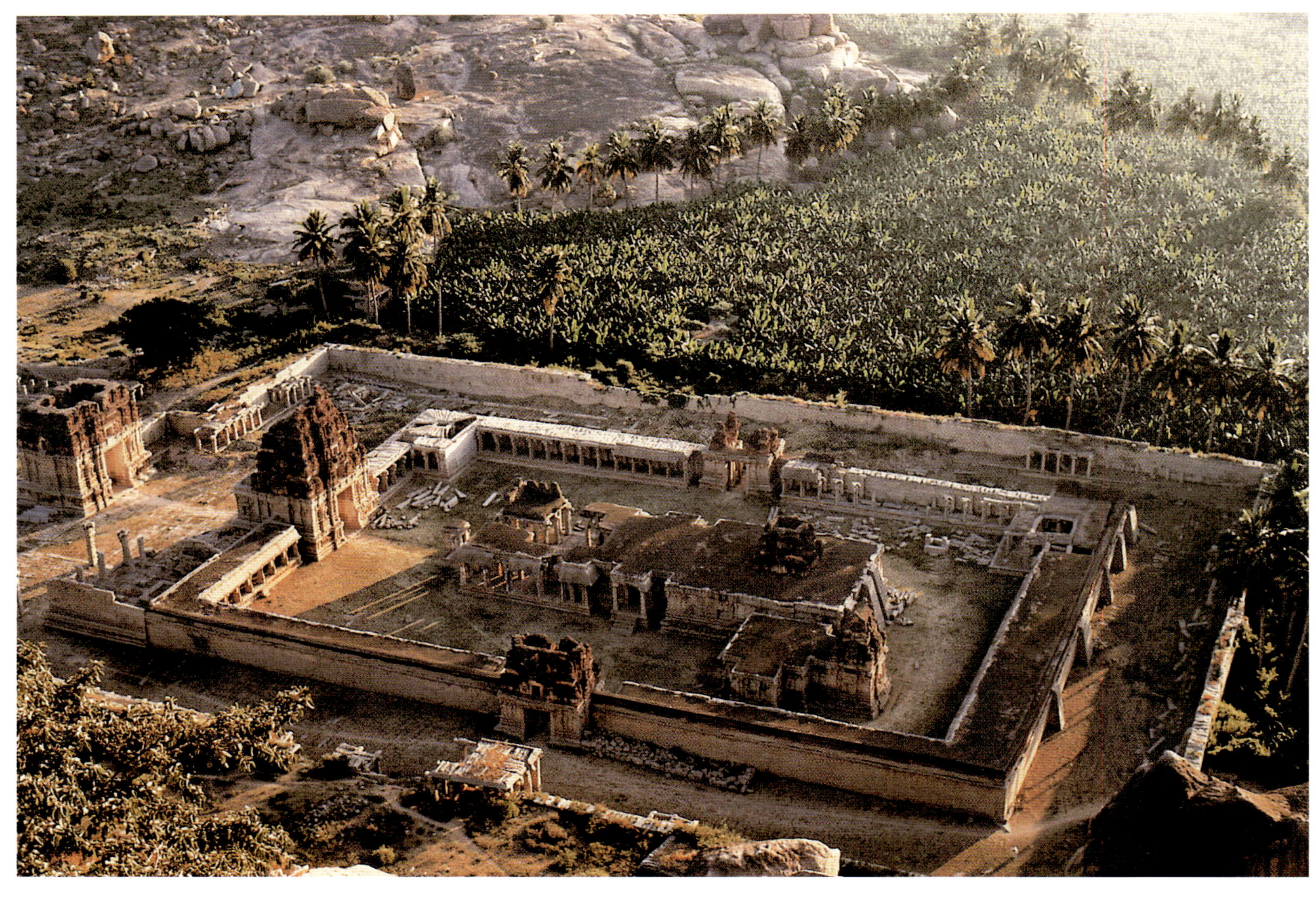

Above: The ruins of Vijayanagar, Karnataka.
Opposite: A *sadhu* in Girnar, Gujarat.

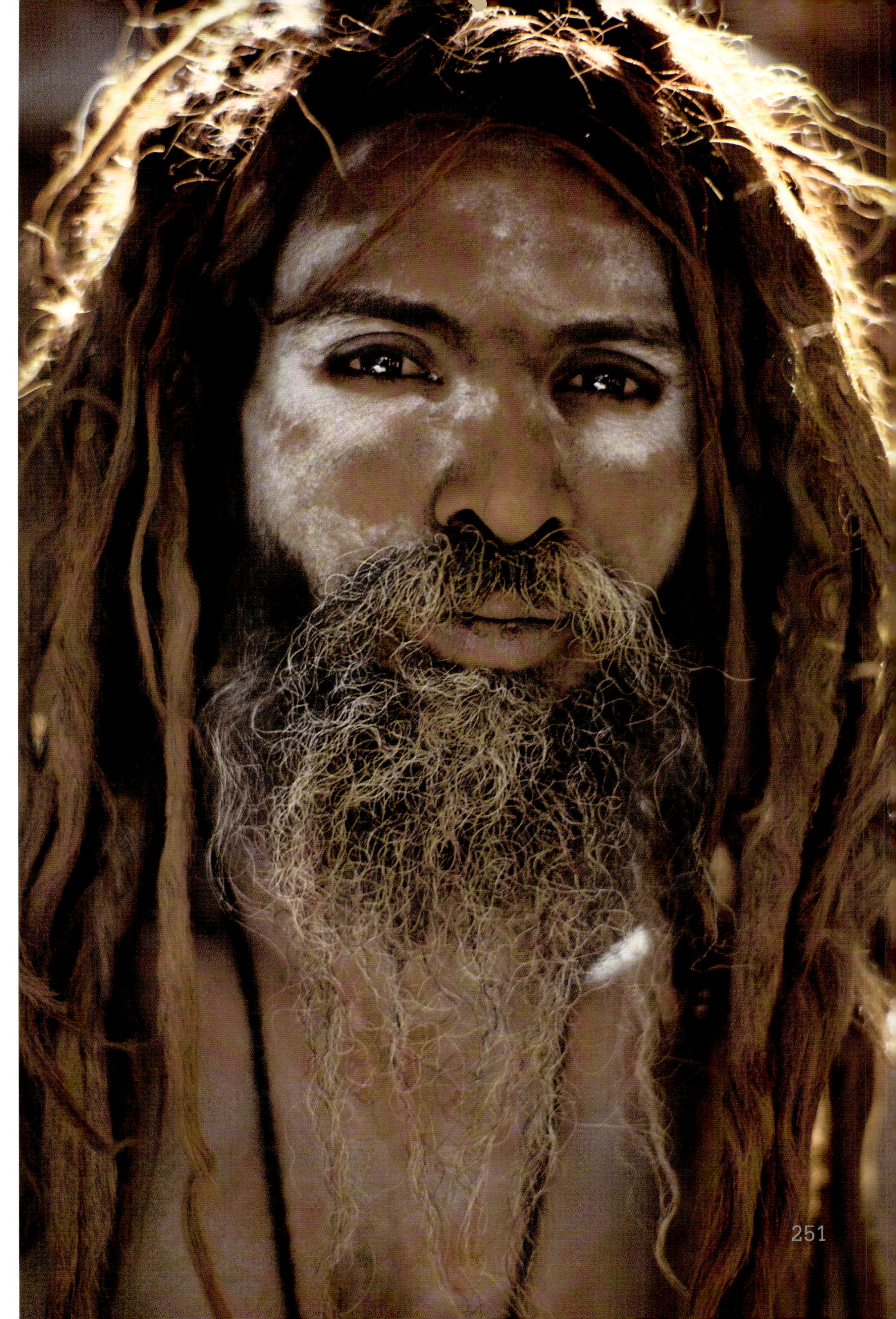

Kerala beach. The sound of the surf, the cries of children, spindrift. If you close your eyes, you could think yourself in Okinawa or Big Sur. A woman walks by. She is barefoot and wears a long red robe that the wind causes to cling to her shape. Her dancing step recreates the world. India is this illusion.

Egmore Station, Madras (Chennai). I had planned to go to a concert, but it didn't happen. I didn't fancy a walk on the beach on this rainy night, even less so in this city that has become violent, but lacks even the raffish charm of Bombay. So I decide to spend the evening at the Egmore Station. It has a long red-brick façade in a style that is a combination of Mogul and Victorian, adorned with columns and cupolas. It looks as if, after a dozen detours, Athens and Byzantium met up here just to give birth to kitsch.

The rain rattles on the tin roofs, the locomotives glisten, passengers enter, their clothing falling into the folds of Greco-Buddhist sculpture. I dash over to watch the departure of the Pearl City Express, which will stop at exactly three minutes past midnight at Ariyalur, where no foreigner may ever have left the train, attracted by the name that sounds like a magic spell. On another track, the Nellai Express will be stopping at Tiruchirapalli between 2:20 and 2:30 A.M., just enough time to grab a doughnut fried in rancid oil and sold on the platform. I sit down Indian-style beside the Chennai Egmore Karaikkudi Nagore Kamban Express no. 6175. A boy of about ten sits at my feet. He touches me hesitatingly, then dashes away. I place my hands on this train that will be stopping at Chidambaram from 1:20 through 1:23 A.M. after a halt at Tiruppadirippuliyur, whose name I would like to hear announced at least once on the nighttime platform.

Chidambaram was the capital of the Cholas from 907 through 1310 and a major center of Shiva philosophy. There is a great temple there that is dedicated to Shiva, Lord of the Dance (*nataraja*). One can still see the sculpted representations of the 108 poses of sacred dance. In a *Nritta Sabha* (hall of dance), a contest was held between Shiva and Parvati, his *shakti*. After the fourth precinct, there are the sanctuaries of the "holy of holies," Shiva in emerald, Shiva in metal, and a crystal *lingam* that is covered with water every evening at *puja* time, just before sunset. When night falls, it is time for fire worship. Man bows before the most intangible element, that should be mollified before it transforms our bones into smoke.

The smoke of the trains that whistle in the night, smoke for the gods who also like blood, smoke of the funerary pyres. Open the palm of your hand and your fingers already herald the smoke. Pfuuiiiit! The Kamban Express shakes itself into action with a loud grinding of metal. People are still hurling themselves at the doors,

children cry, an old man weeps. A man runs along the 253 platform, grabbing at the
last door of the last car with outstretched arms. He hesitates, fails to jump, and
slides off the end of the platform. Has his life been saved? The flames can wait.

20:05: Departure of the Pandyan Express, due in Madurai at 6:40. A very good train.
20:25: The Chennai Rameshwaram, which at 14:25 will reach the tongue of land
        that lies before Adam's Bridge (Rama's Bridge) and Sri Lanka.
20:30: On Track One, a group of five Muslim women dressed as widows stand face-
        less, like statues. Behind one woman's veil there hangs a necklace of jasmine
        flowers like those worn by Hindu women, whose faces are not concealed.
        Seen from afar, the black mass of these women is like a tear traveling upward.
21:45: The Rockfort Express leaves and passes through Ariyalur at 3:00.
        There is a blind man on the platform who has not eaten for a whole day.

Today is Tuesday, I'll wait until 23:30 for the Tiruchi Howrah Express, which
reaches Calcutta on Thursday. It arrives at 23:07.

While it stops for fifteen minutes, I pretend to be looking for someone I had been
waiting for to be my female companion for a night in Madras. When the train
leaves again, a man sympathizes with me: "Your girlfriend wasn't on the train?"

"No. Maybe she'll be on the next one that arrives in two days' time. I'll wait."
The man hands me his newspaper. It's a universal platitude that in India time
isn't the same as it is elsewhere, it passes more slowly. In a moment of insight,
one can laugh at this ridiculous notion. Then one can muse at length upon that
question, especially if one is at leisure to do so.

Sitting in Madurai, for example, above the pool of the great temple, one eventually
realizes that if time had a sovereign existence outside ourselves, its passing would
be the business of each person or each place. That is why it appears to be sleepy
when night falls on Madurai, where everything falls silent in the temple and I find
myself alone in a sort of meditation on the steps that lead to the black, moonless
surface on which tradition advises us to cast our writings. They will float if they are
worthy of attention; if they sink, they should be abandoned. A *Brahman* who knew
what he was doing once told me that there were two ways of making them float.
You should either write lightly or grease god's palm. We shall see.

As for time, which has awoken with the prospect of casting a written wish on
the water, it will perk up again for the procession leading Minakshi to her husband, Shiva, with whom she will spend the night.

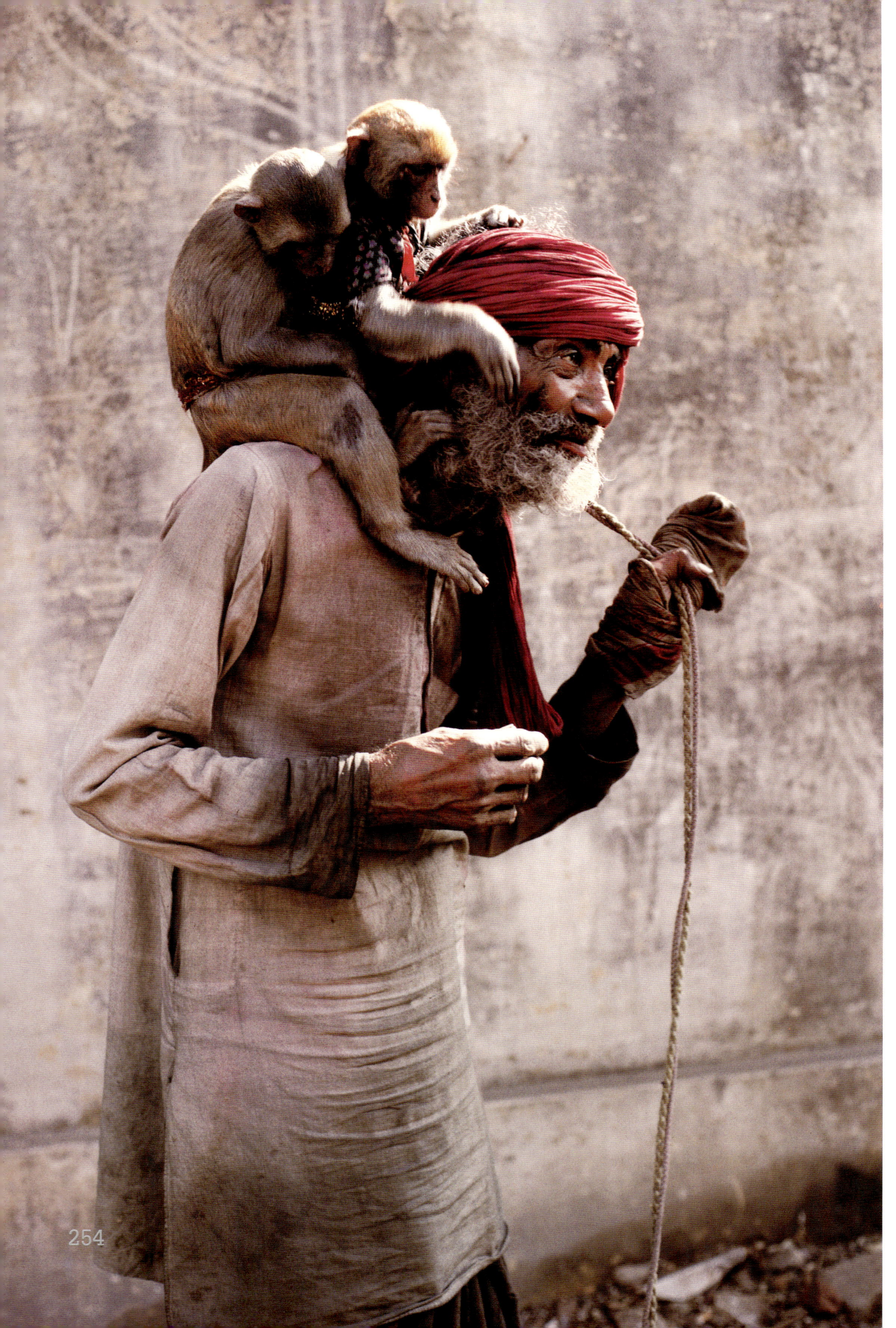

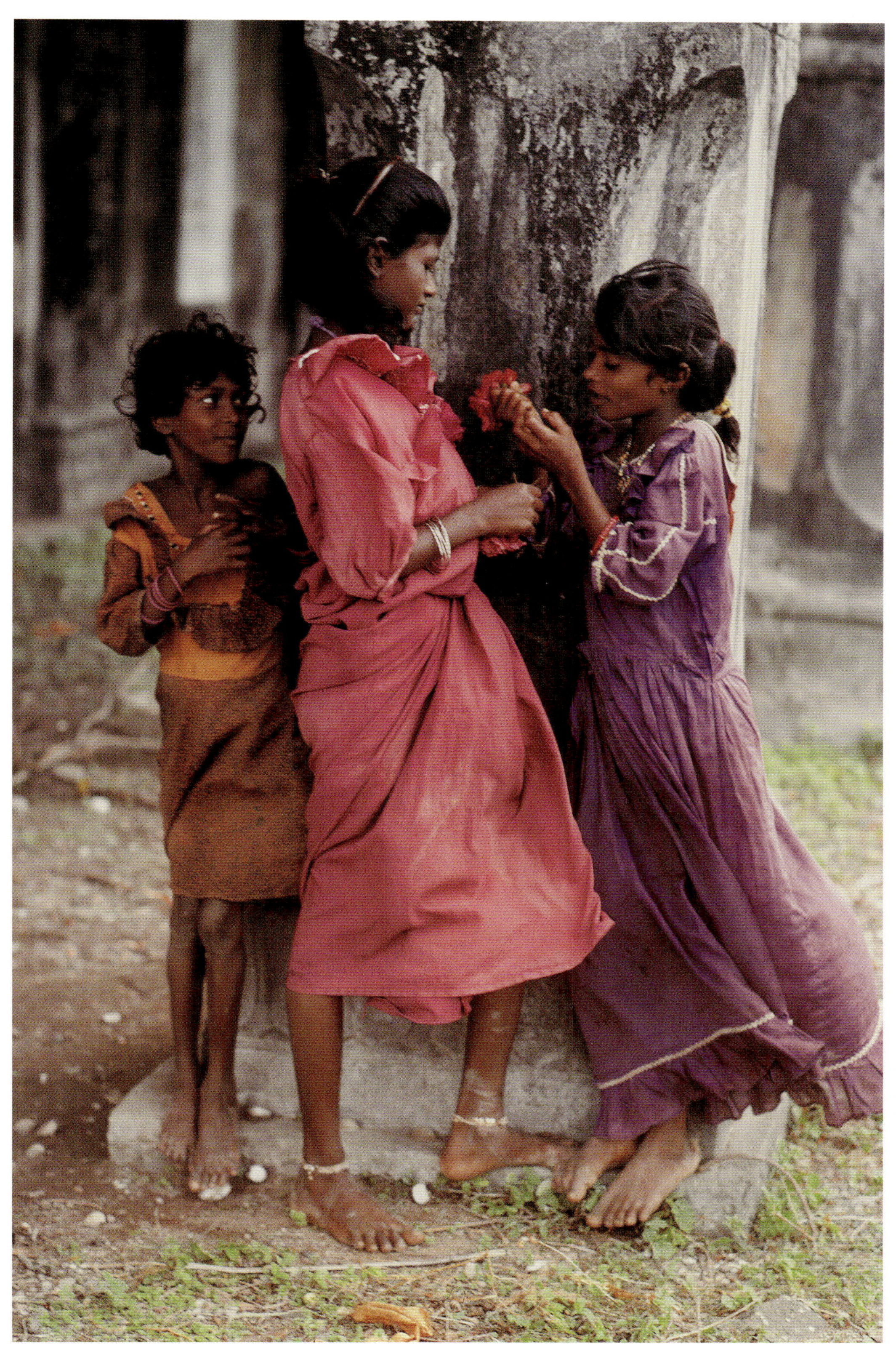

Opposite: Man with monkey, Delhi.
Above: Muslim girls, Maharashtra.

Time will look very different if you are admiring the view from the wooden seats
of the Mayiladuturai/Karaikkundi passenger train as it crosses the plain of Tamil
Nadu, not far from the sea, at its (theoretical) average speed of 18 miles per
hour (28.7 km/h). Time could be said to blink at the rhythm of the sun as it
jumps from one paddy-field to the next. Does time stop during meditation?
That's what they say. The impression it makes on us, in other cases, comes from
its reflection. Would this be unchanging elsewhere? That's one theory. The
music announces that Shiva has left his sanctuary and that he is on his way to
that of Minakshi. Generously—or playfully—time adopts the rhythm of the cymbals. Play (*lila*) is the prerogative of the divinity. Appearances (of which time is
part) is a "game" of the gods. Isn't praying playing together?

*Everything dances and everything is in play at the same time with these women—
their heads, their eyes, their arms, their feet, their whole bodies seem to move in order
to enchant. they're very light and have very strong thighs; they pirouette on one foot
and leap high in another instant with surprising force. Their steps and movements are
so precise that they accompany the musical instruments with the little bells on their
feet, and since their shape is so slender and elegant, all their movements are graceful.*

Maistre de La Tour, *Histoire d'Ayder-Ali-Khan,* 1784

I go back to Ali, the barber whose shop is a corridor in the Muslim quarter of Madras.
He is a meticulous craftsman, who flaps a long cutthroat razor in front of my face and
then slides it over my neck vein. He is content with little. "Is anything wrong sir?"

"Everything's fine." Outside, some children pass by for whom I am tonight's main
attraction. They bid me good day in what they assume is my own language, and I
reply good evening to them in their own southern language, a swift exchange that
they find hilarious. Night falls. A skinny cow laboriously chews on pieces of
coconut. Lamps are lit in the booths. Ali lights an oil lamp that makes me look like a
death's head. I tell him how much I like people who love their work, it is a sign of
wisdom. He hones the razor, his eyes shining with pleasure. He attacks my side-
burns as if he were striking a match. In the broken, badly lit mirror, the blade sends
signals of light. The little genie behind it captures them and hides them in a box.

Outside—but there is no door, the street is fiction—nearby, the children have mul-
tiplied. They are annoyed at having had to wait, they want something that resembles an epilogue, something that can be found in all performances, like a wedding
or a murder. Ali's razor slowly moves from the base of my neck to my chin. I gesture to him. He stops the stroke on the stretched skin. I tell him, "Wait!"

I swivel the chair around toward the children and tell them a story, the story of a monkey who lived in my country, an ancient kingdom of free men. He was well accepted and became accustomed to our habits, which, it must be admitted, are sometimes odd, such as the one that involves always having to know what time it is. He was happy, but he knew that the land from which he came was this southland, where we are now, a forest that faces the setting sun, the mountains of red rock. He wanted to return home, return to his homeland. He worked hard, saved money, bought himself a gray suit, gloves, a suitcase, a red bag for bananas, and an airplane ticket. At the airport, they asked him: "Your ticket, please?" and he held out his ticket without revealing his hairy arm. He was thrilled by the flight—the orange juice, the clouds, the voices of the hostesses, the movie with lots of violence in it.

When he reached the southland, he took his time acclimating to the heat, the food, and the way of nodding and shaking the head for "yes" and "no" that was the exact opposite of what he was familiar with. Then he went to the red mountains, traveling on the roof of a bus. When he got there, he took a joyful leap into the liana-covered trees, those trees that he recognized because he had seen them in a dream. But he jumped too soon, lost his grip, and fell. No one came to his aid, not the little monkey who had shouted such nice words, nor the mommy monkey who was preoccupied with feeding her children, nor even the old man who had nothing better to do. Eventually, humans picked him up and he thanked them; they laughed. They carried him on their shoulders and when they got him home, they killed him. For no reason, maybe just for fun, for the corpse of a little monkey has no value. They threw him on a scrap heap on which cripples foraged. All they kept were his gloves that they had found in his red bag.

The street urchins left before the end of my story. I heard them playing in the distance with an empty tin can. Ali is very sorry. "Don't be angry with them," he begs, "They're just children. They don't know what they are doing."
"I'm not angry with them. I think they were right to leave when the monkey fell out of the tree. I would have left, too."
"You're not too disappointed sir?"
"Yes, I'm disappointed for the monkey."
"But…"
"Your work is perfect," I tell him, "Perfect. You and the razor are one. It's as if you had an extra finger."
"If I had an extra finger, I would have used it to stop the monkey from falling."

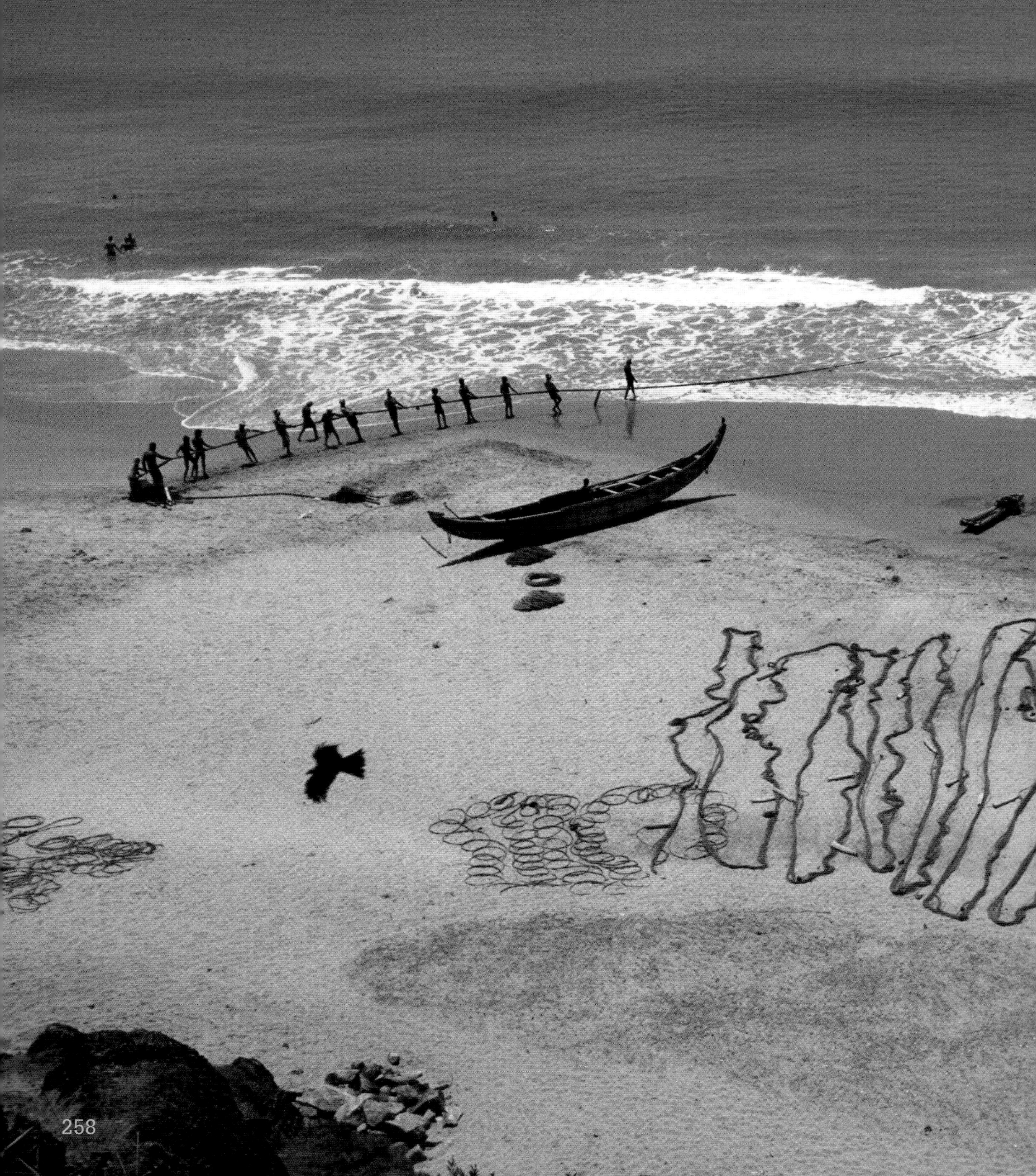

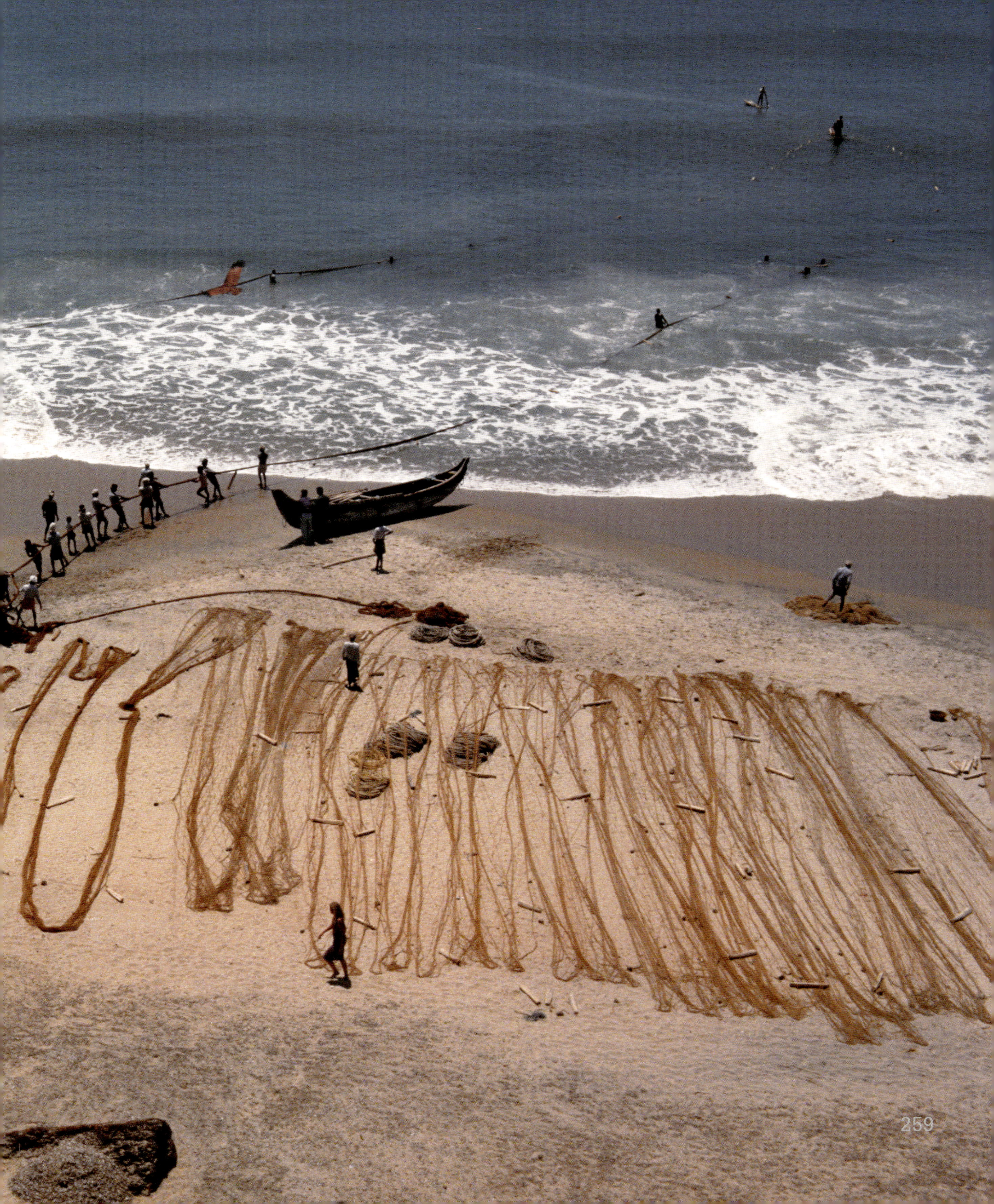

From this remote village in Tamil Nadu there emerges a woman of striking beauty. She does not understand my stupefaction. She does not know that she is beautiful.

M. was once an important center but it is now a small town somewhere on the Karnataka plateau. It is so difficult to get to by bus that it takes us a whole day to travel the sixty or so miles from the city from which we have come. The ancient architecture of the Vijayanagar era is now covered in liana vines. There is a clump of rocks behind the last temple. Did the rulers of the kingdom, whose center was at Hampi, make a pact with these geological masses? The sun is setting. We are joined on a rock by a child whose thigh is marred by an ugly wound. When the sun disappears after blessing the sky and rocks with orange, something is set off in me. I place my hand on the boy's injury. The wound remains. The madman blames God.

Past, present, future, that is how rice is considered here. Ocher splashes of color when the straw dries after cutting, green flames before it is harvested, luminous squares of impeccably combed clumps after resowing.

The tangle of time stretches to the horizon. There is nothing to get excited about. It has always been known that time is like a game of hide-and-seek, concealing and revealing itself at will. From the top of the hill of Tirukalikundram (you have to say it quickly), from where you can see the eagles that fly in from Benares (a legend), the weather has chosen to emulate the rainbow-colored robe of the paddy-fields. Yet another painterly touch is added by the rounded rocks that are scattered over the plain, no one knows why. For the serene visitors who climb the thousands of steps to the hilltop temple, these rounded rocks represent time standing still, a fruitful illusion. For male climbers of a sensual nature, these rocks are the breasts of the earth, swollen between watery stripes.

It is not hard to love the earth, you just need to know how to wait. As for the peregrine falcons of a sensual nature, no word would be subtle enough to explain their relationship to the rounded rocks of immutable appearance. All that remains are the photographers, and they will be disappointed. Between the paddy-fields, the rocks, the groves of palm trees, and the tiny workers in the fields, there are hidden interactions that require a consciousness behind them. One ought to meditate before taking each photograph, not to look for a viewfinder, but for a gift finder. The bicycle ride back is difficult with the sun in my eyes. Having no light with me, I hope to reach my destination before nightfall. Along the road, women dressed in all sorts of bright colors are beating sheaves of rice.

It only takes one of them who is bolder than the others—more liberated, some might say—to get the others to block my path. They want gifts, they want to be photographed, they want to look at my watch, pump up my tires. Farther away, shirtless men who are not interested in the scene are loading bales of rice straw onto carts.

I move on. About sixty feet farther on, I turn around. The women have started work again, as if nothing had happened. I close my eyes, the landscape becomes an abstract painting. The center is empty, but in the upper left corner there are concentric circles, the orange of the sun surrounded by the green stalks of growing rice and the yellow rice straw. Along the edges are the multicolored splashes of the saris, reds and yellows predominating. Between the circles and the edges, the dark blue of the sky is flecked with silver, a black line coming from the skin of the men and a gray splash in which I think I recognize myself. A mandala?

I like Gitta. I find out about her. She comes from a village in Andhra Pradesh. Her family married her off to a husband who beat her. She had two miscarriages, so her husband threw her out. She became a servant to a merchant family. She stole from them, so she was sent to prison in Guntur. When she was released, she earned money from selling her body. (From each customer, she extracted the price of a bowl of rice). She walked all the way to the sanctuary of Tirumalai. She begged for alms at the gates of the temple. Now that she is old, she washes linens for the guests passing through the Dak Bungalow. She sings from morning to night. What a lovely face she has!

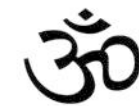

I travel by bus along a dirt road on the Karnataka plateau. It is an arid expanse of red and pink earth on which cows nonchalantly release dung pats that are carefully collected, compacted, and dried to be used as fuel. A herd of bony goats clears a path between the clumps of agave. This is the land of the Serpent King. Our vehicle raises a disturbing dust, the only sign of life for quite a while. Then an oasis restores greenery, a haven against the violence of the light. Above the fences that line the road, sheaves of hay appear to move along on their own.

When the women carrying them appear, they can be seen to be walking in single file, as in ancient Egyptian frescoes. Farther off there is a pond, palm trees, a checkerboard of saris drying on the ground. Paul Klee has added his touch.

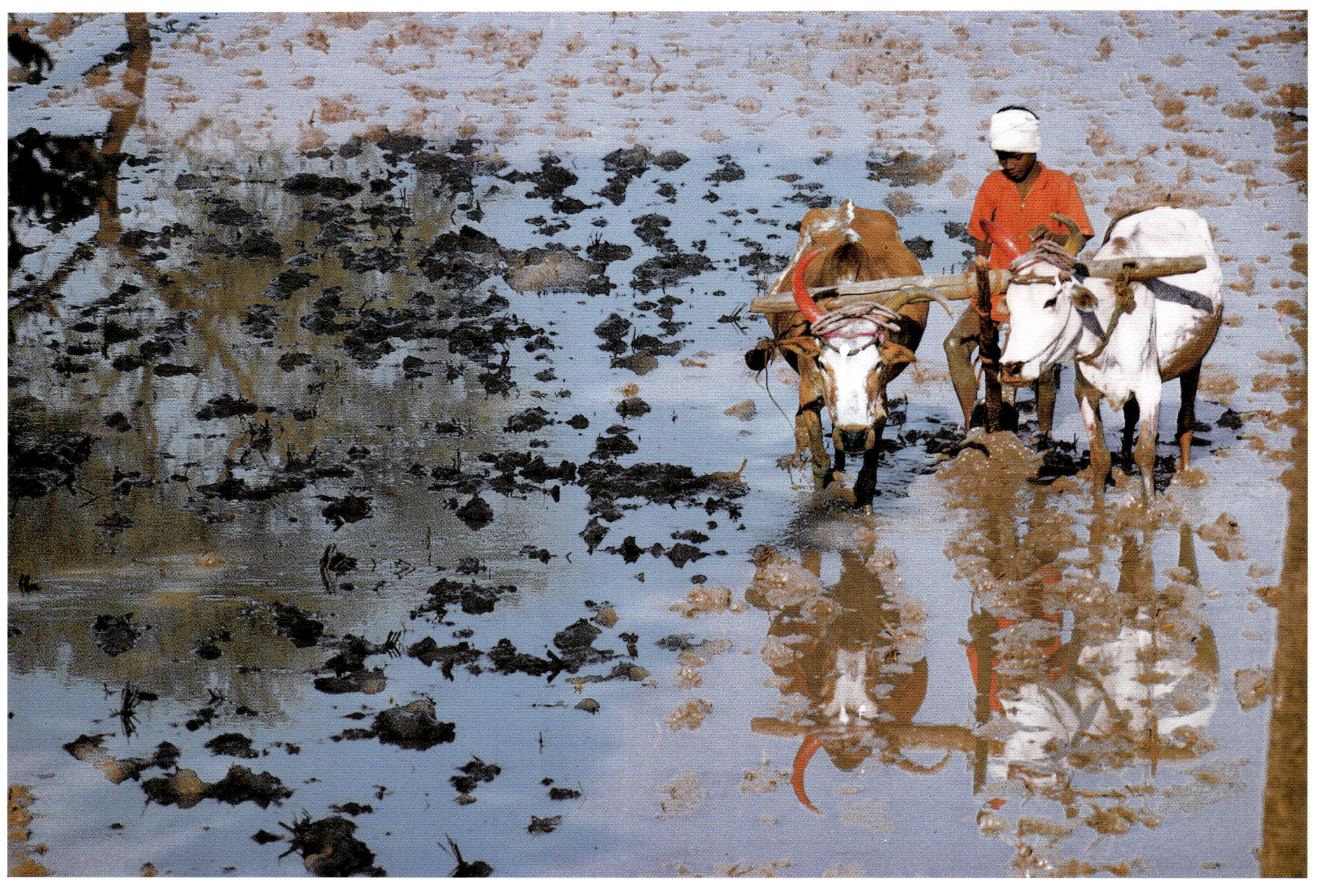

Plowing a paddy-field and replanting it with rice, Tamil Nadu.

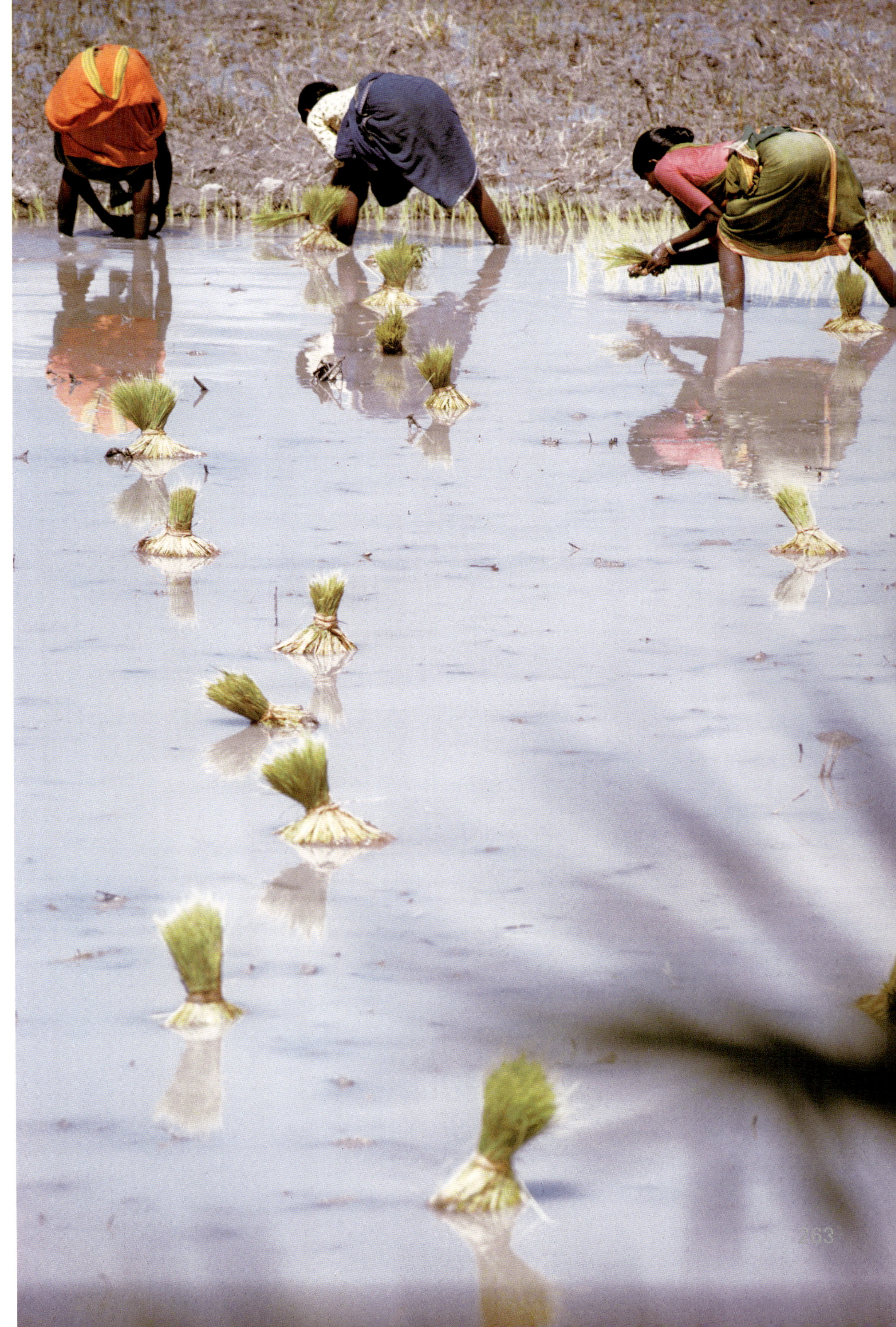

It takes us a whole day and lungs full of dust to reach the village in which Master S. lives. It is three days since we left the ashram of Sri Ramdas on the Malabar coast in northern Kerala.

That evening, the bus drops beside a deserted road near the village, driving away in its yellowish halo. We shake ourselves and rediscover the silence that awaited us in a ditch. As we walk toward the village that can be glimpsed behind a row of trees, we are joined by a child. "He isn't here!" he chants with evident delight. We find good reasons not to believe him, noting his sly expression. But he appears to have been right. In the modest dwelling in which the master lives, a man who seems to be unfinished, confirms it to us.

"When will he be back?
"I don't know."
"Does anyone know?"
"He never says when he is coming back."
"Do you know where he's gone?"
"No."
"How long is he usually away?"
"It varies."
"For instance?"
"Two days, six months. Maybe one time he won't ever come back."
"At the Sri Ramdas ashram, they told us that at this time of year
  he would be here."
"He often is."
"Would you advise us to wait?"
"I think that in your country you don't like waiting."
"OK. And what about tonight?"
"When he isn't here we don't entertain anyone."
"You can go and sleep over there, under the banyan tree behind the road."
"There are hardly any snakes."

Over there, attacked by the mosquitoes, we hear the calls of all sorts of animals for whom hunger is a serious matter.

Then night will be the master.

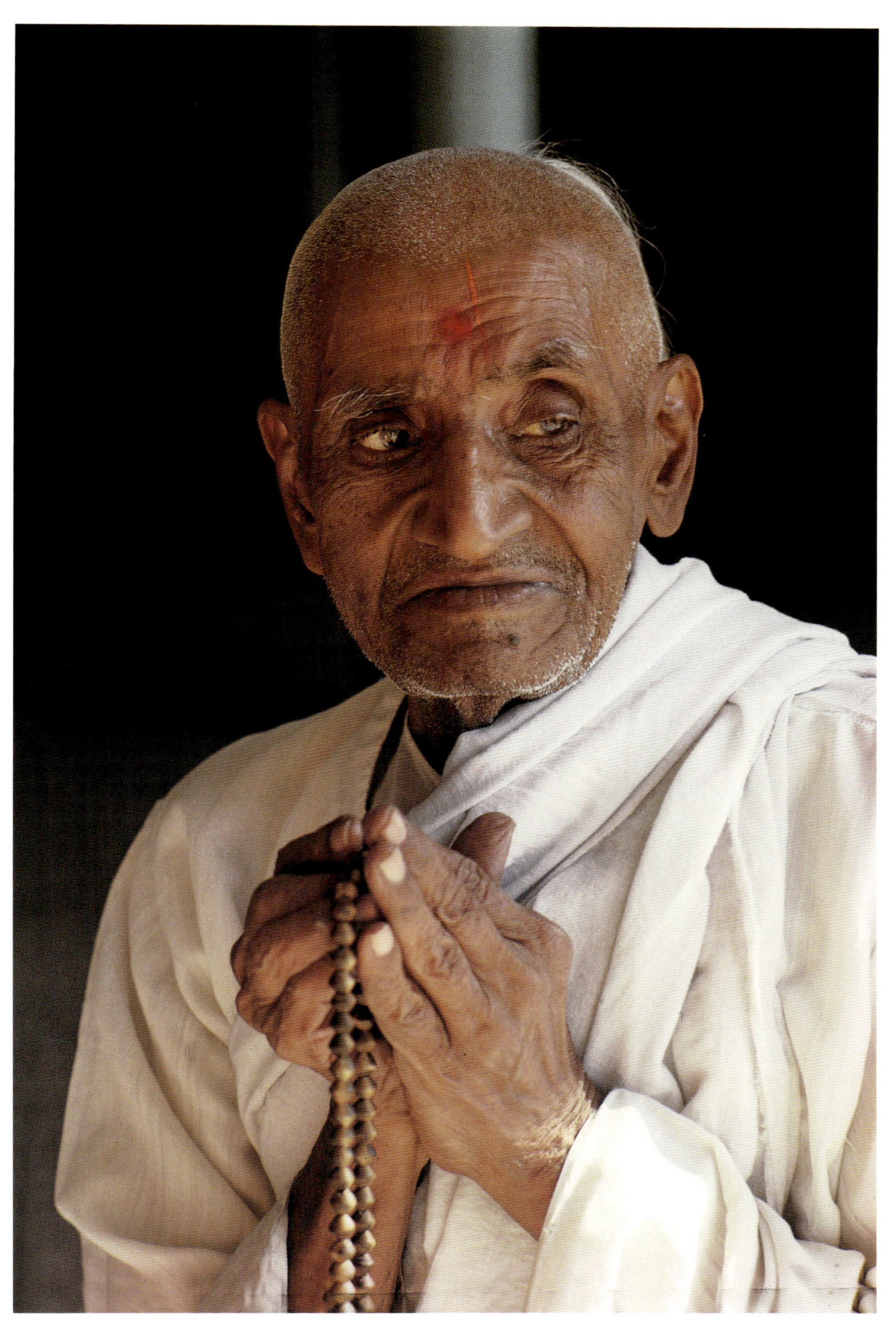

Above: Hindu priest, Ahmedabad, Gujerat.
Pages 266-267: Couple playing in the waves. Dwarka, Gujerat.

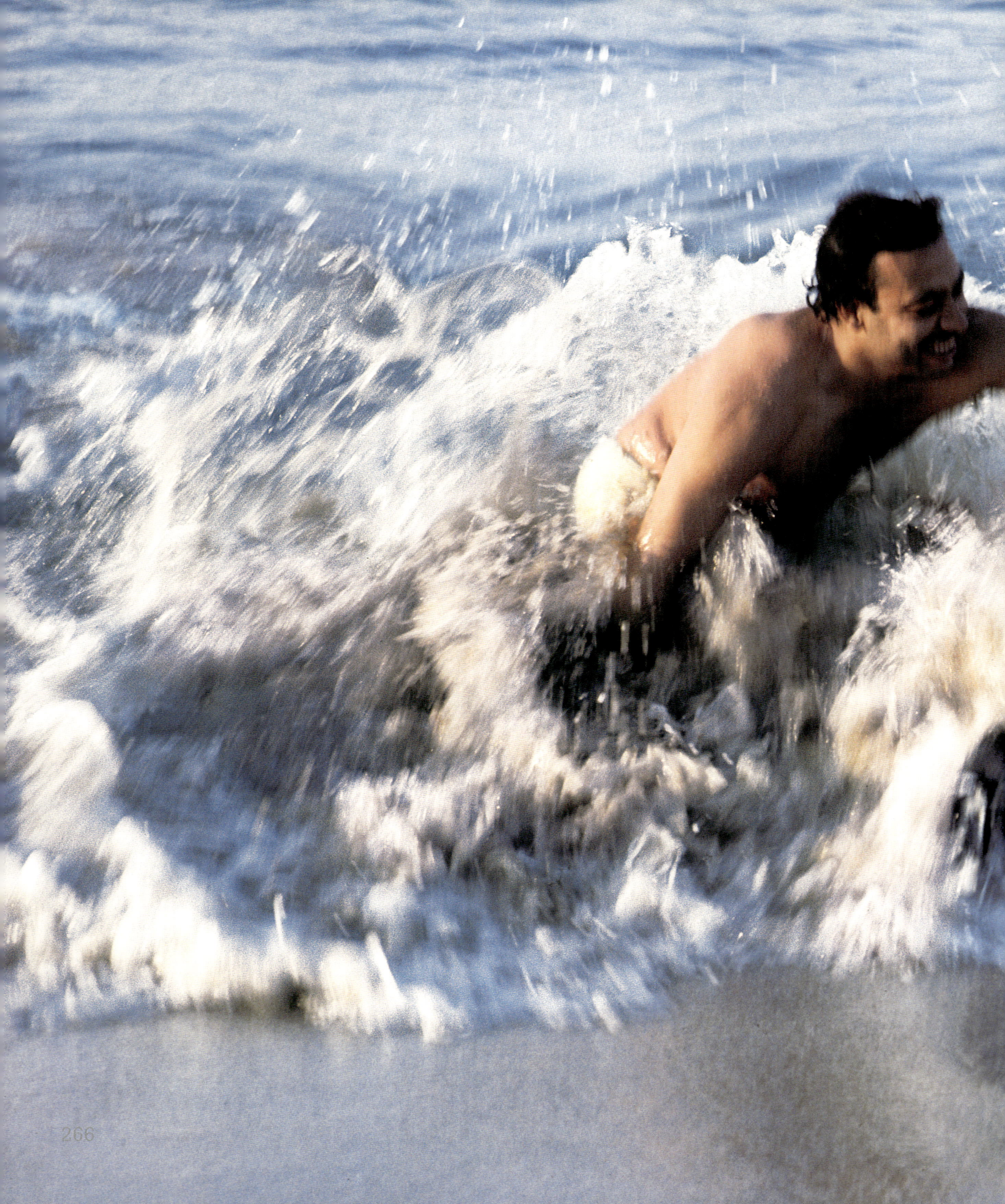

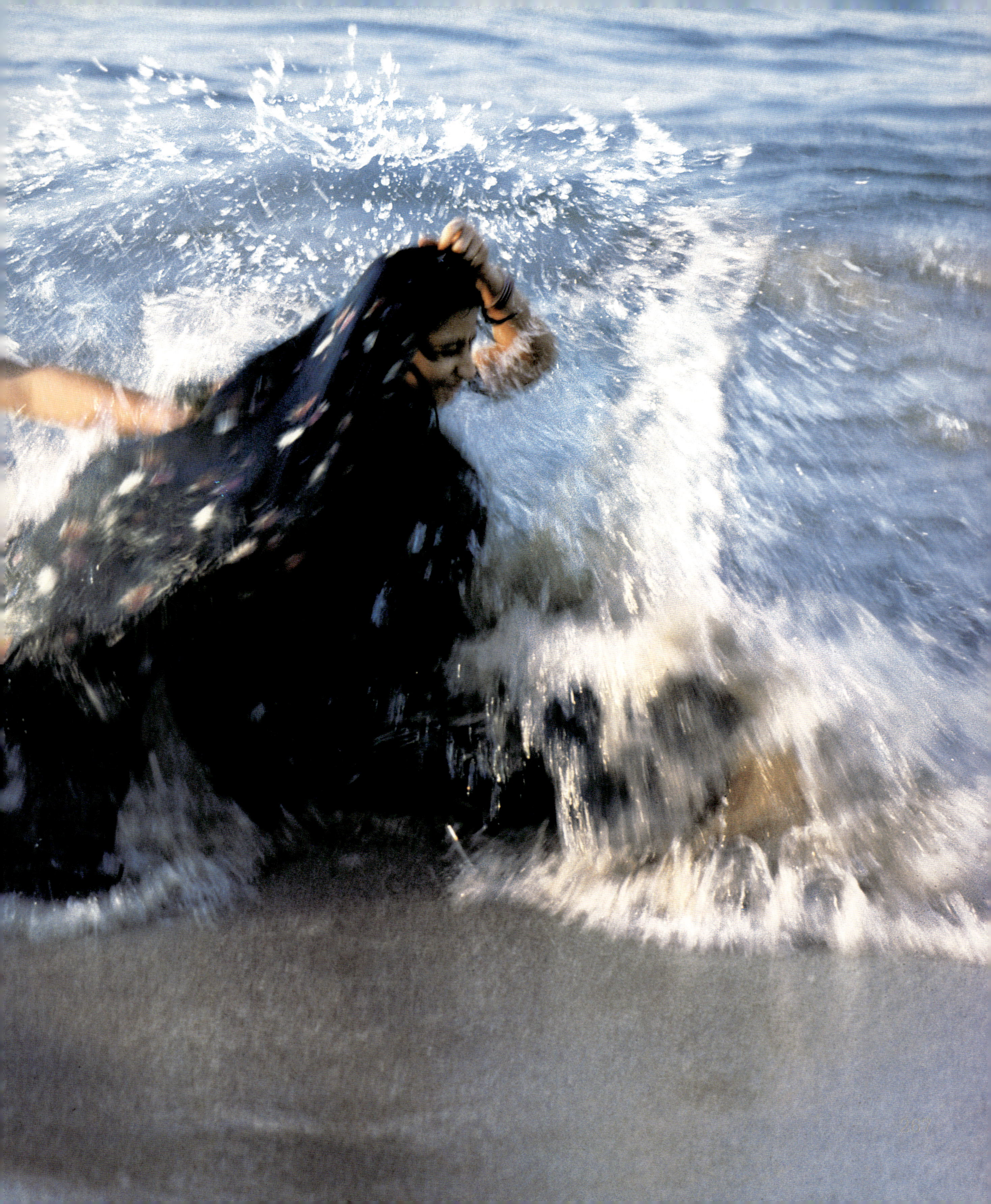

Last word to womanhood

Mahabharata, I:51–52

It would be just as ridiculous to pronounce India "feminine" as it would be to consider the Christian West to be paternalistic. Of course, on the one hand you have the *shakti* (female energy), on the other, God the Father. Yet the *Veda* or *Laws of Manu* are masculine texts, and the three main gods of the pantheon—Brahma, Shiva, and Vishnu—are all men, whereas for more than fifteen centuries the figure of the Virgin ruled a Christianity within which was born courtly love.

The four thousand years of Indian history permit all kinds of diversions. Do not allow simplistic minds to preempt the question of male and female, they will simply flounder. A distinction must first be made as to eras. Between the Indus civilization and the advent of Islam, there have been umpteen ways of perceiving the role of woman, her power and her potential for evil. One must distinguish according to *jati*, to region of India, the age of the woman, and so on. Definitions also need to be agreed. The definition of "equality" cannot be transposed from the West to traditional Indian culture, nor does the concept of "free choice" have any meaning in a society where decision-making is the prerogative of the gods or of custom, but never of the individual.

The Indian woman may not be free according to modern Western criteria, but she radiates and incarnates power, especially as a mother, that the whole of Indian culture acknowledges.

Women are gods, women are life,
Women are finery.
Always take women into consideration.

Vishnu's reply about the aspect of the Buddha in the *Mahacina-Ramacana*

Indian women have a graceful air. This gracefulness comes neither from particularly remarkable features nor from a body like that of the *apsaras*. An Indian woman frolicking in a Californian swimming pool could be beautiful but she will have lost the aura that renders her unique. Her gracefulness emanates from her culture and cannot be transplanted. From earliest childhood, she knows that she contains a sacred principle, and the fact that she is considered in that way gives her a lightness of movement enhanced by the wearing of the sari. The hint of a smile upon her lips, long black tresses, the gait and hands of a dancer, and modesty, combined with a subtle undulation of the hips, she wears an expression of redoubtable innocence—the whole combining to create a work of art that resembles her, familiar yet inaccessible.

Let us dwell for a moment on the concept of woman as living art. In our cultures, we have sung their praises, yet we have (almost) lost them. In the beating of a wing, we can once again find the female companions of Ulysses or Lancelot.

Beware, for the grace of a womanhood has become mythical and cannot be acquired. It fades away if you try to possess it. It is a grace that is there to be admired and is instilled only if carefully cultivated.

Our concept of the traditional Indian woman cannot be discarded. Her freedom is not the ability to develop her individuality, but that of approaching an archetype. On her wedding day the bride becomes a goddess, as her finery proves. She is honored as such, not for her own attributes. The same applies to her children, if she becomes a mother.

And what of the little girls who are married off at the age of eight? And what about barren women who are betrayed by their husbands? And rejected widows? Exploited peasant-women? Raped women condemned to silence? To forget them would be criminal; to see nothing but them would be blindness.

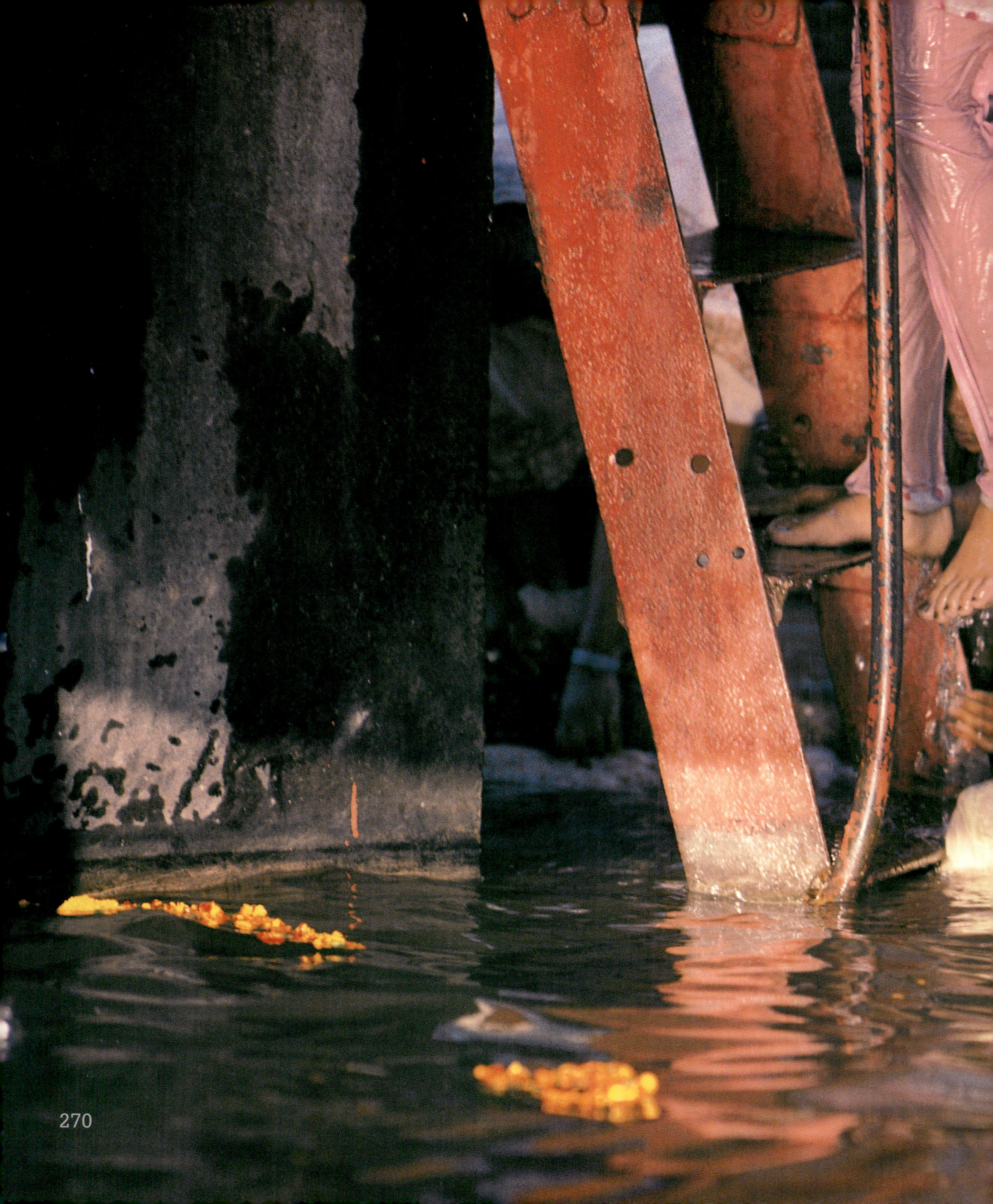

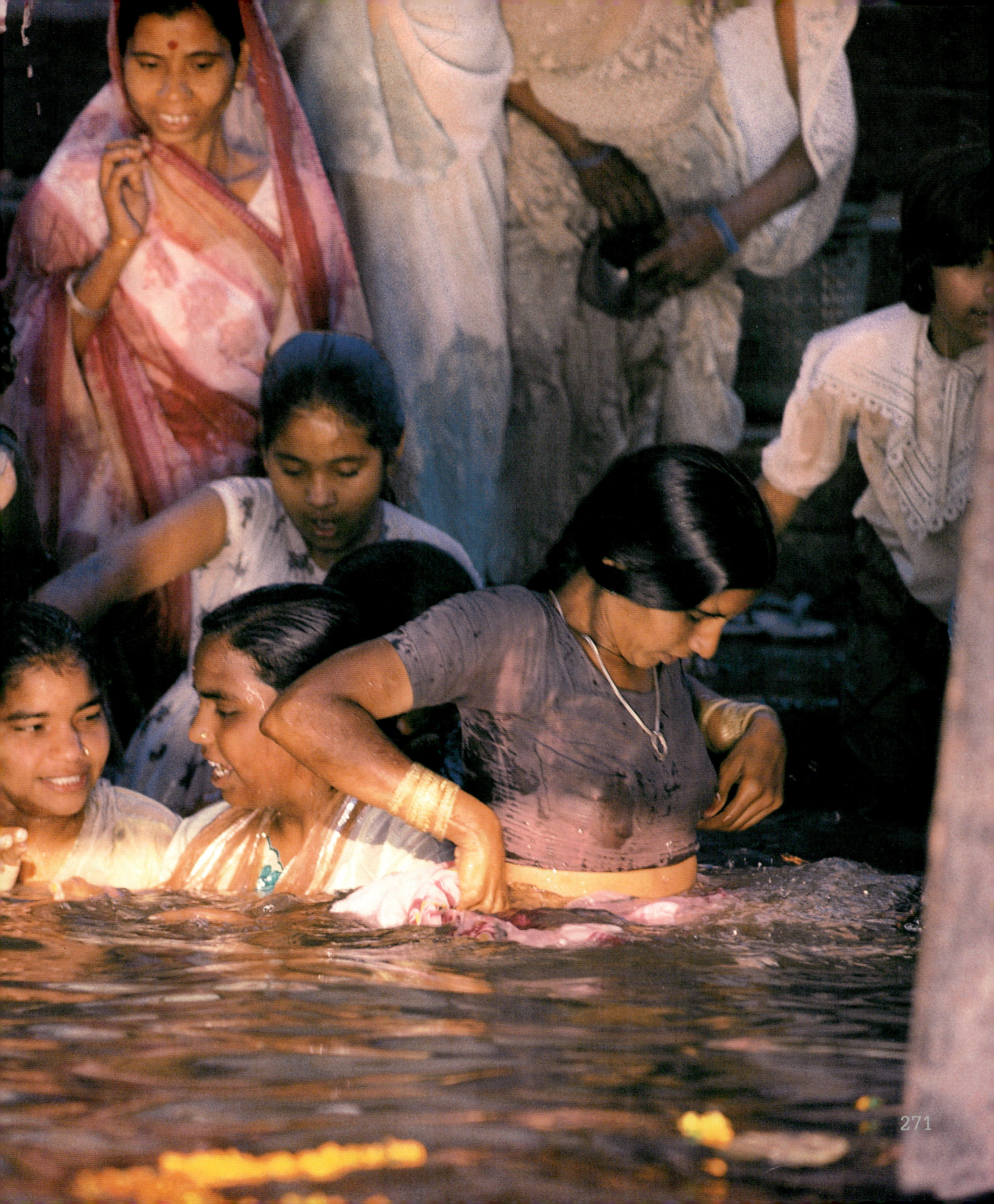

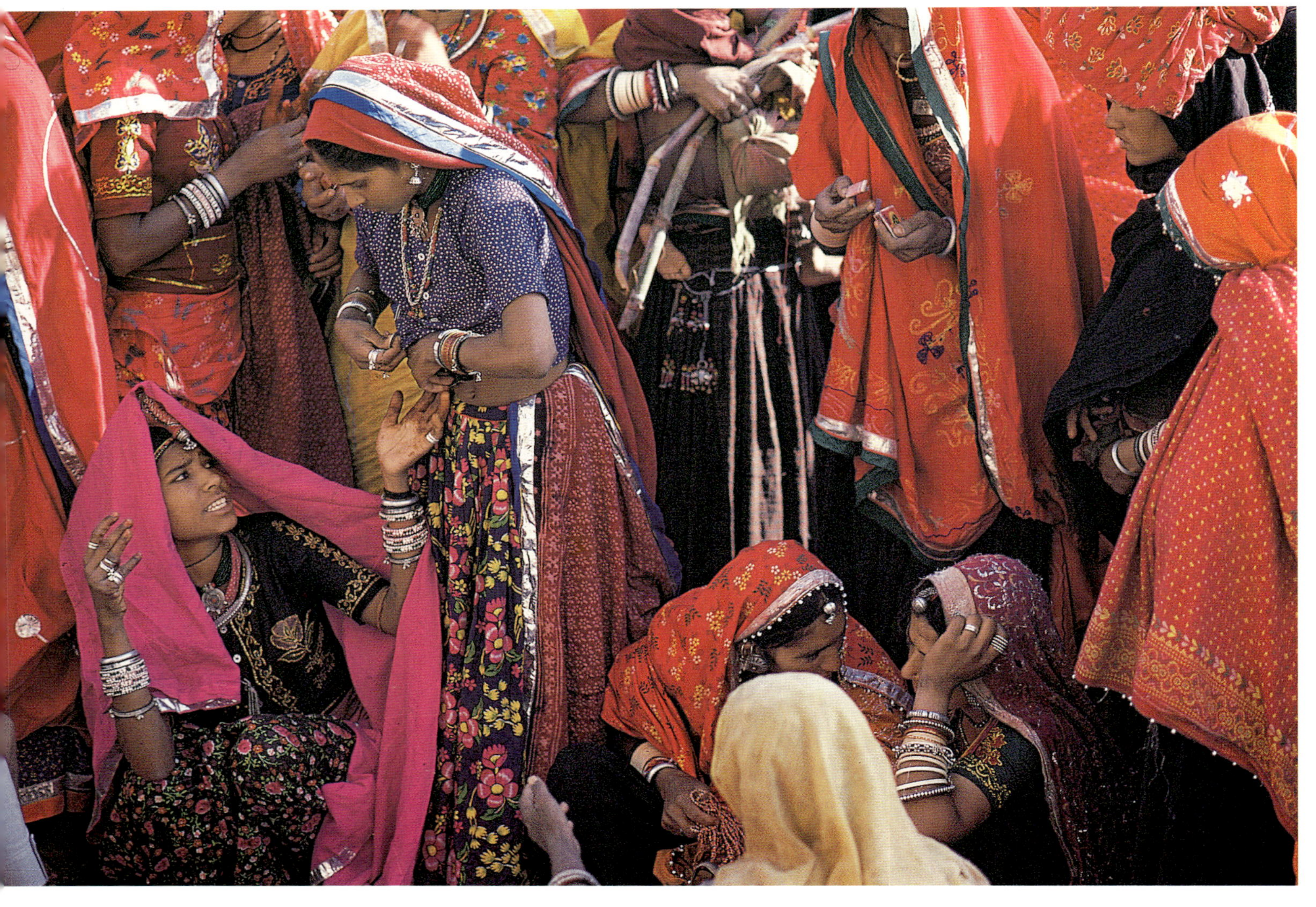

Above: Women at a fair; an elegant villager. Rajasthan.
Pages 273–275: Muslim bride, Rampur, Uttar Pradesh.

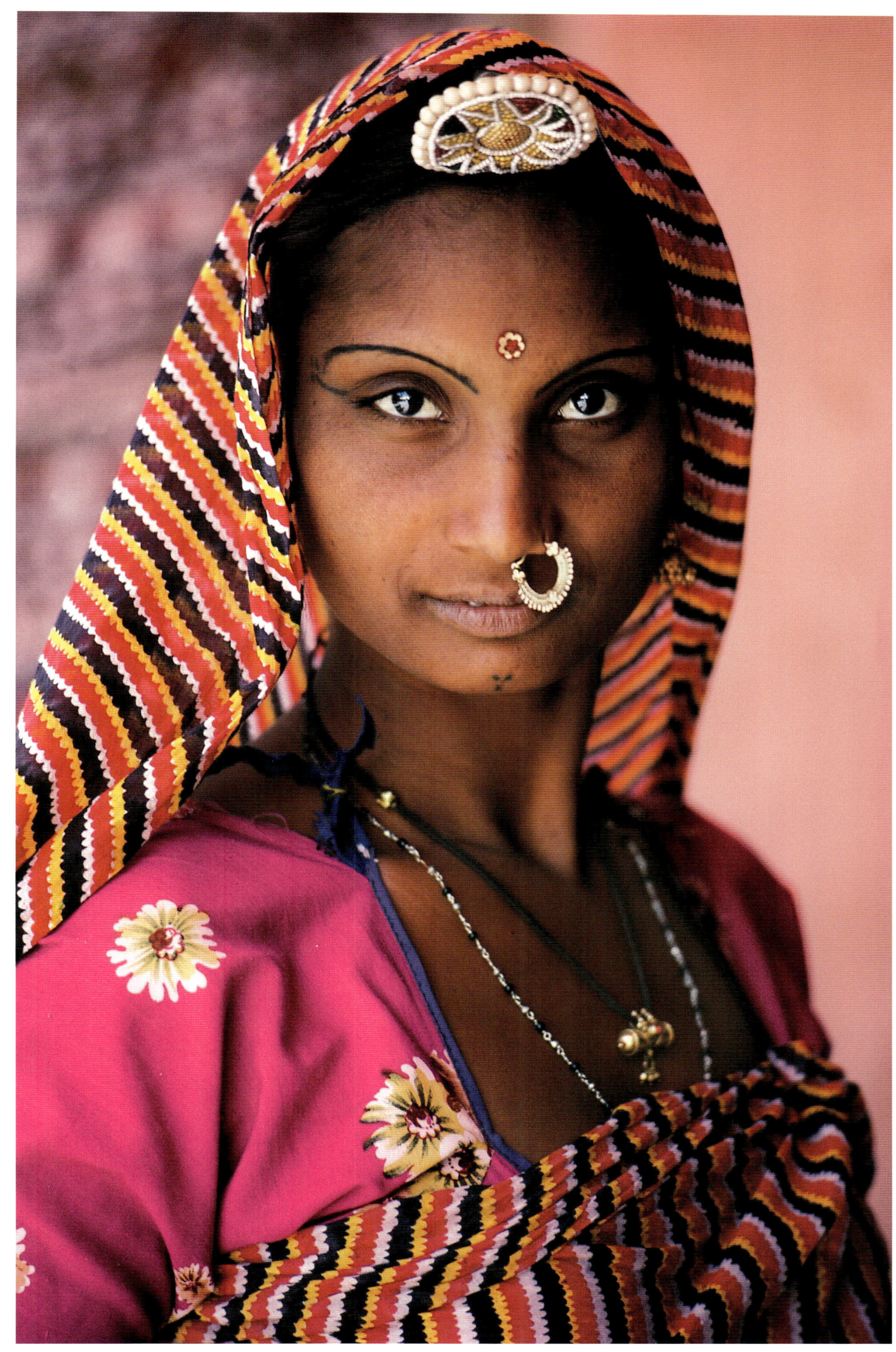

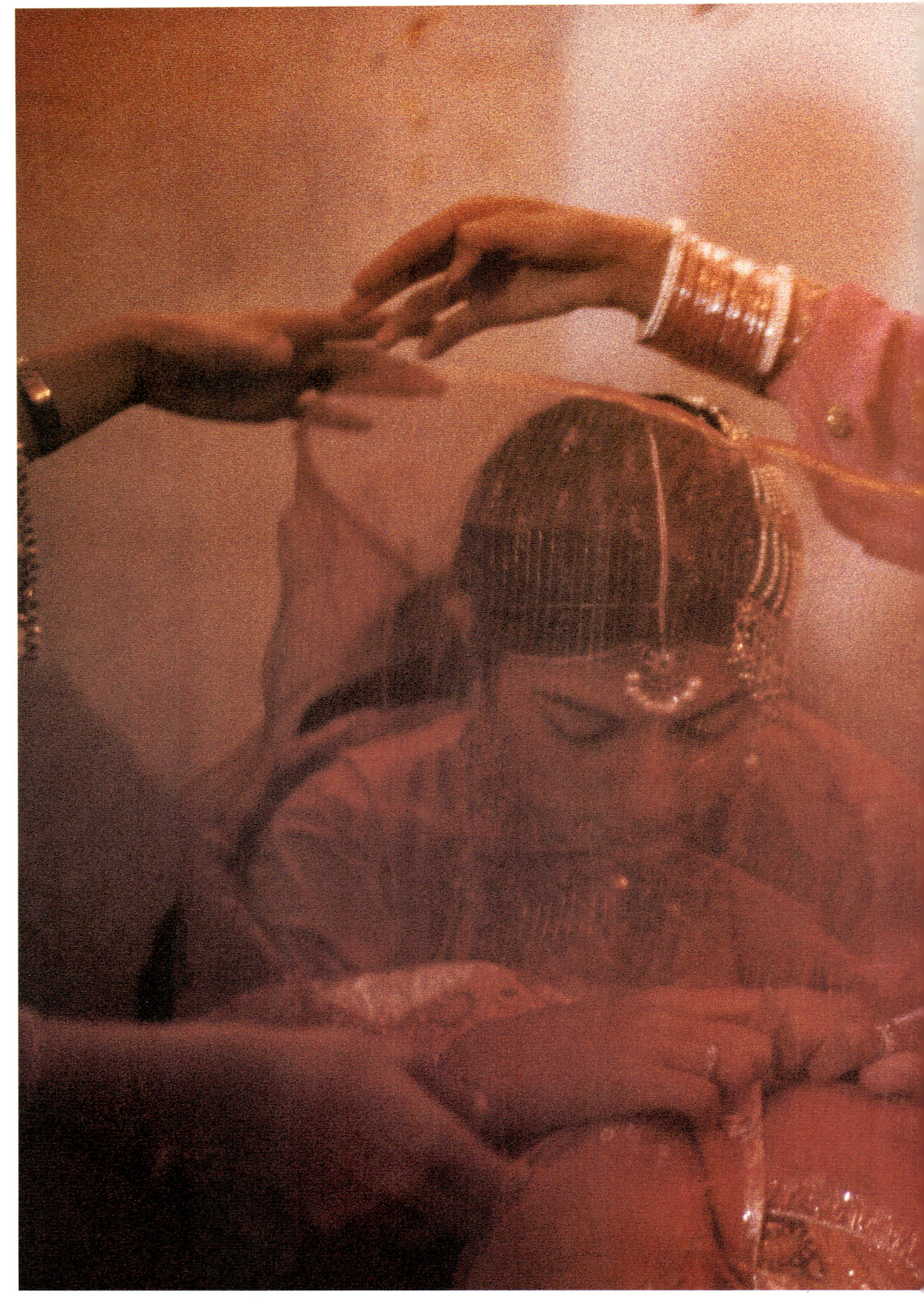

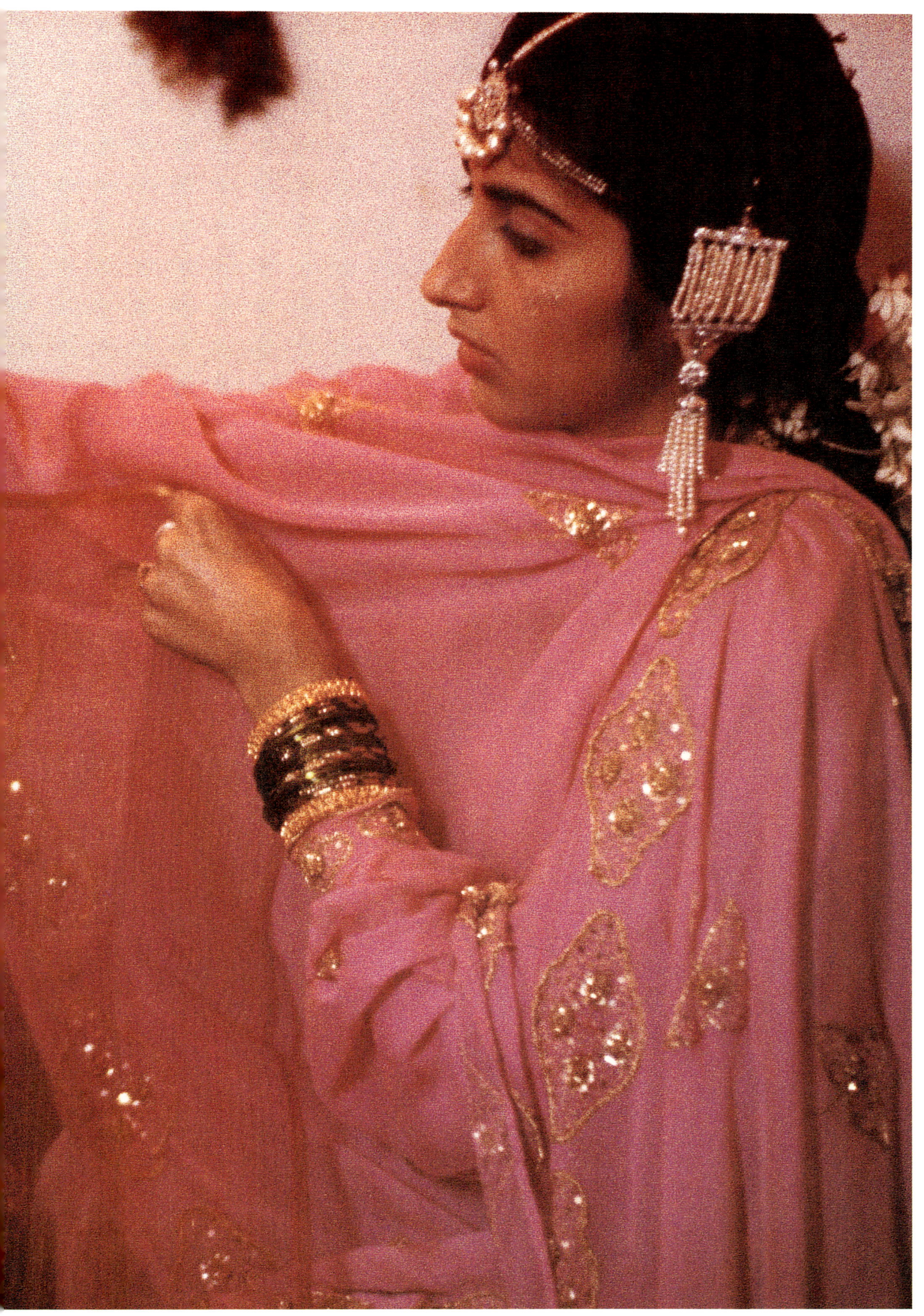

I enter your body:

Thus, united with me, the shakti, become the Lord!
Without me there is no mother,
No woman who will create the effects of the primary cause.
At the moment at which the effect manifests itself, you take on the function of a son.
Without you, there is no father, no man to manifest the effects.
It is you who is my father, and no other than you, ever.
Sometimes you take the form of a father,
sometimes you take the form of the master,
sometimes you accede to the status of son, and
sometimes you are my student.

Kulac udamani Tantra VII:81

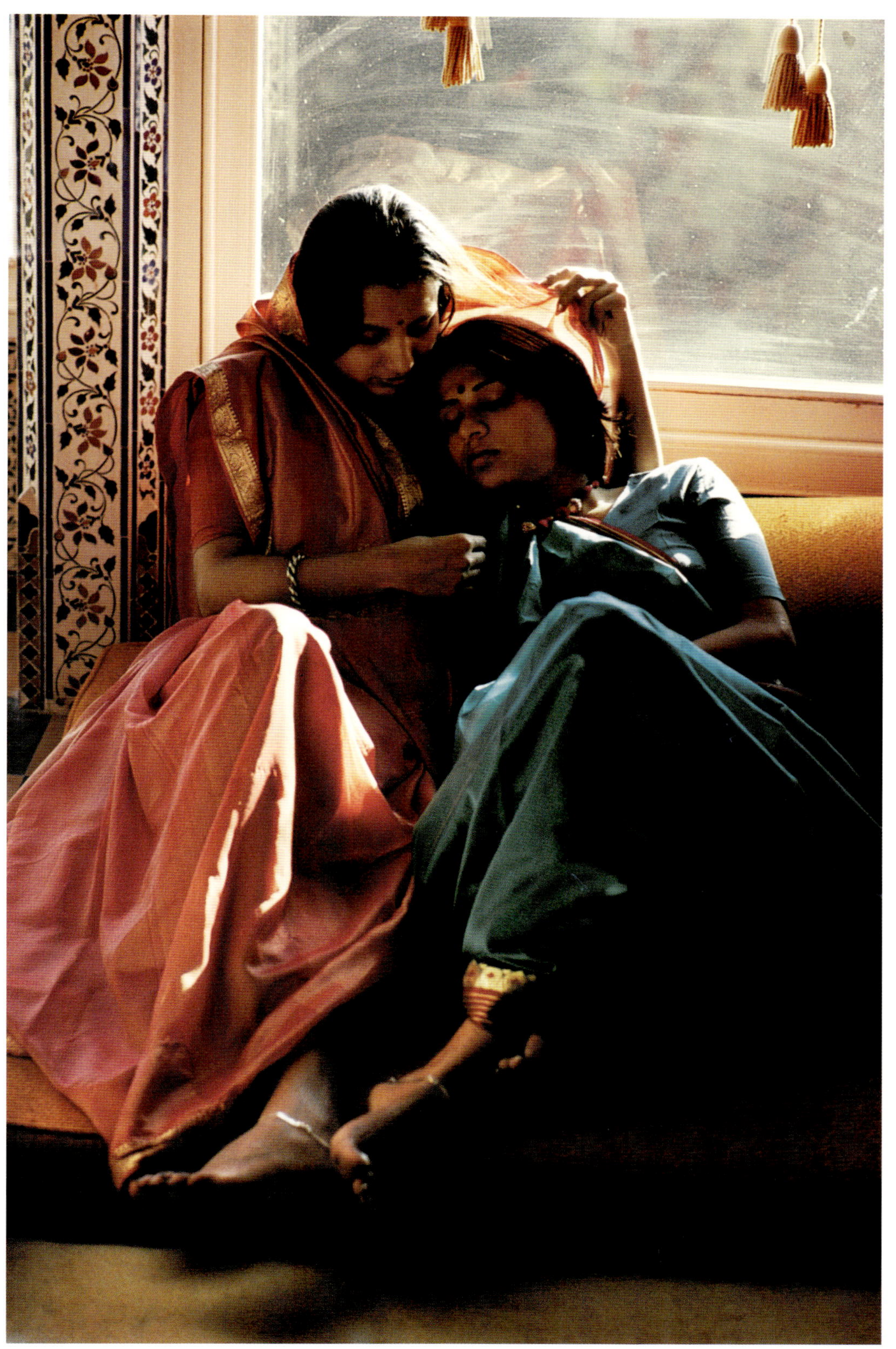

Affectionate scene.

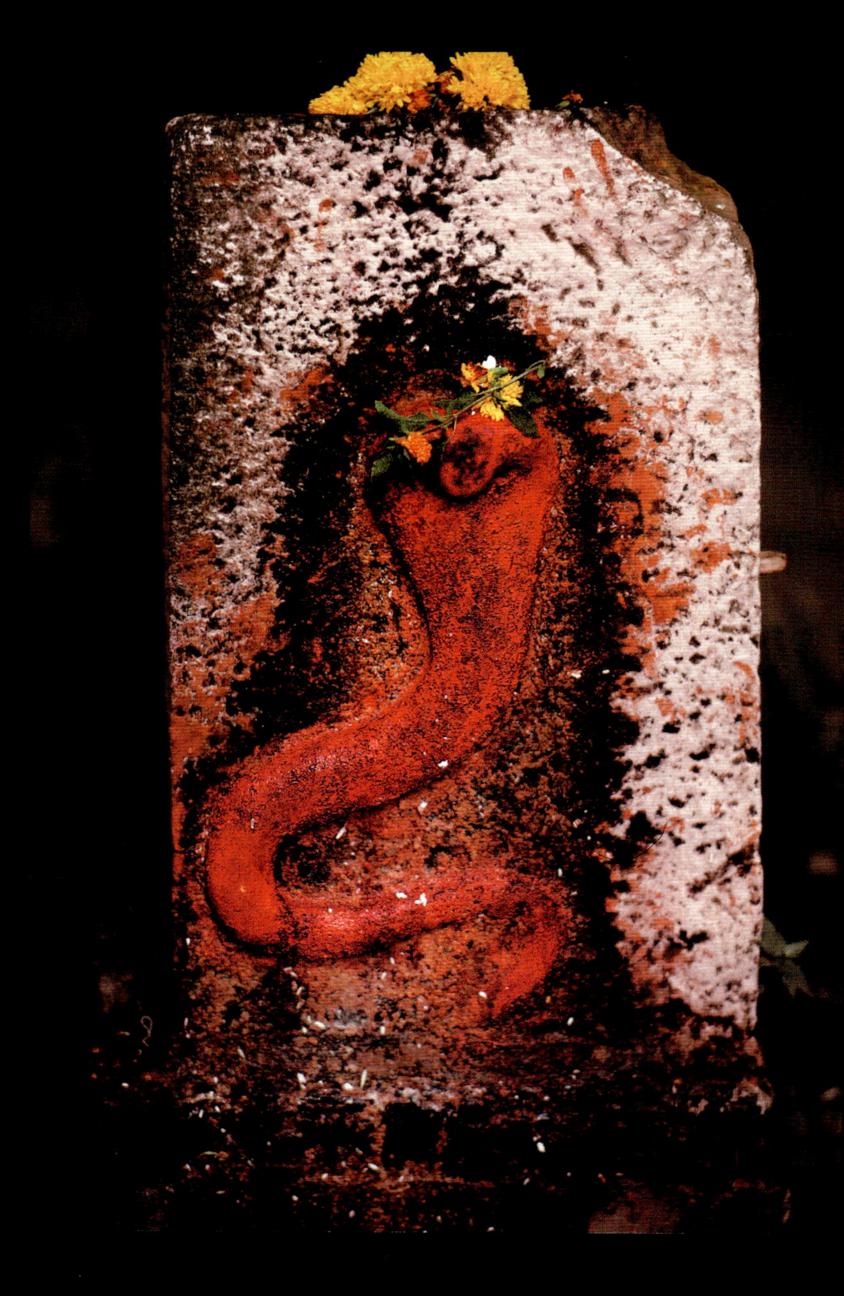

Above: Altar dedicated to the naga. Nashik, Maharashtra.
Opposite: Hairstyle, Tamil Nadu.

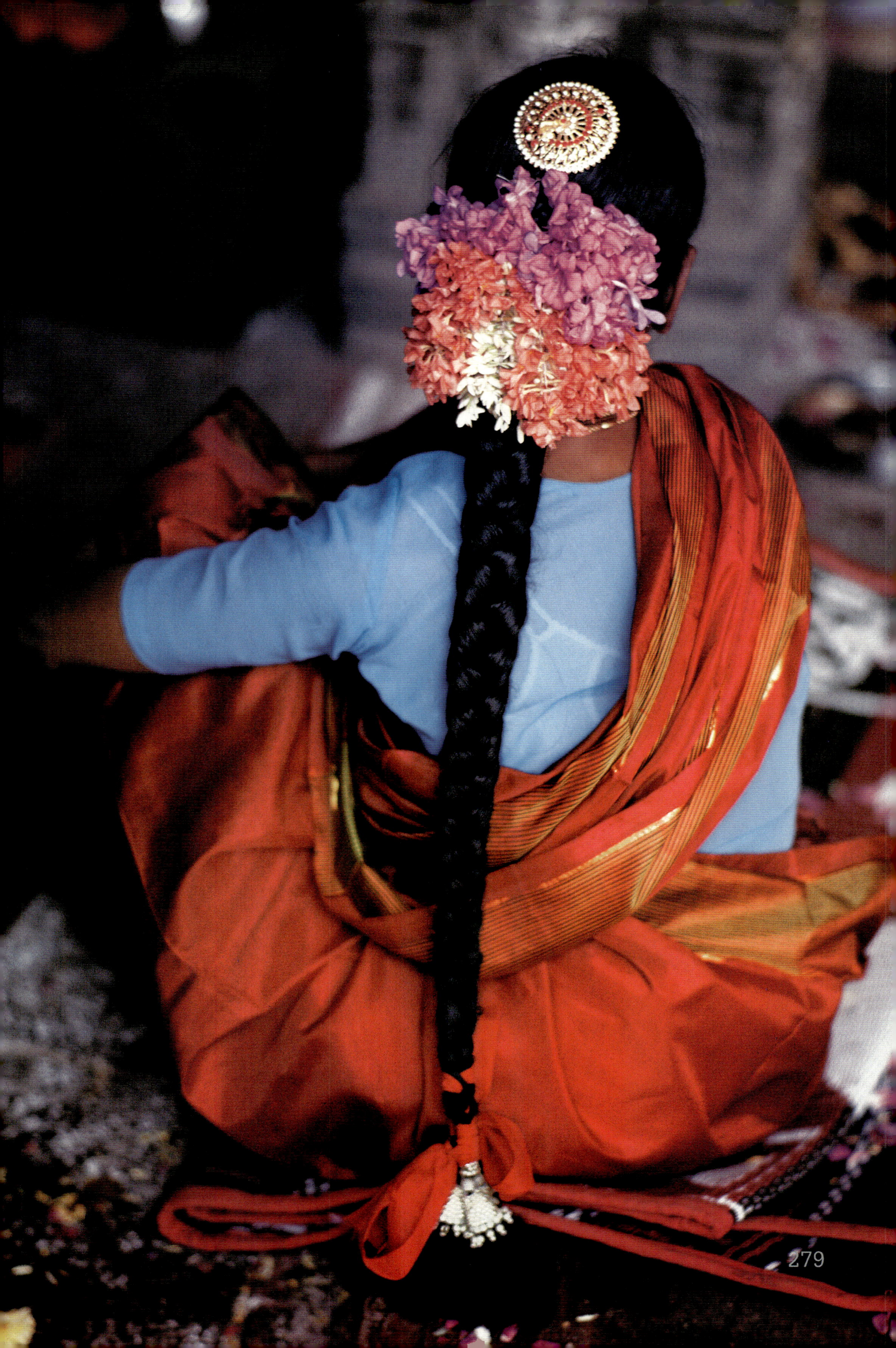

The *shakti* is the creative aspect of the divine. It is the *shakti* that gives form to the world. The phenomenal dynamic is initiated by the *shakti*. Yet it would be ridiculous demagoguery to claim that God is female. God (a Mediterranean concept) is neither man nor woman.

Neither of these two polarities is sufficient in itself. In his *shakti*, the godhead is inert, while the *shakti* is incomplete on its own. Once again we find ourselves in India, faced with moving principles that are intended to encounter another principle.

Every type of union exists in India. Does the woman walking in the dust of the bus station behind a man with a coarse face, whom she must serve and to whom she must sometimes submit, know of the power she has that is enshrined in the sacred texts? Clearly she does. She knows what divine energy flows within her, an energy that innumerable crowds worship in the temples and, better still, through the "mothers" of contemporary India. As for us, we guess that her body and her dreams know it.

Mothers played an important spiritual role in the story of twentieth-century India. They were not mandated by any institution; their recognition has come naturally and by popular acclaim. They radiate spirituality, sometimes from childhood. Disciples and subsequently crowds recognize them and gather around them, An *ashram* is created. After their death, pilgrims continue to gather around their *samadhi*. Note that although certain Indians, profiting from the spiritual aridity of the West, have appointed themselves gurus, although in their case the pocketbook has replaced the soul. No "Mothers" have ever been found to be impostors. Some "Mothers" have withdrawn into solitude. Others teach and distribute their love to those who come close to them.

Those whose influence has been strongest in the twentieth century first include Anandamoyi Ma. Of Bengali origin, she influenced millions of people, including Indira Gandhi. The *ashram* she founded at Haridwar, where the Ganges is still in its youth, attracted many devotees. Mira Alfassa (1878–1973) was a Frenchwoman from Egypt who, after meeting Sri Aurobindo in 1922, became his spiritual assistant in Pondicherry, where they developed one of the main *ashrams* of India. Known simply as "the Mother" and venerated throughout India, she took over the spiritual management of the *ashram* in 1950, when Aurobindo died. She dreamed up Auroville, inaugurated in 1968, a laboratory city for a new breed of the human race that continues to seek its way among trees and birds, under the protection of Matrimandir, an imposing spherical edifice reserved for meditation.

At Auroville, Westerners live in thatched cottages. Some make incense sticks that they sell over the internet; others plant organic cabbages while attempting to approach the supramental state. Still others teach, publish, construct, resell, or just hang out. The new world comes right after the first turning.

Mother Teresa was born in Serbia in 1910, and created her Catholic order of nuns in 1950 in Calcutta, where she died in 1997, having been awarded the Nobel Peace Prize in 1979. The highest authorities in India followed the funeral procession and Indian flags were flown at half-mast. So two of these "mothers" were of foreign extraction; one of them was even a Christian.

At the time of writing, a woman who is still young and from a very humble family in Kerala has created an *ashram* between the sea and a canal that harbors many nationalities. Amma travels to Europe and the Americas every year; she offers everyone all the love she carries within her.

Kama [*desire*] *is the first-born. . . .*
>*Neither the gods, nor the ancestors, nor men can compare with him.*
He is superior to all and will be the greatest forever.

Atharvaveda, 9, 2, 19

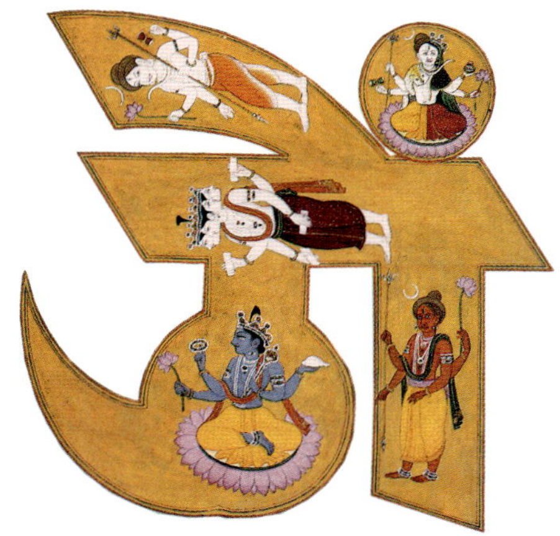

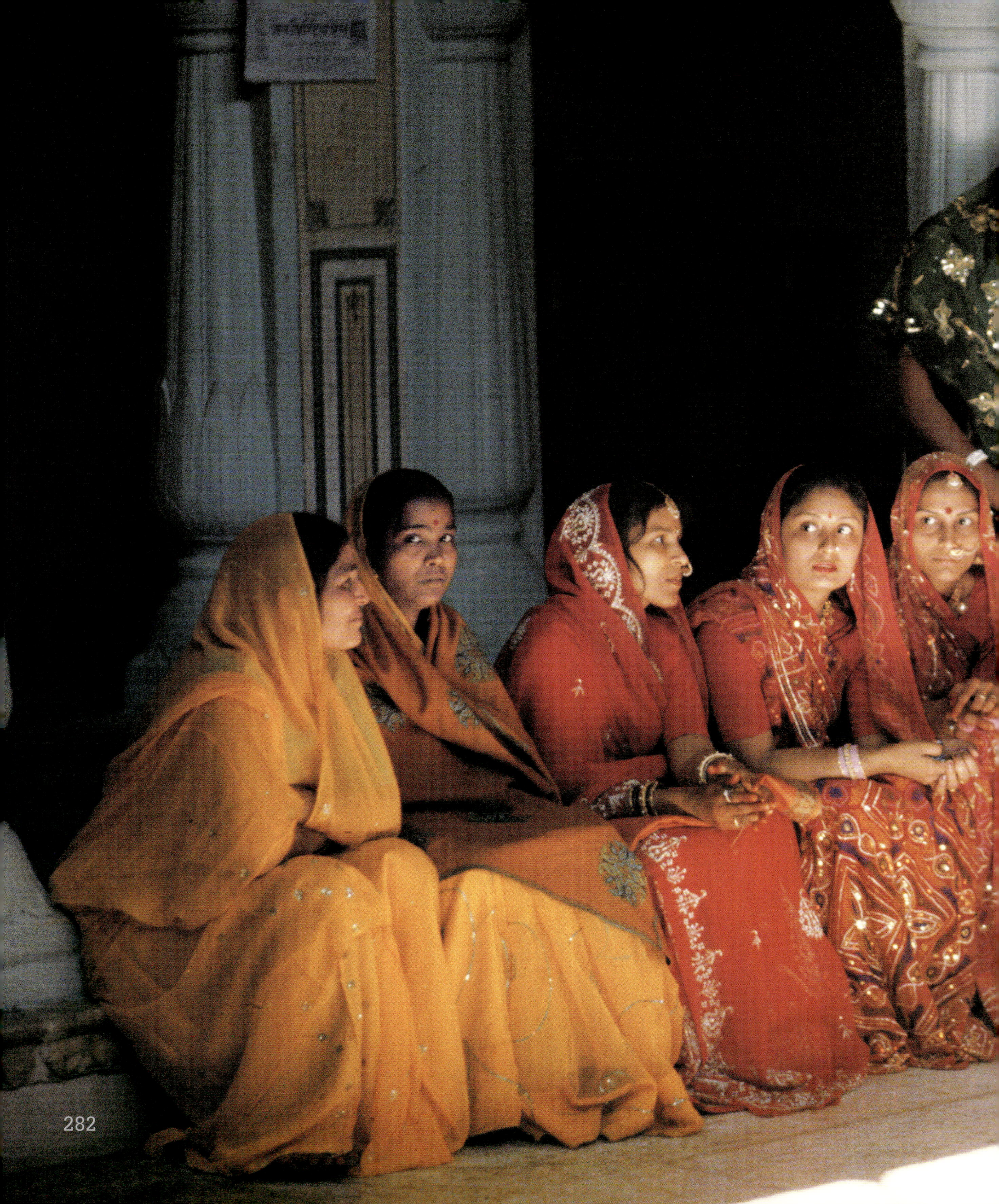

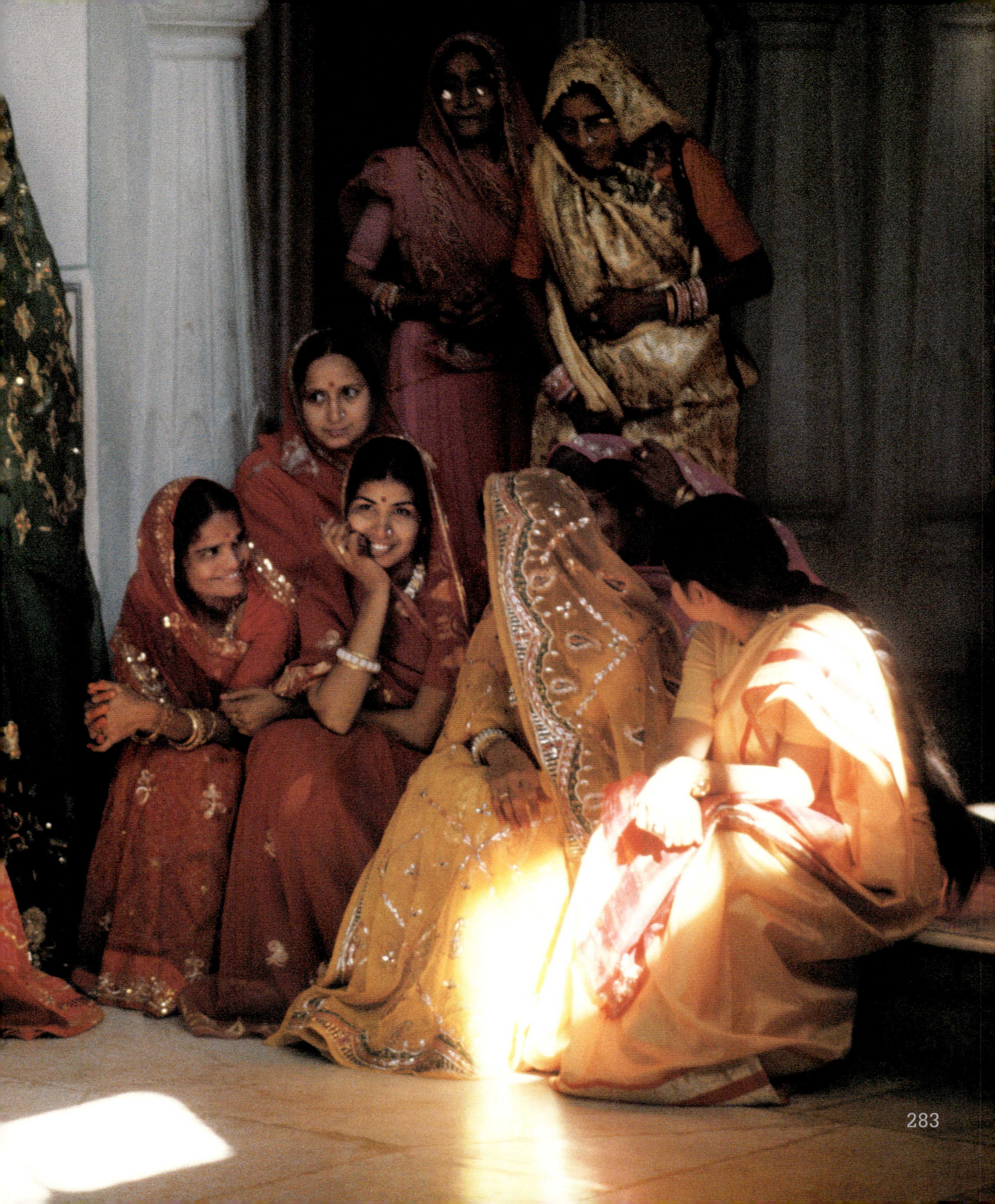

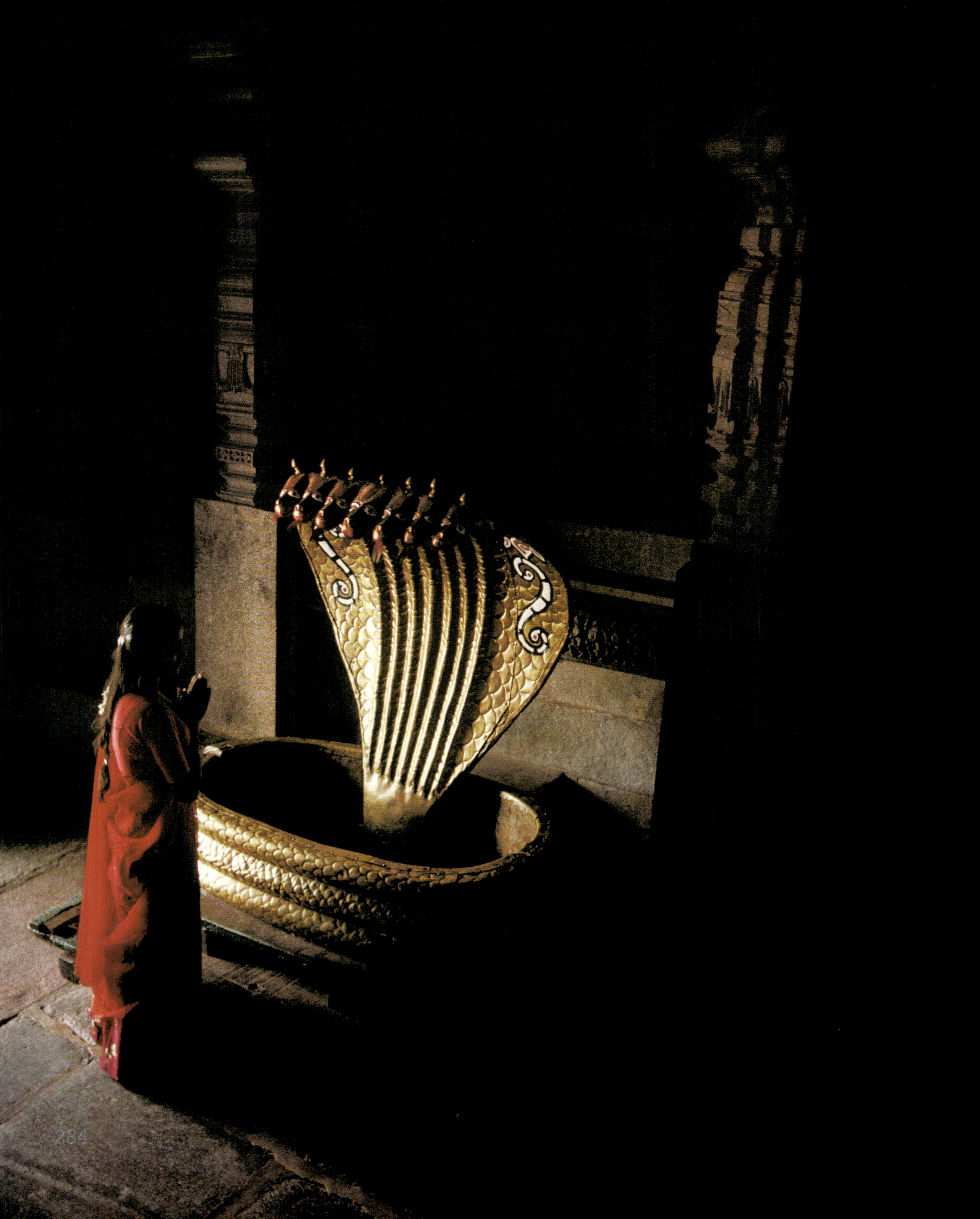

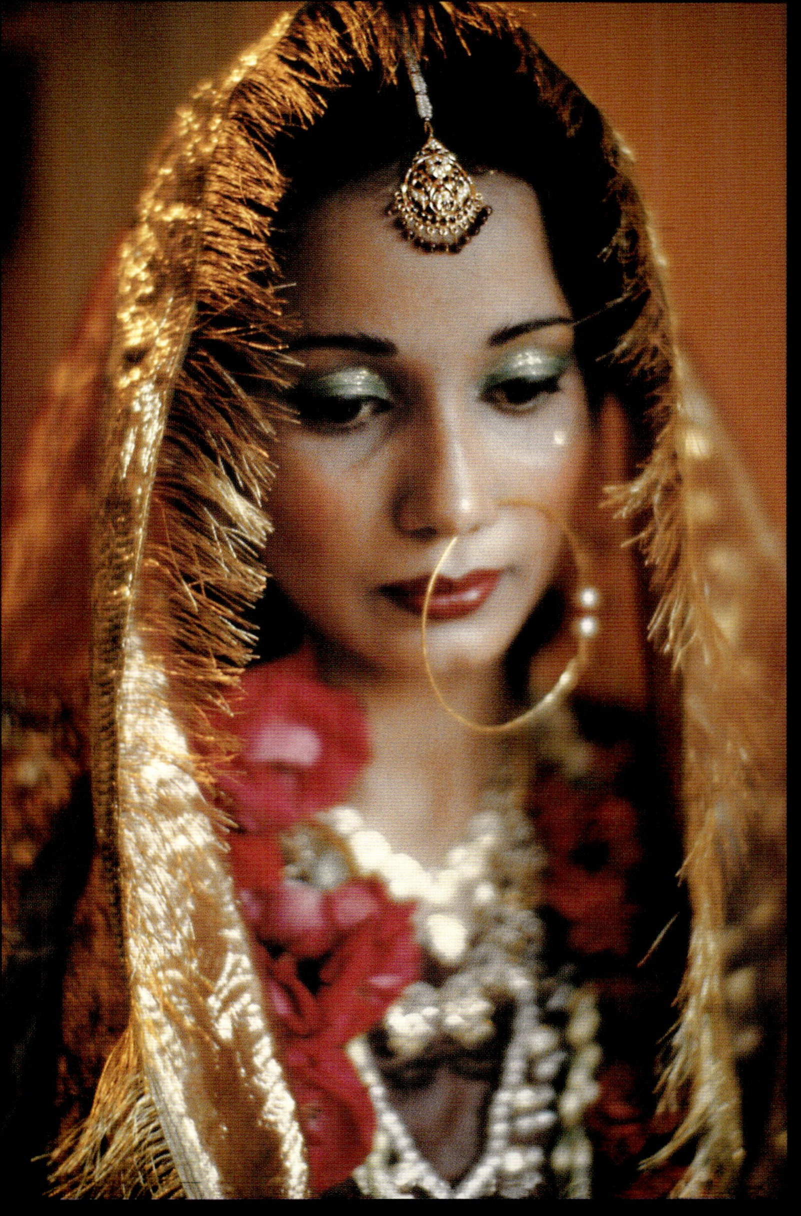

Opposite: Prayer to the naga, Kamataka.
Above: A Muslim bride.
Pages 282–283: Jain women, Rajasthan.

Much has been written about sacred eroticism. It has fueled many fantasies and often disturbs, bothers, or disappoints. This is a field which, while not being exclusive to India, has been developed and practiced there as nowhere else. But anyone who takes these rituals merely for lovemaking to the sound of Om and perfumed with incense will be committing the gravest error. In this aspect of Tantrism, sexual union is the symbol of union with the *shakti*. Tantrism of a sexual nature is reserved for initiates who are bound to keep the secret of the rituals that bring to life energies of such a nature that if they were misdirected could immediately become destructive. No authentic master of this way will ever betray the rule of secrecy that is even more necessary in an era where what is sacred—and this especially—is approached in the same way that one explores a new country. It is not a country; it is an enigma of the source.

These practices, surrounded by silence, are just one aspect of Tantrism, an esoteric movement that emerged in the fourth or fifth century A.D. within Buddhism and Hinduism. It spread throughout India from the seventh century and became firmly entrenched between the ninth and twelfth centuries. The movement is concerned with ritual, magic, yoga, meditation, and so on. There are numerous treatises that explain its principles and practices.

Within Buddhism the influence of Tantrism, is found mainly in the Tibetan Vajrayana and the Japanese Shingon. The *Kama Sutra* is a treatise on sexuality, a practical guide intended for Indians of a high caste, whose authorship is attributed to Vatsyayana, who lived in around the fifth century A.D. Although it is of indisputable historical and sociological interest, it does not tackle the intriguing connection between the erotic and the sacred, leaving the reader with the feeling that it is incomplete. This is a long way from certain Tantric texts, and far from the *shakti* as evoked in the following passage by the Romanian scholar and writer Mircea Eliade:

> *Each naked woman is the incarnation of Nature, the* prakriti. *She should thus be regarded with the same admiration and the same detachment that is accorded to the unfathomable secret of Nature in its boundless capacity for creation. The ritual nakedness of the Yogini has an intrinsic mystical value. If, when confronted with the naked woman, one does not discover in one's deepest being the same terrifying emotion that one feels before the revelation of the cosmic Mystery—then there is no rite, just a profane act.*

> *On Indian Erotic Mysticism*

The evening sun in its red mask. The flame that is raised before Shiva borrows this mask that in its turn animates the circle of flames—the Origin. There is a tapping in the night. Is it that water dripping on a rock? No. Here is the field of the dead. The pyre is hidden behind a briar hedge. It has always been located near a river, whose currents will bear away the ashes.

A child rummages in the embers. He finds a ring that has fallen from the calcined finger of a dead woman who has been hidden. We saw it too, but late at night, when all that is left are ashes, dogs come to feed.

The ember is a living diamond. The red rings it with the speed of blood circulating in the body. Is it possible to worship this red, the same red as that of the womb that receives the semen, the red spot on the forehead's third eye, or that which runs from the severed heads of Kali's necklace?

Blood, sexuality, sun, and wisdom create a circle. Would you like to join it? You must take life in one hand, death in the other. Oblivion? Would you like assurance? Something such as progress or eternity? That's impossible in this dance. India takes life, India takes death, India unites them. Between the two, the only way out is to enter the vermilion spot that is placed by a light finger on the forehead, between closed eyes, the *tilak* that abolishes the shadows.

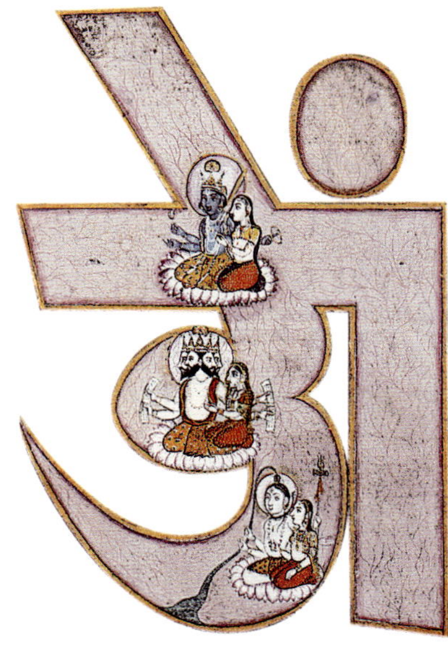

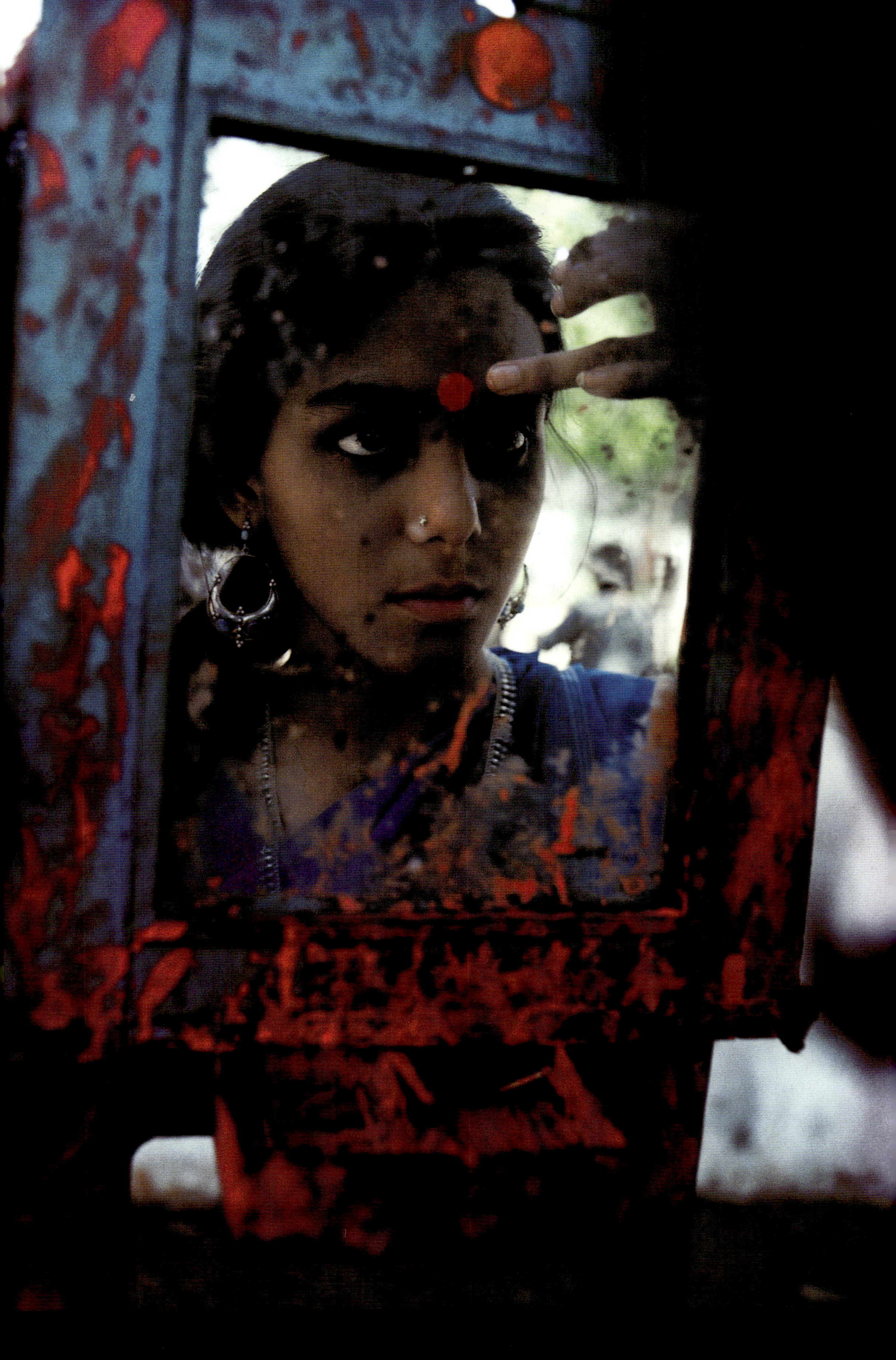

A married woman applying her *tilak*, Ahmedabad, Gujerat.

Notes on the Photographs
by Roland and Sabrina Michaud

Front cover

Kalarippayat. See caption for pages 146–147.

Back cover

Tilak. See caption for page 289.

Endpapers

Jain temples in Politana. See caption for pages 146–147.

2

Camel fair. See caption for pages 102–103.

6–7

Arrival of the monsoon, June 2001

The Agali, The Western Ghats, Kerala. This is when earth and sky are in tumult, preceded by thunder and lightning, when the black rain clouds burst asunder and released their torrents; the Indians talk of the "explosions" of the monsoon. They are a sign that the prayer for rain has been heard. In the words of Rabindranath Tagore: "I beg you, Lord, recall to yourself that silent, dead, deceitful, and cruel heat, that burns the heart with an insurmountable despair." Man breathes again, "the sky opens, the winds are let loose, a laugh makes the earth tremble."

8–9

Monsoon sky, June 2001

Bekal Fort, northern Kerala. As the poet Rabindranath Tagore puts it, the clouds "lean down very low from the sky, like the tearful expression of a mother on a day when a father is angry."

10–11

Pastoral scene in the rainy season, June 2001

Kasargod, northern Kerala. Beneath the monsoon rains, the landscape revives and turns green again; the range of greens and browns expands into a magnificent palette.

12–13

Monsoon rain, July 1977

Galta, near Jaipur, Rajasthan. Cyclists try to take shelter under umbrellas as they pedal along the road to Jaipur.

14–15

Ox-cart race, September 1994

Bhosari region, Maharashtra. Thousands of peasants love the local sport of ox-cart racing. Under a leaden sky, hundreds of oxen harnessed to iron chariots compete on a regulation race course. The atmosphere is electric. In a swirl of yellow dust, the owners throw handfuls of yellow turmeric powder over their beasts to bring them luck. This is an authentic country festival in which one can feel how closely the men identify with their animals as companions at the plow.

16

Road in Tamil Nadu, February 1996

Near Madras. Alongside the "modern" traffic of automobiles, buses, and trucks, Indian roads continue to be clogged with hundreds of thousands of carts and wagons drawn by animals.

18–19

Morning mist, November 1998

Calcutta. A Hatha yoga devotee practices a few positions on the lawns of the Maidan in the heart of Calcutta. This wide, open space was designed to make it easier to shoot at an enemy from within Fort William. Today it is used for horse-racing, political meetings, and cricket matches.

22

Pastoral scene, April 1965

Puri region, Orissa. This is "cow-dust," time, when the herds of cattle return home to the village, leaving a cloud of dust behind them; this special moment is particularly serene and poetic.

23

Sunrise over the trees, February 1966

Darasuram, Tamil Nadu. The bucolic, peaceful atmosphere of deepest India, that of the 600,000 villages that appear to be to be immobile and eternal.

26

Street scene, November 1993

Calcutta. In the Babu Ghat district, the women perform the morning puja ritual in the form of an offering of flowers and fruits to a sacred tree; in the middle ground, a young boy is hosing down an Ambassador automobile under the watchful eye of its owner, a Sikh taxi driver. In India there is no separation between the sacred and the profane.

27

Traditional greeting, February 1994

Tirunelveli region, Tamil Nadu. The guardian of the temple of Krishnapuram continues to hold on to his keys while greeting visitors in the traditional Indian manner. The Indian greeting (namaskar) consists of bringing the hands together over the forehead and heart in anjali, "bouquet of flowers."

28–29

Peasant scene, April 1966

Karnataka. On red laterite soil in a field that has recently been plowed, an old peasant woman collects twigs for kindling that will fuel her fire for the evening meal.

30–31

Pastoral scene, September 1994

Khandava region, Maharashtra. By the end of the rainy season, greenery has replaced the dirty yellow vegetation of the dry season.

32

Herd of Cattle, November 1987

Gujarat. In the arid countryside, a herd of emaciated cattle are moved in search of grazing. The Sanskrit term go, meaning "cow," also means "ray of sunshine" and "spiritual illumination." This last meaning explains the sacred role played by the cow in India, because Indian tradition relates that great sages (the rishi, or seers) were incarnated in cows. The Indian breed of cattle, known as zebu, is different from European breeds due to the hump on its withers, which is also a symbol of the fertile earth, the Divine Mother, who provides five products—milk, butter, yogurt, urine, and dung. Cow's milk is the main source of protein for Indians. Ghee (clarified butter) never goes rancid and is used for cooking and for ritual purposes. Dung is used as fuel for cooking food and villagers mix it with earth and use it as a fertilizer as well as spreading it in the entrance to their houses to clean and purify them. Cow's urine is considered to be purifying, and is drunk by many Hindus as a medicine.

33

Children, November 1987

Gujarat. India is poor, materially speaking, when compared to the prosperous West, but spiritually, it is immensely rich and extremely dignified.

36–37

The Observatory, March 1985

Jaipur, Rajasthan. Jaipur, capital of the state of Rajasthan, was built by the maharajah Jai Singh II (1699–1743) whose name has been immortalized as a politician, city planner, and astronomer. He built five observatories in 18th-century India, including that of Jaipur, which remains the best preserved and the finest. It is constructed of stone and marble in one of the courtyards of the palace. The Jantar Mantar observatory is a brilliant example of architectural strength and technique. Its numerous astronomical instruments are still used by *pandits* (scholars and scientists) to perform astronomical observations and determine the most propitious dates for celebrating certain religious festivals. The circular instruments shown on 36, framed by stone pillars, are made of an alloy of seven metals. Each ring is marked out in 360 degrees and rotates on an axis parallel to that of the Earth. The *pandit* uses a hollow tube laid across the metal diameter of the ring to survey the sky. The position of a star on the graduated circle indicates its position in space. The instrument photographed on 37 represents an armillary sphere consisting of two concave marble hemispheres on a rectangular flint platform. The hemispheres are about 18 feet in diameter and are shown in the celestial sphere upside down. The edge of the hemispheres are divided into 360 degrees, and represent the horizon. The central point at the bottom shows the zenith through which the local meridian line passes. The enormous size of this instrument, called the Jai Prakash Yantra, can be gauged by the pandit who has descended into it. It is a huge map of the heavens, outside in.

38–39

Street scene, December 1983

Old Delhi. This is the great artery that runs from the Red Fort to the Fatehpuri mosque in Old Delhi, an artery choked with vehicles of every kind and lined with temples, bazaars, and movie theaters.

42–43

Traffic jam, December 1983

Old Delhi. This continuation of the Chandni Chowk ends at the Lahore Gate, and is the most overcrowded street in Old Delhi, and possibly on the planet! This is the location of the wholesale flower market and the spice market, with its extraordinary colors and odors. In the picture, the long, narrow pushcarts operated by coolies, rickshaw cycles, and ox-carts are vying for space with trucks and a procession of elephants hired to publicize a brand of detergent.

44

Street scene, December 1983

Old Delhi. The Indian ability to blot out noise and crowds is prodigious. In the middle of the most vibrant hullabaloo, people are able to concentrate on reading a newspaper, drinking tea, or cleaning their ears, and the water carrier and fortune teller carry on with their work. It is hard for a foreigner, especially a photographer, to pass unnoticed and not to have his field of vision blocked by a crowd of spectators staring at him.

45

Beggar, October 1993

Benares (Varanasi), Uttar Pradesh. The justification for the beggar in traditional societies is to enable other people to perform an act of charity.

46–47

Intersection, December 1983

Old Delhi. See captions for 42–43 and 44.

48

Porters, December 1983

Old Delhi. Longshoremen rest for a moment on sacks of merchandise on the pushcart for which they are responsible.

49

Pontoon Bridge, January 1988

Benares, Uttar Pradesh. This pontoon bridge links Benares with Ramnagar on the other side of the Ganges. It is dismantled during the rainy season but during the dry season it makes for better circulation from one bank to the other, at least for light traffic.

50–51

Streetcar, November 1993

Calcutta. The ramshackle streetcars of Calcutta are part of the urban landscape of this city that is full of surprises, in the same way as the rickshaws. In the foreground there is a store selling religious artifacts and exhibiting a representation of Kali, patroness of the city.

54–55

Ganesh festival, September 1994

Bombay (Mumbai). Ganesh Chaturthi (the Ganesh festival) lasts for ten days, and is the most important local event of the year. Huge pottery representations of the elephant-headed god are taken in procession around the city to be finally immersed in the ocean on the beaches of Chowpathy, Worli, Mahim, and Juhu. This festival celebrates the birth of the god who is the son of Shiva and of Parvati and who symbolizes wisdom and prosperity. Ganesh removes the obstacles that lie in the path of every human being. The idols may be very small and are placed on altars in private homes. Gigantic versions are also made which can measure 35 feet in height, weigh several tons, and cost more than 100,000 rupees. Members of the same trade or people living in the same neighborhood get together to collect funds and seek sponsorship. On the last day of the festival, accompanied by musicians, dancers, and street performers, the idols, estimated to number 9,000, are bathed in the ocean at 70 immersion points (cranes are sometimes needed to hoist the statues into the sea and aluminum slipways are set up on the beach to slide them into the water). The number of people who take part in this huge event, singing: "O Father Ganesh, come back to us next year." is estimated at ten million annually.

56

Ecumenical poster, January 1989

Allahabad, Uttar Pradesh. Ecumenism is well represented in India, a traditionally tolerant country. Behind a bicycle parking lot, a gigantic primitive mural shows representatives of all the religions sitting in a circle around a pipal, or sacred fig tree (*Ficus religiosa*) on which the sacred *om* or *aum* mantra is painted.

57

Sannyasin and policemen, October 1993

Benares, Uttar Pradesh. Beside the temple of Vishvanath, a *sannyasi* chats to three police officers. The image symbolizes the two most powerful forces in the world, military and religious, the sword and the spirit.

59

Washing textiles, December 1966

Ahmedabad, Gujarat. This city is the industrial center of India, based on three materials, silk, gold, and cotton. It has the fifth-largest population of any city in India and is famous for its weaving and dyeing industries. Fabrics are dipped in the waters of the Sabarmati, the river that flows through the city and gives its name to the ashram founded by Gandhi in 1918.

60

Offering in honor of Shiva, January 1990

Beraghat on the Narmada River, Madhya Pradesh. A *lingam* is a cylindrical phallic symbol that represents Shiva, the most fundamental image of the divinity whose aim is to put the devotee in the presence of an ineffable Absolute. Every morning, throughout India, millions of faithful offer their favorite god a special form of adoration that can be performed in the open air, in a temple, or at home. For a *Brahman*—member of the highest caste (he can be recognized here by the cord he wears across the chest), the ritual is more complex. Wearing only his dhoti—the traditional loincloth—the *Brahman* seen here is pouring water on a *lingam*. He will perform a series of specific rituals, decorating the *lingam* with a sandalwood paste, placing a garland of flowers over it, and lighting a joss-stick before it.

61

Sadhu meditating, December 1981

Gwalior, Madhya Pradesh. A *sadhu* is normally someone who has renounced worldly goods and temptations in order to dedicate himself to the spiritual life. It is hard for a Westerner to measure the richness of the Hindu tradition in this respect; let us say simply that sages and madmen are venerated throughout India and that there are hundreds of thousands of them. They may be disciples of Shiva, Vishnu, and the Great Goddess; there are sedentary and wandering *sadhus*, those who practice yoga or unbelievable mortification, those who have taken a vow of silence or who live in cemeteries, those who walk around completely naked. The *sadhu* in this photograph is called Sri Baba Ram Ratan Das Tyagi.

62–63

Hindu procession, February 1989

Allahabad (Prayag), Uttar Pradesh. On Monday, February 6, 1989, the day of the new moon in the month of Magh, a procession of holy men and sages walked to the Sangam, where three sacred rivers, the Ganges, the Yamuna, and the mythical Saraswati meet. Here they were to take the greatest ritual bath in India. The astrologers confirmed that the conjunction of the stars had not been as favorable for one hundred and forty-four years. Furthermore, this year, fifteen million pilgrims came here to purify themselves. The great Kumbh Mela is the biggest religious gathering in the world and it only happens every twelve years. Perched on top of a police prowl-car and surrounded by an ocean of humanity, we witnessed and shared the fervor of a nation. The holy men and sages and their disciples are carried on palanquins and are revered with the same veneration as kings or heads of state.

64

Tree trunk representing Ganesh, January 1990

Maheshwar. a city on the Narmada River, Madhya Pradesh. The stylized form of the elephant god, painted vermilion, can be discerned in this tree. All that needs to be added are two pearls for the eyes. This is a Ganesh Svayambhu, i.e. one born of himself who exists autonomously.

65

Wayside shrine, November 1993

Calcutta. Garlands heaped on an altar dedicated to Hanuman, the monkey god, patron of fighters. They were placed there by devotees at a morning offering. The French marigold, *Tagetes patula*, is the most popular floral tribute in Hindu temples because its orange-yellow color symbolizes renunciation.

66–67

Street market, December 1992

Bombay. Crawford Market was opened in 1869, and for a long time, it was the largest wholesale market in the city, selling fruits, vegetables, flowers, poultry, meat, and fish. The reliefs that decorate the outside of the Norman Gothic-style building were created by Lockwood Kipling, father of Rudyard Kipling. The wholesale markets have now moved to New Bombay, Crawford Market, now better known as Mahatma Phule Market, continues to thrive. Merchants reside like high priests over their booths heaped with fruits and deals are made between buyers and sellers by means of a secret set of signs made with the finger beneath a piece of cloth. The paving stones were brought specially from Caithness in Scotland.

68–69

Porters, December 1998

Calcutta. Near Sealdah station, at the Kali Market, porters dexterously maneuver the huge bundles in which the merchandise is transported. Once their mission has been accomplished, they rest from their labors.

70–71

Vultures, January 1988

Uttar Pradesh. Vultures are the super-scavengers of India, the most efficient representatives imaginable of waste disposal who feed on the carcasses of dead animals, cows, water-buffalos, and elephants. They are repulsively ugly when on the ground but fly with remarkable grace and, contrary to received wisdom, they are very timid and cowardly, and will easy give way to dogs and crows. The vulture is traditionally associated with earth and sky. On the earth, since the ancients believed that the nether regions were governed by the king of the vultures. In the sky, because in the form of a mythical creature, half-man half-bird named Garuda, the vulture symbolizes the sun itself. Garuda is the name of Vishnu's chariot.

74

Old woman, January 1967

Ahmedabad, Gujarat. The hands of this old woman are as wrinkled as her face. Life's vicissitudes leave a greater imprint on the poor than on the rich.

75

Returning home from the fields, March 1966

Kerala. The work day in the fields has ended; these farm workers are all smiles and laughter.

78–79

Village in the Deccan, April 1982

Mandu region, Madhya Pradesh. In India, village life sometimes seems to be bathed in an almost perfect serenity, but sometimes it lapses into the most terrible human tragedies.

80

Pipe smoker, July 1987

Samod, Rajasthan. In the 16th century the Portuguese introduced tobacco to India, where it was warmly received. The hubble-bubble dates from more or less the same era and was introduced by the Persians. From a pleasure reserved for the court it spread to the common people, but today it has fallen out of use, except in the country. These villagers are savoring a moment of leisure smoking a simple clay pipe.

81

Returning from the well, August 1987

Madhya Pradesh. Drinking water remains a major problem in India and Indians have always dug wells. Every ruler has tried to provide water tanks and wells, of which there are many types. Access to this well is via a spiral staircase.

82

Village interior, March 1984

Udaipur, Rajasthan. A little girl tries tenderly to distract her mother, who is busy preparing a meal.

83

Winnowing, February 1966

Tamil Nadu. A village girl separates the grain from the chaff using a winnowing basket.

86–87

A moment of relaxation, December 1992

Poona (Pune), Maharashtra. Against the background of a mural gradually fading from the effects of sunlight and inclement weather, citizens relax by reading a newspaper or watching the passing scene. On the left, the scene depicted in the painting represents the construction by an army of monkeys of the bridge destined to link southern India with Lanka (Ceylon, now known as Sri Lanka); on the right, there is the Rama-Sita in which each Indian couple tries to recognize each other.

88

Chess players, November 1989

Udaipur, Rajasthan. On a wall daubed with blue, there are the graphic symbols that represent two Indian political parties (the hand and the lotus). The chess players have found a corner of the sidewalk for themselves and are so absorbed in their game that they are unaware of the presence of the photographer. Chess originated in India. Shesha, Shriram's first minister, wanted to show the king's son, a dissolute prince, that without the support of the people the king was destined to meet an unfortunate end. Shriram was so pleased with this new game that he placed chess boards in all the temples. When the king wanted to know what reward Shesha wanted, the minister asked that a grain of rice be placed in the first square of the checkerboard, that the number of grains be doubled in the second, doubled again in the third, and so on until the last square, when the final measure of grains that resulted would be granted to him. The king protested, saying that such a small reward was inadequate, but Shesha remained inflexible in his request, and the king ordered this to be done. When the king's treasurer worked out the quantity of rice needed, he came to the king trembling and announced that he was incapable of executing the order. He explained that although there would only be one grain of rice in the first square, the sixteenth square would need 32,768 grains, or the equivalent of a pound of wheat; as for the fortieth square, it would need whole granaries to fill it from 16,384 cities. Since there were not that many cities in the kingdom, he could not obey the order. The king was delighted with Shesha's wisdom and heaped expensive gifts upon him declaring that the ingenuity that he displayed in formulating his request was even greater than the talent that enabled him to invent the game.

89

Temple gateway, February 1994

Tirunelveli, Tamil Nadu. Taking a nap in front of the magnificent wooden entrance to a local temple.

90–91

Inn, January 1992

Karnataka. Most of the wayside inns are decorated with crude images of the gods, Bollywood movie stars, and politicians. This inn, where a customer is waiting to be served, is different in its austerity.

94–95

Saffron field in bloom, November 1981

Pampore, Kashmir. Saffron (*Crocus sativus*) is the name given to the pistils of this purple crocus which, when carefully dried, produces reddish-orange strands with a subtle odor and flavor that is faintly bitter. In Kashmir, the flowers bloom in late fall and only grow in the Pampore region. The Mogul emperors who annexed Kashmir, demanded a tribute in saffron, but India was exporting saffron to China as early as the Tang dynasty, and certain Chinese wines, like some Roman wines, were flavored with saffron. The herb is used as a beauty product on the skin, as a medicine to cure headaches, as an aphrodisiac, but nowadays mainly as a spice in the kitchen, since true saffron is rare and expensive.

96

Harvesting chili peppers, December 1983

Kishangarh, Rajasthan. Chili peppers or pimentos are the dried fruits of the *Capsicum annuum.* They play an essential role in Indian cuisine and are cultivated throughout the land. When they are ready for harvesting, a huge carpet of these scarlet fruits dried in the sun. The chilis are ground or crushed and used as a seasoning, either alone or added to other herbs and spices, to make the famous *masala,* the base for all the Indian curries. Chili pepper is an incendiary spice but in the right amount it enriches the flavor of foods. India is the land of spices par excellence, and the people have appreciated their medicinal and other properties for thousands of years, but the famous chili pepper is not native. Chilies come from the New World and were introduced to India relatively late, probably by the Portuguese.

97

Villager girls, March 1984

Udaipur, Rajasthan. Two sisters, attending a fair, enjoy locally made ices.

100–101

Villagers at the fair, March 1982

Chaksu, Rajasthan. India has a host of religious festivals that are celebrated with great enthusiasm. They are almost always accompanied by a fair and a street market. Here village women carrying round terracotta pitchers are enjoying the festival of Shitla Mata, celebrated in honor of the Mother Goddess, "She who refreshes," who protects children and cures smallpox.

102–3

Camel fair, November 1966

Pushkar, Rajasthan. The biggest camel fair in India is held annually at Pushkar, near Ajmer in Rajasthan, at the time of the full moon of the month of Kartik (October/November); it coincides with a major Hindu pilgrimage that provides the fair with around 200,000 visitors. The pilgrims have come to bathe in the holy waters of a magnificent lake.

104

Village encampment, November 1983

Pushkar, Rajasthan. The fair lasts for several days and the villagers sleep there, under the stars, after baking their chapattis (flatbreads) over wood fires.

105

Portrait of a villager, November 1983

Pushkar, Rajasthan. The Rajasthanis are descendants of the Rajputs, the proud warriors who fought the Moguls for so long. Their features are aristocratic and the men wear large mustaches, elegant colored turbans, and often gold earrings and necklaces.

106

Woman on a pilgrimage, February 1989

Allahabad, Uttar Pradesh. There is no particular age for going on a pilgrimage, that is, a visit to a holy place. In Hindi, this is called *tirtha yatra,* i.e., undertaking a journey to a river crossing. There are countless holy places. Pilgrimage is a part of Indian life and requires an effort that is both mental and physical.

107

Smile, March 1984

Chaksu, Rajasthan. A young village girl accompanies her mother to the Shitla Mata festival.

108

The sacred syllable Om or *Aum* represents primordial sound and contains all the other sounds. This syllable is the most abstract symbol of divinity and the instrument of mystical creation. It is a submission which is actually a fulfillment. As a sacred formula of invocation, it is also known as "the ferryman" for it leads to the other shore, that is to say the shores of perception of Supreme Reality.

109

Farmers, November 1983

Family at the Pushkar Fair, Rajasthan. The sight of all these families converging from all parts to attend the fair, arriving on foot, in carts, tractors, buses, etc., and all in their finery is a delight to the heart and the senses, for joy radiates from all of them.

112–13

Ceiling decoration, February 1993
Rameshwaram, Tamil Nadu. The temple of Ramanathaswamy at Rameshwaram is a remarkable example of late Dravidian architecture. It has four impressive walkways lined with sculpted pillars. This is a ceiling pattern from one of the walkways.

114–15

Paddy-fields, March 1987

Kashmir. Arriving by road from the Indian plain and climbing to Srinagar, capital of Kashmir, you reach the Banihal tunnel. You emerge into a landscape of paddy-fields that will delight the most jaundiced eye. Having left the heat and dust below on the plain, this vision of delicious freshness that the Mughal emperors so appreciated indeed seems like a paradise.

116–17

Ceiling decoration, February 1993

Temple of Minakshi Madurai, Tamil Nadu. This is no doubt the most outstanding temple in southern India due to its architecture, the profusion of sculptures that decorate its gopurams, but above all, by the extraordinarily able vibrant life within it. The French writer André Malraux wrote in his *Antimémoires:* "It seems as though peasant piety had erected towers of Babel covered with vegetation of the gods, as it had erected the 299 towers of Chartres cathedral . . . . I discovered that our cathedrals are populated with immobile Christians. I wandered through the endless galleries of a cathedral without a nave, whose nine towers rose unexpected, assaulted by swallows under the solemn flight of eagles." The ceiling pattern is that of a *yantra,* or magical diagram.

118–19

*Landscape in the Western Ghats,
October 1982*

Maharashtra. This is the *Deccan,* in the center of the Indian peninsula, a block of gneiss rock worn down and polished by the weather, until it became a series of plateaus ranging in height between 1,000 and 3,500 feet (300 to 1,000 m), surrounded by the Ghats, meaning "stairs," a ring of mountains. The Western Ghats seen here are around 7,000 feet (2,000 m) high in the south and their steep slopes dominate the plateaus. The predominantly green color indicates that this is the end of the rainy season. It was in these mountains that Shivaji and his Marathi warriors defeated the powerful Mughal Emperor Aurangzeb.

120–21

Ceiling decoration, January 1993

Temple at Chidambaram, Tamil Nadu. The temple of Sri Shiva Kama, Sundasi Ambigai, uses a different *yantra* whose purpose is to concentrate the mind on the idea of divinity.

122–23

The Karakorams, July 1978

Ladakh. These mountains are like dry Himalayas, a lunar-looking landscape consisting of bare mountains rendered even more dramatic by the background of a stormy sky.

124–25

Ceiling decoration, February 1993

Temple of Minkashi, Madurai, Tamil Nadu. The temple is dedicated to Shiva, who is known here as Sundareswara, "the Beautiful God," and to Minkashi, his beautiful wife, the "goddess with the eyes of a fish."

126–27

The Karakorams, July 1978

Ladakh. As in the photograph on 122–23, this is the road leading from Srinagar to Leh, capital of Ladakh, one of the highest and most spectacular routes in the world.

128–29

Mystical diagram, March 1994

Tantric school, Kerala. Painting on canvas representing *Sri Yantra*, the most effective of the *yantras*, also known as *Sri Chakra*, or the Wheel of Fortune. It is the diagram of beauty and harmony, which represents the universal goddess, and widely used in Tantric ritual.

130–31

The Karakorams, July 1978

Ladakh. See the remarks for 122–23 and 126–27.

134–35

Entrance to the Sanchi stupa, *April 1982*

Sanchi, Madhya Pradesh. This is the eastern entrance seen from the front, with a detail of the lower traverse. The scene represents the visit of the Emperor Ashoka to the bodhi tree, under which the Buddha received enlightenment. On the right, Ashoka, accompanied by the queen and his retinue, descends from his elephant; he is shown once again at the foot of the structure on which the tree stands, his hands folded in the attitude of prayer. The stone sculpture was created by craftsmen used to working in ivory, which is why the detail is so fine.

136

Great stupa, *April 1982*

Sanchi, Madhya Pradesh. This *stupa* was built in the reign of the great Emperor Ashoka. The actual *stupa* dates from the 3rd century B.C. but the four magnificently carved entrances, representing the four directions, date from the 1st century B.C.

137

Head of the Buddha, April 1994

Mathura, Uttar Pradesh. This stone head of a Buddha dates from the Gupta period (5th century A.D.) and is in the Mathura archeological museum.

138–39

The Karakorams, July 1978

Ladakh. See remarks for 122–23, 126–27 and 130–31.

140

Tibetan monk, July 1966

Dalhousie, Himachal Pradesh.

141

Novice monk and his master, July 1966

Dalhousie, Himachal Pradesh.

143

The sacred syllable Om or Aum

See comments for 108.

144

Jain temple, April 1985

Mount Abu, Rajasthan. The temple of Vimal Vasahi at Dilwara, which dates from the second century, is a jewel carved out of marble, whose sculpted pillars are linked by garlands of pierced marble. The craftsmen who built this enchanting Jain temple are said to have been paid in the weight of the marble dust that they excavated from a hewn block; the aim was to encourage them to produce endless sculptures. The temple is still in use and the devotees faithfully perform their devotions there.

145

Devotee in a temple, December 1966

Mount Abu, Rajasthan. The temple of Luna Vasahi dates from the eighteenth century but contains sculptures of the same quality as those of Vimal Vasahi.

146–47

Jain temples in Palitana, November 1987

Gujarat. Southwest of the port of Bhavnagar, on the Kathiawar peninsula overlooking the Bay of Cambay and the Arabian Sea, Palitana, the temple city, is reduced to almost a single gateway, leading to Shatrunjaya, Victory Square. From here, there is a climb of more than a mile of staircases leading to a hilltop at 1,000 feet (600 m) that contains 863 temples, almost all of them Jain. When night falls even the priests leave the temples, because the night is dedicated almost entirely to the gods. This little walled city has become a sacred pilgrimage destination for the Jains. These temples were built after the 16th century because earlier temples were destroyed in the 14th and 15th centuries by the Muslims. This is the view from the Muslim sanctuary of Angar Pir, which is littered with miniature cradles placed there by woman who want to have children.

150–51

Jain ascetic at the feet of a statue of Bahubali, December 1993

Shravanabelagola, Karnataka. Every twelve or thirteen years the little town of Sravanabelagola is the scene of a huge Jain festival, the Maha Mastahabhisheka (great anointing), during which a statue of Bahubali, a great Jain holy man, is solemnly bathed in the presence of a crowd of 300,000 pilgrims. This statue of the "handsome lord" is cut out of a single block of granite 69 feet (18 m) high. It represents the perfect Jain, one who has succeeded in liberating himself from desire and illusion in order to immerse himself in the cosmos and become a god. Privileged devotees anoint him with seven precious substances from scaffolding that is slightly higher than the hero's head. At the foot of the statue, a *digambara* or Jain ascetic ("clothed in space"), who lives and travels entirely naked, contemplates the last flower petals falling from the sky to honor the saint.

153

Pilgrim, February 1994

Tiruchendur, Tamil Nadu. Austere face and body of an old pilgrim attending the Masi festival honoring Subramanian, son of Shiva.

154–55

Sadhu *under a banyan tree, April 1982*

Mandu, Madhya Pradesh. A *sadhu* is a wandering holy man in the Hindu religion. This one sits under a banyan tree. *Sadhus* are the most enigmatic characters in Indian society. They have no caste and their position is ambiguous. They are outside society and everything depends on them. It is the very society on which they have to some extent turned their back that feeds and venerates them. They have many privileges and, hierarchically, they are ranked higher than other men.

158
Village mosque, November 1992

Khuldabad, Maharashtra. About a mile and a half from the famous Ellora caves, near the tomb of Aurangzeb, the last great Mughal emperor, this little mosque is redolent of the serenity of Muslim places of worship.

159
Muslim, April 1984

Ajmer, Rajasthan. This dignified vendor of eye lotions based on antimony that are used as cosmetics and to protect the eyes is the archetypal Muslim trader.

160
Muslim woman, January 1984

Hyderabad, Deccan. This young woman is visiting the tombs of the Nizams near the mosque known as Mecca in the heart of the old city.

161
The Great Mosque, February 1965

Fatehpur Sikri near Agra, Uttar Pradesh. This mosque is supposed to be a copy of the Great Mosque in Mecca and is a handsome example of successful fusion between Muslim and Hindu architecture.

162–63
Play of light and shade, December 1981

Fatehpur Sikri near Agra, Uttar Pradesh. Islamic art tries to capture the light and contemplates the world through pierced marble screens such as those at the Taj Mahal, the wooden screens that cover the windows in private homes, or *musharabieh* screens of pink sandstone such as those of Fatehpur Sikri.

164
Muslim, October 1982

Ahmedabad, Gujarat. This Indian Muslim whom we met at the Soerkhej Mosque has hair tinted with henna.

165
The Pearl Mosque, March 1971

Red Fort, Old Delhi. The three elongated domes of the Pearl Mosque inside the Red Fort are seen from an arch leading to the private audience room. This marble mosque was built 1659 for Aurangzeb, opposite the royal baths.

166–67
Lake Dal, November 1981

Srinagar, Kashmir. On a beautiful fall evening, a *shikara* glides over the waters of Lake Dal. The water of the lake is amazingly clear, yet there is no waste water treatment facility, and all the garbage from the floating houses is thrown into it.

168
Caravan, Taj Mahal, December 1981

Agra, Uttar Pradesh. India's most famous monument is photographed here from the opposite bank of the Yamuna, just as a caravan of dromedaries is fording the river. What more can be said about this graceful masterpiece? Yet there are many gaps in our knowledge about it and India has always loved mysteries.

169
Muslim woman, January 1984

Hyderabad, Deccan. The counterpart of the *sari*—the garment worn by Hindu women that emphasizes and embellishes the shape of the female body—for Muslim women is the *burqa*, the huge mantle that protects and hides them. In Hyderabad, however, the Muslim veil is lighter and often transparent.

170–71
Mausoleum of Itimad-ud-Daulah, March 1978

Agra, Uttar Pradesh. Only a mile or so from the Taj Mahal, on the opposite bank of the river, there is another Indo-Muslim architectural treasure, the mausoleum of Itimad-ud-Daulah, which looks like a marquetry jewel box. It is built of white marble encrusted with semi-precious stones. The mausoleum was built by Nur Jahan (light of the world), wife of the Emperor Jahangir and daughter of his vizir, in memory of her father. It has been nicknamed the Baby Taj Mahal by the inhabitants of Agra. The two young Muslim women in silhouette demonstrate the most frequently worn female attire after the *sari*, the *salwar kamiz* or *churidar kamiz*, consisting of loose pants tightened at the ankle or on the leg, worn beneath a long tunic.

173
The Golden Temple, April 1968

Amritsar, Punjab. The Golden Temple, sacred to the Sikhs, is built in the middle of a tank known as the "Pool of Immortality."

174–75
Guards at the Golden Temple, April 1968

Amritsar, Punjab. Sikhism, is a religion founded in 1469 by Guru Nanak. It is based on reformed Hinduism but also contains elements of Islam. The Nihangs (Persian for "crocodiles") who guard the temple are a sort of elite military force. They were founded in 1699 by the tenth and last Sikh guru, Guru Gobind, and often distinguished themselves in combat during the Afghan wars and in fighting against the British. They are almost always armed and are recognizable for their blue uniforms and tall turbans topped with a steel badge. These guardians of the Sikh faith, who right wrongs, evoke images of chivalry and ancient heroism.

176
Flower market, July 2001

Calcutta, Bengal. This photograph of the flower market was taken from the Howrah Bridge. Most of the flowers sold are French marigolds (known in French as Indian carnations) whose bright orange-red color is reserved for the god. Millions of them are offered in Indian temples.

177
The Hooghly River, July 2001

Calcutta, Bengal. The constant movement of the sand banks and shoals make navigation very difficult on the Hooghly. The tide rises about eleven and a half feet at Calcutta.

179
Funeral pyre, December 1966

Ahmedabad, Gujarat. On the banks of the Sabarmati, a funeral pyre unites the friends and family of the deceased. The body is laid on the shore and first purified by immersion to the knees, then laid out on the pyre and covered with dried cow-pats. The eldest son lights the pyre by bringing to it some embers brought from the home. The cremation lasts for three or four hours. It is a true sacrifice offered to Agni, the god of fire. Supplication is made to the organs of the dead body asking them to return to their respective sources, vision to the sun, the *prana* (breath of life) to the atmosphere, the *manas* (mind) to the moon, and the body to the ground. This moving farewell returns the body to the cosmic elements from which it comes. When the body and the wood have been consumed, the ashes are collected and thrown in the river.

182–83
Itinerant barber, December 1993

Sravanabelagola, Karnataka. Many small trades in India are practiced in the street, especially during pilgrimages.

184
Railroad station platform, July 2001

Howrah, Calcutta. Train arriving. Indian trains sometimes have special ladies' compartments. India has the fourth largest rail network in the world, with 11,000 trains running daily, carrying more than 9 million passengers.

185
Muslim pilgrim, March 1985

Ajmer, Rajasthan. Every year huge crowds of Muslims gather at Ajmer to mark the anniversary of the death of one of the greatest Muslim holy men of India, Mu'in ad-Din Chishti— the Friend of the Poor—who lived here in the 12th century.

186–87
Crowd of pilgrims, February 1989

Allahabad, Uttar Pradesh. A veritable human ocean pours toward the banks of the Sangam, the point at which the three sacred rivers, the Ganges, the Yamun, and the mythical Saraswati, meet for India's most important ritual bath. This Hindu religious gathering is held once every twelve years. It is called the *Maha Kumbh Mela*— "Great Fair of the Amphora." The name refers to the amphora of nectar over which the gods and demons fought and of which a few drops fell at the four places that consequently became sacred, Prayag (Allahabad), Haridwar, Nashik, and Ujjain. The fair rotates among these places every three years. This photograph was taken from a police observation tower.

189
Tea break, November 1993

Eluru, Andhra Pradesh. Indian tea is drunk very strong, especially in the north. Indians drink at least five or six cups a day. The tea is boiled with milk and spices and the drinker often pours the liquid into the saucer to cool it, sucking it up loudly and uninhibitedly.

192
Fishing expeditions, July 1977

Malabar Coast, Kerala. These long *pirogues*, known as serpent-boats, whose prow looks like a dragon, are used for fishing on the high seas but also compete in spectacular races on the canals and lakes at the end of the rainy season. Enthusiastic spectators cheer the oarsmen on from the shore.

193
Fisherman, April 1986

Sindh, Pakistan.

196–97
Boatyard, October 1966

Bombay. The ancient boatyard is reminiscent of the world of the legendary Sinbad the sailor when during the monsoon, sailboats were driven by the wind far out into the Arabian Sea eventually reaching the shores of India.

198–99
Boat building, March 1994

Near Calicut, Kerala. Not far from the beach on which Vasco da Gama disembarked on the Malabar Coast in 1498, the little town of Beypore is home to the last boatyard in which traditional craft are built in India. Wealthy Arab ship's chandlers from the Emirates commission them since crewing these vessels that are designed for the high seas requires specialist manpower and plenty of teak wood nearby since this is the only wood used for constructing the boats.

202–3
Ritual Anointing, December 1993

Shravanabelagola, Karnataka. See the captions for pages 150–51. On page 202, the head of the saintly hero is being doused with red kumkum powder. The red powder is sold in all the Indian markets and is used by Indian women to draw the red *tilak* in the middle of their foreheads, a protective mark normally reserved for married women. On page 203, Bahubali is being doused in milk.

206–7
Funeral pyre, September 1987

Ayodhya, Uttar Pradesh. See the caption for page 179. In this religious city, associated with numerous episodes from the *Ramayana*, cre-mations are held on the shores of the Gogra where the name of Ram, the seventh incarnation of Vishnu, is particularly often invoked.

210–11
Shores of the Narmada, January 1990

Nemawar, Madhya Pradesh. The Narmada is particularly sacred; merely seeing it will purify the heart. At sunrise on its shores, the special moment for Hindu ritual bathing is the time for intense religious activity.

213
Temple servant, March 1989

Nathdwara, Rajasthan. The presence in Nathdwara of an image of Shrinathji, the incarnation of the god Krishna at the age of seven, is the reason for intense religious activity in the town. Nearly a thousand worshipers may attend the ceremony. Eight times a day, the *sanctum* is opened for the *darshan*—viewing. This viewing of the god is considered to be such a great spiritual experience that it may lead to enlightenment.

214–15
Temple of Rameshwaram, February 1993

Rameshwaram, Tamil Nadu. Rameshwaram has been dubbed the Benares of the South and is an important center of pilgrimage for Hindus, both Shivaites and Vishnuites. The temple of Ramanathaswamy is the most famous, especially for its magnificent walkways lined with richly decorated pillars. According to tradition, Rama sanctified the place by venerating Shiva after the battle of Sri Lanka.

219
Young boy, March 1989

Girnar, Gujarat. The whole of India swarms with casual sellers of little items that are locally produced, especially toys that are full of charm and character. This boy has just been given brightly colored papier-mâché rattles and noisemakers.

220–21
Preparing for the Kathakali*, March 1993*

Cheruthuruthy, Kerala. This small town, around 20 miles (130 km) northeast of Thrissur, is home to Kalamandalam, the famous Kerala Academy of Arts, founded in 1930, where the traditional arts of southern India are taught. They include the *Kathakali*, an elegant theater of dance in which the ballets feature richly adorned characters representing the gods and demons of Hindu mythology, symbols of the battle between the forces of good and the forces of evil.

222–23
Kathakali performance, March 1966

Irinjalakuda, Kerala. The whole village has contributed so that they can afford a performance that generally lasts all night. All the roles are played by men. The dancers wear elaborate costumes and headdresses; they express through gestures, known as *mudra* and complex eye movements that are used instead of words in their unspoken dialogue. Even the colors are symbolic. Green is the color of the fearless, chivalrous knight; one such knight is Bhima, represented here with his wife, Draupadi.

226–27
Harvesting rice, July 1977

Bengal. For reasons of climate, there is an India of wheat and an India of rice. The rice-growing region extends throughout the regions that have a humid, tropical climate, such as Bengal, during the monsoon.

229
Irrigation system, February 1966

Tamil Nadu.

230–31
Backwaters, March 1994

Vaikom region, Kerala. The Malabar Coast is a swamp land of lagoons and canals known as the backwaters. This is a section between Ernakulam and Vaikom; the barges mainly carry sand which is unloaded in big osier baskets; the bargees use long punts to navigate.

232–33 and 234–35
Kalarippayat, March 1994

Kerala. Kalarippayat is the forerunner of all of the Oriental martial arts. It is always practiced in the traditional manner in Kerala, by both boys and girls, in large rectangular rooms that are half-buried and covered with a thatch of leaves. After vigorous sessions of being massaged with oil, a practice designed to make the body more supple, the master delivers the lesson. The combatants use sticks, swords, and bare hands. Here, two sisters are training at Cannanore and offer an amazing spectacle of beauty and effectiveness.

236–37
South Indian woman, December 1993

Mysore, Karnataka. Indian women, especially in the south, almost always wear flowers in their hair.

238–39
Backwaters, July 1977

Kerala. Under a canopy of coconut palms, *wallams*, the equivalent of Chinese *sampans*, glide along the internal waterways.

240
Vedic school, February 1994

Kumbakonam, Tamil Nadu. The school is dedicated to teaching young *Brahmans*. Those pictured here belong to the two great currents of Hinduism, Shivaism and Vishnuism. The purpose of the Vedic schools is to teach the *Vedas* by heart. These sacred texts have been transmitted orally from generation to generation for 3,000 years. Vedic schools are living libraries of eternal India. For the Hindus, not only the meaning, but even the mere sound of the words, is sacred; the Vedas were "heard" directly from Brahma by the rishi, the seers. They preceded the universe, itself born from the syllable *Om*.

241
Young Brahman, *February 1994*

Kumbakonam, Tamil Nadu. This young Tamil wears the distinctive mark of the Shivaites (three horizontal lines) on his forehead. The sign used by the Vishnuites consists of two vertical lines.

242–43
Vedic school, March 1994

Trivandrum, Kerala. At the age of seven, after the ceremony of accepting the sacred cord, the young *Brahman* has to memorize each note on the phalanxes of his fingers, while learning for ten years how to recite impeccably the hymns of homage to the great divinities. He is taught by a master.

244–45
The Western Ghats, March 1994

Kerala. The Ghats—literally "stairs"—is the mountain chain that stretches for 1,000 miles (1500 km) and gradually descends in steps to the sea. This panoramic view was taken from a peak in the Kumily region, and shows mountains with rounded peaks, the highest of which rises to 9,000 feet. South of the Himalayas, this is the highest mountain in India, and tea is grown on the slopes up to an altitude of 6,500 feet. The Eastern Ghats, which run beside the Coromandel coast, are not nearly as high.

246–47
Site of Hampi, January 1993

Karnataka. In an undulating landscape dotted with enormous rounded boulders, on the shores of the river Tungabhadra, surrounded by fields of sugar-cane and banana trees, stands the little village of Hampi. It is dominated by the 15th-century temple of Virupaksha and its gateway tower or gopura that is 173 feet (52 m) high. From the 14th to the 16th centuries, Hampi, under the name of Vijayanagar—Victory City—was the capital of one of largest Hindu empires in the history of India. At the time, it had half a million inhabitants, and was surrounded by seven concentric city walls. It maintained an army of one million mercenaries. Its wealth came from the spice trade and the cotton industry.

248
Squatted temple, February 1994

Krishnapuram, Tamil Nadu. A Tamil family has squatted in a mandapa—room of pillars—in a south Indian temple. The women are spreading grains of rice to dry on the tiled floor.

250
Ruins of Vijayanagar, January 1993

Karnataka. View from Matanga hill of the ruins of the grand temple of Achyuta Raya with its magnificent sculptures and so-called "musical" pillars that resonate when tapped.

251
Sadhu, March 1989

Girnar, Gujarat. This Shivaite *sadhu* is entirely naked. His hair is normally worn in a bun but is now loose, demonstrating its length, and he has smeared his body with ashes from the ritual fire that he keeps permanently alight, symbolizing the ashes of a funeral pyre. This is an allusion to absolute renunciation of the world and in memory of Shiva who reduced the universe to ashes, then coated his body with them. The *sadhu* is the holy man who is omnipresent throughout India, an enigmatic but revered figure because he has seen what ordinary mortals cannot see and he expresses the reality of the inner peace to which every human being aspires.

254

Man with monkey, January 1988

New Delhi. Monkeys are the funniest and most pathetic domesticated animals because they so easily imitate humans. This one is dressed in a little skirt and has bells on his paws. He dances to the rhythm of a tambourine, shaken by his master. He performs a *kathak*, a court dance of which India's Muslim rulers were particularly fond and which today is still performed by young girls of good families. Trained monkeys beg for money from the spectators by pulling at their clothes until they hand over a few more coins. These street performances continue to be very popular.

255

Muslim girls, June 2001

Murud, Maharashtra. The three little girls are sisters. Zuleikha wears a pink dress, Pushpa a mauve dress, and the youngest, whose name we have forgotten, poses for the photograph without really posing.

258–59

Beach and fishing port, March 1993

Varkala, Kerala. Fishing nets and boats on a sandy beach. Coconut palms overlook the blue sea. Varkala is the very essence of a little corner of paradise on the Spice Coast.

262

Workers in the paddy-fields, February 1966

Tamil Nadu.

263

Replanting rice, February 1966

Tamil Nadu.

265

Hindu priest, November 1987

Ahmedabad, Gujarat. Meeting and greeting in the Swami Narayan Temple in Ahmedabad.

266–67

Couple playing in the waves, November 1987

Dwarka, Gujarat. A young married couple plays among the blue waves of the Arabian sea. As the poet so aptly puts it: "Believe me, it is as hard to become master of a young wife than to make quicksilver stand still in the palm of one's hand."

270–71

Ritual Bathing in the Ganges, January 1988

Benares, Uttar Pradesh.

272

Women at the fair, January 1984

Pushkar, Rajasthan.

273

Elegant village woman, January 1984

Jaipur, Rajasthan.

274–75

Muslim bride, January 1984

Rampur, Uttar Pradesh. Muslim men are permitted to take up to four wives, on condition that they can afford to support them and that they are capable of behaving fairly toward each of them. There is a Mogul proverb to the effect that: "A man should marry four wives, a Persian woman to have someone to talk to, a Khorasani woman to do the housework, a Hindu woman to take care of the children and a Mawarunnahri woman to have someone to beat as a warning to the other three."

277

Affectionate scene, December 1987

Udaipur, Rajasthan.

278

Altar dedicated to the Naga, November 1992

Nashik, Maharashtra. In Indian mythology, the *naga*—a divinity who is half-human, half-snake—is the guardian of the natural riches of the earth and a symbol of fertility. Women who want to have a child pray to it and make offerings before the votive stones representing serpents. After the cow, the serpent is the most venerated animal in India. The cult of *naga* is very widespread. Snakes are fed on milk and fruits and have their special altar in many homes.

279

Hairstyle, January 1993

Chidambaram, Tamil Nadu. See 236–37.

281

The sacred syllable Om or Aum.

Miniature of the Kangra School, 8th century, Bharat Kala Bhavan, Benares. The syllable represented here also contains the three main gods of the Hindu trimurti: the four-headed Brahma, Vishnu (wearing dark blue and sitting on the lotus flower), and Shiva with his trident, wearing the crescent moon as a diadem. See captions for 108 and 143.

282–83

Jain women, February 1982

Jaipur, Rajasthan. India invented the *sari*, the loveliest and most feminine garment in the world, a marvel of elegance, although it is merely a strip of cloth several yards long and about four feet (1 m) wide. The *sari* is worn by most Indian women and there is an infinite choice of fabrics and ways it can be worn. It makes beautiful women even more beautiful, and less beautiful women, modestly and provocatively beautiful.

284

Prayer to the naga, March 1993

Belur, Karnataka. The serpent-god is represented here with three, seven, nine, or ten heads. In the Chennakesawa Temple, a young woman is praying to a seven-headed cobra. Shiva's ambivalent nature, both creative and destructive, is shared with one of his most potent symbols, the cobra, which, despite being venomous, decorates Shiva's neck and wraps itself round his chest and ankles.

285

Muslim bride, October 1981

Lahore, Pakistan. Fariha is of Rajput origin. The different communities on either side of the frontier between India and Pakistan maintain exactly the same customs.

287

The Sacred Syllable Om or Aum

Miniature of the Sikh School, c. 1830–40. Ranjit Singh Museum, Amritsar. This miniature showing the main deities of Hinduism and their consorts—Brahma and Sarasvati, Vishnu and Lakshmi, Shiva and Parvati—is contained in a military teaching manual written in Persian letters. See captions for 108, 143, and 281.

289

Tilak, February 1989

Ahmedabad, Gujerat. See pages 202–3. The *bindi* or *tilak* has long been the distinctive sign of a married woman but this protective dot has now been adopted by all women, except widows. It was once only in red, but it is now worn in every color, and the fashion conscious match the tilak to the sari. The location here is the entrance to a temple dedicated to Hanuman, the monkey-god.

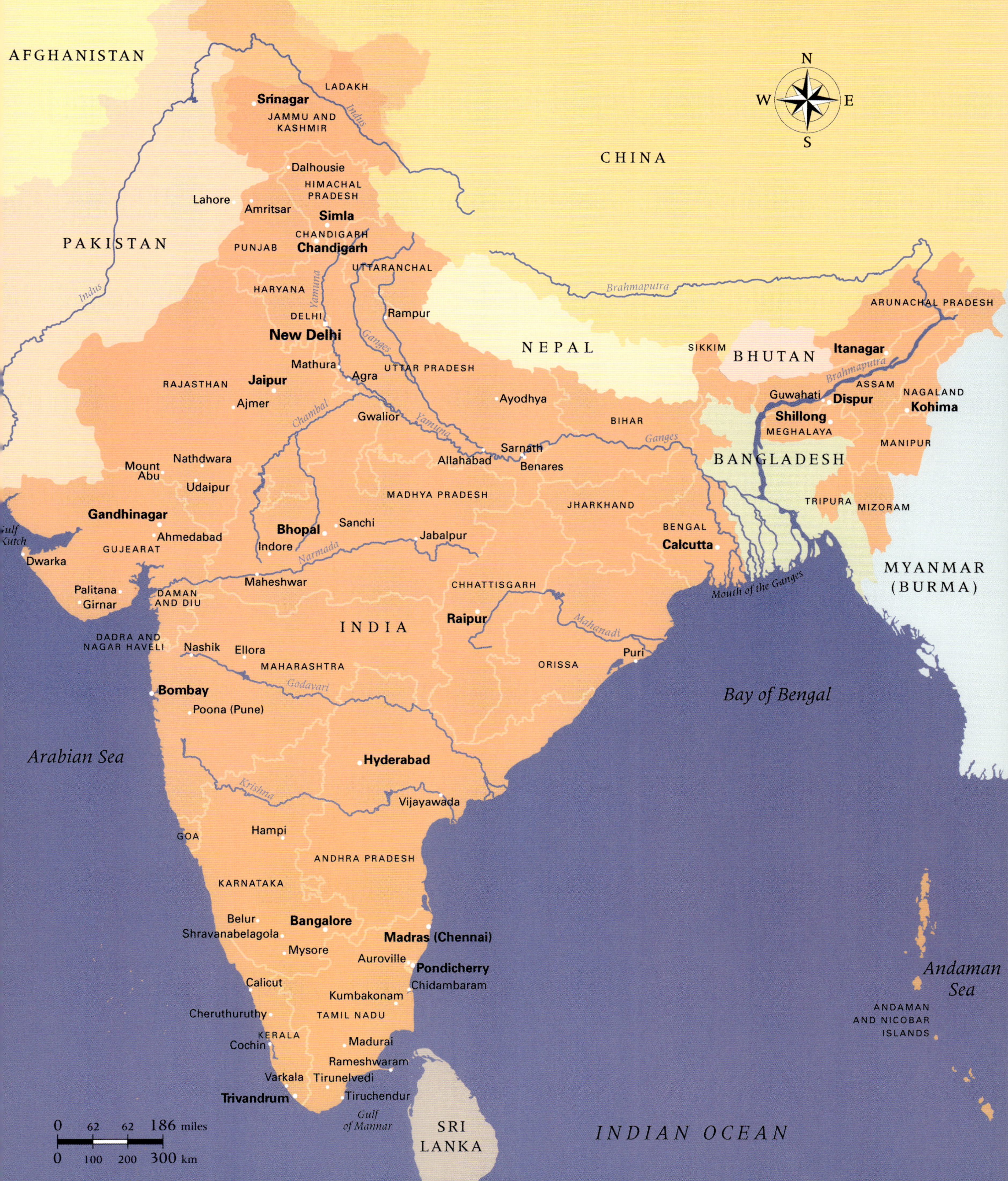

AFGHANISTAN
CHINA
N
W E
S
PAKISTAN
Srinagar
LADAKH
JAMMU AND KASHMIR
Indus
Dalhousie
HIMACHAL PRADESH
Lahore
Amritsar
Simla
CHANDIGARH
Chandigarh
PUNJAB
HARYANA
UTTARANCHAL
DELHI
Rampur
New Delhi
Mathura
RAJASTHAN
Jaipur
Agra
UTTAR PRADESH
NEPAL
Brahmaputra
SIKKIM
BHUTAN
Itanagar
ARUNACHAL PRADESH
ASSAM
Guwahati
Dispur
NAGALAND
Kohima
Shillong
MEGHALAYA
MANIPUR
Ajmer
Gwalior
Yamuna
Ayodhya
BIHAR
Ganges
BANGLADESH
TRIPURA
MIZORAM
Chambal
Yamuna
Sarnath
Allahabad
Benares
Mount Abu
Nathdwara
Udaipur
MADHYA PRADESH
JHARKHAND
BENGAL
Calcutta
MYANMAR (BURMA)
Gandhinagar
Ahmedabad
GUJEARAT
Bhopal
Sanchi
Indore
Narmada
Jabalpur
Mouth of the Ganges
Gulf of Kutch
Dwarka
Maheshwar
CHHATTISGARH
Palitana
Girnar
DAMAN AND DIU
INDIA
Raipur
Mahanadi
Puri
DADRA AND NAGAR HAVELI
Nashik
Ellora
MAHARASHTRA
ORISSA
Bay of Bengal
Bombay
Godavari
Poona (Pune)
Arabian Sea
Hyderabad
Krishna
Vijayawada
GOA
Hampi
ANDHRA PRADESH
KARNATAKA
Belur
Bangalore
Shravanabelagola
Mysore
Madras (Chennai)
Auroville
Pondicherry
Calicut
Chidambaram
Kumbakonam
Cheruthuruthy
TAMIL NADU
KERALA
Madurai
Cochin
Rameshwaram
Varkala
Tirunelvedi
Trivandrum
Tiruchendur
Gulf of Mannar
SRI LANKA
INDIAN OCEAN
Andaman Sea
ANDAMAN AND NICOBAR ISLANDS
0   62   62   186 miles
0   100   200   300 km

Advaita

"Non-duality." A school of philosophy founded on the refutation of the maya, the force that caused the world to develop. It thus claims that Ultimate Reality is not dual in nature. Advaita teaches the transcendental unity of all things. One of its main proponents was Sankaracharya, who lived in the 9th century A.D.

Apsara

A celestial water-nymph who dances and seduces humans, a serious temptation for ascetics.

asana

The seat of divinity and a generic term for yoga postures.

Atman

The individual principle, the ego or deepest being identical to the *Brahman*.

avatar

The earthly manifestation of a god. Vishnu had numerous avatars, including Rama and Krishna.

Ayurveda

"The science of life," traditional Indian medicine.

brahma

The Supreme Existence or Absolute. Its personification is Brahma, one of the three gods of the Hindu trinity (trimurti).

Brahman

A member of the priestly caste.

chakra

"Wheel." The chakras in the human body represent the specific points through which energy passes.

dhyana

Meditation, contemplation. The word became ch'an in Chinese, then zen in Japanese.

jati

Birth, caste. One of the hereditary sub-castes of which India has more than 3,000.

kalarippayat

Martial art form that originates from Kerala and is the origin of the Chinese and Japanese martial arts.

Kama

God of carnal love. The word is also used to designate the desire that leads to creation, which is one of the four purposes of life, the others being *artha* (wealth), *dharma* (law), and *moksha* (liberation).

karma

Deed. It is *karma* (the deeds one has performed in his lifetime) that determines how a person will be reincarnated.

kundalini

"The coiled." Human energy symbolized by a serpent coiled three and a half times at the base of the spinal column.

lila

"Game." The game played by the divinity when he hides behind the maya.

lingam

"Sign." A phallus symbolizing Shiva and, through him, the vital and spiritual spark.

mandala

Graphic representation of the cosmos that serves as a medium for meditation or, in ritual, as a magical diagram in which the divine forces are concentrated.

maya

Energy of the manifestation of the world of which the forms hide the Supreme Reality. Often translated as "illusion."

mudra

Hand gesture, mainly in Buddhist statuary, dance, or yoga. Each mudra symbolizes a particular pose.

nirvana

Extinction. Elevation of the consciousness until it merges with the Absolute. The Buddha's Mahaparinirvana was his great, final nirvana achieved at the moment of his death in Kushinagara.

raga

Coloration. In music, it means a melodic mode, in painting, an emotion caused by outside events or interior states of mind.

Samadhi

State in which the ego is absorbed. Tomb of the Sages.

samsara

Current, flow. The cycle of successive transmigrations, "like a worn garment discarded so as to be able to don a new one" (Bhagavad-Gita).

sannyasi

Wandering ascetic who has renounced the world. Name also given to devotees of a guru.

shakti

Divine energy. The shakti is the female counterpart of a god and his consort.

tilak

The red "third eye" that married women and some devotees wear on the forehead.

Upanishad

Texts that supplement and comment upon the Vedas. They express the zenith of philosophical speculation. They were written between the 6th and 3rd centuries B.C. There are fourteen major Upanishads.

varna

"Color." The four castes of traditional society: *Brahman*, Kshatriya, Vaisya, and Sudra.

Veda

"Knowledge." The name given to the most ancient traditional Indian scriptures, dating between the 12th and 8th centuries B.C.

Vedanta

"End of the Veda." Philosophical principles based on the concept of unity between the individual ego and the universal id.

yoni

Female sex organ represented in temples in the form of an oval receptacle from which the *lingam* rises. Strangely, in Sanskrit the word is masculine.

Chronology

In view of the multiplicity of dynasties that ruled northern and southern India, and the absence of unification before the modern era, this chronology only sketches the most important stages of Indian history, ending with independence.

B.C.

50,000–30,000 (?)	Prehistoric proto-Australoid population groups
c. 2500	The Indus civilization centers on Harappa and Mohenjo-Daro
c. 1500	Arrival in the Punjab of the Indo-Europeans (Aryans), who wiped out the Indus civilization and reached as far as the Deccan
c. 800–600	Magadha kingdom
c. 560	Birth of Siddhartha Gautama, the future Buddha and birth of Mahavira, founder of Jainism
c. 520–515	Persian conquest of the Indus basin
326	Alexander the Great reaches the Indus after conquering the Persian Empire
c. 325–185	Maurya dynasty
c. 270–231	Reign of Emperor Ashoka (Maurya), who supported Buddhism
2nd century	Shunga dynasty
c. 80	The Scythians (Shaka) invade northern and northeastern India

A.D.

1st century	The Kushans defeat the Shaka
Early 2nd century	Kushan dynasty declines
Late 3rd–9th centuries	Pallava dynasty flourishes in southern India
4th–8th centuries	Gupta empire in the north
c. 460	The Huns invade northwestern India
712	Ninety years after the Hegira, the Arabs invade Sindh
8th–12th centuries	The Pala Buddhist dynasty rules northwestern India
10th–13th centuries	Chola empire in the south
11th–12th centuries	Muslim invasions in the north
1192	Creation of the Delhi sultanate
1202	Benares captured by the Muslims
14th century	Muslim conquest of the Deccan and south India

1336–1565   Vijayanagar empire in the Karnataka, last Hindu bastion, defeated by the Muslims at the Battle of Talikota

1526   Mughal dynasty begins with Babur

1556–1605   Reign of the Mughal emperor Akbar

16th–17th century   Europeans (Portuguese, Dutch, British, French) open trading posts on the coasts of India

1658–1707   Reign of the Mughal emperor Aurangzeb

1673   The French capture Pondicherry

1674   Foundation of the Mahratta dynasty in central India, which fights the Moguls and then the British until it is defeated in 1818

1698   The British found Calcutta and annex Bombay

1749   The Frenchman Joseph Dupleix governs most of the Deccan but is recalled in 1754. This marks the end of a major French presence in southern India

1803   Delhi and Agra captured by the British

1857–1858   Sepoy Revolt, after which India becomes a British crown colony

1876   Queen Victoria takes the title Empress of India

1911   New Delhi replaces Calcutta as capital of the empire

1920   Mahatma Gandhi undertakes a huge campaign based on non-violence to oust the British from India

1935   Government of India Act gives India its first constitution

1942   Launch of the *Quit India* movement. The idea of partitioning India between Hindus and Muslims makes progress

1947   Lord Mountbatten, viceroy of India, prepares for its independence, though this results in extreme violence between Hindus and Muslims. The Indian empire is divided among India; Pakistan, which is split into two halves; and Ceylon. Independence is declared on August 15, 1947

1950   Declaration of the Republic of India. Pandit Nehru becomes its first prime minister

Further reading

This list includes general writings about aspects of India as well as some classic novels based on personal experiences of India. Sacred texts, Indian literature, and travel guides are not included.

Auboyer, Jeanine. *Daily Life in Ancient India: From 200 B.C. to A.D. 700*, Phoenix Press, 2002.

Sri Aurobindo, J. *Foundations of Indian Culture*. Lotus Editions, 1981.

Sri Aurobindo, J. *Synthesis of Yoga*, Lotus Editions, 1981.

Basham, A.L. *Cultural History of India*, Oxford University Press, 1999.

Biardeau, Madeleine. *Hinduism: The Anthropology of a Civilization*. Oxford University Press, 1994.

Coomaraswani. Ananda K. *Dance of Shiva*, Farrar Straus Giroux, 1957.

Coomaraswani. Ananda K. *Hinduism and Buddhism*. Greenwood-Heinemann Publishing, 1971.

Coomaraswani. Ananda K. *Introduction to Indian Art*. Theosophical Publishing House, 1956.

Couze, Edward. *Buddhism: Its Essence and Development*. Windhorse Publications, 2002.

Danielou, Alain. *A Brief History of India*. Inner Traditions, 2003.

Danielou, Alain. *The Myths and Gods of India*. Inner Traditions, 1991.

del Droit, Roger. *The Cult of Nothingness: The Philosophers and the Buddha*. University of North Carolina Press, 2003.

Dumont, Louis. *Homo Hierarchicus: The Caste System and Its Implications*. University of Chicago Press, 1981.

Eliade, Mircea. *Pantajali and Yoga*. Schocken, 1975.

Eliade, Mircea. *Yoga: Immortality and Freedom*. Bollingen, 1970.

Filliozat, Jean. *The Classical Doctrine or Indian Medicine: Its Origins and its Greek Parallels*. Munshiram Manoharlal, 1966.

Forster, E.M. *A Passage to India*. Harvest Books, 1965.

Grousset, Rene, *The Civilization of India*. Tudor Publishing, 1931.

Mohandas Gandhi. *An Autobiography: The Story of My Experiments with Truth*, Beacon Press (reprinted edition), 1993.

Jan Gonda, *History of Ancient Indian Religion*, Brill Academic Publishing, 1975.

Keown, Damien. *The Buddha: A Very Short Introduction*. Oxford University Press, 1994.

Jaffrelot, Christophe. *The Hindu Nationalist Movement in India*. Columbia University Press, 1998.

Jaffrelot, Christophe. *India's Silent Revolution: The Rise of the Lower Castes*. C. Hurst & Co Ltd, 2003.

Kakar, Sudhir. *Indian Childhood: Cultural Ideals and Social Reality*. Oxford University Press, 1979.

Lamotte, Etienne. *History of Indian Buddhism*. Institute of Leuven Catholic University, 1988.

Levy, Sylvain. *The Indian Theatre (India-the Land and People)*. National Book Trust, 1971.

McDermott, Robert A. (ed.) *The Essential Aurobindo: Writings of Sri Aurobindo*. Lindisfarne Books, 2001.

Markovits, Claude. *A History of Modern India 1480–1950*. Anthem Press, 2002.

Okada, Amina. *Taj Mahal*. Abbeville Press, 1993.

Padoux, Andre. *The Concept of the World in Selected Hindu Tantras*. State University of New York Press, 1990.

Renou, Louis. *The Civilization of Ancient India*. Susil Gupta Ltd, 1954.

Renou, Louis. *Hiduism*, George Braziller, 1961.

Renou, Louis. *Indian literature*, Walker Books, 1964.

Shayegan, Daryush. *Hinduism and Sufism*. Albin Michel, 1998.

Singh, Patwant. *The Sikhs*. Image, 2001.

Singh, Patwant. *Layayoga: The Definitive Guide to the Chakras and Kundalini*. Inner Traditions, 1999.

Calambur, Sivaramamurti. *The Art of India*, Harry N. Abrams, 1993.

Tagore, Rabindranath. *Sadhana: The Realization of Life*. Kessinger Publishing, 1998.

Tucci, Guiseppe. *The Theory and Practice of the Mandala*, Weiser, 1970.

Silburn, Lilian. *Kundalini: The Energy of the Depths*. State University Press New York.

Varenne, Jean. *Yoga and the Hindu Tradition*. University of Chicago Press, 1977.

Zimmer, Heinrich. *The King and the Corpse*. Bollingen, 1971.

Zimmer, Heinrich. *Myths and Symbols in Indian Art and Civilization*. Bollingen, 1972.

Zimmer, Heinrich. *Philosophies of India*. Bollingen, 1969.

Index

Italic page numbers indicate photographs.

Advaita school, 143, 302
Afghans, 156
Agra, *168*, *170–171*
Ahmedabad, Gujerat, *59*, *164*, *265*, *289*
Alfassa, Mira, 280
Allahabad, *56*, *186–187*
Alleppey, 228
altar dedicated to a naga, *278*
Amaravati, 200, 225
Ambedkar, B. R., 152
Amma, 281
Anandamoyi, Ma, 280
Andhra Pradesh, 224
Aphrodite, 53
apsara, 302
Arab traders, 156
Ariyalur, 252
Arjuna, 112
Arrian of Nicomedia, 92
artha (wealth), 302
Aryan invasion, 58, 224
asana, 148, 302
ascetic, Jain, *150–151*
ashram, 117, 195, 264, 280
Asoka, Emperor, 142
Atharvaveda, 281
Atman, 302
Aurangzeb, 172
Aurobindo, Sri, 143, 280
Auroville, 280–281
avatar, 302
Awakening, 149
Ayodhya, Uttar Pradesh, *206–207*
Ayurveda, 302

Backwaters of Kerala, *230–231*, *238–239*
Bahubali, *150–151*, 200
banyan tree, 20, 25, *154–155*

barbers, *182–183*, 256–257
Battle of Talikota, 249
beggars, 40, 143
Benares, *57*, 191
Bengal, *226–227*
Bhagavad-Gita, 112
Bihar, 152
Blake, William, 180
boat building, *196–199*
Bodhuidharma, 152
Bombay (Mumbai), 54–*55*, 132, 191, *196–197*, 218
Brahma (a god of Hindu trinity), 302
brahma (Supreme Existence), 52, 268, 302
Brahmans (priestly caste), 77, 84–85, 92, 113, 302
Brihadaranyaka Upanishad, 124
British, 58, 132, 156
Buddha (Shakyamuni; Siddhartha Gautama), 20, 133, 200, 303
life of, 148–149, 152
Buddhism, 58, 112, 132, 133–155, 225, 286, 303
decline of in India, 143
schools of, 148
spread of, 152
bus travel, 72

Calcutta, *26*, 124, *176*, *177*, *184*, 191, 253
camel fair, *102–103*
carnal love, 302
Carnatic music, 224
caste system, 40, 58, 77–78, 152, 191, 302, 303
cattle, *22*, *32*
caves, 204–205
chakra, 180, 302

Challes, Robert, 205
Chandigarh, 190
Chennai (Madras), 200, 228, 252
chess players, *88*
Chidambaram, 224, 252
children, *33*, 256–257
chile peppers, *96*
Cholas, 252
Christian community, 132, 133, 281
Christianity, 53, 268
colonization, 58
computers, 190
conquerors, 224
corruption, 40
couple playing in the waves, *266–267*
cuisine, 85

Dance, sacred, 194
Dara Shikoh, 172
death, 112–113, 287
fear of, 124
Deccan, *78–79*
Delhi, *254*
democracy, 40
in villages, 85–92
desire, 111
detachment, 112
dharma (law), 302
dhyana, 302
diparthamba, 121
Dirghagama Lokaprajnapati Sutra, 35
dowries, 40
Dravidian languages, 224
drought, 20
drowning, 24
Dubois, Abbé Jean-Antoine, 93
Dwarka, Gujerat, *266–267*

Ecumenical poster, *56*
Egmore Station, Chennai, 252
elephant, 188
Eliade, Mircea, 286
eroticism, 111–112
sacred, 286
expanding consciousness, 180–181

Fairs, *102–103*, *272*
farmers, *109*
Fatehpur Sikri, *161–163*
feminism, of Southern India, 225
festivals, *54–55*
fire worship, 21, 252
fishermen, *192*, *193*, *258–259*
flower market, *176*
funeral pyre, *179*, 205–208, *206–207*, 216, 287

Gandhi, Indira, 280
Gandhi, Mahatma, 77, 143
Gandhipuram, 98–99
Ganesh, *54–55*, *64*
Ganges, *49*, 121, *270–271*
garbage, 73
Gaya, Awakening at, 149
Girnar, Gujarat, *219*, *251*
Gitta (a woman), 261
gods, 52, 142, 268
Golden Temple, Amritsar, *173–175*, 188
Granth, Guru, 172
Great Mosque, *161*
greeting, traditional, *27*
guards, *174–175*
Gujarat, 156, *164*, *179*
Guptas, 58
gurus, 40, 172, 178

Credits

The publisher would like to thank the following: Editions Albin Michel for their permission to reproduce an extract from *La Tentation des Indes* by Olivier Germain-Thomas; Editions Belfond for the extract from *Narmada Sutra* by Gita Mehta, © Gita Mehta, 1993; Editions Gallimard for the extracts from *Antimémoires* by André Malraux; *Un barbare en Asie* by Henri Michaux, © Gallimard; "The Human Condition," by Kabir, in *Au cabaret de l'amour*, © Unesco/ Éditions Gallimard; Editions L'Herne for the extract by Mircea Eliade from *Sur l'érotique mystique indienne*; Éditions du Relié for extracts from the *Uddhava-Gita*; Editions Les Belles Lettres for the extract from *The Indica by Arrian* of Nicomedia; Editions Denoël for the extract from *L'Odore del'India*, de Pier Paolo Pasolini; Editions Stock for the extract from *The Travel Diary* of a Philosopher by Count Hermann de Keyserling. All rights reserved. Roland and Sabrina Michaud are represented in Paris by the Rapho Agency. They are members of the Leica Foundation.